COMBAT
CREW

John Comer

COMBAT CREW

A True Story of Flying and Fighting in World War II

William Morrow and Company, Inc.
New York

Library of Congress Cataloging-in-Publication Data

Comer, John.
    Combat crew / John Comer.
        p.   cm.   8-90   BT 2200
    Reprint. Originally published: Dallas: J. Comer, c1986.
    ISBN 0-688-07614-9
    1. Comer, John. 2. World War, 1939–1945—Aerial operations,
American.   3. World War, 1939–1945—Campaigns—Europe.   4. World
War, 1939–1945—Personal narratives, American.   5. Flight engineers—
United States—Biography.   6. United States. Air Force—Biography.
I. Title.
[D785.U6C64 1988]   87–28085
940.54′4973′0924—dc19   CIP

Printed in the United States of America

First Revised Edition

1 2 3 4 5 6 7 8 9 10

BOOK DESIGN BY KATHY PARISE

Combat Crew Is Dedicated to the Memory of

James Counce, Corinth, Miss.	*K.I.A. Jan 11, 1944*
George Balmore, Bronx, N.Y.	*K.I.A. Jan. 11, 1944*
Herbert Carqueville, Chicago, Ill.	*M.I.A. Oct 9, 1943*
Raymond Legg, Anderson, Ind.	*K.I.A.*

And to the Memory of All the Men
Who Gave Their Lives
in the Air War Over Europe
That the Rest of Us
Might Continue to Live in Freedom

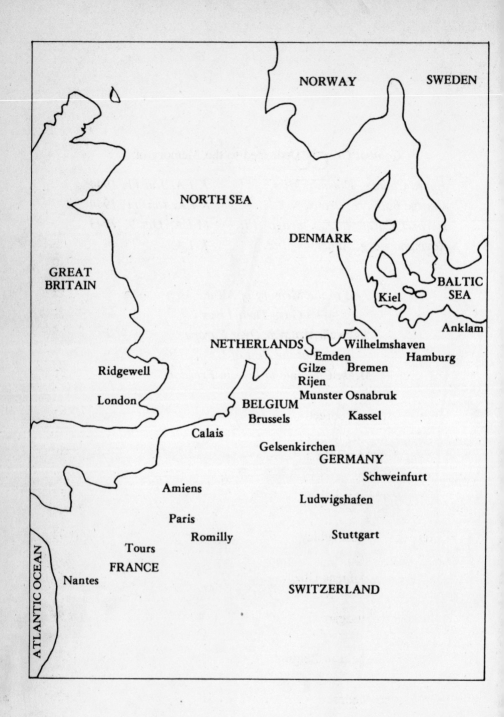

The principal targets for the period covered by this account.

CONTENTS

Contents

PREFACE

The ultimate objective of *Combat Crew* is to make the combat missions come alive for readers of this book. In particular I want the wives, the sons, the daughters, and the grandchildren of the participants to feel that they are experiencing the extreme cold, the constant dangers, and the traumatic events that were common to all the men who manned the Flying Fortresses in the high thin air over the European Continent. To the extent possible my purpose is to take the reader along with us on the combat missions.

This account tells how one combat crew handled the bordeom and monotony of barracks life, all the while sweating out the missions as the air battles unfolded. Every crew was different, reflecting the discipline desired by the pilot. However, I flew with thirteen air crews and found that all experienced crews were far more alike than different. The well researched documentary books about this period may leave the impression that all of the missions were life-and-death struggles. It was not like that: each crew had some very rough missions and some easy ones. Often the accounts of the air battles over Europe are concerned with the commanders and the generals and their agonizing decisions. Again, it was not like that for us: we knew nothing about where we were going or why until two or three hours before takeoff. Once in the air we merely followed the formation, not being concerned about tactics.

What happened to "Gleichauf's Crew" was much like the experiences of men in other crews who succeeded in completing their quota of missions. Each crew could see only part of the action within its range of vision. When our crew had a rough go, sometimes crews in another part of the same battle had it easy. And even on the missions we called "milk runs," almost always some unlucky crews were shot down. Death was never more than a few feet or inches from the men in the Flying Fortresses.

9

FOREWORD

As we approached the site where Ridgewell Airdrome once stood I was overcome with memories. It was June 1972. All at once I was transported back three decades in time. I could hear the raucous roar of Flying Fortress engines revving up for takeoff in the damp predawn cold of an English morning. I could smell that mixture of oil and gasoline that filled the air when engines coughed and started. I could feel again the vibrations of those overloaded aircraft struggling to escape the runway and lift up over the mists. I recalled that uncomfortable feel of an oxygen mask fitted tightly against my face. I remembered the hours I spent recalculating the odds of surviving and the daily realization that they were not good.

Suddenly I shivered despite the warmth of the summer day. I could not shake off the chill of the past. Was this return to Ridgewell going to be a mistake?

One by one I recalled the faces of my crew—a group of young men from diverse locales and backgrounds, thrown together by chance and placed under intense pressure. We were such ordinary men from whom the extraordinary was demanded. We were half trained and woefully inexperienced. Most of our men had been in military service barely a year. We were expected to face the fury of Germany's superbly trained and experienced Luftwaffe and survive. Some of us did. During those months together we formed bonds of friendship I have never experienced before or since.

We were getting closer and I strained to catch a glimpse of something familiar—anything—that would confirm that I had once been a part of this place. Ridgewell had been home, prison, and refuge—the center of my world for so many months. I squinted ahead, secretly hoping for rain, but there was none. That seemed so strange! Ridgewell—without that eternal drizzle and everlasting mud? But that week England played a trick

11

on my memory. The sun made daily appearances and the sky remained uncharacteristically free of moisture. Then it happened! About a hundred yards from the site of the base a gentle drizzle began to fall from skies that up to that moment had shown no hint of rain. It was eerie, as if it had been staged just for me. I was tempted to look upward and say, "Thank you." And I knew I was right in returning to Ridgewell.

Then I was jolted back to reality. The site had long since returned to grain fields. Two old hangars were still standing, but now they were filled with farm machinery. They had traded airplanes for tractors! Part of me knew this was as it should be. Another part reached back through the years remembering how those hangars were once alive with men—and Flying Fortresses needing major repairs. I wanted to regain for a few moments the experiences that could be relived only by those men who flew from this field in that long ago time of war. I stood there silently in the soft rain for a long time, remembering.

My wife and two close friends were with me, but they could not participate in my nostalgia. Nor did they try. To me, it represented the most intensely lived year of my life. To me, this was ground as hallowed as Lincoln's Gettsyburg. Although I flew out of other combat airfields far distant from England, none was burned as deeply into my memory as Ridgewell. It was from here that I had the first traumatic shock of combat. It was from here that so many of my friends, some of the finest men I have ever known, began their last flight.

PROLOGUE

November 24, 1942

A thousand men were assembled on the parade ground at Sheppard Field, Texas, on that November day, just eleven months after Pearl Harbor. A dapper Major strode to an elevated speaker's stand. I will remember him as long as I live. The man was a spellbinder, a military pitchman with superb talents. I listened in hypnotic fascination as he described the adventurous life an an aerial gunner. Carried away by his fiery enthusiasm, I could picture myself holding off a swarm of Japanese Zeroes! With exciting fervor the speaker challenged those of us who had an extra share of guts. Some might, he hinted, be accepted for aerial gunnery. The Major concluded his remarks: "Those of you who want to escape menial assignments for the next three or four years, and live a life of excitement, fall out to my right for physical examinations."

About fifty of us, whose judgment at the moment was questionable, lined up as directed. An hour later I was still sitting in the silence of the reception room at the base hospital awaiting my turn.

The hypnotic spell was beginning to wear off. Men were leaving quietly until there were only a few of us left. What the hell was I doing there? Did I really want to trade a safe aircraft mechanic's job for active combat? Since when had I developed an extra share of guts? Slowly rational thinking returned. I got up and began easing out, and was ten feet from the exit when a hall door opened.

"Comer!"

"Here," I responded automatically.

"That room on the left. Strip down; they'll be with you in a few minutes."

How often the timing of a trivial incident shapes our lives. If that orderly had been five seconds later I would have been gone, and the war for me would have been a vastly different story.

I suddenly remembered the crushing blow ten years earlier when an unexpected visual depth perception change abruptly ended my hoped-for aerial career at the Air Corps Flying Detachment at Brooks Field. I had to conclude that the defect would still be there and I was sure the medical exam would be the same as for pilots.

But now a strange feeling came over me: I wanted very much to pass those tests. And I did great until it came to the depth perception. Once more it floored me. When I showed such obvious dismay at the results of the depth perception gauges, the examining officer asked, "Are you in the Aircraft Mechanics School?"

"Yes, Sir, I am."

"You might qualify for aerial engineer."

"Aerial engineer?" I had never heard the term before.

"Yes, a flying aircraft mechanic who is also an aerial gunner."

It was certainly an interesting new possibility.

"We are not as strict on engineers as on the other gunners. The Colonel might OK you."

When I got to the Colonel he used a new instrument I had not seen in the past—an electric depth gauge. He studied the results, then looked at me.

"Comer, you're close enough that I can waive the defect if you are sure you want to be a flight engineer. It will probably mean combat. Is that what you want?"[1]

I had no time to ponder my decision.

"Sounds great to me!"

"OK. I'll mark your records as medically qualified for Flight Engineer-Gunner. Good luck!"

---

[1] A flight engineer operated a Sperry Computing Sight in the top turret of a B-17. This sight automatically computed the proper lead and all other factors needed to strike the target. All the operator had to do was to spot the correct enemy fighter and feed the wing length into the sight. From that point the sight took over as long as the electric reticles were framed on the ends of the wing of the fighter, and as long as the sight was tracked smoothly. Thus, depth perception was not such a vital requirement.

CHAPTER 1

Arrival at Ridgewell Airdrome

As the personnel truck sped through the wet English countryside my apprehension and uneasiness increased. In a few days we would be facing the fury of the German Luftwaffe. I glanced at the other five men of our crew. Each was silent, immersed in his own contemplation of what the immediate future held in store. It was July 1943, and it was all coming to a head for us quite soon now. What would it be like? Could we handle it? After only ten days of orientation in England, I knew we needed more gunnery practice. The truck slowed down and I saw we were approaching our destination. All day I had been dreading that moment. Most likely the base would be one of those hard-luck outfits who regularly lost high percentages of their aircraft. The worst of all was the 100th Group. Please! Not that unlucky snake-bit command! But logic indicated that the depleted groups would need more replacement crews like us, who had been hurriedly trained and rushed to the 8th Air Force to cover the heavy losses.

It was shortly after dusk, a poor time to arrive at a strange base with no conception of what it would be like. I looked at Herbert Carqueville, the pilot, and he pointed to George Balmore, the radio operator, who was dozing.

"Wake up, George. We're coming into the base."

Carl Shutting, the navigator, straightened his uniform. George Reese, the copilot, looked like he did not have a care in the world. He was like that. Johnny Purus, the bombardier, looked worried—as I was.

The truck wheeled into an obviously quite new base. Looking around, my first impression of the base was prefabricated metal buildings thrown hastily on top of English mud. At headquarters we piled out and unloaded baggage.

A Major took his time examining our papers. There was another crew with us, from the same training command in the States. "I know you are wondering where you are. You are assigned to the 381st Bombardment Group at Ridgewell Air Base."

What a relief that was! The 381st was not one of the high-loss groups we had been hearing about.

"I am sending you to the 533rd Squadron, under the command of Major Hendricks. They are low on crews. A driver will take you to the squadron headquarters. Good luck on your new assignment." From what I had seen since reaching England, we were going to need some luck!

"Major," said Carqueville, "we've heard so many stories, how tough is it? What kind of losses are you having?"

The Major hesitated before answering and studied a large chart on the wall crowded with names. "See that chart? That's the combat roster. We've been here sixty days, and so far we've lost a hundred and one percent of our combat personnel."

That seemed impossible! Did he mean a lot of replacement crews had arrived and were already lost in addition to originals? Surely the Major would burst out laughing in a few seconds. I watched his face for some sign that it was a joke pulled on new arrivals. The smile did not come. The message was clear. I did not know then if that frightful loss figure was factual, or inflated to get across his point that the playing was over. (Those were his exact words! But later I found out that the early losses, while serious, were not that bad.)

The Major continued, "You'd know it anyway in two or three days. I guess it's just as well to let you have it straight right now. Our strength is down and we are happy to have you with us."

I glanced at the other men and noted that the color had drained from their faces. No one said anything as we loaded the baggage into a transportation truck. Each of us was trying to digest the startling high-loss situation and struggling, with scant success, to translate those figures into what they meant to us individually.

At the Squadron Headquarters we were greeted warmly by the Operations Officer. "I'm Lieutenant Franek. Welcome to the 533rd Squadron. We're glad you're here because we have only four combat crews in the squadron, and our minimum strength is supposed to be seven."

Carqueville asked, "Have you any information on our four gunners? They were supposed to arrive about the same time we got here."

"Yes, we do have information," Franek answered. "They're due tomorrow."

That was the only good news I was to hear that day. It was a great relief to know Jim Counce and the other gunners would definitely rejoin us. It would give our sagging spirits a lift just to see them again.

A truck transported us to the combat site, and the driver pointed out the small, metal Quonset huts that would be our quarters. The officers would be in one hut and the enlisted men in another, not far away. The driver said, "Note that here we are widely dispersed to prevent serious damage from German bombing raids. Personnel trucks make regular rounds of the field perimeter during the daytime, and early in the mornings when there is a mission. Combat personnel are quartered separately from the permanent personnel." I picked up the nuance in his voice: what it meant was that combat people were not expected to be around very long.

The driver continued. "You men have a separate combat mess because your hours will be so different from the other men. As soon as you can manage it, I suggest you get into Cambridge and buy a used bicycle. It will make getting around the base a lot easier."

"How far is Cambridge from Ridgewell?" I asked.

"About eighteen miles. A supply truck makes a run every day, and there's also train service from a nearby village."

I doubt if I ever had a more miserable evening in my life. The dingy hut, designed for twelve men, was a dirty, dimly lighted, depressing place. It was bare except for twelve crude cots. A single low-watt bulb hung in the center of the small metal building. I decided on a bunk and opened my bags, but before I could get my gear unpacked, some veteran gunners started drifting in to look us over.

"Where you guys from?" one asked.

Balmore answered, "I'm from New York, and Comer is from Texas."

"That's a helluva combination! You got some more men comin' in?"

"Yes," I said. "Our other four gunners will be here tomorrow."

"Your pilot got a lot of high-altitude formation time?"

"Nope," said Balmore. "Not much."

A second man entered just in time to hear what George had said. "I feel Goddamned sorry for you guys if your pilot can't fly tight formation."

"Oh, I think he can do OK on formation," I offered.

"It takes seventy to a hundred hours of high-altitude formation experience to be a fair pilot in this league. Your pilot got that many hours?"

"Far as I know he's never been in a high-altitude formation, and has only a few hours of low-altitude formation," I said.

"If they don't find you a new pilot who knows what he's doin' at

17

high-altitude formation you're in trouble. Those Jerry sonnuvabitches can spot a new crew on their first circle aroun' the formation and they—''

"They'll tear into your ass on their first attack," interrupted another vet, "cause they always pick the easiest Forts to knock down."

A third man came in. "Don't worry about it, you might make it— sometimes a new crew does get back from its first raid. This week it wasn't too rough: we only lost twenty Forts—mostly new crews!"

Another voice added, "As soon as the Jerries approach us they look for you fresh jokers."

"How can they tell which crews are new?" asked Balmore.

"Damned easy, friend. Green pilots can't stay in tight formation. They throttle-jock back and forth—might as well flash a neon sign!"

A new voice spoke up. "Relax! Don't get lathered up. Mebbe your crew will be one of the lucky ones. We were once new and we're still here!"

"When you hit a German fighter with some good bursts, what happens? Does it break off the attack?" I asked.

The six vets laughed uproariously. "Hell, no! You can see your tracers hit those 190s[1] and 109s[2] an' they bounce off like it's a Goddamned flyin' tank! Those square-headed Krauts keep comin' at you no matter what you throw at 'em!"

The most vocal of the group continued. "The worst bastards they got are Goering's Abbeville Kids—those yellow nose and red nose ME 109s are the roughest you'll ever see." He turned to Balmore. "Hey, kid, you're about my height. What size blouse you wear?"

George replied testily, "None of your damn business!"

"Don't get your guts in an uproar, friend. I need a new blouse, so I spot all you new gunners my size—one of you jokers don't get back, I grab me a blouse before those orderly room pimps get over here to pick up your gear."

One of the vets explained it: "At the 381st they don't issue any replacement clothes. If you tear your pants, or ruin a blouse, you sweat it out until a gunner your size don't make it back."

"That's how we do it over here," said another. "That way ain't no red tape—say, any of you men wear size 38?"

"I do," I replied. "But don't get any ideas—'cause I'm gonna make it!"

---

[1]Focke-Wolfe 190 (F.W. 190)
[2]Messerschmitt 109 (M.E. 109)

"Maybe! But the first rough raid will thin out these huts—a lot of you new bastards won't get back—maybe one of you will be my size."

"Say—there was a nice lookin' kid had that bunk over there for five or six days," one of the vets remarked. "Saw his plane blow up—no chutes!"

He pointed to an empty cot. "The fellow who slept there—they brought him back with no balls."

"Well," a voice added, "that poor bastard don't have to worry no more about findin' a pro station open at four A.M.!"

Ribald laughter reverberated from the thin metal walls, but I couldn't share in their hilarity. My insides were tightening into knots, and I wondered if all those tales were true. I knew they were trying to scare the hell out of us—and succeeding! I kept thinking about those high losses the Major told us about, and realized the vets didn't need to embellish their stories. The plain, unvarnished facts were frightening enough for me.

"Hey, you guys gotta watch those 'lectric fly suits. If a shoe or glove goes out at fifty below zero you can lose a hand or foot."

"But the big thing is an engine fire," from another voice. "When you rookies see that fire you got mebbe thirty or forty seconds before the explosion!"

The vets finally tired of their oft-repeated initiation game and drifted off. George looked at me for a long time without saying a word. He didn't need to for I knew what his thoughts were. Sleep for that night was completely out of the question. The reality of what we faced was almost too much to absorb. Always ringing in my ears were the Major's words: "We've lost a hundred and one percent of our combat personnel." The vets told us we would get in about three missions a month, and the odds stacked up four to one that we wouldn't make it! (Which later proved to be quite accurate.)

Balancing the bad news of the last six hours was my memory of how grand those Flying Fortresses looked in proud formation heading out toward Hitler-held Europe. The second morning we were at Bovingdon, the orientation base near London where replacement crews reported for induction into the 8th Air Force, we were awakened by the roar of many engines. In a matter of minutes the barracks was empty. The Fortresses were passing overhead on their way to strike the Mad Dictator, and none of us wanted to miss the sight. I have had many thrills in my life, but I believe that picture-perfect formation of American bombers headed for a clash with Goering's best was one of the most emotional experiences I have ever had. I wanted to be up there with them. All that day I worried about what those men were going through over the Continent. In the early afternoon I was in an aircraft recognition class when someone whispered, "The Forts are coming back." In one minute the classroom was empty. Where were the proud eagles of the dawn? They returned, but not in the style I had seen that morning. A few were in formation, but most were scattered across the sky. There were feathered engines and many trailed smoke. But where were the other planes? I counted only half of the number that went out that morning. I did not know then that ships in trouble, or low on fuel, broke away from the formations as they approached England, looking for a landing field. For the next half hour, I watched wounded Forts straggle in, a few on two engines.

July 20

There was an agreeable surprise at Ridgewell. The food was good. The combat mess hall was a hundred yards from our barracks. We were in a country where part of the food had to be imported, and all of ours had to come by boat from the States. So those mess officers did a great job with the materials at their disposal.

On the way back from noon mess I said to George, "We're gonna have to get into Cambridge real soon and buy bicycles. I notice all the men here at the base have bikes."

"John, when the other men get here, don't say anything about what the vets did to us last night."

"You mean let 'em get the news on their own?"

"Right! It oughta be interesting to see how they handle it. One thing for sure, they're in for a shock!"

An hour or so later a truck pulled up near the hut and out jumped our four gunners.

"Damn! I thought we were gonna get four good gunners and now you jokers show up again," fumed Balmore. "Come see our Country Club Quarters."

Now that the gunners were back, our crew was all together. James Counce and Carroll Wilson were our two waist gunners. Jim was twenty-three, single, and came from Corinth, Mississippi. He was an engineering student from the University of Tennessee. Jim served as second engineer and was fully as capable as I was, and a very solid man. Carroll Wilson, twenty, from Tulsa, Oklahoma, was assistant to Balmore in the radio room. Carroll was a likable youngster but had not grown up

20

yet. He had married just before leaving for England. The tail gunner, Buck Rogers, thirty nine, was a rugged individual from a small Ohio town. I am not sure of his marital status. He had many rough experiences, but he was a loner and had little to say about some phases of his life. Nickalas Abramo, nineteen, from Massachusetts, operated the ball turret guns. He was an impetuous young man of Italian ancestry.

We were sitting around talking about going to Cambridge to buy bicycles, and the possibility of buying a radio for the hut. Suddenly the door opened and five or six vets entered. "What do you know? We got us some new gunners," one of them said. "Where you guys from?"

I knew what was coming and glanced at George. We sat back in morbid fascination to watch how our four friends responded to "the treatment." A few months later, initiating new arrivals was one of my favorite amusements.

If there was a crew favorite, I suppose it was Jim Counce. Carqueville had a special trick we played on Jim. I would go back to the radio room and make sure he was looking out of the waist window. Herb would put an engine into an extra-inch carburetor position to create some smoke on Jim's side of the aircraft. As soon as Counce saw it he started toward the cockpit, and Herb quickly switched back to automatic lean. By the time Counce reached the cockpit the smoke would be gone.

"Smoke? I didn't see any. John, did you see any smoke?"

"No. You're seein' things, Jim. Are you sure you're OK?"

"I did see smoke from number three engine," he would protest vigorously.

Herb would look at me and shake his head as if to say, "I'm afraid Counce is cracking up."

July 21

From the first night at Ridgewell, it became slowly apparent that Carqueville did not have the experience at high-altitude formation flying to be a first pilot in the big leagues of combat over Europe. It was difficult to understand how the training command in the States could have neglected the one indispensable requirement for a B-17 combat pilot. For the time I knew Herb in training, he was given no high-altitude formation practice. Only two hours of low-altitude formation flying! A copilot should have had fifteen or twenty hours of holding a B-17 in formation over twenty thousand feet.

Late in the afternoon Carqueville opened the door to our hut and stepped inside. I knew instantly he was upset. ''I've been cut back to copilot. I'm takin' Reese's place.'' (Reese had come down with an infection and was grounded for the time being.)

''What!'' Even though I was expecting it to happen, the news came as a shock. ''It's not fair.''

''Wrong! They had to do it. A pilot has to have a lot of formation time, and I don't have it. Believe me, I don't like it one damn bit, but that's how it's got to be.''

Jim spoke up. ''We hate like hell to lose you. Now we'll start all over with some pilot we never saw before. We could have made it with you I'm sure.''

''Thanks, Jim, but Hendricks couldn't permit that risk. He made the right decision. Reese is goin' to be the Assistant Operations Officer.''

Regardless of what he said I knew Carqueville was hurt. Who would be the new pilot? There was much conjecture and concern about what kind of man would take over the crew. The next afternoon Carqueville introduced us to the man who would hold our destiny in his hands. The officers had already met him.

''Men, this is Lieutenant Paul Gleichauf, our pilot. He's got the formation experience we must have if we are going to make it in this league.''

''Lieutenant, I'm John Comer, Engineer.''

''Glad to know you, John.''

The rest of the men introduced themselves and shook hands. It was an awkward moment, with Herb standing there watching his men accept a new leader.

''I'm glad to be your pilot,'' said Gleichauf. ''Looks like we've got good men, so I think we'll do OK.''

There was more small talk but it was mainly verbal sparring while we sized him up, and the pilot got a good look at what he had to work with. Since Herb was to be copilot, it was much like a new football coach keeping the excoach as his assistant. Lieutenant Gleichauf was younger than I expected, but he did fit the image of an Air Force pilot more than Herb.

On the way back to our hut there was silence for a while, then George turned to Counce. ''Well, what do you think of our new pilot?''

''Looks OK. He doesn't talk much but we need the experience he has.''

''John, what do you think?''

''About the same as Jim—only thing, I wish he were a little older.'' (Actually, he was twenty-four, and two years older than I thought at the time.)

Buck said, "That ain't important—we gotta have somebody who can fly tight formation. That's what all the vets say—to hell with the rest of it!"

Paul Gleichauf was originally from Lakewood, Ohio—a suburb of Cleveland. He was a handsome young officer—dashing, slim, and very attractive to women. He came overseas as a first pilot several weeks ahead of us. Just before flying a new Fortress across the Atlantic, a heavy fire extinguisher fell on his foot. He arrived in England with a bad case of hemorrhoids, wearing a moccasin on one foot, and certainly in no condition to handle a B-17 on formation flights. By the time we badly needed a pilot he had recovered enough to resume flying status.

Lieutenant Gleichauf would have been dumbfounded had he fully realized the low level of combat "knowhow" of his new crew. He was aware that Carqueville was short on formation flying, but he had no idea how little gunnery practice the crew had logged before coming to England. He would have been further dismayed had he known that our total experience with oxygen equipment added up to only thirteen hours.

Who was to blame for this woeful lack of training? How could the Second Air Force Training Command have been so ignorant of our needs? I suspect that the Command was overloaded with exeducators who let their passion for classrooms supersede the substance of what was actually needed where we were headed. In a new situation people usually fall back on what they know best. What happened to the communications between the 8th Air Force and the stateside training command? Much time was wasted on classroom trivia and not enough on the essentials necessary for a crew to survive in combat with the enemy.

The 8th Air Force was made up of two units: Bomber Command and Fighter Command. Bomber Command was composed of three divisions,[3] each of which had two wings. Three groups made up a wing. The bomber group was the basic fighting unit of the Command. A combat group had four squadrons who handled the personnel. At that date a group was expected to put up a minimum of eighteen Fortresses on a mission. Sometimes it would be a few more. In most cases a group occupied one air base, and had about two thousand men in combat and support personnel. We found out in the first week that we were in the 8th Air Force, First Division, First Wing, 381st Group, and the 533rd Squadron. The First Wing was made up of the 381st, the 351st, and the 91st groups.

It took me a while to get used to Gleichauf's cockpit procedure. He was as different from Herb as day is from night! He had none of the

---

[3]Later the number of divisions and wings was increased.

easygoing, relaxed characteristics of most four-engine pilots. He was all business from the moment engines started, and prone to issue short, concise orders, which at first sounded irritable on the intercom. But I knew we were lucky to get Gleichauf's kind of experience and ability.

Herb Carqueville was from Chicago, where his family operated a lithographing business. Prior to the war he was quite active in the business, and expected to return to it when the war was over. A good relationship developed between Carqueville and me, partly because both of us had been in the business world for a number of years. Herb's background gave him a different perspective from young men fresh out of college. At twenty-seven, he acted more like a mature man of forty.

Our Navigator, Lieutenant Carl R. Shutting, was from Chattanooga, Tennessee. I had a mental picture of a navigator: he would be a neat, orderly, well-organized person with cold, mathematical efficiency, and precise methodical habits. Carl Shutting was at the opposite end of the spectrum from such an image. He had been married before entering the service, but had recently been the recipient of a "Dear John" letter. Carl was twenty-four, and prior to the war had worked in the post office in Chattanooga, Tennessee.

Johnny Purus, the Bombardier, was from the Boston area. He was in his early twenties, and as dependable as a person could be. He was a bit shy, soft-spoken, and not easy to evaluate immediately. For a short period he had worked as an aircraft mechanic, but not on B-17s. It was good to have another man with mechanical aptitude on the crew. There might come a time in the future when his help would be crucial.

When the war broke out I was thirty-one, married for not quite two years, and living in Corpus Christi, Texas. My education had been at Trinity University and the University of Texas. I was a competent outside salesman for machine tools, equipment, and auto parts. I had a solid background in the field of mechanics and supply, and also some electrical experience (fortunate because a B-17 was operated and controlled mainly by electric circuits). My position was flight engineer and I fired the top turret guns. The turret was mounted in the cockpit directly behind the pilot and copilot.

It did not occur to us that we were already on combat status. No one had told the gunners a single thing about the 381st procedure for gunners. In fact we had not seen a gun since we reached Ridgewell. We were still waiting for the briefing that the Operations Officer promised shortly after we arrived. I understood that we would get at least one gunnery practice flight that would outline the 381st gun armament procedures. We should have asked questions. Where did the crews keep the guns? Where did we get parts or supplies needed on a mission in a hurry? What about the briefing procedures on mission mornings. Did we report to the Briefing Room or go to the aircraft? But military life discourages initiative, so we waited and waited for the instructions, so vital, that never came.

July 29

At 0230 (2:30 A.M.) the lights snapped on and six startled men roused enough to hear the Operations Officer:

"Now listen to this, Comer, Counce, Balmore, Abramo, Wilson, and Rogers. You're flyin' 765 with Gleichauf. Briefing at 0400 hours. Chow's ready now. Come on! Out of that sack!"

"This is a combat raid!" said Counce. "Why didn't they tell us we were on combat status. No one has told us one thing! Do we go to the briefing with the officers?"

"Don't know," I answered. "We gotta catch Gleichauf before he gets to the Briefing Room and get orders."

There were fresh eggs for breakfast but I was too nervous to be hungry. I watched the men come and go in anxious fascination. Our crew seemed to be the only newcomers there. I had a tight feeling in my chest and was beginning to feel nauseated. I envied the confident air of the vets who appeared totally unperturbed. I wondered if I would survive long enough to develop such a carefree attitude. Probably not! I was under no illusions as to what generally happened to new crews. Not many made it back!

Trucks were lined up to ferry us to Operations, and in the dark they assumed ghostly shapes. Men talked, if at all, in subdued whispers. Most were silent except for an occasional curse as some new arrival stepped on a foot. It was a black, gloomy predawn, and our spirits were in complete harmony with the cheerless atmosphere.

Just before the truck pulled out I recalled, with a feeling of panic, that my electric flying suit was back at the hut. I had taken it there to make some needed adjustments. I had no idea if I could survive the intense cold without it, so there was no choice except to jump out of the truck and run through the dark and mud to the hut. When I got back to where the trucks were parked, all had left. I had to run all the way to the Operations Office, following the indistinct shapes of other men in the darkness, and quickly drew my equipment. I found the rest of our men huddled together in a corner of the room, with their flying equipment piled around them.

"What did you find out from Gleichauf?" I asked Jim, who had been the first to get to Operations.

"He was in the Briefing Room before we got here. Everybody who knows anything is in the Briefing Room."

"Don't you see the other gunners are headin' out to the planes?" Jim said.

"Yeah, I see that, but they got orders to do so. We don't. Suppose Gleichauf expects us to be waitin' here," George answered.

About that time the Briefing Room doors opened, and I made a dash for Gleichauf. "Are we free to go to the aircraft?"

"You gunners oughta be there now. Hurry it up or we won't be ready in time!"

We made a run for the trucks and got a new driver who took far too much of our time wandering around the perimeter trying to locate the aircraft. A quick check of the plane showed no signs of any guns. The only man at the plane was a sleepy PFC mechanic.

"Where th' hell do they keep the guns?" I asked.

"Guns? I don't know nothin' about guns," he answered. It was obvious he didn't give a damn, either. "Ain't they in the ship?"

We had only one flashlight and searched everywhere. I was getting very nervous as the time ticked away.

"Don't you know any place the guns might be? We're running out of time."

"Sometimes Armament pulls out the guns while a ship is laid up a spell with heavy damages," he replied.

I hailed an empty truck and the driver agreed to take Abramo and me to Armament, wherever that was. When we got there no one knew anything about our guns. I turned to an officer who had just arrived.

"Sir, we've got to have twelve guns for 765—and real quick."

He turned to a Sergeant. "Get these men some guns and I mean right now!"

"Wait! See those guns in the corner over there, all stripped down? Maybe they're from 765," someone said.

Our ship number was painted on the barrels. Every gun was disassembled and Nick and I tore into them at top speed and got them more or less together. There was no time to make a careful inspection of each gun to be sure there were no missing parts. When we got back Jim checked the guns and asked, "Where are the bolt studs? Didn't you or Nick bring them?" (A bolt stud was a one-inch-long metal device required to insert a round of ammunition into the firing chamber to permit the firing to begin. Unless that round was in place to start the action, the gun would not fire.)

"You mean there are no bolt studs in the ship? Check again. They're supposed to be tied to the receivers," I responded. But there were none in the airplane that we could discover. An obstinate habit of each gunner having his own bolt studs had developed in defiance of regulations to leave them in the airplane. We did not know this at that time. (Before long I was carrying them in my pocket wherever I went.)

An Operations Jeep drove up just then and Carqueville hailed the driver. "Take off for Armament and get us twelve bolt studs. Hurry! You got to get back before we taxi out." The Jeep tore off at high speed. All of the hurry-hurry and confusion was enough to create a panic situation. This was no game we were preparing for! Planes would take off with or without guns in working order! Would he make it? Two minutes before taxi time the Jeep slid to a halt and the driver fought his way through the propeller blast to hand Jim the twelve bolt studs at the waist entry hatch. What a relief that was! Without them, not a gun would have fired.

There was no time for a briefing on the target before takeoff. As soon as we were settled down in the formation Gleichauf came on intercom: "Pilot to crew, Pilot to crew—we're heading for Kiel in Northern Germany. There are several hundred fighters in the area and you can expect a hot reception. Be ready for attacks halfway across the North Sea. This is your first mission—now don't get excited an' let 'em come in on us!"

The formation was far better than I expected. Hour after hour we droned on. It would not be long now: if only we could be lucky enough to get by this one! The way Gleichauf was holding tight formation, I hoped the fighters would not pick us out to be a new crew. Of course I was keyed up to a high pitch and I wondered if I would forget what little I knew about aerial gunnery in the excitement of the first fighter attacks.

Number four engine began to vibrate too much and I watched in alarm as it started slowing down. It looked like either the fuel pump or the magneto had failed. The engine was finished for the day!

"Pilot to Copilot."

"Go ahead, Paul."

"Feather number four." The propeller slowed down and ceased to spin. We were ten minutes from the enemy coast.

For a few minutes Gleichauf tried to keep up, but the formation began to pull away. If we could not keep up it would be suicide, as well as useless, to go on and get knocked off over the target area. Fighters invariably ganged up and finished off the stragglers in comparative safety before they tackled the formation. There was only one thing to do. Gleichauf pulled out of the formation and started the long flight back to England.

"Bombardier to gunners—Bombardier to gunners! Keep alert! We got a long way to go, all alone. Watch for fighters!"

It was a long, tiresome, and frustrating day, and all for nothing! No credit. We still had twenty-five missions to go.

While we were attempting our first mission, six men from the crew of Lieutenant William Cahow moved into the six empty bunks in our hut. Two of them were from Brooklyn, one from Texas, one from California, one from upstate New York, and one from New Jersey. They would become an intimate part of our world for many months to come.

Ugo Lancia was the radio operator and a good one. He was a husky, handsome Italian—loud-speaking and excitable. He had a good singing voice and played numerous instruments, which he somehow acquired in England. The result was that we had the noisiest hut on the base.

Woodrow Pitts, from Houston, Texas, was the engineer. He had a better command of colorful profanity than anyone else in the hut. He needed such an outlet for his temper, especially when he would discover another flat tire on his cranky bicycle. That machine defied all efforts at repairs. Something was wrong every day. Two times that I remember Woodrow picked up an infestation of "crabs" (a tiny licelike parasite that flourished in hair). That caused a frantic trip to the infirmary and a spraying of everything in the hut. Once I picked up the lice from Pitts or from some other unknown source.

Moe Tedesco, a husky Italian from Brooklyn, was one of the gunners. He looked like Brooklyn, and he acted like Brooklyn. He knew little about life in any other environment. His thoughts and interests began and ended back there in the neighborhood where he was born and reared. He said he wanted me to come visit him someday when we got back to the States, and he would show me the real Brooklyn. He gave me his address but also the name of a pool hall. He said they would always know where to find him. Moe was about twenty-five. The Brooklyn accent, tinted with Italian speed, made his conversation interesting. Moe was the kind of man I would want along if I should suddenly end up in a brawl on some dark street in a tough neighborhood.

Hubert (Hubie) Green was the other waist gunner. He was from a city about sixty miles from New York. Like Carroll Wilson, he spent most of his spare time in bed. He had this one big habit—writing letters. That man wrote more letters than anyone I knew in the service. Hubie was tall, dark, slender—very nice looking. He had a good disposition and never gave anyone any trouble. I think he was about twenty-two years old. I didn't know what kind of gunner Hubie was. He always said he merely went along for the ride. I never heard any of his crew complain, however, about his performance not being on a par with the other gunners.

Ray Bechtel, from California, was the tail gunner. He was quiet, easygoing, and cooperative. He rarely had anything to say except when a question was directed to him. Ray was so quiet I would forget he was there for hours at a time. He was a good man to have in our hut because he balanced, to some extent, the noisier characters, of which we had a surplus. I saw Ray in action many times and I know that he handled that position extremely well.

Bill Kettner was Cahow's ball gunner. He was slow-moving, steady, and methodical, which was the opposite of most of his crew mates. The men in our hut were grateful to Bill because of one lucky incident. He was returning from a nearby village one day, and while walking through some woods, he saw a crosscut saw hanging on a tree limb. He immediately appropriated it. That solved our fuel problem. Those long, cold winter nights were made more livable by the fuel we scrounged with that crosscut saw. When the war was over the King's forests nearby were minus a lot of trees, but we had fuel when no one else did. We kept the saw out of sight and only brought it out after dark when some choice trees had been carefully scouted in advance.

For the benefit of those readers not familiar with a B-17 Flying Fortress, five excellent detailed illustrations supplied by the Boeing Aircraft Co., will help in understanding the various sections of the airplane.

The diagrams on the following five pages are printed courtesy of The Boeing Company Archives.

1. The nose section.

This is a B-17 E Model. It does not show the gun on the other side. The navigator fired both guns depending on the direction of the attack. The bombardier's gun fired forward. In the later G Model both side guns were removed and two guns mounted in a chin turret under the bombardier's position. The platform where the Norden Sight was carried in combat can be plainly seen directly in front of the bombardier's seat.

2. The cockpit (or sometimes called cabin).

The two seats for the pilots can be seen clearly. Behind them the flight engineer stood in the top turret. The two turret guns were fired by a Sperry Computing Sight, which automatically compensated for lead and all other aiming factors if it was tracked smoothly and if the wing length of the fighter was properly set into the sight.

The door seen at the rear opened into the bomb bay. Access to the nose section was a constricted space under the pilots' positions.

3. The bomb bay.

Note the narrow catwalk down the middle of the bay. The two vertical supporting beams in the center of the walk created a narrow space that caused the crew men all kinds of trouble trying to squeeze through it due to their bulky high-altitude clothing and the combat gear they all wore. There was not enough space to get through it wearing a chute, so when bombs malfunctioned we had to work on that walk without a chute knowing that if we lost our oxygen supply we could tumble out into the air. The bomb-bay doors down below would open at a weight under 75 pounds.

4. The radio room.

You can see the radio operator's work table at right front (right side of the picture). The door at that point opened into the bomb bay. The door to the rear (left side of the picture) opened into the rear of the aircraft, called the waist. Since this is an early drawing the radio gun is not shown. It was mounted in an open hatch about five feet long and two feet wide. This created an enormous draft of super-frigid air gushing through like a storm. Imagine working a radio wireless key with the air temperature 50 below zero. The later G Model enclosed the hatch space with clear plastic with the gun mounted into it. That saved many R.O.s from freezing injuries.

5. The waist and tail.

The door at the front of the waist opened into the radio room. Just behind this door the ball turret was hung with about two thirds of the turret suspended below the aircraft where the worst of the flak burst. The gun that can be seen is mounted in an open window. With two such openings the wind storm was terrific, causing countless freezing casualties. The later G Model closed the two windows with clear plastic and mounted the guns through the thick plastic. This cut back on frostbite, but the waist guns were no longer as effective as the earlier open window mountings. The tail position was, as you can see, quite crowded. It was so deadly to fighters that they did not attack us very often from the rear.

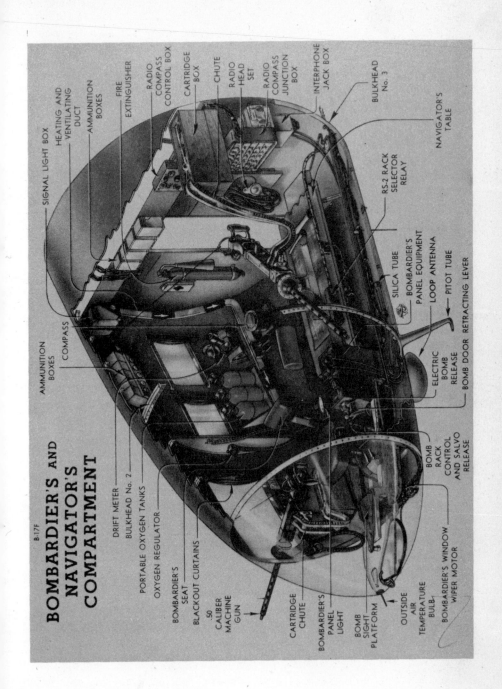

B-17F

BOMBARDIER'S AND NAVIGATOR'S COMPARTMENT

SIGNAL LIGHT BOX

HEATING AND VENTILATING DUCT

AMMUNITION BOXES

FIRE EXTINGUISHER

RADIO COMPASS CONTROL BOX

CARTRIDGE BOX

CHUTE

RADIO HEAD SET

RADIO COMPASS JUNCTION BOX

INTERPHONE JACK BOX

BULKHEAD No. 3

NAVIGATOR'S TABLE

RS-2 RACK SELECTOR RELAY

SILICA TUBE

BOMBARDIER'S PANEL EQUIPMENT

LOOP ANTENNA

PITOT TUBE

BOMB DOOR RETRACTING LEVER

ELECTRIC BOMB RELEASE

BOMB RACK CONTROL AND SALVO RELEASE

COMPASS

AMMUNITION BOXES

DRIFT METER

BULKHEAD No. 2

PORTABLE OXYGEN TANKS

OXYGEN REGULATOR

BOMBARDIER'S SEAT

BLACKOUT CURTAINS

50 CALIBER MACHINE GUN

CARTRIDGE CHUTE

BOMBARDIER'S PANEL LIGHT

BOMB SIGHT PLATFORM

OUTSIDE AIR TEMPERATURE BULB

BOMBARDIER'S WINDOW WIPER MOTOR

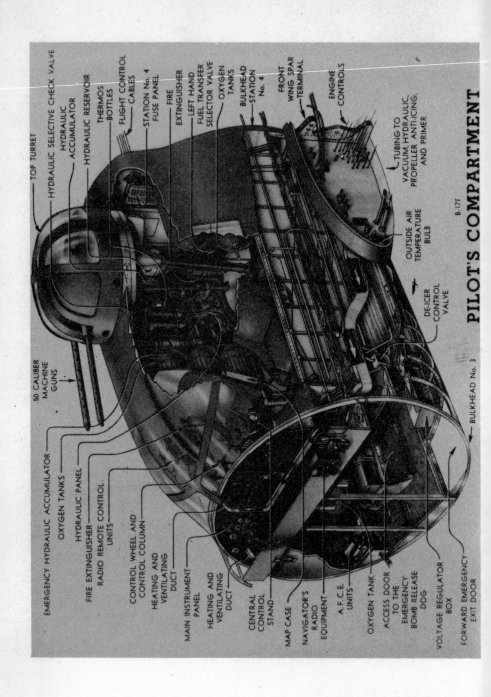

TOP TURRET

HYDRAULIC SELECTIVE CHECK VALVE

HYDRAULIC ACCUMULATOR

HYDRAULIC RESERVOIR

THERMOS BOTTLES

FLIGHT CONTROL CABLES

STATION No. 4 FUSE PANEL

FIRE EXTINGUISHER

LEFT HAND FUEL TRANSFER SELECTOR VALVE

OXYGEN TANKS

BULKHEAD STATION No. 4

FRONT WING SPAR TERMINAL

ENGINE CONTROLS

TUBING TO VACUUM, HYDRAULIC, PROPELLER ANTI-ICING, AND PRIMER

B-17F

OUTSIDE AIR TEMPERATURE BULB

DE-ICER CONTROL VALVE

BULKHEAD No. 3

FORWARD EMERGENCY EXIT DOOR

VOLTAGE REGULATOR BOX

ACCESS DOOR TO THE EMERGENCY BOMB RELEASE DOG

OXYGEN TANK

A.F.C.E. UNITS

NAVIGATOR'S RADIO EQUIPMENT

MAP CASE

CENTRAL CONTROL STAND

HEATING AND VENTILATING DUCT

MAIN INSTRUMENT PANEL

HEATING AND VENTILATING DUCT

CONTROL WHEEL AND CONTROL COLUMN

RADIO REMOTE CONTROL UNITS

FIRE EXTINGUISHER

HYDRAULIC PANEL

OXYGEN TANKS

EMERGENCY HYDRAULIC ACCUMULATOR

50 CALIBER MACHINE GUNS

PILOT'S COMPARTMENT

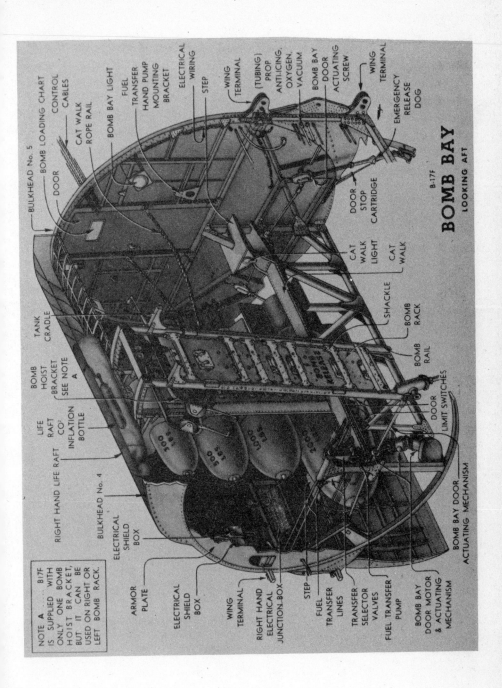

BULKHEAD No. 5
BOMB LOADING CHART
CONTROL CABLES
CAT WALK ROPE RAIL
BOMB BAY LIGHT
FUEL TRANSFER HAND PUMP MOUNTING BRACKET
ELECTRICAL WIRING
STEP
WING TERMINAL
(TUBING) PROP ANTI-ICING, OXYGEN, VACUUM
BOMB BAY DOOR ACTUATING SCREW
WING TERMINAL
EMERGENCY RELEASE DOG
DOOR

DOOR STOP CARTRIDGE

CAT WALK LIGHT
CAT WALK

SHACKLE

BOMB RACK

BOMB RAIL

DOOR LIMIT SWITCHES

BOMB BAY
LOOKING AFT

B-17F

TANK CRADLE
BOMB HOIST BRACKET SEE NOTE A
LIFE RAFT CO₂ INFLATION BOTTLE
RIGHT HAND LIFE RAFT
BULKHEAD No. 4
ELECTRICAL SHIELD BOX
ARMOR PLATE
ELECTRICAL SHIELD BOX
WING TERMINAL
RIGHT HAND ELECTRICAL JUNCTION BOX
STEP
FUEL TRANSFER LINES
TRANSFER SELECTOR VALVES
FUEL TRANSFER PUMP
BOMB BAY DOOR MOTOR & ACTUATING MECHANISM

BOMB BAY DOOR ACTUATING MECHANISM

NOTE A   B-17F IS SUPPLIED WITH ONLY ONE BOMB HOIST BRACKET, BUT IT CAN BE USED ON RIGHT OR LEFT BOMB RACK.

33

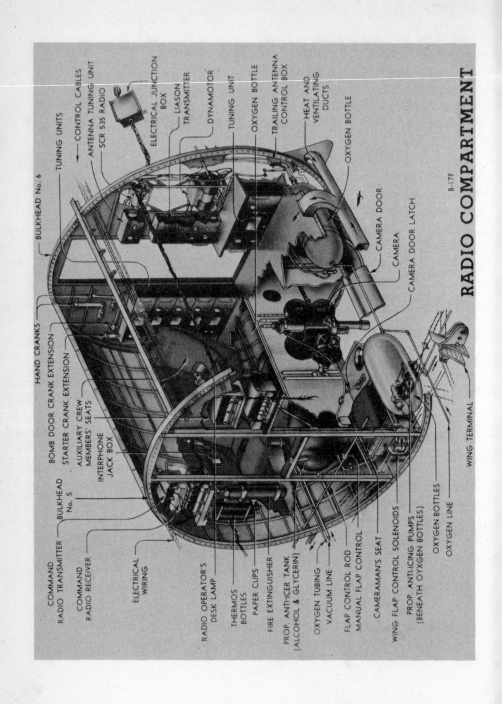

COMMAND RADIO TRANSMITTER

BULKHEAD No. 5

COMMAND RADIO RECEIVER

ELECTRICAL WIRING

BULKHEAD No. 6

TUNING UNITS

HAND CRANKS

BOMB DOOR CRANK EXTENSION

STARTER CRANK EXTENSION

AUXILIARY CREW MEMBERS' SEATS

INTERPHONE JACK BOX

CONTROL CABLES

ANTENNA TUNING UNIT

SCR 535 RADIO

ELECTRICAL JUNCTION BOX

LIASON TRANSMITTER

DYNAMOTOR

TUNING UNIT

OXYGEN BOTTLE

TRAILING ANTENNA CONTROL BOX

HEAT AND VENTILATING DUCTS

OXYGEN BOTTLE

OXYGEN BOTTLE

CAMERA DOOR

CAMERA

CAMERA DOOR LATCH

RADIO OPERATOR'S DESK LAMP

THERMOS BOTTLES

PAPER CUPS

FIRE EXTINGUISHER

PROP. ANTI-ICER TANK (ALCOHOL & GLYCERIN)

OXYGEN TUBING

VACUUM LINE

FLAP CONTROL ROD

MANUAL FLAP CONTROL

CAMERAMAN'S SEAT

WING FLAP CONTROL SOLENOIDS

PROP. ANTI-ICING PUMPS (BENEATH OXYGEN BOTTLES)

OXYGEN BOTTLES

OXYGEN LINE

WING TERMINAL

B-17F

RADIO COMPARTMENT

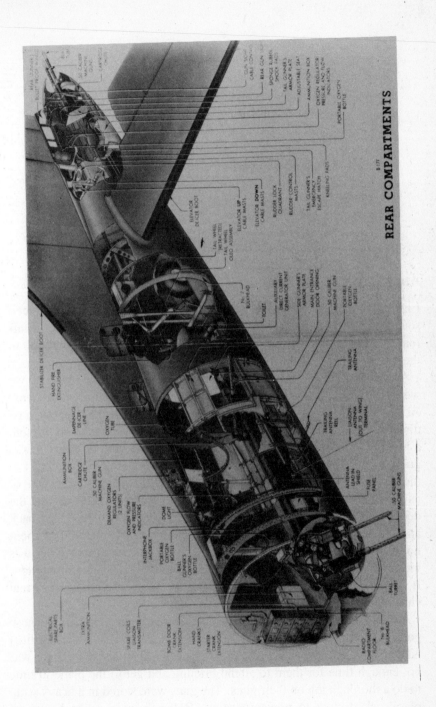

REAR COMPARTMENTS

B-17F

35

CHAPTER II

Mission to Brussels

August 10

I heard the Jeep stop outside a little after 2:00 A.M. I could never sleep soundly when I thought a mission was likely. I would listen to the far-off roar of aircraft engines and shiver at the thought of where we might go in the morning.

We had learned a lot from that first aborted mission, and this time we were ready when the officers arrived. Each Group had different systems. At the 381st they considered it to be more important for the gunners to go directly to the aircraft and get it ready for the mission than to sit through a briefing. Really, all we wanted to know was the kind of target it was going to be. The rest of the briefing information was of little interest to the gunners. We worked out an easy way to evaluate the target. One of us would stand outside the door of the Briefing Room. As soon as the doors were closed, the curtain covering the target map was pulled back and the reactions of the officers could be plainly heard; that told us about how rough the target was going to be. If an extra-rough mission was indicated, we wanted advance notice. One thing was extra ammunition. It was against regulations, but I wanted more ammo if there was any real chance we might need it.

At the aircraft we would get our own guns ready, then prepare the nose guns so that the Navigator and Bombardier had only to make the final adjustments and slip them into receivers when they arrived. There was not enough time for them to attend briefing and get to the plane in time to do a thorough job on their guns. The guns were stored in a heavy wrap of oilsoaked cloth to prevent rusting. Before a mission the heavy oil coating had to be removed because it might absorb moisture and cause the guns to freeze at high altitude. A light oil film was rubbed on for the mission.

The target for the day was Hamburg. The R.A.F. had firebombed it during the night and we were to increase the holocaust. We were flying as spare and would fill in if any ship had to abort over the North Sea. I had mixed feelings about bombing that city. I had once spent three pleasant weeks in Hamburg. I recalled the evening I was carried along by a crowd into one of Adolf Hitler's fiery rallies—but being warned there might be street fighting, I turned away at the edge of the crowd. At that time the name Hitler meant nothing to me.

No aircraft aborted the formation, so when we reached the turnaround point, Gleichauf headed back toward England. It was a long, wearisome trip and I was concerned that fighters might spot us. But the size of the invading formation pulled all of the German interceptors inland and we saw nothing but water. Again, there was no credit for a mission.

August 15—Brussels   *Aircraft 765*
                                        Nip and Tuck

It was a little after three the next morning when I heard the crunch of heavy shoes on the gravel walk outside. The lights came on and Lieutenant Reese roused us from sleep.

"Get up, you bastards! You're flying 765 with Gleichauf: Comer, Counce, Rogers, Abramo, and Wilson . . . Wilson!—Wilson!"

Wilson raised up in bed.

"Come on! Let's go—and Good luck!"

Jim and I went on ahead of the others and got out to the ship early. We had plenty of time to get the guns ready. When Gleichauf got to the aircraft he called us for a briefing.

"We're hittin' the port docks at Brussels today—it will be a short run. S-2 [Air Force Intelligence] says they have a hundred fighters close by and moderate flak, but very accurate. Ought not to be too bad. Any questions? OK. Let's climb in and get ready to go."

Major Hendricks, our Squadron C.O., was leading and we were flying as right wing in the second element of the lead squadron. As we headed out over the North Sea and the English coast faded from sight, several feints were made in fake directions and we returned to England and started over again. As early as 1943 the Allied strategy was to provoke Goering into putting his fighters up at the wrong time and at the wrong place. That would divide and reduce the interceptors that could attack us, and also force Germany to use up her precious fuel supply. The Germans did not have the vast oil resources of the Allies.

Surely, on our third attempt we ought to get a mission credit! How long was it going to take to get in twenty-five missions? But now clouds began to form heavily underneath the formation and halfway over the North Sea it became a solid blanket.

"Pilot to Bombardier."

"Go ahead, Paul."

"Can we drop in this soup?"

"No way—I think Hendricks will try an alternate."

"Navigator to Bombardier—I'm sure the alternate is covered, too. Don't think we're gonna drop anything today."

Oh, no! Not again! Would we ever manage to get in a mission? We had what seemed to be an easy one—and now! Three attempts and all that work for nothing! The rule for a mission credit was that the formation must do one of three things: fly the course all the way and drop on the target, drop on an alternate target, or engage the enemy in combat. The latter included encountering flak; however, it was never intended to include a sporadic burst or two I am sure.

"Navigator to crew—the lead ship reported flak! We've got us credit for a mission!"

"Bombardier to crew! Did any of you see flak? I didn't see any."

"Navigator to crew! Dammit, don't argue with the Brass! They're gonna give us a mission!"

"But there wasn't any flak, Navigator."

"Pilot to crew—if the C.O. says there was flak, you can be sure there was flak. Now don't raise any questions at interrogation." (The debriefing of the crews after a mission.)

That was the smart thing to do, of course. So—ring the bells! Beat the drums! We had a mission credit!

What a difference one mission made! We were now allowed to join in a conversation without someone saying, "What th' hell do you know about it?" I felt one hundred percent better because of that one mark on the mission tally board. We were lucky to ease into combat with sorties, because each time we had learned some valuable lessons, gained confidence, and increased the odds for surviving the first few real fights.

Only one of the eighteen crews that we trained with in the U.S. came with us to the 381st. The day after we arrived their navigator was pressed into service, because navigators were in short supply. We were all at the hardstand to meet him on his return, and were stunned to find that our friend was dead. It hit Carl hard because the nose of the plane was so vulnerable to heavy flak fragments or fighter projectiles. The ball turret operator on that crew was so badly wounded on the Hamburg raid that he will probably never walk again. But the worst was yet to come for Carl: two days later a navigator had his testicles shot off. Shutting never fully recovered from the trauma of that shock! He lived in deadly fear that it might happen to him! He persuaded the people at Armament to cut and shape some special armor plate to fit around his genital area. Holes were drilled in the edges so that it could be tied in place with four heavy cords. It took two men to assist in tying Carl's shield in proper position, and it became the matrix of his protective armor. Shutting was the only navigator in the United States Air Force with specially made genital protection armor plate. In addition, he placed two sheets of armor plate on the floor where he would stand at either gun.

The B-17E was being replaced with the B-17F, but a new crew could expect to be assigned one of the older, more undesirable airplanes. The main thing that bothered me was the small fuel capacity of seventeen hundred and fifty gallons, compared to the extra nine hundred gallons of the newer Forts. I hoped that whatever plane we were going to get, it would be soon. It would be better knowing what we would have to work with on a mission, than to draw a strange aircraft each trip.

On our first two sorties, I noticed that Gleichauf stayed on the Command radio frequency while Carqueville remained on the intercom to keep crew control. That freed Gleichauf to concentrate on formation flying, which used his experience to our best advantage. Paul let Herb take care of the rest. It was a good combination that worked out quite well.

August 15

Jim and I rode into Cambridge on the morning run of the supply truck, and started looking for bicycle and radio shops. There was no restriction on the sale of used items, and even new appliances could take on a used look very easily. We made our purchases and shipped the two bicycles to a nearby town by train. We carried the small radio. I doubt that any of us ever got more pleasure from a one pound investment ($4.13 each) than we received from the purchase of that radio. It made a big difference in our lives. We had the full range of the British Broadcasting Company, which offered excellent music and world news. We listened regularly to the Allied Forces Network that broadcast the things Americans wanted to hear. While in England we became aware of a young singer named Frank Sinatra.

Our radio introduced us to a new type of program—very interesting, even though it was pure propaganda. We soon learned when to tune in to the German English-language broadcasts. They had an announcer with an exaggerated British accent. His name was William Joyce, but he was called Lord Haw Haw. To a newly-arrived combat group at an English airdrome, he would beam something like this: "Welcome to the 381st Bomber Group at Ridgewell Airdrome. We wish you good luck and look forward to meeting you over the Continent very soon. By the way, please correct the clock at your Officer's Club. It is five minutes slow!" And sure enough, on checking, the clock would be five minutes slow! That left the impression that German agents lurked everywhere.

CHAPTER III

Mission to Le Bourget

August 16—Le Bourget Aircraft 765   *Nip and Tuck*

Soon after daylight the formation was crossing the gray-green water of the English Channel. My anxiety and tension mounted, as I knew we would face the fierce German fighters, for on this clear day we would invade the lair of Goering's best. The veterans had made certain we knew what usually happened to new crews on their first meeting with Jerry. They were not expected to come back—it was as simple as that.

The intercom came on: "Tail to Copilot, Tail to Copilot."

"Go ahead, Tail."

"Fighters five o'clock low."

"Ball to Copilot. Looks like the escort."

I spotted a long line of specks closing in fast from the north. It was the escort of fifty P-47 Thunderbolts. Good! I felt better because they could keep the enemy fighters away for a little while. However, the P-47s had a short fuel range, as the disposable belly tanks available at that time only held seventy-five gallons.

"Navigator to crew—Navigator to crew! Enemy coast five minutes away."

"Bombardier to crew! Watch out for fighters!"

Scared? Where do you draw the line between fright and intense nervous anticipation? Nothing in civilian life had prepared me for the feeling of kill or be killed. Our meager gunnery training was laughable compared with the skill and experience of the veteran German fighter pilots.

The briefing on the target earlier that morning kept turning through my mind: "We're hitting an aircraft plant at the edge of Le Bourget airfield—near Paris. The fighter opposition will be plenty rough! This is your first real taste of combat so—!" The Abbeville Boys meant Goering's personal squadrons, the roughest Germany had to offer.

When I saw the French coast pass by underneath, I became more tense and keyed up. We had been warned repeatedly that German fighters liked to lurk in the area where we would have to look directly at the sun to see them. They would attempt to slip in on us undetected by most of the formation gunners. It was my responsibility not to let it happen. From my turret I had the only unobstructed view of the sky above in all directions. George Balmore, in the radio room, could see part of the area above and to the rear.

"Bombardier to crew! Bombardier to crew! Fighters twelve o'clock low! Can't make out what they are, but don't look like 47s!"

I stood up in the turret, looked down, and counted twenty or more that could be seen from my position. They were German fighters, all right! The enemy pilots knew that the P-47s were at the end of their short fuel range, and were patiently waiting for them to turn back. In a few minutes the escort dipped their wings as if to say, "Good luck! See you in England tonight," and they were gone. I felt a knot in my stomach as the big Thunderbolts vanished to the north.

Immediately the enemy pulled up to our level and began circling to pick out positions for attack. Of course I was excited! It was my first time to see hostile aircraft in the sky!

"Copilot to crew! Throw the lead at those fighters if they come in!"

"Copilot to Turret."

"Go ahead."

"Keep your eye on those three fighters three o'clock high—I'll watch high and forward."

"Copilot to Tail. See anything trying to sneak in back there?"

"No, clear below and behind."

Suddenly Carqueville screamed over the intercom: "Fighter coming in twelve o'clock level—get him! Get him! Get him!"

I was tracking four suspicious fighters at nine o'clock and wheeled around just in time to get my sights on the fighter attacking us. It was headed straight for our nose spitting deadly 20mm cannon shells and 30 caliber machine-gun bullets. I was so fascinated by the sight that I froze! Did not fire a shot! Neither did the Bombardier nor the Navigator—the only other guns that could bear on a frontal attack! Light flashes from the leading edge of the fighter signaled how many cannon shells were being fired at us. I could hear some projectiles striking the airplane. It was a spectacle that drove deep into my memory. The fighter turned his belly to us and slipped into a beautiful barrel roll under our right wind and dived out of range.

Carqueville was boiling mad! He exploded over the intercom: "What th' hell's the matter with you sunnuvabitches? You're supposed to be gunners! Why didn't you shoot? That fighter could've knocked us down! You let one more come in like that and I'll personally work you over— all three of you!"

He was furious and he should have been, because there was no excuse for failure to fire. I have relived those traumatic moments many times, and I can still feel the mesmerizing power that prevented my hand from pressing that firing switch. Why didn't we fire? I will never know for sure. We were seized by the paralysis so typical of what happens to a deer hunter the first time he gets a buck in his gun sights (or the commandment "Thou shall not kill!").

The intercom came to life again. "Bombardier to Navigator and Turret: We blew that one! I don't know why but we did. But, believe me, it's not gonna happen again!" And it never did.

We were lucky to sustain that first attack with little damage, because the enemy had minimal opposition to divert his aim or tactics. There were three simultaneous attacks which cut down the fire that each fighter drew. The Germans were smart in choosing which way to come in, relying mainly on head-on confrontation. When several fighters attacked at one time the concentrated fire of the formation guns was divided, reducing the opposition to each fighter and disrupting the defensive tactics of the formation.

"Ball to crew—B-17 going down on fire four o'clock low!"

I looked down and it was sickening. Long streams of flame extended beyond the tail. I kept screaming to myself, "Why don't they jump? Jump! Jump, dammit! For God's sake, get out before it's too late!" But it was already too late. It was my first time to see men die in combat and it was a shattering experience. My stomach turned over at the thought of those ten men hurtling down to certain death. I wondered what flashed through their minds on that terrifying plunge to earth in their burning, spinning airplane.

Suddenly the Bombardier called out: "Flak nine o'clock low!"

"Ball to crew—flak at eleven o'clock low."

Huge puffs of black smoke began to burst around the formation. So that was flak! It was thicker than I expected, and a lot closer.

"Bombardier to Pilot—over."

"Go ahead."

"We're on the bomb run."

That meant the planes had to fly a straight and steady course for several minutes to provide a stable platform for the Bombardier and the Norden Bomb Sight.

Bam!

The ship rocked and I saw a nearby burst of orange flame followed by boiling, black smoke. I had been told that the crew would not hear the shells burst. Well, I heard that one! Mostly I saw only black smoke explode into large globs and heard pieces of shrapnel striking the aircraft whenever a shell burst too close. Flying through the floating smoke made the field of fire seem worse than it was.

One battery of guns below began to move in closer and closer. They seemed to choose us as their special target and were firing five 88mm shells at a time. As the bursts crept ever closer I could feel the hair on my head trying to push up against my helmet. All the German gunners needed to do was make one final correction, and they would have had us bracketed dead center.

"Radio to Copilot—can't we take some evasive action?"

"Hell no! We're on the bomb run."

I prayed a little, but who knows whether it helped or not. At the time, a man with a religious background felt that it could help, and in that sense perhaps it was useful. Later, when I looked back on such moments more rationally, I wondered why I believed that through the mysterious phenomena we call prayer the Supreme Being could be induced to alter the Laws of the Universe—His Own Laws—just for me. Was I some special favorite? Was anyone praying for the protection of the innocent people who lived and worked too close to where our exploding bombs were landing? How strange and paradoxical for men to pray selfishly for their own lives, while doing everything in their power to kill other men, who in turn perhaps were praying to the same God.

I was suddenly jolted back to the urgency of the moment as I heard, "Bombs away!" The unexpected upward lurch of the aircraft, as the bomb weight fell away, startled me momentarily. As we turned left away from the target, I got a glimpse of several columns of smoke rising from the bombed area.

"Pilot to Tail."

"Go ahead."

"Did we hit the target?"

"Where we hit looks like factory buildings—don't know if that was our target."

I dropped down out of the turret just long enough to have a quick look at the fuel gauges, and got a shock when I saw that we only had a third left. After hasty calculations of probable consumption going back, with the aid of letting down from high altitude, I felt that we could make it back to Ridgewell.

"Copilot to crew—Copilot to crew. Stay alert! They may hit us goin' back. Turret!"

"Go ahead."

"Put on your sunglasses and watch that area around the sun. We don't want them slippin' in on us."

Ten minutes later: "Fighters ten o'clock low!"

"What are they doin', Ball?"

"Only two of 'em—not tryin' to come in."

"Bombardier to Navigator."

"Go ahead."

"When are the Spitfires due?"

"In about ten minutes."

Some time later. "Ball to crew—ten fighters six o'clock low—could be Spits."

"Navigator to crew: I think they're Spitfires, stayin' low to keep the Jerries from gettin' to us."

The Navigator was right because no more Bogies climbed up to our level. Before long I could see the gleam of sun on water up ahead and I began to relax because we had our mission almost made. As soon as we were over the Channel, the likelihood of another attack faded out.

At Ridgewell Airdrome, nine happy men climbed out of aircraft #765. Jerry was better than we expected, and flak was much worse. Regardless of our initial failure, we had met the enemy and returned safely . . . something many new crews failed to do.

The tenth man out of the plane was the Copilot, but he definitely was not happy. He was still fuming about our miserable performance on that first fighter attack. Carqueville glared at me, and stalked off without a word, but I got his message: "I expected more from you! Of all the people on this crew, I didn't expect you would screw up on your first combat action!"

After a plane returned the crew was not through. A truck carried the men to Operations for interrogation. Hot coffee, hot chocolate, and Spam sandwiches were waiting, one of the few times Spam ever tasted good! All of the crews gathered in the waiting room and milled about, swapping stories and checking up on other crews' versions of incidents. The Colonel was there, looking the men over:

"Nice going, Jim."

"Good formation, Lieutenant."

"Nice shooting, Sergeant."

If he spotted a man who looked shaky, he often patted him on the back with some remark to boost him up. Colonel Joseph Nazzaro was a fine Commanding Officer. He had the respect of the men in his command. The Colonel was from a military family, but no typical brass hat. He was the quarterback on the 1933 West Point football team that lost only one game—7 to 6 to Notre Dame. (He later became a four star general and succeeded General Curtis LeMay as head of the Strategic Air Command.) The Colonel was my idea of what a combat commander should have been. I never heard one bitch about him from anyone in his command that made any sense.

In our Group Interrogation Room the atmosphere was loose and free from any kind of restraint. Here the complete picture of the raid was placed on paper. No one crew could see everything accurately, so the final group picture of the mission was composed from the data supplied by various crews. Often there were new items to report which set in motion the network of Air Force Intelligence (S-2) which was constantly striving to stay ahead of the enemy. A new defensive weapon or method was pounced upon as soon as it showed up, in an effort to find the best counter-method before the Germans had time to exploit a temporary success.

If a gunner thought he had shot down a fighter he had made his claim at the interrogation, where the briefing officer could get confirmation from other gunners who might have seen the incident. Wilson was positive he had badly damaged a fighter.

"What kind of fighter was it, Sergeant?" asked the interrogation officer.

"F.W. 190, an' I got in three heavy bursts. I could see 'em hittin' it an' pieces flyin' off."

"Well, Sergeant, the enemy fighters who intercepted us today were all M.E. 109s with liquid-cooled engines. The F.W. 190 has an air-cooled engine, but the only fighters today with air-cooled engines were our P-47s—did you hit one of them?"

"Oh, no! I'm sure it wasn't a P-47 . . . I—uh—maybe there wasn't as much damage as I thought. I—uh—withdraw the claim."

Balmore said, "Go ahead with your claim, Wilson. Maybe you can get credit for downing a P-47."

It was after interrogation that fatigue really hit me. But the day's work still was not over. Wearily, we went back to the aircraft because the guns had to be cleaned and checked for worn parts, and stowed in oilsoaked cloths. They must be ready for another raid the next morning in case one was scheduled. It was twilight when I got back to our hut. Total exhaustion, such as I had never experienced before, so numbed me that I did not bother to go by the mess hall or take the time to wash. The long hours since the call at 2:30 A.M., the debilitating rigors of high altitude, the intense cold, and the wearying fatigue from fear and tension combined to hit me hard. I literally fell into bed, with part of my clothes on, and in two minutes was oblivious to everything, including the noise and hubbub of men coming and going.

After that first combat experience, I realized a peculiar phenomenon of the mind: it is more traumatic to listen to a factual telling of a hair-raising experience than actually to go through the same thing yourself. The difference is that when listening to such a story, one has no escape mechanism. However, when living through a harrowing experience, the mind is too occupied with defense and physical actions to provide full accommodation for fright.

Originally I had some reservations about Nick Abramo, because the ball was so important to the crew. Hanging down there all alone, cut off from the rest of the aircraft, was an unenviable position. By the time we got back from Le Bourget I was satisfied that we had a reliable man guarding the approaches to our plane from below. I guarantee that no other man in the crew would have voluntarily entered that risky, cramped, overexposed contraption. The ball required the knees to be brought upward on each side of the Sperry Computing Sight. Over a long flight the gunner became uncomfortable due to the inability to stretch out his legs to relieve cramped muscles. He was more exposed to the fury of bursting flak shells than anyone else on the aircraft. Almost three quarters of the ball hung suspended in space, creating a horror of exposure from which there was no protection.

Unknown to the bomber crews, the English and American Air Commands were at odds over the basic concept of how to conduct the air offense against Hitler-held Europe. In August 1943, the skies offered the only path the Allies could use to reach the heart of Nazi territory.

The R.A.F. was certain that night saturation bombing of industrial centers was the best method. The Americans were equally convinced that for them, with the more heavily armed B-17s, daylight strategic bombing of selected targets (by virtue of their importance to the German war machine) was a better use of men and machines. True, the R.A.F. certainly had far more war experience, and had tried daylight raids early in the war with disastrous losses. Their night bombing was built around the excellent Lancaster Bomber, which was fast, long ranged, and carried

47

a heavier load of bombs than the B-17s. It was lightly armed, however, and not very rugged. The R.A.F. system was to send over fast target-marking planes early in the night to outline the target area with incendiary bombs that would glow brightly for hours. The Lancasters followed, one at a time, avoiding German fighters under the cover of darkness. Such tactics resulted in a saturation type of destruction hoping to hit war plants, cripple the cities, and demoralize the German workers as well.

The Americans favored the use of rugged, heavily armed bombers at high altitude because they would be above the worst flak and the effective ceiling of some of the older German fighters. They thought that the highly accurate Norden Bomb Sight would permit pinpoint accuracy of bombing against Germany's most vital military targets. The American view was that on night raids so many of the bombs fell outside the main target area that their effectiveness was doubtful, as far as reducing the German capacity to produce war materials.

Based on their own experience with daylight bombing raids, the R.A.F. commanders were sure that when the American bombing fleet became strong enough to begin daylight raids deep into Germany, the losses would be so disastrous that they would be unacceptable. On one night of bombing, however, the R.A.F. lost ninety-six Lancasters! So what was an acceptable loss?

General Ira Eaker, Commanding Officer of the 8th Bomber Command, was getting ready to put the high-altitude strategic bombing concept to a series of crucial tests. At a secret meeting in North Africa, President Roosevelt had given way to Prime Minister Churchill's argument that night bombing was the best use of Allied aircraft.[1] But Mr. Churchill, in a meeting with General Eaker, gave him a little more time to prove the American bombers could invade heavily defended targets deep inside Germany (where we had not yet attempted to raid). The implication was that if those test raids failed, the American Air Force would begin a shift to the English night raid concept.

Our crew went on combat status ten days before the first of those really decisive missions was scheduled. In other words, we had arrived in England at the worst possible time of World War II for a bomber crew.

---

[1]As explained in *Decision Over Schweinfurt,* by Thomas Coffey—David McKay Co., Inc.—New York.

The conference was in January and General Eaker was anxious to make good on his promise to the P.M. But he had an unexpected blow: some of his Groups were transferred to the North African invasion. So he had to wait several months for more aircraft. Meanwhile the 270 single-engined fighters available to meet the Fortresses over Europe in early April increased to over 600 by the end of July.

CHAPTER IV

Schweinfurt #1

THE BALL-BEARING PLANTS

August 17

It was to be one of the most storied air battles of this or any other war.
Some critical pages from my journal did not survive. The pages where I
recorded the names, pilots, and aircraft numbers of the men in my hut
who were on that raid were lost. In my early days in England I could find
no writing paper of the size I needed, so I had to use the back sides of
bulletins or other printed sheets. At that time I had not procured cover
binders to hold these sheets together, so several pages somehow got
away. Thus, I had no record of which men from the Gleichauf or Cahow
crews were on the mission. The only men I was sure of were Jim Counce,
Carroll Wilson, and Buck Rogers. In addition, Purus, Shutting, Abramo,
and George Reese may have been involved. All of these men were flying
as spare crew men where such were needed to fill in. Jim Counce wrote
down quite a few notes for the journal and all of them are included.
Therefore I decided that the best way to get across to the reader what
happened was to take a writer's privilege and tell the story in the first
person, covering the highlights of the action. This is a composite from the
accounts of the men of both crews as they told it after the mission.

An ominous groan came from the Briefing Room. I knew then we were
in for a rugged day. We were still groggy from the mission of the
previous day, and not in the best physical condition. "The crew I was
assigned to had a great deal of experience. They were all strangers to me,
and I'm sure they would have preferred having a more experienced

gunner. The radio operator cornered me and offered me some advice. 'We got a peculiar pilot,' he said. 'He's tops when the going gets tough, but he has the habit of cursing the gunners, and raising hell over the interphones. When fighters attack he will call you every kind of sunnuvabitch he can think of. He don't mean a damn thing by it—nothing personal. It's just his way of keeping his gunners under control. After the mission he won't remember a word he said, so don't let it upset you.' '' (From an account by James Counce written for me the day after the raid.)

The weather was so foggy that I doubted we would get underway, or if we did get off, it would be mid-morning. When the pilot arrived, he called us together. ''All right, men. We're in for a wild one today! We're hittin' some ball-bearing plants at a town called Schweinfurt in Bavaria. The route will force us to fly over the middle of Germany, goin' in and returning. Those plants make more than half of Germany's ball bearings, and if we destroy 'em, our raid will be a success—even if only a few of us get back.''

There was an audible groan from the crew.

''The altitude will be 23,000 feet and we will try to divide the opposition. The Third Division will go first, hit Regensburg close by, and then fly on to North Africa. The other two divisions will hit Schweinfurt and return to England. Let's hope the plan works, 'cause if we don't fool 'em we could see three to four hundred fighters. The First Division will lead the attack on Schweinfurt and the 91st will be in front. The 381st will fly the low group position.''

The hated word ''low'' prompted more comments and considerable bitching because the low group always caught the worst attacks.

''Knock off the bitching! This is gonna be one hell of a raid, and I don't want to see one Goddamned round of ammunition wasted! You gunners hear me? Not one wasted round! You'll fire only when the enemy is close enough to hit, and only when they're attacking our plane! We gotta make that ammo last, and don't you forget it!''

Either Hitler's military staff, or the influential Albert Speer, had become alarmed at the continuous build-up of American bombers, and the prospect of an increasing flow of new bombers from U.S. factories. Unknown to the Allied High Command, General Adolf Galland, commanding the German fighter defense, had pulled back some of his crack fighter groups in France. He had also withdrawn some air units from the Russian Front to form a better defense system. Until then he had a fighter defense protecting Northern Germany, but little behind it. Now the Germans placed reserve forces strategically about Germany so they could battle the Fortresses coming into and going out of the Fatherland. The

General felt that he could make the penalty so costly for deep daylight bombing missions that the Americans would be forced to give it up, an opinion shared by the R.A.F. Command.

The weather overcast hung doggedly on, but Colonel Curtis LeMay's Third Division managed to get airborne and the mission was on. The air historians and writers emphasize the Third's ability to get off in the soupy weather. LeMay said it was because he made his pilots practice instrument takeoffs. I doubt if the Colonel could have made successful instrument takeoffs that day with the number of inexperienced pilots we had in the 381st Group. The aircraft would have been so scattered when they came out above the bad weather that too much fuel would have been used up to continue so long a fight. The distance was close to our maximum range.

When takeoff time came, the fog blanketing the area was even more dense, so we waited, and waited, and waited, and were almost sure the raid would be scrubbed. As the minutes ticked away, the hoped-for advantage in dividing the fighter interception was slowly eroding. By the time the fog decreased enought to take off the Third Division must have hit the target at Regensburg and no doubt was on the way to North Africa. Instead of helping, by dividing the fighters as expected, it had alerted the German Fighter Command to an all-out battle.

On the climb upward the fog began to break at about one thousand feet. By 1030 hours the 381st was in the air. The formation converged quickly and headed for the Continent. Little time was wasted with feints, and they were up to twenty-three thousand feet altitude approaching the German border. A few minutes beyond the border an unexpected layer of heavy clouds blocked the path. A formation could not fly into clouds, so Colonel Gross, commanding the First Division, had a tough decision to make. He had three choices, none of which was desirable. One, he could pull up over the cloud cover to 27,000 to 28,000 feet, but the target might well be covered by the same clouds when he got there. Two, he could switch to an alternate target, which would upset all the planning and action already underway. Three, he could go under the cloud bank between 17,000 and 18,000 feet, giving the Germans an unusual advantage. That was the choice he decided to take. There was much criticism of his decision later, but those so quick to blame him were not up there that day, faced with an immediate choice from the hard alternatives open to him. Colonel Gross was in an extremely difficult position. Based on his possible choices, I think most Commanders would likely have made the same decision.

The formation descended to 17,500 feet and plowed steadily on into

German airspace. For a while we had an escort of R.A.F. Spitfires, followed by fifty P-47s. They were of little help because of their limited fuel supply. The interceptors were waiting, fired up and ready. The lower altitude was very much to their advantage. The fighting characteristics of the F.W. 190 and the M.E. 109 were extra good at 17,000 feet. They had two other hefty advantages: one, they had more fuel for attacks—two, they could reach the bombers faster after takeoff.

For ten minutes after our fighters left, nothing happened. Then the Ball Turret called out: "Ball to crew—Ball to crew! Fighters at eight o'clock low! Looks like about seventy of the devils!"

They came rushing up to intercept us and before long the low group was surrounded by a swarm of snarling fighters. They appeared from all directions and quickly showed their intention of a "give no quarter" battle. They just came in and kept on coming in. The German pilots were intense in their attacks and paid little attention to their usual cautious tactics. Attacks were from all angles during the run to the target, but the high nose attack seemed to predominate. At times it looked like the entire Luftwaffe was lined up at twelve o'clock high. The outcome was very much in doubt. The Jerries gave no thought to personal safety in their zeal to teach the Fortress crews a devastating lesson. Fighter losses were high but if ten of their planes went down in flames it seemed like twenty more came up to take their places. Every time two or three fighters were knocked down, a Fortress would go too. "The plane flying on our left wing was hard hit, lost control, and went down. I did not see what happened to the crew. A little later the plane on our right caught fire and exploded. For this kind of fight we had the right pilot. He flew like he had the controls of a fighter craft. He was throwing the ship up and down and from side to side in wild lunges, as the fighters roared in for the kill. The Germans were trying to finish off this squadron before exterminating the next one. There is no question but that we were extraordinarily lucky. It was a combination of a wild pilot doing things not usually done in a formation and pure luck—whatever that is—that kept us from extinction. Evasive action helped, but I wondered what it was doing to the formation." (From the account of Jim Counce.)

Colonel Hall, Operations Officer, said that one hour from the target he was not sure that any bomber would reach the objective.

Much to our surprise, enemy planes were waiting for us all along the briefed route with mathematical precision. At the time, we thought someone had talked too much, not realizing that we were encountering a new fighter defense in depth for the first time. "I remember distinctly how the pilot cursed and screamed at us over the intercom, exhorting us to stay on the ball,'' Counce recalled. '' 'Left Waist! You see those bastards at ten o'clock high? Watch 'em! Here they come! Shoot the sonnuvabitches! Kill them! Blow their asses off! Knock 'em down!'

'' 'Right Waist, you no good sonnuvabitch. I've told you a hundred times not to shoot when they can't hit us. Dammit, that fighter was rolling away from us.'

'' 'Crew! Crew! If you keep on wasting your ammunition we'll be out of ammo before we get to the target! Goddamn it, don't shoot 'til you can hit th' bastards! Don't waste one single round. You think some damn ammo truck's gonna fly up here an' give us some more bullets? Watch your ammo!'

''A few minutes later: 'Get those three bastards eleven o'clock high! Shoot! That's it—blow 'em out! Don't let 'em hit us!'

''The pilot kept telling us, over and over, that when a fighter quit firing at us to forget about him, and concentrate on the one that was coming in next. He said. 'Don't waste any Goddamn attention tryin' to confirm claims for some gunner. Keep up the fire when they come in, an' catch th' next one—hit 'em while they're comin' in—foul up their aim.'

''A plane flying near us was hit and caught fire. The flame streamed beyond the tail, and down it went. Likely no one got out. About twenty minutes later, as we crossed over the Rhine River, the Squadron lead plane lost an engine. A little later a second engine began smoking. The plane dropped back, and the tail gunner reported that three fighters finished it, but he saw three parachutes.

''The intercom came on, and a shaky voice said, 'I'm scared! I want my mama!' ''

Jim reported the following conversation from the aircraft he was in. ''Navigator to Pilot! Aren't we out of formation?''

''Out of formation? Can't you see we're the only one left in the squadron?''

Jim continued: ''The enemy fighters were trying doggedly to finish us off, and the pilot was taking heavy evasive action. It threw me all over the waist and my ammunition flew out of the ammo cans and got fouled up. Once we almost collided with a fighter, but they didn't get us. We maneuvered over to a squadron still in fair shape. One plane was throttle-jockeyin'—fallin' back, catching up, fallin' back. When it fell back too far, we sat down in its place. A few minutes later I saw that ship catch five fighters, and down it went.'' That may sound ruthless and coldhearted, but if someone ahead of you was hit and got out of tight formation and then began to straggle, it was accepted procedure to move right into his place.

Our route in was slightly west of Koblenz, where the Moselle River joins the Rhine. At the time the Germans probably guessed that Frankfurt was our target. By the time we had passed that city they must have realized with great anxiety that the bombers were headed for their most essential war plants—the bearings factories at Schweinfurt.

"Navigator to Pilot."

"Go ahead."

"You can see Wurzburg ahead and a little to your right. We'll make a ninety degree turn to the left and be on the bomb run in five minutes."

There was another flurry of attacks, and then I saw bursts of flak nearby.

"Bombardier to Pilot, we're on the bomb run."

"OK, Bombardier."

The flak was moderately heavy. The fighters kept away, as always, when we went through the field of fire approaching the target.

"Bombs away!"

We breathed a sigh of relief that we were rid of that weight. The group had sixteen aircraft left at the halfway point. Suddenly, either a rocket or a flak shell made a direct hit on one of our Forts nearby, and it blew up.

Right after the target, fighter activity slacked off, and I mistakenly thought the worst was over. North of Frankfurt they hit us with one of the heaviest attacks of the day. The 381st was losing one plane after another. I thought the fighters would leave us soon and take on the incoming Second Division. There were plenty of fighters, however, to handle the Wings going in and coming back.

The pilot was listening to every burst of fire and keeping up his unending harangue: "Keep watchin' that ammo! We're gettin' closer. Make that ammo last a little longer. Dammit, we're gonna make it! The worst is over!"

A little later we lost another B-17. Several others were in serious condition. Suddenly, I realized that the fighters were fading away. I was well aware that we didn't have much ammo left. Was it really over? Or were we due for another mauling? A great feeling of relief swept over me as the minutes ticked off.

Jim said that he looked around at the 381st and tried to count the losses, but he did not know how many ships the group put up to start the mission. From what he could see, his guess was twelve to fourteen missing, but that did not mean all of them were lost.

When the coast slipped by I felt mighty good. We definitely were going to make it! Troubles for the 381st were over, I thought—but not quite:

one of our aircraft was in serious trouble and dropped down, down. Just before we reached the English coast it hit the water.

"Ball to Copilot."

"Go ahead."

"Beautiful ditching below us—I can see the crew climbin' out. I think they'll be safe this close. Air-Sea Rescue oughta find 'em before dark."

Carroll Wilson said after the mission:

"The coast of England had never looked so good, and the white chalk cliffs were a welcome sight. We began to let down and those miserable oxygen masks came off. How I hated those masks!"

It was approaching dusk as we set down at Ridgewell Airdrome. A weary and beaten crew climbed out, thankful that they were privileged to get back. All of the aircraft were damaged, many quite heavily. The 381st lost eleven out of twenty-four aircraft and one plane aborted, the highest loss of any group. The leading 91st Group lost ten ships.

Interrogation was long and detailed. Official claims contended that the target was half destroyed. In truth, something like thirty-five percent of the capacity to produce bearings was destroyed.

The 8th Bomber Command had taken a frightful, shocking loss. Sixty B-17s shot down! Twenty-seven other Fortresses were damaged too severely to be repaired. Another blow dealt us at this time was the incredible failure of Air Force planning to coordinate the facilities in North Africa with a reasonable expectation of the need for repairs. Colonel LeMay found, to his amazement, that the only service he could get would be refueling![1] There were no available parts, and no mechanics to repair the heavy battle damage his division suffered—which was comparable to our own.

The combined Schweinfurt-Regensburg casualties were:

60 B-17s shot down—16% of the total force
27 Damaged too much to be repaired
60 B-17s left in North Africa due to no facilities for immediate repairs (what eventually happened to them I do not know)
147 Total Aircraft

Morning brought a severe letdown in morale. At breakfast very few men showed up. The long rows of empty tables took away my appetite. Only yesterday men were crowding in line waiting for seats. That day there were too many unoccupied seats. The usual chatter and banter was

---

[1]The only account I have seen about this incident was in *Decision Over Schweinfurt*, by Thomas Coffey.

absent. Men ate in silence and left quickly. I found myself looking around for faces that I knew I would never see again. What about the future? Was yesterday a preview of what we could expect? That question hung heavily over Ridgewell Airdrome on the morning of August 18.

It seemed to me that it would be a week before we could get enough replacements to make up the minimum requirements of a Combat Group. Nevertheless, that evening I made a trip to the base canteen to check out the faces. The people I looked for were there, so that meant nothing was shaping up for the next day, as I read the signs. The men who loaded the bombs were called Armorers. If none of them were at the canteen we knew that bombs were being loaded and made mental preparations for the next morning. Many times last-minute weather changes would make raids possible. Three favorable conditions had to exist simultaneously: visibility over the target had to be fair, local conditions had to be favorable for takeoff, and visibility had to be assured for landing a large group of planes on the return.

The Americans and British had a decided advantage over the German weather forecasters, because of the Allied weather stations in Greenland and Iceland. The weather forces that determined what conditions would prevail over Europe developed in the Arctic regions. It was helpful to be able to tie in the long-range forecasts with on-the-scene reports from Allied weather planes sent out over the target areas. Also of great value was the Turing electronic machine. It quickly unscrambled the German military and diplomatic code, and could read the German weather reports broadcast to their military and air units each day.

The 8th Air Force officially claimed 288 German fighters were shot down on the August 17 Schweinfurt-Regensburg mission. The R.A.F. throughout the war was positive that American claims were grossly inflated. I certainly agreed. There was really no reliable way to determine accurately the number of aircraft shot down. Probably one-third would have been closer to being correct.

The problem in claiming fighters shot down was that it was rare when only one position fired at a fighter. Sometimes twenty guns were involved and in a few cases as many as fifty. At times several gunners thought they shot down the same fighter and put in claims for it, so the claims ballooned. Also, enemy fighters were so heavily armored that they could shake off heavy hits and keep coming.

At the command headquarters General Eaker's staff that morning pondered deep and searching questions. What was the lesson learned at Schweinfurt? Had the R.A.F. been correct in their predictions about daylight Fortress raids deep into Germany? The General, very likely, reached two conclusions: one, the Fortresses could battle their way to any target in Europe regardless of German all-out opposition; two, the Bombers must have long-range escort fighters to hold the losses to an acceptable figure when making deep thrusts to well protected targets.

The questions were: What fighters did we have that could go with the B-17s to distant targets? When could we get such fighters delivered to England? The proposed new modified P-51, with Merlin Rolls Royce engines, was not released yet for full production. As far as we knew, the only other fighter with enough range was the P-38 Lightning. Was the P-38 a match for the excellent M.E. 109s and F.W. 190s? The P-38 was a good fighter, but not great, and I'm sure the General wanted something better. We, the bomber crews, knew nothing of Bomber Command's urgent appeal for long-range escort. We would have slept better had we known how strenuously they were pleading with General Arnold, in Washington, for immediate help.

After the Schweinfurt showdown the Colonel no longer had to exhort his experienced pilots to stay in tight formation. Those who got back had learned a lesson they would never forget. They saw what the Jerry fighters did to "throttle jocks." There were a number of reasons why a tight formation was so essential to standing off German fighter attacks. A bomber could not concentrate much fire power against a fighter except on tail attacks. The Germans knew that, so they mainly hit with a frontal charge. A single Fortress could bring to bear only three guns on a head-on attack (the nose gun and the two top turret guns). The navigator could fire only if the attack was approaching at an angle to the nose. The top turret guns could not be brought down quite level, so a German fighter charging straight in at the nose could sometimes get under the trajectory of the turret, leaving only the Bombardier's single gun to oppose him. (When the B-17G model was brought out in October of 1943 the single nose gun was replaced with two guns in a chin turret and the navigator side guns were eliminated.) That meant three 50 caliber machine guns versus four 20mm cannon and two to four 30 caliber machine guns—quite an unequal match-up if the fighter was opposed by only one B-17. (German fighters, varied in the kind and amount of armament.) So the chief defense factor was a large number of guns from adjoining aircraft, exceeding the fire power of the attacker. The tighter the formation was, the more fire it could bring to bear against the enemy. Even so, the Bogies had armor plating protection around the engine and cockpit, which cut the chances of our 50 caliber projectiles getting to the pilot and the most vulnerable parts of the aircraft.

Attacks from the rear were infrequent because very early the Jerries learned that to attack a B-17 from the rear was not the way to remain alive and healthy. First, the lethal tail guns were assisted by the top turret, the ball turret, and sometimes the radio gun. Second, the fighters overtaking the bombers had a slow rate of closure. That meant the B-17 guns could begin firing at one thousand yards and do a lot of damage before the Germans got close enough to fire their cannon, which had a shorter range of six hundred yards. Thus, a tight formation was the ultimate defensive tactic of a bomber force beyond the range of fighter escort.

That night Jim said to me, "Do you remember that time when we were flying alone over the mountains and number one engine burst into flame?"

"Sure, I remember it. We didn't know enough to realize it was highly dangerous. We know now."

"If it happened tomorrow the whole crew would be rushing to the nearest escape hatch."

That incident did not disturb us a bit. Herb calmly retarded the throttle, then opened it up and sucked out the blaze as if it were an everyday occurrence. But I would never again remain calm with an engine fire. I had seen what happened, and how fast, after engines caught on fire.

August 18

For the first month at Ridgewell the mental strain of not knowing what to expect with the dawn of each new day was severe. No amount of training, and especially the kind we had, could prepare one to step from a sheltered civilian life to the chance he would face death, or an injury even worse, in the next twenty hours. All of a sudden my priorities had undergone a traumatic shift. The small anxieties I used to worry about seemed so trivial. Did I once worry about making my sales quota? Or about paying the monthly bills? How absurd! It boiled down to revising my mental priorities to accept a new way of looking at things—a new mental attitude that would have been alien and totally unacceptable six months ago.

I turned to Balmore: "George, I've begun to study the men with the most missions, and I can see some common characteristics among them."

"Like what?" asked Wilson, who came awake long enough to hear part of the conversation.

"Well, the best way I can explain it, they act like they don't give a damn what happens! Haven't any of you noticed that?"

"Now that you mention it, yes. Some of 'em do act that way," replied Nick.

"Is it an act? Or do they really feel that way?" asked George.

"My guess is it starts out as an act—a sort of front to mask their real feelings—then they work themselves into a mental state where they really don't worry much about tomorrow. It's the old philosophy that you can make yourself be what you think you are. I guess that's what we need to copy. I remember that General Pershing once said that when he wanted his best troops he went to the guardhouse and let them out."

"The men who raise enough hell do let the tension work off," said Rogers.

"Well, I know for sure, cautious civilian thinking isn't going to work over here. I don't know how much I can change my mental outlook—or how fast—but I am starting to try right now."

After making my decision, I began consciously to try to drive out contrary thinking. "Why worry about tomorrow? There is no tomorrow—there is only today. Quit thinking about tomorrow or next week or next month. You can't control what will happen tomorrow, so why spend the precious time you have today worrying about it? The only time you have for sure is now. Today is real. So forget what the future may bring and learn to enjoy to the fullest extent what you have now. When life is threatened, each hour becomes more irreplaceable. Today you are alive and well, so be grateful. For all you know this may be your last day! Don't ruin it by morbid forebodings of burning airplanes and horrifying plunges out of the sky. To hell with tomorrow!"

I began to grope my way slowly, with twists and turns, and a few detours, to controlled thinking. I went a good way toward that objective during my stay in England but it was during another tour of combat duty, in a different area of the conflict, before the process matured, and a combat raid for me became just another day at the office (15th Air Force, Foggia, Italy—50 missions).

I think the best soldiers in combat develop a mystic feeling of immunity to death. Sure enough "others all around me may get it, but the bullets and shrapnel will miss me! I've got this special thing going for me. What special thing? I have a strong feeling I'm going to make it, no matter how hopeless it seems, or how rough it gets."

On days we weren't flying, we tried to find things to do to fill the idle hours. I began keeping a record of the things we did, and included some of our conversations. I kept detailed accounts of our raids, gathering together eight or ten men—some of them from different aircraft—going over what happened after each mission. I gradually began to record not only the combat raids, but what went through the minds of men under combat stress. There also developed for me a new pleasure in simple things. When the continuity of life was threatened, the reality of what life was became clearer. After all, one achieves an exalted state of existence only at rare moments. The rest of life is the daily sequence of one small insignificant thing followed by another. If one stands aloof waiting for another mountaintop experience, and fails to find zest in the small matters that comprise most of life, he or she will miss a majority of the best life has to offer.

CHAPTER V

Mission to Gilze-Rijen

August 19—Gilze-Rijen   *Aircraft 003*

I heard the Jeep stop outside and that surprised me, because I was so sure we could not mount a mission with our recent heavy loss of aircraft and our damaged planes.

Counce bounced out of bed. "I thought you said we wouldn't go out for another week."

"I didn't think we could! How many ships can we put up?"

"Not more than one squadron 'til they get some more patched up," Nick Abramo answered.

"I'll bet they're puttin' together a force from two or three groups," said Wilson.

An annoying sensation plagued me some mornings. I shook and shivered while dressing. Was it the early morning cold, or just my nerves? By the time I was on my way to the mess hall the shakes were gone.

I saw Gleichauf at Operations before briefing. "We're goin' to have an extra passenger along today," he said.

"Who we takin'?"

"Lieutenant Cohler, one of the Flight Surgeons, will be riding with us in the nose."

"Good idea! They need to know what it's like."

Jim and I got to the plane early. Only the loud stutter of the small engine operating the electric generator broke the silence. The crew chief had finished his daily inspection and was asleep in the cockpit. Soon other men arrived and the sounds of clanging metal and hand charging reverberated through the aircraft.

Buck Rogers was not with us. He was badly shaken up on the Schweinfurt raid, and was now in the hospital. He suffered internal injuries from the severe bouncing he took in the tail of the plane during heavy evasive action. Buck was probably a little too old for combat gunnery, although he was a tough guy. A new man, Raymond F. Legg, from Anderson, Indiana, had replaced Rogers for the time being on the tail guns. Legg came from a rural area. He was twenty-one years old— quiet, good-natured, steady, and a nice looking young man. I liked him on first sight, but how he would do on the tail guns was yet to be seen. That day was an ideal mission to break in a new man.

Balmore was grounded again with frostbite, and an operator named Brophy was with us in the radio room. It was almost time for the officers to arrive, when it suddenly occurred to me that Wilson was missing.

"Has anyone seen Wilson since we left the hut?"

"I thought he was gettin' up when I went out the front door," Counce said.

About that time a truck stopped and out climbed Wilson, not overly concerned about being late. He arrived just ahead of Shutting.

Paul gathered us into a circle to hear the briefing. "The target today is Gilze-Rijen, in Holland. Not too bad! We will put up three composite squadrons made from two groups. We will have fighter escort all the way in and out. Flak will be moderate to heavy. We could see some fighters, so don't get the idea that this is gonna be a milk run! The Germans have two hundred fighters close enough to intercept. This is Lieutenant Bernard Cohler, one of our Group Flight Surgeons. Lieutenant, you'll fire the right side nose gun. Jim, show the Lieutenant what he needs to know about the gun."

Shutting turned to Cohler. "If you have any trouble with the gun, let me know quick, an' we'll switch guns."

What a contrast to our last raid! This one showed promise of being a snap. The 381st furnished one squadron, and the other two came from the 91st Group. I did regret that I had to participate in a raid against the Dutch and their lovely country. Years before I had spent some pleasant days in Holland. How unfortunate that it happened to be located between Germany and the North Sea!

The formation got underway after a long, drawn out flight across England in an attempt to confuse the Germans. The fighter escort was to meet us a little short of the Dutch coast. Not much fighter action was expected in view of the escort protection and the short time over enemy territory.

"Radio to Turret. Radio to Turret."

"Go ahead."

"Something wrong with my oxygen regulator."

"What th' hell is it this time? You radio jocks always think you got oxygen trouble!"

"The gauge wiggles."

"Wiggles? Are you sure you're sobered up from last night?"

"I'm perfectly sober—the thing flutters—wiggles."

"I think you're imagining things. How do you feel?"

"I feel OK."

"If you feel good, don't worry about the gauge. You're gettin' enough oxygen, or you'd know it."

"Turret to Waist."

"Go ahead."

"Keep an eye on Brophy. Can you see him from where you are?"

"I can see him."

"If he shows any signs of trouble go take a look, quick."

"OK. We won't be on oxygen very long today, anyway."

When it was fairly certain that the mission would not be canceled, I called Purus. "Turret to Bombardier."

"Go ahead."

"Are you ready for me to pull the bomb fuse pins?"

"Yes, I think so—go ahead."

So I took a walk-around oxygen bottle and went back to the bomb bay and pulled the pins out of the bomb fuses. That meant that when the bombs fell out, an impellor would quickly spin off (caused by the wind), leaving the striker pins free to hit on impact with the ground and trigger the explosion.

"Turret to Bombardier."

"Go ahead."

"The bombs are armed. Rack switches are on."

"OK, Turret."

The flak started coming up as we approached the coast. Lieutenant Cohler had a ringside seat for some close-up views. I knew how he was feeling, seeing it for the first time. That plexiglass sure looked agonizingly thin when the shells exploded.

"Bombardier to Pilot."

"Go ahead."

"We're on the bomb run."

It soon became obvious that the bomb run was too long.

"Pilot to Bombardier."

"Go ahead."

"Why the hell didn't we drop?"

"Don't know, Paul. Either his position was off or the Sight wouldn't line up. We're starting a three sixty."

"We'll be twenty minutes coming around for another run. If we fool around over this target they'll get some fighters up here."

A few fighters had been reported flying low and to the left. I suppose that some silly new gunners became confused and cut loose at the 47s thinking they were 190s. The escort immediately retreated to an altitude well above our fifty caliber range. Twelve to fourteen 190s saw the opportunity and slipped in under the escort and raced toward the formation.

"Copilot to crew! Copilot to crew! Fighters eleven o'clock high—comin' in! Blast 'em! Shoot th' hell out of 'em!"

I could see my tracers hitting the first one but he kept right on coming. Lieutenant Cohler had the excitment of a head-on attack, and one fighter whizzed by him so close that the pilot's bright red scarf could be plainly seen. The formation leader was shot down, and I saw two more Fortresses explode and go hurtling toward the ground far below. Lieutenant Alexander, one of our squadron pilots, was a lucky man that day. A 20mm cannon shell ripped through the cockpit side window, brushed him lightly on the head, and zoomed out through the other side without exploding. Unbelievable!

I could hear Legg firing from the tail, and twice I zipped around to see what the action was back there. He looked like he was doing all right from what I could see.

"Bombardier to Pilot."

"Go ahead."

"We're on the bomb run again."

"Hope we drop this time!"

Three or four minutes later: "Bombs away! Let's go home!" from Purus.

I felt the load release, and the formation made a left turn and was soon back over the North Sea.

The next morning Balmore was at the station hospital and overheard the men kidding Lieutenant Cohler about his "mission." One of the orderlies said, "Lieutenant, how was it yesterday? Rough?"

The reply was, "Yeah, it was rough all right, but you sonnuvabitches will never know how rough!"

The opposition on our last mission was the Fock-Wolfe 190. Most B-17 men considered it Germany's finest fighter at that time. It performed well between twenty and thirty thousand feet. On balance I thought the

P-47 and F.W. 190 were evenly matched on a plane-to-plane basis. The 47 was superior above thirty thousand feet, and I thought the 190 was better from about twenty-two thousand and lower. The advantage the 47 had as an escort aircraft was in tactics. It could fly high above the formation and swoop down with an altitude and dive advantage when the 190s attacked the Forts. The way it worked out, the F.W.s had to become the aggressor and run the risk of being attacked, while the P-47s became the defensive force and could choose their time to attack when they had a height advantage.

On August 20, the loudspeaker on the base came on in the middle of the morning. "All combat personnel report to Operations—all combat personnel report to Operations." It continued at intervals—every fifteen minutes.

On the way to Operations there was much bitching among the crowd.

"Why can't those Operations nitwits leave us alone?"

"Another one of those aircraft recognition classes! I know what a 190 and 109 look like!"

"They keep us on alert all th' time, an' on a day we don't have to go out they gotta dream up some horse shit to look good on their reports to headquarters."

At Operations there was gloomy silence until we were all assembled, and then we didn't really believe what we heard. "This is goin' to be a real surprise! We're giving every combat man a four-day pass, and we'll have personnel trucks ready to leave at 1:30. We'll take you to the outskirts of London where you can catch a tube into the city." When the cheering died down, the voice continued: "You men need some free time—now is our chance to give you four days off while we get our damaged planes repaired. This pass will be mandatory unless excused by the Flight Surgeons."

Someone in the crowd said, "But some of us are broke! Hell, we can't take off for London with no money!"

"We thought of that. The Finance Officer is standing by to issue an advance on your next pay, for all those who need it."

The whole thing was organized superbly. The Command obviously wanted all of us away from the base, away from the empty tables at the combat mess, away from the empty bunks in the huts. They wanted us to rid ourselves of whatever tensions had built up inside. Someone at headquarters was smart enough to know that the best therapy was a big blast—a wild weekend that would let it all come out. Those in charge were concerned about the morose attitudes and glum faces after Schweinfurt.

There was a scramble to get ready, but no man in the 381st was going to be left behind when those trucks took off. We were in London before dark, and the celebrating got off to an early start. We took full advantage of our good fortune for we might not get another four-day pass for a long time.

London was an exciting place to be in 1943. Throngs of men, far from home, were seeking pleasures of various kinds, trying to find some escape from the stifling military confinement. The area along the Strand and near Trafalgar Square was especially crowded. There is a statue of Admiral Horatio Nelson on the square, along with two huge stone lions, one on each side of the Admiral. According to legend, the lions roar whenever a virgin passes, which is not often.

When the drinking establishments opened to provide the stage for the evening festivities, downtown London was crowded with men in many kinds of uniforms. From open doorways one could hear snatches of lusty songs from groups well along with their drinking. Although the nightly blackout was strictly enforced, up and down the streets there would be the flare of a cigarette lighter so some soldier could get a look at a girl standing in a darkened doorway. From those doorways there was a lingering odor of cheap perfume that attempted to camouflage the need for a bath. Soap and warm water were rare luxuries in wartime England. There were swarms of men walking arm in arm, sometimes fifteen abreast, headed for some bistro. Here and there one could see a soldier and a girl walking along, perhaps toward her room in some shabby hotel or flat. Would the soldier discipline himself to hunt up a pro station at 3:00 A.M. or run the risk of a venereal disease?

By 10:00 P.M. the favorite bars of the soldiers were crowded and getting wound up. The noise was deafening but no one minded. There was camaraderie and loud talk, but seldom any brawls. Soldiers swapped favorite tales and enjoyed a few hours away from military confinement. Then someone with a commanding voice would get up and pound for attention, and start singing:

"Roll me over, in the clover,
Roll me over, lay me down,
And do it again."

And the favorite barroom song of wartime England would roll on and on. There were endless stanzas, and each participant could make up his own. The singing would go on until the singers grew tired.

During the war years drinking establishments in England were rigidly regulated. At the nighttime closing hour, soldiers were just getting started. To circumvent the restrictive hours, private clubs opened up. One of those was the Bazooka Club, near the Strand and patronized mainly by the R.A.F. An English friend sponsored Jim, George, and me and I do not recall any other American members. That place became a favorite and convenient hang-out for us when we were in London. The club was a lively place. The members were mainly connected with Allied Air Forces. There were Australians, South Africans, Canadians, and a small number of men from the Free French and Free Polish Air Forces. Those nationalities mixed surprisingly well, and many pleasant evenings were spent swapping tales with the men who manned the Lancaster Bombers or flew the Spitfires. One night I was with three R.A.F. men at the Club. One of them asked me, "You Yanks really think you tagged out two hundred and eighty-eight Jerries on your ball-bearing raid?"

"No," I replied. "We probably got a hundred, maybe a few more. The claims get duplicated."

"Those Jerry chaps don't scratch out easy, ya know."

"You're damned right they don't! All that armor plate! Say, what's it like up there all alone over a German city at night? I think it would scare the hell out of me."

"Some nights it's a piece of cake—some nights it's a rough show!" said one.

"The worst time is when we get caught in those searchlights! We are stone blind until we get clear of those bloody lights."

One man turned to a handsome young chap, with blonde hair and a curling mustache. "Bill, tell him about that night you fell out of the open hatch."

Bill wasn't eager to talk about it, but after some persuasion, he began: "We were in a Wellington Bomber, ya know. The rear entry hatch cover becomes part of the walkway through the waist. I was operating the wireless when we flew through some flak and took a bit of a hit mid-ship. It banged the craft around, ya know, and the pilot called me to take my torch and see if the control cables were OK back there. I picked up my torch, but the thing wouldn't light up. I stepped back into waist, flicking the switch, and dropped out into bloody space. The flak had knocked off the hatch cover! I grabbed the rim of the hatch with one hand and hung on—no parachute, you know."

"You mean you were hanging out in space with one hand?"

"I couldn't get a good grip with my other hand, and I knew I couldn't hang on very long. The wind blast was terrific. My mike was still snapped on 'cause we have a long cord, but I couldn't talk, just gurgled and made choking sounds. The pilot heard those funny noises and rushed someone back to see what was wrong. He followed my mike cord back to the hatch, and grabbed me just before I was slipping off. It took two blokes to pull me back into the aircraft. A bit of a show, ya know!"

The temperature in the room that night was about fifty degrees, but Bill's forehead was dotted with big beads of perspiration as he recounted, for my benefit, his frightening experience. I never heard a more hair-raising tale throughout the war.

The last night of our four-day pass was a real bash! It must have been 4:00 A.M. when we hit the sack. By the time we got up the next morning it was too late to find any place open that served breakfast.

"Why don't we go back to the club?" George asked. "Maybe they'll have some doughnuts or pastries left over."

There was no intention to start drinking so early in the day, especially on an empty stomach, but one round wouldn't hurt. That was how it began and before long we were off on a super bender until it was time to leave for Waterloo Station and get a train back to Ridgewell. I did not recognize my condition until I took a few steps, and everything went blank. George and Jim had matched me drink for drink all day, but those were the only men I have ever known who never showed any visible signs of intoxication. Big George picked me up and staggered down the stairs and got us into a cab. At the huge Waterloo Station, he managed to get me through the crowd and aboard the train, avoiding the Military Police.

August 21

George had a good friend, a radio operator named Feigenbaum, who came from New York, not far from where the Balmores lived. "Feig" spent a lot of time in our hut because of Balmore. He had a companion we called "Brooklyn," and the two were always together. They paired off well: Feig was the comic, and Brooklyn was his straight man. Together, those two could entertain a barracks for hours, with just normal conversation. Feig had an unusually husky voice with an inclination to stammer. He loved to stumble in at two in the morning and wake up the entire hut to tell about his date. Anyone else would have had practically everything in the hut thrown at him, but Feig was in a class by himself.

The day after our last sortie, Balmore came back from Operations, visibly shaken.

"What's wrong, George?"

"I can't believe it—I just can't believe . . ."

"What can't you believe? What is it?"

"They say Feig got a direct hit in the chest with a twenty millimeter—gone instantly!"

"Oh, my God! Not Feig! His first mission?"

"Yep, his first lousy mission! John, I can't believe a man like Feig will never be around any more. Just last night he was here in the hut with us!"

George was low for several days and we all had Feig on our minds, for he was an unforgettable man.

August 22

That morning Gleichauf and Carqueville came by our hut shortly before noon and gave us the latest news. "We've been assigned 765. It's not too bad as B-17s go," Carqueville said.

"For an E model, it's OK. It's about as good as we can expect," I answered.

"That's right. New crews don't get the choice aircraft, John," Gleichauf added.

Herb suggested that we take a good, hard look at the aircraft and see what we could do to improve it.

"OK, Jim and I'll get to work on it right away."

The E Models held only seventeen hundred and fifty gallons of fuel, while the newer planes could take on nine hundred more gallons with the addition of the Tokyo tanks added at the far ends of each wing. On long missions we would have to sweat out the fuel consumption, knowing that the leaders would have another nine hundred gallons to play with and might forget about us jokers dragging up the rear.

August 23

That damp night at the hut we were talking about combat crews and how they got together at the various training centers in the States.

Tedesco asked, "You and Jim been together since gunnery school?"

"Longer than that," Counce answered. "We first met at the Boeing Aircraft Engineering school at Seattle."

"But how did you get assigned to the same crew? That's a hundred to one chance," Tedesco insisted.

Jim said, "It wasn't chance. It was an unusual situation. We were at Gowen Field at Boise, Idaho, for assignment to combat crews. One day Comer and I got to wondering if they had made up crew lists yet and we decided to find the chief clerk and see what he would tell us. The chief was a decent guy, so I asked him, 'How do they go about assigning engineers to combat crews?'

" 'Oh, the Head Engineering Instructor does that—two of you to a crew.'

" 'You mean there will be two engineers on every crew?'

" 'That's right—a first engineer and a second engineer.'

" 'What's the difference?'

" 'The first fires the top turret and gets another stripe. The second fires a waist gun.'

" 'When will they start assigning us?'

" 'Maybe the engineers are already paired off. What are your names?'

" 'Comer and Counce.'

"He looked through the pile of papers and pulled out a sheet.

" 'All right, here you are. Both of you are on this list. Go ahead and look at it.'

"John and I were both listed as first engineers.

" 'Well, what do you think about your second engineer?' I asked John.

"He said, 'He won't be worth a damn. I don't want to be on any crew with him—what about you?'

" 'Look who they put with me! The lousiest gunner in the class at Vegas, and a screw up along with it!'

"I turned to the chief clerk. 'Could you—uh—accidentally switch names and put both of us on the same crew?'

" 'I guess I could—I doubt if anyone would notice it—but if I did . . .'

" 'If anyone did notice, it was only a typing error—right?' I cut in, and we both took out a five-dollar bill.

" 'Sure. Just a typing error. These new clerks we got here are always goofing things up. Which one of you is going to be first engineer?'

"I said, 'Want to flip for it?' John won the toss and we slipped the chief the two fives."

CHAPTER VI

Mission to Villacoublay

August 24—Villacoublay *Aircraft 765*
Nip and Tuck

I was awake when I heard the Jeep outside. As usual, it took some effort to get Wilson out of bed, but the others were up quickly. At Operations, the sound from the Briefing Room were mixed, so I had no clear idea what to expect until the pilot arrived.

"Here's the deal for today. We're hittin' an aircraft workshop factory at Villacoublay, which is south of Paris. The altitude will be twenty-five thousand and the temperature forty below. An escort of P-47s will go halfway to the target. You know that Jerry has his best fighter groups protecting the Paris area, so we can expect a hot reception. Keep a sharp lookout and start firing as soon as you can reach 'em—hammer at 'em all the way in—louse up their aim."

I turned to Jim. "It's gonna be a balmy day in th' waist—only forty below. Imagine that!"

"Damn, I forgot my shorts!"

"I hope those red and yellow nose bastards don't show today."

"If they do, start prayin'," Nick said.

"They're no meaner than those checker-nose devils," added Balmore.

No words could adequately express our admiration and appreciation for the American escort pilots. Few of us in the 8th Bomber Command would have escaped either oblivion or a prison camp in 1943 without their help. Bad news about crews we knew at Boise and Casper kept seeping through, which highlighted the fact that we had been lucky so far. So when I saw those escort fighters approaching, I said to myself, "Thanks for your help—I hope I see you at the pub tonight and can buy you a drink.''

George was back with us in the radio room and I felt better, because he was the best I knew at that position. Balmore had two phobias: one, aircraft fires; two, oxygen troubles—some of it purely imaginary. I knew in advance that on every mission he would find something wrong with his oxygen system.

Soon after takeoff Gleichauf went on intercom: "Pilot to crew—I forgot to tell you that we are the spare today. We will trail the formation at high left. If no one aborts before we reach the coast of France, we turn around and come home.''

The bomb load was thousand pounders, which I liked better than the five-hundred pounders. They were heavy enough to fall out if the release shackles operated at all. Sometimes during that period bombs remained hung-up in the racks. Bomb-rack malfunctions were common with the E and F Models but were rare with the later G models. When there was a hung-up bomb or two it was my signal to go into the high-wire bomb-releasing act on the ten-inch catwalk between the radio room and the rear cockpit door. Two vertical supporting beams halfway between the two doors restricted the walk-through space so severely that it was almost impossible to get through it wearing a parachute. So I had to work on the narrow walk without a chute; it was like a high-wire performer with no safety net. Oxygen supply was from an unreliable walk-around bottle good for four minutes with no bodily exertion or excitement that could double the need for oxygen. An oxygen failure on that open walk, with nothing below but five miles of air, was something I tried not to think about.

The formation came together on time and turned toward the English Channel. We were flying parallel to a higher group that was behind the 381st, so we could spot an abortion quickly. Suddenly I caught a glimpse of something white floating by. I whirled around too late to see what had happened. There was a parachute with no one in it. Pieces of wings, tails, and fuselages littered the sky. Where there had been several aircraft a moment before, there was nothing but empty space and falling debris. I caught a brief glimpse of one ship going down. The fuselage had torn off flush with the trailing edge of the wing. All four engines were still running and the ship was revolving rapidly, like the way a rectangular piece of paper will do when released in the air. It was a nauseating sight. Forty or fifty men were wiped out in a matter of seconds. I saw another ship emerge below in one of those flat, Flying Fortress spins. A B-17 when out of control often went into a shallow circling descent that was neither a dive nor a spin, as we normally use those terms. I saw it so often that I coined the word ''flat spin'' to describe it. My first reaction was that fighters had slipped across the Channel and jumped us from out of the sun when we weren't expecting them. I searched the sky wildly for some sign of enemy aircraft, and noted other turrets doing the same thing.

''Copilot to Turret—do you see any fighters?''

''No—nothing above us. It must have been an explosion.''

''Copilot to Navigator, did you see what happened?''

''No, I was looking to my left—didn't see a thing 'til it was all over.''

''Copilot to Ball. Nick, what's happening down below? How many planes were lost? See any chutes?''

''Air's full of pieces and parts of planes! There were four or five that got it! All but one broke up. I see three chutes.''

''Oh, Lord! Five ships and only three chutes?''

''That's all I see. They're goin' to land in the water, an' the rescue boats are already headin' out to pick 'em up.''

''Copilot to crew—Copilot to crew. Four or five ships were torn up, we don't know why. Either an explosion or collision. Stay calm! It wasn't caused by fighters.''

Whatever caused the tragedy, I wondered if it could have been avoided with better disciplinary control of the group. The puzzling part of the catastrophe was that we were flying very close to the planes that were lost, yet we had felt no concussion or unusual air currents. In a few minutes the remainder of that group aborted and returned to their base.

Ten minutes from the French coast, Shutting called the Pilot, ''Paul, Paul!''

''OK—go ahead.''

''There's a wing ship at three o'clock in the second element pullin' out!''

''I see it.''

A few minutes later we dropped down into that vacant position.

''Bombardier to crew—flak, nine o'clock low.''

''Flak, eleven o'clock high.''

The fire was moderate and caused no damage.

''Radio to Turret—Radio to Turret.''

''Go ahead.''

''Something's wrong with my oxygen!''

''What's th' problem?''

''I don't feel good.''

''Turret to Waist—Jim, go take a look at Radio's regulator.''

Counce was back on intercom quickly. ''Nothing's wrong with your

73

regulator, Radio. I think you imagine you're not getting enough oxygen and are breathin' too heavy. Relax! Breathe normally an' you'll be OK.''

"Tail to crew—escort catching up with us—high at six o'clock.''

"This is the Navigator—they sure look good to me!''

"Bombardier to crew! We're gonna need 'em real quick. Bogies at eleven o'clock low, comin' up!''

The P-47s had numerous clashes with F.W. 190s trying to get to the formation. I counted ten enemy craft that might have been shot down. I didn't know for sure unless I saw a fighter explode or the pilot bail out. If any of them crashed, we were too far from the scene by that time to see the impact.

I wonder if there has ever been a sight—show or drama—as thrilling as watching a series of dog fights between good pilots, with all of them aware that death awaited the losers. It was such a fascinating sight I sometimes forgot briefly that I was a part of the drama. At times I almost felt like it was a highly realistic war movie in which I was a bit player.

"Navigator to Pilot—over.''

"Navigator to Pilot.''

"Navigator to Copilot.''

"Motion Paul to get on intercom.''

"Go ahead, Navigator, this is Paul.''

"Five minutes to the I.P.'' (Initial point.)

"OK.''

Several minutes later Shutting called the pilot again. "There's the I.P. down on the right, about one o'clock.''

"I see it—hard to miss the Eiffel Tower.''

"Navigator to Bombardier.''

"Go ahead.''

"On the bomb run in three minutes.''

"Ball to Copilot.''

"Go ahead.''

"Flak—six o'clock low.''

The Tail called, "Flak—five o'clock level.''

Wham!

That burst was mighty close! Then four more bursts—all close. The aircraft was now on the bomb run and had to fly straight and level. Another four bursts were so nearby I could hear the shell fragments strike the aircraft hard!

"Copilot to Waist.''

"Go ahead.''

"Anybody hurt back there? Any serious damage?''

74

"Some good-sized holes behind me—not serious—so far."

That flak battery of four guns had us in their sights and were bursting salvos all around us. Each salvo crept closer.

Bang!

The ship rocked and pitched from the concussion of the nearby shell explosion. They weren't far off target—that was certain! I grudgingly acknowledged and admired the accuracy of those German gunners so far below. When I could hear the "whoosh" sounds of the shell bursts and see the orange flame in the center of the explosions, that told me they were getting much too close! For the second time German flak gunners had us so well targeted that they needed only one more very small correction to lay that salvo right on us.

"Bombs away!"

That was always sweet music to my ears.

"Radio to Bombardier."

"Go ahead."

"One bomb's hung up in the bomb bay."

"Turret to Bombardier—I'm goin' back and try to release it."

"Hold your position, Turret. We can't drop that bomb 'til we get clear of French territory," said the Copilot.

Recently a new ruling had been posted forbidding any plane to jettison bombs or equipment over occupied Europe. There was a left turn and a wide circle and we were heading back toward England.

"Ball to crew—three fighters four o'clock low—190s, I think."

"Copilot to Tail."

"Go ahead."

"Can you see the fighters?"

"No, they're outa my view."

"Can Waist see the fighters?"

"Left Waist to Copilot—cannot see them."

"Ball to Copilot—they're comin' up from underneath."

I heard the ball gun open up with one heavy burst after another. In a little while the firing stopped.

"Tail to Copilot—I see those fighters now—they're droppin' down an' away."

"Tail, this is Nick. They changed their minds when four Balls opened up. I hit one of 'em real good. One broke off without firing."

I expected a sharp clash with the red and yellow nose meanies near the target, but they failed to show. I knew we would meet them somewhere before long.

"Bombardier to Copilot."

"Go ahead."

"Fighters one o'clock high."

"Navigator to crew—could be Spitfires—they're due right away. Be careful!" The Spits looked like 109s at a distance.

As soon as we identified those sleek R.A.F. beauties, the ones mainly responsible for saving England from Goering's bombers in the Battle of Britain, I felt certain we had no more worries about fighters for the day. The Spitfires were beautiful airplanes in the sky and deadly to tangle with. Their R.A.F. pilots were veterans of countless sky battles. The Spitfire was designed to meet German bomber attacks over England. They could land, rearm and refuel, and get back in the air rapidly for the next wave of bombers. Large fuel tanks were not needed and would have been a handicap for the fighting over Britain. The small fuel tanks, however, reduced their effectiveness as escort aircraft.

"Ball to crew—flak ten o'clock low."

"Tail to crew—flak six o'clock level."

It turned out to be light and inaccurate. The formation began a gradual letdown as soon as we neared the English Channel.

"Turret to Bombardier—I'm goin' back and release that bomb."

"OK—need any help?"

"No, don't think so."

On the catwalk I discovered with relief that the stuck bomb was in an easy position to reach. With a long screwdriver I tripped the shackle that held the bomb and it tumbled out. I watched until it struck the water with a gigantic splash, then returned to the cockpit.

"Turret to Bombardier. Bomb bay clear, you can raise doors."

"Thanks, Turret—Bombardier to Radio."

"Go ahead."

"Are doors comin' up?"

"Doors are up."

The 381st didn't lose a ship that day, but some other groups behind us caught it much rougher.

There was a famous B-17 that took part in the raid on Villacoublay. The *Memphis Belle* was the first American aircraft to survive twenty-five missions. Its crew was the first combat crew on a B-17 to fly twenty-five missions over Europe. The World War II movie *Memphis Belle* was filmed partly in England. It played up the Villacoublay mission, and one scene showed wounded men being lifted from B-17s at the end of that raid. The movie helped to sell war bonds and became popular during the war period. The *Memphis Belle* and her crew flew back to the U.S. and toured the country in support of the War Bond Drive.

At interrogation many questions were asked about the horrible tragedy that wiped out four or five planes. The next day the official version was released. Two B-17s were caught in a propeller blast, due to a sudden shift of position of a lead ship. That meant the air turbulence, created by that unfortunate move, caused two pilots momentarily to lose control of their aircraft. I could visualize their frantic efforts to avoid a collision, and the helpless feeling they had as the wind blast forced them together. When they collided there was a violent explosion that wiped out two other aircraft close by.

On August 25 new B-17Fs with their crews arrived and were assigned to the 533rd Squadron. They were indeed welcome because the squadron was under strength, which kept all crews on constant battle call status. We were happy to see the new men, but even more delighted to get the new Fortresses, with their increased fuel capacity and better performance.

August 28

Carroll Wilson was the number one goldbricker I knew in the Service, and I knew a lot of accomplished ones. But he had a redeeming quality to balance it. He had the natural ability to con people into things the rest of us could never have managed. In the States we would send him to the Orderly Room for passes because he rarely failed to talk them into it. But there was one incident in which Wilson was the principle actor that topped all of the ludicrous stunts I saw in my Air Force years.

The Bomb Sight incident began one morning when we were in crew training at Casper, Wyoming. We took off to let the Bombardier do some practice drops with a Norden Bomb Sight. Soon after takeoff the oil pressure on one engine dropped off too much and we returned to the base to have a relief valve replaced. Now the Norden Bomb Sight was guarded with elaborate security. The Sight was the cornerstone of the high-altitude concept and elaborate means were taken to insure that it did not fall into the hands of the enemy in time for it to be duplicated and used against us. Bombardiers were held responsible. When Purus checked out a Norden Sight for a practice flight he was required to wear a .45 automatic and keep that sight under surveillance at all times.

When Herb landed the aircraft and pulled onto the hardstand I saw right off that the crew chief was alone. I told him the bad news. "I'm afraid we're gonna have to replace a relief valve on number three engine. You want me to start taking it out while you go get a new one?"

"That would speed things up. I oughta be back in twenty to thirty minutes."

When the crew chief took off for Aircraft Supply, Herb asked, "How long we going to be tied up?"

"Forty minutes to an hour," I answered. "We'll have to run up the engine and check out the pressure after the valve is changed."

Herb turned to the other men. "Come on, let's go to the club for coffee. We have plenty of time and we don't need to hang around here."

Purus shook his head. "I can't go, Herb. I've got to guard this damn Bomb Sight."

"Aren't you a commissioned officer? Well, order one of these sergeants to guard the sight while we're gone."

Purus hesitated. "I don't know . . . well, I guess it would be all right. Here, Wilson, buckle on my forty-five and stand where you can see the sight up in the nose at all times. Don't let it out of your vision—and *no one* is to enter this aircraft 'til we get back. And remember, this gun is loaded! Be careful!"

I was working high on an engine repair stand with my head up behind the engine most of the time. A few minutes later I looked down and saw Wilson practicing fast draw with that forty-five.

"Wilson! Put that gun back in the holster! You know better than to play with a loaded gun!"

He meekly agreed to do so. Five minutes went by and I glanced down. He was at it again!

"Wilson, you're gonna kill someone! Put that gun where it belongs!"

I felt someone tap my foot and looked down. There was one of the sight technicians I had seen at the bomb-sight vault several times when Purus checked out a Norden Sight.

"Sergeant, we got an inspection due today on the sight you're carrying. How long will you be here?"

"Another thirty minutes, I guess."

"Good! I'll have the sight back in less than thirty minutes."

"Don't talk to me! See that Sergeant with the gun? He's in charge of the sight. Talk to him about it."

I went back to work and assumed he cleared it with Wilson. In a few minutes I had to come down for a tool and could see the technician in the nose of the plane, removing the sight. He was clearly visible through the plexiglass, and I saw him leave the aircraft carrying the Bomb Sight and walk off close enough to Wilson that I thought sure he saw him.

I heard the rest of the crew returning. When Purus looked up at the nose of the plane his face went white.

"Wilson!" he screamed. "Where's the Bomb Sight?"

Carroll whirled around and stared in utter disbelief at the gaping, empty space in the nose, where the sight should have been. His mouth popped open and he went into shock. He couldn't say a word—just blabbered incoherent sounds. That was when I realized that Wilson didn't know where the sight was.

Carqueville ran over to me. "John! You must have seen something! Where's the Bomb Sight?"

"No idea," I said, "I was busy and had my head up in the engine nacelle. How could I see anything?"

Stark tragedy had suddenly struck Purus and Carqueville! They had succeeded in losing the Air Force's top secret device. A prison sentence was altogether possible. The crew chief returned just in time to catch the last of the act. He glanced at me, saw that the sight was in safe hands, and said nothing.

Purus turned his fury on Wilson. "You stood there and let someone walk off with the Norden Sight!" He was almost hysterical. "Don't you know what that means? The Germans would pay a million dollars for that Norden Bomb Sight!"

Carqueville sat down on a box and buried his face in his hands. I heard him muttering, "Why couldn't I get nine sane men like the other pilots do?"

Wilson finally recovered his voice. "I only looked away for five seconds—whoever got it had to work mighty fast!"

Balmore yelled, "Hey! Isn't that someone carrying a Bomb Sight?" He had spotted the technician who was now about forty yards from the bomb-sight vault.

"That's him! Catch the sonnuvabitch! Don't let him get away! Catch him!"

All nine of them took off like the Keystone Kops after Charlie Chaplin. It was a scream to watch! Wilson was leading the way, determined to redeem himself, waving the forty-five and yelling, "Stop, you sonnuvabitch! Stop! Or I'll drill ya!" Even Carqueville put on a burst of speed that amazed me.

When the unfortunate man heard all the commotion he turned and was astonished to see a madman flourishing a lethal forty-five and eight more hostile men bearing down on him. He started to make a run for the safety of the vault, but realized he couldn't make it carrying the heavy sight.

"Hands up! Hands up!" screamed Wilson, and he leveled the gun as if to shoot. The technician quickly put the sight down and raised his hands. They swarmed over him and pinned him to the ground and held him there.

"We got him! We got him!"

Our brave men had captured the dastardly spy! Attracted by the noise, five or six men from the vault ran quickly to the scene, and from the distance I saw the man get up and several men help brush the dirt off of his clothes. There was a short conference and nine sheepish, subdued men headed back to the aircraft. That rukus over the Bomb Sight was funnier than anything I had ever seen on a movie screen. The crew chief went into such hysterics that he lost his balance and fell off the engine stand. Fortunately I was there to break his fall. The returning heroes did not appreciate the uncontrolled mirth of the crew chief and me.

"What's so damned funny?" growled Counce.

Balmore was inordinately sensitive about anything that made him look silly. I could see that he was getting angry, and about ready to take a swing at me, so I quickly got out of range. "Go ahead and laugh," George fumed. "We were trying our best to get the Bomb Sight back, and you guys think it's a joke."

Carqueville had regained his composure and turned on Wilson. "You had only one thing to do," he said, "and that was to guard the Bomb Sight, yet you let a man walk off with it!"

"Honest, Sir, I never took my eyes off that sight," Wilson insisted, "except for a few seconds when I lighted a cigarette."

The truth was that Wilson never once glanced at the Bomb Sight. With his glib tongue, however, Carroll could get out of anything! I listened to his spiel, still laughing, but said nothing about his Billy the Kid act. I owed him something for his lead role in a real-life comedy so memorable that it still lingers in my memory as one of the funniest things I have ever seen.

Carroll had another characteristic that was not so funny. On training flights he would find a comfortable spot in the waist or radio room and sleep for two or three hours at a time. He would wake up and get bored with the long flight and wander around the airplane trying to find something to do. One night he wandered into the cockpit while Jim and I were running down an open circuit. Jim was holding the large cover of the main fuse box and I was trying to locate a burned-out fuse. Wilson decided we needed help so he turned to Jim. "Here, let me hold that while you help John." In his awkward movements he jammed the cover against the open fuses and shorted out almost every electrical circuit on the airplane. A ball of blue fire rolled out of the fuse box, between the Pilot and Copilot, and against the windshield before it burned out. The only lights left in the cockpit were a few luminescent instrument figures. Carqueville was so infuriated that if he could have reached Wilson at that moment he would have inflicted physical damage. Fortunately, we had two flashlights.

August 30

By the end of August the crew had settled down into a routine that was predictable. Carl Shutting was the clown, and every crew needed one. The ground crew was always grumpy in the cold, predawn hours when the combat personnel arrived at the aircraft. But when Shutting dumped out his gear at the hardstand the mechanics gathered around him to chuckle at his antics and wisecracks. He always had something missing from his equipment bag. It might be a mike or an electric glove he had neglected to replace from the last mission. Some mornings I would have a spare of what he needed. Other mornings it was not unusual for Carl to have one of the ground crew rushing to get something. He refused to enter the nose of an aircraft without his special armor plate on the floor. When he donned his testicle protective armor he had no problem getting two volunteers to assist in tying it in place. The mechanics followed him around until time to enter the ship. It was the only show on the base at that hour. Shutting set out to create a character behind which the real Carl Shutting could hide. He was never as slaphappy as he often appeared to be. All of us built up a wartime pose which made us appear different from what we were in civilian life. Carl carried it two levels beyond the norm. He adopted a homespun manner of talking similar to Bob Burns, an early-day Bing Crosby radio character (who coined the word "Bazooka" to describe the odd musical instrument he played). Gleichauf told me Carl had a special cap that he wore at night to keep his bald head warm that created mirth and kidding.

CHAPTER VII

Missions to Amiens-Glizy
and Romilly

August 31

Woodrow Pitts made an early trip to the Grog Shop and was back within
a couple of hours. "They're loadin' those damn bombs."

"Are you sure?" Green asked.

"Hell, yes—twelve five hundred G.P.s" (General Purpose Bombs).

I turned to Balmore, "Where did Abramo and Wilson go? Anybody
know?"

"They took off for the pubs two hours ago."

"You know Nick never leaves 'til they close the pub—somebody has
to go find them an' tell them to break off."

Counce spoke up. "I'll do it. Anyone want to go along? We don't want
Nick to piss in his pants tomorrow."

They were back in time to listen to the late news from B.B.C. There
was no point in going to bed until the newscast was over and the noise and
lights died down. I lay in the sack a long time before sleep would come,
wondering where we would go in the morning and how rough it would
be. I could never resist the question before a mission: "Which of us will
not be here this time tomorrow night?"

August 31—Amiens-Glizy

Aircraft 765
Nip and Tuck

The next morning I stood outside the Briefing Room with Counce until
we heard the reaction to the target when the map curtain was pulled back.

Jim said, "About average—probably somewhere in France."

"That's how it sounds to me."

The weather looked questionable, but there was always the chance it would break before sunup. We were happy to have George back with us in the radio room after a layoff to recover from frostbite again. Raymond Legg was doing well as a replacement for Rogers, whose future status was unknown.

Gleichauf called us into a circle for the crew briefing. "We're hittin' Amiens-Glizy in France. There are two hundred and fifty fighters that can intercept. Flak will be moderate, and fifty P-47s will pick us up at the coast. Colonel Nazzaro will lead the Wing flyin' with Colonel Gross, the Wing Commander."

The Group got off on time and the climb and assembly were flawless. It seemed to me that things always went smoother when Nazzaro was leading. By the time the three Groups were assembled into Wing formation we were over heavy clouds with ground visibility zero.

"Bombardier to crew, Bombardier to crew—oxygen check."

"Turret OK."

"Radio OK."

"Ball OK."

"Tail OK."

"Pilot and Copilot OK."

"Waist OK."

"Bombardier to crew, test fire guns."

One by one I listened to the positions rattle off a short burst. For ten minutes the formation droned on toward the Continent.

"Pilot to Navigator."

"Go ahead."

"Is this cloud cover goin' to foul up the drop?"

"If it stays like this it will—got two alternates but they may be covered, too."

"Turret to crew, flak three o'clock high."

The anticraft fire was light and inaccurate.

"Waist to crew, Waist to crew—fighters four o'clock high. Looks like the escort."

The cloud cover held on but there were a few breaks in it.

"Navigator to Copilot. Tell Paul if these clouds don't open up real soon, we won't hit the primary target—we're gettin' close to the I.P. now."

Gleichauf switched from Command to intercom at the Copilot's signal.

"Navigator says it don't look good for the main target."

As we approached the drop area, visibility was nil and there was no possibility of executing the primary plan. I suppose most leaders would have turned around and headed for England. But with plenty of fuel Nazzaro intended to use all possible means to inflict damage to Germany's ability to wage war. We flew around for a long hour with the lead Navigator searching for an alternate or a suitable target of opportunity. Our 47 escort was excellent until they had to turn north toward England. Suddenly there was a break in the clouds and an enemy airfield loomed straight ahead. I do not know if the Lead Bombardier recognized it or not.

"Bombardier to Pilot."

"Go ahead."

"There's an airfield and we're going to drop on it."

"Radio—watch the doors down."

"This is Radio—doors are down."

After a short run I felt the bombs drop away.

"Navigator from Pilot—what did we hit?"

"Don't know—didn't recognize it."

"Bombardier to Tail, how did the strike look?"

"Looked good to me—covered the field."

We were lucky to get a quick bomb run and an excellent strike pattern. The mission was an example of good leadership turning a failure into a success. The return flight was uneventful until we neared the home base. Visibility was far too poor for a sizable force of planes to attempt to land at the same time. So each ship was on its own to feel the way down and hunt holes in the mist, at the same time avoiding a collision with other aircraft.

September 2

Lieutenant Purus never changed from the way he was the first day I met him. Quiet and soft spoken, mild in manner and disposition, he was a solid man to have on the crew. What I remember best about Purus was that he managed always to look neat and clean even in the English mud. The Bombardier was responsible for the bomb load as soon as the aircraft moved away from the hardstand. Those bombs had three safety devices to insure against an accidental explosion: (1) a cotter key had to be removed by hand from the fuse mechanism of each bomb; (2) an arming wire had to pull out of the fuse assembly when the bomb fell from the aircraft; and (3) an impellor had to spin off of the fuse assembly from the action of the wind on the drop. As long as any of those three safety measures was in place, the bomb was supposed to be inert and no more dangerous than a block of concrete of the same weight. Any of those devices would restrict the striker pin from igniting the explosion at the moment of impact with the ground.

Our practice was to remove the cotter pins as soon as we were reasonably sure the mission was going as planned and a few minutes from the enemy coast. Since I was nearer to the bomb bay than Purus, I performed the pin-pulling assignment. If the mission had to be canceled later, the pins had to be reinserted before the ship could land, a much harder task than removing them.

Balmore worked at a table adjacent to the bomb-bay door. He could open the door and see into the bay. So he reported doors up or down and when the bomb load released. If one or more bombs failed to release, the radio operator immediately called the Bombardier. By arrangement with Purus I took over the task of working the stuck bombs free, because I was closer to the bombs and had the only tools on the aircraft. Ordinarily I could trip the bomb shackle with a long screwdriver and quickly get rid of it. But if we had an unusual situation with several bombs in difficult hang-ups to reach, we kept the bomb-bay doors open until we were at sixteen-thousand feet, letting down on the return. At that point Purus and I went back and did whatever was necessary to get those bombs out of the ship. Once a bomb failed to release from a rack the aircraft was not permitted to land until that bomb was ejected one way or another. Believe me, it was not a fun thing to work out on that narrow catwalk with the doors open below.

While the bomb was theoretically supposed to be inert with any of the safeties in place, I would not have wanted to wager any money on it. But one night a guard was sitting in the cockpit of a B-17 that was loaded with bombs for a mission the next morning, and somehow in fooling around with the switches and controls he accidentally dropped all twelve bombs out of the airplane. They knocked down the bomb-bay doors and hit the pavement of the hardstand and rolled in every direction. None of them exploded, but we had a white-faced guard who thought for a few seconds it was his last moment on earth. The strange thing was that he should not have been able to do this without pulling the salvo ring, which was an emergency release for the bombs in case the electrical system should fail.

September 3

In early September our gunners began to get the foolish notion that we were a hot crew. Our slight combat experience did not justify such arrogance, but as silly as it sounds, we began to get cocky. It was like a boxer who has won his first two fights and thinks he is ready to take on the champ. So when Jim Counce found a can of red paint, Nick came up with a great idea: "Why don't we paint the engine cowlings red? It'll give our ship a special look."

The suggestion was quickly OK'd. Didn't a hot crew need a hot airplane? Something a little different from the other crews? We borrowed a paint brush and without checking it with the Pilot spent the afternoon changing the appearance of Aircraft 765. Standing at a distance to admire our work, we thought it looked sharp.

September 3—Romilly

Aircraft 765
Nip and Tuck

I listened to the Briefing Room noise and judged it medium tough, and decided to put aboard an extra thousand rounds of ammunition. The standard load was seven thousand rounds, and it was against regulations to add more. But we had a special friend, Vernon Chamberlain, who was the armorer for 765 (as well as a number of other aircraft). He could always get more ammunition when I wanted it, which was every time a mission sounded like it could turn out extra mean. Vernon was from a small town in Arkansas, and our relations with him were unusual, to say the least. He did extra things for us over and beyond his assigned duties.

I listened intensely as Gleichauf spelled out the hazards for the day: "The target is Romilly, an ammunition factory, about fifty miles east of Paris. One Group of P-47s will meet us ten minutes inside the coast. Now watch your fire! Don't let me see any of you shooting at the 47s! We need them close to us. If you fellows keep shooting at them, they are gonna stay the hell away from us. Altitude will be twenty-eight thousand five hundred feet and the temperature will be forty-five to fifty below. Watch out for frostbite. OK, let's go."

Some of the P-47 pilots had visited our base three days earlier, and we had a discussion about the difficulties in distinguishing between P-47s and German F.W. 190s. At a distance they did look alike. Sometimes the 190s painted their engine cowlings white to look more like 47s. The main distinguishing difference was a bulge of the nose of the 190s and the shape of the wings in silhouette. We told the 47 pilots they must never, never point the nose of their fighter at a Fortress unless in an obvious turn, because the Fortress gunners became extremely nervous when they saw the lethal guns of a fighter pointed directly at them.

Purus distributed the "bail-out kits" and we climbed in and closed the hatches. The kits contained a tiny compass, a rubber map of the area we would fly over on that mission, a rubber water container, and water purification tablets. There were also concentrated chocolates and benzedrine tablets to help overcome the shock of bail out and the long glide down in the chute. After each raid the kits were turned in. The thinking was that if a man did bail out and avoided capture upon landing, the kits would be helpful for the first week of flight from the area toward the nearest locations that would provide some chance to make contact with the Underground. We knew the parts of France where the population was sympathetic to underground resistance, and also the Bulkans presented an opportunity to tie up with resistance forces.

The temperature was unusually bitter and my feet were numb for hours. Most gunners wore the thin felt electrically-heated moccasin and pulled on fleece-lined flying boots over them. Then they tied their regular shoes to the parachute harness. It was a precaution in case they should have to suddenly bail out. No one wanted to land on the Continent minus shoes! That would have been a disaster, captured by the enemy or not. It was impossible for me to tie my shoes to the chute harness because there was not enough room in the turret, so I passed up the electric shoes and wore my heavy leather shoes with the flying boots on top of them. I had to suffer through many hours of agony when temperatures were extra low and often had to keep exercising my feet for extended periods to avoid freezing.

Major Hendricks did a good job of guiding the formation around flak areas as we crossed the French coast. Soon after entering enemy territory the intercom came on.

"Ball to Copilot—another Fort aborting! That's three of them in the last five minutes."

"Dangerous this far inland, Ball."

Meanwhile Cahow's crew was in trouble. This is the way Lieutenant Cahow told it: "We lost an engine at the worst possible time. We were too far into enemy territory to abort. The big worry was that we had to pull out the stops and draw full emergency power on the three engines that were left to try to stay up with the formation. All the engineering data said this kind of power could only be used for five minutes, but we had to pull that excessive power for hours. Both my copilot, Stanley Parsons, and I kept hearing all of those strange noises that straining engines make—and a lot of other noises that we imagined. We kept the bomb-bay doors up until the last minute. Even then the drag was too much but we caught up with the formation soon after bombs were away. The three remaining engines kept getting noisier and rougher. We could see the engine cowlings shaking from the strain. I didn't know whether we would make it back to our base or not.''

"Tail to crew—escort five o'clock high.''

"Copilot to crew, they are stayin' high to keep out of your range, an' I don't blame them.''

"Ball to Copilot.''

"Go ahead.''

"Can you see that Fort trailin' us by about a thousand yards?''

"No. Can't see it from the cockpit.''

"The markings look odd.''

"Keep your eye on it. Call me if it does anything strange.''

"Bombardier to crew—oxygen check.''

All positions checked in except the Tail.

"Bombardier to Tail—Bombardier to Tail—come in.''

"Bombardier to Right Waist.''

"Go ahead.''

"Can you see the tail gunner?''

"Yes. Looks OK to me.''

"Go back an' signal him to get on intercom.''

Three minutes later: "Tail to Bombardier, my phones got unhooked. Sorry.''

"Navigator to crew—fighters at ten o'clock low.''

"Bombardier to crew—they're 109s.''

"Waist to Copilot.''

"Go ahead, Wilson.''

"Two fighters flyin' like an escort for that trailing Fort. They're not 47s but could be Spits helpin' us out on their way back from a sortie.''

"Navigator to crew—get ready for the fighters—the 47s are at the end of their range.''

"Waist to Copilot—I can see those two fighters better now—they are 109s. Hey! That Fort is shootin' at us!'' (Germany had some captured B-17s.)

"Copilot to crew—those sonnuvabitches are throwin' twenty millimeter shells at us.''

"Turret to crew, P-47s are diving on that Fort. Hope they shoot the bastards down.''

That was the only time I watched a B-17 shot down with glee. I saw brown Jerry chutes pop out and the Fort went into one of those typical flat spins that told me it was out of control.

"Waist to Copilot—the 109s are comin' up to mix it with the 47s. They must feel mean today.''

The German pilots usually waited until the escort turned back. I knew that was going to happen any time. Perhaps the enemy pilots were inexperienced and too eager for action. It was a hell of a fight. I saw two P-47s shot down for certain, and another possible. It was hard to tell when a Jerry fighter was knocked down unless it was seen to explode or the pilot bail out. I saw five that might have been knocked down, although some of them could have recovered. Most of the heaviest action took place four to eight hundred yards from us at various levels. It was some show! The 47s hung in there longer than I expected and when they finally had to break off and head for England, the German ships had used up too much of their fuel to hit us hard with direct attacks. Some parts of the formation did get some fighter action, but we escaped most of it.

I kept watching Cahow and he was holding in tight. There was no sign that any of his remaining engines were developing trouble, in spite of the continuous high power he was drawing.

"Navigator to Pilot."

"Navigator to Copilot—tell Paul the I.P. comin' up in five minutes."

There was silence on the intercom for a few minutes. Then Purus called, "Be on the bomb run in three minutes."

"OK, Bombardier."

"Copilot to crew, flak twelve o'clock level."

The antiaircraft fire turned out to be mild—off just enough to miss our elevation. Did I love that! Flak, while not nearly as dangerous as fighters, scared the hell out of me. When it was bursting around us I stood in my turret and cringed and shivered. I never did get used to it. If I had been occupied with necessary activities, lining up a sight or flying the aircraft, perhaps I could have ignored it. But with nothing to do, unless we were facing attacks, I could not help watching the bursts explode, and I became somewhat of a coward. I could visualize those white-hot pieces of jagged cast iron zipping by my unprotected rear! I don't know what thoughts the other men had during those agonizing moments, but I may not have been the only coward on board when the bursts came heavy and accurate.

A new swarm of enemy interceptors approached from the south.

"Bombardier to crew—Bogies at twelve o'clock high—get ready!"

The fighters showed us some new tactics by adopting a pecular pattern from five o'clock high. Wilson got in some excellent bursts; I saw him strike two of them hard. I had some dandy shots but at longer range. I thought I was reaching them but, if so, the fighters showed no signs of it and came roaring in. The M.E. 109 was a super-rugged airplane with ability to shrug off punishment that would down most airplanes. The attackers eventually ran low on fuel and were replaced by a fresh group. They annoyed us with pecking attacks most of the way to the coast, but were not the hot pilots we usually saw near Paris.

"Navigator to Copilot."

"Go ahead."

"Fighters coming up from below. They look like Spitfires—we're not supposed to have any escort on the return."

"This is the Pilot—I don't give a damn why they're here—just glad to have them."

And so was I! Those Spits must have been on the way home from a mission and saw us up above surrounded by fighters. That finished the attacks for the day, and soon I could see the coast ahead. The formation began a slow letdown.

"Turret to Copilot—looks like Cahow has it made now."

"Right! I was worried back there when he had to feather that engine so early."

We were halfway across the Channel: "Tail to Copilot."

"Go ahead."

"A B-17 turning back towards France."

"You mean we had one of those bastards in our formation?"

"I guess we did. Where else could it come from?"

"No wonder the fighters kept finding us so easy. Those bastards were right in the middle of us radioing our position all day."

"Pilot to crew. Pilot to crew. I want all of that damn red paint off of this airplane before you hit the sack tonight. It was drawin' fighters in on us today! We don't want anything on this airplane to attract the attention of enemy fighters."

Now let's switch back to Cahow's crew: "I thought we had it made when we approached our base, but the tower ordered us to proceed to a repair base not too far away. When I banked the plane to turn on the downward leg number one and number two engines both quit, either out of gas or worn out with that heavy power for so many hours. I never found out which. I kept the plane in a steep bank and landed more than one half way down a very short runway, and had to ground loop it when we ran off the end. The tower officer came screaming out to the plane, hardly before the dust had settled, wanting to know who in the hell the dumb SOB was that would make a landing like that! He really backed off and became quite nice when my crew came tumbling out, all in combat gear, looking like gorillas. Moe Tedesco, Ugo Lancia, Hubert Green, Ray Bechtal, and my bombardier, John Levrette, were all heavy weights, and over 6 feet tall."

September 6

If someone was looking for the Gleichauf or Cahow crew, they listened
for a cacophony of discordant sounds and located the noise cnter. If they
heard no loud reverberations disturbing the airwaves, they knew that both
crews were either on a pass or flying a mission. Let me describe a typical
evening at ten. Lancia was blasting away on his trumpet, accompanied by
another instrument handled by a man from a nearby hut. In his off-key
voice, Tedesco was trying to sing the Italian song they were playing.
Across the room from this bedlam, Carroll was sleeping as soundly as if
at home in a quiet bedroom. Under his cot was a pile of dirty socks and
underwear.

Balmore was doing a tap dance to the rhythm of the music and looking
around for an approving audience like he was a young George M. Cohan.
No one paid any attention to him, because it was the only routine he knew
and we had seen it before. Hubie chose this moment to leap out of bed
and start penning another letter, probably the sixth or seventh of the day.
Who in the hell did he write all of those letters to? Did he have that many
girl friends back home?

Rogers was trying to read but, distracted by the noise, he beat against
the metal wall in protest, then gave up. In disgust he turned up the volume
of the radio to attempt to compete with the sound from the other end of
the hut. Bill Kettner got up and added a piece of green wood to the
struggling fire in the small metal stove, wood recently purloined from the
King's forest under cover of night. An outsider strolled in and picked up
one of Lancia's idle instruments and superimposed his unwanted contribution onto the sounds already shaking the hut. The metal walls vibrated
from the pulsating sound waves and in turn amplified the volume.

Outside the weather was cold even though winter had not yet arrived.
Jim stepped out to study the weather and forecast what we can expect by
morning. His meteorological discourse attracted scant attention. Woodrow Pitts was absent, which meant he had not returned from his nightly
scouting trip to the canteen. I was writing in my notebook, trying hard to
capture on paper the feel and pulse of this odd hut and describe the
assortment of characters.

There was a loud banging on the metal wall from outside, and two men
from an adjoining hut opened the door and demanded that the noise level
be lowered by several decibels. They were ignored because who cared
what they wanted? It was getting late, but going to bed was out of the
question until the occupants wore themselves down.

The sound of a heavy crash against the wall overpowered the music volume. Jim said to me (the only one who was close enough to hear him), "Pitts hit the hut with his bicycle. Must have tanked up pretty good."

"I wonder what he found out."

An explosion of classic profanity—not the ordinary timeworn barracks expletives, but a flow of words with expressive character. The door opened and Pitts entered.

"Hey, Pitts!" said Counce, "Did ya step in the big mud hole in the dark?"

"Or did you have the crabs again?" asked Kettner.

"Hell, no. I don't have the crabs! I went over my boot top in the stinkin' mud. And my bicycle has another flat." That triggered one more outburst of colorful adjectives.

"All right. All right. Knock off the noise. Let's hear what Pitts found out," said Tedesco.

The sounds faded out and we looked at Woodrow. "Well, I talked to three armorers. They're loadin' thousand pounders. All the signs say go in the morning."

"In that case," I said hopefully, "let's hit the sack an' get some sleep."

Such a silly suggestion was unworthy of consideration. Lancia turned to Pitts. "New Jersey raises more vegetables than your whole state of Texas."

"Bullshit!" Pitts roared in rebuttal. "The Rio Grande Valley grows more in a week than your two-bit New Jersey farmers grow in a month!"

We were off on one of the nightly arguments. Ray Bechtel said, "California grows more than Texas and New Jersey put together."

Pitts and Lancie turned on Bechtel, and Pitts looked to me for support of the Lone Star State. I declined to join the fray because none of us knew anything about growing statistics. Barracks arguments are won by the loudest voice.

Wilson stirred and opened one eye. "What time is it?" he asked.

"About midnight," someone answered.

"Why didn't somebody wake me up for chow?"

"I got an extra Hershey Bar if that will help," I volunteered.

Kettner interrupted, "Hold it! Hold it! It's time for the late news."

He switched on the radio to B.B.C. "This is the news: Royal Air Force Lancasters are out in force over the Continent tonight. Flight Officer Leahigh-Smith, flying a Mosquito, reported he could see a huge column of fire sixty kilometers from Cologne. The sounds of heavy gunfire in the Channel could be heard today east of Southampton. . . . The Admiralty admitted the loss of a freighter from a convoy south of Iceland . . . Air raid sirens are wailing over the Midlands tonight. . . . Continued mopping up actions in Italy against slight opposition. There are unconfirmed reports that the Italian Military Forces are on the verge of surrender. . . . The Prime Minister said in Parliament today that we will drive the Hun from France and the soil of Belgium and Holland, but let the Hun guess when and where our forces will strike.''

CHAPTER VIII

Mission to Stuttgart

September 6, 1943   *Aircraft*
Stuttgart, Germany   *Tinker Toy*

The noise of the Jeep outside woke me up. I flipped on a flashlight and looked at my watch: it was 0230 hours . . . an early start! What did that mean—an extra-long mission? As I heard the familiar footsteps on the gravel walk, going from hut to hut, I was halfway hoping it wasn't my morning to go. When I heard the steps go on past our door, however, I became resentful that they were passing me up. Now what did I really want? That sound of crunching feet on gravel put me in an ambivalent mental state: the dread of going versus the prospect of excitement. The door opened, and I listened with little enthusiasm to the reading of the battle roster.

On the way to the mess hall George said, "I wonder how the Operations Officer feels when he reads out our names—he knows some of us won't make it back.

"Someone has to do it, George. Which would you rather do? Take the risks yourself? Or have to choose which men may die?"

"I could never send men out to fight, John, and maybe to die. . . . I would feel responsible for those who didn't get back."

At Operations I waited with Jim and George for some signal from the Briefing Room.

"I wish they'd start the Briefing—Oh! Oh! Listen to that!" Jim grimaced.

There was a deep and prolonged groan followed by silence! My insides constricted because the pilots thought we had a super-mean one coming up.

Balmore said, "I hope it's not Schweinfurt again—or somewhere worse."

"Where th' hell could that be?" asked Counce.

An hour later I had the extra ammo on board and was about finished with the guns. Someone stuck his head up in the hatch under the nose and called, "Put the guns away, leave 'em right where they are. Grab your equipment—hurry!"

"What's wrong with those knuckle-heads at Operations? Don't they know we can't change planes this late and get ready on time?"

Then I realized it was Gleichauf down below. "The Operations people aren't knuckle-heads!" he said. "I made the aircraft change! Where we're goin', 765 can't make it on gas."

"I'm sorry . . ."

"Forget it. Grab your stuff, and let's go! Hurry up!"

In the back of the speeding truck Gleichauf gave us the story. "We're hittin' Stuttgart, in South Germany—another ball-bearing plant. It's the longest raid B-17s have attempted. Some aircraft will have twenty seven hundred gallons of fuel, but we will have only seventeen hundred and fifty. It is gonna be close on fuel. No way 765 could make it on gas. P-47s will be with us a little way, then we go it alone. We'll be over enemy territory five hours."

It was the big league for sure. When the truck stopped and I saw the aircraft it was another blow! *Tinker Toy!* Many of the gunners thought it was a jinx ship. They thought that somehow she attracted fighter attacks, because of the consistent battle damage that had become her trademark. Sitting there in your easy chair reading this account, and insulated by both time and distance, you may smile indulgently at the idea of a jinx. But men in combat tend to become superstitious. They go to great lengths to avoid whatever they suspect to be unlucky. And they cling to lucky charms or some clothing that they have always worn on missions, or to anything they associate with luck. There were some pilots who liked to fly *Tinker Toy* because the ship handled well and was easy on fuel. But her reputation with the gunners continued to grow.

Balmore looked like he had suddenly become ill.

"Oh, now, George, an airplane couldn't really be a jinx—that would be like believing in ghosts," I countered.

Gleichauf walked by. "Cut this talk about a jinx and get this airplane ready! We only have ten minutes until time to start engines!"

We were running woefully short of time, and I was shocked at the poor condition of the guns. All we could do was to keep working on them, mainly to remove the rust from the working parts, after the plane got into

95

the air. We were almost across the Channel before my two guns were ready.

There were no bail-out oxygen bottles in the aircraft, but I had six that I always carried in my equipment bag for emergencies. They were steel cylinders wrapped in piano wire and filled with oxygen compressed to eighteen hundred pounds pressure.

Gleichauf knew Purus had picked up a case of diarrhea during the night. Johnny made a hurried exit into the darkness, and when he returned Paul asked, "Are you gonna be able to make it?"

"That was the third crap since midnight," he answered.

"If you shouldn't go, I'll call Operations to try to get another Bombardier."

"Not enough time for that," Purus replied. "I'll go—but I may get more calls."

Shutting had a suggestion. "Take along one of those metal ammunition cans. If you have to crap you can throw it overboard on the Krauts!"

Carl was to regret that advice a few hours later.

The formation came together quickly, to save fuel, and then set out over the cold waters of the English Channel.

"Radio to Turret."

"Go ahead, Radio."

"My oxygen is leaking."

"Here we go again! What's th' problem this time?"

"I already told you," Balmore replied testily. "My oxygen's leakin'."

"How do you know that?"

"Because the right system is goin' down too damn fast!"

Before I could leave the turret to go to the radio room the pilot came on intercom: "Turret, stay where you are! We're too close to the French coast."

"Pilot to Right Waist."

"Go ahead."

"Jim, take a look at the Radio oxygen system."

"OK, Pilot."

Five minutes later Jim called, "Waist to Pilot! Waist to Pilot! There's a slow leak in the right aft oxygen system—no telling where it is."

"Copilot to crew—Copilot to crew! All positions in the rear switch to the right oxygen system—use it up first."

That was all we could do for the moment. The route was over France to the Rhine River. We crossed the coast at a lower level than usual and were still climbing.

"Waist to crew—B-17 pullin' outa th' formation—can't see anythin' wrong with his engines. What the hell is he trying to do?"

The escort had already turned back to England and it was still a long way to the target.

"Waist to crew. Fighters—six o'clock low, comin' up fast! May be 190s."

For a few minutes the B-17 trailing us flew along unmolested. I think the Jerries were puzzled and may have suspected a trick.

"Tail to crew! Three 190s jumpin' that Fort behind us."

"Waist to crew! Th' wing's on fire—why don't they jump? Oh, I see some chutes now!"

There was heavy smoke and another Fortress was on its way down.

"Bombardier to Copilot."

"Go ahead."

"That was stupid! Why do you think he pulled out of the formation?"

"Some new pilot, nervous and inexperienced—thought it would be easier to fly all by himself."

As we approached the Rhine River, George called again.

"Radio to Turret—pressure's down to a hundred pounds."

"Even so you should have enough . . . your left system is OK and you can kick off of oxygen at sixteen thousand feet coming back."

Tinker Toy was an old ship, an E model. It had small oxygen tanks in each turret that had to be refilled from the main system tanks on long flights. We were used to that, as aircraft 765 was an E model.

"Ball to Waist—my oxygen tank's gettin' low. Be ready to fill it in a few minutes."

"OK, Nick. Let me know when you're ready," Counce answered.

"Bombardier to Navigator."

"Go ahead, Johnny."

"I got another call—got to use that damn ammo can! Take over my gun until I'm through."

The forward nose gun was much more vital to our defense than either of the side guns in the nose.

"OK," Shutting said. "I'll take over your gun, but you're gonna freeze your butt at 35 degrees below!"

"I know that but it's better than lettin' it go in my pants."

"Copilot to Nose—keep the intercome clear!"

"Waist to Ball. Ready for me to fill your tank?"

"Yeah—soon as I swing around. I'll hold steady 'til you tell me it's clear."

My earphones were not the best and the higher we climbed, the worse they were. I could make out only fragments of the intercome conversation.

Jim finished filling the ball turret tank from the left rear system pressure. When he removed the filler hose there was a loud spewing noise, and Jim realized that there was moisture in the oxygen system, no doubt caused by the condensation of moisture during those prolonged periods when that aircraft was out of action for repairs from battle damage. Hard ice had formed to hold both valves open, letting the precious oxygen pour out of both the ball and the left rear system tanks. He frantically tried to reengage the ball valve but the ice was too hard. In desperation, he ran to the waist for the nearest walk-around bottle and quickly hammered it onto the system valve. But he could do nothing to stop the drain of the ball pressure and it dropped to zero. Most of the system pressure in the rear of the aircraft was now gone.

"Waist to Copilot . . ."

I could not make out what Jim was saying.

"Copilot to Ball—Copilot to Ball, come in."

"Go ahead."

"Get outa that Ball quick, Nick. Jim says your oxygen pressure is gone."

"I'm comin' out of the Ball."

"Copilot to Radio."

"Go ahead."

"Help Nick out of that ball and hook him up on your spare hose."

"Paul—Paul!" Herb motioned for Gleichauf to switch over to intercom. "Got a bad problem in the back. Th' ball oxygen is gone an' not much left for the other men. How about sending Nick to the nose? He's in the radio room now."

"Nick, can you hear me?"

"Go ahead, Pilot."

"Move to th' nose right away. Got to save what oxygen we have back there."

"Copilot to Abramo—don't forget your chute!"

Meanwhile Purus had completed his uncomfortable session with the ammo can, but the Navigator did not hear the order for Abramo to hasten to the nose, because his earphones were disconnected as he changed back to his regular gun position.

"Copilot to Turret—watch Nick through the bomb bay."

It was very easy to get hung up in the center of the bomb bay. A stocky man like Nick, in heavy flying clothes, had trouble squeezing through the narrow part of the catwalk where two vertical beams supported the weight of the bomb load. I got out of the turret and looked into the bomb bay to see Abramo struggling valiantly to break through. With a violent lurch he broke free, but dropped his parachute. He made a grab for it, but accidently caught the rip cord! A cloud of white silk flooded the lower bomb bay. His chute was finished, so he stumbled groggily into the cockpit and on down to the nose, ignoring the oxygen hose I held out to revive him. He was too far gone for his mind to function normally, and was struggling against collapse. Shutting, unaware that Nick was coming, had the entrance to the nose blocked. Nick crashed into him and down went the Navigator, knocking over the Bombardier's recently used ammunition can before the contents had time to freeze. The smelly mess spilled liberally about his clothes.

"Navigator to Pilot."

"Go ahead."

"I've got Johnny's shit all over my clothes!"

"What! You say Johnny shit on you?"

"No! No! His ammo can turned over on me! What we gonna do about my clothes?"

"What you're gonna do is get back on those guns. Right now! Worry about your damn clothes when we get back to Ridgewell."

"Navigator to Nick."

"Go ahead."

"You all right now?"

"Yeah, I'm OK."

"Look what you did to my clothes."

"Copilot to Nose! Cut the talk an' keep that intercom clear!"

"Turret to Waist—my earphones are real bad. Tell me what the situation is back there. Talk very slow."

"We—got—oxygen—for—one—hour."

"One hour?"

"Right!—One—hour."

We had just crossed the Rhine River and that meant real trouble if all we had was an hour of oxygen left in the rear at twenty-six-thousand feet.

"Copilot to Bombardier—the Jerries are sendin' up everything that can fly—even some 187s."

"First 187s I've ever seen—and they're using JU 88s, too." Purus answered.

The 381st was flying a tight formation and that saved us some attacks. The enemy fighters were not as aggressive as I had anticipated over that part of Germany. I suspected that most of those fighters were trained for night fighting against the R.A.F.

"Navigator to Pilot."

"Go ahead."

"Ten minutes to the I.P."

Two M.E. 109s hit us but they were caught with a heavy converging fire, and I thought both were badly damaged. Cahow's crew was in serious trouble. Their aircraft had sustained some heavy hits, and the ball turret door had blown off. But down in that ball Bill Kettner obstinately refused to leave his gun position. Despite the enormous wind blast at thirty-five to forty degrees below zero, he hung in there for the next three hours! It was bad enough to be in that ball on any mission, but that terrific force of wind, when he had to face directly into it to meet an attack, was an ordeal beyond the call of duty. I do not know how he survived it.

"Bombardier to Copilot—Herb, motion Paul to switch to intercom."

"This is Paul."

"Bomb run is coming up. I hope those clouds floatin' over th' target don't mess up the drop."

Unfortunately for us, one small cumulus cloud did obscure the target from the direction of our approach. The lead Bombardier could not line up his sight.

"Pilot to Bombardier—are we goin' to drop?"

"No. I think we're goin' to come around on a one eighty."

"Oh, hell! That will ruin us on fuel!"

The formation executed a slow, costly half circle and another try for the target. Again the cloud obscured the main objective. The situation was so confused that I'm not sure what target we hit. It may have been an alternate. One good thing: I was greatly relieved to get rid of that bomb load!

"Radio to Bombardier."

"Go ahead."

"Three bombs hung up in the racks—don't raise doors."

"Turret to Bombardier—I'll go back and get rid of 'em."

"Pilot to Turret—stay on your guns—too many fighters around us now."

"Turret to Copilot. How do your fuel gauges read?"

"Between a third and a quarter—closer to a quarter. Not good!"

"It's gonna be damn close on gas!" I answered.

"We're on auto lean—th' flaps are pulled down. Not much else we can do 'till we can drop out of formation and slow down," Carqueville explained.

"We have about five hundred gallons—three hours using our altitude," I answered.

"Navigator to Copilot. We're three and a half hours to Ridgewell. We might make it to some airfield on the coast."

"Doubt we can make it to England if we stay at this high altitude all the way to the Channel," I answered.

I felt that if there was moisture in the aft oxygen tanks we probably had the same in the forward system. I made a test by filling a walk-around bottle. Sure enough, when I unhooked the bottle the filler valve was frozen wide open. I hammered the bottle back onto it and stopped the drain. Being forewarned by Jim's earlier problem, I was ready and knew what to do.

"Radio to Pilot."

"Go ahead."

"Oxygen pressure about gone back here. What we gonna do?"

"Turret to Pilot—I got six bail-out bottles—should be good for thirty minutes each, if they're careful."

"Rush 'em back real quick. Herb will take over the turret 'til you get back." It required some time to distribute the bottles and coming back to the cockpit I got hung up in the bomb-bay racks. There was no oxygen left in the walk-around bottle I was using, so I knew that I had to break free quickly. I could feel myself slipping. With a final effort I tore loose and barely made it to the rear door of the cockpit. I fell partly in, with my legs dangling into the open bomb bay, and passed out. When I came to, I was plugged into the spare oxygen hose. I got back into the turret and called the Copilot.

"Turret to Copilot—thanks for pluggin' me in—I was lucky to make it to the cockpit."

"You're wrong, John. You plugged yourself in," Carqueville replied.

"No way I could do it! I was completely out when I fell into the cockpit door."

"Well, no one helped you."[1]

"Then we got Gremlins aboard! Hey, Gremlins—thanks for pluggin' me in."

"I wish your Gremlins would help us out on oxygen and gasoline!"

How I got connected to the cockpit hose still remains a mystery.

Wilson, Counce, and Balmore took two bail-out bottles each. That left

---

[1] I was actually beyond walking down the catwalk. I lurched toward the cabin door like a drunk on a diving board. It was a very close thing! Carqueville insisted then and later that no one helped me. But I have seen too many men in that same state of anoxia, and none of them could have made such a connection after they became unconscious. Either the copilot or the navigator had to help me, but neither would admit it.

the remainder of the system oxygen, plus one bail-out bottle they found in the waist for the Tail Gunner.

"Pilot to Copilot. Three things we can do. We can make a run for Switzerland. We can try to dive down to a lower Group. Or, we can bring one more man to the cockpit and let the other three bail out when they use up their oxygen . . . Switzerland sounds like the best bet to me."

"I think so, too," answered Carqueville.

"Tail to Pilot—there are fifty to sixty 187s between us and Switzerland."

"Then forget about Switzerland."

A few minutes later: "Pilot to crew. We're goin' to try to drop down to the lowest Group. Ought to help on oxygen—watch out for fighters."

For the very first time being in a low Group sounded good. Gleichauf dropped the plane down and pulled into an opening in the formation, barely in time to avoid a swarm of fighters that tried to cut us off.

"Turret to Copilot."

"Go ahead."

"Got to refill the turret oxgyen tank. It may freeze like the ball did. If so, I can't save it, but I can keep the main pressure from leaking out."

"Any options?"

"Well, I could try to operate the turret from the cabin oxygen hose . . . I couldn't turn the turret much without unhooking the hose."

"Try filling the turret tank."

The same situation existed as had happened earlier. I jammed on a walk-around bottle and pounded it into position which saved the forward system pressure, but I could do nothing to keep the turret oxygen from spewing out. I quickly switched to the spare cockpit hose, but I could not turn the turret very much unless I dropped the hose. So when I had to meet fighter attacks I cut loose from the oxygen hose. When the attack was over, I dropped to the deck and re-engaged the oxygen hose before I lost consciousness. The supply of oxygen was barely adequate. I vaguely remember once when the intercom was blasting: "Get him, John! Top Turret! Top Turret! He's comin' in at twelve o'clock high. Shoot th' sonnuvabitch!" With all that going on I was half-conscious and strangely undisturbed. I didn't give a damn if half the Luftwaffe was coming in as a unit! Lack of oxygen (partial anoxia) causes a curious mental sensation. The ability of the body to execute commands from the brain drops in proportion to the drop in the oxygen supply. Example: when off of oxygen one could not place the hand on the nose as directed; it might touch the left shoulder.

"Copilot to crew—over France now, so we can't get rid of those three hung-up bombs 'til we get to the Channel."

That meant carrying some extra weight we did not need, and to make matters worse, the bomb-bay doors had to be left down, causing an extra drag and higher fuel consumption.

Bail-out bottles were never intended for any use other than bailing out at very high altitudes. I usually carried five or six in my equipment bag for oxygen use if they should be needed. That day the extra bail-out bottles saved several men. Three of them would have had to bail out or risk dying or suffering brain damage. The mission to Stuttgart was the only instance I know of where men at twenty-six-thousand feet were able to retain consciousness with such crude equipment for an extended period. A valve had to be opened with each intake of breath and closed while exhaling. George made one bottle last for forty-five minutes.

I got out of the turret long enough to look at the fuel gauges, then refigured our estimated consumption. "Turret to Copilot—it looks like we're gonna shave it extra close on fuel. Depends on how much we got left when those gauges show empty."

"And that won't be long!"

"Pilot to Navigator."

"Go ahead, Paul."

"Why we swingin' so far west?"

"Don't know—makes no sense to me . . . this headin' will take us close to Paris," Shutting answered.

"Isn't Paris out of our way?"

"Hell, yes—it's not the shortest route," fumed Shutting. "They're sittin' up there in the lead plane with plenty of fuel, forgettin' about us in these old planes with small tanks. Paul—my uniform stinks!"

"I don't give a damn about your uniform, Navigator. We got real problems—don't they know some of us won't make it if we go a hundred miles out of the way?"

Wilson finished his last oxygen bottle and refused to leave his gun position. In a few minutes he collapsed. George brought him to and moved him forward to the radio room. It must be remembered to Wilson's credit that in a very bad spot he was determined to do his job to the end.

"Radio to Copilot—we're down to th' last of our oxygen—if you want us to bail out we got to do it before we all pass out."

"Hold it, George! I think the formation is going to let down to twenty-one thousand feet to save fuel," Carqueville answered.

At that altitude men would live, even if they passed out. Soon it was twenty, then nineteen, and at sixteen thousand the formation leveled off. The men were perfectly safe now. Jim had been off oxygen since he gave up his bottle to revive Wilson.

"Copilot to Turret."

"Go ahead."

"Pilots are calling the leader about runnin' out of gas. We're not the only one in trouble."

The intercom was silent for a while, then the Copilot called, "The fuel warning light for number two engine just flashed on."

"And that's Paris far off to our left," the Navigator added.

A fuel warning light meant that the engine tank had less than fifty gallons left. The normal cruising consumption of gasoline was about fifty gallons per hour for one engine. When holding in a formation the consumption increased due to some jockeying that was inevitable, but as soon as the formation began a gradual letdown the rate would drop considerably.

"Copilot from Turret, when will they start to let down?"

"Not much 'til we approach the Channel."

Ten minutes later: "There goes the last warning light!"

"Pilot to Turret, you think we can make it over the Channel?"

"Not unless we got a little more fuel than those gauges show. Some of the older E models have a slight reserve when they read empty. Let's hope *Tinker Toy* is one of them. That's our only chance of making it over the water."

"I think I can see the coast ahead about five minutes. All of our gauges are reading empty," Carqueville interposed.

"Ask the crew if any of them want to bail out now over land. We got some altitude to play with—our chances are about fifty-fifty of making it to an airfield on the English coast," replied Gleichauf.

All crew members elected to stay with the aircraft and take the risk; they knew that if we ran out of fuel and had to ditch without power, the chances of being able to set down on the water successfully were poor.

As luck would have it that day, we could do nothing right and crossed where it was a wide stretch of water. Now Gleichauf could drop out of the formation and slow down. Three other B-17s pulled out and fell in behind us. They must have thought we had a definite English airfield in mind. We cut far back on power, using our 10,000 feet of altitude to drop slowly downward.

"Pilot to crew—Pilot to crew. Jettison everything heavy—get those bombs out quick so we can raise the doors."

The ammunition was the first to go because it was heavy. Jim Counce picked up full boxes of fifty caliber ammo and tossed them out of the window like they were matchboxes. He was that strong. Carqueville released the three bombs while I removed the turret guns and heaved them out. At last we could raise the bomb-bay doors that had been down since the bomb drop.

"Pilot to Radio."

"Go ahead."

"Stay in contact with Air-Sea Rescue frequency 'til we're over land. Don't know when these engines will quit."

"Radio to Copilot—lots of Forts calling Air-Sea Rescue—sounds like eight or ten will have to ditch." (Land on the water.)

"Tail to Navigator—those three B-17s are still tailin' us."

"Pilot to Navigator."

"Go ahead."

"Pick the nearest English airstrip you can find on your chart."

"Can't pinpoint where we are exactly—but there should be some some airfields anywhere we hit the coast."

"Pilot to Bombardier. Soon as you can see the coast, watch for a place to land."

We were still letting down, drawing so little power that the engines were barely above idling R.P.M., and I expected them to quit at any moment.

"Bombardier to Pilot—I can see the coast ahead, very faintly."

"Pilot to Navigator. Do you see an airstrip? Which way?"

"Navigator to Pilot—don't see any airfield. Never crossed the coast before without seeing two or three!"

We had inadvertently picked out the only spot on the English coast, or so it seemed, that did not have a number of landing fields. It could not go on much longer. My mind was in turmoil: "These engines have to have gasoline to keep running and the tanks are down to fumes! Where are all of those landing strips I see every time we come over the English coast? Either we find one in a matter of minutes or we put this big airplane down in some farmer's backyard! We are too low to bail out! I hope all of us survive the crash landing, but that is not likely! Come on engines! Hang in there a little longer. There's got to be a landing strip nearby. Where? There are a thousand airfields in England. Well, one way or another we're going down in the next few minutes. There is no way this can go on!"

"Navigator to Pilot! Look over to your left at ten o'clock. Isn't that a small airfield?"

"I see it! Thank God! We're gonna make it! John, fire the emergency flare when we get close enough that they can see us comin' in."

By that time I was at my usual low-altitude position—between and slightly behind the pilot and copilot. The flare would alert the airfield that we were landing without normal landing procedures. The copilot turned to me, "Pump any fuel we have left from number two and number three engines to number one and number four. We need one engine on each side for the approach."

I sucked the remnants in the inboard tanks to the outboard engines. As we slowly dropped down to the small runway I "ceased breathing," hoping those two engines would not quit until we got near the short landing strip. "Keep going, engines! Just another thirty seconds! That's all I ask—another thirty seconds. We almost got it made."

The wheels touched down and I resumed breathing. Gleichauf quickly braked the speed and pulled off the runway to let the trailing B-17s land. Then one of our two remaining engines quit! It was that close!

We had landed at a small R.A.F. Spitfire base. Nick's parachute silk was partially streaming out of the bomb bay and that drew a crowd right away. They probably thought someone was hanging on the end of the chute!

I could not bounce back to normal all at once; far too much had happened in a short period of time. The hazardous experiences of the day had brought us perilously close to disaster. And now to be safe again was almost too much to take in. Slowly the tensions evaporated and my sense of well being returned.

Some R.A.F. officers came out to invite Paul and his officers to their club. Gleichauf asked me, "Have you seen Shutting?"

"No," I said, "not since right after we landed."

It was odd that Carl could have vanished so quickly. I found him hiding in the tail. "Go on, John," he said. "Act like you don't see me."

"No, Gleichauf's lookin' for you—might as well come on out."

Carl had peeled off his outer coveralls, but it didn't help much. He was right about one thing: *he did stink!* Off he went to where I presume he had a table to himself. True, his charisma that day left something to be desired, but he had lived through unbelievable hours in one of the storied Flying Fortresses of World War II, known as *Tinker Toy*. Nothing had gone smoothly or as planned that frantic September day for Carl R. Shutting. Yet there he was, alive and uninjured, and back on friendly soil. So what else really mattered? He could have his clothes cleaned.

I never knew a mug of ale could taste so good! The English were very hospitable and wouldn't let us pay for a thing. Meanwhile the ground crew found enough gas in five gallon cans to get us back to our base. A little before sunset we took off for Ridgewell. At the 381st the men were surprised to see us, because we had been reported lost over France. A few more hours and all of our clothes and personal things would have been gone.

We lost forty-five Fortresses and four hundred and fifty men (except those men who were picked up before dark by the Air-Sea Rescue people), on that poorly planned, poorly executed mission to Stuttgart. In addition to the heavy loss of lives and planes, a half million gallons of fuel (uselessly consumed) transported at high cost in men and materials across perilous sea routes, bristling with submarines. All for nothing! That was the worst waste of Air Force power that I saw in World War II. Far too much was risked on a paper-thin margin of fuel consumption. Seventeen B-17s[2] went down in the Channel from lack of fuel, and we barely escaped being one of them. The excellent Air-Sea Rescue Service saved many of the downed men, but no figures were released on the exact number picked up from the water. I doubt if I will ever completely forget the anxieties and frustrations that besieged us during the raid on Stuttgart. The only thing we did right all day was to get back to England. The amount of damage to that weird aircraft was far below what *Tinker Toy* usually suffered on a combat mission. Was she a jinx plane? I don't know. What we call a jinx must surely be a state of mind. Some 381st men said that they heard Lord Haw Haw (the German propaganda broadcaster) say that they were going to shoot down *Tinker Toy*. It was strange that he would know that aircraft by name and reputation. Did the enemy have some special vendetta for her that would explain her apparent attraction to the fighters?

I have read no explanation of the unnecessary longer return route from Stuttgart, when so many of the aircraft were desperately short of fuel. It seemed to me that someone in command made an error in judgment, but then we were not privy to all the facts. There may have been good reasons, such as a large fighter force waiting for us on the more direct return route. The story of war is a mixture of good command decisions versus poor ones. On the whole, Bomber Command provided good leadership. Once in a while, like September 6, 1943, nothing went right. It must have been the bleakest day in General Eaker's life. Fortunately for us, such days were rare in the air offensive over the Continent.

It was on the Stuttgart raid that Carroll Wilson came of age. When the chips were down, he showed me special qualities that were impressive. He proved that he had courage beyond the ordinary. I had always felt that it was not a question of ability with Carroll—that he could do whatever he set his mind to do. After all, he was only twenty when he came with our crew, and he had some growing up to do.

That night when the lights were out my mind slipped back to that

---

[2] The number of planes lost in the waters of the Channel varies with different reports. Edward Jablonski in *Flying Fortresses* (Doubleday & Company) states that 118 men were plucked from those frigid waters by the efficient Air-Sea Rescue teams.

frantic day in Nevada when I fired a gun from an airplane for the first time. Each gunner had to have at least eight percent hits on the tow target sleeve to qualify. Even on perfect shooting most of the projectiles will miss a small target when fired from a distance because of the spread-out shot pattern. The aircraft was a single-engine craft with two open cockpits. Before takeoff the pilot gave me his instructions:

"When we get near the firing range I'll give you five commands: One, hoist the ammunition can over the side an' secure the gun—don't drop that can! Two, feed the ammunition into the receiver. Three, hand charge. Four, fire until finished or I tell you to stop. Five, clear the gun and stow it. One more thing: keep your gunner's safety belt fastened at all times 'cause it's going to be real rough up there today."

All the way to the firing range I struggled feverishly with the safety belt. It was so tight that I couldn't budge it, and was a foot and a half too short for me to stand up in the cockpit to fire. I had no microphone to tell the pilot, so it boiled down to working in that super-rough air without a safety belt, as risky as that would be. The intercom was impossible! All I could hear was loud babbles of static.

"Squawk—awk—eek—ug—."

I supposed that was command number one. I lifted the heavy can of ammunition out into the slipstream and at that moment the aircraft lurched upward and I came close to dropping my ammunition. I hooked the can onto the gun and relaxed for a moment. That was a mistake! When I looked back at the can I was horrified to see the ammunition belt streaming rapidly out into the air! With a desperate lunge I caught the end of the belt—it was whipping and gyrating in the slipstream like a long, angry snake. I dragged it slowly back into the can and asked myself the question: "What in the hell ever made you think you wanted to be an aerial gunner?" I looked at the pilot's mirror and he was shaking his head and frowning.

Loud intercom static blasted my ears: "Squawk—eek—awk—."

I could not make out one word so I hooked the ammo belt into the receiver of the gun. It was one of the few things I did right all day—that is, it would have been right with the safety belt on. I was leaning out over the gun when the aircraft pitched violently downward and I was thrown up and almost out of the open cockpit. I could feel myself going overboard. I reached down frantically but was too high by that time to grab anything. At the last second one foot caught a projecting edge down below, and it was enough, but just barely, to make the difference. At that low altitude I wouldn't have had time to find the rip cord of the parachute. Before my breathing returned to normal the intercom exploded again. I caught the word "charge" so I hand charged a round into the gun chamber ready for firing.

More static: "Gurk—gook—awk."

That meant fire,—but at what? More loud squawking and the wings shook violently! Where was the damn target? More static! Then I saw it—so far away it looked like a postage stamp. Did they expect me to hit anything that small and that far away, out of a bouncing airplane?

My first burst was too high. Then the gun stopped! My mind went blank about gun stoppages. In the excitement I automatically hand charged and the gun resumed firing. That told me it was either a short round or a badly worn gun. In all, I had seventeen stoppages, and seriously doubted I had ever touched the target sleeve. Finally I stowed the gun in disgust! Instantly there was a furious babble of static. What was the pilot trying to tell me? Then I remembered! I had forgotten to clear the gun, and there was one live round left that could have killed someone on the ground! Pilots had the authority and the obligation to ground gunner candidates who were not suitable to handle weapons in the air. After my inept performance that day I thought he was likely going to wash me out on the spot. When we landed he took his time getting out of the front cockpit, and I cringed as he approached me.

"You almost lost your ammunition two times! Your cockpit procedure was the worst I ever saw! You failed to clear the gun and could have killed someone! But, in spite of all that, I think you got some good hits on the target. Now tomorrow, calm down and you'll be all right."

He started off, then turned back. "Sergeant, one time I saw you bounce too high. Your safety belt was much too long. That's dangerous in rough air."

"Yes, Sir, it was—uh—too long. I'll watch that next time."

Waiting for the scores to be posted was agony. I hoped that I hit the target sleeve at least once. When nineteen percent was posted by my name—one of the highest scores of the day, I was stunned. I had lost seventeen percent of my ammunition because of rounds that wouldn't fire, and still hit nineteen percent? That score triggered a transformation. I imagined myself an aerial Doc Holliday and swaggered a little on my way to the barracks—like I thought Doc would do.

September 7

The next morning it was great to awake at a reasonable hour and look forward to a day of unruffled simplicity. The morning after a rough raid

I always felt in tune with the universe. I had once again thumbed my nose at the odds and was still there. Even the small, everyday tasks that might otherwise seem menial were pleasant to contemplate. It was good to polish shoes or do some routine repair on flying equipment. When one lives on the brink of extinction, his outlook on life undergoes a change, for he realizes that life is a fragile and precious gift. I had a full day at my disposal and I intended to enjoy every moment of it. Nothing was going to louse up my day!

Counce looked haggard when he got up and started dressing.

"How you feel?"

"Terrible! Got a bad headache."

"You were off oxygen far too long yesterday."

Surprisingly, at this early hour of the day, Wilson stirred and sat up. "Anybody got some aspirin? I've had an awful headache for hours."

I handed him an aspirin bottle and a cup of water.

"It will probably take three or four aspirin to knock this one," he said.

"No, don't take more than two, Wilson. If that won't do it, go see the Flight Surgeon."

Jim said, "I hope this headache is the only damage I got from yesterday."

"Have you noticed any dizziness?"

"No, just this blasted headache. Being out of oxygen was my fault . . . I should have had a bottle on hand and somethin' to hammer it on with."

"That's ridiculous," insisted Wilson. "How could you have known there was water in the oxygen system?"

"Well, I should've been ready for an emergency like that, and I wasn't."

"If it makes you feel any better, Jim, go ahead and blame yourself, but no one else does," I answered.

Counce and Wilson took off for the base hospital, and I pedaled to Operations to do some work on my electric suit. I felt so good I was even glad to see Lieutenant Franek. To my surprise Carqueville was there, in animated conversation with Reese and Franek. I could tell he was pleased about something and wondered what was goin' on.

"John, guess what?"

I waited for him to continue.

"I've been made first pilot again."

"Hey! That's great! When will you take over your crew?"

"Today! Believe me, I hope they give me some good men. I'm so used to all of you, but I can't expect to get men like Gleichauf has. I'll get whatever is available from the spare gunners, navigators, and bombardiers . . . I'm gonna miss you, John, and Balmore and Jim."

I deeply regretted that the relationship with Herb would be broken, but I was happy for him because I knew how much he wanted to get back to first pilot status. That evening we pedaled into Great Yeldham to celebrate Carqueville's sudden elevation to first pilot position. Nearly all the crew went along. Balmore joined some villagers in a dart game. He was very good and could beat any of the crew with no effort. In fact, he could hold his own with the English who had played the game since childhood. Some of them were real experts. They arrived at the pub with their special dart cases, and had a great time competing with their friends and engaging in village gossip.

September 10

On a mission, the navigator in the lead plane did the Group navigating. But if the formation broke up on the return, or we had to fall out of it to conserve fuel, Carl had to quickly pinpoint our position. With only an occasional glance at his charts, he wasn't always able to recognize our exact position instantly. That's where Balmore entered the picture. A good radio operator was priceless to a navigator. George could attempt either a position fix or a Q.D.M. A fix[3] would provide Shutting with our latitude and longitude at a given time. A Q.D.M. would give him a compass heading directly to the radio station Balmore contacted. Either one would put the navigator in excellent position to bring us over Ridgewell Airdrome even if the weather was foul.

---

[3] A fix was a matter of triangulation—a known distance (between two radio stations) and two angles (created by the angles of the radio beams reaching the two stations).

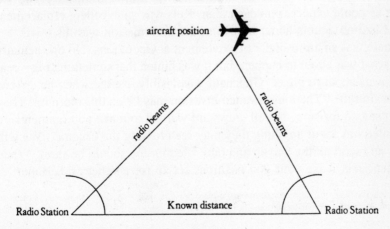

CHAPTER IX

Mission: Airfield in Belgium[1]

September 9—Airfield in Belgium   *Aircraft 765*
Nip and Tuck

Buck Rogers was back with us again and that made me feel better. I felt safer with Rogers in the tail than any tail gunner in the 381st. Raymond Legg, who had been flying in the tail while Buck was recuperating, was a nice kid. I liked Raymond, but Buck was the best I had seen in that position at that point.

Now that Carqueville was a first pilot with his own crew, Lieutenant John M. Kels, from Berkeley, California, was assigned as our copilot. He was easygoing and relaxed, quite a contrast to Gleichauf's tense concentration. Kels was twenty-three years old, a large, well-proportioned man who made a good appearance. We could not expect him to be another Carqueville right off. It would take a while for him to know the crew, and what he could expect from each man. Kels was an excellent replacement and I had no doubts about him from the first mission with us.

There was an atmosphere of excitement at Operations. No one actually said what was about to happen, but it was hinted that something big—real big—was about to break. Gleichauf was visibly excited when he arrived at the aircraft. "The long-awaited invasion may be on this morning. They don't say so for sure, but all crews are warned to make no comments on the intercom about anything they may see crossing the Channel. We will have an escort all the way in and out. The mission should be short. When we get back, leave your gun positions set up for another raid. Report to

---

[1] The official roster of missions shows Lille-Nord on this date. My diary shows an airfield in Belgium. Perhaps different formations hit both targets that date.

interrogation quickly and be ready for a second mission if they call it.''

Takeoff time was early. Before dawn the planes were lined up on the taxi strips. A night takeoff was a fascinating sight. The darkness was spotted with moving lights as the aircraft moved steadily into position. There were sudden stabs of bright illumination as pilots hit a landing light to help outline a tricky turn. The aircraft pulled up close together near the end of the runway and the throb of engines dwindled to a steady rumble. The lead ship was in place. One minute . . . two minutes . . . three minutes . . . there was the signal flare. Four engines opened up with a deafening roar. The ship trembled. Brakes were released and the aircraft sped down the runway appearing as a series of fast-moving lights, the turbo superchargers gleaming blue-white from the heat, an eerie glow under the wings. The next plane followed, then another. Eventually our turn came. When we pulled into place Kels put the cowl flaps in trailing position. On takeoff I stood between and slightly behind the pilot and copilot where I could see the instruments clearly. I did not get into the turret until we were nearing the Channel or North Sea.

''Tail wheel locked—light is out,'' said the copilot.

Gleichauf glanced at me and I nodded. A last look at the controls and the four engines opened up. Paul held hard brakes until the engines reached full takeoff power of twenty-five-hundred R.P.M.s

''Brakes off.''

The ship lurched forward as the four engines grabbed the air—Paul jockeyed the throttles momentarily for control, then commanded, ''Lock throttles!''

''Throttles locked,'' replied the copilot moments later.

My eyes were glued to the engine instruments. They jumped rapidly from one engine to another until I was satisfied they were going to hold. Then a hasty look out of the right and left side windows at the gas tank vents. Sometimes they siphoned out fuel into the air on takeoff. Back to the instruments: still OK. I had time now for a fleeting look at the runway. By this time speed was coming up and I started calling out the air speed, ''Sixty . . . sixty-five . . . seventy . . . seventy-five . . . eighty . . . eighty-five . . . ninety'' so the pilots would not have to look at the airspeed indicator.

Gleichauf pulled back the wheel and released it, starting a series of gentle bounces that would tell him when there was enough lift on the wings to pull the plane into the air.

''Ninety-five . . . one hundred . . . one-oh-five . . .''

The aircraft lifted smoothly from the runway. ''Wheels up.''

''Wheels coming up,'' responded the copilot.

"Hundred and ten . . . hundred and fifteen . . ."

The aircraft was gathering speed. We hit some propeller wash from a preceding aircraft and there was a risky moment or two. Kels said, "Wheels are up—lights out."

"Hundred twenty . . . hundred twenty-five . . ." I relaxed because there was nothing to worry about for the present. It was still dark but in the east there was a faint hint of dawn. Far ahead were lights we must follow carefully. Gradually darkness gave way to predawn light. The Squadron formed in proper order, ready for Group rendezvous. I was keyed up for this raid, expecting big things to open up. After the climb to high altitude we headed out to sea toward the target. I suspected that the object of the raid was not so much bombing damage to a target as a diversionary action to draw off enemy air interference with the naval craft if indeed the invasion was underway.

"Navigator to Bombardier."

"Go ahead."

"Look at all those ships."

"Pilot to crew—Pilot to crew, make no comments about anything you see below. Sometimes intercom talk leaks through to Jerry." (By freak electronics.)

Sure enough, ships were strung out in a long line from the British coast halfway across the Channel. It looked like the invasion was on, but I could hardly believe we were strong enough then for an all-out attempt against the Continent. It was an exhilarating view, but I had to cease sightseeing and turn my attention to the business at hand.

"Navigator to Pilot! Navigator to Pilot!"

Kels motioned to Gleichauf to switch to intercom.

"This is the Pilot."

"Enemy coast in five minutes."

"Pilot to crew—keep alert."

"Bombardier to crew, oxygen check."

"Tail, rajah."

"Ball, OK."

"Radio, rajah."

"Turret, OK."

"Cockpit, OK."

"Ball to Copilot—Ball to Copilot."

"Go ahead, Ball."

"Flak, eleven o'clock low."

Boom! A real close one! I heard fragments strike the aircraft hard, but could see no damage from my position.

"Copilot from Ball."

"Go ahead Ball."

"Sir, I am wounded."

There was a momentary lag on the intercom. I was not certain I had heard Nick correctly.

"Copilot to Ball, will you repeat that?"

"Sir, I am wounded."

We never used the word "Sir" on the intercom and Nick seldom used it on the ground unless a high-ranking officer was present. What induced Nick to become so formal when he was wounded?

Kels motioned Gleichauf to get on intercom. "Nick was hit by that heavy burst of flak."

"Pilot to Ball—Pilot to Ball! Where were you hit? How bad is it?"

"Got me in the leg an' foot. Goin' numb, but hurting some."

"Can you move your foot?"

"I can move it OK."

"We are just now enterin' enemy territory. Think you can stay on the guns until we get back over water? It won't be long."

"Yeah, I think so."

"Good! We'll get you out of the ball as soon as we're back over water."

"OK, Pilot—I can make it."

"Radio to Ball, turn your heated suit up high to hold down shock."

"OK."

"Bombardier to Ball, use pure oxygen, Nick. We got plenty today."

"OK, Bombardier."

"Pilot to Ball, if you start feeling dizzy let us know an' we'll get you out of there quick."

"OK—I'll make it."

"Navigator to Bombardier. There is the I.P.—be on the bomb run in five minutes."

"Waist to Turret."

"Go ahead, Waist."

"Number three engine is throwin' a little smoke."

"OK, Jim."

"Turret to Copilot—is number three on auto lean?"

"No, it was runnin' a little hot, so I put it on auto rich."

"Suggest put it back on auto lean and open cowl flaps enough to keep it about two fifteen [215 degrees cylinder head temperature]."

"OK, John."

A few minutes later the Waist called, "Number three has quit smoking."

"Good! Remind me to tell the crew chief when we get back."

"Bombardier to Pilot—we're on the bomb run."

"Tail to crew. Flak five o'clock low."

"Waist to crew, flak three o'clock low."

The flak was mild and not very accurate, which was welcome to me, and no fighters were in sight, which was unusual.

"Bombs away."

I felt the load drop off and the aircraft surge slightly upward.

"Radio to Bombardier, bomb bay clear."

"OK, Radio, doors coming up."

"Doors are up."

"Pilot to Ball—Pilot to Ball."

"Go ahead."

"How are you feeling?"

"Foot's hurtin' worse. Get me out soon as you can."

"We'll have you out in a few minutes now."

"Bombardier to Radio, get the blanket ready to wrap up Nick when we get him in the radio room."

"Bombardier to Ball, I'll be back as soon as we leave the coast and help you out of the ball. I can see the coast up ahead now."

The fighter escort was perfect. No enemy planes were sighted. Flak was meager. Nick was unfortunate to catch a flak fragment from the only burst that was close to us. The formation began letting down and Purus went back to help Nick, who was in pain but not enough to justify a morphine shot. Purus decided it would be best to leave the foot and leg wrapped in blankets and not try to bind the wound. The bleeding seemed to have stopped. It was much too cold to expose the foot to outside air temperature. All they could do for Nick was keep him warm and as comfortable as possible. Gleichauf broke from the formation to get fast medical help for Nick. At lower altitudes the intercom was unneeded in the cockpit. Paul turned to me. "Fire a red flare on the approach."

When I was sure they could see it, I fired the flare that signaled wounded man aboard. Shortly afterward I saw an ambulance head for the taxi strip we were expected to use.

As soon as the aircraft stopped Nick was lifted gently onto a stretcher and into the ambulance. As it pulled away I had a depressed feeling. I had come to admire Nick. He was a brash young man, but he had been a mainstay down in that ball, where none of the rest of us would have ventured by choice. It took a special kind of man, with a tough mental attitude, to handle the anxieties of that position amid the bursting flak. Herb Carqueville was waiting when we climbed out of the ship and very much upset about Nick. Captain Ralston, the Flight Surgeon, was also there. I knew Nick would get the best of care and treatment.

At interrogation we learned nothing more about the ships we saw in the Channel. Orders were to leave the guns mounted in the aircraft and stand by for the possibility of another mission. It never came. All afternoon we stayed close to the radio waiting for a news flash. Not a thing was said about an invasion. The next morning newspapers carried a story of an invasion rehearsal—no doubt a part of the continuous effort to confuse the enemy as to when and where the invasion would come. The code name for the exercise was "Starkey."

I had serious reservations about the ethics of dropping bombs on the Occupied Countries. All of us understood the necessity of destroying submarine pens, harbor facilities, and war plants. But the civilian population of Belgium and Holland were caught between the grinding forces of two ruthless military machines. Make no mistake about it—the Allies were ruthless and had no hesitation to sacrifice innocent people to achieve military objectives. Did the bomber crews have any accountability for raining death from the skies on helpless populations who had nothing to do with starting the war? Edward Cayce, the noted psychic reader, is reputed to have been able to describe the events of previous lifetimes by some psychic ability to read directly from the pages of what he called the "Akashas Records." I prefer to think that no such celestial archive exists. Nevertheless, I was bothered by my part, as insignificant as it was, in the impersonal fury of destruction poured down on Europe from above. And I think that most of the men who manned the bomber crews were uneasy whether they admitted it or not.

Across Europe the portraits and statues of military commanders look down from positions of honor. Their names and deeds have been encased in a mantle of glory. But war is not glorious—or noble. War is incredible brutality and inhumanity beyond description. Too soon the cruelty and terror of the campaigns are forgotten. The faces of the conquerors hang alongside the portraits of saints and are only a little less honored.

September 11

During the early part of September the 8th Air Force was reorganized. General Carl Spaatz assumed command of all American Air Force Operations in Europe. Major General Ira Eaker moved up to command the 8th Air Force. The 8th Bomber Command was put under General Frederick Anderson. The rest of the command shaped up as follows:

First Division	Brig. Gen. Robert Williams
Second Division	Brig. Gen. James Hodges
Third Division	Brig. Gen. Curtis LeMay

Divisions were increased on paper to four wings, each composed of three combat Groups. The combined strength was to be built up to that structure in the immediate future. Such plans would mean larger formations and improvement in the odds for survival for each man. Whether the buildup would take place soon enough to be of any help to me was yet to be determined. The casualty rate was so high at that period that even large numbers of new crews and aircraft would build up the force less rapidly than expected.

When I began to feel sorry for myself in reference to the heavy odds I remembered that I could have been assigned to the 100th Group—the hard luck Group of the 8th Bomber Command. That unfortunate outfit had earned the undying hatred of the German Luftwaffe. Whenever their group insignia was recognized the Jerry pilots were instantly infuriated. One story explaining the circumstances that brought this on kept circulating so persistently that it must have had the elements of truth. According to that story, the 100th was under intense attack over the Continent and in desperation one Fortress lowered its landing gear. That is the internationally recognized signal for surrender. When the German fighter pilots pulled in close to escort the surrendering craft down, some of the Fortress gunners suddenly opened fire at the unsuspecting fighters while they were out of position to return fire. Several fighters were shot down and some pilots lost. From that moment on the 100th was a marked Group and the sight of that hated insignia inflamed the German pilots to turn full attention to the 100th.

September 13

Sam Spivak was one of the early crew chiefs in the 381st and a good one. He was the brother of Charlie Spivak, a well-known orchestra leader of that period. When Sam and Gleichauf got together it was old friends meeting again. It was reassuring to have that kind of man in charge of keeping our aircraft in top condition.

One bitterly cold day Sam was working alone, high up on an engine stand with his head in the nacelle space behind the engine. Electricians, armorers, and other specialists were coming and going. Sam heard another vehicle stop but paid no attention to it. An English voice said, "Yank, how do you like our English weather?"

No American liked the miserable winter-spring weather of 1943 in England, and Sam thought he was talking to one of the English runway workers. His reply was a volley of profanity that clearly expressed what he thought of English weather in very definite and colorful terms. When he did not hear any reply, Sam stooped down to where he could see to whom he was talking. He got the shock of his life: there stood King George VI, flanked by British and American military brass! Sam tried to stutter an apology but the king cut him short. George VI was laughing heartily and said, "Forget it, Yank. I had it coming. And I've heard better profanity than that many times. I'm an old navy man, you know."

CHAPTER X

Mission to Nantes

September 16—   *Aircraft 765*
Nantes, France   *Nip and Tuck*

Carqueville was flying his initial mission as a first pilot with a crew newly
put together. He would be on the right wing and we would be on the left
wing of the second element of the squadron.

✈ ✈ ✈ First element
✈ ✈ ✈ Second element

I saw Carqueville at Operations early that morning and he said, "John,
my men are nervous and scared, as all of us are on our first raid. We may
need some help if fighters hit us hard. Keep your eye on us."

Jim cut in, "Keep tight formation and the fighters won't pick you out
as a green crew."

The target was submarine installations at Nantes, on the Loire River,
a few miles from the Bay of Biscay, on the west coast of France. Takeoff
and wing assembly were smooth and on schedule. A short time before we
reached the enemy coast Purus called me.

"Bombardier to Turret—pull the bomb fuse pins."

"OK, Bombardier."

"Ball to crew, fighters six o'clock low—can't make out what they
are."

"Tail to crew, they are P-47s."

The escort flew crisscross patterns above us and for an hour nothing
happened. Then the Navigator spotted trouble.

"Navigator to crew, 109s eleven o'clock low—looks like about fifty
of them."

Reliable Jerry had timed the range of the escort perfectly and approached the formation at the time when the 47s would have to turn back. When the Thunderbolts were gone the enemy interceptors pulled up to our altitude and began the usual circling tactic to pick out the best angles for attack. We could never be certain what they looked for, but a ship with signs of mechanical trouble or a straggler was sure to be high on the hit list. We also knew they looked for the weakest formations and suspected that they tried to spot green crews. Perhaps certain groups had earned a reputation of being rough on attack. Other groups may have been easy targets in the past and when they recognized the opposition by the insignias, they may have changed their tactics.

"Bombardier to crew, fighters are hitting the high squadron."

The attack screamed by us at about two hundred yards and we let go with burst after burst. There were seven fighters attacking in a single file.

"Tail to crew—109 comin' in six o'clock high."

I whirled around to help Legg and we hammered hard at the 109 and another right behind him.

"Ball to Turret."

"Go ahead."

"I think you an' Tail got one—I can see it going down smoking."

I saw us hit it with a dozen bursts, but I think Legg did the most damage. This was the kind of fight I liked. We were never swarmed by fighters but there were enough attacks to keep us busy. By that date I had enough combat experience to be keyed up to maximum performance by fighter action.

The fight slowed down, but ten or twelve interceptors were still buzzing around the formation. A fighter was leading three other Bogies and circling us at about twelve hundred yards.

"Navigator to Turret."

"Go ahead."

"Hey, John, think we could hit that sonnuvabitch at four o'clock high?"

"He's a little out of our range, but we might fire high an' lob a few rounds into him if we're lucky."

"Let's dust him off for the hell of it."

"OK—fire away."

I set my elevation several degrees above his flight path and took a long lead. Both of us squeezed off three or four bursts. We picked the wrong man to mess with. He was not bothering us and we should have left him alone. His wings wiggled as if out of control for a few seconds then he went into a dive and came straight at us with the other three fighters following his lead. We had a full thousand yards to fire and the nose and turret guns poured a deadly hail of lead and steel all of the way. We were assisted by other gun positions in adjoining ships. One after another those fighters barrel-rolled under our right wing, and I heard Jim open up as they flashed by his position. Then Legg cut loose as they dived down out of range. The 109s were so rugged they could absorb a lot of punishment and keep right on coming in. Well, one of us did hit the lead ship with an improbable shot.

"Navigator! This is the pilot. That was damned stupid! That fighter wasn't botherin' us an' you and John made him mad. Those four 109s could've knocked us down. Don't either of you ever pull a stunt like that again."

Gleichauf was really hot and he had a right to be. We should not have instigated that attack. Fortunately, he did take effective evasive action while the four of them were coming in on us. That was probably why we did not take any damage.

As soon as the fighters dived past us I whirled around to see how Herb was doing. Two fighters were zooming by his aircraft and severe damage was clearly evident.

"Turret to crew, Herb's badly damaged. His ship is riddled from the waist back an' looks to me like the Copilot and Top Turret are wounded."

"Waist to crew, Herb is all right as far as I can see."

It was typical of Jerry tactics to mount two or three simultaneous attacks to divide the defensive fire. In this case it worked well because we were tied up with our own problems. When Herb needed some help we could not give it to him.

"Navigator to Pilot."

"Go ahead."

"The I.P. is just ahead of us."

"Bombardier to crew, flak twelve o'clock high."

The fire was light and inaccurate, which was great with me. I hated that damn flak. The bombs released on time and the formation made a right swing out over the Bay of Biscay. Two aircraft had release problems but they got rid of their bombs as we passed over a harbor nearby. I watched the boats making frantic movements in an attempt to avoid the bombs they could see falling directly on the harbor.

"Bombardier to Pilot. I think Herb is goin' to be able to hang on. His Copilot is sitting up in his seat now."

The flight back to England was long and tiresome. When we landed Major Hendricks, the Squadron Commanding Officer, sent for Shutting and me. The Major was usually a mild-mannered man, but when we reported he was steaming.

"I've seen some asinine things in my day, but you two men drawing four fighters in on our squadron for no sensible reason takes the prize for stupidity. Don't you have sense enough to leave fighters alone who are not bothering us? If I ever hear of any such irresponsible action from either one of you again there will be severe disciplinary measures!"

When we were out of range of the Major's hearing Shutting whispered, "I never knew Hendricks had such a temper. Good thing we both kept our big mouths shut."

"Damn right! If we were not so short on combat personnel he would have thrown the book at us."

Well, it did sound like a good idea at the time. The action was getting a bit dull and we thought dusting off that fighter would liven things up. And that is exactly what happened, but not the way we anticipated. I still wonder, when I think of that day, which of us hit that fighter. It was one hell of a shot.

A gunner who wore size thirty-eight did not make it back from the mission and my blouse problem was solved. It was an excellent fit and I had a full uniform again. I hoped the unfortunate man got out of the ship in time.[1]

September 18

When the combat action slowed down, the 381st resumed their endless classes, not only because the information might be useful, but also to fill the vacuum between raids. The aircraft recognition classes were a matter of repetition. Pictures showing the silhouettes from different angles of vision of all the enemy aircraft we were expected to see would be flashed on and off of the screen. In time we came to recognize an aircraft at a distance the same way we recognized a Ford or Chevrolet without conscious thought.

The prisoner-of-war classes made a lasting impression on my mind. I can recall the lecturer saying something like the following: "Never resist an armed soldier because he is looking for an excuse to kill you after what you are doing to the cities of his country. German civilians are worse than the soldiers. They have been known to shoot men parachuting down. German soldiers will follow the prisoner-of-war rules of the Geneva

---

[1] I had ruined my only blouse on a recent bicycle accident on the way back from the pubs one very dark night.

Convention. So if you have a choice, surrender to soldiers rather than to civilians. If you are captured, your orders are to tell the captors your name, rank, and serial number and nothing else. Give the enemy no other information no matter how trivial it may sound to you. Your second order is to attempt to escape if you can. Don't do anything foolish. Remember that as a prisoner of war you are costing the enemy food, housing, materials, and manpower. Dead, you cost the Germans nothing. You will be questioned to extract whatever information they can get out of you. The Germans are skillful at interrogation. You might be ushered into a comfortable office where a smiling officer offers you a cigarette and a chair. He might have a glass of beer brought in. There could be small talk about the U.S. Perhaps the officer has visited our country. This could go on until he thinks you are disarmed. Then the questions will get closer and closer to what he is probing for. If you are not careful, you will spill information the enemy can use to put together a better picture of what we are doing and how we are doing it . . .''

Sometimes the lecturer was an escapee from a prison camp and we listened with intense interest. ''Your third order is to obey the orders of the enemy as long as they do not aid the enemy war effort. You will refuse to work in a war plant or to do anything that will work against your country. You have little to fear from the German soldiers in the way of physical abuse. No matter what you have heard, we have no confirmed cases of torture of American or English soldiers. Herr Hitler still feels he is going to win this war, and hopes to create a working relationship with the U.S. and England after the war.

''Your fourth order is that you will be under the command of the senior Allied officer in your prison camp. The enemy will issue most of their directions through him. Never wear or carry anything in clothes or equipment that is not definitely a military issue. If the enemy finds anything on your person other than military or aircraft paraphernalia, you might be considered a spy or a saboteur. If they suspected you were an agent, you would be turned over to the Gestapo, and rest assured that the Geneva rules would not apply. They would put you through torture to extract useful information . . .''

September 21

When a four-day pass was available we always made a strenuous effort to get into London early enough to find a hotel room. My favorite place was ''Prince's Garden,'' the site of the Eagle Squadron Club of Americans who served with the R.A.F. before the U.S. was drawn into the struggle. It was located far enough away from the beaten path of soldiers on leave that rooms were usually available up to mid-afternoon.

One night in London I bumped into Johnny Graves in a bar near Trafalgar Square. He joined me at Sheppard Field that day when a few of us were conned into volunteering for aerial gunnery. We were together at the Boeing Aircraft Engineering School, at the Las Vegas Gunnery School, and the various training bases where combat crews were put together and developed. I was struck immediately by the change that had taken place in Johnny since I had last seen him. The look in his eyes and the lines tightly drawn across a face too young for such lines told me he had been through some harrowing experiences. This is what he told me: "We were badly damaged and had no chance to make it across the North Sea. The radio operator got in touch with Air-Sea Rescue, and as we headed down to ditch, there was enough power left to control the ship. We hit hard and bounced some before settling. Two of us were out real fast and got the rafts launched, and managed to cut loose before the ship sank. Right quick I saw we were in trouble 'cause the raft I was in began to deflate. There was a leak, either a defect in the raft or some battle damage. I got the hand pump going and me and one of the waist gunners kept that raft inflated. It was almost dark when we hit the water and we knew our chances of being rescued before the next morning were almost nil. The other raft drifted away in the dark and was never found. In a very short time we were soaking wet from the wind blowin' spray on us and so cold—so cold. I was worried the hand pump would wear out before morning, but the two of us stayed with it all night. When dawn came the other three men were dead of cold and wet exposure. The exercise of pumpin' was just enough to keep two of us alive all that awful night . . ." Graves paused, unable to go on and tears welled up in his eyes. In a few minutes he recovered. "You'll never know what it was like. Looking at them cold and lifeless was terrible. They were almost like brothers. That morning a patrol boat spotted us and the ordeal was finally over. I'm OK now, John, on another crew, but it won't ever be the same for me again. I'll keep remembering how they looked . . ."

There may have been other overnight survivors in the North Sea, but Johnny Graves and his crewmate were the only two I heard about. That leak in the raft turned out to be the difference between life and death.

There were not nearly as many air raids against London in late 1943, but one had to be prepared for an air raid any night. If an air raid warning sounded, I followed the crowds to the nearest shelter and waited it out. But one night I was opposite Hyde Park when the sirens began to shriek. That eerie, baleful sound always made shivers ripple through me. There was an anticraft battery in the Park, so on impulse I decided to forget the shelter and watch the show, reasoning that I might not get another opportunity to watch antiaircraft fire close by at ground level. I gazed with intense fascination as the huge searchlights stabbed the sky with brilliant beams of light. It was awesome to see those batteries fire and the orange-red bursts high in the sky. A bomber got caught momentarily in the converging beams of two searchlights and gleamed bright in the sky like a lighted billboard. I tried to visualize the blinding terror of the men in the bomber, knowing as they did that they were a perfectly outlined target for the R.A.F. night fighters.

Suddenly pieces began dropping around me and I realized that jagged chunks of cast-iron shell fragments could strike me any second. Quickly I ran into the shelter of a large overhanging doorway until the sirens sounded all clear.

"Good show?" came a voice out of the darkness.

"Yes, indeed," I replied, "quite fascinating to watch the batteries fire."

"It might be so to me if I hadn't seen it so many times, you know."

"Do you often stand here rather than go to the shelters?" I asked.

"Oh, no, tonight I was going to visit friends. When the sirens opened up I was not near a shelter I knew about and I saw this big doorway" was the answer.

We stood talking for a while, then he asked, "Were you headed somewhere special when the raid started?"

"Just back to Picadilly to see if I can find any of my friends."

"Would you like to go with me to visit my friends for a little while? And see how some of us Englishmen live in wartime London?"

"That would be interesting. I can go to the club later."

The friends were a couple with two children living in a nearby flat. They talked at length about the difficulties and trauma encountered in rearing a family surrounded by the terror of war. Both of the men were ex-soldiers who had sustained wounds and were now working in war plants. I felt a warm glow of comradeship with those people who were so hospitable to a man they had never seen before. On my next trip to London I used all my rations at the P.X. and carried numerous scarce items to this fine family. The children were delirious with excitement over the candy and the mother was delighted with several bars of soap and some sugar I conned the Mess Sergeant out of.

September 22

When an air crew had been in heavy combat action, and appeared to be shaken up, they became eligible for one of the rest homes maintained in England. It was not a matter of the number of raids, but the mental condition of the crew. The Flight Surgeon kept a watchful eye on the men before and after missions. He alone decided when a crew needed a week or two of respite from the war.

Carl Shutting organized a campaign of odd behavior by the crew for the benefit of the Flight Surgeon, Captain Ralston. He had it worked out well, carefully orchestrating the act to catch Ralston's attention, but I had no confidence it would work. The elated Navigator came to our hut in fine spirits that afternoon: "We did it! Ralston thinks we are on the edge of bad nerves. We're leaving for the rest home in the morning for a whole week away from this rat race."

"Where are we going?" asked Jim.

"Some village on the upper Thames River—that's all I know. Maybe we can get out of this mud for a week anyway."

"We got you to thank for this. I didn't think our little act would work. You know there isn't a damned thing wrong with any of us."

"We know that, John—but Ralston don't—and that is what counts."

"It sounds great."

We left for Cholsey in fine spirits. The day was clear and cold, which was exceptional for the time of the year. It was too bad that Wilson was in the hospital for frostbite, and Rogers was not included because it was evident that he was not going back on combat duty. George, Jim, Shutting, Purus, Gleichauf, and I were the lucky ones.

At Cholsey Station a personnel truck met us. It was a short ride to our destination. When we pulled into the long driveway, I was surprised at the layout. It was a magnificent old manor house, beautifully covered with ivy. The house was four stories high and the lovely grounds were spacious and well kept. Green lawns, attractive hedges, and bright flowers were a welcome sight.

The staff met us at the door. "Welcome to Buckeley's Manor! We hope you will have a pleasant stay here. Each man will be assigned a room to himself. The schedule for meals is posted on the bulletin board, and you can dine any time during the hours listed."

We went upstairs and were shown our rooms. Imagine having a room all to myself.

"Here are your sheets."

Sheets? I had forgotten about such things.

The bathrooms were down the hall.

"What time of the day do you have hot water?" I asked hopefully.

"Oh, it's always hot until ten P.M. Then we turn it on again each morning at seven o'clock."

Unbelievable! How long had it been since I had a hot bath?

"Let's go downstairs and fit you men with tweed trousers and pullover sweaters," said one of the staff members. "You are free to wear these clothes instead of your uniform while at Buckeley's."

After dinner that evening all of us were issued passes for the week.

"You are free to do what you wish with your time while here. We have tennis courts, a trap or skeet range, badminton courts, and there are golf courses nearby. Or you may enjoy archery and horseback riding. You will be issued a bicycle so you can ride into the villages or explore the countryside. The beautiful Thames River is close by and we suggest you take a boat trip up the Thames. A boat runs a regular schedule every day. Enjoy yourselves while here. Forget about the war. If you have any other requests, please let us know."

The Thames River upstream is quite different from the muddy, commercial estuary a traveler sees at London. The Thames I saw was a beautiful river, clean and sparkling. Fine old estates bordered each bank, and their well-kept grounds sloped to the edge of the estuary. Most of the homes had private piers and boats; it was England at her finest. The stream wound between inviting lawns and over-hanging trees for mile after mile, becoming more picturesque as the boat moved farther upstream.

At Buckeley's there were men from many groups in the Air Force, and some recently from North Africa. I noticed that most of the latter were recovering from wounds or nervous shock. Late at night we sat around huge open fireplaces and swapped experiences—experiences that no doubt were expanded in the act of retelling. Each morning our routine included some fast tennis to limber up, then a bicycle ride around the back roads until lunch time. In the afternoon we would shoot skeet for a while, then take off for another ride through unspoiled rural byways. We were lucky to find a pleasant pub at Wallingsford, a village remote from major cities. Uniforms were nonexistent except for us—too rural for soldiers. That pub gave me an insight as to how the villagers lived. I listened to intimate political discussions, and learned for the first time that England had a fast-growing movement toward socialism and some tendency toward mild communism. I learned that, although the English strongly supported Churchill, many of them were opposed to the Tory party. They wanted him for the war, because strong leadership was required, but I listened in amazement to what they wanted in the future. They did not want a Churchill government after the war. They were determined that England was not going back to a government dominated by the aristocracy. (After the war when Americans were shocked that Churchill was turned out of office, I remembered Wallingsford and knew why.)

The time spent at Buckeley's Manor was one of the most pleasant weeks I have ever experienced, because it was such a contrast to Ridgewell Airdrome. It was a week's interlude of tranquillity in the midst of war.

At the Cholsey Station Shutting said, "We won't have another week like this one in England—it has been great! I hate like hell to go back to the war."

"Same here," Gleichauf replied.

Late that afternoon we reached the village station and rode the rest of the way on our bikes that had been checked in at the station when we departed a week earlier. It was almost dark but we could see the Fortresses returning from a mission.

Back at the hut Jim asked Lancia, "What's gone on since we left?"

"We made a run on Emden—got in an easy one."

"And we used a new radar gadget that lets you see through the clouds," Pitts added.

"Wait a minute," I said, "there's no such thing."

"No bullshit! The navigator sees right through the fog," Pitts insisted.

"How did the drop come out?"

"Not too good, but this was our first time to use it. Give them a chance to work the bugs out of it. Sounds good to me," Lancia replied.

"What do they call this new thing?" George asked.

"The Limeys call it Pathfinder."

That was one of the early American attempts to use the radar device that we later called Mickey.

"There's a rumor that one of the Squadron Commanders tried to quit flying this week," said Kettner.

"Who was it?" I asked. "Not our C.O., I hope."

"The story is this Squadron Commander got fouled up mentally— broke down—said he couldn't take it any more. We don't know who it is."

"They're tryin' to keep it hush-hush," Tedesco added. "I heard they won't let him quit flyin'—would be bad for the morale of the men."

"How would you like to fly a raid with that commander leading it?" Jim asked.

CHAPTER XI

Mission to Emden

The temperature was warmer, so Balmore joined me for the long bike ride into Ridgewell. The White Horse Tavern was a favorite watering station for soldiers and civilians. Three men from the base came in and took over a table next to us. After a while I could not help overhearing their conversation, perhaps because it dealt with a common subject high among the gripes of combat personnel.

"Why can't we get better flyin' equipment?" one man asked. "They keep improvin' the goddam airplanes, but they screw us with lousy equipment."

"The bastards who designed it don't never have to wear it in combat—that's one reason," said another.

"Wonder why they can't copy the R.A.F.? They been improvin' their stuff for years. Some of it is damn good."

"Harry Houdini couldn't get out of one of our chutes if he landed on water! He'd drown like a rat caught in a fish net," added a third voice.

"But the R.A.F. has a quick release so they can cut loose the chute just as they hit the water."

"Or in a high wind."

"OK! Why can't we copy them?"

"But my big bitch is that lousy oxygen mask. I think the Gestapo must have designed it."

"I know what you mean. How did they manage to get that extra thing in it that makes your nose start to run as soon as you put it on?"

"I don't know, but after a couple of hours in that wind back in the waist, the Copilot calls me up an' says, 'What's the matter with you? I can't unnerstan' what you are sayin'.' How the hell can I talk plain with a mouthful of snot?''

"Where did they dredge up those bastards they call engineers who design this stuff?''

"Some 4F draft dodger not worth a shit for anythin' else. But even those no-goods should've come up with better electric gloves. Why in the hell did they put the heat in the palm of the hand? Don't need it there! It's the fingers that freeze holdin' metal at fifty below. But no, the bastards never thought of that.''

"If one of them had to fly a few missions in the waist or radio room, he would come up with some electric overshoes real quick instead of those silly electric shoes we have to wear. If we had to bail out we would be on the Continent without any shoes! How would you like that?''

I turned to Balmore. "Electric overshoes! That's exactly what I need. You know what, I think I could make a pair of them. The idea of how to do it just hit me. I'm glad we came here tonight. I'm going to start huntin' up the materials first thing in the morning if we don't get a call.''

George looked at me but said nothing. I could tell by his look that he thought I was hallucinating. The possibility of making something like that out of scraps with crude tools was not in the realm of his understanding.

October 2—Emden   *Aircraft 765*
Nip and Tuck

Two weeks had gone by since we had last been out on a mission and I did not expect one that morning. I was groggy when Reese turned on the lights.

"Wake up! You guys been loafin' long enough.''

The combat mess hall was getting crowded again with the influx of new men. One real rough raid would take care of that! It was easy to pick out the recent arrivals. I could see the anxiety written on their faces and in their gestures. After a while, if they lasted long enough, they would be able to mask their fears. Only a few men, who were born with less than the normal sensations of fear, could quickly become accustomed to the frightening proximity of death, which was a companion one had to accept on every mission. As men became more experienced in combat action, their confidence increased along with each successful raid, but twenty-five missions was insufficient to form a protective mental armor against constant danger. If they sustained enough combat time it would eventually become a way of life, overcoming most of the fear and anxiety. For me this happened in the 15th Air Force when I had about sixty missions. A man learned to hide his thoughts behind a facade of cocky bravado—an image often displayed at the mess hall before a mission. A veteran looked like it was a breeze, not a care in the world, but inside his stomach was churning. The main difference between beginners and experienced men was that the latter knew they could take it, and the new men did not yet have that mental shelter. I studied the faces with an ambivalent mixture of amusement and compassion.

At Operations the Briefing Room reaction was moderate. Jim said, "Doesn't sound too bad."

We threw our heavy bags of equipment into the personnel truck. On the ride out to the aircraft, Legg said, "You don't think this one will be another Stuttgart?"

"From the sounds I heard we are not goin' that deep today," I answered.

Wilson came awake. "John, do you think *Tinker Toy* is really a jinx ship?"

"I don't know. What is a jinx anyway?"

Someone from the dark interposed, "You're damn right she's a jinx! All that damage, raid after raid."

"Maybe so, but how can metal, wire, and plexiglass take on a personality? Yet I have to admit there is somethin' different about that plane," I replied.

There was plenty of time to get ready. When Gleichauf arrived he gathered the crew into a circle out of the hearing range of the ground men. "Not too bad today. It's Emden—a short run over the North Sea. We may see a hundred fighters, if the Germans figure out where we're goin' fast enough. We'll have a P-47 escort over the target. The flak will be mild and the temperature about thirty-eight degrees below."

The weather over England was favorable for takeoff and the Wing formed on schedule. The flight over the North Sea was tiresome; the formation was loose and erratic, reflecting the large number of new crews. We were ripe for a heavy fighter attack. The route was parallel to the enemy coast for a while. I saw the Island of Helgoland to our right.

"Bombardier to crew, oxygen check."

Each position chattered away with the routine procedure that assured that no one was in trouble out of sight of the others.

"Navigator to Pilot."

"Go ahead."

"We're going to swing right in five minutes, then make a ninety degree turn to come over the target downwind."

132

"Turret to crew—Turret to crew—the escort five o'clock high."

"Tail to Copilot, those 47s look good up there. I bet we don't see any Bogies today."

"This is Ball, flak four o'clock low." It was scattered and ineffective.

"Tail to crew, I was wrong—fighters at six o'clock low—look like 190s."

The formation pulled in a little tighter. The Jerries made some quick passes close by, but I saw no B-17s sustain damage. The 47s dived into them and that was the end of the attacks for a while.

"Bombardier to Pilot, we're on the bomb run." That meant the aircraft had to be level and steady for the bomb drop. At this point the bombardier in the lead aircraft took charge. The other bombardiers watched his bomb bay and the moment they saw the first bomb fall from the lead ship they released their loads. On the bomb run the lead bombardier was in control of the ship through the Norden Bomb Sight. It connected into the automatic pilot. When the moving indices of the sight lined up properly, the bombs were released. The Norden Sight computed air speed, altitude, wind drift, and all other factors that could influence the accuracy of the bomb strike.

Immediately after the bombs were released on the shipping docks and submarine pens, the Wing made a long, slow left turn and headed for the North Sea.

"Turret to Navigator."

"Go ahead."

"How would you like some more easy raids like this one?"

"Suit me fine except it has been a little dull."

"Not too dull for me," Gleichauf cut in, "I like 'em dull."

Bomber Command announced we had lost twenty-eight ships on that easy mission to Emden. To me it was almost a milk run. Why? There was only one answer: too many pilots throttle jockeying back and forth lousing up the formations so that they were vulnerable to fighter attacks. Who do you think the fighters would choose to hit: the tight, well-disciplined formations or the loose ones signaling green crews? The Wing was a sorry looking operation on the Emden mission, and if we put that kind of show against a tough target, I shuddered to think what would happen.

October 3

I was eager to put my idea of electric overshoes to work. Fortunately I found everything I needed in the discarded equipment bins. In two or three days I had the design worked out. What it amounted to was cutting up a number of old electrically heated felt shoes into sections large enough to fit around my regular G.I. shoes. With some help from the Parachute Department, where they had experts in sewing and the equipment, the sections were joined together. The heating wires were placed on the outside of the overshoes for easy access in case repairs should be needed. A pair of extra-large flying boots was split and enlarged enough to fit around the overshoes to protect the heating wires from damage in use.

The overshoe design worked even better in high-altitude extreme cold than I expected. My feet felt exactly as if I were on the ground in mild weather. There was no sensation of either heat or cold. They were durable enough that no repairs were needed for the remainder of my missions. The design made so much sense that it was difficult to understand why the Air Force equipment experts stayed with those too-hastily-designed electric felt shoes that were not what combat crews needed.

October 5

The training classes continued concerning bail-out procedures and escapes from enemy-occupied territory. I can still hear the instructor droning: "Now when you see a wing fire, that means gasoline or oil is burning. Sometimes a wing fire will burn itself out but that is rare. When you see the flame streaming back from the wing, get ready to bail out. You will not have much time to ponder the situation. There is no need to panic. Snap on your chute and wait for the bail-out order. Grasp the ripcord in one hand, fold your arms against your body, and fall out. Count at least twenty and pull the ripcord. Never pull it too quick because it might blossom up an' hang on the tail of the airplane."

Then questions would interrupt the instructor. When the order was restored, the speaker would continue: "Don't worry about passing out in the thin air. You will revive when you get down to ten or twelve thousand feet. When you get close enough to see the ground clearly, look in all directions for dense woods or some other place to hide until dark. Determine if any army or civilian patrol is on the way to where you will land. If they are, do not resist or attempt to run away. If you do you will be shot on the spot."

Each instructor had different ideas about how to land safely. I liked the following because it was the same system I was taught at Brooks Field many years earlier: "At about a hundred feet from the ground reach out and grab as many parachute shroud lines as you can grasp in each hand. Just before you hit the ground, bend your knees slightly to avoid breaking a leg, and pull down hard on both groups of shroud lines in order to help break the impact of your fall. Immediately after hitting the ground, turn loose of the shroud lines with one hand and use both hands on the other lines. Pull hard enough to spill the air out of the chute and prevent the wind from dragging you. If you are not apprehended, stuff the chute under some bushes then take off fast for the nearest place to hide. Swallow one of these benzedrine tablets from your escape kit to prevent shock. Stay hidden until dark, then move out to put some distance between you and any patrol that may be looking for you.''

If an escaped airman was picked up by the Underground Resistance people, as often happened, he would need an identification picture for forged papers. All civilians in Europe were required to carry identification papers with a picture attached. The Underground could easily forge a set of false papers, but no photographic paper or film was available to civilians in occupied Europe. So each crewman carried an escape picture of himself made under harsh light to make him look haggard. Since the combat groups were strictly military units they had a limited number of civilian jackets for those pictures. On the following page are seven pictures, all showing exactly the same jacket. The Germans learned to identify captured fliers by the jacket in their escape picture.

I remember a lecture from an airman who had bailed out and made his way to Spain and eventually back to England. ''Most Frenchmen will recognize who you are, but Germans in France may not. Never force a conversation with a Frenchman because you do not know if it is safe for him to speak to you or recognize you for what you are. A French family caught aiding an escaped American or English airman is executed. If you reach the point where you desperately need help, try to find a remote village. Watch it from a distance for signs of Germans or officials. If there are none, then just before dark saunter slowly through the town without speaking or nodding to anyone. Let the people see you. Keep right on walking down the road so they will know where you will be after dark. If it is safe, they will notify the Underground. Leave it entirely up to them.''

CHAPTER XII

Mission to Bremen

October 8

The nightly raids against England continued but were a civilian threat, not a military one. The Germans did not have the accuracy to pinpoint military sites at night. Hitler had given up the idea of attempting to invade England, and knew that his forces could not destroy her with the weapons presently available. The German air raids were as much in retaliation for the nightly R.A.F. destruction raining down on Germany as they were to wipe out war production.

If we thought Hitler was about to give up on the idea of subduing England, we were very much wrong. He could not accomplish it by means of conventional weapons, but his excellent scientists were working hard to develop new means of terror for the stubborn British. The Allied Commanders had no means to know how close to success they were, but alarming rumors were filtering into Allied intelligence centers. Some came from agents on the Continent. Other information of a highly disturbing nature was picked up from the secret Turing Machine (code-named Ultra), a marvelous machine. It was developed by a brilliant Englishman named Alan Turing, and could decode the supposedly unbreakable German cipher as easily as the Germans could do so with their code books. The German high command never suspected that their cipher had been broken and the Allies read their secret messages throughout the war. Mr. Churchill thought that "Ultra" was one of the most decisive advantages that the Allies possessed. Thus the Allies knew the threat of new super weapons was not just an idle boast of the German propaganda machinery. In English-language broadcasts we heard direct allusions to terrible instruments of death and destruction that would turn the tide of victory to Germany. We knew the Germans were capable of creating new machines of death if they had enough time. Even though we dismissed the threats as so much propaganda, we did not take the enemy lightly. I would not have been surprised at any time that some new weapon was thrown at us. We assumed that the Allies were working on super weapons, too, but there was the haunting fear that the German scientists were ahead of us because they could have started as far back as 1935 or 1936 and might be nearing success.

October 8—Bremen   *Aircraft 755*

"OK! Wake up. Let's go! Listen to the roster: Comer, Counce, Balmore, Legg, and Harness flyin' 755 with Gleichauf . . ."

"Wait! You mean 765," I said.

"No! 755 like I said."

"But 765 is our ship," I replied.

"Not today. Some other crew is flyin' it. Good luck."

Reese was gone before I could say anything else.

Jim exploded. "Damn those clerks at Operations! Giving our ship to some other crew an' makin' us fly one we've never seen before."

"It's an error in typing but too late to do anything about it. George, how about you standing by the Briefing Room door while Jim and I get to the aircraft early? I don't remember aircraft 755."

The aircraft was in excellent condition. An hour later I said to Jim, "Things are going too well this mornin'—not normal. We must be overlooking something."

George came out on the next truck. "Didn't sound too bad. I'd say medium tough."

"You think we need more ammunition?"

"Don't think so."

A Jeep pulled up and the Flight Surgeon stepped out. "Rub some of this salve on your face where the mask does not cover it. I hope it'll cut down on frostbite." Captain Ralston was a good one. He never succeeded in finding an ointment to prevent frost bite but he kept trying.

The crew chief drew me aside. "How long you fellows been here?"

"Since July."

The chief looked relieved. "Who is your pilot?"

Examples
of
Escape
Pictures

Note that every man used the same jacket.

138

"Gleichauf."

"Oh, good man."

Paul was well known to the veteran crew chiefs. They took pride in the condition of the aircraft assigned to them. When necessary the ground crews put in long hours. They became upset when an inexperienced crew abused an airplane. The chiefs, of course, expected battle damage, but they were incensed when planes returned with unnecessary wear on brakes and engines caused by pilots who did not have enough experience or did not care. Gleichauf had a reputation for respecting an aircraft and the men who kept them in good condition.

When the pilot arrived, I started sounding off about some other crew assigned to our airplane but Gleichauf cut it short. "Some clerk made an error. Forget the bitching and let's get ready to start engines." He waited for the rest of the men to gather around him. "We're goin' to Bremen today. The fighter opposition is not expected to be too rough. There are two hundred and fifty flak guns—very accurate. There are two hundred fighters in the area, so it could turn out rougher than expected. P-47s will go with us nearly to the I.P. The target is submarine installations."

As we approached the enemy coast I went into my regular ritual. "Oh, God, be with me today and keep me from danger . . ." Instantly my brain received a message as clear as if it had come routinely over the intercom system, except it was not audible. "German pilots rising up to meet you are asking the same thing. How can you be so misguided, understand so little?" Where did the message come from? I put small credence in prayer in the sense of physical phenomena. It had always been for me more of a ritual or historical practice of Christianity than a direct communication with a higher power. I had never really expected a positive response. My mind reeled from the impact of a new dimension with which it was unprepared to cope.

"Navigator to crew, fighers nine o'clock. It's the escort right on time."

"Waist to Turret."

"Waist to Turret—come in."

I recovered when I realized that someone was calling my position. "This is the Turret—go ahead."

"Number four engine is vibrating too much—could be detonation."

"Turret to Copilot, what's the temperature of number four?"

"Two fifteen."

"That oughta be OK if the gauge is accurate. You can try two things: switch to automatic rich or open the flaps and drop it down to about two hundred."

I saw the cowl flaps open slightly and in a few minutes Jim called again, "Number four looks OK now." I made a mental note to tell the crew chief to check the cylinder head temperature gauge for number four engine.

We crossed over the edge of the Low Countries and entered the air above Germany. The P-47s dipped their wings and turned back toward England. What went through the minds of the men who flew the P-47s when they had to break off and leave us alone to face the fury of Goering's vicious fighters?

"Tail to crew! Fighters at six o'clock. More fighters low and coming up."

"Copilot to Tail, let us know what they're up to back there."

"Tail to crew—four fighters closing fast at six o'clock high."

"Radio to crew, I think they're gonna come on in."

"Turret to Copilot, watch forward an' call me if anything shows up—I'm goin' to help the Tail."

"OK, Turret."

When I spun around I could hardly believe what I saw. Four fighters were flying so close together they looked like one enormous four-engine aircraft. Surely they did not intend to attack us that way! The greenest German pilot should have known better, but they kept coming. At six hundred yards I saw the first flash of cannon fire which was the signal for the formation gunners to let go with a furious assault. Every fifth round was what we called a tracer. It was a projectile with a magnesium insert in the rear, which would ignite and glow brightly as it flew through the air. Immediately the sky was ablaze with tracers. Almost all top turrets, some balls and all tails poured a heavy barrage at those four unfortunate fighters. The enormous mass of fifty caliber slugs was so devastating that there were four puffs of black smoke and a sky filled with debris that erased four poorly-trained German pilots. They made two horrendous mistakes: one, flying so close together that they gave us a single target; and two, choosing the worst possible angle of attack where they would have to face the maximum fire power a B-17 formation could bring to bear.

"Tail to Turret, they were crazy. They didn't have a chance."

"A good way to commit suicide."

A curious thought ran through my mind. "Perhaps in their twisted Teutonic thinking they were reaching for Valhalla—if so, I hoped they found it."

"Navigator to crew, fighters—nine o'clock level—eleven o'clock level."

They came at us from four directions. A Jerry defense commander must have stirred them up and they were breathing fire—mean and rough. It might have been what they saw us do to those four green pilots. For the next fifteen minutes it was a savage fight as intense as I can remember.

We were in the low location, called "purple heart corner." On the first heavy fire the turret clutch kicked out of position, stopping the action. I jumped out, removed the cumbersome glove from one hand, reached high up into the maze of cables and reset the clutch. The turret was quickly back in operation. The next burst of prolonged firing kicked the clutch out again.

"Turret to Copilot, the damn clutch keeps jumping out! Must be a weak spring. I've got to try to wire it in position."

"Hurry it up. If the turret is out of action too long, the fighters will notice it."

As fast as possible, I re-engaged the clutch and wrapped copper wire around it to hold it in position—I hoped. As I climbed back into the turret, a fighter zoomed by spraying us with machine-gun fire. A slug knocked out my intercom phones. I did manage to repair the mike, but the earphone system was dead.

As we approached the target the enormous field of flak ahead was unbelievable. And frightening! My thoughts were "Good God! Can anything fly through that?" I knew how accurate the flak was over Bremen. The German gunners had excellent radar control. Intense antiaircraft fire was far less dangerous than fighter attacks, but more scary: there was no way to fight back at bursting shells.

Wham! The heavy crashing noise came from below me. I dropped down to survey the damage. My first fear was that one or both pilots might be seriously injured, but as far as I could see with a quick look, both were OK.

"Turret to Copilot, over."

"Go ahead."

"Are either of you hurt? My earphones are dead, so give me some sign."

I leaned down enough to see them and he shook his head, which told me there was nothing too serious. Several fighters were circling high and to my left and I was watching them closely. I turned to the right for a quick look and was petrified! A huge rectangular mass the size of a large car was flying alongside, not far from me, glistening in the bright sunlight like a thousand diamonds. "What is that monstrous thing?" I said to myself. "Some fantastsic new weapon the Germans are throwing at us? If that mass explodes it could blow us out of the sky." I hid on the opposite side of the computing sight to take the small amount of cover available, and peeked around it at the terrifying apparition. It began to lose speed and broke up into shimmering reflections that fanned out behind into a luminous cloud of particles. How could that huge mass have gotten twenty-five thousand feet up in the sky? What was it?

Fighters were streaking in straight ahead too low for me to get any shots. We caught a direct hit on number three engine and it began to vibrate heavily. I heard a loud smash underneath and suddenly my intercom was working. (Like a radio that you kick and it resumes playing.)

"Copilot to Ball."

"Go ahead."

"Can you see any oil leaking from number three engine?"

"It's throwin' oil real bad."

"Pilot to Copilot—feather number three."

The engine slowed down and eventually stopped.

"Copilot to Ball—is number three still leakin'?"

"It's about stopped."

I felt the bombs fall out and soon we were clear of that awful flak! I looked back and the sky was a solid mass of boiling black smoke. How in the hell did any of us get through it?

There was a loud bang from number two engine. It must have taken a hard smash from a cannon shell or a big piece of flak. I waited for smoke or heavy vibrations but when, after thirty seconds, it was still running smoothly, I relaxed. Had we lost another engine it would have been extremely hazardous for us alone among all of those snarling fighters. We could not have kept up with the formation on two engines.

Another attack came and I heard something strike the radio room with a sound of tearing metal.

"Copilot to Radio—Copilot to Radio—come in."

"Copilot to Waist, can you see Radio?"

"I can see him. Got some equipment damage, and he's rubbing his ass like he may have been zipped there, but don't think it is too serious."

"Go check out Radio an' call me back."

"He's OK now, Copilot, he's motioning that his intercom is knocked out."

"Waist to Copilot."

"Go ahead Wilson."

"765 has been hit—looks bad—don't think she can keep up with us."

I watched 765 fall back with mounting apprehension. Soon she was out of my range of vision.

"Ball to crew—765 is gone! No chutes. Damn!"

After a few minutes the Ball continued. "Six fighters tore her apart. Looked to me like they had time to jump."

Our faithful old aerial warhorse was finished! As she rolled back within my sight far below, I felt stabs of anguish. It was like losing an old friend with whom I had shared both escapades and harrowing experiences.

A fighter zoomed up from below and cut loose at us with cannon fire.

"Tail to Copilot, a twenty millimeter shell damn near got me. Knocked off one of my boots an' crashed on through without exploding."

Aircraft *Tinker Toy* moved into the space that 765 had been holding.

"Tail to crew, look at *Tinker Toy*. She's riddled from the ball to the tail."

"That's *Tinker Toy*—same old thing!" said the bombardier.

"Copilot to crew, two fighters comin' in eleven o'clock high. Let 'em have it Turret! Hey, Navigator, blast the bastards."

They were going for *Tinker Toy* and hit her dead center of the cockpit. I saw a small explosion.

Counce called, "They got the pilot! Copilot is hit, too. The engineer is trying to move the pilot's body so he can get in his seat."

"Turret to Copilot, I think I just saw the engineer put *Tinker Toy* on auto pilot until he can try to get control."

Kels motioned for Gleichauf to switch over to intercom.

"What is it?"

"Keep your eye on *Tinker Toy*. Pilot is dead. Engineer put her on auto pilot. He's trying to move the pilot's body. The copilot is slumped in his seat—can't tell how bad he's wounded."

"We'll watch her—don't want a collision with *Tinker Toy*."

The fighters kept striking her. One wing was badly torn and an engine cowling knocked off. But she flew on. In my imagination I could hear her taunting the fighters: "Yah! Yah! You kraut pimps! You can't knock me down. Go ahead! Try it! You square-headed bastards ain't good enough to get me. Yah! Yah! Yah! Go ahead and try to shoot me down! Yah! Yah!"

The wounded copilot raised up in his seat momentarily and helped the engineer with a control then collapsed again. How could the two men in the cockpit withstand that awful blast of super-frigid wind blowing squarely in their faces without windshields?

Suddenly I realized my left hand was so cold it was becoming numb. That was normally a sign that the electric glove had burned out. I looked down at the hand. It was bare except for a thin silk glove. Where was the electric glove? Oh! I had removed it to wire the turret clutch in place. At thirty-five below, I was handling the metal gun controls with a hand covered only with the light silk glove normally worn under the electric outer glove. Impossible! My hand would have frozen solidly in a very few minutes. Yet, I was looking at the numb hand and the electric glove was resting where I took it off much earlier—before we reached the target. There was only one explanation: in the excitement of the action my blood pressure had gone sky high, pushing a large quantity of warm blood to the hands which replaced some of the lost heat.

When the fighter attacks finally faded out my relief was quickly punctured by the antics of number three engine. It suddenly unfeathered and began to revolve out of control. It required engine oil pressure to hold a propeller in a feathered position with the blades flat to the wind. If the oil pressure failed, the blades would shift to an angle, and the strong wind would rotate them. That was called windmilling, and with no means of control, the propeller revolutions would rev up to fantastic speeds. With no lubrication the engine would get hotter and hotter until it became red hot. The danger was that it might tear off of the aircraft with severe damage. The engine revved up and up beyond the twenty-five-hundred R.P.M. red-line limit. I watched with a sinking feeling as it shot up to three thousand. Then, to my immense relief, and for no reason that I could think of at the moment, it began to level off, then started slowing down. Eventually it stopped and resumed a feathered position again.

"Turret to Ball."

"Go ahead, Turret."

"Check number three again for an oil leak."

"No oil leak from number three engine."

"Pilot to Turret. What's wrong with number three prop?"

"Not sure. Could be a fracture in the oil pressure system in the prop hub that opens and closes. Ball says no oil leak down below so far. If it starts squirting out oil we'll have a runaway prop."

"Turret to Waist. Jim, how does this sound to you?"

"Don't see how it could be anything but a pressure leak."

Five minutes later the process repeated. All of the way back to Ridgewell that propeller would race up to three thousand revolutions and, having made its point, return to zero. Each time the speed zoomed upward my blood pressure went up with it.

We could have caught fighters again, but fortunately nothing else happened. *Tinker Toy* had serious landing problems but ended with nothing worse than slipping off the runway into sticky mud. A crowd gathered quickly to see what new horrors she had thrown at her crew. And again the question: Was she really a jinx ship? For the men who flew combat raids in her it was more than a wartime superstition. It was a series of nightmares! That day her nose was blown off, both windshields were wiped out, one wing was battered, and she was heavily damaged from the radio to the tail. The cockpit was splattered with blood, bits of flesh, and hair—a horrible sight to see.

When I climbed out of 755 the crew chief was waiting. "You had better put in a call for some sheet metal men, you will probably need two new engines, the radio is shattered, you will need two windshields, and one wing flap. The tail is also damaged. I think all of the main fuel tanks will have to be replaced because they are bound to be perforated . . ."

The 381st sent out twenty-one ships and lost seven. The 100th had another bad day and lost eight. The total loss for the raid was thirty-seven Forts. Of the returning aircraft, seventy-five percent were damaged.

As soon as we were on the ground, I asked Gleichauf and Purus about the huge mass of shining particles I saw near the target. It turned out to be a new way to confuse the enemy radar by dumping out bales of thin aluminum foil fragments. The light pieces floating in the air confused the enemy radar by appearing to be aircraft. What I saw was a compressed bale of foil that had not yet begun to break up. Later on it was thrown in bulk from several aircraft regularly and was called "chaff."

After the mission I hit the sack, weary, exhausted, and in a state of confusion. What did the message I received on the way to Bremen mean and where did it come from? I never expected to get an answer to a prayer, if indeed, that is what had happened. There was absolutely no doubt but that I did get a communication. The question was, "Where did it come from?" A simplistic answer would have been straight from God. I could have accepted that except it seemed too simple—too easy to draw such a conclusion as fact. I tried to think about it in rational channels, although I realized that at some point any religion steps beyond logic or reason into mystical or metaphysical phenomena. The danger faced each mission made me ready to turn to any spiritual assistance that was readily available, but I needed to separate the real from the dross that had accumulated in my mind.

CHAPTER XIII

Mission to Anklam

October 9—Anklam, Germany   *Aircraft 719*
                                                       Hellcat

It was difficult for me to get out of bed that morning. I felt tired and low on energy, which was unusual for me. When I got to Operations, Gleichauf was waiting. "They've given us a new airplane, John—one of those G Models that arrived two days ago—the number is 719."

"That's great! Now we will have twenty-seven hundred gallons of fuel. I wish we could have had one flight before we take her up for a combat mission. I hear there are a lot of changes."

"Oh, I don't think the changes will make much difference," Paul replied, "but get on out there as fast as you can and look it over. Find out what you can about those new electronic supercharger controls they told us about."

When Jim arrived I called to him. "We've got a new airplane—one of those new G models. Get your equipment quick and let's get out there and see what she looks like."

An ominous groan from the Briefing Room sent a shiver down my spine. Jim looked up, "Listen to that! We must have a real bitch today!"

"Wherever we're headed, it's gonna be mean. That much is for sure," I answered.

"I hope Chamberlain is on hand with plenty of extra ammunition, 'cause it sounds to me like we're goin' to need it."

In the personnel truck on the way to the ship Jim asked, "What do we know about the changes in the new models?"

"The main ones are the electronic supercharger controls and the new chin turret."

146

Tinker Toy as the aircraft looked after the October 8 mission. On top of the plane is mechanic Dean L. Carrier, who later became a flight engineer-gunner. The officer in the picture is Capt. Greewood. Sgt. Carrier is pointing to the hole where the 20mm cannon shell entered the aircraft and killed the pilot.

"Don't forget about those enclosed waist windows and the radio hatch cover. No more of that storm of cold wind gushing through the waist and radio room. The electronic supercharger controls are near my position. I'll check them out with the crew chief and see what we can do in an emergency."

The early E and F models of the B-17 had open waist windows with guns mounted in those openings. The radio room upper hatch was removed and a gun was placed there. In most groups the rear radio room door was also removed, since it served no purpose in combat. The combined open spaces created an enormous suction causing a terrific frigid wind blast to roar through the radio room and the waist. This hazard was responsible for untold casualties of freezing and frostbite. The new G model replaced the open spaces using clear plexiglass windows with the gun mounts built into them.

"OK—we'll both check out the new turret for Purus. The guns have probably never been fired. I hope that remote-control sight works out well."

"It will take Purus a while to get used to it—sounds awkward to me—but it ought to help up front where we need more fire power."

Chamberlain was there when we arrived and I asked him for four thousand extra rounds in case we needed them. How did he always manage the extra ammo? There wasn't supposed to be any surplus around the flight line.

I was waiting anxiously for Gleichauf to begin the briefing: "All ships will have twenty-seven hundred gallons of fuel today for the first time on a mission. Three Wings will cross Denmark at thirteen thousand feet and attack different targets. We will fly a little way over the Baltic Sea then turn right into Northeastern Germany to hit an airframe factory at Anklam. S-2 thinks the different routes, the unexpected lower altitude, and timing will upset the opposition and divide the fighters. They estimate the opposition will be light. Jerry does not know we can strike a target this deep."

The crew was delighted at the lower altitude and mild temperature. My enthusiasm waned when I had time to reflect on the long route over Denmark so close to the German border. I found Purus examining his new turret. "You say S-2 doesn't expect much fighter opposition?"

"That is what they told us."

"Suppose S-2 is wrong? We'll be within close range of German fighter bases for six to seven hours. Every fighter they have can easily get to us at thirteen thousand feet."

"You're right. We could catch a long, rough fight in and out."

148

I turned to Gleichauf. "I don't buy S-2's estimate of the fighter opposition. There are too many fighter bases close to our flight path. We could catch half of the fighters in North Germany and we better put on all the ammunition we can carry."

"I don't like to carry more weight than we need," he answered.

He did not give me a flat no, so I put aboard more ammunition, raising the total load to thirteen thousand five hundred rounds. It was almost double the regulation seven thousand rounds.

When our turn came to takeoff, we roared down the runway and at ninety miles per hour Paul felt out the lift of the wings. Nothing. At a hundred miles per hour, still nothing. At a hundred and ten he tried again with no response! We should have been in the air at a hundred and five. At a hundred and fifteen the ship still would not begin a bounce. Kels glanced at Gleichauf with a questioning look. The end of the runway was rushing toward us. It was too late to abort the takeoff. Big beads of sweat broke out on Paul's face. At a hundred twenty-three miles per hour, there was a feeble bounce.

Paul screamed at Kels, "Raise landing gear!"

That desperation move lowered air resistance just enough to permit the aircraft to stagger drunkenly into the air. I have never been so frightened in my life! We barely skimmed over some trees and rose unsteadily to a little over sixty feet. Then the airplane started sinking, in spite of all Gleichauf could do and what should have been a safe airspeed. For the only time in my life I gave up all hope of survival. I knew that no one survived a crash on a takeoff with an overloaded airplane. We cleared some trees and reached a large open area of fields as the aircraft sank toward the ground. I expected at any second to spin off to the right or left and crash. That is what airplanes normally do when they cannot maintain flying speed on takeoff.

Paul yelled to Kels, "Lower landing gear!"

John quickly flipped the gear switch and the main wheels came down before the plane struck the ground. The ship hit hard and bounced back into the air thirty or thirty-five feet.

"Raise landing gear."

Up came the wheels and we hung precariously in the air for a few seconds. Slowly the plane began to sink again. We got down to twenty-five feet and steadied. The engines had been wide open all that time and airspeed was up to a hundred and thirty. Now the aircraft began to inch upward. I saw some trees ahead and we were able just to clear them. Ever so slowly the ship rose on up to a safe height.

Lucky! Lucky! Lucky! Nothing but pure, unbelievable, and

undeserved luck saved us from a complete wipe out! Ten men got a reprieve from what seemed certain death. Why? The aircraft was mushing on takeoff because of too much tail weight, upsetting its aerodynamics. Too much extra ammunition weight? I did not think so. The ships we had been flying could have handled it. Up to then I had not considered that a G Model, with the chin turret disrupting the air flow a little, might not have as good takeoff characteristics as the older ships. That may have had something to do with it, but was not the main reason for the near disaster.

I hurried to the radio room to check the weight distribution of the extra ammunition. I had placed as much as I could against the forward wall of the radio room next to the bomb bay and the center of gravity of the airplane and the rest as far forward as possible, along with some in the cockpit and nose. To my shock the boxes of reserve rounds were far back in the waist and some stacked right against the tail gunner's position. I was furious. "Are you guys crazy? You damned near killed us. You never move weight to the rear of an airplane!"

Jim knew better so why did he let them do it? Then I saw the Tail Gunner getting out of the tail. "You were in that tail on takeoff? No wonder we were so tail heavy." I was so incensed I could have choked Legg on the spot. "Get those boxes of ammo back against the radio room forward bulkhead an' leave them there until they are needed."

In the cockpit I explained to Gleichauf what happened. "The crew back there pulled most of the extra ammunition to the waist. And Legg was in the tail with all of his equipment on the takeoff. We were thirteen hundred pounds too heavy at the tail." That must have been the worst successful takeoff since Orville Wright made the first one.

The length of the mission cut out the usual feinting tactics. We formed up quickly and headed out over the North Sea toward Denmark.

"Bombardier to crew—Bombardier to crew—test fire your guns."

I listened to the guns chatter.

"Navigator to Copilot. How about this? No oxygen mask—and a decent temperature."

"I wish they were all like this," Kels answered.

"Pilot to crew, cut the unnecessary talk. Keep the intercom clear."

"Navigator to Pilot. Danish coast in ten minutes."

"Bombardier to crew, we're close enough that fighters could hit us. Keep alert."

The coast passed by underneath. We were flying parallel to the German border. Denmark looked green and peaceful below.

"Bombardier to crew, fighters at eleven o'clock level."

I counted thirty-two M.E. 109s. They made numerous attacks but were cautious and showed inexperience in opposing B-17 formations.

"Waist to crew—more fighters coming up—look like M.E. 210s."

"Bombardier to Navigator, my guns have jammed. Take a look at the ammunition chute."

The G Model eliminated the navigator side guns and placed two guns in the new nose turret. The Navigator had the responsibility of reloading the small ammunition cans by removing a section of the deck above the ammunition chutes. The long chutes were assisted by electric motors activated by the firing trigger.

The attackers were wary of the formation guns and we kept them at a distance with good protective fire coverage. Some large twin-engined craft came up and flew along with us on both sides of the formation just out of our gun range. Some gunners were firing at them.

"Bombardier to crew. Do not fire at those ships. They're out of range. I think they're trying to get us to use up our ammunition."

Over the Baltic Sea there was little opposition. We passed directly over a German naval base. I could see frantic action below as boats hurriedly attempted to clear the harbor before the bombs they expected started falling.

"Navigator to crew, watch those Krauts tryin' to get out of the harbor."

"Ball to Bombardier, lower the bomb-bay doors and scare the hell out of 'em."

"Pilot to crew! I told you to keep the intercoms clear!"

The formation made a sweeping turn to the right into Northern Germany. Perhaps then the German Defense Command could narrow down the possible targets and alert the fighter airfields protecting those installations. The enemy could not be certain until we made the final turn toward the objective.

"Bombardier to Navigator, my guns are jammed again."

Later Shutting called Purus. "Your ammunition keeps jamming up in those long chutes. Must be somethin' wrong with the design."

"Copilot to crew, watch the F.W. 190s one o'clock high. They're comin' in but not on us."

We helped out another squadron with protective fire at long range.

"Bombardier to Pilot."

"Go ahead."

"We'll be on the bomb run in five minutes."

"Flak nine o'clock low—flak ten o'clock level."

When the doors came down the fighters stood away from us as they always did. I never figured out why. Were they afraid of our falling bombs? When the load released cleanly, I felt much better because the mission was half over. It would be a long ride back, but the Germans usually hit us harder before the target, so going back should not be too bad. That extra ammunition was not likely going to be needed. Gleichauf would probably give me hell about loading on too much ammunition: all of that extra weight for nothing.

Ten minutes later Purus called the Pilot. "Looks to me like we are goin' to be hit harder on the way back. By now every fighter in North Germany knows where we are and how long we'll be in their range."

Wilson came on the intercom. "Copilot, check ten o'clock level —is that a four-engine Dornier bomber with all of those guns sticking out?"

"I've never seen anything like that before—are they trying to use that big ship against us like a fighter?"

The formation continued the steady fire and it was effective. At that rate, if fighters kept showing up, we were going to have an ammunition problem before long. I changed my mind about the extra ammunition. We were going to be glad we had it aboard.

"Bombardier to Copilot, look at twelve o'clock! A small open-cockpit training plane comin' right at us—must be gunnery students."

I could scarcely believe what I was seeing! No doubt they were German students on a gunnery practice flight with a single small-caliber gun. They were taking on a Flying Fortress formation bristling with heavy-caliber guns . . . Teutonic Don Quixotes cheerfully facing impossible odds. (I thought that the little plane went on through the formation, but I rarely glanced at an aircraft once it passed by and was no longer a threat. Woodrow Pitts said he saw the aircraft shot down. I hope that the youngsters in it managed to bail out—they had unusual courage.)

"Bombardier to Navigator, my guns are jammed again. This is the fourth time."

On the return over Denmark the fighters came up in relays. When one group ran short of fuel another group arrived to take over. One Fort after another was hit and lost.

"Copilot to crew—two fighters coming in twelve o'clock high."

The nose and turret poured heavy fire at them from a thousand yards out all the way in. Both the M.E. 210s were burning when they flashed by us very close.

"Pilot to Turret—did we get either one?"

"Both are badly damaged."

"Waist to Pilot, the pilot bailed out of one of them."

"Turret to crew—slow down on the ammunition. Some of the Forts are already out of ammo." Not many put on extra ammo. But at least one aircraft did. Ed Klein said his plane had 14,000 rounds aboard.

"Copilot to crew—Hendricks is hit. Don't know how bad. He's losing an engine, I think."

We were halfway across Denmark and I thought Hendricks had a good chance to make it to the coast where our escort was supposed to pick us up.

"Tail to Copilot, some M.E. 210s at fourteen hundred yards behind us, a little high. They're gettin' in some kind of a formation."

"Turret to Tail, what are they doing back there?"

"Nothin' yet, but they must be up to somethin'—I see what looks like big tubes under their wings."

Flak began to burst around the formation. It was larger in size than what we were used to seeing.

"Copilot to Navigator, where is that flak coming from? I don't see any cities or plants down below."

"There is not supposed to be any flak in this area."

The bursts got more consistent.

"Tail to Copilot, those 210s are firing something at us. The flashes are bigger than cannon fire."

I turned around to watch. Flashes of flame were coming out of those funny looking tubes. I looked closer—there was a faint vapor trail coming from a fighter and I followed it into the formation where it burst like a flak shell. Rockets! Jerry's much heralded rocket defensive weapon.

"Turret to crew. Those ships are throwing rockets at us. It's not flak. It's rockets."

"Tail to Pilot! Quick! Pull left—fast! A rocket is heading straight for us."

Gleichauf responded and the rocket passed a few inches from the horizontal stabilizer, then slowed down to our speed.

"Turret to crew, look at that damned rocket! It's spinning like a huge disc."

It was not more than twenty-five feet from my turret. Another ten feet and it would have struck the right wing. I took cover, expecting it to explode any second. The rocket slowed some more and spun away from us before it exploded. It was the first time I actually saw a lethal projectile clearly aimed at me.

We had experienced a few rockets before. We knew the Germans were working feverishly to get them in shape to try to stop the Forts on daylight raids.

"Turret to Bombardier, that last rocket was much too big to fit in those tubes under the wings of the 210s."

"You saw a malfunction, Turret. It was spinning end over end. That's why it moved so slow and looked like a big disc."

"Pilot to Tail, any way we could reach them with our guns?"

"Turret to Tail, let's aim high and try to lob some rounds into them."

We tried numerous elevations, but it was too far—we had a thousand yard trajectory with our guns. Beyond that the projectiles lost velocity rapidly. Jerry had the distance figured exactly right.

The 533rd Squadron began slowly falling behind and as a result we were drawing more of the rocket fire. Purus kept warning us not to waste ammunition, because we did not know how much longer the fight would continue. It seemed to me that seventy to eighty percent of the gun positions were out of ammunition already.

Major Hendricks was in the lead ship and we were on his left wing. I saw him leave the cockpit and go toward the bomb bay. A few minutes later he returned to his seat. Immediately he dropped down out of the formation. Perhaps he hoped to get close to the ground, below the radar, and try to slip through. I doubted he could make it. There were too many fighters circling about us. A lump came into my throat and I said to myself, "Take a good look at Hendricks—I doubt if we will ever see him again."

"Ball to Pilot, is Hendricks trying to surrender? His landing gear is down."

"No, that's his signal for the deputy lead to take over."

Gleichauf moved up to take over Squadron lead and I lost sight of Hendricks.

I could sense the pain in Gleichauf's voice. He and Hendricks were good friends and it was hard to lose a friend in plain sight with no chance to help him.

Kels called the Pilot. "Hendricks saw he was slowing down the Squadron and did what he thought was the right thing for the Squadron."

"He didn't have to do it—we could have made the coast. The escort will meet us there."

"Legg to crew, four 210s trailing us—may come in."

"Turret to Tail—if they start in, fire two quick bursts an' I'll turn around and help you."

When I heard Legg open up I whirled around. Two 210s were closing fast at six o'clock slightly high. Both of us threw burst after burst at them and they broke off the attack. The other two 210s must have absorbed some hits, too, because they also turned suddenly away and vanished from sight.

"Ball to crew, 210 trying to come up at us."

Harkness tore that ship apart. The Ball had a large advantage when a fighter tried to sneak in from below. A J.U. 88, used that day as an interceptor, tried the same thing and Harkness drove it off, but the 88 took all he could throw at it with no outward signs of damage. It was a rugged ship.

"Tail to Waist, any ammunition left?"

"A full box. I'll shove it back to where you can reach it."

"Navigator to Bombardier, most of our planes are out of ammunition."

"Copilot to crew, don't talk about ammo—it might leak through to Jerry."

The fight was showing no signs of abating. Ammunition became deadly serious. By that time we were one of the few aircraft with ammunition. I realized that if Jerry discovered we were defenseless, few of us would make it through the day because to ditch, or bail out, in that ice-cold water would amount to a slow death.

A few minutes later, when I saw the fighters fade away to the south, I thought we almost had it made because the rendezvous time for our escort was a few minutes ahead. Five minutes later the Bombardier called, "Bombardier to crew, the escort at nine o'clock high."

They were a welcome sight. It had been a long day and now we could relax and let them worry about the fighters, if any more showed up. All of a sudden I saw something odd. What in the hell were those 47s doing? They knew better than to dive on a B-17 formation! Oh, my God! They were F.W. 190s! If they knew about our ammunition, we were done for. (F.W. 190 fighters did look like P-47s at a distance and they had appeared at the same time and same direction that we expected P-47s.)

"Turret to Waist—Wilson."

"Go ahead."

"They're comin' in on Cahow. Let's give him some help."

I fired so close over Cahow's head that he might have preferred the fighters if he had a chance. There could not have been much, if any, ammunition left in the 381st Group—certainly not enough to hold off another attack. Until the P-47s arrived we were helpless. The German fighters made one run through the formation, then pulled away and began circling us. All they had to do was drop flaps to slow down to our speed and blast us out of the sky. Never before had Jerry had a formation of B-17s of this size on the ropes. Any minute the slaughter would begin. Wait! What was happening? Were they really turning away to leave? It was hard to believe. Didn't they know they had us whipped? I watched with a combination of amazement and jubilation as those fighters vanished into the haze. I will never know what saved us. It is possible that the fighters intercepted us at the outer limit of their fuel range.

"Waist to Copilot, you think they're gone for good?"

"You better hope so."

Five minutes later I called Jim. "We are not out of the woods yet, but it's looking better every minute."

The formation droned on toward England and I watched the Danish coast fade away to the east. Was it over? Where was the escort? What had happened to Hendricks? I would have prayed for him and his men if I had known how, or what to say. For the next fifteen minutes I anxiously scanned the skies to the south and east until I finally felt that the long air battle was over.

When I heard about Carqueville at interrogation I went numb. The information was meager: "He was last seen with engines smoking heavily headed downward but still under control." Herb was with another squadron and I did not know he was on the mission until after interrogation. We went by Operations to ask if there was any word about Carqueville or Hendricks. Nothing!

In the hours before dawn, after a sleepless night, my thoughts turned back to Carqueville. Did he make it to Sweden? Did he go down in the ice-cold Baltic Sea? Maybe he bailed out over land. I wanted desperately to believe he was all right, but somehow I had the feeling he did not make it. There was that sickening sensation deep within me that told me Herb was gone.[1] How did such a communication reach my brain? I frankly do not know. But during the days in England, I developed a psychic ability to perceive things about some people in combat unrelated to facts from the sensitory world. Although he was not a great pilot, Herb Carqueville was my friend. How often we use the word "friend" when we really mean an associate or a neighbor. Often it is because of eccentricities or shortcomings that the attraction develops. The pain of losing a friend never subsides. Could it have been only last April when our crew first came together? It seemed much longer.

---

[1] No trace of Carqueville or Hendricks was ever found. In 1982, while attending a memorial service at the beautiful American Cemetery near Cambridge, I found their names carved on the long white stone wall dedicated to all of the service people who were missing in action in that part of the war. I looked at those two names a long time, and memories, long buried by the passage of years, came flooding back.

October 10

Bomber command sent another large force against Munster and caught heavy opposition and lost thirty Fortresses. The 381st was bypassed no doubt to permit more time to repair damaged aircraft. The unlucky 100th Group had another disaster. They lost all twelve of their ships. A sizable consignment of new planes and crews arrived at our base during the day and they were indeed welcome. Our strength was below par, which put a strain on the crews and repair personnel. I watched the newcomers at the mess hall that evening and could not help wondering how long they would last. Which ones would be shot down before we had a chance to learn their names?

Johnny Purus and I were greatly disturbed by the jamming malfunctions of the chin turret guns on their first test under combat conditions. We got by with it the day before only because the attacks, while strung out over five or six hours, were at no time an intense action of fighters coming in right behind each other; we had time to get the jammed ammunition straightened out between attacks. We could not afford to have the nose turret out of action in an all-out fight. We carefully re-examined the new weapon and concluded that the problem was caused by the assist motor in the ammunition chute. The electric motor was put there to help slide the ammunition along an extra long chute. The idea was fine, but as we saw it, the motor continued to revolve for a few seconds after the firing ceased, causing the ammunition to jam tightly in the chute, creating a stoppage. We decided that if an adjustable restrictor could be fitted into the chute behind the motor it could be adjusted to exert just enough back pressure to relieve the problem. I borrowed a ruler and we took careful measurements. That night at the barracks I prepared a drawing to proper scale of the modification we thought would work. The officers at the Turret Shop and Armament studied it and agreed it might solve the problem. They sent it to the machine shop with a rush order for four of the devices to install on the two G Models on our base.

My other concern stemming from the Anklam Raid was the rocket fighter menace. Most of the men on the mission were not that worked up about it, because the enemy did not have spectacular success with the rockets. Jim told Lieutenant Adkins, the Gunnery Officer, that the pattern of the rocket weapon was very good. I agreed. It was, he contended, merely a matter of time until Jerry would apply it against us with ten times that many rocket carriers. I felt that it worked much too well for a new weapon and we could expect accuracy to get better. They already had the distance worked out perfectly.

Adkins said, "We've got people smart enough to develop a new weapon with a two or three thousand yard range, but it would take a year to get it to us. We need it now."

Jim replied, "Then you think the only fast answer is long-range fighters?"

"Yes! I do not see anything right now that will work except fighters who can stay with you fellows to the target."

That was discouraging news because, if Adkins was right and our only practical defense was long-range fighters, where were they coming from? Did we have such fighters?

One other worry had been solved the day before. When Nick was wounded, it meant a new man in his position. Harold Harkness showed me over Denmark that he was a top-notch ball gunner. We were lucky to draw a man so solid and steady from the unassigned gunners on the base. When lethal flak shells were exploding around the ball, it took some kind of man to hang in there calm enough to do his job. The shells were fused to burst under the aircraft, so the ball always caught more of it than the rest of us. There was no place for Harkness to take cover. Of course, there was little cover anywhere in an airplane, but for most positions there were barriers that flak shrapnel had to penetrate from at least some directions. The rest of us donned heavy metal-lined flak vests when we approached the flak areas, but it was impossible in the ball, due to the restricted space. Harold had traded a farm tractor for a weird glass-and-aluminum ball hanging under the belly of the B-17 like a single giant testicle. Did he wonder at times if the ball was securely fastened to the aircraft? I would have. Suppose the plane took a heavy hit! Could he get out of that awkward prison in time to jump? Nick was impetuous and unpredictable. Harkness was the opposite: steady and methodical. I often speculated about the problem of an overflowing bladder in the ball. What did the gunner do? I suspected that I knew the answer, but never discussed it with Harold.

That night Jim said, "How in the hell did we get by with that takeoff? When it sunk to the ground I thought we were all gone!"

"So did I? No way we could have cut it thinner!"

"That's the second time we almost got it on takeoff. Remember that night at Boise when Captain Glenn almost got us killed?"

"I'll never forget it," I answered.

Pitts spoke up. "You say some Captain almost crashed the plane?"

"No, we were scheduled for a night instrument takeoff check for the pilot. I got to the ship ahead of the others and Captain Glenn, the instructor pilot, was already there and impatient to get the flight over with. He told me he had already done the preflight inspection, so let's get the engines started. I climbed into the copilot seat and reached for the checklist.

" 'I've already been through the checklist—don't need it again,' he said.

" 'But I thought we had to do . . .'

" 'Sergeant, I told you I have already been through it! Now start those engines!'

" 'Yes, sir!'

"When Carqueville got there the Captain told him, 'We've already done the checklist. We'll get the hood in place and take off.' (With the hood in place, the pilot could see only the instruments.) The flight was an instrument check. A few minutes later we roared down the runway and at ninety-five I saw Herb pull back on the elevator controls. Great Gods! The elevator was locked! I was standing alongside the copilot (Captain Glenn had his seat) directly over the elevator locking device! Both of us instantly dived to the deck to try to unlock it in time for the aircraft to get airborne before we ran out of runway! All we managed to do was knock each other out looking very much like a Stan Laurel and Oliver Hardy comedy. Herb jammed brakes, released them, and jammed them again and again. Near the end of the runway he revved up an outboard engine and skidded the aircraft around. We slid sideways up to the end of the runway. We ruined the brake system and both tires and were lucky to get by with nothing worse."

Balmore said, "I think that day we almost crashed into the mountain in Oregon was the closest thing we've had. It was worse than the takeoff this morning."

Counce added, "You're right! We were seconds from a head-on crash and it looked like there was no way to avoid it."

Jim was talking about a hazardous incident that took place on a training flight over the Pacific Ocean. I was not on the flight and Jim was serving as engineer. It was a check out of the Navigator and Radio Operator on over-water procedure. In a short time we would be heading out over some ocean for an overseas assignment. The flight started at Marysville, California. Soon after takeoff, fog closed in solidly up to twenty thousand feet. The Operations Tower directed them to continue the flight as planned because there would be no break in the fog for several hours. That put Lieutenant Shutting on a pure dead-reckoning course with no means of checking his position for wind drift until the fog dispersed. Carl did fine for the first five hundred miles over the water. Radio contact indicated that they passed over a check point on time. But the Navigator listened to considerable radio talk from ships and decided that the wind had shifted direction from the early morning briefing. After an hour or two on his changed heading (he had shifted the heading some to allow for the supposed change in the wind direction), he realized that the change was probably in error and he could not pinpoint where they were. The Navigator had downed too many cups of coffee and had to take time to go to the bomb bay to urinate. But he found the perchant tube hard frozen. He located Jim in the cockpit.

"What am I going to do? Let it go in the bomb bay?"

"Here, take one of these paper bags the lunches came in. Urinate in this and throw it out of the waist window." Jim solved his problem. It worked fine until Shutting tossed the sack out of the window; the swirling wind caught the sack and flung it back into the Navigator's face. There was not much Jim could do for him except offer a handkerchief.

In the radio room Balmore was trying to make contact with any station that might help. At that time of crew training, the radio operators had not yet been instructed in how to get a "fix" or a "Q.D.M.," but fuel was running low and they had to know exactly where they were. George raised a Coast Guard station and the operator suggested a fix. An officer was called in and explained the procedure to Balmore by Morse code. A few minutes later he was able to give Shutting his exact position at a given time. With that definite information, the Navigator brought them over the Air Base at Eugene, Oregon. The fog was still solid over the western part of the U.S. Visibility was near zero and fuel too low to proceed east far enough to clear the fog. Below were rugged mountains. An instrument letdown in unfamiliar mountain surroundings was beyond the experience of the pilot.

Carqueville turned to Jim. "How much fuel do we have left?"

"Less than an hour."

"We're goin' to have to do somethin' before long, even if it means takin' some risks."

The control tower at Eugene understood the gravity of the situation and called Carqueville. "We can hear your engines so we're going to try to talk you down by sound. Keep circling and start lettin' down an' we'll call your turns and headings. Let down at two hundred feet per minute."

"OK—we're ready."

"Pilot to crew. The tower is goin' to talk us down. We will be lettin' down in mountains, so everyone get in position an' keep a sharp lookout. If you see anything up ahead call me quick."

"Navigator to crew. We'll be lettin' down in a valley with mountains on each side. You know what that means."

160

Cautiously they began easing down, following the instructions from the tower. The tension was intense. Every eye strained into murk, hoping to spot an obstacle in time. Surely there is no experience in flying more nerve wracking than to know you may, at any second, hit a mountain head on.

Down! Down! Down! Down!

"Pilot to Navigator, we're below the height of the mountains on either side of us now."

"Mountain—straight ahead," screamed the copilot.

"Oh, my God."

Out of the gloom was the sight that all pilots hope never to see coming at them from close range! Carqueville jerked the nose of the aircraft sharply upward so that they were flying parallel to the sloping side of the mountain, almost brushing the tree tops. They could not maintain that steep angle of climb more than a few more seconds before the ship stalled out. Then number three engine could not take the strain of prolonged high power and conked out. That appeared to seal their doom, if it was not already certain! Seconds before stalling out, the ship cleared the top of the mountain and Herb quickly leveled off. There is no way it could have been nearer to a disaster!

Suddenly Wilson roused himself.

"Hey, John, remember the day we left Boise? We were about ready to clear the field, and a horrible accident took place right in front of our eyes?"

"I certainly do remember—I'll never forget it!"

When First Phase Training was over, our crew, along with another crew, were ordered to proceed to Casper, Wyoming, by train. There was a delay on the morning of our departure, however, because the pilot of the other crew had to be pressed into duty as an instructor for a two-hour flight. Men of both crews were waiting together, in front of an orderly room. Fifteen minutes later we heard the roar of a B-17 taking off. Then suddenly, there was the earth-shaking sound of a horrendous crash, followed by intermittent explosions.

"Look at that parachute!" shouted Jim.

How weird! I saw a parachute billow into the sky with no one in it! The next second the air was filled with debris, flames, and smoke. We were stunned! The pilot we were waiting for was in the aircraft that just crashed! The plane ran wild on takeoff, veered from the runway, and streaked across the parking ramp, crashing into several B-17s. It ended up in a pile of burning wreckage against one of the school buildings where our training classes had been held. Two men were pulled from the flaming wreckage and seven others died.

It was so pathetic. The lives of seven young men wiped out instantly, either due to a pilot error or some mechanical failure of the plane. I could visualize the arrival of telegrams, and the tears of grief and anguish! I could see the flag-draped coffins and the solemn services. I could hear the lovely haunting echoes of "Taps," bidding the young men a final good-bye. I knew that after a short time the memory of those men would begin to fade. In a little while only their families and a few close friends would remember. The rest of the community would soon forget them. After a year or two, most of the people who once knew them well would have a hard time recalling exactly what they looked like.

The triangle "L" insignia that identified the 381st bomb group.

The Joker—a well known aircraft of the 381st group.

—*Air and Space Museum, Smithsonian Institution*

Boeing Flying Fortress B-17 G that was modified to add more fire power up front. Note the extra-large side windows in the nose and guns in those windows. It must have had some special use.

Lockheed Lightning Fighter P-38. It was the first escort fighter that could go deep with the Flying Fortresses into the heart of Germany.

—Air and Space Museum, Smithsonian Institution

Republic Thunderbolt P-47 Fighter — the escort that was most often used to help the Fortress formations in the high thin air over the European continent.

—*Air and Space Museum, Smithsonian Institution*

The Mustang P-51 Fighter—most experts agreed that it was the finest fighter of the war. The aircraft could hold its own in combat performance against anything in the air and with disposable fuel tanks could go with the bombers on their deepest missions.

—*Air and Space Museum, Smithsonian Institution*

Royal Air Force Spitfire Fighter—as good as any fighter of the war in combat action. The small fuel tank limited the Spitfire for escort service.

—Air and Space Museum, Smithsonian Institution

German Focke-Wolfe 190 Fighter—probably the best fighter the Germans had for the early stages of the war. There was a bulge of the nose that does not show up in this picture that made it easier to identify.

—*Air and Space Museum, Smithsonian Institution*

German Messerschmitt 109 Fighter—when the 109G model was activated in late 1943 it probably became the best propeller-driven fighter that Germany developed.

—Air and Space Museum, Smithsonian Institution

German Messerschmitt Fighter—often used to carry rockets.

CHAPTER XIV

Second Mission to Schweinfurt

(BLACK THURSDAY)[1]

Johnny Purus was an unusually good man to have on a crew. He was as steady in the nose as Jim Counce was in the rear of the aircraft. The rest of us would screw up at times, but Johnny never did, except on that first fighter attack when three of us failed so miserably. He entered the service as an enlisted man and had some aircraft mechanical experience. Purus could handle the controls of a B-17 well enough to get back to the base if something happened to the pilot and copilot. Counce showed natural flying ability, and I had flying experience also. That was good insurance for the crew.

Coming out of the mess hall at noon, I found Purus waiting for me. "Paul's got a flu bug an' a bad case of the G.I.s, so Captain Ralston has grounded him for the rest of the week an' sent word to Operations that none of the rest of the crew has to fly any missions 'til Gleichauf recovers."

Jim spoke up, "Well, maybe we can get a four-day pass to London."

"Go ahead an' try, but John can't go 'cause he's goin' to be busy with me putting in those two restrictors in the chin turret."

"You mean they're ready?" I asked.

"They'll be finished today. I was at Armament this mornin' checking on them."

By mid-morning the next day Purus and I were working with an

---

[1] The name of a book written about this mission by Martin Caiden.

armament mechanic on the tricky job of installing those hastily made assemblies at the best positions. We did not know how much back pressure would be needed to correct the malfunctioning of the ammunition, or at what point too much restriction would interfere with the movement of the ammunition to the receiver of the gun. Late in the afternoon the Major who commanded Armament, which included turret maintenance, came out to 719. After examining the installation he remarked, "Looks to me like you're about finished."

"Another thirty minutes will do it," Purus answered.

"How do you know how to adjust it?" asked the Major.

"We don't," Purus said, "that will have to be done under fire."

"That's what I thought. If 719 goes out in the morning, who is goin' to do the adjusting?"

There was complete silence while the Major waited. Then he looked at me. "Wasn't this your drawing? Isn't this your ship?"

"Yes, sir."

"Well, I think I can get you on it as Navigator—OK?"

"Wait! Wait! I'm not on combat status for the rest of the week," I answered.

"What's wrong with you?"

"Nothing. Our pilot is sick an' Captain Ralston gave the rest of the crew time off 'til he recovers."

"But you could go?"

"I suppose I could."

"I think you should—it's your ship an' you're the engineer. We don't want some damn navigator foulin' up this test and that is what we're going to get unless one of you does it. I never saw a navigator who knew anything about guns except which end the bullets come out." (That wasn't quite fair to navigators. Even though they did not have as much opportunity to fire the guns, some navigators did take their gunnery seriously.)

"You got a good point there, Major."

"Well, how about it?" he answered.

"I'd like to, but hell, I—uh—you know what happens when you volunteer. You get the shaft ever' time."

He laughed. "Oh, that's just barracks talk—let's go to Operations and see what they say."

At Operations Franek said, "You can go if you want to, but you got a medical excuse for the rest of the week. It's your choice."

The Major asked, "Can't you give him some hint about where we might go in the morning?"

"We don't have the target yet an' couldn't tell him or anyone else if we did know where it was. But you have the bomb load. You could tell him what your men are goin' to load tonight."

He turned to me. "I'm not supposed to talk about the kind of bombs, but I guess it won't hurt to tell you. We're loading block busters."

Block busters? Where did we use those two-thousand-pound big ones? Wheels turned in my brain. Lights flashed on and off. Submarine pens! That's the only place we had ever used them. Where were submarine pens? On the coast! It was going to be an easy target somewhere on the coast. I was not about to let a milk run get by me. The easy ones counted the same as the mean ones.

"OK, Major, I'll do it."

Turning to Lieutenant Franek I asked, "Can you put me on 719 as Navigator if we go out in the morning?"

"I guess I could this one time. I hope to hell 719 don't get lost with you doin' the navigating." He paused for a moment. "I'll put Cahow on 719 'cause his navigator's sick."

"That's fine with me."

Franek called as I started out the door, "Not a word to any of Cahow's men until wake-up call if we go in the morning. Got that straight?"

"OK, not a word."

October 14— Schweinfurt Ball-Bearing Plants

Aircraft 719
Hellcat

At three-thirty, George Reese turned on the lights. "Pitts, Lancia, Tedesco, Green, Bechtel, Kettner, and Comer flying 719 with Cahow— briefing at 0530 hours—good luck."

"Hey, wait," said Lancia. "Comer is not on our crew."

"He is today," Reese replied. "He's your Navigator."

"Navigator! That bastard, a navigator?"

"I've been taking a correspondence course in navigation for the last week," I answered.

"Come off the bullshit! What are you doin' with us?"

"Seriously, the chin turret guns jam up real bad on these new G Models. Yesterday, we put some special-made restrictors in the ammunition chutes. I'm going to adjust them in action an' see if they work."

"You think they'll work?" Tedesco asked.

"You better hope so, 'cause Franek told me he is goin' to assign the other G Model we have on the field to your crew."

Pitts moaned, "God! I hope we don't get lost today with you up there in the nose."

They had decided that this mission was going to be an easy one, probably because Operations assigned me as navigator. As they saw it, I would not be up in the nose if it was going to be a long, tough raid. So no one on the crew stood by the Briefing Room that morning to catch the reaction when the curtain was pulled back revealing the target. We had the usual early morning murk, but there was a good chance it would break by takeoff time.

In the briefing room when the curtain was pulled and they saw that long string pointing straight to Schweinfurt, the pilots let out one long obscenity in unison—the last place on earth any of them wanted to go.

Dawn found the gunners in a breezy mood. The copilot, Lieutenant Stanley Parsons, got out of the personnel truck looking glum.

"Where are we goin' this morning?" asked Pitts.

"Schweinfurt," Parsons replied.

"Very funny," said Lancia, "where are we really going?"

"Now listen, you've had your fun! Get this straight! We're goin' over the middle of Germany to Schweinfurt an' back." He hesitated a moment, then added, "If we get back."

My mind recoiled in disbelief. "No! No! No! Not Schweinfurt! Was this some kind of joke? If so, it was on me. But I thought we were going on a milk run! Thought? If I had done any thinking, I would have been back at the hut," I said to myself. "Anyone stupid enough to volunteer for a combat mission deserves exactly what you are going to get today." I looked around at the other men. The silly grins had faded out. Tedesco tried some comic remark. No one laughed. Only the sound of the electric generator broke the silence. Gunners started drifting back to the aircraft. A little more head space for heavy firing. More ammunition. The oil buffer could be adjusted to allow more rapid firing. I came out of my shock and decided to recheck the two nose guns I had already set up for the bombardier, Lieutenant John Leverette. They had to be right for what I knew was coming.

When Cahow arrived I wondered if he was as calm as he looked. "I see that you already know what the target is. No need to tell you about the fighters. You know what to expect, so be careful with ammunition. Don't waste one round 'cause we're going five hundred miles into Germany. Three divisions will participate on this mission. The First Wing will lead the attack and the 381st will be the low group . . . ."

That drew heavy moans and sarcastic remarks. "Here we go again! Is the 381st on the Wing shit list?"

"Knock off the bitching and listen to what I am telling you. We'll have an escort going in—P-47s—as far as their fuel will permit . . ."

The whole thing sounded ominous. A low position against the heavy opposition we knew would be waiting meant a brutal fight for survival for hours over Germany. The thought went through my mind that many of our 381st men would not survive the day.

At engine starting time the fog was expected to be no higher than four thousand feet, but we had to grind up slowly through ten thousand feet of murk before breaking clear of it. I recall how bitterly I cursed that miserable English weather and the ever-present chance of a sudden collision in the soup. By the time we pulled out on top of the fog the Group had to circle and circle until our widely scattered planes could be gathered into a formation. They were always in confusion when climbing that high through fog. Meanwhile, other groups in the Wing broke into good weather at four thousand feet and were on schedule, but we lost too much time collecting our scattered aircraft and were late. Major George Shackley, leading the Group, set out to try to intercept the Wing over the Channel. But we were not the only group that missed their rendezvous. The 305th was behind time and their Wing was out of sight. When the 305th commander sighted the 1st Division with the low position open he pulled into it. A little later, when Shackley caught up with the Wing, he was astounded that our assigned position was occupied. At that time I did not know what group had usurped our position or why.[2] The 91st was leading and I noticed that they appeared to be understrength. I watched with delight while the 381st pulled up to a position adjacent to the high group. It was a peculiar combat formation but certainly a fortunate one. (Recently George Shackley told me he made that decision.) The escort arrived much too early, in another failure of timing, and therefore was of little help, because they had to turn back before we passed Aachen. As we started angling in toward the Rhine River, various gun positions began to call out warnings of approaching fighters.

When it was time for the escort to leave us I watched with growing apprehension as enemy fighters gathered in unusual strength for the opening attacks. I had other things to do when the fighting began so I could not estimate how many fighters hit the Division. One report said that the Germans threw two hundred interceptors against us early in the fight. The action was a lot like the August 17 mission. They came in from all angles but what I remember most is that they seemed to line up in groups of three to six and come head on, thus dividing the defensive fire

---

[2] Until I read *Decision Over Schweinfurt,* by Thomas Coffey.

of the formation. Once while looking down at the heaviest action the thought struck me that it was an aerial version of cavalry tactics. I saw single-engine fighters carrying rockets that were fired from close range. Fortunately for me most of the worst action was below the high position of the 381st. I could not see the 305th very well but the reports of the Ball and Tail indicated that it was being struck hard. I could not keep from remembering that our group was supposed to have been down there. One Fortress after another was reported as hit. Some I could see, but most were out of my viewing range. Some blew up. Others were set on fire. Possibly a third of the men were able to bail out in time. The battle was as furious as any I saw over Europe.

During the early firing action I was lying face down on the deck watching the ammunition slide in the chute and tinkering with the restrictor adjustment. The device worked perfectly and the ammunition jamming problem was solved. From that point on, my main responsibility was to reload the chin turret cans when the ammunition ran low.

The pilot described the action as he saw it from the cockpit: "When I saw the fighters go through the formations ahead and come at us without breaking off, and seeing Fortresses going down everywhere I looked, I knew our chances for survival were not too good. But the luck of the Irish and a few side-slips as they came at us helped. I had a theory that if I slipped a Fortress up or down, and into the fighter's attack curve just as he started firing, it might throw him off just enough to miss us in the few seconds of his pass. But if the fighter was not aiming at our plane I flew a level path and gave the gunners a better crack at him."

At first I did not pay much attention to the Ball and Tail reports about two-engine fighters standing back out of the Fortress gun range and steadily throwing rockets into the formations.

"Ball to Pilot."

"Go ahead."

"That low group is takin' a helluva beating—they're getting rockets and fighter passes at the same time."

"Waist to Bombardier."

"Go ahead, Waist."

"When the rockets explode it looks like they throw out something like hand grenades that also explode."

"Bombardier to crew—watch those rocket explosions. Tell me if they are throwing out other explosives."

"This is Radio! M.E. 109 is right above us—something is hangin' below it—on a long cable. The sonnuvabitch is tryin' to drop a bomb on us."

Fortunately, the bomb fell through the formation and exploded too far below to do any damage. The rocket-carrying twin-engine fighters increased in number as we battled deeper into Germany. The rockets were hurled steadily into the formation with devastating results. A few made direct hits, but mostly Forts were damaged too much to be able to stay up with the formation. When they fell behind, away from the protection of the concentrated defensive fire, the single-engine fighters ganged up on them, and their chances for survival were slight.

We turned toward the target at Wurzburg, Cahow called the Tail Gunner: "How many Forts has the low group lost?"

"Eleven I think—don't know if any of 'em are gonna make it."

With that final left turn, the Germans knew for sure where we were heading. They must have suspected that the ball-bearing plants were the objective thirty or forty minutes earlier. The modest city of Schweinfurt now lay straight ahead. The fighter fury intensified; their attacks became more savage. In the distance, sunlight reflected from a maze of red-tiled roofs. There was a slight haze and some smoke, but visibility was excellent. At that point I could not pick out the bearing plants for certain, but I did see sizable buildings along the Main River that wound through Schweinfurt, and I suspected they were the targets.

Flak began to burst all around the formation and I could hear heavy shrapnel striking the ship. To my surprise the fighters kept on coming after us in the middle of that inferno of fire and smoke. The enemy showed great tenacity in defending those plants that were so vital to their military production. I knew there were three hundred 88 and 105mm antiaircraft artillery pieces in the Schweinfurt defense perimeter. With no guns to fire, I felt stripped of protection. The act of doing familiar things provides some sense of security in combat. In a strange position with little to do, I was shaking as if I had a chill. There was too much time to look and think about the paper-thin aluminum sheet metal and transparent plastic separating me from the hideous white-hot shrapnel. I wished I had Shutting's special armor devices.

Below, and to my right, I noticed several Forts trailing us on a strange bearing that would cause them to miss the target if maintained. There was no heavy damage that would explain why the Fortresses were out of formation. They must have been remnants of some badly mauled outfit. It was soon evident that they knew the turn we would take after the drop, and were cutting the target short in order to pull into one of the groups low on aircraft. (It was the only time in seventy-five missions over the Continent that I saw, or heard of, undamaged Flying Fortresses deliberately bypassing the target.) None of the documentary accounts I have read mention that incident. It was one of the few times I was in position to see the bombs strike the target. The drop pattern blanketed what I thought must have been the bearings plants. The strike looked real good, but I wondered if it was really worth the high price we were paying. There had been strikes before that we thought to be excellent, but the plants were back in production in a few weeks.

The 381st fared better than I expected, only because we were high up in the formation escaping the worst of the rockets and fighters. The lowest group was always easier to attack because the enemy fighters performed better lower down, and the defensive fire was reduced. Halfway back to the coast the two remaining aircraft of the ill-fated 305th Group pulled into empty positions in the 91st. Thirty minutes from the coast the interceptors faded out. Were they really gone? I searched the sky for a while then slowly unwound from the high tension that had gripped me for the last seven or eight hours. It was the first time I relaxed since I heard the dreaded word ''Schweinfurt'' early that morning.

Counce, Balmore, and Wilson were waiting at the hardstand when we climbed out. They had heard what the target was and knew only too well what we were catching. They told me that Purus was on the mission with Hutchins and his crew and their plane was reported missing. My elation at getting back was short lived. The interrogation was long and tedious, but I barely listened, wondering what happened to Johnny. I felt numb, almost devoid of energy, my vitality drained down to empty.

The way I saw it, on October 14 the Germans achieved a victory over the Fortresses. The enemy losses in planes shot down were small in view of the intense action. The rockets were devastating. Standing back just out of the gun range of the Forts, the Jerry pilots had tremendous success throwing rockets into the Fortress formation. At Luftwaffe headquarters they must have been elated that at last they had a weapon that would either stop the American attacks, or wipe out the attackers if they persisted on deep missions into Germany. Albert Speer described Goering's triumphant report to Hitler about the success of the rocket defense against the Fortresses earlier in the day—sixty bombers smashed out of the sky.[3] Goering was positive that long-range fighters could not be designed or built with the technology of that period, as were many other aviation experts. Without deep fighter escort, the German Defense Command thought that they now had the much needed weapon to stop deep raids into Germany in daylight. And in the weeks following, it looked that way to the American flight crews also.

---

[3] *Inside the Third Reich*, by Albert Speer.

Back at the hut a long time later, I hit the bed quickly and closed my eyes. The station loudspeaker came on: "Now hear this—now hear this—Lieutenant Hutchins landed at an English airdrome on the coast with all crew members safe." It was a good day for me after all. But I vowed that I would never again volunteer for anything as long as I was in the service.

The official losses were:

Sixty-two Forts shot down.

Seventeen Forts damaged too much to be repaired.

Ninety-nine enemy planes shot down.

Thirty enemy planes probably shot down.

Thirty-six Forts damaged but could be repaired.

A day later the damaged figure was raised to one hundred forty-two. Which figure was correct, if either was, I did not find out. Perhaps it depended on how to define "damaged."

Unpredictable factors, impossible to foresee, sometimes decide the fate of men, or shift the course of history. For me—and the 381st Group—that high bank of fog hovering over our air assembly space that morning was an incredible stroke of good fortune. Although we bitterly cursed the fate that put us in that ten thousand foot layer of murk, it turned out to be the difference between acceptable losses and disaster! Had we been in our assigned low position, the odds against getting back would have been twelve to one (based on the losses of the 305th Group).

In the days that followed the second Schweinfurt Raid, it received widespread publicity, ranking alongside Doolittle's Raid on Tokyo, and the sensational raid on the oil fields at Ploesti. Mr. Roosevelt had to make a public statement about the raid to soothe over the disastrous losses. It represented to me the zenith of German aerial resistance to the American Air Forces. Never again was Goering able to achieve an out-and-out victory over the Fortresses. There would be days when the B-17s would suffer losses of comparable numbers in the future, but against much larger fleets with a far lower loss percentage.

Some persons can point to a spot in their lives—a name perhaps—that represents to them an intangible emotional height beside which all other days pale. The name of the obscure Bavarian town "Schweinfurt" means nothing to most Americans but a name on a map of Germany. But the men who endured the fury of either of those historic battles will never forget what air combat, at its epitome, was like. Some historians contend that the collision of those two large forces over Germany marks the highest point that aerial combat has ever reached—the greatest air battles of all time. That is, of course, merely an opinion. There is no way to compare the great naval engagements of the Pacific involving carriers and their planes with the savage conflicts over the Continent. In the Pacific, the great air battles covered vast distances and sometimes lasted several days. The two Schweinfurt raids were a powerful, determined offensive air fleet clashing with an equally potent defensive force in a restricted air passageway in a time span of four or five hours. There had never been anything like them before. Never again will two air forces of such magnitude collide head on in a single afternoon.[4] By some criteria the October 14th mission was the most savage in the history of the Air Force. It depends on how a historian looks at it: there was a devastating 19 percent loss of the aircraft participating.

October 15

No matter what the conversation started out to be, sooner or later it would inevitably shift back to the thing most on our minds. The raids were flown over and over. Bits and pieces that were missing fell into place because other men in different aircraft saw things I could not see. I could reconstruct the whole action only by gathering the observations of others who were in different positions, and fitting them in with my fragmented memories of what happened. In the process of doing this, there was a tendency to combine the ideas and impressions of others with my own in such a manner that a month later what I actually saw could not be separated from what I heard from them. I am sure that I have some vivid memories of incidents that I did not see so indelibly imprinted in my mind that now I think that I personally witnessed them.

There was a divergence of opinion about how the odds for survival worked out. Rogers led one school of thought on the subject and I was the foremost proponent of a different way of looking at it.

"Now, Buck, you say that ever' time I fly another mission my luck and chances for survival stretch thinner?"

"That's right. The more raids you get, the more the odds catch up with you."

---

[4] Long after the war I visited Schweinfurt. It was a beautiful Sunday morning. The burghers were on their way to church. The city was so quiet and tranquil that it was hard to imagine the carnage that once rained down on it. The streets and buildings looked as if nothing had disturbed them in the last hundred years. The bearings factories were still there, now turning out assemblies for Mercedes Benz and B.M.W. vehicles, instead of Hitler's fierce war machines. I rode slowly through the city and let my mind drift back in time to August 17 and October 14, 1943. The faces of fine men lost those two days flashed through my mind; some I could recall distinctly and others would not quite come into focus, like a television picture out of adjustment. So many men lost and so many families bereaved! Did those two gigantic efforts of men and machines really shorten the war and save far more lives than they cost? There was no answer.

"You mean to say that the odds on my twentieth mission will be twenty times more against me than on my first mission?"

"You're damn right, if you make it to twenty missions. Those odds stretch and stretch. That's why so many men go down on their last two or three missions."

"The way I see it the odds start all over every day or every mission," I answered.

"I can't buy that. The more you fly, the closer you get to the breakin' point. Then bang! They catch up with you," Rogers said.

"The laws of chance don't change just because we're talkin' about missions," I insisted.

"Sure they do," said someone, "they're bound to catch up with you."

"Look, you take a pair of dice—you roll them and the mathematical chance to get a seven or eleven will repeat every time you throw those dice. It's the same for a mission. What's already happened doesn't count. It's a new ball game ever' mission morning."

Jim cut in, "You are right. But each raid you learn something new, so you can change the odds a little in your favor with experience."

But Balmore disagreed. "Buck's right, your odds keep stretching like a rubber band—unless you are lucky, one day the rubber won't stretch any more an' it snaps."

"I can't figure your thinking. You're trying to tell me that if I roll dice ten times the odds for me to make a seven get less each time I pick up the dice. The professional gamblers sure wouldn't agree with you. And the laws of chance are a matter of mathematics. It makes no difference if it's cards, dice, or missions."

Neither side would budge from their positions and the arguments went on month after month.

October 16

It was a cold night, too rainy to get far from the hut. The small depressing building was quiet for a change. Only four of us were there. Woodrow Pitts walked over to my bunk.

"Comer, how did you like your ride with us to Schweinfurt?"

"I felt strange. I was out of place. It was like a bad dream when I suddenly find myself in some public place with no clothes on."

"Because you didn't have any guns?" he asked.

"Partly that—an' I couldn't see the action behind us. I heard all those comments about the rockets on the intercom and could not see them from the nose.''

"You had a lotta time to look around. Could you see the strike?''

"Yes,'' I answered, ''I could see the strike OK—one of the few times I ever saw them hit—an' I saw too many Forts on fire or out of control.''

"I saw too many of those myself.''

"Woodrow, I used to feel nauseated an' sick when I saw a Fort go down an' no one get out. But that day I watched them fall with a cold, impersonal feeling—like there were no men in them.''

"You're just getting used to it. When you see so many lost, you quit thinking about it.''

"Are we becomin' so callous we don't care when we see our own men trapped in a falling airplane?'' I asked.

Jim Counce spoke up. "Don't you think it's nature's way of conditioning a man for what he has to do? People can get used to worse than what we've seen.''

"In combat you have to become accustomed to death all around you or you'll blow up inside,'' Pitts added.

"Think how much worse it would be if we were fighting hand to hand with bayonets. But we could get used to that, too, if we were in it long enough,'' Jim said.

Of course they were both right and it was a good thing. One could not dwell on what happened to other men—even those he knew well—and maintain his sanity.

October 18

After lights were out that night and I thought the others were asleep, Lancia muttered into the darkness: ''We've gotta have long-range fighters.''

He was voicing the thought uppermost in the minds of all personnel in Bomber Command, from the Commanding Officer down to the newest gunner. Without some way to stop those rockets we were all but finished as an effective deep offensive force.

"Where ya goin' to get 'em?'' came from a voice at the other end of the hut.

"They could send us some P-38s.'' I recognized Pitt's voice.

"But are they good enough to go against the 190s and that new 109G?'' I asked.

"That leaves us nothing but the P-51s—the new models we've heard about. But no one has seen them in combat yet, so we don't know what they can do," Pitts added.

"Well, the P-38s would be a lot better than nothing," said Jim. "They could tear up those rocket-carrying fighters—that's for sure."

October 22

On days that missions were not scheduled, Operations often called crews for wearisome practice flights, or to slow-time aircraft with new engines. There were also flights to test repairs that could only be checked out at high altitude. With a shortage of crews, we caught a lot of those assignments if Operations could find us. We developed a sensitive ear for the sound of the Operations Jeep, and if we heard it in time escaped quickly to other locations. If they could not find us, they picked up others less fortunate, especially flight engineers, radio operators, and pilots.

Ridgewell Airdrome was located at about fifty-two degrees latitude, which corresponds with the lower end of Hudson Bay and Labrador. Only the warm waters of the Gulf Stream make the British Isles a decent place for people to live. But the Northern latitude meant that long winter nights were rapidly approaching. Our crude metal hut was ill equipped to withstand the ordeal soon to descend. So Jim and I went into Cambridge and managed to procure wire, receptacles, lamps, and insulators to install individual lights for each bunk. We also got caulking compound and sealers to plug up the cracks that let the north wind blow in unhindered. The English electrical system was two hundred twenty volts requiring more care in installation than our one hundred ten system. We made some crude chairs from wood we could scrounge, and a table for the poker games and for writing. A few pin-ups of nude women provided the remaining touches, and we were more ready for the cold days and long nights of mid-winter.

Balmore was on pass in Cambridge doing some shopping the day we nailed shut the back door and sealed it securely. Early the next morning George heard the Jeep coming. He hastily grabbed his jacket and coveralls and made a run for the back door. While he was frantically trying to open it, Lieutenant Franek, the operations officer, came in the front door.

"Well! Well! Where you heading so eagerly? Do you always run around in your long handle drawers? Maybe we can find something for you to do. Be at Operations at nine hundred hours for a slow-time."

He turned to go, then came back to George's bunk. "I'm glad to know we have such eager men who leap out of bed so early in the mornings. We will try to find some more interesting flights for you, Balmore.''

After Franek left George glowered at the rest of us who were shaking the hut with loud laughter. Lancia said, ''How about that? You are getting to be Franek's favorite boy.'' And he rolled out of the way of the vicious kick he knew was coming. Balmore could be pushed just so far and that temper would explode!

''What the hell is the matter with that back door! I couldn't budge it.''

''No wonder,'' Counce replied. ''Me an' John nailed it up yesterday.''

''You could have told me about it, instead of lettin' Franek catch me with my pants down. Now he will have me on one of those miserable slow-times for two or three days a week.''

October 23

In Washington doubts were developing about the ability of the Fortresses on daylight strategic combat missions into Germany, where it really counted. The R.A.F. Command was still unconvinced about the accuracy of the bombing or the ability to resist the certain fierce attacks on deep daylight missions. General Eaker was unshaken in his feeling that the American concept could hit the enemy harder with fewer men and materials. What had the October raid on Schweinfurt proved? One, that the Fortresses could severely damage any target in Germany regardless of enemy opposition. Two, the losses of men and machines were too severe for continuous attacks into Central Germany without long-range fighter escort.

It is unfortunate that the Lancasters and the Fortresses did not concentrate their bombing offenses jointly on a few key German industries, using daylight and night raids to obliterate them. Eaker could never get the R.A.F. to help destroy the bearings production, regardless of the fact that the enemy only had five or six locations that could have been eliminated with better cooperation and understanding of what such a blow could have done to German military production. Then there were the oil and transportation industries, and they were almost as vulnerable. An oil refinery or large storage tank site was difficult to conceal. In late 1943 it seems to me that the Allies had the combined air strength to wipe out at least one or two of those industries. No modern army could fight long if deprived of any of them. Instead of concentrating on a few vital targets, we scattered our air strength over so many kinds of targets that in truth we succeeded in destroying none of them. German war production continued until the Allied armies broke into the interior of the Fatherland.

October 25

There was some free time that morning. At the hut I asked, "Anyone want to join me? I'm headin' for the bath house."

"You better hurry and get in line," Green said.

Jim chipped in, "I do like the big windows in the bath house—such a good view. We don't really need any glass in the windows—better ventilation an' no mildew."

"Well, is anyone else comin'?"

"Hell, no! Not me. I'm not gonna freeze my ass in that ice box," Buck answered.

"You know somethin'? You guys from the north are always the first to bitch about being cold. In all barracks you will see men from Maine and Michigan near the stove an' the men from Texas an' Florida at the end of the room."

The bath house was located in the middle of the personnel huts but in winter it was shunned as if the plague lurked in its murky interior. An icy north wind blew unhindered through the open window spaces. This is what went through my mind: "Why don't I put it off? Hell, I had a bath last week. No! You got to get on with it. Won't be any warmer tomorrow. Well, here we go! Get undressed—that's it. Hang your clothes on those nails. Forget about that freezing wind. Now off with those shoes. All right, go ahead and yell! That cold mud is hell. Come on, let's get it over with before pneumonia sets in. Over to the shower—now turn on the water. That's it, leap back when the water starts squirtin' out. Now hold the wash rag in the water and get it lathered up real heavy. OK, now soap down all over. Quit shaking; the blue skin will recover in ten or fifteen minutes. You are committed now! You've got to get under that shower to get the soap off. All right! Step under the shower. No! There's no hurry. Yes there is. Now get under that water! Owwwww! Yell louder! You're not going to disturb anyone. Do those yells actually make me a little warmer or is it my imagination? That's enough. Get out of here, you're wasting water. Turn it off and make a run for the towel. Where in the hell did I hang the clean underwear? Oh damn! It fell off into the mud on the floor. Well, put on the dirty underwear. Now on with the shirt and pants. You are feeling much better now. Right? Sure you are. Now rinse off the mud from your feet. You feel great! Just great! It was worth the ordeal, wasn't it? Tell that to the boys back at the hut!"

October 29

George, Hubie Green, and I were lingering over a last cup of coffee at the mess hall. The building was almost empty as most of the men had departed.

"Hey, look comin' in—some brand new officers," I said.

"Yeah," said Green, "you can see that look on their faces. They must have arrived today."

Five minutes later they had their trays and were seated at a table next to us. The temptation was too much to resist: it was time to start their initiation. Immediately we launched into a morbid discussion of combat raids in drastic detail, explosions, aircraft fires, dead crewmen, amputations, planes falling in spins out of control. We made it a point to act as if we did not realize they were listening. When the conversation was particularly gory, there was no sound of knife or fork from the next table. I noted with satisfaction when we left that the newly arrived officers were no longer hungry. It was our warm and friendly welcome to the 381st Combat Group and Ridgewell Airdrome.

November 1

There were nights when we could hear the faint sound of air raid sirens from the east toward the coast. We would lie there quietly listening to the spine-tingling wails, hoping they would fade away to the north or south. But some nights sirens closer to us would open up, then the nearby towns would come alive, and we knew the German bombers were coming in our direction. There were no air raid shelters at the base. There were some slit trenches near each hut, but they were always half full of water and mud. Most of us had rather chance the bombs than the freezing water and mud. If the weather was clear, men swarmed outside to find a vantage point and try to catch a glimpse of the action. Sometimes a dark shape of a bomber could be seen in the sky, silhouetted against a searchlight beam or the moon. On those rare occasions when a Jerry plane was caught by a blinding searchlight beam, it would shine brightly in the night sky, a perfect target for the R.A.F. night fighters. One night in October, eight parachute flares burst into brilliance over the base but floated over an adjacent village and burned luminously. It was clear that the bombers were after the 381st that night.

CHAPTER XV

Mission to Wilhelmshaven and Gelsenkirchen

November 3—   *Aircraft 719*
Wilhelmshaven, Germany   *Hellcat*

The weather looked questionable when I left the hut. The first man I saw at Operations was Chaplain Brown watching each man as he arrived. What did he look for? And if he pinpointed a man who appeared shaky, what did he say to him? Did he say, "God will watch over you and protect you," knowing that the man was on his way to kill and destroy?

When Gleichauf arrived at the aircraft, I had no idea what kind of mission we would face for the day. "We're hittin' Wilhelmshaven in Germany. Fighter opposition will be about the same as we get over Bremen, which can be rough. Flak is estimated from medium to heavy concentration. We'll pick up fifty P-47s at the coast on the way in. But the big news is we will have P-38s with us over the target."

There were whoops of joy! We were completely unaware that P-38s had arrived in England until that day. The Lockheed Lightning was powered by two liquid-cooled engines and had a double tail boom. Its main feature was long range and strong construction. Fighting characteristics were good, but not great. It had performed well in the North African campaign against German aircraft, but how it would stack up in the rarified air of twenty-five to thirty thousand feet, against the best pilots the enemy could muster, was yet to be determined. But even a fair performance on those long penetrations, with the rocket menace hovering in the background, would be a tremendous help. There was no doubt that they could easily handle the rocket-carrying fighters with those awkward chutes hanging under each wing.

A few minutes after the P-47s turned back toward England, the Tail gunner came on intercom: "Tail to crew—here come the Bogies—five o'clock low."

The fighters climbed rapidly to our altitude and began circling to look us over as they usually did.

"Turret to crew—Turret to crew—those Germans got a big surprise coming. P-38s at four o'clock high."

I watched a P-38 lead plane pick out a target and go into a steep dive. To my surprise the P-38 caught a blast of fire from somewhere and broke into two pieces and fell away in flames. The other P-38s pulled back up and decided to look things over a bit more carefully.

"Navigator to Copilot."

"Go ahead."

"Did you see what happened to that P-38?"

"He got caught by a 109 he never saw—it'll take a while, but they'll learn to use the P-47 tactics—get careless with those 109s an' they'll blow your ass off."

German and American fighters were evenly matched in numerical strength. I noticed that 38s seemed to fight in elements of two, while the P-47s used elements of four. But the 38s did better than I expected on their first encounter with the more experienced foes.

"Ball to crew—fighters comin' up at us from below."

I heard his guns chatter again and again. No one could help him down there. Attacks I could not see always worried me.

"Bombardier to Pilot—Bombardier to Pilot. Over."

"This is the Pilot . . ."

"We're on the bomb run."

"Tail to crew—flak at eight o'clock level."

It was spotty, but what they threw up was devastatingly accurate. Numerous Forts took hits, but none that I saw had to pull out of the formation in our Group. That Wing following us was not so lucky.

On the return P-38s chased away the few Jerry fighters who came up to our level. No rocket-carrying craft showed up. Actually, I would have liked for Jerry to have attacked us with rockets to see what the P-38s would do to them. On the way back I began to calculate the way long-range escort was going to shift the odds of survival for me. Until that day I tried many times to compute what the odds really were, using the total number of men who participated on raids since I arrived against the total casualties. This figure I projected over twenty-five missions. But the statistics I played with were too unreliable to have real meaning. My guess was that from July through October the odds must have been at least four to one that we would not make it. With the P-38s those odds were going to improve. That was the great news of the day. How much they would improve would depend on how many P-38s were in England then and how fast the force would be built up. At that time no airman at the 381st had succeeded in completing twenty-five raids. It was past the time that some of the earliest arrivals should have been through. For the first time I began to feel a cautious optimism that before long the 381st was going to turn out some graduates.

November 4

The Flying Fortresses were originally designed to fly as individual aircraft at high altitudes up to thirty-eight thousand feet using the accuracy of the Norden Bomb Sight. In practice this concept turned out to be impractical for two reasons. First, thirty thousand feet was found to be the highest altitude that crews could stand with consistency, due to the crude oxgyen equipment and the intense cold in some areas of the airplane. Two, the opposition was so fierce from enemy fighters that the bombers had to attack in tightly flown formations to concentrate defensive fire.

In late October some officials of Bomber Command raised the question as to whether the Fortresses needed a highly trained navigator and bombardier in the nose. Could one officer be quickly trained to perform enough of the duties of both so that a well qualified gunner could be used up front where the main attacks were? Some bombardiers proved to be top-notch gunners, like our Johnny Purus, but others could not get over the notion that their main job was to drop the bomb. That was important, of course, but I can tell you for certain that the primary thing nearly all of us had in mind was to get back to England one way or another. Some training toward combining the two positions had already been started. After all, a navigator was needed only when an aircraft was separated from the formation or lost in murky weather on the way home. The navigator in the lead plane did the rest of the navigating for the Group. And the bombardier in the lead aircraft did the work with the Norden Bomb Sight. All of the other bombardiers watched for the first bomb to fall from the leader, then instantly released their load. But if the aircraft became separated deep in enemy territory, a bombardier would be needed to find some target of opportunity to keep the mission from being a total failure for that aircraft.

Shutting and Purus took this idea as a big joke. "Why we need you, Johnny?" Shutting asked. "I can toggle out those bombs when the stud bombardier lets go, and we can get us a good gunner on those nose guns."

But Purus retaliated, "No! It's you we don't need any more. If we get lost comin' back home, all I gotta do is call Balmore an' ask for a fix or a Q.D.M.—why we need you?"

(The concept of a singler Bombardier-Navigator never caught on. A great deal of time had been spent in the training of both positions, and resistance to combining the two positions was too strong to overcome. After a few weeks we did not hear any more about it.)

November 5, 1943—Gelsenkirchen   Hellcat #719

On the way to the mess hall that morning I could hear the last of the Lancasters up above, returning from a night raid against the Germans. I wondered where they had been and what it was like up there alone at night. They had to have a hell of a navigator to find the target and the way back to their base in the dark.

The briefing sent a shudder up my spine: "We're heading for Gelsenkirchen in the Ruhr Valley. We'll have a P-47 escort at the coast—the navigator will give you the rendezvous time. Spitfires are due on the way out. Be careful not to mistake the Spits for 109s. There are seven hundred gun emplacements in the Ruhr so the flak will be intense, rougher than any we've seen so far."

There was an audible groan.

"Ball, keep a watch underneath for flak damage. There can be up to two hundred fighters, but they may not be too eager to come after us in all that flak."

After the briefing Kels said, "We got us two Navigators now, so which one of you jokers is gonna give us the headings today?"

Balmore stepped up. "I've got the solution to that problem." He presented small bail-out compasses[1] to Carl and Johnny. With a serious expression on his face he said, "I'm giving compasses to both of you, so when the pilot calls for a new heading, the one who comes up with it first gets to call it in."

Shutting and Purus solemnly shook hands with Balmore and accepted their tiny compasses.

---

[1] Fingernail-sized compass included in bail-out kits.

"Balmore, your thoughtfulness is greatly appreciated. Now each of us has his very own compass!" responded Shutting.

At the coast the Tail came on intercom: "Fighters at six o'clock high."

"Radio to crew—they're 47s."

"And right on time," added the navigator.

The P-47s were using some larger disposable belly tanks made from pressed paper by the British that extended their range considerably. A few fighters broke through the escort cover but were ineffective. Losses to the bombers were slight, but the flak was awesome. There seemed no end to it and the accuracy was unbelievable. Numbers of times we were bounced about by the concussion of close ones. I heard frequent shell fragments crash into the aircraft, and could see some damage from my position. Lieutenant Butler's ship was hit, and he began to fall back. One of his engines was smoking. Then Colonel Nazzaro's ship was hit and the engine trailed black smoke for two hours.

Wham! A big piece of shrapnel slammed through the accessory section of number four engine.

"Turret to Copilot."

"Go ahead."

"How do the instruments look on number four?"

"Instruments are normal."

"All we can do is hope there is no fire."

The wings were perforated with holes to the right and to the left. My greatest concern was an oil or fuel system rupture that would ignite from the red-hot exhaust collector-rings of the engines.

"Turret to Ball—can you see any serious damage under the right wing? Look for fuel leaks."

"I see a lot of holes, but no leaks yet. Maybe they self-sealed."

A large chunk crashed under me and was deflected by an oxygen tank. Another slashed through the narrow space between the turret and copilot, and on out of the aircraft.

"Bombardier to Pilot—Bombardier to Pilot! We're on the bomb run."

"Drop 'em quickly so we can get out of this damn flak!"

A few minutes away from the target coming out I heard an extra-loud clang down below. A close one had showered the ball turret.

"Ball to Copilot—Ball to Copilot!"

"Go ahead."

"The Ball was hit an' both my eyes are full of glass. I can't open 'em to see."

"Are you hit anywhere else, Ball?"

"No, just my eyes full of glass slivers."

"You want us to get you out now, or wait 'til we're over water?"

"You can wait. I'm as well off here as I would be in the radio room."

Number too engine took a heavy hit squarely on the propeller hub, but continued to operate normally. A hunk of flak, a lot bigger than most of the fragments, tore through the empty bomb bay with a fearsome noise.

"Bombardier to crew—fighters at one o'clock level—109s, I think. They don't seem too eager . . . ."

"If you were a Jerry would you want in this damned flak?"

"Hell, no!"

The Spitfires scheduled for the return escort did not show, although they could have been flying low cover below us. When the coast hove into view, a small flak field opened up. The Colonel expertly moved the formation around it. Lieutenant Butler was having double trouble. He was in doubt that he could make it over the North Sea. Later he insisted that the copilot gave orders for the crew to bail out while over land without his knowledge or consent. The navigator, four enlisted men, and the copilot jumped, including a special friend of ours named MacGinty. "Mac" was often a visitor to our hut. We would miss him. He had thirty-three raids with the R.A.F. and this raid would have made a total of forty-two. Lieutenant Butler, with only three of his crew left, made it back to Ridgewell.

As soon as we got to lower altitude, and the threat of fighters had eased, I got out of the turret and looked for any damage I could see. After checking the hydraulic system I stood where Gleichauf and Kels could hear me.

"We got trouble with the hydraulic system. No pressure! We won't have any brakes on landing."

Paul asked. "Are you sure we can't raise any pressure temporarily?"

"Yes, the fluid is gone."

"Pilot to crew. We will have to land without brakes. I'll try to touch down at the end of the runway, then rev up number one and two engines. If we can ease off into the sticky mud to the right of the runway, that ought to stop us."

On the final approach Paul brought #719 in as slow as he dared—aiming at the end of the runway. What he saw ahead was unbelievable! Kels screamed out, "Paul, look at those damn people, lining both sides of the runway!"

"What are they doin' out here in our way!" Paul was frantic with helpless rage. "We can't turn off the runway and kill a dozen people!"

When the wheels touched down, Kels opened his side window and leaned far outside, trying to attract the attention of the people lining the runway. He frantically motioned the crowd to get out of our way. They smiled brightly and waved back at Kels. Gleichauf was infuriated! "Those stupid people are gonna make me wreck this airplane! We can't stop! Who the hell let them out here?" The pilot was turning red with rage. Kels was still trying to signal the crowd to get out of our way. Total failure! The high speed of the aircraft meant nothing to them! Then it was too late! The end of the landing strip was coming up fast and we were still rolling at considerable speed with no possible chance to make the turn onto the taxi strip.

Number 719 sped toward rough ground, roads and ditches, but little soft mud needed to slow us down. This was long before a pilot could reverse the propeller pitch to slow down an aircraft. (There was a large field of sticky mud to the right side of the runway, if only we could have turned into it.) I asked many questions about why that unwanted crowd of people was lining the runway, not only in the way but in danger from the damaged aircraft coming in to land, some of which were without the usual landing controls. No one would tell me why the men were there, or who was responsible for an absurd situation that defied common sense. I suspect some officer ordered the men out to welcome "the boys back home." It might have sounded like a great idea to someone in an alcoholic daze.

The aircraft was coasting toward a country lane when I saw an English soldier blithely pedaling along on a certain collision course apparently unaware of impending doom. I watched in horror! At the last moment the man looked to his left and saw those huge whirling propellers coming right at him. Then he passed out of sight under the wing and I felt a slight impact as if we had struck something.

I said to Paul, "I'm afraid we got him!"

"Oh, God! I hope not!" Gleichauf replied.

"Last I saw he was about ten feet away with number four prop headin' right into him."

We bounced crazily this way and that, over more ditches and obstructions, slowing down. I saw with dismay that we were heading straight for a barnyard and two elderly ladies were sitting on a wooden fence directly in our path. There was a sizable ditch and the wheels dropped into it, throwing one wing into the ditch, and the other up at a grotesque angle. The aircraft came to a lurching halt, with the nose of the plane resting about where I saw the two women sitting a few seconds earlier. Among the crew our only serious injury was to Harkness.

Paul leaned out of the window and called to some men nearby. "Did we hit those ladies sittin' on the fence?"

"No, it was a bit of a scramble, but they made it, you know."

That was a relief. The soldier on the bike was the only casualty. There was nothing we could have done to have prevented killing him. Number 719 was a sorry mess and it was all so stupid and unnecessary. A man killed and a new airplane wiped out for no sane reason! We should have gotten by with nothing more serious than a lot of sticky mud and perhaps a twisted landing gear.

The medical team arrived quickly to take Harkness to the hospital and get that glass out of his eyes. Those Medics were always efficient and fast when we had wounded men aboard. A crowd gathered around the plane, but I was concerned about the extent of damage to #719. One wing tip would have to be replaced and the landing gear was destroyed. The bomb bay was in sad shape and the bomb-bay doors would definitely have to be replaced. One engine was shot, and possibly a second from the collision with the ditch. While I was climbing around estimating the repairs that would be needed, a muddy English soldier walked up and tapped me on the shoulder. His clothes were badly torn and he looked like he had been in a fight.

"Your bloody machine nearly got me, Yank," the soldier said.

"What's that?" I turned to stare at him.

"The propeller damned near cut me haid off—and I fell between the wheels—smashed me bike to bits. Bloody ruined!"

"I thought we killed you, soldier. Don't know how you escaped."

"I was on my way to the pub. I look up, and was never so scared in me whole life. I see that bloody propeller comin' right at me!"

Shutting climbed wearily out of the airplane with his briefcase of maps and his bag of flying equipment. He looked around until he located the radio operator. "Balmore, you saved us today!"

"What do you mean by that?" George responded.

"If it hadn't been for this little Boy Scout compass you gave me early this morning we couldn't have made it back. All my instruments were shot out!" His voice was almost breaking with emotion as he continued. "No compass. No drift meter! No nothing except this little doo-dad. So I says, 'Carl, this is it! The whole Wing is depending on you to navigate us home,' so I brought 'em back with this little Boy Scout compass. I want to thank you for giving it to me, Balmore."

George and Shutting shook hands solemnly. Those of us who were close enough offered our solemn congratulations. Of course, all of this was pure nonsense! Shutting had no more use for a compass that day than I did. Our plane merely followed on the Colonel's left wing all day, while the lead navigator did the navigating. But unknown to us, an Associated

Press reporter was in the crowd writing down this insane foolishness word for word. The next morning the A.P. all across the U.S. carried a front-page story of the incident. The account hinged on Shutting's supposed heroic leadership in navigating a wing of Fortresses home by means of a Boy Scout compass. It made big headlines in all the hometown papers of the crew. Within two weeks some of us began getting letters from home asking about the crash. Was anyone injured or wounded? At first it sounded like they had us confused with some aircraft that crash-landed in England. Then Shutting received a letter containing a clipping from a Chattanooga newspaper. It read: "Carl Shutting Leads Forts Home With Scout Compass" in big, black, front-page headlines. Before Carl could recover from his shock, someone spirited the clipping out of his hut, and the next day it was pinned on the 381st bulletin board. That embarrassed our bashful navigator no end! It looked like Carl had been sending home some fanciful stories of his heroism.

Carl Shutting Leads Forts Home With Scout Compass

Chattanoogan in 700-Bomber Raid Falls Back on Small Guide After Instruments Ruined

A U. S. BOMBER BASE IN BRITAIN. Nov. 5 (AP)—Lt. Carl R. Shutting. 107 North Seminole Drive, Chattanooga, Tenn., used a Boy Scout compass to lead his division of Flying Fortresses home safely from the 700-heavy bomber raid over western Germany today.

Navigator of the "Hell Cat," Lt. Shutting used the small compass to keep on the beam after the regular navigating instruments had been rendered hors de combat by enemy fire. As it was, the "Hell Cat" was forced to make a landing which sent it bounding over two ditches and through three fences because the hydraulic brake system had been shot up.

(Lt. Carl R. Shutting is the son of Mr. and Mrs. Rudolph Shutting. His father is a well-known commercial artist and map maker in Chattanooga.)

The Fortress with the lofty name, "Spirit of Franklin County, Mo.," which citizens of that county bought with their war bond purchases, led another division and stoutly maintained the lead position all the way back to the English coast although badly shot up.

With one engine out, gas flowing from the left wing, the windshield cracked and the fuselage

LT. CARL SHUTTING

perforated from antiaircraft fire, the "Spirit" reluctantly turned over leadership to another plane and

See Page Two, Column Seven

November 6

One man that I remember so well was always welcome at our hut. We saw him nearly every day. His name was Pete Ludwigson. It was a relief to see such a clean and wholesome young man untouched by the sordid aspects of war. We had traveled the same path since the days of the Engineering School at Boeing Aircraft, Seattle. His crew and ours went through training procedures at the same time, and we ended up at the 381st on the same day. Pete did not let anything bother him. He was always the same. When the rest of us would get worked up over some fancied abuse, Pete would say, "Quit bitching. It's all part of the game. A week from now you won't remember what you're so hot about now." And he was right: gripes, shortages, inconvenience, dirt, mud, cold, military orders that made no sense, fear, and above all, sheer boredom, were the things that made up the military life. I wished that I could be more like Pete and take things of no real importance less seriously. On the mission yesterday our good friend Ludwigson was lost somewhere over the Ruhr Valley. That was all we knew because there were no witnesses to what happened after the aircraft had to drop out of the formation and fell far behind us, struggling along on two engines and a third operating at half speed. I had a hard time going to sleep last night wondering what Pete endured and if he made it out of the plane when it finally gave up. We knew that the Fort did not get back to England. It was a blow to lose a man like Pete. We hoped that he was able to bail out in time. Often I could achieve a psychic feeling about a crew that was lost, but in this case I had no impression about their fate.

In early November we began to hear more rumors about super weapons being hastily developed by the Germans. Hitler made numerous veiled references to frightening new instruments of destruction that he said would turn the war in Germany's favor. Goebbel's propaganda machine turned these dire predictions to advantage in raising the spirits of the German workers. Allied Intelligence slowly accumulated more specific information as to what German scientists were attempting. None of this leaked through to our level, except the disturbing worry that if some super weapon did emerge from the war, Germany would be most likely to come up with it because of the seven or eight year head start they had with preparations for a war.

After lights were out I made the following remark to whoever was awake and listening: "This afternoon I talked to Lieutenant Atkins [the Gunnery Officer]. He says there are rumors that Hitler's boys are workin' on a gigantic rocket that they can fire across the Channel."

Rogers said, "It sounds like one of Goebbel's pipe dreams to me."

"The trouble is, Buck, these people have the brains an' the knowhow to do it, if they get enough time," I answered.

Jim added, "They've probably been at it since 1936."

Lancia said, "Those Germans are damned smart. We can't sell them short. Ever' raid I look around an' halfway expect to see something new thrown at us."

"Me, too," I said. "I've seen two extra-large explosions recently up high. They had a brownish color and looked big enough to blow a group out of the sky if it burst in the middle of a formation. Has anyone else seen this thing?"

No one had and I hoped it was my imagination.

Pitts asked, "Well, suppose they can make a huge rocket. How are they goin' to hit anything with it fired from a distance?"

"It could be controlled by an aircraft near the target like a model airplane," Counce added.

"They think the Allied Intelligence will find out soon where it is being tested," I said.

Then there was silence except for an occasional snore, and the faint sound of engines on the distant flight line. Did it mean a mission in the morning? I never could sleep well when I thought a raid was shaping up.

CHAPTER XVI

Mission to Wesel

November 7—Wesel, Germany   *Aircraft 808*

I wanted to get in a mission because the weather had slowed down the air offense. George Reese read the roster and the aircraft was number 808 from another squadron.

I asked George, "What kind of ship are we flyin' today?"

"It's a new G—only been on two missions."

Jim peeped outside, "Don't see much low hangin' mist—we might get off this morning."

I asked Counce to wait outside the Briefing Room while I went on out to the aircraft. Anytime it was a strange ship I wanted more time to look it over and talk to the crew chief, as all aircraft had peculiarities that it was good to know about. It was a very dark morning and my flashlight quit working. I knew those planes well enough to feel my way along in the dark. I thought I was the first one on the plane. As I groped slowly forward in the waist area suddenly something very hard struck me on the head just above my eyes. I fell flat on the floor and counted a dozen stars from the pain. A flashlight came on and Wilson helped me to my feet.

"John! I'm sorry! Didn't know anyone was in the plane but me."

"What did you hit me with?" I inquired in a shaky voice.

"I jerked out my gun barrel just as you walked by in the dark."

"My head throbs! An' both eyes feel like they're swellin' shut. This is the first time you've been early since we got to England. From now on go back to bein' late."

I was still woozy and hurting when Gleichauf arrived. "What's the matter with you? Been in a fight?"

"Our brilliant waist gunner hit me in the head with a gun barrel in the dark."

"Can you make it today?"

"I'll make it—going to have two shiners—nothin' worse, I hope."

The rest of the crew arrived and it was time for the briefing. "The target is Wesel, in Germany, on the far edge of the Ruhr Valley, but we'll cut across the valley and try to miss the worst flak. The temperature will be near fifty below, so watch yourselves for frostbite. We'll use the Pathfinder System[1] today, so we can drop through fog and not have to worry about clear weather at the target. We're glad to have Trapnell with us in the radio room. Once more—watch out for the low temperature."

At twenty-eight thousand feet, I became concerned about the bitter cold.

"Turret to Navigator."

"Go ahead, Turret."

"How cold is it?"

"Minus forty-eight centigrade."

"Turret to Bombardier—with this low temperature, we may get some ice in oxygen masks—you might want more frequent crew checks."

"Good idea, Turret. We'll have one ever' twenty minutes."

The escort was on time and gave us perfect coverage. What fighters came up, if any, were quickly turned away and the formation was untouched. The bomb run was twelve minutes long, double the usual length.

"Bombardier! Are we goin' to drop or not?"

"No, we missed it, Paul. Looks like we're going around again."

"Hope he drops this time—we stay around here too long an' fighters will get to us."

"Bombs away" was good news.

"Radio to Bombardier—Radio to Bombardier—bomb hung up in the bomb bay. Keep the doors open."

"Turret to Bombardier—I'm goin' back to take a look at it."

The hung-up bomb was high on the outside rack and difficult to get to the shackle with a screwdriver. The problem was to keep the bomb from knocking me off the catwalk when it fell free. On my fourth attempt it released.

---

[1] The lead aircraft in each group, and the deputy lead also, was equipped with the special Pathfinder radar to aid the Navigator. Waves bouncing back from the ground were converted into a scan of the surface below that could be interpreted by a trained operator. He could in effect see the ground through clouds or darkness. Later the Americans dubbed the process Mickey.

"Turret to Bombardier, the bomb bay is clear. You can raise the doors."

"Radio to Copilot—I think I'm gettin' frostbite on one hand—it's numb—no feeling."

"Is your 'lectric glove workin' on that hand, Radio?"

"It's workin' but the heat is not on the fingers where I need it to handle cold metal."

My mike went silent and after a hasty change to a reserve mike, I called the Radio Operator. "Radio, can you hear me?"

"I can hear you."

"This ship has 'lectric gun heaters—turn on the gun heat and put your hand where the heat is."

I liked the idea of the Pathfinder System if we learned to hit a target with it. We would know after photo planes came up with a good picture of the damage in a day of two. That equipment showed promise of opening up the air offensive in poor weather. I could feel both eyes swelling almost shut and my head ached from the blow. The return to England was painful and tiresome. But I would trade two classic black eyes and a throbbing headache for an easy mission like that one anytime. I was not going anywhere on pass for a while anyway, so I did not let the jibes and wisecracks bother me. The incident did not increase my affection for Carroll Wilson.

November 8

Jim Counce had girl problems that worried him. He had broken with a girl he had been seeing for a long time before his last furlough and became engaged to a girl he did not know very well. He was a bit bewildered by the speed at which it came about, but was serious, and had every intention of carrying out his pledge. He worried that there should have been more time to get to know each other better, but he was glad that his mother approved his choice.

Counce was our mainstay in the aft section of the aircraft. We needed at least one solid man with top-notch mechanical aptitude back there. Balmore was excellent at his radio position, but he was helpless with some sudden mechanical problem for which there had been no specific training.

Wherever we were situated for a few weeks, Counce would find a temporary girl friend. He was the kind of man that women are attracted to. By late August he had two girls close enough to the base that no pass was needed. One interesting and unexpected entanglement worked out. An English mother liked Jim as much as her daughter did. He talked about that development with George but never mentioned it to me. Why? Perhaps he thought I would disapprove of the bizarre situation. I suppose that I never quite shed the image of being a little square.

November 9

Rain! Rain! Rain! It was bitterly cold and there was no fuel for the tiny stove. We had our hoarded crosscut saw, but it had to be kept out of sight. We could cut the King's trees only at night and when weather allowed. Did you ever try to saw wet wood? When the rain let up enough, two or three men would pedal into the nearby village and bring back copious amounts of cider and ale. Enough ale and the cold was less difficult to handle.

November 11

Stimulated by the success of my electric overshoes, I made a much better pair of electrically heated gloves. The heat was placed where it was needed instead of in the middle of the palm. Having to keep the fingers in constant contact with metallic controls, at temperatures that varied from thirty-five to sixty below zero centigrade, should have required that the electric heat be concentrated on the fingers where the contact was. But the equipment designers apparently had no conception of high-altitude gunnery needs and put the heat in the palm of the hand. Of course, it was much better than nothing, but at the lower temperatures handling metal for extended periods overtaxed the crude design. My new gloves were ideal and for the remainder of my combat missions never needed repairs.

No matter what the conversation was, or the location, the bull sessions always led back to the one thing uppermost in the mind: Where would we go tomorrow? How rough would it be? and the ultimate question: Would we make it? I never deliberately let that question come up, but it was there in the subconscious mind day after day. The boredom for stretches of days at a time, the endless waiting for action we knew was coming, and too much time to think all combined to draw the nerves ever tighter.

November 13

Allied weather forecasters had a complex task in trying to decide what could be expected a day or two in advance with enough accuracy to guide

Bomber Command in their planning. European weather is changeable and clear periods such as we are accustomed to are infrequent. For stretches of days at a time, clouds hover over the area of the European Continent. Sometimes a mission would take off with questionable visibility, and an hour later the operation would be scrubbed. One day during that period we were scheduled for a raid over Germany and so much murk settled in that there was no chance of the mission. The fog increased and created hazardous flying conditions. Three wings of airplanes were blindly groping their way down, hoping for a break in the clouds. We were lucky and found a hole in the swirling mists with a welcome airdrome in view. When we pulled up to an empty space, Counce said, "Look! Yonder is *Tootsie Snoots,*" our one-time airplane. Her name now was *Dottie J* but to us she was still *Tootsie*. At that time she had twenty-five missions to her credit without a turn back for mechanical problems. In the 381st, few aircraft made that many missions. I examined the ship from close range for a long time with Jim and let my thoughts drift back to Herb Carqueville, and the high hopes of that day when we landed *Tootsie* on English soil. So much had happened that it seemed a long time. It was almost certain by now that Herb was gone. If he had bailed out and survived we would have heard about it. Every time I had to face that harsh reality I felt a dull stab of pain.

November 14

The call came at 2:00 A.M. Jim was ahead of me and when I got to Operations he said, "There's somethin' different in the air this morning. The Brass looked tense when they went into the Briefing Room."

"Any idea what may be comin' up?"

"No. But you can bet it's gonna be a rough one! Go on to the ship an' I'll wait until they pull the curtain."

When Jim arrived on the next transport truck, I was waiting anxiously. "What did it sound like?"

"The worst groan you ever heard—then dead silence—not another sound."

"Where do you think we're goin'? Schweinfurt again?"

"Could be Schweinfurt—or some other place just as bad."

When Gleichauf arrived I could see that he was keyed up. "Today it will be *Berlin*!"

"Is this some kind of a joke?"

He shook his head.

Counce said, "We're not really goin' to Berlin?"

"We sure as hell are. There may be two thousand fighters close enough to hit us. This will be the first daylight raid ever on Berlin. S-2 says to 'expect the Luftwaffe.' It will be rougher than anything we've seen so far."

I had difficulty believing that Bomber Command would attempt what seemed to me a foolhardy venture. There were so many fighters in the Berlin area that the forces we could put up would be overwhelmed as I saw it. Perhaps in a few months, with two or three times as many B-17s and a swarm of long-range escort fighters, hitting Berlin in daylight would become feasible. But we did not have that kind of strength then and I think most 381st men knew it. George Reese assigned himself as our copilot. Either he knew something the rest of us did not know, or he had more courage than brains.

Two new gunners were flying our tail and ball positions. I did not resent them personally, but why did Operations have to stick us with two inexperienced men on a raid like this? Both of them were already so numb with fright that I doubted either would be worth much to us. I got Shutting, Counce, and Balmore together for a minute and said, "Those rookie gunners are scared so bad that the color has drained out of their faces. We got to do something to relax them." Turning to Shutting: "Couldn't you put on a comedy act with your testical armor? Get them to help you assemble it. We got to get them over the shakes. The best way is some horseplay."

Carl was at his best. "They're gonna be after me today! They think they goin' to shoot off my balls. No way! I got 'em fooled. They don't know about this armor doo-dad. I get it tied like this then stand on my armor plate."

"But what if the flak bursts on your left side instead of below you?" I asked.

"I got that figured out. If they burst on the left I get on the right side of the Bombardier. If it's on the right I get on his left side—use him for armor plate—we got a surplus of Bombardiers."

George had some chalk and inscribed each bomb "Herman," "Adolf," or "Goebbels" and obscene remarks about what we would like to do to each one of them personally. I watched the tension fade and the color return to the two young gunners. When they could laugh at the wisecracks and foolishness I felt much better about them.

Thirty minutes went by while crews waited for the signal to start the engines. Suddenly I heard cheering echo across the field. The mission to Berlin was canceled. Did Bomber Command really intend to strike Berlin that day? I still have doubts. Was it a morale thing to break the monotony of idleness caused by bad weather and a slowdown awaiting a build up of long-range fighters? I thought so.

November 17

Two times recently we had been on missions flying #730 that had to be called off for weather reasons. On both flights number three engine developed heavy smoke, becoming increasingly denser as the aircraft climbed to higher altitude. At sixteen thousand feet the ball operator could see a suggestion of raw flame from the exhaust. To me this was a clear case of a malfunction in the air fuel mixture system, probably in the bellows valve of the carburetor, which adjusted the amount of fuel as the altitude increased and the outside air pressure being sucked into the carburetor became lower. I rarely had differences with the efficient ground crews at Ridgewell, but locked horns on that malfunction. The crew chief insisted that nothing was wrong because the engine ran fine at ground level. I don't think he understood the function of the bellows valve and unfortunately his line chief backed him up. I was dead certain they were both wrong!

That morning Major Shackley, the Squadron Commanding Officer, was leading the Group and riding with us in the copilot's seat. I knew the aircraft would not make it to the bombing altitude and managed to catch the major outside operations.

"Major, 730 won't make the mission! It has a bad bellows valve but the crew chief says I'm wrong an' won't change it. I thought you would want to know it."

"I'm leading and can't run the risk of an abortion. We'll switch planes. Stand by for a change."

The mission was canceled over the North Sea but not before 730 got into serious trouble. At seventeen thousand feet number three engine blew off the cylinder heads and scattered broken parts over the sky. Her crew was lucky to escape more damage or a fire. The ground crew blew it that time, but it was one of the few instances of a mistake so serious that should have been avoided. I don't recall what crew was flying #730 but I was glad it wasn't us.

CHAPTER XVII

Mission to Norway and Mission to Bremen

Norway—Johnny Purus Only   *Aircraft 878*
November 16

Johnny Purus was drafted to fly with a new crew on their first mission. What did he do to deserve such an unenviable assignment? He must have become crossways with Franek because bombardiers were not in short supply. I am sure Franek would not have done that to most of the experienced bombardiers. It was one of those days when nothing went right. The first error was the faulty weather forecast. The second error was the information on the target, which was a plant in Norway located over a mine. The briefed altitude was thirteen thousand feet, but halfway across the North Sea they hit a weather front that was unexpected, and had to circle and circle up to nineteen thousand to get over it. When they reached the target area neither the lead navigator or bombardier could find anything resembling the plant supposed to be there. The intelligence relied on by Bomber Command might have been planted by the Germans. Both sides tried to lure the other into costly misadventures to waste manpower and materials. In frustration the Group made a wide three sixty swing back over where the target was supposed to have been. Again nothing!

But the boneheads for the day were not finished! The pilot was too inexperienced to realize the need to stay in formation so he was trailing along behind. Ten minutes from the Norwegian coast the pilot made what turned out to be the fourth error of the day. He left the cockpit and headed for the radio room to confer with the radio operator. Pilots do not leave the cockpit in enemy territory without a compelling reason! On the catwalk near the door to the radio room he was shocked by the rattle of fifty caliber guns in action and a twenty M.M. cannon shell tore through the bomb bay, somehow missing the bombs, and took off part of his flight jacket sleeve. Eight enemy fighters had jumped the formation and hit the stragglers first as they always did. Another slug crashed into the top turret. The copilot belatedly decided to get into the formation and did a good job of flying to pull quickly into the protection of the defensive fire coverage. That was how new crews got shot down! They listened to the stories about fighters and did not buy them. "All of that junk about tight formation was for the birds!" Purus was lucky to survive.

November 26   Bremen

The raid was called on a raw, windy morning. Outside the sky was a mass of shifting clouds and blowing fog. After a quick look I went back into the hut and said, "We got weather problems today for sure. It'll surprise me if we get off the ground."

Balmore was still grounded for frostbite injuries, but he sat up and remarked, "Hope you fellows don't get another one of those blind climb ups through fog."

"If we go at all it looks like that is exactly what we will draw," I answered.

Balmore continued, "I'd rather have fighter attacks than sweat out those climb ups in fog."

Gleichauf gave us the story for the day: "The target is going to be Bremen. You know what the flak will be like! The weather over the Continent will be ice-forming so some of the fighters may not be able to get to us. The altitude will be twenty-six thousand feet and the temperature will be about fifty below." Shutting added, "There is a strong wind blowing at a hundred and forty miles per hour at our altitude. It is one of those winds that can shift directions and cause problems."

Gleichauf had one more comment: "The Copilot and Engineer must keep an eye on the engines for carburetor icing."

It was a bleak outlook. The biggest mistake of the day, and there were many, was the weather forecast. I knew there would be mixups in such turbulent skies. The takeoff proceeded on schedule thirty minutes before dawn. I was invariably fascinated by the sights and sounds of a group takeoff in the dark. There was an element of the theatrical with airplanes groping toward the lineup at the end of the runway. Pilots detested the severe risks of collisions or mishaps because B-17 formations were not really suitable for night flights.

Paul followed the flight course as briefed: A specified rate of climb and speed for so many minutes, then a forty-five degree turn, repeating the process until out of the murk. Theoretically the planes should come out in the clear close together so that the squadron could form quickly. If the fog was a thousand to fifteen hundred feet, the tactic would work fairly well. But if the overcast was up to eight or ten thousand feet it would create chaos.

"Pilot to Navigator."

"Go ahead, Paul."

"Can you see anything ahead?"

"Nothing! Blind as a bat."

"John, get in the turret an' watch out ahead. Lots of planes in this soup."

A little later: "Pilot to Navigator—what is our rendezvous altitude over splasher four?" (A radio beam projecting upward to aid navigation.)

"Five thousand feet."

At that height there was a clear space between banks of heavy clouds and the 381st was supposed to assemble over this radio beacon. Some aircraft were already there.

"Bombardier to Pilot."

"Go ahead."

"There's our signal light color high at seven o'clock."

"Good. I see it."

When we pulled close to the aircraft flashing the signal light that was intended to identify the 381st Group, it turned out to be another group, and a mixup on the signal light colors. It was just one of a number of mistakes the pilots would have to endure for the next two hours. Another aircraft with the familiar 381st Triangle "L" was also lured by the false signal. The pilot saw we were from the 381st and moved in on our right wing and stayed there.

"Hey, Paul, we got company," said the Copilot. "It's from our Group, but I don't recognize the ship."

"I wish to hell he'd get off of our wing! We got more fog comin' up."

But the aircraft hung in on our wing tight, much to our consternation. It was bad enough being in the soup with so many other ships flying blind. Later we found out the reason: that wing aircraft was without a navigator, and the confusion and awful weather was driving the pilot to desperate measures. It seems odd that Operations would have permitted a ship to take off under such conditions without a navigator.

"Pilot to crew—we're goin' on up to nine thousand feet—hope we can catch the 381st there—everyone watch out for other airplanes—Navigator! Navigator!"

"Go ahead."

"Let me know when we are approaching the rendezvous point."

Sometime later: "This is the Navigator. We're getting close to where they told us to go—can't see anything in this soup."

"This is one big mess, Navigator. I'll try to contact the Wing."

After another five minutes: "Pilot to Navigator—OK, they say go to twelve thousand feet over splasher four."

At twelve thousand feet it was the same—fog—fog—fog!

"Pilot to Navigator—this is no good either! Can't see anything. Let's try thirteen thousand."

But another thousand feet did not help, and we lost radio contact with the Group leader.

"Radio to Pilot—Radio to Pilot."

"This is the Pilot."

"Blasingborn says the 381st will pass over splasher four at fifteen thousand feet at nine hundred hours."

At the scheduled time we were over the radio beacon at the correct height and it was the same story—just blinding fog!

"Pilot to crew—we're goin' on up until we break out of this soup. Ships this high have lost contact—no telling how many lost planes are up here. Watch out for other aircraft."

The overcast broke at nineteen thousand feet. There were many aircraft milling around in confusion looking for a formation to join. The long climb up to this altitude had undoubtedly used up a lot of fuel.

"Turret to Copilot, do we have enough gas to join a formation without knowing for sure how long the mission will be?"

"'Copilot to Pilot."

"Go ahead."

"We've burned up a lot more fuel than we expected. We got enough for a short mission, but not for a long one."

"I don't see any formation to join anyway. If we should find one later we would run a risk on gas! Navigator—Navigator."

"Go ahead, Paul."

"Give me a heading for Ridgewell."

Shutting knew that the wind might have shifted in the several hours since the weather briefing, but without visibility he had no means to check for drift. "Start letting down in wide circles, Paul, and I'll keep calling out the headings."

A long time later the aircraft broke under the clouds. We were over land near the North Sea.

"Navigator to Pilot, we were lucky. We could've come down far out over the sea the way these high wind currents can shift direction."

On this same goofed-up mission attempt George Reese was assigned to Lieutenant Deering's crew as copilot on their first mission. Operations thought that with Reese in the cockpit Deering could stay out of trouble. The rookie navigator must not have paid much attention to the briefing because he evidently did not catch the hundred and forty mile per hour wind. It was odd that he could miss such navigational data, probably due to the fear and trauma of a first combat mission. When it was decided that it was impossible to proceed with the mission, the Navigator had to rely on dead reckoning[1] to get back to the base. The strange story came from George Reese: "We were at twenty-one thousand feet when I told the pilot that the mission was scrubbed. I didn't pay too much attention for the next hour as the ship eased down through fog; I was worried mainly about a collision in the soup. I remembered that a high wind was blowing but I could not recall the exact direction from the briefing. Once or twice I called the Navigator to ask if he was allowing for the drift from that high wind, but could not get anything out of him. I was a little uneasy that he might be confused, but at that time there did not seem to be any good reason to ask the radio operator to get us a Q.D.M. I expected that we would need one when we broke clear of the fog. There were no holes in the ceiling and we came down blind. At six thousand feet the Ball called, 'Ball to crew—land below us.'

" 'Pilot to Copilot, do you recognize the area? See anything familiar?'

" 'Don't recognize it—Navigator.'

" 'This is the Navigator.'

" 'Watch for some landmark you can recognize from your charts.'

"Deering dropped down to a lower altitude. Sanford, a waist gunner, had quite a few missions, but neither of us could pick out anything, familiar. Suddenly a tower appeared to the right. I recognized immediately that it was a German flak tower, but before I could say anything, a furious burst of shells exploded around us.

" 'Get the hell out of here—we're over the Continent.'

"But where over the Continent? It could have been East or West

---

[1] Dead reckoning means navigating strictly by instruments, speed, time, etc., without any chance to correct the course for changes in wind direction or velocity.

France, Holland, Belgium, North Germany, or possibly Denmark. Stanford and the tail gunner did have the pleasure of strafing the German tower—one of the few times I know of that Fortress gunners could shoot back at the enemy manning those flak guns.

"We flew north for ten minutes until we sighted what I thought was the North Sea. Suddenly twelve bursts of very accurate flak caught us almost dead center. I quickly grabbed the wheel and ducked out of that spot fast. I threw the ship up and down and took as much evasive action as I thought the crew could stand.

" 'Copilot to Navigator, we've got to find out where we are so you can give us a heading for England.'

" 'Copilot to crew—Copilot to crew. Watch for fighters. They're goin' to hit us if we don't get out of here quick.'

"Back in the waist, tail, and radio room, the ammunition had been thrown out of the cans and the men banged up a bit by the drastic evasive action. The gunners were frantically trying to get the ammunition straightened out. Deering turned west and flew parallel to the coast in the hope that Stanford or me would see something familiar. Thirty minutes of this and we turned southeast. High and inaccurate flak came up. A few minutes later a lone F.W. 190 appeared and made two passes. Fortunately both were against the tail where we have our best defense. Deering did a good job of evasive action.

" 'Copilot to Tail, good going back there! Let 'em have it when they come in.'

"Deering turned into land again. 'Copilot to crew, two fighters at two o'clock high—pour the lead to 'em if they try to attack us.'

"The pilot dodged into a cloud bank before the fighters could strike.

" 'Good work, Pilot. Stay in this cloud until we shake those fighters, but we got to find out where we are—we can't hang around here all day.'

" 'Copilot to Radio.'

" 'Go ahead.'

" 'Do you know how to get a fix?'

" 'I think we're too far away for a fix.'

" 'I was afraid of that. Try anyway.'

"When we came out of the clouds, Deering turned inland again and headed for a sizable city in full view. Without warning all hell broke loose! Flak and small arms fire came up in a hail of lead.

" 'Copilot to Pilot. I know where we are. That is Calais! Let me have the controls.'

"I took more evasive action but not fast enough. I heard a loud noise underneath the aircraft. 'Copilot to Ball, where did we get hit? Any bad damage?'

'' 'The bomb-bay doors were knocked down.'

'' 'Copilot to Top Turret, go back an' see if you can hand crank the doors back up.'

''The doors would not come up, but it was not important. We had plenty of fuel.

'' 'Pilot to Navigator, give us a heading for Ridgewell and be sure to allow for that heavy wind current.'

''Deering took over and climbed to six thousand feet. Two more F.W. 190s came up from the rear. Both had belly tanks and one had a rocket chute.

'' 'Copilot to Tail, watch that fighter with the rocket. When you see the rocket fire, follow the vapor trail 'an tell the pilot which way to move the airplane.'

'' 'Pilot, this is the Tail. It's gettin' in position about fifteen hundred yards behind us, slightly high. He fired it! It's comin' straight at us! Pull up! Pull up!'

''Deering jerked the aircraft up an' the rocket passed under us real close.

'' 'Tail to crew, fighter comin' in five o'clock level.'

''I could hear the tail and waist guns hammering an' saw the fighter flash by below my window. It pulled up high and tried a nose attack.

'' 'Pilot! Evasive action!'

''The attack failed and the two fighters disappeared into the mists.

'' 'Copilot from Top Turret, I think we hit that fighter—maybe knocked it down.'

'' 'I doubt it. Those 190s are heavily armored and can take a lot of punishment.'

''The radio operator had been feverishly attempting to pick up a fix. He got a response all right, but the station failed to answer his challenge for the day. He knew then it was a German station trying to lure us in for a kill. That was a trick used by both sides. (The radio operators used Morse code, which was easy to fake.) Actually we were a little too far away for a reliable fix. Halfway across the water that same F.W. 190 our gunners thought they had shot down appeared again. That persistent bastard followed us all of the way to the English coast. Radio finally got in contact with a home station and established a Q.D.M. At the coast a Spitfire showed up and the F.W. 190 took off for Germany in a hurry. I was much relieved to see the outlines of Ridgewell show up. There was one final error: Radio was confused about the damage to the aircraft and had radioed ahead that our landing gear was shot out. When we came in to land I saw to my surprise ambulances, crash wagons, and fire trucks standing by. The Old Man was plenty teed off! He blamed me for the mixups and damage to the plane.''

November 18

During this period the 381st was constantly being infused with new crews, who had yet to learn the hard lesson that tight formation was as essential to their well-being as blocking is to a football team. We received new crews, but continued to lose experienced ones, and that meant an exhaustive effort to keep the quality high. Training went on but too many replacement crews lessened our ability to fly good formations consistently. Either the new pilots arrived with some high-altitude formation experience or they had to start learning it on combat missions. Sure, we flew some formation practice, but there was no way that the 381st could provide the training that the crews were supposed to have had in the States. For quite a while the Group was losing as many men as it was gaining from new arrivals. We did not have the time, or the aircraft, or the fuel to retrain those new arrivals.

November 27

The rain clouds cleared and there was a part of a moon. Eight or ten of us pedaled into a nearby village and enjoyed an evening at the pubs. At closing time we started back to the base. The men in the lead used their flashlights and the rest of us followed along in the dark. Between the local road and our quarters there was a swift-running stream spanned by a narrow bridge. We were strung out in single file behind a Captain in the lead. Suddenly the Captain dropped his flashlight and everything went dark. I heard a wild yell and a splash as something hit the water. I switched on my light in time to see an officer's cap floating jauntily downstream bobbing gently in the water like a toy boat.

Someone yelled, "Where's the Captain?"

Four flashlights scanned the empty water rushing by. An authoritative voice took command. "All right! Jerk off your blouses! All of you! Now! Get in that creek! Couple of ya go downstream and work back. We gotta find him—and quick!''

The frigid water sobered me real quick. In one or two minutes someone located the Captain and we pulled him out of that freezing water. Fortunately he did not take on much water internally, and in ten minutes he was recovered enough to be out of danger. I was shaking with a bad chill by the time I got to the hut and into some dry clothes. The temperature was thirty-five degrees.

CHAPTER XVIII

Mission to Paris and Leverkusen

The month of November was frustrating because the weather kept the B-17s grounded for a week at a time. When a mission was called we fully expected it to be canceled before takeoff, or in the air before we reached enemy territory. If clouds were almost certain to cover the target, there was no point in continuing the mission unless the drop was scheduled to be by Pathfinder equipment. Since the middle of the month we had taken off eight times back to back without getting in a mission. That was hard on morale. Being confined too much of the time to the small metal quarters, we became irritating to each other. Sometimes Lancia's noise became abrasive and Wilson's disorderly bunk was always revolting to a person like me, who wanted things neat and shipshape. There were days when Rogers withdrew into a morose silence and ignored the rest of us. When he was in one of those moods it was better to leave him alone. Tedesco's continual harping on Brooklyn and New York got on my nerves. Hadn't he ever been anywhere else before he was drafted into the service? The least offensive occupant of our hut was Hubie Green. He was such a nice, gentle young man I could find little to resent about him.

December 1—Leverkusen, Germany   Aircraft 730

Jim climbed wearily out of bed and groaned, "Another false alarm I suppose. Will we ever get in another mission?"

"We haven't flown a completed raid since early November," I said. "At this rate we'll be here another year."

Harkness added, "But we've been in sight of enemy territory four times before we turned back."

Gleichauf intercepted me at Operations. "We're carryin' a General with us this mornin' so get things in good shape before we get there."

I did not like the idea of high-ranking brass on a mission. It meant extra trouble and having to be more careful over the intercom. As soon as I examined the cockpit of aircraft 730 I made a run for the perimeter road and was lucky to hail down a passing Jeep. "Get word to Operations real quick that aircraft 730 has no extra cockpit oxygen outlet—cannot handle an extra passenger in the cockpit."

When Gleichauf arrived he said, "They switched the General to another ship. The target is Leverkusson, at the edge of the Ruhr Valley."

There were groans from the crew.

"Cut the bitching. Major Hall, the Group Operations Officer, will lead the 381st." He turned to Harkness. "Watch close for flak damage under the engines."

With Hall leading I knew it would be a smooth, well executed mission if the weather permitted. The takeoff was efficient and on time. The weather had improved so much it looked like we might be able to proceed with the operation.

"Pilot from Navigator."

"Go ahead."

"We'll hit the coast at eleven hundred hours. Fighters can show any time."

The P-47 escort arrived as we crossed the coast and shortly afterward the intercom came on: "Ball to Copilot—fighters at four o'clock low comin' up."

"Tail to Ball, what are those fighters tryin' to do? I've never seen them circle around down below us before."

"Don't know. Maybe it's a new tactic against the 47s."

"Copilot, I can see at least thirty from the turret."

I looked up in time to see eight 47s streaking down at high speed followed by the remainder of the escort. For a few minutes there was a marvelous view of about forty P-47s tangling with about fifty M.E. 109s. It was the biggest dogfight I ever saw—a gigantic, twisting, turning, diving battle that was soon out of my range of view.

At the I.P. I saw the first B-17 go down from a fighter attack. Suddenly ice began to form inside the turret glass and cut my vision to zero. Where was the moisture coming from? The cockpit windows and windshield were clear.

"Copilot to Turret—Copilot to Turret—four fighters crossing in front of us at ten o'clock high—let 'em have it."

I scraped the ice furiously. When I could see, they were too far away to get in my sights. Gleichauf was caustic. "Why in the hell didn't you shoot? They were right in front of you!"

"Ice! The turret glass is iced up—barely see out of it. Scraping it off as fast as I can. Don't know where the moisture came from."

The aircraft was another of those old E models with small Ball and Top Turret oxygen tanks. "Ball to Waist. Ball to Right Waist—It's time to refill the ball oxygen tank."

"OK, Ball, turn it around forward and hold it there. Don't move that ball until I tell you it's clear."

"Got it, Jim."

Remembering what happened the day we flew *Tinker Toy*, Jim had George standing by with a walk-around bottle in case ice should form and hold the valves open. When he tried to remove the filler valve it would not release. Realizing that he would have to run back to the waist and get a screwdriver to prize it off, Jim went on intercom: "Waist to Ball, do not move the ball—repeat—do not move the ball, until you hear me say clear."

All Harkness heard distinctly was the word "clear." "Thanks, Jim," he said, and whirled the ball back into action and snapped off the filler line. The oxygen pressure in the left side aft system of the Waist and Tail vanished as the gas spewed out. Fortunately the pressure in the ball held firm.

"Radio to crew. Radio to crew. The left rear oxygen system is gone. Switch to the right system."

My earphones were so poor that I could not pick up what was going on in the aft section of the ship. Really it was no serious matter, as the mission was relatively short. We had plenty of oxygen but Sanford, flying left waist, failed to hear the warning and keeled over and passed out. Counce quickly switched his hose to the right side regulator and he revived.

"Bombardier to Waist."

"Go ahead."

"Is everything OK back there?"

"I think so. I can't tell about Legg. I think he's OK 'cause he looks like he's sitting up at his position."

"Bombardier to Tail."

"Bombardier to Tail—Bombardier to Tail—come in."

There was no response.

"Waist?"

"Go ahead."

"Go back and check out the Tail Gunner."

When Jim got to where he could see Legg clearly he realized the tail gunner was in very serious condition, and had to have oxygen fast or he was going to suffer brain damage or worse! Jim struggled valiantly to untangle the gunner's hose and switch him to the undamaged right side system, but Raymond had collapsed so that he was lying on his hose. There was only room in the tail for one man. Counce knew that man had to have oxygen quickly. Without a moment's hesitation he unhooked from his portable bottle and plugged Legg into it. He knew he would probably pass out before he could get back to his waist position, and he did. But Sanford quickly revived him and no harm was done.

"Tail from Waist—Tail from Waist."

"This is the Tail, go ahead."

"Are you all right?"

"I guess so—a little dizzy—but I'll make it."

"Keep your regulator on the right side system. The left system is empty."

"OK—Waist—that's what the trouble was? Thanks for straightening me out."

While Legg was unconscious he suffered a severe electrical burn on his leg where the electric suit pressed too tightly against him. When off of oxygen for an extended period, the bodily resistance to high or low temperature plummets.

"Ball to Copilot, my electric heat has gone out—hope I can keep from freezing a foot or hand."

"Use straight oxygen. That'll help some."

In the ball the gunner had less room for bulky clothes so he depended more on his electrically heated equipment than the rest of us. I felt the bombs fall away. It told me we would be free of that miserable flak in a few more minutes. That was the main thing I wanted right then.

"Turret to Ball, exercise your hands and feet as much as you can. A little exercise can stave off frostbite."

"Turret to crew. Turret to crew—fighters at one o'clock high."

The attacks were directed to the high squadron and I did not have a good opportunity to fire.

"Tail to crew, another Fort going down at eight o'clock low—four chutes."

A Fort nearby caught heavy damage to number three engine. An oil or fuel line was ruptured and a long stream of flame shot back as far as the tail. Several men dropped out of the waist hatch. One unfortunate crewman pulled his ripcord too soon and the silk blossomed up into the flame. It instantly began to blaze. I watched in stunned horror as the condemned man started his terrifying plunge toward Earth five miles below!

"Copilot to crew—that's the third Fort I've seen go down so far."

The fighters kept circling the formation making sporadic passes. They were by no means a hot interceptor group. I suspected they were green German pilots. It was time for the attrition of war to begin decimating the excellent pilots with whom Germany had started the war. Ten minutes from the coast the intercom came on: "Tail to crew—another B-17 dropping down at five o'clock."

"Copilot to Ball—do you see it?"

"Yes. I see it. No chutes so far. It looks to be under control." After some more questions Kels announced, "That must have been Nixon's plane. I guess he knew he could not make it across the Channel."

The way I saw it, Nixon decided to give the crew a chance to bail out rather than risk a water ditching. Those men were old friends and it was depressing to see them lost. Well, it would be better for them to jump if they couldn't make it to England. With bad visibility shaping up, the chances of getting picked up from the water before dark were poor. Few survived a night drifting on the cold Channel.

The total loss was twenty Forts, which was too high in view of the moderate opposition.

December 5—Paris   Aircraft 730

Jim Counce and I were scheduled to ride with the crew of Lieutenant Deering, the pilot George Reese was with when they accidentally came down over the Continent. I suspect that the assignment was to give Deering a little experience in his crew, but there was not always any particular reason for assignments. The raid would be Deering's second attempt and I was leery of him as a pilot. Of course Jim, as well as myself, was annoyed at being put with a green crew. The Paris area always threatened to throw Goering's crack "Yellow Nose" squadrons at us, and they were as mean as fighters could be. If they caught us near the target, with a pilot throttle-jockeying the formation, it would send out a clear signal of "green crew—hit it first."

Riding in the rear of the personnel truck in complete darkness to the perimeter where the aircraft were parked was a different experience each mission morning. Some days the men were morosely silent, lost in speculation of what the next few hours would be like. Or they were gabby, covering their anxieties with the bravado of inane chatter. That morning I did not see them get into the truck so they were only voices in the darkness.

"Why the hell didn't they send someone to tell us they were loading bombs last night? We closed the Goddam pub. I feel like hell."

"Some pure oxygen will snap you out of it—always works for me when I got a hangover."

"The way you soaked up the ale last night I bet you piss in your pants down in the ball today."

"Hey, you remember that red-headed broad we saw at the pub last week?"

"Yeah—she looked good."

"I had her out two nights ago."

"How was it?"

"Allllll right! Her ole man only gets home every three weeks and she can't wait that long."

"We got us a new boy flyin' Navigator today. Our Navigator's got the clap—on that last pass to London I guess."

"They can cure the clap easy now with that sulpha stuff—dries it right up."

"Let's hope it stays dried up."

We got out at aircraft 719 and as the truck pulled out I could hear the conversational drivel still going on. "Hey, let's go to Ridgewell tonight—there's a blond bitch you'd go for . . ."

The crew chief headed my way with a glum look on his face, "Sorry, but 719 is redlined for today."

"Damn! We draw a green crew an' now the airplane's canceled out."

Jim asked, "What's wrong with it?"

"Number three is vibrating too much—real rough."

"Did you call Engineering?" I asked.

"Yeah, they're sendin' a truck to pick ya up."

Jim growsed, "Another one of those delays—not enough time to get the guns ready—and on top of that a new crew."

The wait for the truck wasted precious time needed to get the aircraft, whatever one it would be, ready for a mission. When we finally piled out at the replacement airplane it was near engine starting time. Deering arrived at the same time we did.

"Pilot," I said, "we don't have time left to get the guns ready. How about calling Operations and telling them that we will be late taking off because of a last-minute change of aircraft?"

Operations told Deering to try to catch the formation over the Channel and set up a rendezvous time. Of course formations were rarely that close on timing. A minor mechanical problem added another ten minutes to the takeoff delay.

When the aircraft finally became airborne we were twenty minutes late. It was time consuming for the process of squadrons to gather their planes, then for the groups to form and the wing to assemble into proper positions. Deering had instructions to head straight for the final rendezvous over the Channel. When we got to the Channel the 381st was in sight but so far ahead that to try to catch up was impractical. We trailed the rest of the way over water midway between two groups. I think Deering still hoped to overtake the 381st.

"Top Turret to Pilot."

"Go ahead."

"Fighters can show up anytime now. Not good being out of a formation."

He did not reply.

Ten minutes later he still had made no move to get into a formation. That was how aircraft got shot down. Flight Engineers do not tell pilots what to do, but something had to be done right away.

"Top Turret to Pilot."

"Go ahead."

"There's a vacant spot in the high group to our left—it's always better to be in the high group if fighters attack."

"Good idea—don't think we can catch the 381st."

"No chance of that."

A few minutes later Deering pulled into the high group and I felt a hundred percent better about the situation.

"Pilot to Copilot."

"Go ahead."

"I hope they don't raise hell about us bein' in the wrong group."

So that was what had been worrying him. I suppose he did get chewed out for that episode with Reese and he did not want to get back on the carpet on his next flight.

"Top Turret to Pilot. Don't worry about that. Planes fly with other groups all the time when they can't find their own outfits. You got a good excuse. Operations didn't really expect you to catch our Wing when they saw you take off twenty minutes late."

"Thanks."

After that Deering relaxed and did what I thought was an excellent job for a pilot with so little formation experience. We got off in such a hurry that all I knew about the target was that it was an aircraft plant somewhere near Paris.

"Copilot to crew—I've got good news for you. Today we're gonna have a P-51 escort. How about that?"

Super news! At last we were getting what had been billed as a long-range fighter that would be a match for the best Germany could throw at us. We would soon find out if the P-51s were that good.

"Tail to crew—fighters at six o'clock high."

As soon as they were close enough I saw what they were. "Top Turret to crew—they are P-51s."

They were beautiful airplanes. I wondered if the Germans knew we had P-51s in England and what they thought about them. The secret had been well kept from the bomber crews. I watched with glee as the 51s drove off a handful of Jerry fighters and stayed with us to the I.P., where a group of P-47s with the larger disposable fuel tanks took over escort duties. Shortly afterwards seven F.W. 190s came poking up toward us. The 47s dived after them and the action moved beyond my vision. As far as I saw there were no fighter attacks against the formations. Visibility was zero over the target. The weather forecast missed completely.

"Pilot to Bombardier—we going to drop the bombs?"

"Not on this target—they may try an alternate."

The soup covered Europe, and by that time Bomber Command in .England knew it. The B-17s turned back to England with no blow struck against Adolf. It was a frustrating day, with so much effort expended for no results. At one-thirty we touched down at Ridgewell Airdrome. Seven more raids would put me over the top. With those P-51 beauties, my prospects looked far brighter.

The P-51 Mustang Fighter began as a mediocre low-level fighter used mainly for strafing. The original Allison engine was replaced with the Rolls Royce Merlin engine. Other modifications were made and it emerged as the finest propeller-driven fighter plane of World War II. With disposable fuel tanks, the plane could go with the bombers to the deepest targets.

After the landing I singled out Lieutenant Deering. "I want to compliment you for the way you held tight formation today. That is the best I've seen for a new pilot since I arrived in England. If you keep that up, your crew will be OK."

December 6

When newspapers from the U.S. occasionally found their way overseas, there were distorted stories and statements about the war that were irritating. I remember one silly news article: a U.S. Senator said the

German Air Force was almost eliminated. That was 1943 when the Luftwaffe was at its height. A Congressman orated that the war would be over by June, the date of the Normandy landing. An American newspaper was an object of both nostalgia and derision at some of the fanciful tales.

December 8

If a Sunday was free I sometimes attended Chapel Services on the base. The Chaplain was named Brown and he got along well with the English people who lived nearby. I can remember the familiar sight of the farm families from close by walking down the runways on Sunday mornings to church. One Sunday about time services were to begin, a large, awkward soldier in oil-stained coveralls and muddy shoes stumbled down the aisle and took a front seat. Obviously, he came directly from work. That was certainly all right, but it seemed to me he should have taken a back-row seat in his soiled clothes as the civilians were dressed in their best. A few minutes later that big bear of a man with grimy hands stood and faced the audience. Suddenly he was transformed: the notes of the "Lord's Prayer" in a powerful and beautiful baritone voice filled the Chapel. It was a magnificent solo, as good as any of the top rated baritones of that day could have done. When the last notes died away, his shoulders sagged and he was once again a weary G.I. mechanic. He nodded to the Chaplain and was gone. Who was he? With such a voice he had to be a highly trained professional singer. I never discovered his name or saw him again around the base. In this time of war any man in uniform might have been a well-known name that one did not recognize among the thousands wearing military garb that made us all look a little alike.

Eight months earlier, when we were a newly formed flight crew at Boise, Idaho, I arrived at the aircraft site for a night flight ahead of the rest of the crew.

The instructor pilot was already there, so we went through the preflight inspection procedure, and I picked up the aircraft flight form to write in the names of those on the flight.

"Sir, may I have your name, rank, and serial number?"

"Oh, let me have it and I'll fill it in. That way I know I'll get the serial number right," he replied.

There was a wearisome two-hour flight with six of us crowded into the cockpit space. A week later I was in the P.X. barbershop getting a haircut when the same instructor pilot came in. I noticed that he went out of his way to nod to everyone nearby.

"That officer must be a politician in civilian life," I whispered to the barber.

"Don't you know who he is?"

"Sure. The name is Stewart—instructor pilot."

"Don't you recognize Jimmy Stewart, the movie actor?"

CHAPTER XIX

Mission to Emden

December 11—Emden, Germany   *Aircraft 719*
                                       Hellcat

Our aircraft was ready to fly again, we hoped, and the question was, would it handle as well as it did before the damage? It was snowing when Gleichauf pulled the wet nose of 719 into the air and the thick gray soup. Pilots detested that nerve-wracking procedure that could at any time so easily end in a head-on crash with another plane. The flight of airplanes could not be held precisely to the exacting specifications of the briefing plan, and especially with so many pilots short of flying experience.

"Pilot to crew—keep alert—it's going to be thick today—Bombardier."

"Go ahead, Paul."

"Watch ahead—if you see anything call out quick."

He turned to me. "Get in the turret and help us look—keep a sharp eye above us."

"I know how many green pilots are taking off this morning all over England. That's what bothers me most in this stuff," I said to George Reese, who was our copilot for the mission.

"Bothers both of us," he replied.

"Pilot! Pilot! Eleven o'clock level—that dark blob! What is it?"

After intense scrutiny it turned out to be a splotch of darker cloud. But with nerves drawn tight we were ready to see the dark form of an aircraft on a collision course.

At nine thousand feet we broke through into brilliant sunshine and a sparkling sky. The world atop the fleecy billowing clouds was one apart

232

from the winter drab and mud below. I had not seen the sun in so long it was reassuring to know it was still shining, and that the sky was as blue as I remembered it.

"Navigator to crew—Navigator to crew—the temperature will be only thirty-eight below today. We'll have an escort of P-51s at the German coast and we'll sic them on those Jerry fighters and sit back and watch the fun."

The target was the port facilities at Emden, Germany, from an altitude of twenty-three thousand feet, lower than usual. We were scheduled to fly with a high composite Group made up of elements from several groups in order to add extra strength. The slow climb to nine thousand feet through fog disrupted the timing enough that our squadron missed the Group we were supposed to be part of. That left the decision of what to do to the Squadron Commander and he elected to go on alone.

A little before ten o'clock we started across the North Sea toward Germany bucking a strong head wind that required heavy power on the four engines. Even so, the crossing consumed two hours, because the velocity of the head wind subtracted from the airspeed of the ship.

Emden was not regarded as a difficult target, but the formation that day turned out to be ragged, with aircraft throttle-jockeying back and forth.

"Damn these new pilots—I can't keep up a steady airspeed—one minute I'm drawing too much power and the next minute we're barely above stalling," fumed Gleichauf.

"Klein's raisin' hell every time you dogleg," said the Copilot.

"Navigator to Pilot, there's the Frisian Islands right at one o'clock."

A voice cut in on the intercom. "Hey, Bombardier, drop some bombs on that seaplane ramp and watch the Krauts scatter."

"Copilot to crew, cut the unnecessary chatter."

"Bombardier to crew, single fighter coming from the south at nine o'clock high."

The solitary M.E. 109 circled us cautiously for a few minutes.

"Bombardier to crew—flak at twelve o'clock level."

Fortunately it did not amount to much, then the Navigator spotted something. "Fighters at ten o'clock—about thirty-five of them."

The enemy interceptors came in to five thousand yards and after a few minutes pulled away to the left and were soon out of sight. For some reason not known to us they elected not to attack. It could have been that they were at the far end of their fuel range.

"Pilot to Navigator, where did you say the escort would pick us up?"

"At the coast, Paul. If they are comin' we oughta see 'em soon. In five minutes we'll swing to the right inshore then make two left turns to come in over the target downwind.''

Fifteen minutes went by and Purus called. "We're starting the bomb run.''

"OK, Bombardier.''

Flak began popping at us as we approached the target. There was a loud crashing sound from the rear section of the aircraft.

"Copilot to Waist, anyone hurt? Any damage?''

"This is Jim—big chunk struck where I was standin'. The armor plate deflected it. Otherwise would have got me. No serious damage.''

"Bombardier to Radio, stand by to watch bomb-bay doors down.''

George, as usual, was standing with the front radio door open to watch the bombs fall out. "Radio to Bombardier—Radio to Bombardier, over.''

"Go ahead, Radio.''

"Three bombs hung up in the racks. Thousand pounder stuck on the bottom rack an' two five hundred pounders on top of it.''

"Turret to Bombardier, I'm goin' back to release the bombs.''

"OK, John—Radio, stand by to see if Turret needs any help.''

The bomb load was mixed. Thousand pounders were carried on the lower racks while five hundred pounders were hung on the middle racks. Above those were clusters of either incendiaries or fragmentation bombs held in place by small steel cables. The situation in the bomb bay was a weird mess. One thousand pounder had failed to release on a rack well below the catwalk. Resting on top of it two five-hundred pounders were also hung up on the loose cables used to hold the fragmentation bombs in the racks. To trip the rack shackle on the lower bomb a screwdriver had to be used, but access to the shackle was blocked by one of the five-hundred pounders directly on top of the big one. I caught a glimpse of Balmore in the radio room motioning me to return to the cockpit.

"Turret to Bombardier, it'll take two of us to clear the bomb bay.''

"OK. We'll wait 'til we are down to fifteen thousand feet.''

It would have been foolish to attempt the release at high altitude because of the limited working time of the portable walk-around bottles, and the risk of losing oxygen and tumbling out into space. A few minutes later I called Purus again. "The thousand pounder is stuck on the lowest inside rack below the catwalk. The two five hundreds are resting on top of it and tangled up in the loose cables from the frag cluster.''

"When we release the thousand pounder, will the two fives fall free?''

"It's impossible to tell for sure. We may have to cut them loose,'' I answered.

"How can we cut those steel cables?"

"I always carry some hacksaw blades, Bombardier. One of us is going to have to hang down below the walk and slip a screwdriver between the big one and the fives on top of it."

"I'm smaller than you so I'll do it while you hold my legs."

"OK. I will straddle the catwalk and lock my legs around it. You hang down in front of me so I can get a good hold on your legs. We got to be careful that when that big one falls out the fives don't knock us off of the catwalk."

At fifteen thousand feet we cut loose of oxygen and began the risky procedure that had to be done. An airplane could not land at an airfield with hung-up bombs. The risk was too great to the other aircraft and base facilities. I sat on the narrow catwalk and locked my legs around it. Purus climbed over me and slid head down so I could grasp his legs. There was barely enough room between the bombs to work. Johnny carefully pushed the long screwdriver, working by feel in the cramped space between the bombs. When he got the tool in position to attempt the release he looked back at me, and I increased my grip on him and the narrow beam we were sitting on. We did not know which way the two upper bombs would move and had to be ready. When he pushed the shackle release the big one let go smoothly and the other two bombs shifted their hang positions slightly but not enough to endanger us. That was a tremendous relief! But not for long! The two five hundreds began to swing back and forth on the cables, striking the vertical support beams on each swing. Theoretically they were not supposed to explode as long as the impellor was in place, but I would have preferred not to put the theory to a test.

Now it was my turn. With Purus holding me I leaned far out and began sawing away at the steel cable holding the closest of the two remaining bombs with a hacksaw blade. Meanwhile we were speeding across the North Sea assisted by a terrific tail wind that Purus and I had forgotten about. At the moment the first five hundred pounder broke off and fell free I caught a frantic signal from Balmore at the door of the radio room. He pointed down: to my horror that bomb was headed straight for an English seaplane base on the coast of England. All I could do was watch in shocked consternation. As it neared the base the bomb appeared to the eye to veer slightly seaward and struck the water fifty yards from the ramp. It was frightfully close to a disaster! Gleichauf turned back over the sea and circled until I cut the last bomb hazard loose.

When I returned to the cockpit Gleichauf was visibly upset. "What were you trying to do? Wipe out an English base?"

"We forgot about that strong tail wind."

"We had been trying to stop you back there," he replied testily.

"You can't hear much in an open bomb bay with that deafening wind noise."

"We'll get chewed out when we get back to Ridgewell—maybe some disciplinary action—you can bet on that!" And he was right. We knew the English would get our aircraft number and lodge an angry complaint.

When the Bombardier raised the doors a limit switch failed to shut off and the circuit began to sputter and smoke, but fortunately I was nearby and saw it quickly. That circuit fuse should have blown out instantly, breaking the current connection. I had no choice but to reach in with my fingers and pull out that hot fuse to avoid a fire. It was painful and I had bandaged fingers for a week, but was far better than what a cockpit fire could have done to us. It would be interesting to know what the odds were against two malfunctions on the same circuit at the same time.

Forts out ahead of us ran into trouble and fourteen B-17s were lost. Our gunners claimed the ridiculous figure of one hundred and thirty-seven German fighters shot down. My guess was that thirty-five would have been a high kill. With so many duplicated gunner claims our figures for enemy aircraft shot down were becoming a joke. No one who knew firsthand how tough those fighters were paid serious attention to our extravagant claims.

An incredulous Major at Group Operations the next day was caustic!

"You say a thousand-pound bomb stuck on the lower racks and two five hundreds on top of it tangled in loose cables from the fragmentation clusters carried on the top racks?" the Major asked.

"Yes, sir."

"And you just happened by some odd chance to have some hacksaw blades on hand? Is that what you expect me to believe?"

"Yes, Sir—we always have hacksaw blades."

He looked at us in disbelief. "You always carry hacksaw blades! No other crew in England does! You expect me to repeat this wild tale to the English?"

"But we are telling you the straight truth, Major," Purus insisted.

That night I repeated the conversation to Counce at the hut. "I wouldn't have believed it either," he said, "if I was in his position. Two bombs hangin' up on cables at one time must be a million to one chance."

"Jim, do you remember how we wondered why the people at Boeing Aircraft recommended a half dozen hacksaw blades as part of what flight engineers should carry on missions, along with the other tool list they made up at our request?"

December 12

One very cold night in London I was with Jim in a cab about 2:00 A.M. returning from Kensington to our hotel. The night was exceptionally dark under the blackout common at that period of the war. The two small slits in the headlights that were permitted gave the driver little illumination to negotiate the maze of twisting streets. I had no idea where we were and do not see how Jim could have known either. He turned to me. "Pay the driver my part of the fare and I will repay you tomorrow. I'll meet you at the club about noon. OK?"

I looked at him in amazement. "What are you talking about?"

"Driver, let me out here, please."

He got out and disappeared into the blackness of the bitterly cold night. "See you tomorrow."

Had he completely gone off of the deep end? There was no way he could have known where we were. There was not a thing open at that time of night in the area he chose to get out. The next day he met me at noon in a bright, cheerful mood as if nothing unusual had happened. He made no move to explain his unorthodox behavior and, since it was none of my business, I did not ask him. Neither of us ever mentioned the incident. Jim was like that. When I thought I had him figured out he would shock me with some bizarre act totally out of context with his character or usual habits. Jim shared my taste for good music so we saw some excellent musicals at the Prince of Wales Theater. One evening we were fortunate to get tickets to a fine performance of the opera *La Traviata*.

CHAPTER XX

Mission to Bremen

December 13—Bremen   *Aircraft 730*

Reese flicked on the lights and his voice broke the silence: "All right! Let's go! Out of that sack! Lancia, don't screw up today—this is your twenty-fifth—good luck."

Green asked Lancia, "How do you feel?"

"Lousy! Couldn't sleep last night—wide awake—but I'm gonna make it today."

Ugo had been sweating out this mission for several weeks because of some illness that had him temporarily grounded. As we left the hut everyone shook hands with Lancia and wished him the best of luck. The trip would make twenty missions for me and should have been good news except for a strange phenomenon: luck ran out for so many men in the 381st Group in the final quarter of the game. We have talked about a jinx airplane and for a while it looked to us like the 381st might have been a jinx group. Why was it so difficult for a 533rd man to complete twenty-five missions? Why had nearly every man who approached the finish line met with disaster? Only a handful had succeeded in running the twenty-five-mission hurdle. Was it merely coincidence? What about the Fortress taking off with nearly all the crew on their twenty-fifth and exploding? It was like an evil force hovering over the 381st ready to cut men down just as they neared success. That day Ugo was on a crew composed mainly of men reaching for the elusive last raid. We were anxiously awaiting the verdict, hoping they broke through the hard-luck syndrome we had seen too often. Rogers and Balmore were still adamant that it was the odds catching up that explained the heavy loss of men nearly through. Regardless of what the real reasons were, a psychic wall was slowly developing in the minds of those who were getting close to the magic number. Combat men tended to be superstitious and watched with dismay as the pattern repeated so many times that it no longer appeared to them to be a series of coincidences.

Takeoff time was nine o'clock into a dense cloud bank fifteen hundred feet high. Above the weather was bright and clear.

"Pilot to Navigator—that fog was extra thick—you think it will dissipate by the time we get back?"

"I hope so, but it don't look like one that'll burn off as soon as the sun heats it up."

There was no use worrying about it. If it hung on until we returned it would create pure chaos with so many planes trying to land in a short time period. At eight thousand feet the Wing turned out over the North Sea and began a steady climb to the scheduled altitude.

"Pilot to Navigator—why are we making a left turn?"

"We're starting a three sixty to balance the timing of the Wings because we're fifteen minutes early."

After the formation circled the Copilot came on intercom: "The wing ahead is gettin' hit by fighters—I can see the cannon flashes."

"Turret to crew—they lost a Fort at nine o'clock low—I see two chutes."

"Ball to crew—two more chutes opened up before it exploded."

"Bombardier to crew, three Forts aborting the wing ahead—I don't see any feathered engines or smoke."

I watched them drop down just over the cloud layer, as if they intended to use the clouds if necessary. The abortion looked suspect to me—a severe breach of discipline. Meanwhile the formation passed Bremen to the right and made two left turns to pick up downwind currents over the target for maximum airspeed. We knew what the flak would be like and I am sure the rest of the crew was dreading it as much as I was.

"Waist to Turret."

"Go ahead, Jim."

"My gloves an' shoes just went out an' we got a long way to go before we come down."

"Try to find out which unit is burned out and use your short circuit plug." (The heated suit electrical system was a series circuit, like old-time Christmas-tree lights. If one unit burned out it broke the circuit and knocked out the rest of the units. I made some special plugs that could be used to shunt the current around a defective unit to restore power to the other units.)

"The plug is in my electric suit. Remember that they couldn't locate my suit at Equipment Check Out this morning and gave me this spare?"

"I'll pass my short circuit plugs back to Radio an' you can get them from him—Radio?"

"Go ahead, this is Radio."

"Meet me on the catwalk."

Ten minutes later Shutting called: "Navigator to Pilot."

"Go ahead—this is the Copilot—Paul's on command."

"Tell him the I.P. is coming up right away."

I expected the usual flak spectacular but this time special tactics were used in an attempt to reduce flak damage. Three wings were sent over Bremen at closely timed intervals and widely varying altitudes to confuse the antiaircraft gunners.

"Bombardier to crew, flak ahead—it's coming up all over."

The expected flak intensity was there, but the plan did work. Even though the volume of fire was as heavy as usual, the accuracy was nothing like the last time we were over Bremen.

"Navigator to Copilot, look at that formation of B-24s at twenty thousand feet—they're taking a lot of flak off of us."

"Bombardier to crew, fighters ten o'clock low."

"Ball to crew, Focke-Wolfe 190s six o'clock low."

"Turret to crew, vapor trails very high catching up with us—P-47s, I think."

"Waist to crew, Fort goin' down at three o'clock low—Jerry fighter on fire and out of control."

Dogfights erupted at high and low levels. Fast thinking saved an unknown P-47 pilot. A Jerry fighter got on the tail of the 47 and hung there; the pilot had an inspiration. He dived straight down toward the edge of the Fortress formation with the Jerry still on his tail and unaware of what awaited. When the 47 flashed by us at short range, fifty guns slammed into the enemy fighter turning it into flaming debris.

"Tail to crew, B-17 pulling out of formation—engine feathered. Hey! Wait a minute! Three 47s are coming down and slowing to his speed—they're flying alongside to give him protection."

The 47s stayed with that crippled ship until the formation pulled so far ahead that I could no longer see them.

"Waist to Turret, Ugo just about has it made."

Twenty more P-47s arrived to relieve the first Thunderbolt escort. It was hard to remember that only a few weeks ago the short-ranged escort was ineffective. Now with long-range fighters and larger disposable fuel tanks it was a different war. I would have liked to have bought a drink—

a big double—for every escort pilot who helped keep the Bogies off of us.

"Bombardier to Copilot, I can see fighters hitting the wing ahead of us."

"This is the Navigator, there goes another Fort."

I saw only four Forts go down that day. It must have been some kind of record. The total loss for the mission was eleven aircraft, which was modest in view of the tough target for the day.

"Waist to crew, I know Lancia has it made now. We're nearly to the coast. He's going to break the jinx."

"There will be a big celebration tonight," Wilson added.

When the aircraft landed the procedure was normal. I turned around to pick up some equipment and the brakes failed. Gleichauf turned off into the mud to let it stop the aircraft. It was a muddy mess but there was no damage to the ship. Later the crew chief told me that a hydraulic fitting snapped off from the landing impact.

The celebration started before I got back to the barracks, after the guns were put into good order for a possible raid the next day. Some men from the 533rd Squadron had finally completed twenty-five missions! It could be done! The black clouds dispersed and a collective sigh of relief rolled over the Squadron. That night the nearby pubs were packed with celebrants and glasses were raised to the six men who swept away the barrier. There was now little doubt in my mind that I would soon join the selected band. I expected Ugo to put on a wild demonstration, but to my surprise he was quiet and somber. Perhaps the full impact had not yet had time to come through to him.

Air-Sea Rescue (No Mission)   Aircraft 765
December 14   Nip and Tuck

The night before, the Royal Air Force made a raid against Germany and encountered heavy opposition. On the return a number of Lancasters were forced down at sea shortly before dawn. Any R.A.F. men who made it into rafts might have survived that day, but they had small chance to last out that night. The area covering all of the water where they could have ditched was divided into search areas by grid lines. One aircraft was assigned to each search area. The plan was an exacting one for the Navigator, Lieutenant Smith. He certainly was a busy man, carefully calling out headings to the pilot so that all of the area was checked. The constant staring at the waves became nauseating. For hours we were just above the wave tops, peering intently at the water for some signs of a rubber raft.

"Pilot from Nose—Pilot from Nose, what's that black spot at nine o'clock?"

"I don't see it."

"I see it from the turret."

We came around over the spot and it was a water-soaked piece of timber. Later the Tail called, "There's somethin' at five o'clock—I think—not sure—it looks like—well, I don't know—."

It proved to be nothing except a dark blob of water and an imagination.

"Navigator to Pilot, if there are any rafts out here I hope we can spot them."

"I guess we are all thinking the same thing—next time it might be us out in that cold water," replied Gleichauf.

We knew that whoever was there and still alive had only an hour or two of daylight left and would never survive the night if not found before visibility faded out. For eight hours we scanned the waves. Nothing! Just empty water! At sometime during the day we were not too far from the coast of Denmark. The danger was slight because we were too low for radar to spot us and it was highly unlikely that there would be armed patrol planes over the area. By dusk every man on the ship was half sick. The sensation was similar to seasickness. The unfortunate R.A.F. crews who were hopefully waiting for rescue were not located. Perhaps none of them made it out of the Lancasters in time. The big British bombers were less sturdy than the Forts and more likely to break up in the process of ditching. We were more than glad to help in the rescue act because the R.A.F. pilots frequently provided escort for us, and without some escort the bomber groups would have suffered an intolerable casualty percentage.

December 17

Ugo Lancia left for the port of embarkation to the U.S. and in spite of his noise and gusto, I was reluctant to see him leave. Without his lively spirit the hut would not be the same, indeed it would be too quiet. Instead of the wild celebrating I expected him to do, Lancia was restrained and quiet his last days at the hut, as if torn between relief that combat duty was over and a sense of belonging with the rest of us. Until then I had relished the idea of more peace and quiet, but now I would have traded it for the noise and confusion Ugo created. I had become fond of that big, brash Italian but I never got around to letting him know it.

There was an unspoken feeling among men who have lived together and fought side by side that has no parallel in civilian life. We all went to the train to see Ugo off. I realized that barring some unforeseen coincidence I would never see him again. Oh, we mumbled words like "we'll write and keep in touch" but it would not happen, and we knew it. Separated by time and distance, the letters and cards we intended to write would get sidetracked until the relationships would fade out. Tucked away in a far corner of the mind a flicker of remembrances would surface at odd moments, but by then the addresses would be lost or obsolete.

That night things were depressed after the departure of Ugo's exuberant personality. Tedesco remarked, "Well, it's the beginning of the end for Cahow's crew."

Someone asked, "How many missions does Cahow need?"

"I don't know for sure—three I think," Tedesco answered.

Jim Counce and I had the same number of missions completed, but Balmore trailed by five, due to recurrent frostbite injuries that grounded him three or four times.

"John, you and Jim will finish way ahead of me, and I'll end up as a spare radio for whatever crew needs one."

"Now wait, George Reese is your friend and he'll see that you get on decent crews."

"But you and Jim will go back to the States and we will get separated an' you know what that means."

"You're probably right," Counce added, "but I know the three of us will keep in touch and get together now and then after the war is over."

December 18

Three days earlier Carroll Wilson had been on a rough raid with another crew and he suffered internal injuries from the banging around in the waist caused by the pilot taking severe evasive action to blunt the effectiveness of fighter attacks. In spite of his goof-offs, which were legion, he was a likable youngster with good potential. All he needed was some responsibility to bring out his merit. When the going was extra tough, Wilson reached back into the reserve that some people are born with and came up with whatever was needed for the day to see it through. Compared to that, what else really mattered? He was transferred to a recovery hospital at another base and it was depressing to see him go. I knew there was a good chance I would be gone from Ridgewell before he returned.

CHAPTER XXI

Mission to Bremen

December 20—Bremen   *Aircraft 730*

Harold Harkness was back with us in the ball turret after recovering from the painful glass in his eye injury. It was good to have a competent man watching things below the aircraft. Raymond Legg was grounded, due to burns suffered when he became unconscious for too long in the tail. Wineski, a member of the Free Polish Air Force, was with us on the tail guns. He had escaped from Poland when the Germans invaded his country and joined the R.A.F. for a while before he was transferred to the American Air Force. He was an experienced gunner and we were glad to have him. La Buda was on the left waist guns taking Wilson's place.

The aircraft lifted from the runway at eight thirty, just as dawn was breaking. Shutting called the Copilot. "Did you ever see a more beautiful sunrise?"

Before he could answer Gleichauf cut in, "Keep the intercom clear—no personal conversation."

"Navigator to crew—Navigator to crew, the altitude today will be twenty-nine thousand, five hundred feet and the temperature will be sixty below. Watch yourselves for frostbite."

It turned out to be the coldest temperature I have ever had to endure. At nine thirty we went on oxygen and the long climb began. At ten thirty the Wing headed over the North Sea toward Germany. The target was Bremen again, with that awful flak. When I saw the coast approaching, I called the Navigator. "What is our altitude and temperature?"

"We are at twenty-seven, five hundred and the temperature gauge is against the stop—low as it can register—sixty-two degrees below."

244

"Navigator, how cold is that on the Fahrenheit scale?"

"About eighty below—an' we got another two thousand to climb. It's goin' to be between eighty and ninety below Fahrenheit at our top altitude—real balmy—you can take off your shirt and get a good suntan in the turret."

"Turret to crew, at this temperature if any of your electric units go out, it will take heavy exercise to keep from freezing, so watch it."

"Bombardier to crew, we'll take more frequent oxygen checks today."

Fifteen minutes into Germany Purus came on intercom: "Oxygen check—report in."

"Turret an' cockpit OK."

"Radio, rajah."

"Ball OK."

"Navigator OK."

"Waist OK."

"Bombardier to Tail—come in."

"Bombardier to Tail—Bombardier to Tail—report in."

There was no response.

"Bombardier to Waist."

"This is Jim, go ahead."

"Go back and check out the Tail."

"Rajah, will do."

Counce snapped his mask into a walk-around bottle, picked up a reserve constant-flow oxygen container and headed for the tail. Jim found Wineski passed out and immediately started working on him. Then his own regulator froze and cut off his oxygen supply. The demand-type regulator was supposed to be impervious to freezing at any temperature, so Jim thought his mask had frozen and hastily went through the procedure to clear a frozen mask. By that time he was too far gone and collapsed on top of the tail gunner. La Buda, the other waist gunner, could not see into the Tail with Jim blocking the view.

"Bombardier to Waist, what is Counce doing? Everything OK?"

"Something is wrong back there! Counce is not moving—repeat— Counce is not moving!"

"Waist! Get back to that Tail quick an' revive those men."

"Radio!"

"Go ahead."

"Take over the waist guns and let us know what is happening back there."

Three to five minutes went by and a frantic Balmore called, "Bombardier! Bombardier! La Buda just passed out an' fell on Counce. For God's sake, send John back there quick! I don't know what to do. Don't let these men die!''

"I'm on my way, Radio. Calm down and keep your mask clear of ice. We can't have another man down.''

"Pilot to Copilot, get in the turret until John gets back.''

My mind was in a turmoil. I kept asking myself, ''What is happening in that tail that has knocked out three experienced men? Anything different today from other days? Yes, the temperature. But that shouldn't cause major trouble. The demand regulators are not affected by low temperature.[1] But what if the regulators are freezing?'' Those thoughts raced through my mind as I got out of the turret and plugged into a walk-around bottle. Instantly my oxygen failed. Hastily I switched back to the turret hose and tapped the walk-around bottle several times hard with a heavy screwdriver. I switched back to the bottle and it worked. So that was the problem! The demand regulators were freezing.

"Turret to crew—Turret to crew—listen carefully. The demand regulators are freezing! Repeat: the demand regulators are freezing! If it happens to you, tap the regulator several times with anything handy, screwdriver works fine.''

Grabbing four or five bail-out bottles and two walk-arounds, I went aft as rapidly as possible. I kept telling myself, ''You must not make any mistakes—if you do some people are going to die—watch what you are doing—no mistakes—.''

I heard the nose and turret guns chatter over and over. ''All right, keep your mind on what you're doing. Forget the fighters.'' George was slowly going insane with three men needing help so badly. He had the mental ability to know that if he rushed back to the tail, there would be four men unconscious in short order. When he saw me he was like a man reprieved. I could see a change come over him as he regained his mental composure.

When I reached the tail, La Buda had to be revived first to get him out of the way so I could get to the other two men. Both of their faces were black as coal. The tail gunner looked like he was dead and Jim looked almost as bad. I poured oxygen down La Buda continuously until his color returned and he revived enough for me to clear his regulator and readjust his mask. With La Buda on his feet and helping, we pulled Jim

---

[1] The demand-type oxygen regulator opened and closed by means of inhaling and exhaling. Up to that time it had been considered impervious to freezing, but the temperature that day was extremely low, perhaps a little beyond the capacity of the regulator to handle. It was the lowest I encountered in seventy-five missions over Europe.

out to where I could get to him. He was awful to look at. The unreal blackness of his usually pale face was terrifying. I had never seen a person off of oxygen that long at thirty thousand feet. "Oh, God," I whispered as a stream of oxygen coursed down his throat, as much as I felt he could stand, "let him come back—please! Don't let him die!" When I saw the first signs of color returning, I felt a surge of joy. He was going to make it! As soon as he came to enough to move, we got his mask in position and his regulator working. I sent La Buda to help Jim back to the waist and turned hurriedly to Wineski. There was no doubt in my mind that the tail gunner was dead. His face was coal black, like something out of a bad dream. He was not breathing, because the slightest breath could be seen in that intense cold, and he had already been off of oxygen longer than the medics told us a man could continue to live at thirty thousand feet.

La Buda returned and helped me pull him out of the cramped tail space. Hopeless or not, I had to make every conceivable effort to revive him. I rammed a tube down his throat and injected extra-heavy doses of oxygen for a full minute with no success. I knew that if he had the slightest chance it would require some desperate measures! I increased the oxygen pressure, deliberately running the risk of serious if not fatal injury. Those bottles held eighteen hundred pounds of pressure and too much could have ruptured his lungs. It seemed to me that the risk was necessary. That went on for another minute and I had given up all hope when I had a vague feeling of slight movement. At first I thought it was my imagination playing tricks. No! He did move! I was sure I felt something. Then there was a sharp twist of his left leg, and there was no longer any doubt. The man was going to revive. I would not have given him one chance out of a hundred a few minutes earlier. The color slowly returned to his face and I reduced the amount of oxygen and timed the intakes to coincide with my breathing rate. It was a great feeling to see a man return from what I believed to be death. When his color became normal I began working on his regulator with my free hand, while continuing to keep oxygen flowing with the other. Physically, he was coming along well, but I could see from the wild look on his face that he was mentally disoriented. I hoped that it was not a matter of brain damage. Suddenly he drew back his fist and struck me hard on the jaw. I failed to see the blow coming and it knocked me backward and my head hit a metal joint so hard that for a couple of minutes I was mentally out. Counce, who by now was fully recovered, ran back and straightened my mask and helped me up. Meanwhile, Wineski had passed out again when he lost the oxygen I had been feeding him. We got his mask in place and the regulator working normally and watched him closely until sure that his brain was once again functioning. In another five minutes he was back on the tail guns, OK as far as I could determine.

The aircraft was bouncing around so I knew we must be in the middle of the flak. I hoped we were past the target and would quickly get out of the antiaircraft gunners' range. I was working my way forward carrying an armload of empty oxygen containers. To enter the radio room from the waist, one used the top of the ball turret as a step because it was directly in the way. Harkness chose that exact moment to whirl the ball around. Both feet went out from under me and I took a nasty fall. The worst part was that two of the heavy cylinders bounced into the air and struck me on the head with stupefying force as I lay prone on the deck, feeling like a losing fighter just before the referee stops the fight. Two knockout blows in ten minutes—it was not my day!

When I climbed wearily into the turret we were past the target on the way home. I knew from the sounds of gunfire that there was a brisk battle while I was in the tail. The report said that sixty fighters jumped us and I missed the action. The only good thing about the mission was that I did not have to look at the detestable flak over the city of Bremen.

"Radio to Turret."

"Go ahead, George."

"It was close. You got back there just in time. Little longer, an' both Jim and Wineski would have been gone. Right?"

"Yes, it was close for Wineski. He was partly inside the Pearly Gates—or that other place."

"Tail to Turret, was it that close?"

"At first I did not have any hope you would come out of it—how are you feeling?"

"OK, except for a bad headache."

"Navigator to Turret, *Tinker Toy* got it while you were in the tail."

"Was it flak or fighters?"

"A 109 slammed into her waist and both ships went down locked together, turning end over end."

"It's hard to believe. I thought *Tinker Toy* would always make it back."

"Turret to Navigator, were we supposed to have P-38s on the return?"

"Yes, but they didn't show."

A strong head wind was slowing down the return.

"Bombardier to crew, fighters at twelve o'clock low."

The enemy made two passes and vanished without doing any damage.

"Tail to crew, that B-17 strugglin' behind the formation is about to get it—four fighters are ganging up on her."

I turned around to watch that Fort put up a furious battle and hold off

248

the attackers. I believe it was the only time I ever saw a B-17 survive a fight with that many interceptors. The American papers were full of stories about wounded Fortresses holding off ten or fifteen fighters. Most of those stories were purely imaginary. In the real life of combat over the Continent, it simply did not happen against experienced fighters.

Halfway across the North Sea the tail gunner reported, "Lone 109 closin' fast from the rear."

"What is he goin' to try?" asked the Bombardier.

"Don't know—but he's goin' around to our left."

That audacious fighter pilot pulled ahead of the formation, circled to eleven o'clock, and with guns blazing whipped straight at us.

"Navigator to crew, look at that bastard—did you ever see such guts?"

What did a military formation do to a gallant airman blithely taking on deadly odds? The book said shoot him down, but that went against the grain of American admiration for courage beyond the ordinary. And in a hopeless cause. We easily could—and perhaps from a military point of view should—have destroyed that fighter. But there was some chivalry left in the American makeup. Without a word of consultation with each other, all of our gunners came up with the same decision: they held their fire. The formation opened up to let him blaze through. How could we kill a man with such foolhardy courage? It is seldom that men see an example of pure nobility. That German expected to die on his assault. It was foolish of course but, like the British cavalry's "Charge of the Light Brigade," it was a thrilling spectacle to watch.

Landing time was 3:00 P.M. and I was saddened to learn that a top turret gunner died during the mission from oxygen failure. Bomber Command listed twenty B-17s lost to fighter attacks. I saw little of the action so could not judge if the loss was excessive.

Jim Counce sustained a frozen hand when he removed a glove to try to clear ice he thought was in his mask. The damage was severe and it was certain that he would be grounded for several weeks to a month. He was depressed when he found out about the damage, because it meant that he would be grounded for an extensive period and would drop far behind in his missions.

December 21

After Jim left for Braintree Hospital, I felt lost and depressed. We had been together so long—well, not that long by the calendar, but so much had happened in those eleven months that it seemed more like years.

"George, I hated to see Jim leave. I may be finished and gone before he gets back to Ridgewell."

"I'm afraid you're right. The doctors told Jim his hand is in bad shape. You know, there is a chance it will have to be amputated."

"Where did you hear that?"

"Jim told me last night after they finished examining the hand."

"It's not gonna be the same, with him gone, in this hut."

"Before long, John, I'll be the only one left in this hut out of the two crews. You an' all the rest will get through before me. How many missions you need now?"

"Four. Shutting needs four, and Purus needs three. Don't know about Gleichauf. I think he needs either two or three."

"It will be lonesome around here when all of you guys are gone. Cahow's men will be finishing too, but I'll be here with a hut full of new gunners."

Later that day I went to the flight line to do something to 719 and passed by the empty hardstand where *Tinker Toy* had been parked since the 381st arrived at Ridgewell. At times I had imagined that she thumbed her nose at me as I pedaled by her when I was new to the base. She seemed to say, "Another one of those screwed-up gunners they send over here to ruin good airplanes like me." Her end was as weird and spectacular as her reputation. A ship with such a bloody and storied record could not have had an ordinary ending like other airplanes. The Copilot saw her go. "That fighter spun out of control. It hit *Tinker Toy* in the waist just behind the ball—it went halfway through her like a giant arrow! They tumbled end over end—I saw flame and about a thousand yards down she exploded and I could see metal and bodies all over the sky."

The stars were out that night. I liked that very much because it meant a hard freeze and out of the mud for at least two or three days. Also, it sent a message to the combat crews: get ready for a mission in the morning. With that in mind I set out my mission clothes and equipment. Most combat men developed superstitions about clothes or some special talisman they always carried on a raid. I remember one gunner who wore the same coveralls each trip and refused to have them washed. Somehow the unwashed coveralls had become his security blanket.

After turning in, I lay in the sack and let my mind replay the events of the last six months. There was one strange thing I had problems understanding. In that cold, damp climate, and many hours at extreme altitudes and temperatures, I had been remarkably healthy. There had been no colds or sinus difficulties such as I had expected. Barring a hangover I awoke each morning feeling exceptionally good.

CHAPTER XXII

Mission to Osnabruck

December 22—Osnabruck   *Aircraft 419*

Pitts was the first man up when the call came, "Aw right! Get outta that sack. This is Cahow's twenty-fifth."

Tedesco muttered, "He's been so nervous all week that I hope he doesn't screw up something today."

"That's not like Cahow," I said. "I remember how cool he was on the raid to Schweinfurt."

Green added, "When they get down to one or two they all start to sweat—they've seen too many blow it at the end."

"After this run, five or six of us are goin' to start sweating," Pitts remarked.

George waited to pick up the sounds from the Briefing Room so I could go on to the aircraft. We were flying a ship I knew nothing about. When I unloaded at the aircraft I asked the crew chief, "Does 419 have any peculiarities I ought to know about?"

"Yes, there are two things. You got to keep the cylinder head temperature of number two below two fifteen or you'll get detonation. And there's a vibration between seventy an' eighty on takeoff. It don't hurt nothing, so don't worry about it."

I always wanted words with the crew chief because every plane, like every flier, had its own eccentricities.

The target was Osnabruck, known to me previously for its cheese. Gleichauf was leading the squadron and we were flying the low position in the Group.

"Well, we got the purple heart corner again today," said Balmore.

251

The first ship got off at ten thirty and pulled steadily up through an overcast. The tail gunner flashed a red "L" signal with a bright lamp to guide other aircraft to form on the lead plane with less loss of time.

"Bombardier to Turret, pull the bomb fuse pins."

A few minutes later, "Turret to Bombardier, pins are pulled—rack switches are on."

"Radio to Turret."

"Go ahead."

"My oxygen regulator is not right."

"What's the problem?"

"It just don't look right. I don't think it is working."

I knew it would be better to get George settled about his oxygen system before we reached enemy territory.

"Turret to Copilot, I'm going to the radio room for a few minutes."

A mechanic had hooked up the regulator backwards, but it made no difference. It was working fine. As soon as I got back to the turret, I called George.

"Your oxygen supply is OK. It does look odd but don't worry about it."

At twenty thousand feet we headed out over the North Sea. The temperature was minus forty-two degrees, but otherwise it was a nice day for a mission. The clouds thinned and visibility was adequate below.

"Tail to Turret, my electric heat went out."

"Which circuits are gone? Hands and feet or the body circuit?"

"All of them are out."

"Check the plug on the end of the cord. You may have a poor connection."

"Can't see anything wrong with it—I've tried plugging it in and out several times."

"One other thing you can try—scrape the prongs on the plug with any kind of metal you have back there. A screwdriver will do fine. Try to get any corrosion off the plug."

"Bombardier to Tail, it's going to be better than forty below at our full altitude today. You think you can make it?"

"I'll make it—some way."

"Copilot to Tail, exercise those hands and feet."

"Not much room in the Tail to exercise, but I'll find some way to do it."

"Turret here, now keep up that exercise no matter what. One mission I had to go up and down for four hours to keep my feet from freezing."

"Copilot to Turret, the damn airspeed indicator went out."

"What's the altitude?"

"Twenty-two thousand."

"It could be in the instrument or it could be that some trash in the air caught in the pitot tube. Can Gleichauf fly lead with no airspeed?"

"It will be rough. We would be better off flying a wing position. If Paul can't cut it, we'll drop back and let the deputy lead take over."

"Navigator to Pilot, enemy coast in ten minutes."

"Bombardier to gunners, test fire your guns."

I listened to the chatter of the guns as each position rattled off a burst and thought how lucky I had been to be with such a solid crew of ordinary men who became extraordinary when they had to. It all boiled down to three things: a first-class pilot who was good at tight formation, a good crew, and those much appreciated escort pilots.

"Radio to Turret, I'm getting dizzy. I told you this regulator wasn't working right."

"George, listen to me. I think you're imagining trouble and are over breathing. Now relax. Breathe normally and quit taking in deep gulps of air. Try it and see if you feel better."

"OK, I'll try it."

"Bombardier to crew, fighters at eleven o'clock low."

"Copilot to crew, don't let them slip in on us."

Sleek 109G fighters, the latest German interceptor to appear against us, circled the formation warily and made several passes but none directly against our Squadron.

"Tail to crew, the escort at six o'clock high."

"Copilot to Navigator, look at those dogfights! How I'd love to be flying one of those fighters."

I could think of many things I would prefer to do. The fight between the 47s and 109s was a swirling panorama of tracers, cannon flashes, and smoke plumes. Then the Bogies vanished and for a little while we had the 47s overhead. When they reached the end of their fuel range, they dipped wings and turned away. P-38s were due in a few minutes and I hoped more Bogies would not hit us in the interval. I was already starting to worry about my last three missions.

"Copilot to Navigator, this formation is so lousy, a group of hot fighters could tear us apart. How long to the I.P.?"

"About twenty minutes."

"Navigator to crew, fighters at nine o'clock low."

They climbed to our level and began to circle the Group picking out targets.

"Copilot to crew! Fighter coming in twelve o'clock high."

I had some good shots but could not tell if I inflicted any serious damage. I could hear the ball guns hammering away below. When the firing ceased, I called Harkness. "Are you all right down there?"

"I'm OK—they keep coming up at us—I spray 'em an' they break off the attack."

The 381st took a beating as we approached the target and three Forts went down. I saw one chute but the unfortunate man pulled his ripcord too soon, and the silk flared out quickly and hung on the rear of the Fortress. It was a sickening sight to watch that pitiable drama that could end only in a prolonged agony of terrifying struggle and a horrible death unless somehow that silk shook loose from the tail where it was caught. The last I saw of the stricken Fort, that doomed man was still trailing along helplessly in the slipstream. Nearby, two P-38s blasted a 109 and I noticed a brown parachute blossom from it seconds before it went into a dive out of control. One of those P-38s had to execute a frantic turn to avoid flying into that chute.

"Navigator to Pilot."

"Go ahead."

"They are sure cracking that wing ahead of us."

Balmore picked up the three words "cracking the wing" and his blood pressure went out of sight. In the radio room he could see little of the action. About that time the aircraft caught some propeller wash from a plane ahead and lurched sickeningly. George thought the wing was coming off and grabbed his chute and headed for the exit door in the waist. La Buda, flying as waist gunner for us that day, stopped him, but George insisted on examining the two wings from the waist windows before he would return to his position.

"Radio to Turret, is something wrong with one of our wings?"

"Not that I know of—why do you ask?"

He did not reply, but I could sense his relief.

"Turret to Copilot, is the airspeed still out?"

"Yes—shows nothing."

"How is the Pilot doing?"

"Rough. He's estimating the speed by watching the squadron ahead. Could the pitot tube be frozen?"

"It could be, or something in the air clogged it up. Or the instrument may have gone out."

"Bombardier here, did you see those two 109s up above try to throw their bellytanks at us? They'll try anything."

"No, couldn't see it from the waist, but two Forts at three o'clock high came damn close to colliding. That could've knocked out half of the squadron. A 109 just clobbered a 38 at four o'clock low.''

''This is the Copilot. I saw it. The 38 got careless. You can't do that with those damn Krauts.''

''Bombardier to Pilot—Bombardier to Pilot.''

Kels motioned Gleichauf to switch from command to intercom.

''Go ahead, Bombardier.''

''We're starting the bomb run.''

Flak began bursting around us. It was not heavy, but it sure was accurate. As usual, I cringed when the shells burst close by.

Wham! It was jut below us.

''Copilot to Ball—are you all right?''

''I'm OK—it was close but didn't hit me—we got damage between the waist and tail.''

I felt better when the bomb load fell free.

''Radio to Bombardier, the bomb bay is clear.''

''Tail to crew, the fighters are fading away—fuel getting low is my guess.''

''Navigator to Pilot—Cahow has about got it made.''

The formation droned placidly along with no opposition. I kept alert for another fighter group to come screaming up, because we were vulnerable with our loose erratic formation. This time, the 533rd Squadron was throttle-jockeying like the rest because Gleichauf was guessing at his airspeed.

''Navigator to Pilot—ten minutes to the coast. Now I know Cahow has it made.''

I knew his men were happy for him and so was I. He was one of the best. The coast slid by and the North Sea was a welcome sight, like the causeway when I was coming back to Corpus Christi by way of Aransas Pass. We were almost home again.

I relaxed and began removing some of the equipment, especially that uncomfortable oxygen mask. After five or six hours, my face was raw from the pressure of the mask and the low temperature. I found out early in the game that a mask was worse when the whiskers needed shaving. If I thought a mission was likely, I often shaved at night to lessen the discomfort. The realization came over me that I was tired. It was not the usual exhaustion of the early missions; I had become acclimated to the routine. It was a built-up weariness of months of altitude and combat tension. For the first time I understood why twenty-five missions was set as the completion point of a combat tour. It was the time when crews would begin to lose mental and physical effectiveness. I suspected the accumulated fatigue was due more to mental strain than to physical weariness.

As we approached Ridgewell, Kels punched me and pointed down. "Cahow is buzzing the field." Indeed he was. At the 381st it was customary to permit a pilot returning from his twenty-fifth mission to buzz the field in celebration of a job well done.

That day we lost seventeen Forts to German fighters. To my thinking the loss was excessive. It was the familiar pattern of late: loose, erratic formations inviting Jerry to attack. The accumulated losses in men and aircraft during the summer and fall of 1943 were staggering and beyond expectations. The replacement crews were put through speeded up training procedures, by no means as thorough as the original 381st received. The predictable result was that inexperienced pilots and crews predominated, and the price we paid was higher casualties than should have been necessary. In the air as on the ground, raw troops rarely fare well against seasoned battle-hardened forces. But an attrition factor was working for us: we were thinning out the experienced pilots of the Luftwaffe. When a veteran German pilot with eight or ten years of training plus experience in numerous campaigns was lost, they could not replace him any faster than we could create his counterpart in the U.S. or England. The advantage in attrition gradually shifted to the side with the largest manpower and industrial facilities. Fortunately, that was the combined might of the Allied Forces.

December 23

Lieutenant Cahow had finished his twenty-five missions! The dangers were all in the past. He had nothing more to worry about now except getting back to the States. However, Operations assigned him, along with Pitts (Engineer), Parsons (Copilot), and Dubois (Navigator) to take a B-17 to a Modification Base 30 or 40 miles away. They were to return another B-17 that had been modified back to Ridgewell. There was a solid overcast at 500 feet but no problem. The navigator gave Cahow a heading of 190 degrees going over. Coming back, the navigator gave him another heading of 195 degrees. The pilot should have recognized that to be an error, but it was a fun flight and they were all joking on the intercom, not paying too much attention to what they were doing. All of a sudden Cahow began getting interference on his headset. It got worse and worse. Something was definitely wrong with the radio—the noise became increasingly louder. Suddenly Cahow saw that he was flying between heavy steel cables that would have sawed the wing right off an aircraft that hit one of them. To his horror he realized he was in the middle of a balloon barrage near London! He could not see the balloons because they were hidden in the overcast above. That loud noise was his IFF (Identification Friend or Foe) sending out a warning signal of the balloons and cables, and the flak guns down below, ready to blast any unidentified aircraft from the skies. Lieutenant Cahow turned that big Fortress around like it was a fighter plane and carefully dodged those cables until he was back in the clear.

There were few signs of Christmas on the base at Ridgewell Airdrome. Some cards and a few packages had arrived, and some scattered decorations were hung here and there. It was a half-hearted effort to do lip service to the Prince of Peace while we went about the grim task of killing and destruction. I had a good idea of how I would spend Christmas Eve, no doubt in dropping off a Christmas package for Uncle Adolf. Our gift would be twelve giant firecrackers a bit larger than the ones I used to explode Christmas mornings. Peace on earth and good will toward men would have to wait until the killing was finished.

It was extremely cold and it had been weeks since the last distribution of coal to our area. During the morning we tramped the nearby woods searching for small trees that might be sneaked out for firewood without attracting attention. There was a risk if caught, but weighed against no heat in the middle of winter, it was a slight deterrent. Most of the woodcutting with our crosscut saw was done at night to lessen the chance of getting into trouble. Two hours after dark we had a sizable stack stashed away for the next two weeks. With the fire going again that night, it was cozy in the hut. Balmore asked, "John, you are down to three missions?"

"That is correct—three and I got it made."

"How many does Purus need?"

"Two I think—not sure."

"I noticed he's been nervous the last week. That's not like Johnny."

"They all go through that emotion. Gleichauf will finish one raid ahead of me so I will have to fly my last one as a spare—and I don't like to think about the possibility of having to do the last raid with a new crew," I added.

George continued, "I wish I was up there with you. I need so many missions, I'm bound to draw some lousy crews."

Watching others approaching twenty-five missions, I had seen the tension building up, but I did not expect it to happen to me. I was older than most of the men flying combat missions and I thought that I had more disciplinary control over my mental processes. I resolved that I would not let it happen to me.

CHAPTER XXIII

Mission to Calais[1]

December 24—Calais   *Aircraft 730*

When I heard the Jeep coming some distance away, I got up and started dressing, because the signs were clear the night before that we would go out today if the weather cooperated.

"You would think we could do without raids on Christmas Eve," growled Balmore. "What we do today isn't going to change the war much."

"But Mars is more powerful than Jesus—I don't think the burghers are goin' to like the presents we have for them today," I answered.

We waited outside the Briefing Room after drawing equipment. A loud cheer echoed through the closed door.

"It must be a super milk run," George said.

"That's fine with me. I hope my last three runs are milk runs."

An hour later Kels arrived with a grin on his face.

"All right! Let's have it. Where are we goin' today?"

"Maybe I should wait an' let Gleichauf tell you," he toyed.

"Come on! Where we goin'?"

"Today we raid Calais!" he answered.

"Calais! I can't believe it."

"It is Calais—we will go over in small nine-plane formations to try to destroy some construction sites the Allied Command thinks the Germans are building to launch long-range rockets across the Channel. There can be a lot of fighters but Spitfires and P-47s will fly low cover to keep them

---

[1] The official roster of missions shows Cocove, France. My diary shows we went to Calais Dec. 24, 1943.

from getting up to us. Major Fitzgerald will be flying as Copilot and I will go along as Observer.''

''I've heard about observers but you are the first live one I've ever seen. What the hell are you supposed to do?''

''Try to see what the bombs hit an' how much damage they do.''

''We already got a whole squadron of tails and balls who can see the bomb drop a lot better than you can see it from the cockpit.''

At 1:00 P.M. the Squadron cleared the English coast and turned toward the Continent. It was a beautiful day for wintertime Europe and the altitude was only twenty thousand feet.

''Bombardier to crew—stay alert—don't get cocky an' think we can't get hit over Calais—test fire guns.''

''Navigator to crew—heavy flak ahead.''

Calais had a large number of flak guns and I dreaded the barrage at our lower altitude, because all of their antiaircraft guns could reach twenty thousand feet with accuracy. The squadron circled to the right slightly in an effort to go around the main field of fire. All at once the bursts caught us dead center. With perfect visibility and the low height, the Jerry gunners were at their best. Burst after burst exploded in the middle of the Squadron. It was incredible that with so much accuracy and so many shells thrown at us, no direct hits were made. The fuse timing was perfect: every burst was exactly at our level. It was the best example of the art of antiaircraft fire I ever saw. At times the other planes in our small formation were obscured by the smoke of the bursting shells. Only pure luck prevented one or more of the Squadron aircraft from taking a direct hit. At times I cringed down behind the Sperry Computing Sight, as if that would do any good. There was no way to guess which way the lethal fragments were coming from.

I heard a loud crashing noise on the right wing. A heavy fragment struck it under a main fuel tank.

''Turret to Ball—do you see any serious damage like a fuel leak?''

''No—nothing that amounts to anything.''

Flak struck the armor plate that Balmore was standing on and knocked him to one side. A few seconds later a fragment caromed off the rim of the radio hatch a few inches from his head.

''Radio to Copilot—they're dustin' me off from two sides—that last one missed my head by two inches.''

Four pieces of large shrapnel smashed through the cockpit to my rear with a fearsome noise. I turned around to look for damage and another piece whistled by my ear; it slammed up from below, went through the turret, and out the top, sounding like a cannon exploding when it pulverized the plastic glass above me. Fortunately, I had on sunglasses. One lense was broken and the other scarred by the flying glass fragments.

"Copilot to Turret—are you OK."

"I'm OK."

Bam! A huge chunk struck where number two main tank was located. I held my breath for several seconds waiting for the telltale signs of fire.

"Copilot to Ball—can you see sign of a fuel leak?"

"No—I guess we are lucky."

"Sometimes they self-seal an' sometimes not."

Wineski was on his twenty-fifth mission and it was almost his last day again. Big hunks of flak tore by him so close they damaged his clothes.

"Bombardier to Pilot—we're not going to drop—a small cloud has the target covered—we'll have to do a one eighty and come back over it."

"I wish that we could get out of this damned flak," Gleichauf muttered.

The second bomb run was better, although I did not know what the target was. My concern was that fighters would arrive if we stayed around too long. But once the bombs were released, we were quickly over the Channel on the way home and raid number twenty-three was tucked away.

The remnants of Cahow's crew were with Schultz on our right. They picked up two hundred holes. We had only fifty-five, but many of ours were exceptionally large for flak shrapnel and in vulnerable spots.

Bill Kettner and Ray Bechtel finished their twenty-five that day. What a great Christmas present for them! No question but that tension was mounting more than I expected. How could I suppress it knowing that so many good men had failed at the finish line? The question kept coming back: Was it purely coincidence? No doubt it was, but at the time imagination, frustration, and superstition allowed phobias to build up.

Recently two men were reputed to have predicted their own deaths with accuracy. What mental processes were involved that defy rational understanding? There must be undiscovered capacities of the brain that perhaps someday we will understand. But how did they know what was coming for them? It is possible that many men made such predictions in error. When one of them turned out to be correct, it attracted intense interest. But such instances were bewildering and unsettling. They were shocking and the mind groped for a reasonable explanation. The recognitive phenomenon confused and fascinated at the same time.

My experience was in the opposite direction. I had tried to psyche myself to help provide a basis for courage that might otherwise have been lacking. I just somehow knew—or made myself think I knew—that I would make it through the war. I felt that if I had to jump, I knew parachutes well enough to make it down safely. I was confident that if I could avoid capture upon landing I could make it back to Allied territory, because I had some familiarity with European customs.

December 25

Christmas Day! It turned out wet and foggy, so no missions were planned. All day the station loudspeaker resounded with Christmas music, but the best thing for me was the return of Jim Counce. His hand turned out to be better than first expected. Jim was depressed because the rest of the crew was getting ahead of him and would be breaking up after one more raid by Gleichauf.

Anne had sent a full-sized fruitcake loaded with nuts in a tin container with the lid soldered. There was no other way a cake could have made the trip. Whatever food goodies came from home were shared with the others in the hut. That cake was the big event of the day.

While we were opening packages I heard some unusually loud profanity from Bill Pitt's corner. When it died down he sputtered in a rage, "Look what my Aunt sent me—a five-pound can of spam!"

The day before, several men not on the battle order for the day went into Cambridge on the supply truck and brought back large sacks of ale and hard cider bottles from one of the wholesale liquor houses. So mostly that day we sat around the little stove, drank ale, and listened to Christmas music on the radio. And of course talked about the raids. We could never stay off of that subject very long. Late that night the President's Christmas message was rebroadcast: it was a typical Roosevelt speech, with his magnetic warmth and assuring us that right would prevail over tyranny.

Bill Kettner and Ray Bechtel spent the day packing and giving away accumulations too bulky or heavy. They had sold their bicycles and we refunded their share of the radio. Whoever took their bunks would have to cough up part of the common ownership of the radio. Watching them, I realized that two more missions would put me in the same position. I had seen Gleichauf that morning and he was noticeably nervous and tense.

Christmas Day 1943 was the most somber one I can remember. Mostly the men were withdrawn, lost in memories of happier times. Americans were asked to stay off of the trains and public transportation facilities during the season so that the English soldiers and war workers would have an easier time getting home for a few hours. It was a reasonable request because we had nowhere special to go.

December 26

Weeks ago huge boxes were placed in the Post Exchange and other spots about the base for men to drop in candy or presents suitable for the English children who could expect little for Christmas. I watched men file by and drop all of their P.X. rations of candy and chewing gum, which the children loved, into the boxes. Many of the English youngsters had no recollection of prewar days. I was on a mission when the party for the nearby village kids was given. Trucks brought them to the base. Jim was there and told us about it. "You should've seen those kids. When they saw the candy and chewing gum and other things, they squealed and danced with joy." Many of them had never seen such an abundance of goodies. At least we did one thing right during Christmas week.

December 29

Bechtel, Cahow, Bell, and Wineski left that day for transportation to the United States. It was my impression that Wineski, a citizen of Poland, was being granted special status for American citizenship because of his service in the Allied and American Air Force. He deserved it but almost did not survive to make it two times I knew of. He would be an asset to our country—no question about that. We shook hands and said the usual things about keeping in touch.

The weather was decent enough the last two days but I was bypassed. The main thing now was to get those last combat missions over with. But the pace seemed to have slowed down recently. That day General Doolittle succeeded General Eaker as Commander of the 8th Air Force. Although it was unfair to the new Commander, the news was received with misgivings. All we knew about Doolittle was the raid on Tokyo that seemed to us like a publicity stunt, with the certain loss of aircraft and men not remotely justified by the insignificant damage one such puny raid could inflict.

CHAPTER XXIV

Mission to Ludwigshaven

December 30—Ludwigshaven   *Aircraft 730*

The call was welcome because I was anxious to put the last two missions behind me. I looked outside and said, "You won't believe this—it's clear outside. We're going to get in a mission today."

Jim raised up in his bed and said wistfully, "I wish I was goin' with you—hell, I don't know when they'll turn me loose to fly again."

"Just two more, Jim, two more an' my war is over."

Counce could have stayed in bed, but he got up and went out to the airplane with us. It was a habit hard to break.

When Gleichauf arrived, he gave us the pertinent information. "It's Ludwigshaven! We're goin' for the I.G. Farben Chemical Works. You know what the flak will be. We could draw two hundred fighters but there will be three groups of escorts—Spitfires goin' in—P-38s over the target—and P-47s comin' back—you all know this is my twenty-fifth so don't screw up on anything today."

I could tell Paul was nervous because he was easily irritated. It was harder to tell about Purus. He was so much the same day after day. I will wager he had spent some sleepless nights in the last week.

Shutting turned to Purus, "If those Jerries intend to hit your ass they better get with it. I hear they have been putting in special gunnery practice this week. They know it's your last mission."

"You've only got two to go—who are you goin' to give your special testical armor to?"

"Some Navigator who don't want his voice to change suddenly."

The first streaks of dawn lighted the horizon as the ships took to the air and the sunrise was beautiful. Thirty minutes later the formation began to climb up to high altitude. My mind tried to cover all possibilities. "We must be careful! Watch what you are doing. Above all else don't let any Jerry fighters slip in on us out of the sun—you know how many men have been lost on their twenty-fourth or twenty-fifth—but I'm different—I'm going to make it—I can feel it—yeah? Those men who got it probably had the same feeling. Calm down! I know Gleichauf is nervous and not at his best but he'll be good enough for today. But what if he gets too tense and screws up? Forget it. We're one of those crews that had the sign from the first raid that we would survive. Oh, come now! You know better than that. You say you've got something special going for you! You can't believe that—not really. Oh, yes, I do!"

My inner dialogue was interrupted as we made several diversionary turns then headed in the direction of the target. I expected a rough day. Two times before in that area the opposition had been fierce. A cloud cover underneath worried me, because I could see no Pathfinder planes, and that meant enough visibility was necessary to drop visually. We would be the first group over the target, so whatever reception the Germans planned we would likely catch the worst of it.

As the flight passed east of Calais and the enemy coastline, I expected fighters to intercept us in the next few minutes. Surprisingly we droned on for a while without opposition. A fifteen degree turn to the right brought us in line with the I.P. and at that point, General Galland's defense commanders could narrow their estimate of the possible targets we could strike. If our strategy was good enough it gave us two advantages: one, it forced Jerry to put fighters over several targets, thus reducing the number that would intercept us. The second thing it did was to force Jerry to use up his dwindling fuel.

"Pilot to crew—Pilot to crew, a large formation of fighters is due to hit us in a few minutes—get ready for them."

The information must have come from the Wing Commander. Did it mean that the ban on radio silence was being lifted? I hoped so. It seemed to me that we had carried the ban too far. What difference did radio silence make when Jerry had us on radar?"

"Navigator to Pilot—Navigator to Pilot."

"Go ahead."

"We'll cross the German border in about five minutes."

"Bombardier to crew—fighters at eleven o'clock low."

"Ball to crew—about seventy fighters—they look eager."

At first the interceptors circled the formation, searching warily for the weakest spots. Gleichauf pulled in tighter. At all costs he did not want to attract attention on his last mission.

"Bombardier to crew, three fighters coming in head on twelve o'clock—let's get them."

They barrelled through us with cannons blazing, were hammered by seventy guns, and turned into flaming wrecks. No flying machine could withstand that kind of punishment and continue to be an airplane.

"Navigator to crew—Spitfires high at eleven o'clock."

When the Spitfires approached, the German fighters surprised me by taking off for safer territory. Perhaps they did not have enough fuel left to mix it with the R.A.F. pilots. No other Bogies showed up and the Spit escort stayed as long as they could.

"Bombardier to Pilot—we're approaching the bomb run."

"Radio."

"This is Radio."

"Watch the bomb doors down."

"Doors are down."

"Copilot to crew—flak at ten o'clock level."

Antiaircraft gunfire was mild and scattered but devilishly accurate. We were bounced around from the concussion of some close ones.

"Copilot to Pilot."

"Go ahead."

"That new joker on our left wing is hangin' in tight. He's going to be a good one."

"Right. I told him to stay the hell on that wing—an' he's doing it."

"Bombs away."

"Radio to Bombardier—bomb bay clear—you can raise the doors."

We were improving! Another drop with no bomb release malfunction. The bomb shackle release problems were finally getting under control.

"Copilot to crew—Paul just heard that the radio operator on the plane to our right died from an oxygen failure."

Death from any cause was final and irreversible. It seemed to me it would be preferable to be able to report to the family that the man died from enemy fire in the defense of his country. I would have been reluctant to write his family and have to tell them he died by accident from an equipment failure. I remembered how close we came to losing Wineski from the same kind of failure.

"Bombardier to crew—the P-47 escort is with us."

Purus and Gleichauf almost had it made now. Kels called, "Paul take a look at France. Next time you see it maybe you'll be a tourist."

The Navigator came on intercom: ''Hey, Johnny! Those Krauts only got a few more minutes to hit your ass.''

Ten minutes later I could see the glistening water ahead. They had made it. There was no way that Jerry was going to hit us with an escort above and friendly water below. We came out southwest of Le Havre.

As soon as he saw the English coast, Gleichauf began to whoop and sing snatches of songs. He was a happy man. It was something to lift the tension of combat flying and put it in the background. That was the only time I saw Paul Gleichauf act up in the cockpit of a B-17. After we crossed the coast the men from the rear came forward to congratulate Paul and Johnny. Both were popular, not only with our crew but others on the base. Paul broke out of the formation and began his triumphant buzzing of the airdrome and an unexpected thing took place.

''What's the matter with that left wing ship? Can't he see I'm going to buzz the field?'' Gleichauf asked in exasperation.

''You told him to stay on your wing and that is exactly what he's doing,'' Kels answered.

''But he oughta know I didn't mean on a buzz.''

''You didn't mention the buzz and he thinks this is some special test for him.''

''Well, he'll break out of it when I go into the dive.''

He was wrong! That persistent wing man hung in tight and cozy down to fence-height altitude. I do not know what he thought was going on, but it was probably the only time in 381st history that two B-17s zoomed over the field at ten-feet elevation flying in tight formation. I imagine there were explosions of unprintable words in the control tower.

Jim, Legg, Chamberlain, and many others were waiting when the aircraft stopped. Gleichauf was popular with the ground crews because he always treated them with special respect. Most of the crew chiefs showed up to offer congratulations. The Squadron C.O. and the Operations Officer were there. Major Shackley had a bottle of good scotch and passed it around in honor of the event.

While our celebration was starting, the friends and associates of two hundred and nine men were numbed by their loss. Twenty Forts were missing, one radio operator was gone, and eight escort pilots paid the price.

That night Gleichauf and Purus celebrated wildly. Those of us still on flying status had to break it off and get to bed at a reasonable hour because we were subject to call the next morning. My sweat-out of mission twenty-five started in earnest the next day. I went to Operations and cornered George Reese. I wanted to know what kind of crew I could expect on the last raid, now that I was unfortunately just a spare top turret operator.

"Now look, John, we're goin' to get a first-class crew trying to finish up and a good pilot—isn't that what you want?"

"You're damn right that's what I want. When?"

"I can't tell you the date now. Give me time to work it out."

"Well, don't keep me on the fence too long."

"Oh, how would you like Ferrin for your pilot?" he asked. "You know him well?"

"Real good. Who else?"

"What's left of Cahow's crew an' I'll dig up some more who are ready to finish."

"That will be great if you can arrange it."

"Now just relax and leave it to me."

He was right and I would do that. No need to worry about a thing. Reese was working up the best deal available. I would not allow myself to get in a sweat. It was just one more mission. I tried to make myself believe I could forget about it until the morning they called me for the last one.

December 31

That night as I lay in the sack my mind went through fanciful twists: "Good-bye 1943! And thanks for your help. I hope 1944 will be as good to me as you were. I am not listed in *Who's Who*, but I am listed in *Who's Still Around*, which is more important. I want to thank you for that, 1943. It could so easily have been a different story! Do you have any influence with 1944? You do! Great! Please do me one more favor and ask her to give me the same breaks. You know I will likely be back in combat somewhere in 1944, so ask her to keep my luck simmering on the back burner until I need it. Again, 1943, thanks for your help!"

The first thing the next morning I was back on that twenty-fifth mission syndrome. There was too much time to think about it. "Will it be tomorrow? Will it be a good solid crew, or will Franek make up the assignments and throw me on a new crew that needs a gunner? I don't want to wait forever. Let's get it over with. I have been very lucky so far. Will my luck hold one more time? How can I sleep tonight without knowing if I am on the battle order? Now wait! Here I go again, overplaying this thing. Remember it is only one more raid. Why not calm down and take it like all the other raids? Sure, that is what I'll do. Not going to let it bother me. I will forget the whole thing until they call me. George promised he would get a good crew together, but I haven't heard a word from him. He may have forgotten all about it and I am just a spare gunner on the extra board waiting for whatever the dice roll . . .''

We went into the village that night and I caught the bartender diluting our scotch with cheap potato whiskey, which was common later in the evening when we would not notice it, and got into a heated argument. But George cooled it down and we moved to a table with some more men from the Air Base.

"You are sweating out your last mission? No wonder you are so edgy—I've only got five—how I wish I was in your shoes," one of them said.

"But Operations won't give me that last call. What am I supposed to do? Why don't they let me get it over with?"

"When was your last raid?" the other gunners asked.

"December 28."

"That was only three days ago. You missed two runs and now you're bitching about it? Give them time to put you on a good one."

Jim said, "That is what I keep telling him—cool it down. Let it come when it comes and quit worrying about it."

January 2, 1944

I was wide awake when the Jeep stopped outside to wake up the crews. I flipped on a light to catch the time and saw it was an early call. Did that mean a long mission? For hours I had been unable to sleep. The far-off sound of engines being run up kept telling me a mission was shaping up. Normally I would not have heard it. Hopefully waiting for the call to come, I heard the Operations people pass our hut and familiar noises as nearby huts came alive. That made the third time they had passed me up. Why? Maybe they did not have a mission mean enough! What were they waiting for? Another Schweinfurt or Berlin? My mind was operating in an irrational manner. Operations was doing me a big favor by holding me off until a good mission developed if such a thing existed. I should have been grateful, and in moments of lucid thinking I was, because extra considerations were uncommon in military operations. But the opposite pull was an almost insatiable desire to get it over with.

About mid-morning Jim came back from Operations with bad news. "A Fort blew up on takeoff this morning and killed the whole crew.

Three men were on their twenty-fifth. The others were on their twenty-third.''

"Did we know any of them?"

"They were from another squadron but we've seen them many times around the mess hall or Operations. They must have got here about the same time we did."

"What a hell of a thing to happen! Makes you sick to think about it."

"John, suppose you had to write to their families. Would you tell them it was just a lousy accident?"

"They are just as dead, no matter how it happened," George added.

"Yes, but think about the families wondering about how the accident came about, if it was carelessness on the part of someone."

"Why are you holding your neck so stiff?"

"I don't know what it is—maybe it's a kink that will be OK tomorrow. Today it's dealing me a fit."

"You better go to the infirmary and see the Flight Surgeon. You don't want to come down with the flu or some bug an' get yourself grounded for two or three weeks."

"Man, I can't get grounded now—the worst thing that could happen. You are right. I'll go see what the Infirmary says."

The Flight Surgeon examined me and asked a lot of questions: "How many missions do you have?"

"Twenty-four, Sir."

"Are you getting nervous about the twenty-fifth?"

"Oh, not much—some men sweat it out, but it doesn't bother me."

"All right, Comer. I think I know what your problem is. I'm going to give you some pills. Take one when the pain bothers you and before going to bed at night."

He went into the adjoining room, but I could see him reflected in a mirror over a lavatory. He was laughing! An orderly handed him a bottle and he resumed a serious expression and returned to the room where I was waiting.

"Here you are. Now take these and I'm sure you will be OK in a week or two."

That laugh told me all I needed to know. My problem was nerves. The pills were no doubt some harmless concoction. They went into the first trash can I passed. The only pill that would help me was one more mission. The pain in my neck and shoulders got worse. It was painful to turn my head either way. Well, I had to live with it a little longer. Otherwise they might ground me for a while if the Infirmary found out how bad it really was. That night I had the greatest difficulty finding any position where the pain would permit sleep. I heard every noise in the area for hours, but it was not a matter of expecting a call. The signs, as best I could read them, said no mission in the morning.

January 3

The pains were definitely worse when daylight finally arrived. I remembered all of those futile resolves: "All of those great words! It was not going to get to you like other people. Where was the discipline? The Flight Surgeon spotted it right away. I hope it doesn't hang out for everyone else to see."

Reese was busy when I arrived at Operations. When he slowed down I asked, "Are you going to be able to work out that special deal for us?"

"Got it all shaped up. All I'm waiting on now is a target that won't be too rough. Just be patient a few more days."

"With Ferrin?"

"Right. With Ferrin."

That afternoon I pedaled into the village with Moe Tedesco to get some exercise and a couple of beers. The weather was quite cold, but we were used to that.

"John," Moe said on the way back, "if they keep putting me off, I may get so nervous I'll crack up."

"We'll get the call the first time Reese thinks it's a good run. He's looking after us and I'm damn glad. I would hate to draw another Schweinfurt."

"Or Berlin!"

"In five or six months they can hit Schweinfurt with five hundred Forts surrounded with P-51s all the way to the target. Things are changing fast, but it won't do us any good."

"You know where I would like to be right now?"

"Where?"

"Ebbetts Field watching the Dodgers beat the hell out of those damn Giants. You've never seen a ball game until you see those two square off. They hate each other. The Dodger fans hate the Giant players and scream at every Giant batter who comes up."

"You really love Flatbush, Moe?"

"Greatest place on Earth! I know that city. Her sounds are music to me 'cause I've heard them all my life."

"I think this ale helps the pain in my neck some. Not quite as bad as it was earlier today."

"What's wrong with your neck?"

"Nerves—from sweatin' out that last one."

"With me it's tryin' to sleep. I lie awake—doze off—wake up—catnap all night."

"About the same with me—haven't had a good night's sleep in a week."

January 4

The pains were becoming so severe that I could barely turn my head, but I was determined to ride it out, because I could not afford to get grounded and have to keep putting off the final raid. I kept saying to myself, "How long can I hold out? I need pain pills now and do not know how many more days . . ."

Since exercise helped a little yesterday, I talked Jim into the long ride to Ridgewell. The pains eased up a bit after two or three beers. Riding back to the base the clouds parted and it turned into one of those rare winter nights of clear weather.

"Jim, tomorrow is the day. I can feel it. Look at that sky and you know it will be clear in the morning. I'll get that last call."

"Don't bank on it. Franek has you working on that electric gadget he wants for the Operations Office and he may keep you waiting until you finish it."

"What are you saying? He wouldn't do that to me."

"He might if he thinks about it."

"When do you think you'll be released to start flying again?"

"I think it will be this week."

"That soon? You'll catch up real fast," I replied.

"Don't know about that, John. Me an' George are extras now and never know when they'll call us or who we will fly with."

CHAPTER XXV

Mission to Tours

January 5, 1944—Tours, France   *Aircraft 514*

I had a strong feeling it would be my day. From midnight on I heard every sound in the area. There was loud talk in the adjoining hut when two of the residents staggered in from a night at the pubs. On the distant flight line there was a faint roar of engines being revved up. It was an ominous sound that suggested "in the morning we go." Every hour Tedesco or I would sit up in bed and light a cigarette. The pains in my neck were so bad that aspirin no longer helped.

An hour after midnight I heard the faint wail of air raid sirens far to the east. Which way were they coming? I hoped the invaders would go to the north, but the next ring of sirens opened up closer to us. I lay there and pondered the situation as the sirens became louder. It began to sound like the target might be Ridgewell. "Well, Comer, what's it goin' to be? Are you goin' to stay here in the warm shack and bet they can't hit you? If you climb out where will you go? The slit trenches are full of water an' by now have a sheet of ice over them. Hell, you might as well stay in the sack . . ." Then the antiaircraft guns and sirens in the nearby town opened up. The metal walls rattled and vibrated loudly and I knew a bomb had exploded somewhere not far away, but too distant to hear the sound of the explosion. The eerie sounds of German bombers overhead faded out and the sirens signaled all clear.

Then came dead quiet. But sleep for me would not come. If I was going out in the morning sleep was desperately needed. Just two or three hours of partial slumber would help. I tried all of the tricks to induce sleep I could remember, to no avail, and I lay there staring morosely into the dark. The seconds ticked slowly by. I flipped on a light long enough to look at my watch. The thing must have stopped running. It had to be later than that! No, the second hand was still operating. Would that night never end?

I caught the sound of the Jeep a mile away as it sped toward us. I followed the course of the noise as it halted on the loose gravel nearby. There were sounds of steps on the gravel paths between the huts. Muffled noises floated through the metal walls. I could hear the sound of voices and a cold water tap turned on. Someone tripped over a parked bicycle and knocked it against our hut with a crash. I heard cursing but could not recognize the voice. The steps headed our way. "Great! They're coming for us." The steps passed by on the gravel. "No! No! They're passing me by again! What is the matter with Reese and Franek? Have they forgotten I exist? The first thing in the morning I'm going to see Major Shackley—wait—the steps are coming back—hold it—maybe . . ." The door opened.

"All right! We gotcha a good one. Come on and get up you lazy bastards—Comer, Tedesco, and Green—you're flying with Ferrin in five one four. This is it—good luck."

I bounced out of bed, although every move meant stabs of pain. Hubie Green and Tedesco were up with grins on their faces. "One way or the other this will be the big one," Green said. "That was the longest night of my life."

Moe answered, "I didn't sleep much either an' I saw John get up and smoke a cigarette two or three times."

"Let's check over that ship extra good and no foul ups—no mistakes today."

"Hey, Jim. What're you getting up for?"

"How could I sleep with that damn air raid, then you guys making noises all night? I might as well get up an' see you off."

So he went to the aircraft with us and helped get the guns ready for the Bombardier, who was also on his last mission. Jim said, "What I really came out here for is to watch Shutting put on his testical armor for the last time. I wish I had a picture of it for the *Chattanooga Times*."

Ferrin and the rest of the officers unloaded and I waited expectantly. "OK, the target is Tours—about eighty miles southwest of Paris. We will have a fighter escort in and out." He was interrupted with cheers. "The altitude will be twenty-two thousand feet and the temperature will be twenty-three below. Stay alert. Nothing is going wrong today. We're all going to make it."

Opposition was expected to be mild so it sounded like a good mission for us. The Wing formation turned out over the Channel and the operation was finally on the way. Almost no chance existed now that it would be canceled or called back.

"Navigator to crew—enemy coast in five minutes—start watchin' for fighters."

"Bombardier to crew. Let's have an oxygen check."

I listened to all positions report in.

"Turret to Bombardier."

"Go ahead."

"Do you want me to pull the bomb fuse pins?"

"Yes, go ahead an' pull them."

Five minutes later I was back in the turret:

"Turret to Bombardier, pins are pulled—bomb rack switches are on."

"Thanks, Turret."

The run going in was without incident. Believe me, no other crew on that mission was so alert and ready for trouble if it materialized. A few minutes inside enemy territory the P-47s appeared as briefed. They were a beautiful sight to me. Some persons might think the big Thunderbolts too heavy and massive to be pleasing to the eye. I saw them from a different perspective. They saved my life many times and I would never lose my gratitude to them and the men who flew them.

"Navigator to Pilot."

"Go ahead, Navigator."

"The I.P. in ten minutes. We'll do a sharp turn to the left and the bomb run will come up fast."

"Bombardier to Radio, when we go on the bomb run, watch the doors down."

Ten minutes went by and the Ball reported flak. It was light to moderate.

"Bombardier to Pilot, we're on the bomb run."

When I saw and felt the bomb load fall out, I felt good. All we had to do now was get back to England and it would be all over for me.

The Bombardier screamed over the phones: "Fighters! Twelve o'clock level!"

His call came too late. None of us saw them in time! They must have dived down out of the sun and were a hundred yards away before the first man spotted them. That is what happened on a mission when it was seemingly too easy and the Fortress crews relaxed their normal alertness.

"Copilot to crew! Fire! Dammit, fire!"

Three 109s screamed through the formation and caught the lead B-17 with a rocket directly in the cockpit. The Fort burst into flame and in seconds was on the way to oblivion. No one escaped from the doomed craft.

"Waist to crew—fighters are circling to get in front of us again."

"Copilot to crew—the sonnuvabitches are coming in! Fire! Fire! Fire! Pour the lead to them!"

They turned around and attacked again with cannon fire blazing from their wings. The aircraft shuddered from the impact of heavy firing. I could see my tracers striking the lead fighter.

"Tail to Copilot. Fort exploded behind us."

"Ball to Copilot, another Fort at four o'clock in bad shape."

The fighters vanished to the south as suddenly as they had appeared.

"Copilot to Turret, do you have sunglasses?"

"Yes, Copilot."

"Put them on an' watch the sun area."

For an hour nothing happened and I relaxed. The mission was about over and I exulted in the smug knowledge that I finally had it made. But Jerry had one last goodie in reserve to throw at me! Oh, hell! More 109s straight ahead! Where did they come from?

"Turret to crew! Turret to crew! Two 109s one o'clock high coming in!"

The fighters swooped down and leveled out too low for my guns to reach them. Two times on that mission Bogies had slipped in almost undetected. Two more Forts caught heavy damage. Suppose one of them had hit us a lethal blow less than twenty-five minutes away from the coast. It almost happened.

"Bombardier to crew, fighters eleven o'clock low."

"Navigator to crew, they are Spitfires—our escort home."

Well, I thought, surely I have it made now, with those R.A.F. beauties crisscrossing below, ready to take on anything that looks German. A little later the sunlight reflecting on the Channel began to sparkle in the distance. It was almost over, but I wouldn't risk jinxing the crew by saying so—yet. I watched the coast slowly slide by below with mixed feelings. When it faded into the haze I knew for sure it was all over.

"Turret to Navigator, we got it made. We got it made."

"Pilot to crew, keep the intercom clear an' stay on your positions until we cross the English Channel. We are not taking any chances."

We had broken the 381st jinx again (if there was a jinx) and that would make a good many men feel better. Jim, George, and the others waited with congratulations. There was no way I could describe my relief and exultation. I turned to Shutting. "You made it without losing your balls."

"Yeah, but a couple of times it was close."

"What are you going to do with your special armor?"

"I'll find some deserving Navigator."

"I got a better idea. Take it home and hang it on the wall."

On the way to interrogation Jim asked, "How does it feel to have twenty-five made?"

"It would be great if I didn't have these miserable pains ever' time I move. It was murder when I had to look straight up today—like a knife stabbing me in the neck."

"You better go have it looked at."

"I will, first thing in the morning."

After interrogation, I had to go out to the plane and clean and stow the turret guns. With fair weather holding another day they might go out again the next morning. On the perimeter truck to the personnel site, I suddenly realized that I felt different. What was it? Then it dawned on me that the pains were gone. Just like that. It took an hour and a half after the mission for my ragged nerves to return to normal. The Flight Surgeon knew it would happen. Now I felt just great! Never before had I any concept of what effect tight nerves can create in an otherwise healthy body.

The celebration that night lasted until 2:00 A.M. and when the pubs closed, it resumed at the hut. I was through! The fighting part of the war was over for me! Now and then I would glance at Jim or George and it was clear that they felt left out of things now. But I had no doubt that both of them would come through fine. Reese would put them on the best available crews, so I did not let their gloom dampen my elation.

January 9

It was now a matter of awaiting orders for the port of return to the States. It was a proud moment to report to Colonel Nazzaro and receive the Distinguished Flying Cross, awarded to men who survived twenty-five missions at that date. Studying the decoration, I pondered why my luck had held up and tried to recall the faces of those I knew well who failed. What was luck? Was it an inexplicable thing available to a few at times, but withheld from most men? Or was it a series of pure coincidences? Looking back at it today the latter seems far more likely, but I am not sure. In wartime some men and some crews wore a charm one could almost see. I could spot them around the Operations area or the mess hall. I could spot others that I felt certain would never make it. How could that be? I developed the ability to sense those things. It was strange and puzzling to me that I could feel those predictions in advance and I never discussed it with anyone else. Of course, the majority of our combat crews fell into neither class. Only a few, on the opposite sides of what I call luck, generated those psychic impressions.

The feeling of elation at completing a combat tour was starting to wear thin. I was so bound to those men and to that place that I felt sad and a little depressed at leaving. Something inside me said, "You belong here until this thing is over," and I suppose a part of me will always remain at Ridgewell. One could not go through those experiences and walk away cold.

Meanwhile Carroll Wilson had recovered and arrived at the hut on combat duty again. It was good to see him once more before I left, because from the time he joined the crew I had a warm feeling for that complex and immature young man. As always, he was broke, so I loaned him another ten pounds in addition to what he already owed me. (When he returned to the States he sent me every cent of it.)

The weather turned nice and most of the men were out on a mission. The ground was dry enough for the English farm children to play outside our huts. A gunner named Pope was trying to teach seven or eight of them how to throw and kick a football. I can still remember his happy-go-lucky grin and cocky mannerisms. Kids took to him readily. When Pope entered a room the atmosphere changed. He was one of those people who had the knack of placing themselves in ridiculous situations. He had the look about him that suggested he would try anything at least once. I know he had been a star athlete somewhere but he never talked about it. His Georgia drawl lingers yet in my memory. The next day he failed to return from a mission. There was no report about what happened to the aircraft. I hope he got out in time.

That night George, Jim, Carroll, and I were in a somber mood. We talked about our early crew days and the scary situation when we arrived at Ridgewell. Those men were more like a family than could have been expected from ten persons drawn from so many divergent backgrounds and parts of the country. I was reluctant to see it break apart and scatter us about over the country.

I thought about a funny thing that happened on one of our missions. We were bouncing around in some flak and all of a sudden I was startled to hear the radio gun behind me cut loose with heavy firing. I whirled around expecting to help George hold off fighters diving down on us. Evidently a piece of flak had hit the inflating valve on one of our two life rafts. The big, bright yellow raft automatically inflated with gas and

277

pushed out of the upper storage compartment, in front of the radio hatch where George was standing at his gun facing the rear. It tumbled into the slipstream, and the blast of air propelled it directly over the radio position. I turned just in time to see George pouring furious bursts at it as the huge contraption zoomed beyond the tail.

"Radio from Turret."

"Go ahead."

"Did you get that big yellow fighter?"

"Go to hell, Turret."

I developed such a brotherly love for that big man with his infectious Irish grin. He had so many strengths balanced with small weaknesses. One of the things I remember best about him is the one tap dance routine he knew and his soft voice singing, "Mary, Mary, plain as any name can be . . ."

After lights were out I said, "Jim, do you remember that night at Las Vegas when we got out of that bar just before the fight broke out and the M.P. patrol wagon arrived?"

"Yeah, I recall the incident."

"What happened?" asked Wilson.

"One night we were having a drink in a small casino and bar and Jim went to the rest room. He returned in a hurry and told me to pay for the drinks quick and get out of there. From across the street we heard the sounds of a sizable brawl break out, and watched the paddy wagon cart off twenty or thirty civilians and servicemen."

George inquired, "How did you know the fight was going to break out?"

"Because I started it," Jim replied. "Some soldiers and sailors were arguing in the rest room. When I left I turned off the lights and pushed them together."

January 10

It was quiet my last night at the airdrome. I volunteered to check the canteen for signs of a mission shaping up for the next morning. It was the last thing I could do for them.

"Well, the key faces are missing so you can expect a call in the morning," I reported.

"You mean those who will go—they may not call us," said George.

"Or we may draw a green crew. Who knows what to expect from now on?" Counce added.

"I don't think either of you will have to wait long. I don't see any surplus gunners or radios around."

Jim had been returned to combat status that day and was in better spirits, with a chance to run off the four or five missions he needed quickly. The door opened and Vernon Chamberlain walked in.

"I heard you were leaving tomorrow and wanted to say good-bye, John."

"Vernon, you have been a faithful friend to our crew and we appreciate it. You took chances many times to slip us the extra ammunition we needed," I said.

"I don't know what it was, John. At first it was Gleichauf, then all of you. Your crew became my team. I've been sweating out you guys so long it's going to be odd not to have someone on the missions that I feel a little bit responsible for. You guys were always the same, no matter where the mission was. Other crews came out to the plane nervous or silent or bitching about the guns when nothing was wrong with them. But you fellows always arrived in a good humor, kidding each other or some kind of horseplay. You were just different from the others—my kind of people, I guess . . ."

It was going to be difficult to leave all of those friends, not knowing if I would ever see them again. Certainly we planned to get together after the war, but would it really happen? Or would the occasional letters eventually die out?

Jim looked at me, "We have talked often about mental attitude—about fear. Tell me something honestly, John—have you overcome fear in combat?"

"No. I doubt if anyone ever does completely. But starting with the way it was when we arrived here, I have gone seventy to eighty percent of the way toward controlling it. That damn flak still bothers me at times."

"I haven't done near that well," said George. "I doubt if I have gone fifty percent of the way."

"It depends on what you mean by fear," I answered. "How do you tell when it starts and when it ends?"

"I don't follow you," Balmore said. "I'm either scared or I'm not."

"Look at it this way: you are flying along knowing that fighters are going to hit you. When? Where are they? Hope we see them in time. You build up anxiety, the first stage of fear. I wish the escort would get here before they do! We got to be careful and not let them slip in on us out of the sun! Tension builds up. There they are! About sixty of them. Where's the escort? The sensation of fear wells up. Here they come! Look at those cannon flashes! You pour bursts at them and excitement crowds out fear.

The adrenaline is flowing. At two hundred yards your bursts get longer and closer together. Excitement increases. The fighters are now at one hundred yards, using their full assortment of weapons at you from close range. Your bursts are three times as long as they taught you at gunners school. You do not care if the barrels burn out. You are keyed up to your maximum performance—exhilaration! It's an emotional high that is a heady sensation unlike any other emotion you have ever experienced. A gunner could become addicted to it with enough experience. In time he might crave the kill-or-be-killed thrill as some people crave strong drugs. Maybe that's why some men become professional soldiers of fortune. Civilian life is too tame for them after years of combat and the high excitement that goes with it."[1]

There was silence for a while and Wilson said, "You're getting close, John."

Counce added, "I never thought about it the way you break it down, but it's true that all of those emotions are involved in a fighter attack. I guess we all have a secret desire to flirt with danger, but each of us thinks that others will pay the price—not him."

"What do you say to all this, George?" I asked.

"In the radio room I hardly ever get to see any of the attackers until it's over and they flash by. Most times they roll under the wing and I don't see them at all. I hear the intercom scream, *'Coming in.'* I hear the bursts getting longer and longer and I'm petrified back there, seeing nothing that is going on! If I had more chances to fire at the fighters, it might be different."

That last night at Ridgewell I was caught in an ambivalence of twisted emotions. Of course, I was glad to have escaped the hazards of air combat. But the attractions of exhilarating combat experience lingered in the subconscious mind. Stateside military duty, whatever my assignment might be, by contrast with Ridgewell would, I knew, be too dull and stagnant. And there was regret at having to leave these men, with whom I had relationships that could not be repeated in civilian life. After lights were out I lay there in a state of gloom. What should have been a happy contemplation had turned sour.

---

[1] If Sigmund Freud were alive I think he would agree that combat fatigue is caused by the traumatic memories buried in the subconscious.

CHAPTER XXVI

Good-bye to Ridgewell

January 11—
James Counce and George Balmore Only—
On different aircraft

At 5:30 A.M. the lights came on and roused me from a deep sleep. I listened to the roster: "Counce flying 888 with Klein—Balmore flying 912 with Crozier . . ."

I raised up in bed. "Those are good crews. Right?"

"We could have done a lot worse," Counce answered.

"Well, since I'm already awake, I might as well go out and see you jokers off."

The personnel truck let George out first. "Good luck! I'll see you back in the States when this thing is over." A handshake and he was gone.

I helped Jim get the guns ready until it was time to start engines. "Good luck, Jim. Let me know where you are stationed when you get back to the States."

He gave me that big grin and closed the hatch. I watched the ship pull away and almost wished I was going with them.

I had to hurry to get my bags ready for the truck that was to take us to the nearby station. Just before the train arrived, I looked up as I heard a formation overhead.

"Take a good look, Carl. That's the last time we'll see the 381st in action."

"Good luck, boys," he said. "Go get 'em."

It was a long, slow train ride across England to Chorley, on the west coast, the embarkation point for service personnel who were returning to

281

the United States. Nearly all of these men were wounded, or for some other reason were no longer needed in the combat area.

When men completed a tour of combat duty and returned to the States, quite a few of them did become highly nervous for a while. The condition was brought about by too many traumatic experiences buried deep in the subconscious mind and seeking an outlet. The excitement, and the motivation created by the need to defend all that was good in our civilization, was abruptly withdrawn, and replaced by a hum-drum military existence. The change was too sudden and drastic for the mind to accept it right away. So those men continued to dwell mentally in the immediate past for a while. The falling aircraft, the explosions, and the hideous flak were strongly imprinted and needed to be worked out of the subconscious mind. In time, the nervousness would wear off for most of those who were affected. The need to talk about the war would fade, to be replaced by the daily trivialities of civilian life, from which they had escaped for a brief time into high adventure. For the majority of those men there was no lasting damage. Slowly they returned to what we call normal. For a few, perhaps more sensitive than others, the memories were too indelibly planted. For them, more time and treatment were needed. In severe cases of neurosis and continuing anxiety, injections of sodium pentathol were used, along with the help of a psychologist, to pry troublesome memories out of the subconscious mind. The patient was induced to talk at great length, in response to questions about those lingering nightmarish experiences. The drug helped to release the deeply buried tensions. Most times it worked.

January 14

I was standing in the snack bar at Chorley when I saw Lieutenant Ferrin walk in. He was a few days behind me getting away from Ridgewell.

"When did you leave the 381st?" I asked.

"Yesterday. Got here this afternoon."

"I read that the January eleventh mission had high losses. How did the 381st come out?"

"There was a mixup and the planes were called back. Some of 'em didn't get the message and went on and got clobbered."

"How many did the Group lose?"

"Quite a few. I didn't get the exact number, but it was bad!"

"You know Jim Counce and George Balmore."

"Sure, I know 'em."

"They were with Crozier and Klein on that mission. Did both of those ships get back OK?"

"The loss startled Colonel Nazzaro because it was unexpected."

"How about Klein and Crozier?" I sensed he was avoiding my question.

Ferrin took a deep breath and looked me in the eye. "Crozier and Klein both went down, Comer."

I listened in a state of shock and disbelief. For a minute I could not say anything.

"Were there any chutes—either plane?"

"Crozier's plane was seen to explode.[1] There was hardly any chance for a survivor." There was an icy feeling in the middle of my chest. When I recovered enough, I asked almost in a whisper, "And the other plane?"

"Klein's ship was last seen badly damaged and engines burning—it is not known if any of the crew got out. No chutes were observed."

At least there was a chance that Jim had time to jump, but I knew too well how fast the explosions came after engines caught fire. If anyone got out, surely Jim would be one of them, for he was close to the waist escape hatch.

"Have you seen Shutting?"

"Yes, I ran into Carl an hour ago."

I turned away from Ferrin and stumbled blindly from the crowded bar. He followed and told me the meager details that were known. But I had quit listening. My mind was in shock. Right then I could not talk to anyone. The night was bitterly cold and it was raining. I walked blindly in the rain without cap or raincoat for a long time because a man does not cry in front of other men; I walked until I was soaked and shaking with the cold. What Ferrin said kept coming back. "The 533rd Squadron was almost wiped out—lost six ships! The mission was called back but the First Division did not get the message. So it went on to the target and was hit with a devastating fighter attack!"

There was no possible sleep for me! All night I stared into the blackness and groped for the means to accept the inevitable. At such times the mind tries to find ways to avoid the truth when it is too bitter to accept. There is some mistake! They will turn up! The word will seep back that they got out and are prisoners of war.

---

[1] At a 381st Reunion in San Antonio I met Gordon Crozier, pilot of the aircraft that George was in. Gordon told me that all of the crew was able to bail out except Balmore. He personally examined Balmore and confirmed that he was dead. All other crew members survived as prisoners of war.

January 15

It was a bad day for me. The weather was cold and rainy. I kept thinking about Jim and George. I supposed that it was futile to keep trying to delude myself that George got out in time. I had to accept the facts, and they were that the aircraft was seen to explode and no chutes were reported. But surely Jim had a chance. He was in the closest position to an escape hatch. No one saw the aircraft explode and it was under control at the last report. Yet, I had a strange feeling—some extra sense—that Jim was gone! It was the same psychic premonition that I often felt about combat crews and was almost always correct. No matter how I tried to rationalize his escape, I knew there was no hope.

January 16

In a state of depression I looked up Shutting. I had avoided him the day before because I could not talk to anyone about it until I accepted the facts.

"I tried to find you yesterday, John," he said. "That was terrible about Balmore and Counce. They were the best."

"It hit me hard. One of them would have been bad enough, but both the same day on different planes!"

"Maybe Jim bailed out."

"No! He's gone. Don't ask me how I know, but I do. I'll try to see Mary Balmore if we land in the vicinity of New York and the Counce family later when I can."

"John, we were just lucky that we made it. Think about how many we knew who didn't."

January 20

In the dim predawn light, I stood high on the stern deck of the S.S. *Frederick Lykes* and watched the shoreline of England dissolve in the distance. As I stared into the dark swirling mists, memories began to cloud my vision. Once again I saw the Forts flying in perfect formation with long trails streaming far behind them in the sky. Once more I heard the distinctive drone of Fortress engines. And I saw faces—unforgettable faces I would never see again: Herb Carqueville, Pete Ludwigson, Major Hendricks, Feigenbaum, Pope, and many others. All lost over Europe.

More than anything, I saw Jim and George. I could almost hear their voices, those comically contrasting accents of the Bronx and Mississippi. We had shared a unique and special brotherhood, forged by circumstances and tested by adversity. It was a gift of friendship beyond anything I had experienced before. And I knew it could not be replaced.

As I remembered them, I felt an overwhelming sadness, and turned away from the others nearby to hide the tears that I could not blink away. At that moment I experienced an intuition of startling clarity. Suddenly I realized that we would meet again. I did not know how or when, but I knew! "Death is not the end, but only the beginning of a new dimension." How many times had I heard that Christian refrain? But I suppose that I had never fully accepted its meaning until that moment. There was no longer any doubt. I felt a certainty and a peace. The sense of gloom lifted and I was a different person.

Yes, we would meet again. And until we did, I vowed to keep my memories of them from fading. I named my firstborn son James Balmore Comer. And because of them and their families, I wrote this book.

EPILOGUE

I have often been asked: Why did you volunteer for more combat? The story is that when I returned from England to the U.S. I had no idea I would soon be on the way back overseas. I was assigned as a flight engineer instructor at a new combat crew training base at Gulfport, Mississippi. They put three of us together as a team: an excellent instructor pilot, myself, and a veteran radio operator. Each day we would get a new group of four or five new copilots and radio operator students. The radio people did their thing back in the radio room. I took these green kids out to the aircraft and gave them practice starting engines. Then the major came out and we gave these youngsters landing and takeoff practice for four or five hours. None of these men had ever been in a big airplane before so they were confused about the controls and instruments. I would stand over them and tap their hand if they made the wrong move or got confused over which control the pilot was talking about.

A B-17 has a large horizontal fin that tapers quite high as it gets to the tail. A cross wind blowing against this very large surface will push the tail crosswise on landing unless the pilot exerts extreme rudder pressure. We always had a crosswind at that field so those kids were in trouble on almost every landing. You would not believe how often we had to suddenly pull up and go around for another try. And you would not believe how often we came sliding in with the nose 15 to 25 degrees angle to the runway. I got to where I would yawn if it was only 15 degrees.

One day after an extra-hazardous landing and two shaky takeoffs I ran into an instructor pilot I knew well at Operations and complained, "One of these days one of those kids is going to wipe me out! It would be safer back in combat!" He replied, "I have been trying to get transferred to combat—if you could find some more gunners that want to go back I think they would let us make up a new crew."

That night at the barracks I passed the word around and six of us agreed to give it a try. Sure enough it worked! Within a week we were on our way across the Atlantic, flying a new B-17 to Italy.

And it was safer over there than waiting for some green kid to end my days.

AFTER THE WAR

Paul Gleichauf, Pilot: Remained in the Air Force and retired as a Lt. Colonel. When I located him he was living at El Paso, Texas. When I finished the first rough draft of *Combat Crew,* I took the first copy to him. I was very sad to learn that he had a brain tumor and could not last much longer. He died two months later. We keep in touch with his wife.

Herbert Carqueville, Copilot: M. I. A. No trace of the aircraft or crew was ever found.

Carl Shutting, Navigator: Became a practicing psychiatrist at Chattanooga, Tennessee, where he died ten years ago from a heart attack.

John J. Purus, Bombardier: After a 1951 reunion in New York with the Comer and Balmore families all contact was lost.

George Balmore, Radio Operator: K. I. A. January 11, 1944.

John Comer, Flight Engineer-Gunner: Was a sales manager, then a zone manager for a large manufacturer retiring at Dallas, Texas, where he still lives.

James Counce, Waist Gunner: K. I. A. January 11, 1944.

Carroll Wilson, Waist Gunner: Retired as a Master Sergeant in the Air Force with some rough later experiences. He was an air attaché with army that was hit by that devastating attack by the Chinese and had to fight their way out under difficult conditions. We visited with him a year ago at his home at Nashville, Tennessee.

Nickalas Abramo, Ball Turret: Was wounded, recovered, and resumed combat action. He was wounded again, had to bail out, and became a P. O. W. Unconfirmed information is that he died several years ago.

Harold Harkness, Ball Turret after Abramo was wounded: He is now retired from the U.S. Post Office and now lives at Aztec, New Mexico.

Buck Rogers, Tail Gunner: He was grounded when he did not recover from severe injuries early in his missions. After the war no contact.

John Kels, Copilot after Carqueville became a first pilot: No contact.

George Reese, original Copilot: Operations officer during the action and once in a while our Copilot—a lawyer in New Orleans.

Raymond Legg: After I left England, Raymond was shot down with another crew. All of the crew got out of the aircraft safely but were killed by enraged German civilians in the vicinity of Berlin.

Mitchell La Buda, Waist Gunner: He is retired and lives at Northfield, Illinois.

Bill Brophy, Radio Operator: Presently lives at Philadelphia, Pennsylvania.

I kept up a long relationship with the Balmore and Counce families. Both of the Balmores have passed on. I attended Mr. Balmore's funeral at N.Y. I have visited the Counce family many times. Last year we saw Mr. Counce at Corinth, Mississippi, just three weeks before he died. We still stay in touch with Jim's younger sister, Amy.

When we lived at Nashville, Tennessee, a few years after the war, the Carl Shutting family also lived there. We became very close friends with Carl's wife (after the war), Mary Katharine Shutting. Carl Shutting, the onetime clown and other things, was now a practicing psychiatrist—a walking example of all the virtues (as so often happens to one who was not that great when younger).

William Cahow stayed in the Air Force and retired as a Lt. Colonel and presently lives at Fresno, California. I see him at all the 381st reunions and of course we refly the October 14 raid to Schweinfurt.

Woodrow Pitts retired as a Master Sergeant in the Air Force with a long record as flight engineer. He lives at Pasadena, Texas, and we get together once in a while and relive those days in England.

I located Hubert Green one month too late. He had just passed away. Hubie retired as a police captain at Middletown, New York. His lovely wife and two sons and their wives attended the reunion at Asheville, North Carolina, last year.

It was the same thing with Bill Kettner. I located him too late. But Mrs. Kettner came to the Asheville meeting last year from her home in Florida.

Ugo Lancia lives in New Jersey and ran a successful oil business until recently. His health has not been good lately, but we hope he will be at the Boston reunion. We have exchanged letters and talked by phone. He told me that Tedesco passed away a few years back.

The
Over-the-Counter
Securities Markets

A REVIEW GUIDE

Second Edition

LEO M. LOLL, JR. / JULIAN G. BUCKLEY

Prentice-Hall, Inc., Englewood Cliffs, New Jersey

Library of Congress
Catalog Card Number 67-22419

Current printing (last digit)

10 9 8 7 6 5 4 3 2 1

PRINTED IN THE UNITED STATES OF AMERICA

Prentice-Hall International, Inc., LONDON

Prentice-Hall of Australia, Pty. Ltd., SYDNEY

Prentice-Hall of Canada, Ltd., TORONTO

Prentice-Hall of India Private Ltd., NEW DELHI

Prentice-Hall of Japan, Inc., TOKYO

Preface

        This book is specifically designed to help anyone who desires to enter the securities business, on either a full-time or a part-time basis. It should be particularly helpful to anyone wishing to pass the examination required for qualification as a registered representative or registered principal of a securities firm. The book was revised with special emphasis on the 1966 NASD *Study Outline for Qualifying Examination for Registered Representatives and Registered Principals.* Most of the topics covered in the NASD *Study Outline* are fully described and indexed.

This second edition of our book has been greatly expanded over the first. Chapters have been added on economics, taxes, and stock market techniques. The areas of municipal bonds, investment management, and the money market have been greatly expanded. The sections covering federal and state securities laws and the regulations of the National Association of Securities Dealers, Inc. have been updated and enlarged. Investment companies are discussed extensively, and their advantages and disadvantages are explored along with the federal and state regulations governing their distribution and use.

Newcomers to the securities industry are from all walks of life. Some are building full-fledged careers in their newly chosen occupation. Others are employed on a part-time basis, generally as mutual fund salesmen, and they view their new job as an interesting and productive way to spend their spare hours and supplement the family income. In the past many new securities salesmen entered the field with little or no knowledge or experience in the securities business. As early as 1956 the National Association of Securities Dealers, Inc. imposed minimum membership requirements for the registered representatives of its member firms. These requirements included the passing of a written examination. Since that time the entrance standards have been raised and the examinations have become progressively more difficult.

This revised edition should help the candidate meet these tougher standards since it is closely geared to the 1966 *Study Outline*. For registered representatives this book provides a useful tool in solving the complex investment problems that confront securities salesmen daily. It is a valuable reference guide for information on the Investment Company Act of 1940, the SEC Statement of Policy regarding investment company sales literature, and other important federal and state laws in the securities field. Included is a detailed discussion of the Rules of Fair Practice and the Uniform Practice Code of the National Association of Securities Dealers, Inc. Also described is the Net Capital Rule for a securities firm, with examples of how to compute a firm's net capital. In addition, the book gives a summary of the important principles of corporation finance and investments.

We are grateful to John Dunsmore of the Wall Street Journal, Dr. Allen O. Felix of the New York Stock Exchange, Robert N. Schilling of the American Stock Exchange, Jonas H. Ottens and Dr. Henry Kaufman of Salomon Brothers and Hutzler, Herbert Filer, Jr. of Filer Schmidt and Co., Inc., Walter C. Levering of Carlisle and Jacquelin, and John J. Bowler of First Investors Stock Fund Inc. for their help. Our deepest appreciation is expressed to John H. Hodges, Jr., Bruce J. Simpson, James W. Ratzlaff, and George J. Bergen of the National Association of Securities Dealers, Inc., for their close cooperation, helpful suggestions and constant encouragement throughout the revision period. We are indebted to Professor Lawrence S. Ritter, Professor Joseph A. Mauriello, David Sortor, and C. B. Allen of the Graduate School of Business Administration of New York University.

L.M.L. / J.G.B.

Contents

Business Organizations

Chapter 1

One of the first problems in starting a business, whether it is selling securities or locomotives, is the selection of the best form of business organization. There are a number of forms of business organization, but the most important include: the sole proprietorship, the general partnership, the limited partnership, and the corporation. There are many small securities firms which are sole proprietorships, but the bulk of the larger firms are partnerships or corporations.

The advantages and disadvantages of the various forms of business organization are varied and complicated. Anyone starting a business should consult a lawyer in order to find the most suitable form for his individual situation, and to have the necessary papers drawn and filed in order to avoid serious complications and losses. For instance, any firm, regardless of its form, which is in the securities business must file with the Securities and Exchange Commission if it is engaged in interstate commerce; many state authorities also require that securities firms register or file papers.

It might be important for a securities firm to become a member of the National Association of Securities Dealers and perhaps of one or more of the stock exchanges. The regulations of the National Association of Securities Dealers will be discussed in Chapters 8 and 13–17.

The Proprietorship

The proprietorship is a business organization owned by one individual. All earnings after expenses belong to the owner or proprietor of the business. The owner has exclusive control of the firm—he is not answerable to someone else for time spent working, retirement, or complying with numerous rules. A proprietorship is easier to form than a partnership or a corporation. The use of the proprietorship form of business organization also might result in some saving in federal income taxes. The owner must report the income of the proprietorship along with any other income but the tax rates are no larger than he would pay as an individual. The tax liabilities of a proprietorship will be compared with those of a corporation on page 6.

The proprietorship form is suitable for business providing service of a highly personal nature. It is flexible and gives the proprietor an incentive to work. Any profits resulting from his efforts are his alone and do not have to be shared with partners or stockholders.

The most important disadvantage of a proprietorship is the owner's complete liability for all the debts of the proprietorship. Another potential disadvantage is the fact that if a sole proprietor dies, the company ceases to exist. Even when customers and goodwill have been built up over the years, it is often difficult for a successor to hold the business. It is difficult for a sole proprietorship to raise a large amount of outside capital. No stock or bonds are issued by a proprietorship.

A General Partnership

In a general partnership, two or more individuals agree to operate a business. As in a sole proprietorship, no stock is issued, but its formation is a little more complicated.

The partnership agreement should be in writing; although no form is prescribed, it usually includes:

 a. The nature of the business
 b. How the profits are to be divided
 c. The amount of capital contributed by each partner
 d. How long the partnership will last
 e. The duties of each partner
 f. How disputes will be settled

This agreement constitutes a *contract* between the partners.

The partnership has to file a federal, and in most cases a state, income tax return. The partnership as such, however, does not pay income taxes. Instead, each partner includes in his income tax return his share of the partnership profits (whether or not it is withdrawn from the partnership) along with other personal income. He then pays an income tax based on the total amount, at regular individual tax rates.

A partnership is a flexible form of business organization in which each partner may specialize in a particular branch of the business and yet share in the common profits. It is suitable to business of a *personal* nature such as brokerage, law, and accounting. Once a partnership has been formed, no new partners may be added without the consent of all the partners. A partner cannot sell out his partnership to a new partner or leave his share to a relative without permission of the other partners.

He can, of course, leave his interest or sell it; but the heir or buyer can only collect the assets. In short, individuals cannot become partners without the permission of the other partners.

The general partners are liable jointly and severally for the debts of the firm. This means that if the partnership fails, the creditors may look to all or any one of the partners for the unpaid debts of the firm to the extent of their assets, subject to the priority of personal creditors. If the partnership agreement states how the debts may be shared, the creditors usually will respect this agreement provided the assets are sufficient. If the assets of the general partnership are not sufficient to meet the claims, the creditors look to the partners' personal assets; the liability of a general partner is *unlimited*. The tax liabilities of a partnership and of a corporation are compared on page 6.

A Limited Partnership

A limited partnership is a business organization of two or more individuals, with at least one of them a general partner who manages the business, and at least one a limited or special partner. The formation of a limited partnership is subject to state law. Usually publication of the agreement is required; in some states it must be published and filed with the local county official.

The liability and duties of a general partner in a limited partnership are the same as in a general partnership. However, the liabilities of the *limited* partner are generally limited to the amount of money he has contributed.

A limited partner must take great care to avoid being classed as a general partner and hence becoming liable for the debts of the firm beyond his contribution. Among other things, he must take no part in determining the policy of the firm or in any other functions of management. He may work for the firm but only under the direction of the general partner. Also it must be indicated that the limited partner is a limited and not a general partner. That is, the firm must publicize the fact that he *is* a limited partner. This is to avoid giving the impression to the public and to creditors that the full extent of the assets of the limited partner are available to creditors. If, for example, the partners' names are listed in a directory of securities firms, the limited partners should be clearly designated as limited partners. The same would be true if the partners were listed on the stationery of the firm. A limited partner usually may withdraw his capital with proper notice, provided there are sufficient assets for the creditors.

The great advantage of a limited partnership is that it enables a moneyed partner to leave some of his funds in the firm without incurring the unlimited liability of a general partner.

The Massachusetts Trust

The Massachusetts or business trust is not a form of business organization that one starting a securities business would normally consider, but a number of investment companies are Massachusetts trusts.

A Massachusetts trust is usually formed by individuals who desire their property to be managed by a board of trustees. These individuals turn their real estate, securities, or cash over to a board of trustees who might hold the property or sell it in exchange for other property. The trustees charge a small annual fee for management. They issue transferable trust certificates or stock to the individuals who have entrusted to them their property. Thus an investment company such as the Massachusetts Investment Trust of Boston receives cash in return for stock. These shares (sometimes called trust certificates) represent proportionate interest in the company. Usually an investment company will redeem its shares on demand of the stockholders at their liquidating value.

The trustees of a Massachusetts trust are usually *not* elected by the shareholders and cannot be removed by them except for some major cause such as fraud. When one trustee dies or resigns, the other trustees usually elect a successor. In almost all cases the stockholders or certificate holders of a Massachusetts trust are not liable for the debts of the trustees or the trust. This is particularly true if the shareholders have no voice in the management of the trust or the selection of the trustees. The legal status of the Massachusetts trust differs in the various states, leading to possible complications. For this reason most of the investment companies formed in recent years have been corporations.

The Corporation

The corporation is formed by a group of individuals, usually three, called incorporators. They apply to the state authority, usually the Secretary of State, for approval of a charter. The charter is the birth certificate of the corporation. Information required in charter applications vary from state to state. Usual requirements are:

a. The exact title of the corporation
b. Details of the type of business
c. The names and addresses of the incorporators and directors
d. The number of shares and par value of the common stock

Some corporate charters also provide for preferred stock. (After the charter has been approved by the state authorities, the directors and the officers are elected and the corporation is born.)

Thus the corporation is formed under state laws and is a creature of the state. Its *status* is that of a *legal entity*, distinct and apart from the officers, the directors, and the stockholders. It can sue and be sued in its own name. Its life, as long as it stays solvent, is perpetual in most jurisdictions.

A company is considered a *domestic* company in the state where it is incorporated. A company can send salesmen to other states and sell there, but in *other* states it is considered a *foreign* corporation and may have to qualify as such. For example, if a corporation established a large warehouse to distribute the goods, the corporation might have to satisfy relevant state laws, which might require filing documents and paying certain taxes.

An *alien* corporation is a corporation formed abroad with head offices and management also abroad but operating in the United States; for example, a factory. For instance, the Volkswagen firm of the Federal Republic of West Germany has factories in this country and is considered *here* an alien corporation.

The directors are elected by the stockholders and in turn elect the officers who manage the corporation. The directors have many duties and obligations. They declare dividends, appoint officers, approve capital budgets, set salaries, and authorize suits. Their number is set by law, usually at a minimum of three. Their liabilities are, in general: (1) for malfeasance, which is doing something bad such as stealing, (2) for misfeasance, which is doing something that ordinarily is legal but is wrong in a particular case, such as declaring a dividend which will impair capital, and (3) for nonfeasance, which is neglect of duty; for example, failure to attend directors' meetings over an extended period.

A corporation has a number of advantages. It can expand by borrowing money and, with the approval of the stockholders, sell more stock. Thus it can obtain large sums of capital and engage in large-scale operations. Also, the corporation is a legal person. It is separate and apart from the stockholders and even the directors. All the stockholders and directors could die, yet the corporation might go on, since its charter usually states that it is perpetual. Another advantage is that in the event that the corporation runs into financial difficulty, the stockholders are usually not liable to the creditors for the debts of the company as they are in the case of sole proprietorships or general partnerships. This is true if there is no fraud involved and if the stock is fully paid.

There are times when a corporation has a distinct tax advantage over other forms of business organization. In order to determine relative tax advantages of a corporation on the one hand and a sole proprietorship or partnership on the other a comparison might be made between the federal income taxes levied on the two categories.

Federal income taxes will be discussed again in Chapter 3, but basically they are:

22% on taxable corporate income *up to* $25,000
plus
48% on taxable corporate income *over* $25,000

Income from partnerships and sole proprietorships is reported along with the recipient's other personal income on Form 1040 and is taxed at regular personal income tax rates.

Applying corporate tax rates and personal income tax rates to a taxable income of $10,000, the following rates will have to be paid by a taxpayer if single, and if married:

	Single		*Married*
Taxable Income	$10,000		$10,000
Taxed as Corporation			
22% × $10,000	2,200		2,200
Taxed as an individual			
Base Tax	1,630		1,380
Plus 28% or excess of		Plus 22% or excess of	
$8,000—(28% × $2,000)	560	$8,000—(22% × $2,000)	440
Total	$ 2,190		$1,820

On the basis of the above calculation it seems to the advantage of the taxpayer with a taxable income of $10,000 to use the partnership or sole proprietorship form.

The following figures show the taxable income up to $200,000 and the federal income taxes (1966) that would be levied on a married couple, on a single individual, and on a corporation:

PROPRIETORSHIP AND PARTNERSHIP

Taxable Income	Married	Single	Corporation
$ 11,000	$ 2,040	$ 2,510	$ 2,420
14,000	2,760	3,550	3,080
19,000	4,100	5,620	4,180
25,000	6,020	8,530	5,500
50,000	17,060	22,590	17,500
100,000	45,180	55,490	41,500
200,000	110,930	125,490	89,500

By examining the above figures one can clearly see that a *married* person would pay lower taxes on a sole proprietorship or a partnership than as a corporation until his net taxable income reached about $19,000. At this point the taxes on a proprietorship or partnership are $4,100 or a little less than the taxes on a corporation. But as the married person's income goes higher there is a distinct advantage in the corporate form.

In the case of the *single* individual, if his income is $11,000 or more, the tax advantage seems to be in favor of the corporation.

In the above examples it is assumed that the corporation retains all its earnings. If dividends were paid out by the corporation, the individual receiving them would have to pay personal income tax on the dividends. This fact might make it more favorable to have a proprietorship or a partnership. However a lawyer should always be consulted before the individual makes a final choice. Until April 14, 1966, a proprietorship or a partnership could elect to be taxed as a corporation. But on that date this privilege was repealed by Congress, effective January 1, 1969. In the interim between April 14, 1966 and January 1, 1969 no new election will be permitted.

While there are still some disadvantages in a corporation, such as closer regulation, there are a number of advantages as well. For example, a corporation can raise large sums of capital, expand operations, and impose only limited liability on the stockholders.

Every time you buy a security—a stock, a bond, or shares of an investment company—you become a part of a corporation, either by owning a part of it or by lending it money. Therefore, it is important that the investor understand the fundamentals of a corporation: its balance sheet, its income statement, the types of securities it issues, and the regulations under which they are traded.

REVIEW QUESTIONS

1. What are the basic characteristics of a proprietorship?
2. What are the advantages and disadvantages of the partnership form of business organization?
3. Discuss the most important considerations in selecting the form of a business organization.
4. Contrast the risk assumed by a general partner, a limited partner, a sole proprietor, a shareholder of a Massachusetts trust, and a shareholder of a corporation.
5. Distinguish between a domestic corporation, a foreign corporation, and an alien corporation.
6. Explain the liabilities of a director of a corporation. What are his duties?
7. What are the major advantages of the corporate form of business organization? Are there any disadvantages?
8. Explain the reason why considering taxation is so important in making the decision to select the form of business organization. Illustrate by using the table on page 6.
9. Describe the usual state charter of a corporation. What is its legal status?

The Balance Sheet

Chapter 2

The balance sheet shows the financial condition of a company on a particular day, usually the last day of the year. We call it a balance sheet because all the assets equal, or balance with, all the liabilities plus the stockholders' equity. The balance sheet shows a fixed condition of the company; the income statement shows where the money came from, how it was spent, and what is left. While the balance sheet is related to the income statement, it is distinctly separate from it.

Below is a simple balance sheet. The *assets*, listed on the left-hand side, include cash, inventory, accounts receivable, and property, making total assets of $1,000,000. The *liabilities*, listed on the right-hand side, include the *debts* of the company to bondholders, to the United States government, to the trade, and to the long term creditors. These debts total $700,000.

Now, we have assets of $1,000,000 and liabilities of $700,000. Clearly, the assets do not balance with the liabilities. The difference of $300,000 belongs to the stockholders. We call this *stockholders' equity*. In other words, if all the assets were sold for $1,000,000 and the creditors paid the $700,000 due them, the owners or stockholders would get $300,000. The $300,000 is a liability, in that it is due the stockholders, but in another sense it is a *balancing item* between the assets and the liabilities. Thus, a balance sheet is intended to show the financial position of a business as of a certain date by listing the items owned, the items owed and the equity of the owners.

The table illustrates how these items balance.

8

December 31, 1966

Cash	$ 200,000	Taxes	$ 200,000
Accounts Receivable	100,000	Accounts Payable	200,000
Inventory	200,000		
Property	500,000	Bonds	300,000
			(700,000)
		Stockholders' Equity	300,000
Total Assets	$1,000,000		$1,000,000

It is suggested that the reader look at the more detailed balance sheet of the Lobuck Corporation on page 18 and keeping in mind the three main categories: assets, liabilities, and stockholders' equity. We will now discuss the items of this balance sheet in detail.

Assets

The assets of a business are the items of value it owns. There are three main types of assets: current assets, fixed assets, and other assets.

Current Assets usually include cash on hand, or in banks, United States Government securities, marketable securities, accounts receivable, sometimes notes receivable, and inventories. We call them current assets because they can be turned into cash in the normal course of business, usually within one year. The statement of the Lobuck Corporation on page 18 shows the following current assets:

Item		
1	Cash	$ 400,000
2	United States Government securities	200,000
3	Accounts Receivable	500,000
4	Inventories	400,000
5	Total Current Assets	$1,500,000

Cash (item 1) is clearly a current asset. United States Government and marketable securities (item 2) can be sold within a few days time. It is reassuring to see on a company's balance sheet a large amount of cash and marketable securities in relation to the amount of current liabilities. This means a company can easily pay its current debts. Also, a company with large cash resources can expand its own business or even buy another business.

Accounts receivable (item 3) is the amount of money due to a company from its customers. Companies often sell goods to customers in return for promises to pay. The evidence of such a promise is the order, either verbal or in writing. Sometimes customers do not pay their bills promptly, or default on their payments. To cover an actual or possible loss, a reserve is set up for bad debts; this amount is deducted from the accounts receivable, and only the net is carried as a current asset. In good times, the losses on accounts receivable are small, and a company usually has little difficulty in turning the accounts receivable into cash. Sometimes *notes receivable* appear as a current asset. Here the customers have signed papers or notes promising to pay their debts. This is usually done when the terms for payment are long, running into several months.

Inventories (item 4) include, first, raw materials which the company has purchased, such as steel, lumber, cloth; second, goods in process or partly finished products; and third, finished products, such as automobiles, furniture and suits, and so forth. Inventories are usually the least current of the so-called current assets. Trouble often occurs when a company is unable to sell its old inventory. We can spot this if the inventory over the years increases, when compared with current assets or sales. Comparison should only be made with companies in the same fields, since in some businesses companies traditionally carry high or low inventories.

The cost of inventories may be determined by a number of different methods, but the most common are *last in first out*, or LIFO, and *first in first out*, or FIFO.

Under the LIFO method, all sales are *assumed* to be made from inventories acquired most recently, and the value of the inventory left on hand is prorated back to the earliest purchases.

Under the FIFO method, all sales are *assumed* to be made from inventories acquired during the earlier periods, and the inventory left on hand is prorated back to the most recent purchases.

Thus, in a period of rising prices the LIFO method is the more conservative, since it understates the profits and inventory value. The reverse is true with the FIFO method.

The following example will illustrate this under the LIFO method:

Assume Sales of 30 Units @ $100 per unit = $3,000

Inventory for Sales Assumed To Be Taken From the Most Recent Purchases

December 10	purchase	10	units	@	$90	per unit	$ 900
November 15	purchase	10	units	@	$70	per unit	700
October 12	purchase	10	units	@	$60	per unit	600
							$2,200
Balance							$ 800

Inventory on Hand Prorated Back to the Earliest Purchases

Sept. 10	purchase	10	units	@	$60	per unit	$ 600
July 8	purchase	10	units	@	$50	per unit	500
July 10	·purchase	10	units	@	$55	per unit	550
Inventory Value							$1,650
Balance							$1,350

But under FIFO the opposite would be true. The inventory taken for sales would be valued at $1,650 instead of $2,200 giving a balance of $1,350 ($3,000 — $1,650 = $1,350) instead of $800 under LIFO.

The inventory left under FIFO would be $2,200 instead of $1,650 under LIFO.[1]

Quick Assets are a little different from current assets in that they *exclude* inventory. In other words, *quick assets* include cash marketable securities and accounts and notes receivable.

Fixed assets usually include property, plant, buildings, and equipment. Companies sometimes show these items separately but more often as a single figure, as in the Lobuck Corporation item 6 on page 18 as follows:

Item		
6	Property, Plant, and Equipment	$1,400,000
7	Less Reserve for Depreciation	700,000
		$ 700,000

The property, plant, and equipment are the assets from which the company obtains its main source of income. Sometimes companies own valuable patents or copyrights which yield a substantial income in the form of royalties.

It is difficult to evaluate fixed assets. Almost all companies carry their plant and equipment *at cost*. This means the amount of money the plant and equipment cost the company either to build or to buy. But the cost figure may be meaningless if the plants were built when prices were much lower. Every year, a prudent management customarily writes off, by a charge against income, a part of the cost of the plant, buildings, and equipment. This charge to income is called depreciation. Depreciation as well as depletion and amortization will be discussed in Chapter 3. At all events, the sum on page 18 of all these annual charges to depreciation for the Lobuck Corporation is $700,000. As shown above, this reserve for depreciation is carried as a deduction from a fixed asset. Thus, the net property, building, and equipment is figured by deducting the accumulated reserves for, or provision for, depreciation from the cost of the fixed assets. The actual value of the fixed asset might be much more or less than the net amount.

Other assets usually include investments in subsidiaries, and intangible assets such as trademarks and patents. In the balance sheet of the Lobuck Corporation, on page 18, the following are the other assets.

---

[1]For more complete explanation of LIFO and FIFO, see John H. Prime, *Investment Analysis, 4th Edition* (Englewood Cliffs, N.J.: Prentice-Hall, Inc., 1967), pp. 356–57.

Item		
8	Investments in Subsidiaries	$174,000
9	Patents, Trademarks, and Goodwill	20,000

Investments in subsidiaries (item 8) usually include investments in operations which complement those of the parent company. For example, the General Motors Corporation owns a subsidiary called the General Motors Acceptance Corporation. This subsidiary handles the financing of automobiles and other products of the parent.

Also, many companies, such as the Ford Motor Company and the International Harvester Company, have large investments in subsidiary companies operating in foreign countries.

Intangible assets include patents, trademarks, brand names, and goodwill. They are usually not a large item. Many companies carry them on the balance sheet at $1. A *patent* (item 9) is an exclusive right given by the United States Government to a device or a process. The life of a patent is seventeen years. For example, Sanford L. Cluett some years ago invented a process for preshrinking linen before it was tailored. This patent had considerable value to Cluett, Peabody & Co., Inc.

A *trademark* (item 9) is a picture, drawing, or design used by a manufacturer to distinguish his goods. A trademark does not have a legal life and can be used by a company as long as it is in business. A well known trademark is the flying red horse of the Mobil Oil Co., Inc.

A *brand name* is simply a special name given by a company to one of its products in order to make it better known. Thus the American Tobacco Company hopes that the public will ask for a "Lucky Strike" cigarette.

Goodwill (item 9) often appears on the balance sheet of a company which has bought another company at a price in excess of its book or net asset value.

Sundry deferred charges (not shown) are sometimes called prepaid expenses. Examples are fire insurance premiums or rent paid in advance.

Liabilities

Liabilities are the amounts owed by a business and include *current liabilities* and *long-term liabilities*. Although stockholders' equity is carried on the liability side of the balance sheet, it is not strictly a liability which must be paid. The stockholders receive their equity only if the company is liquidated and after all creditors are paid.

Current liabilities are called "current" because they are debts which usually must be paid by the corporation within one year. They include accounts payable, notes payable, taxes payable, wages payable, and long-term debt due within one year. In the Lobuck Corporation, on page 18, the following are the current liabilities:

Item		
11	Accounts payable	$200,000
12	Notes payable	150,000
13	Accrued taxes	250,000
14	Accrued salaries and wages	25,000
15	Other current liabilities	75,000
16	Total current liabilities	$700,000

Accounts payable (item 11) are the amounts owed for goods received or for services rendered. They are usually paid promptly.

Notes payable (item 12) are often necessary where a company must borrow from a bank to purchase inventories or supplies, or to pay wages over a seasonal peak. When the finished products are sold, the bank loans are paid. Almost all bank loans are of short-term nature. That is, they are due within one year. Sometimes a company will buy supplies and equipment and give notes to the manufacturers.

Accrued taxes, or *reserve for accrued taxes* (item 13), are one of the most important of the current liabilities. Corporations, like most individuals, must pay income taxes to the United States Government. For most large corporations, this amounts to about half of their income after expenses. The companies calculate the taxes which will be due based on estimated earnings. In addition, most companies owe money for state taxes and local real estate taxes. Clearly, all of these are liabilities which must be paid within a year. Also, payroll taxes, frequently substantial, are carried as a current liability.

Accrued salaries and wages (item 14) are, as the name indicates, the amount of money due the employees of the company. Most of the employees are paid on a weekly or semi-monthly basis. Thus the accumulated wages are usually not large.

Other current liabilities (item 15) would include interest accrued on bonds, dividends *declared* but not paid, and installments on long-term debt due within one year. Accrued interest and dividends declared are usually not large amounts, but debt installment can be an important item. Often industrial companies issue bonds and agree to pay off a substantial part of these bonds every year.

For example, on December 31, 1964, the Union Carbide Corporation had outstanding $495,410,000 of long-term debt of various maturities and interest rates. But a substantial part of this debt was due serially—that is, a part was to be paid off each year. At the end of 1964, the current debt installments were $18,667,000, which sum was carried as a current liability.

As we have shown above, current liabilities are debts that the corporation must pay within a year. *Long-term liabilities,* or funded debt, are debts that are not due until after a year's time. They usually include all types of bonds: mortgage, debenture, and refunding bonds, as well as equipment trust certificates and serial bank loans. They do *not* include reserve for depreciation, or common or preferred stocks. A more complete discussion of these bonds is given in Chapter 4. Essentially, a bond is a written promise of the corporation to pay a fixed sum in the future, usually over five years, plus interest. In the Lobuck Corporation, on page 18, we show the following:

Item		
17	First Mortgage Bonds 4% due June 1, 1981	$400,000

This means that the Lobuck Corporation on June 1, 1981 must pay $400,000. In the meantime, it must pay interest at the rate of 4 per cent a year or $16,000 (4% $\times$ $400,000). Bonded debt is also called funded debt. Bonds are sold by corporations in order to buy land, build plants, purchase equipment, and so forth.

We also class *term loans* of commercial banks and insurance companies as long-term liabilities. Here the company may borrow from banks or insurance companies to buy fixed assets, to add to current assets, to retire debt, and so forth, but the company agrees to pay the term loan in installments over a period of from three to five years.

Stockholders Equity or Net Worth

Stockholders equity usually consists of capital stock and retained earnings or surplus.

The *capital stock* is the preferred and common stock originally subscribed by the stockholders. When a corporation is formed, a stated number of common shares is authorized, and sometimes preferred shares are authorized. A part or all of these authorized shares may be issued and sold. The authorized but unissued shares are not part of the capitalization but are held in reserve for a future time. Common and preferred shares usually have a par or stated value.

In the balance sheet of the Lobuck Corporation, page 18, we have set forth the following:

Item		
18	Preferred Stock (3,600 shares—5%—$100 par)	$360,000
19	Common Stock (100,000 shares—$4 par)	400,000
20	Retained Earnings (or Earned Surplus)	434,000
21	Capital Surplus	100,000

The *preferred stock* (item 18) on the balance sheet has a par value of $100 which is the usual par value for preferred stocks. The number of shares outstanding can be obtained by dividing the par value into the dollar amount outstanding. Since our balance sheets show $360,000 of preferred stock outstanding, the number of shares would be $360,-000/100 or 3,600 shares. Par value of $100 does not mean that the stock is worth $100. Also, the company is in no way obligated to pay $100 a share on the preferred.

The *common stock* (item 19), like the preferred, is usually carried at a *par value* or a *stated value*. As in the case of the preferred stock, the number of shares may be obtained by dividing the dollar amount of the common stock by the par or *stated value*. This would be $400,000 divided by $4.00 par value or 100,000 shares. As will be explained in detail in Chapter 7, the par value has no relation to the market or intrinsic value of the stock. Par value is simply an arbitrarily assigned figure.

However, there is a distinction between par value and stated value. *Par value* is the arbitrarily assigned amount at which the stock is carried on the financial statement. It is sometimes called face value. It it also the amount which the company must receive for each share of stock issued. Most state laws provide that this par value—$1, $5, $10, or $100— has to be fully paid when the original or new stock is sold, in order for the company to have fully paid and nonassessable stocks. High par values make it difficult for companies to sell new stock, particularly if business has declined and the market value is below the par value.

Hence, *no-par* laws have been passed in a number of states. These laws permit corporations to issue no-par stocks without face value, but they require that such stock have a *stated* or *assigned* value, usually at least $1. Under no-par law, assigned value has to be paid into the corporation, and any excess can be called surplus.

Retained earnings or *earned surplus* (item 20) is the accumulation of earnings over the years that has not been paid out to the stockholders in dividends. These earnings have been "plowed back" into the company. That is, the officers of the company might have used these excess earnings to buy more inventory, to add to plant, to buy more equipment, and so forth. For this reason, the investor should not take the term retained earnings too literally. These retained earnings are not held in cash which could be paid out to the stockholder. In almost all cases, the retained earnings are invested, wisely or unwisely, in the business. Sometimes a company may have a large retained earnings account, but due to poor earnings or a weak financial condition can pay only small dividends to the stockholder. An example of this situation is the case of the New York Central Railroad Company. This railroad reported *surplus* (retained earnings) of $369,943,000 at the end of 1964 but could pay only a small dividend. The New York Central Railroad Company uses the term surplus instead of retained earnings. This is the older form and is still followed by some companies. The American Institute of Certified Public Accountants prefers the term *retained earn-*

ings. Sometimes companies use the terms reinvested earnings, earnings employed in the business, or earnings retained.

Capital or *paid-in surplus* (item 21) occurs where the stockholders pay to the company for stock at the time of issuance an amount in excess of par or stated value of the stock. This excess amount is carried as capital surplus on the liability side of the balance sheet but is invested in the business just as earned surplus is. For example, the Lobuck Corporation might start with 100,000 shares of $4 par value or $400,000. The subscription price to the stock might be $5, or a total of $500,000 (100,000 shares times $5). This would mean that $400,000 would be carried as the capital and $100,000 as capital or paid-in surplus. Sometimes managements wish to start their companies with an extra amount of surplus. This gives the company a chance to get started and to absorb initial losses without invading the capital stock account. Normally, operating losses are not charged to capital surplus or paid-in surplus, but rather to earned surplus. It will help the investor to keep in mind that *retained earnings* is a balancing item between all of the assets on the one hand and the liabilities plus stocks (common and preferred) on the other. It is not a store of available funds.

The *capital structure,* or the *capitalization* as it is sometimes called, is the total amount of funds invested in or at work in the business. The buyers of the bonds when they were first sold supplied funds to the corporation. The subscribers to the common and preferred stocks also supplied funds to the corporation. But only those initial subscribers to the bonds and stocks supplied capital. To buy a bond or stock in the market adds nothing to the funds of the company after it has been sold initially. In short, the capitalization or the capital structure of a corporation is the stocks (common and perhaps preferred), the bonds, the retained earnings (or earned surplus), and the capital surplus. The authorized but unissued stock is *not* part of the capitalization. The capitalization of the Lobuck Corporation shown on page 18 is the funded debt, the preferred and common stock, and the surplus, as follows:

Item		
17	First Mortgage Bonds—4% due June 1981	$ 400,000
18	Preferred Stock—3,600 shares—5% 100 par	360,000
19	Common Stock—100,000 shares—$4 par	400,000
20	Retained Earnings (or Earned Surplus)	434,000
21	Capital Surplus	100,000
	Total capitalization	$1,694,000

Sometimes a corporation will set up *reserves* for contingencies. This entails segregating funds from the surplus account for possible loss, possible plant addition, and so forth. While this sum is not an actual liability, as is a *reserve* for federal income taxes, it earmarks the surplus in a sense and prevents its being paid out in dividends.

The *book value*, net asset value or net worth of a common stock is the theoretical amount per share which a stockholder could receive if the corporation went out of existence by distributing all of its assets less debts to the stockholders. In other words, it is the liquidating value.

We figure that the theoretical book or liquidating value of the Lobuck Corporation equals $9.34 a share as follows:

Item		
19	Common Stock (100,000 shares @ $4 par)	$400,000
20	Retained Earnings (Earned Surplus)	434,000
21	Capital Surplus	100,000
	Total equity for the Common Stock	$934,000

Per share of Common equals $934,000 divided by 100,000 shares of Common equals $9.34

It should be stressed that this is the *theoretical* book value. Book value as such is not an accurate figure because of the difficulty in determining the intrinsic worth of many assets. Further, in almost all cases the book value of a stock bears *no* relation to its *market* value. For example, at the end of 1964, E. I. du Pont de Nemours & Company had a book value of $39.66 a share compared with a year-end 1965 market value of $237 a share. But the New York Central Railroad Company on the same date had a book value of $195.77 a share compared with a year end 1965 market value of $80 a share.

Liquidating value means the amount a stockholder could realize if the company were liquidated—that is, the assets sold and the debts paid. This amount could be more or less than the so-called book value. It is largely a theoretical concept, because a company is almost never liquidated unless it is in difficulties. In this event, the amount realized in liquidation is almost always substantially less than the net worth or book value as shown on the balance sheet.

Treasury stock is not shown in the above illustration but is important and will be discussed on page 80.

Analysis of the Balance Sheet

Perhaps the easiest way to analyze a balance sheet is by the use of balance sheet ratios. A balance sheet ratio is the relationship of one part of the balance sheet to another.

The *current ratio* is the relationship of current assets to current liabilities—it is the current assets divided by the current liabilities. In our balance sheet on p. 18, total current assets (item 5) are $1,500,000 and current liabilities (item 16) are $700,000. Thus the current ratio is $1,500,000 divided by $700,000, or 2.14. Usually we like to see a current ratio of 2.00 or more, depending on the type of business. In the case of a public utility or a railroad, a current ratio is not particularly important. Also we should always look at the proportion of current assets. For example, if inventories have been increasing over the years, it may mean that a large part of the current assets are in unliquid inventories. This would mean that company might not be able to meet its current liabilities as they mature. In a similar manner, accounts or notes receivable might increase sharply and become unliquid.

Cash items to current liabilities is a useful comparison. It shows how much cash and government securities the company has available to meet its current debts. In our balance sheet below, cash (item 1) of $400,000 plus U.S. Government securities (item 2) of $200,000 equals $600,000. We should compare this with current liabilities (item 16) of $700,000. Thus, cash items of $600,000 divided by current liabilities of $700,000 gives a ratio of 0.86. Usually a satisfactory cash items ratio is between 0.50 and 0.75.

THE LOBUCK CORPORATION

Balance Sheet

Assets		December 31, 1966
1	Cash	$ 400,000
2	United States Government Securities	200,000
3	Accounts Receivable	500,000
4	Inventories	400,000
5	Total Current Assets	$1,500,000
6	Property, Plant and Equipment	1,400,000
7	Less Reserve for Depreciation	700,000
		$ 700,000
8	Investments in Subsidiaries	174,000
9	Patents, Trademarks, and Goodwill	20,000
10	Total Assets	$2,394,000

Liabilities		
11	Accounts Payable	$ 200,000
12	Notes Payable	150,000
13	Accrued Taxes	250,000
14	Accrued Salaries and Wages	25,000
15	Other Current Liabilities	75,000
16	Total Current Liabilities	$ 700,000
17	First Mortgage Bonds—4%—due June 1, 1981	400,000
18	Preferred Stock (3,600 shares—5% $100 par)	360,000
19	Common Stock (100,000 shares—$4 par)	400,000
20	Retained Earnings or Earned Surplus	434,000
21	Capital Surplus	100,000
22	Total Liabilities	$2,394,000

Working capital or *net working capital* is simply the excess of *current* assets over *current* liabilities. On our balance sheet on page 18 it would be current assets (item 5) of $1,500,000 less current liabilities (item 16) of $700,000, or $800,000. Large working capital, or net current assets as it is sometimes called, means that the company has free liquid funds. These funds can be used to acquire new assets to improve credit standing by making prompt payments to creditors or by paying funded debt.

The *debt working capital ratio* is the relationship between the net working capital and the debt. In this case, working capital of $800,000 divided by debt of $400,000 (item 17), or 2.00. This is a very satisfactory ratio. Customarily, in an industrial concern we like to see at least a ratio of 1.00. This means that working capital is equal to debt. This should not be considered a hard and fast rule. Companies in the aluminum and aviation fields have a low ratio of working capital to debt. These companies are expanding through sales and earnings at a rapid rate and can support large debt. Nevertheless, a low working capital to debt ratio should be investigated.

The *acid test* of a balance sheet is the ratio of current assets *less* inventory or quick assets to current liabilities. In our balance sheet, it would be current assets of $1,500,000 less inventory of $400,000 equals $1,100,000 divided by current liabilities of $700,000 or 1.57. Usually a satisfactory acid test ratio is about 1.00. This is called the acid test because inventory is the current asset which fluctuates the most. Inventory can be old and very unliquid. Therefore, to exclude it from current assets leaves cash, United States Government securities, which clearly are liquid, and accounts receivable, which *usually* are liquid. These can be tested by the income account, as will be shown in Chapter 3.

The *percentage of debt to the total capitalization* is another measure to determine the strength of the company. Usually, in an industrial concern, we like to see debt amounting to no more than 33 per cent of the total capitalization, in electric public utilities 55 per cent, in natural gas companies 65 per cent, and in railroads 40 per cent. If a large part of the capitalization is debt it means that the bondholders are putting up most of the funds for the business.

The debt percentage in the case of the Lobuck Corporation may be calculated by referring to page 16, which shows total capitalization of $1,694,000. The debt-capitalization percentage is figured by dividing the debt of $400,000 by the capitalization of $1,694,000, giving 23.6 per cent.

Mergers, Consolidations, Recapitalization, Receivership, Watered Stock

These bring about drastic changes in the capitalization of a corporation.

A *merger* is the acquisition of one company by another company, sometimes by outright purchase or exchange of stock. For example, the Marine Midland Trust Company of New York merged with the Grace National Bank. The Marine Trust was the surviving corporation under the name of Marine Midland Grace Trust Company.

A *consolidation* is the turning over of assets by the companies involved to a *new* concern, usually with a new name. The old companies are usually liquidated.

A *recapitalization* is a readjustment of capitalization by approval of the stockholders. For example, the United States Steel Corporation in 1966 offered holders of each non-callable 7% preferred, $175 a share in 4⅝% bonds of 1996. This should not be confused with *refinancing*. Refinancing is the term customarily used when a company pays off an outstanding debt by selling new obligation. For example, a company might refinance its short-term bank debt by selling long-term bonds. That is, long-term bonds would be sold and the proceeds used to pay off the bank's debt.

A *receivership* occurs when a company gets into serious financial trouble. The court appoints a receiver who attempts to liquidate the company and pay off the creditors. More often, however, the court will appoint a trustee who will attempt to keep the company going by working out an arrangement with the creditors under Chapter X and XI of the Bankruptcy Act of 1938. Financial difficulties are often caused by excessive debt in the capital structure.

Watered stock is an old term going back to the days when farmers drove their cattle to market. First the unscrupulous farmer would feed the livestock salt, then let them drink from a river. As a result, the cattle weighed more when sold, but the added weight was only water. Today the term means that the stock a company is issuing and selling cannot be backed by assets or earnings. Sometimes a company will sell stock as fully paid but only receive part of its par value. For example, a company might issue $10 par stock, of which only $5 would be paid in. Such stock can be called watered.

REVIEW QUESTIONS

1. Distinguish between current assets and current liabilities. Mention four possible current assets and four current liabilities.

2. Explain the difference between FIFO and LIFO in determining the cost of inventories. In a period of rising prices, which is the more conservative? Explain.

3. Distinguish between a patent, a trademark, and a brand name. What is the general term for these assets?

4. What are the most important fixed assets? How are they carried on the balance sheet of a corporation?

5. Distinguish between par value, no par value, and stated or assigned value of common stock.

6. Explain the calculation of the following, giving in each case the desired ratio:

    a. current ratio
    b. cash items ratio
    c. debt/working capital ratio
    d. acid test or quick ratio

7. What is the difference between a merger, and a consolidation, a recapitalization, and a receivership?

8. Describe in detail the components of stockholders' equity. How is the book value of common stock calculated? What is the relation of book value to market value? Illustrate.

The Income Statement

Chapter 3

As we have seen in the preceding chapter, the balance sheet shows the financial strength and the general condition of the company on a stated date. The statement of income and expenses, frequently referred to as a *profit and loss* statement, shows where the money comes from, how it was spent, and what remains for the owners or stockholders for the period of a *fiscal* year. The *fiscal* year may be the same as the calendar year, ending December 31. Sometimes the fiscal year is based on the normal business year for the industry. For example, the *fiscal* year for the retail trade industry ends on January 31 and for the United States Government on June 30.

Every income and expense statement, no matter how complicated, may be divided into three parts: revenues, costs, and net earnings. If the reader will examine the income and expense statement of the Lobuck Corporation on page 28, he will see these main parts, as follows:

Item		
1	Revenues	$5,000,000
2, 3, 4, 5, 6	Costs	4,458,000
7	Net Earnings	542,000

It is easy to see that the company has earned $542,000 on sales of $5,000,000, or 11 per cent. This appears to be a good profit margin, but it should be compared with the profits of other companies in the same field and with previous years' profits of the same firm. In this way we can see if the affairs of the company are improving or getting worse. While past earnings are not an infallible guide to future earnings, the buyer of a security of a company with improving past earnings feels more confident than if the earnings were declining or remaining steady.

A more detailed discussion of the items of the income statement of the Lobuck Corporation might be helpful.

Item		
1	Net Sales	$5,000,000

Net sales (item 1) is the amount of money which the company has collected by cash sales or expects to collect by credit sales. The term net sales means the net amount collected or due after allowance for discounts and for returned goods. On rare occasions a company will report both gross and net sales. But the difference between gross and net sales is usually small. A few industrial concerns, such as the oil companies, as well as all railroad and public utility companies, use the term *operating revenues* instead of sales.

Item		
2	Cost of Goods Sold	$3,430,000
3	Selling and Administrative Expenses	300,000

Cost of goods sold (item 2) includes wages, cost of materials, and maintenance of plant and equipment. These are called the basic costs of operating the business. Clearly, labor must be paid, materials must be bought, and equipment must be maintained. If the cost of goods sold increases faster than the sales, it is possible that the management is not alert to rising costs. Perhaps the company should increase the price of the product or control expenses.

Sometimes a company will list separately its cost of materials and supplies, its salaries and wages, its maintenance, and even its research. But the usual practice is to lump them in one item: cost of goods sold or cost of sales.

Selling and administrative expenses (item 3) include all the expenses of selling the goods and services. Some of the more important items are the training of salesmen and the salaries or commissions of salesmen. A well-trained and alert sales force can be an important growth factor. One of the reasons for the success of the International Business Machines Corporation is its highly trained and active sales force. Another important selling expense is advertising.

Item		
4	Depreciation	$200,000

Depreciation (item 4) is the means by which the cost of plant, buildings, and equipment is recovered. Let us assume a manufacturer has bought a piece of equipment worth $15,000. He expects that this equipment will last for five years. Therefore he must recover the cost of this

machinery over its life. He sets aside an equal amount each year in the
form of a depreciation reserve, or $3,000 each year; this is the so-called
straight-line method of depreciation. The reserve is used to reduce
the cost of the fixed asset (see Lobuck Corporation, item 7, page 18.)
Depreciation is sometimes called a noncash charge. The manufacturer
has the use of this money in his business. Depreciation should not be
confused with earnings; the money is simply set aside to recover the
cost of the fixed asset over the years. But almost never are these funds
kept in cash, nor are they available to the stockholder. They are, to
repeat, used in the business. This would include the purchase of new
equipment and plant construction. Depreciation is treated as an expense
of operating a business. It is thus a deduction before federal and state
income taxes.

There are other ways of calculating depreciation but perhaps the
best known is the *sum of the years digits* or SYD. The following table
compares the depreciating of an asset costing $15,000 with a five-year
life using the straight line SL method and the sum of the years digits.

Year	S L	S Y D
1	$ 3,000	$ 5,000
2	3,000	4,000
3	3,000	3,000
4	3,000	2,000
5	3,000	1,000
15	$15,000	$15,000

To find the sum of the years digits simply add the years: $5 + 4 + 3 + 2
+ 1$ equals 15. Then divide $15,000 by 15 or $1,000. Then start with
the *largest* digit or $5 \times \$1,000 = \$5,000$, then $4 \times \$1,000 = \$4,000$, then
$3 \times \$1,000 = \$3,000$ etc., etc.

It will be noted that in the earlier years the changes under the SYD
are much larger but in the later years lower.

Depletion is a term—and a tax allowance—generally used by natural
resources companies whose assets are constantly being exhausted or
depleted. Under the federal tax laws, these companies can make charges
against income to allow for their wasting of these assets. For example,
the petroleum-producing companies can charge for depletion $27\frac{1}{2}$ per
cent a year of the value of their productions. To a lesser extent, the
copper, sulfur, clay, asbestos, and brick companies can make charges
of depletion.

Amortization means to set aside money regularly to retire debt or
write off an asset. The most frequent use is to retire or amortize debt
through sinking fund payments. That is, regular payments, usually
semi-annual, are made by the company to a trustee who retires the
bonds either by purchase in the market or by drawing by lot according

to the numbers on the bonds. Assets usually retired by amortization include intangible assets (see page 12).

Obsolescence is the process of an asset's becoming out of date or obsolete. It might be losing its value due to technological changes. For example, a new type of machine to make rubber tires might lead to the obsolescence of the old machines.

Item		
5	Interest	$40,000

Interest (item 5) includes the interest paid by a company on its bonds, on its long-term payable notes, and on its bank loans. In railroads, the term *fixed charges* is used and includes not only interest on the railroad's own debt but interest on guaranteed bonds, dividends on guaranteed stocks, and rentals for leased lines and properties. In an industrial company, interest charges are usually not an important item. But if interest charges are large compared with the operating income, the company may be operating on a thin margin. This means it is vulnerable to a decline in general business activity. As we will explain in Chapter 4, the operating profit should be several times the interest or fixed charges. Interest charges of public utility companies are a large item in the income statement. But the revenues of these companies, due to their nature, are more stable than most industrial concerns. Interest or fixed charges is an expense of operating a business, and therefore is a deduction before taxes.

Item		
6	Taxes (Federal Income)	$488,000

Taxes (item 6) generally include income taxes paid to the United States Government. In addition, companies pay substantial real estate taxes to the city or town, as well as the state, where the properties are located.

In the Lobuck Corporation the federal income taxes are calculated as follows:

Item		
(B)	Operating Profit	$1,070,000
5	Less interest on Bonds	40,000
	Taxable Income	$1,030,000
	Federal Income Taxes	$ 488,000

Federal income taxes in 1965 on corporations were divided into (a) normal taxes of 22 per cent on all taxable income, and (b) surtaxes of 26 per cent on all taxable income in excess of $25,000. On most large corporations, the rate is about 48 per cent of the taxable income. The above federal income taxes of the Lobuck Corporation are calculated as follows:

Normal tax equals 22% of all taxable income (22% × $1,030,000)	$227,000
Surtax equals 26% of all taxable income in excess of $25,000 or	261,000
(26% × $1,005,000) equals (result rounded)	$488,000

There are times when corporations pay less than 48 per cent (the sum of the normal and the surtax) of their taxable income. This happens where corporations have tax losses from previous years which are carried forward and used to reduce current taxes. Also, a corporation might have holdings of municipal securities. As will be explained in Chapter 4, the interest on these securities is exempt from federal income taxes.

Other income sometimes appears on the income statement of companies. It includes income from securities, from real estate not used for operations, and from investments in subsidiary and affiliated companies. In most cases, other income of industrial companies is not large.

Item		
7	Net Income	$542,000

Net income is the most interesting item on the income statement. It is the amount which results from the deduction from the net sales of all the expenses. It is also *in theory* the amount which is available to the stockholders. We say in theory because the stockholder rarely receives *all* of the net income. The amount the stockholder receives in dividends depends on the board of directors. In the five years ended in 1965, 177 industrial corporations in the United States paid out an average of 52.4 per cent of their net income in dividends.

From net income, however, the analyst can determine the amount earned per share of *preferred*, if there is preferred stock outstanding. After deducting the preferred dividends from the net income, the analyst can also calculate the earnings per share of common stock.

From the income statement of the Lobuck Corporation, on page 28, the net income per share on the *preferred* stock is calculated as follows:

Item		
7	Net Income	$542,000.00
11	Per Share Preferred Stock	
	($542,000 divided by 3,600 shares	
	equals per share)	$150.56

Since the Lobuck Corporation had net income of $542,000, the earnings per share of preferred are figured by dividing the number of shares of preferred into the net income. Although the Lobuck Corporation earned $150.56 per share of the preferred, this does not mean that each share of preferred is entitled to $150.56. The maximum amount the preferred stockholders of Lobuck Corporation could receive each year is $5 a share (5% × $100 par equals $5). As will be shown in Chapter 5, the per-share earnings are merely one indication of protection or coverage of the preferred dividend. The maximum dividend paid depends on the stated rate, which in this case is $5.

The earnings per share of common are obtained by dividing the number of shares of common into the net income, *after deducting the preferred* dividend as follows:

Item		
7	Net Income	$542,000
Less		
8	Preferred Dividend (3,600 shares of preferred	
	× $5.00) =	18,000
	Balance for Common	$524,000
Item		
12	Per Share Common $524,000 divided by	
	100,000 shares =	$5.24

Thus, the per-share earnings of the common of the Lobuck Corporation are $5.24.

The dividend paid on the common amounted to $3 a share, or 57 per cent of the net income per share of $5.24. This is usually called the *dividend payout* ratio or sometimes simply the payout ratio. The *dividend payout* ratio, therefore, is simply the percentage of the common earnings paid out in common dividends. Some companies, such as the automobile companies, pay a large percentage of their earnings in dividends. Others, such as the drug companies, pay out a much smaller percentage. In 1965, 177 leading companies had a payout ratio of 52.4 per cent.

Finally, we have the *retained earnings* of $224,000. This is the net income which the company does not pay out to the stockholders. It is retained in the company and added to the surplus or retained earnings account in the balance sheet. It might be used to buy more inventory, to buy equipment, or to expand plant. In the Lobuck Corporation, on page 28, the retained earnings are figured as follows:

Item		
7	Net Income	$542,000
Less		
8	Dividends on Preferred Stock	18,000
9	Dividends on Common Stock	300,000
		$318,000
Item		
10	Addition to Retained Earnings this year	$224,000

LOBUCK CORPORATION

		Item	1965
Revenues			
$5,000,000	1	Net Sales	$5,000,000.00
	2	Cost of Goods Sold	3,430,000.00
	3	Selling and Administrative Expenses	300,000.00
	4	Depreciation	200,000.00
Costs	–	(A) Operating Expenses	3,930,000.00
$4,458,000	–	(B) Operating Profit	1,070,000.00
	5	Interest on Bonds	40,000.00
Net Earnings	6	Taxes (Federal Income)	488,000.00
$542,000			
	7	Net Income	542,000.00
	8	Dividends on Preferred Stock	18,000.00
	9	Dividends on Common Stock	300,000.00
	10	Retained Earnings	224,000.00
	11	Earned per Share (Preferred)	150.56
	12	Earned per Share (Common)	5.24
	13	Dividend per Share Preferred	5.00
	14	Dividend per Share Common	3.00
	15	Number of Shares of Preferred	3,600.00
	16	Number of Shares of Common	100,000.00

Analysis of the Statement of Income and Expenses

The analyst can make a number of comparisons between the items in the income statement. Comparisons with previous years' statements are particularly helpful. They enable the analyst to see the progress or deterioration of the company. Some of the parts of the income statement which he should examine and compare not only with previous years but also with other companies include: net sales, operating profit, and net income.

Net sales growth is very significant. A steady year-to-year increase in sales is usually a good sign. Also, a consistent decline in sales is almost always a bad sign. A company must sell its goods and services to make profits. The growth of sales can be measured and compared in several ways.

One of the easiest ways is to take a simple base year, for example, 1958. This year should be compared with the net sales of a more recent year, such as 1965, in order to determine the percentage increase. For example, the net sales of the United States Steel Corporation in 1958 (a poor steel year) were $3,438,000,000. In 1965, sales were $4,400,000,000. This is a gain of $962,000,000 or 27.9 per cent. ($962,000,000 divided by $3,438,000,000 equals 27.9 per cent.)

Inland Steel Company in the same period gained 47.5 per cent, Republic Steel Company 50.8 per cent and seven leading steel companies gained 42.8 per cent.

But sales comparison between one year and another in the past can be misleading, particularly if the past year is an abnormal one. A better comparison would be to take the sales of an average of several years, say 1957, 1958, and 1959, and show the percentage increase of sales of a recent year over the average sales. For example, the average sales of the United States Steel Corporation in the years 1957, 1958, and 1959 were $3,804,000,000. The sales in 1965 were $4,400,000,000, a gain over the 1957–59 period of 15.6 per cent. The comparable gain for the Inland Steel Company was 37.5 per cent and for the Republic Steel Company, 28.4 per cent. Thus, Inland Steel showed a sharp gain from a bad steel year (1958 to 1965) but also the best gain from the average period. This indicates that Inland is maintaining its improving trend in the industry.

The comparison of *capital expenditures* to sales growth is helpful to the analyst in determining the effectiveness of capital expenditures. If a company spends a large amount of money over a period of years on new equipment to plants, the sales should increase in rough proportion to the expenditures. A rule of thumb might be that for every $2 of capital expenditures, sales should increase $1 over the period. For instance, a company that makes capital expenditures of $20,000,000 in a given period should show an increase in sales of about $10,000,000. This is particularly true of the chemical industry. For example, E. I. du Pont de Nemours & Company between 1961 and 1964 spent $1,109,000,000. During the same period sales increased $564,000,000. Thus for every $1.93 of capital expenditures, Du Pont realized a gain of $1 in sales (capital expenditures over the period of $1,109,000,000 divided by gain in sales of $564,-000,000 equals $1.93). Allied Chemical Corporation spent $2.44 for every dollar gain in sales and Union Carbide Corporation was the most efficient, spending only $1.50. *Net Sales* are also used to measure the turnover of inventory and the age of accounts receivable.

The *turnover of inventory* is often measured by taking net sales divided by inventory. In the Lobuck Corporation, net sales of $5,000,000 divided by inventory of $400,000 (see pages 18–28) would be 12.5 times. Any slowing up of this turnover would indicate that inventory is accumulating faster than sales. Also, it might indicate that some of the inventory is getting old and less marketable.

The *age of accounts receivable* is measured somewhat in the same way. Net sales are divided by the accounts receivable and then translated into number of days. For example, net sales of $5,000,000 are divided by accounts receivable of $500,000 (see pages 18–28, or 10 times.) This in turn is divided *into* 365 days, giving 36.5 days as the age of the accounts receivable. An increase in the number of days of accounts receivable indicates that the accounts receivable are becoming less liquid and collections are slowing up.

Operating profit is an important item in the income statement. It shows the amount of money which the company has made on its sales before taxes and interest. In the Lobuck Corporation on page 28 it is figured as follows:

Item		
1	Net Sales	$5,000,000
Less		
2	Cost of Goods Sold	$3,430,000
3	Selling and Administrative Expenses	300,000
4	Depreciation	200,000
Item		
A	Total Operating Expenses	$3,930,000
B	Operating Profit	$1,070,000

Here we deduct from the sales of $5,000,000 the operating expenses of $3,930,000 to obtain the operating profit of $1,070,000. Sometimes the sales of a company will increase, but at the same time the operating expenses will increase at a faster rate. As a result, the operating profit may remain the same or in some cases decline. This may mean that the company is taking on more business but is cutting prices. Also it may mean that the expense of obtaining the orders or producing the goods has increased.

But when sales expand it is encouraging to see the operating profit expand at a faster rate. This reflects maintenance of selling prices and control of expenses in the face of expanding volume.

Sometimes a company will be so inefficiently operated that it will report an operating deficit. In other words, it cannot earn enough to pay its out-of-pocket operating expenses. This might be a temporary situation due to prolonged strikes such as have taken place in the airlines or in the newspaper field. On the other hand, the analyst should avoid a company which, for no explained reason other than inefficiency or inherent weakness, reports deficits.

The *operating margin* is the relationship between the operating income and the net sales. It shows, in effect, the percent of net sales that are brought down to operating income. On the basis of the above figures, the operating margin may be obtained by dividing the operating profit of $1,070,000 by the net sales of $5,000,000, giving 21.4 per cent. Thus, on every dollar of sales the company has an operating profit of 21.4 cents. Again we stress that trends are important. An improving operating margin is obviously to be favored over a declining margin. Also, comparisons might be made with similar companies *in the same industry*. In this way, the analyst can obtain an appraisal of relative efficiency.

Perhaps a better way to measure the operating efficiency of a company is to determine the operating profit *before* depreciation, federal income taxes, and interest. This may be done by subtracting from net sales *only* the cost of goods sold and the selling and administrative expenses. The net amount then can be divided by the net sales to show the percentage earned on sales. Referring to the Lobuck Corporation, on page 28, the percentage earned on sales *before* depreciation, federal income taxes, and interest would be figured as follows:

Item		
1	Net Sales	$5,000,000
Less		
2	Cost of Goods Sold	$3,430,000
3	Selling and Administrative Expenses	300,000
		$3,730,000
	Operating profit before depreciation, Federal income taxes and interest	$1,270,000

Percentage earned on sales ($1,270,000 divided by $5,000,000) equals 25.4%.

This method enables the analyst to compare more accurately the relative operating efficiencies of companies before special charges. For example, one company might arbitrarily make higher depreciation charges than another. Thus, all things being equal, the company making higher depreciation charges might show a lower profit margin after depreciation than a company which was not so conservative and is writing off the cost of its assets over a longer period.

Net income is perhaps the most important item on the income statement. A study of the growth of net income in capsule form gives the progress of the company. Further, it is a reasonable means of forecasting its future. If a company is showing a good trend in net income over the years, it is reasonable to assume that it has good management, that its capital expenditures have been wise, and that its expenses are controlled.

We can measure net income growth by comparing a recent year with a past year or an average of three years in the past in the same way we measured sales on pages 28–9. For example, in 1965, E. I. du Pont de Nemours & Company earned $8.63 a share compared with $4.71 in 1958 (excluding income from General Motors Corporation), a gain of 83.2 per cent. The gain of the 1965 earnings over the average for the years 1957, 1958, and 1959 was 52.2 per cent. The following shows the comparison of the net income per share of three chemical companies in 1965 and in the 1957–1959 period.

	Earned per Share			% Gain 1965	
	1965	1958	1957–9	over 1958	over 1957–9
Allied Chemical Corporation	$3.14	$1.64	$2.05	91.3	53.2
E. I. du Pont de Nemours	8.63	4.71	5.67	83.2	52.2
Union Carbide Corporation	3.76	2.08	2.39	80.8	57.3

An examination of the table shows that all three companies have exhibited improvement in earnings over the 1958 year. But Allied seems to show the largest gain. Comparing the 1965 earnings with the base years of 1957–59, Allied's performance is not quite as good as Union Carbide's. However taking both periods into consideration, Allied seems to outperform the better-known chemical companies. Further, it will be shown on page 95 that Allied is selling at a lower price/earnings ratio (cheaper price) than either Du Pont or Union Carbide.

The *percentage earned on sales* is another useful means of comparison. In the case of the Lobuck Corporation (page 28), it is calculated by dividing the net income of $542,000 by the sales of $5,000,000 to equal 10.8%. It should be stressed that comparisons should be made with the percentage earned on sales in previous years and with other companies in the same line of business. In this way it can be determined if the percentage is increasing or decreasing on a comparable basis.

As we have explained in Chapter 2 (page 16), the capitalization of the Lobuck Corporation consists of the funded debt of $400,000 plus the preferred and common stock of $760,000 plus the surplus of $534,000 for a total of $1,694,000. Thus the *percentage earned on the capitalization* for the Lobuck company showing a net income of $542,000 would be 32 per cent ($542,000 divided by $1,694,000 equals 32.0%). Again, trends are important. In particular the analyst should observe the expansion policies of a company. For example, a company might expand its plant and equipment. To do this it might be necessary to sell bonds or stocks. In this case, earnings should be compared with increased capitalization in order to determine the wisdom of the expansion policies.

Cash Flow is simply the sum of the net income plus the depreciation charges. In the case of the Lobuck Corporation, the following would be the cash flow calculation:

Depreciation	$200.00
Net Income	542.00
Total Cash Flow	$742.00

Some security analysts use incorrectly the term cash flow earnings and reduce it to a per share figure. This should be done with great caution if at all. Most analysts consider depreciation a method of recovering the cost of an asset and not available as earnings to the stockholder.

In our analysis, we have assumed that the earnings as reported are accurate. One of the best ways to check this is to be sure the accounts are audited by a recognized firm of certified public accountants. This is true of almost all large concerns. There are, however, different ways of treating depreciation, taxes, and inventories which might change the net income of a company. Therefore, the security analyst should always check these items when comparing one company with another in the same field.

Debit and Credit

The terms *debit* and *credit* are used in accounting transactions. A debit is an entry on the lefthand side of an account, and a credit is an entry on the right.

A debit, for example, is made to an account whenever an asset or an expense is increased, a liability is decreased, or net worth is decreased.

A credit is therefore made whenever a liability is increased, an asset or an expense decreased, or net worth is increased.

The following might illustrate some of these transactions:

(1) Inventory purchased for cash. (Asset increased, asset decreased)

	Debit	Credit
Merchandise Inventory	$1,000	
Cash		$1,000

(2) Inventory purchased and notes receivable given.

(Asset increased, liability increased)

	Debit	Credit
Merchandise Inventory	$5,000	
Notes Payable		$5,000

(3) Wages paid. (Expense increased, asset decreased)

	Debit	Credit
Wages	$5,000	
Cash		$5,000

(4) Note payable for inventory met at maturity.

(Liability decreased, asset decreased)

	Debit	Credit
Note Payable	$5,000	
Cash		$5,000

REVIEW QUESTIONS

1. Define net sales, cost of goods sold, and selling and administrative expenses.

2. What is depreciation? Explain in detail two methods by which it may be calculated.

3. Distinguish between depletion, amortization, and obsolescence.

4. Given a taxable corporate income of $2,000,000, calculate the federal normal tax and the surtaxes.

5. After you have calculated the above taxes, *find the net income per share* *of common stock,* assuming 100,000 shares of 5% $100 par preferred, and 200,000 shares no par common stock. (see page 27)

6. Why is the growth of net sales significant? How can sales growth best be measured and compared?

7. How is operating margin or margin of profit calculated? In what way may it be used by the analyst?

8. Explain two ways in which changes in earnings per share may be measured.

9. Describe cash flow. In what way should the terms *not* be used?

Bonds

Chapter **4**

A bond is an engraved certificate indicating that a corporation has borrowed a fixed sum of money and promises to repay it at a future date. Also, for use of this money, the corporation agrees to pay at specified intervals (usually twice a year) interest at a stated rate. When bonds are issued, the maturity date or the date the company must pay the principal of the bonds is usually a long time in the future: twenty or thirty years. Bonds are usually issued in $1,000 denominations, but denominations range from $50 to $10,000. Bonds in denominations of less than $500 are called *small* or *baby* bonds. The interest rate is stated in percentages on the face of the bond. In short, a bond is evidence of debt, and the bondholder is a creditor of the corporation. A stockholder, as we shall later see, is a part owner and holds evidence of ownership in his stock certificate.

The company *must* pay the interest and principal on bonds when due and in full. With the exception of income bonds (discussed later) there is no option as to the amount or the time of the payments. Failure to pay interest or principal when due almost always means insolvency and often the appointment of new management. Therefore, corporations make every effort to live up to their contracts by paying principal and interest.

The bondholder, as long as he receives his interest on principal, does not have any voice in the management.

The obligations of the corporation are set forth in the deed of trust or indenture drawn when the bonds are issued. The trust indenture outlines the duties of the corporation, such as the payment of interest, the maintenance of sinking funds, and keeping the property insured and in satisfactory condition. Also, it outlines the rights of the bond-holders in the event of default. It also sets forth the duties and qualifications of the institution i.e. bank or trust company with capital funds

35

not less than $150,000 which must act as trustee for the bondholders. Above all the trustee must be independent of the issuing corporation. This indenture usually must be drawn in accord with the Trust Indenture Act of 1939 summarized in Appendix. Basically, this act is aimed to protect the bondholder by the appointment of an impartial, solvent and competent institutional trustee. However, the trustee does not in any way guarantee the bondholder against loss. A weak corporation that fails may cause severe losses to the bondholder no matter how strong or able the trustee. Therefore, bonds should by no means be considered riskless securities.

Many of the large bond issues are listed on the New York Stock Exchange. A few issues are traded on the American Stock Exchange, but most bond issues, whether listed or not, are traded over the counter—that is, they are traded over the telephone between securities dealers (see Chapter 11).

Bond Quotations

Railroad, public utility, and industrial bonds are called *corporate* bonds. These are quoted in *per cent of face amount or $1000*, using fractions of $\frac{1}{8}$, $\frac{1}{4}$, $\frac{3}{8}$, $\frac{1}{2}$, $\frac{5}{8}$, $\frac{3}{4}$, and $\frac{7}{8}$. (Sometimes instead of face amount the term *par* value is used, since it is the amount which is stated on the face of the bond.) Since face amount for bonds is almost always $1,000, the following would illustrate the relationships between the quotation and the dollar price.

Quotation	Dollar Price
103¼	$1032.50
102⅛	1021.25
105½	1055.00
97½	975.00

An easy way to calculate the dollar price is to extend the round numbers and then take a fraction of $10. For example, a bid of 103¼ for a $1,000 bond would be figured $1,030 plus ¼ of $10 or $2.50, making $1,032.50.

In the case of new issues, the dollar price is often stated in decimals rather than fractions. For example, late in 1959 the Florida Power and Light Company offered to the public 5¼% bonds due 1989 at 101.519, or $1,015.19 per bond.

United States Treasury certificates, notes, and bonds (discussed later in this chapter), are, like corporate bonds, quoted in per cent of face amount. But the fractions are stated in 1/32nds. Thus a United States Treasury bond quoted at 101.16 would have a dollar price of $1,015. This is calculated by extending the round number 101 to $1,010 and adding

16/32 of $10, or $5. This would amount to $1,015. Treasury bills are sold and quoted at a discount on a yield to maturity basis.

It is difficult to understand or even talk about bonds without having a clear understanding of bond yields.

Bond Yields

There are three types of yields: the nominal yield, the current yield, and the yield to maturity.

The *nominal yield* is usually the interest rate shown on the face of the bond. It is stated in round percentages: 4%, 5%, and so forth, or in fractions of ⅛ths or ¼ths. For example, a corporation on August 31, 1959, might issue $1,000,000 or 4% bonds due August 31, 1979. This would mean that the nominal yield is 4% or $40. It is seldom equal to the current yield or the yield to maturity.

Interest payments, generally, are made every six months. In this case, the company would pay $20 twice a year. If the interest rate were 4⅜%, the company would pay $43.75, or about $21.87 twice a year.

The *current yield* is almost always different from the nominal yield. In some cases bonds sell at a premium—in excess of $1,000—or at a discount—below $1,000. If a 4% bond sells at a premium over par, the current yield will be less than 4%. For example, if an investor buys a 4% bond at 105 or $1,050, he is investing $1,050 but is only getting $40 a year. Simple inspection will show that the current yield is less than 4%. The current yield may be obtained by dividing the *price of the bond into the interest rate*, as follows:

$$\text{Current Yield} = \frac{\text{Interest Rate}}{\text{Price of Bond}} = \frac{\$40.00}{\$1,050} = 3.809\%$$

The yield to maturity is a little more complicated to compute than the current yield, yet it is important for the investor to understand its principle, because the yield to maturity is the yield most generally used when deciding to buy or sell a bond.

The yield to maturity, calculated by the approximate method, is the average percentage return taking into consideration the eventual gain or loss of principal through payment of $1,000 at maturity. Take our example of a 4% bond selling at $1,050, due August 31, 1979. The investor knows that between August 31, 1959, the date he buys the bond, and August 31, 1979, when the bond matures, he will lose $50 or $2.50 a year over the twenty-year period, since the bond is paid off at maturity at par or $1,000.

Therefore, the interest rate should be adjusted to take care of this loss. On an annual basis, it amounts to $50 divided by twenty years, or $2.50 a year loss. The adjusted coupon is $40.00 *less* $2.50 or $37.50.

The average price can be obtained by taking an average of the cost price of $1,050 and the maturity payment of $1,000, giving $1,025. Now we are ready to calculate our yield to maturity. In this case, we use an adjusted interest rate and the average price to obtain the yield to maturity by the approximate method, as follows:

$$\text{Yield to Maturity} = \frac{\text{Adjusted Interest}}{\text{Average Price}} = \frac{\$\ 37.50}{\$1,025.00} = 3.658$$

A more accurate method of calculating the yield to maturity is by use of the *bond yield tables.* (But for all practical purposes the approximate method is surprisingly accurate.) For example, using the bond table, the *exact* yield to maturity on a 4% bond selling at $1,050, due in twenty years, is 3.646%. The bond yield tables are useful when it is necessary to calculate the yield to maturity when the maturity is not in an even number of years.

The following example shows how the bond yield table is interpolated. The bond yields are arranged by years and coupon rates. For example in order to arrive at the above yield you should turn to the page in the Bond Yield Book which shows the yields on a 4% bond due in twenty years and see the nearest yields to the price of 1050.

	4%
	20 years
104.94	3.65
105.00	X
105.67	3.60

Thus we see that a bond selling at 105.67 yields 3.60 and at 104.94, 3.65. Therefore we know that the yield on the bond selling at 105 is somewhere between 3.60 and 3.65. We can solve the problem by taking a proportion or percentage of the difference represented by the difference between 105.67 and 105.00 or 67 as the numerator of the fraction and the difference between 105.67 and 104.94 or 73 as the denominator. Thus:

$$\frac{67}{73} \text{ of } .05 = \frac{335}{73} = .046$$

This we add: 3.60
                          .046
Final yield   3.646

We add .046 because the price of 105.67 yields 3.60. Therefore the price 105 is lower and yields $\frac{67}{73}$ of .05 or .046 per cent *higher.*

In summary, we have the following yields *which are all different:*[1]

---

[1]For a more complete explanation of yields, see John H. Prime, *Investment Analysis, 4th Edition* (Englewood Cliffs, N.J.: Prentice-Hall, Inc., 1967), pp. 79–87.

1. Nominal yield	4.000%	
2. Current yield	3.809%	
3. Yield to maturity		
By approximate method		3.658%
By the bond yield table		3.646%

In the event that the corporation fails to pay interest or principal, or fails to live up to its agreements, the bondholder has certain rights. These rights are set forth in the Deed of Trust or Indenture which is written when the bonds are sold.

The deed of trust or indenture is a written agreement describing the rights of the bondholders, the duties of the corporation, and of the trustees. The corporation agrees, in addition to paying interest and principal, to keep the property insured and in good repair. Also, there are a number of other clauses or covenants to which the company agrees, such as the amount of the bonds to be sold, and the amount to be retired by sinking fund.

The trustee, in turn, agrees to see that the rights of the bondholders are protected. That is, the trustee checks on the payment of interest, the principal, and all the other covenants of the indenture. When the company fails to live up to its agreement, the trustee must take legal action to protect the bondholders.

A more detailed discussion of the indenture will be under the Trust Indenture Act of 1939 in Chapter 15 and in the Appendix.

The Issuance of Bonds

Bonds are issued in three forms: (a) coupon bonds, (b) fully registered bonds, and (c) registered as to principal but not as to interest.

Coupon bonds have interest coupons attached to each bond by the corporation which issues it. They are also called "bearer bonds." For example, a company might issue 4% bonds due in twenty years. This would mean that attached to each bond would be forty coupons for $20 each. On the due dates for the interest, the owner clips the coupons and presents them to the authorized bank for payment. Also, the principal, when due, is payable to the holder or bearer of the bonds. In other words, the bond owner should take great care of his bonds. If they are lost or stolen, the company is in no way responsible for the payment to the rightful owner. In short, losing a coupon bond is the same as losing a $1,000 bill.

When a new bond issue is sold, the corporation usually issues *temporary certificates*. These are similar to bonds since they have the promise to pay at maturity the stated amount. But they often have only two or three coupons. This gives the company time to have printed the so-called *definitive* bonds with all the coupons attached. The bondholder must exchange the temporary certificates for the *definitive bonds* as soon as the coupons on the temporary certificates have been paid.

Fully registered bonds, registered in the name of the buyer on the books of the issuer as to principal and interest, are held by investors who are afraid they might lose coupon bonds or do not wish to bother with clipping coupons and presenting them to the paying agent. Registered bonds have the name of the owner written on the face of the bond. Also, the company or its authorized agent, usually a bank, has a record of the name and address of the owner. The interest, when due, is paid to the bondholder by check. If the bonds are lost or stolen, the rightful owner may obtain a new bond from the company, but care must be taken even of registered bonds. The owner of a registered bond will have to go through a considerable amount of paper work and perhaps expense before a new bond is issued. In most cases, registered bonds sell at a slightly lower price than bearer or coupon bonds. One reason for this is the time and trouble required to transfer them.

Bonds registered as to principal but not as to interest are self-explanatory. The principal is registered in the name of the owner on the books of the company in the same manner as fully registered bonds. At maturity, the company or its agent sends a check for the principal amount to the holder of record. But the bonds are *not* registered as to interest. In other words, these bonds have coupons which might be detached and presented by the owner or bearer. Thus these bonds, like the coupon bonds discussed above, are also sometimes called bearer bonds.

Types of Bonds

Mortgage bonds are perhaps the oldest type of bond. Here the corporation makes the usual promise to pay a stated sum at maturity plus interest. In addition, the corporation states that the bondholder has a specific claim for mortgage on a part or all of its assets. In other words, a mortgage bond is evidence of indebtedness which is secured by a mortgage or other lien on some underlying real property of a corporation. Many first-mortgage bonds were issued to build the railroads in this country. These usually had a first claim on specified miles of railroad before all other creditors. An example of this type of bond is the Morris and Essex Railroad Company first-mortgage $3\frac{1}{2}\%$ bond due December 1, 2000. This bond has a first claim on 126 miles of main line from Hoboken to Philipsburg, N.J.

In many cases, the railroads needed additional funds for expansion and sold more bonds. But the claim of these bonds is junior to that of the first-mortgage bonds. It is a second mortgage or, as often called, a general mortgage. A general mortgage is a promise by the railroad to pay a fixed sum backed by a blanket or second-mortgage claim on all of the corporation's fixed capital. An example of a general mortgage is the Pennsylvania Railroad Company issue of general-mortgage 4½% bonds due in 1995. Sometimes a railroad will issue a bond that has a first mortgage on one part of the railroad line and a general or second mortgage on another part. An investor should always beware of titles, particularly in the case of railroad bonds. It is not always true that a first mortgage is a safe investment. As will be shown later, the safety of a bond depends more on earnings and other factors than on its mortgage position.

Public utilities often use mortgage bonds, but their capital structure is usually simple. Industrial concerns, however, seldom use mortgage bonds.

Mortgage bonds may be open-end, closed-end, or limited open-end. An *open-end mortgage* means that a corporation under the mortgage may issue additional bonds. But the open-end mortgage indenture usually provides that the corporation can issue more bonds only if the earnings or additional security obtained by selling the new securities meet certain tests of earnings and asset coverage. This might be illustrated as in the table.

	A	B	C
Property Value	$200,000	$200,000	$300,000
Amount of Bonds	100,000	150,000	150,000
Number of Bonds	100	150	150
Property Value per Bond	2,000	1,333	2,000
Rate of Interest on Bonds	5%	5%	5%
Interest	$ 5,000	$ 7,500	$ 7,500
Earnings before Interest	20,000	20,000	30,000
Interest Coverage	4.0	2.66	4.00

Under Column *A*, $100,000 of bonds—100 bonds of $1,000 each—have been issued.

Each bondholder would have property value of $2,000 per bond—$200,000 property value divided by 100 bonds equals $2,000.

The interest on the bonds is 5% times $100,000, or $5,000.

If earnings before interest were $20,000 the interest charges would be earned 4 times—$20,000 earnings divided by interest of $5,000 equals 4.

In Column *B* the company has issued $50,000 of additional bonds bringing the total to $150,000 under its open-end mortgage.

It can be seen that the property value per bond of the original issue has been *reduced* from $2,000 per bond to $1,333—$200,000 property value divided by 150 bonds equals $1,333.

Also, the interest coverage has been reduced from 4.00 to 2.66. But almost always, the indenture of the mortgage provides against a substantial reduction of the property per dollar of debt by stipulating that additional property must be included under the mortgage as the amount of the mortgage is increased. Also, an earnings test often provides for the maintenance of the same or substantially the same interest coverage.

In Column *C* it will be noted that the debt has been increased $50,-000 to $150,000, but additional property worth $100,000 has been acquired, bringing the property value to $300,000. This might be accomplished by the sale of bonds and of stocks. At all events the per-bond assets behind the bonds in *C* are the same as *A*—$2,000 per bond ($300,-000 property value divided by 150 bonds equals $2,000 per bond).

The new property will also increase the earnings to an estimated $30,000. This will mean that interest will be covered four times ($30,000 earnings divided by $7,500 interest—the same as in Column *A*).

This illustration is an oversimplification of a few ways in which the bondholder is protected in the indenture against dilution or an over-issue of bonds in an open end mortgage.

In a *closed-end mortgage,* the company agrees to issue at one time a stated amount of bonds. After these bonds have been issued *no more may be issued* under the mortgage. Additional bonds may be sold, but they rank as junior to the first-mortgage bonds. In other words, the original issue has priority on claims and may not be issued beyond the specified amount of the issue. An example of a closed-end mortgage bond was the Pennsylvania Railroad Company's 4½% consolidated mortgage bonds due August 1960.

In a *limited open-end mortgage,* the indenture provides that a corporation may issue a stated amount of bonds *over a period of years in series.* For example, the indenture might provide that a corporation could issue up to $100,000,000 of bonds. The corporation might issue at once $25,000,000 of 5% Series A due 1980; sometime later it might sell $50,000,000 of 5% Series B due 1983, and so forth. All of the series issued under this indenture would have the same claim on the assets.

Refunding bonds are usually a new issue of bonds sold by a company to pay off an old issue, most often to save interest. For example, in the late 1940's a number of bonds were sold with coupons as low as 2½% to pay off bonds with coupons of 4%. In 1966, a number of good companies had to sell bonds with coupons over 6%. If and when interest rates go down, these bonds will be refunded. (However, some of these bonds have call restrictions of five years or more).

On occasion, a company will refund an issue at maturity in order to extend the payment of its debt. This is usually done by direct exchange. Generally, the issue offered for exchange is more attractive, with a higher coupon rate, sinking fund, etc.

Debenture bonds are written promises of the corporation to pay principal at its due date and with interest. While these promises are as binding as mortgage bonds, debenture bonds are not secured by any pledge of property. They are sold on the general credit of the company.

In short, debentures have no specific collateral behind them; they are simple promises to pay principal and interest, and their security depends on the assets and earnings of the corporation.

In addition, it might be mentioned here that United States Government bonds are debentures. Since they are backed by the general credit of the United States Government, they are considered prime investments.

Debenture bonds are used extensively by industrial concerns, sometimes by utilities, but to a lesser extent by railroads. In many cases, the debentures of the industrials and utilities are better investments than the mortgage bonds of many of the railroads. For example, the General Motors Corporation, the United States Steel Corporation, and the American Telephone and Telegraph Company have sold large debenture issues which have high investment standing.

Convertible bonds, as the name implies, may be converted *at the option of the holder* into a specified number of shares of common stock. On rare occasions, a convertible bond is convertible into preferred stock. The terms of conversion are explained in the indenture. Sometimes the indenture might state that a $1,000 bond may be converted into a specific number of shares of common stock. For example, if a convertible bond selling at $1,000 is convertible into twenty shares of common, it would mean that the stock would have to sell at least $50 a share to make conversion worth while: a stock at $50 a share times 20 shares would equal $1,000. If the stock went to 75, the bond would be worth about $1,500 or 75 times 20 shares. Quite often the indenture of a convertible bond will say that the bond is convertible into common stock at a *price*. For example, a *conversion price* of $50 would mean 20 shares of common or $1,000 divided by 50 equals 20 shares. In many cases, the conversion terms change with the passage of years. For example, a convertible bond due in 1975 might be convertible into twenty shares until December 1, 1965, into eighteen shares until December 1, 1970, and not convertible from December 1, 1970 to maturity in 1975.

Conversion parity simply means that the value of a convertible bond and the shares into which it may be converted are the same, or on a parity. For example, if a convertible bond is convertible into twenty shares of stock its *conversion ratio* is 20. If the bond is selling at $1,000 and the common at $50, the conversion value would equal 20 × $50 or $1,000. Thus the exchange value of the bond and the stock are equal, or at parity. The investor would have little trouble in finding the exchange value of the bond which is referred to as *parity price of the bond*. All he has to do is multiply the number of shares that his convertible bond permits him to buy times the price of the common stock, i.e., 20 × $50. However, the *parity price of the stock* is a little more difficult. For example, let us assume that a convertible bond is selling at $1,500, the *parity price of the stock* is found by dividing the price of the convertible bond by the conversion ratio or the number of shares the convertible bond receives on conversion. In this case, $1,500 ÷ 20 equals $75. Thus the common stock would have to sell at 75 to justify the price of $1,500 for the convertible bond.

Almost always, the holder of a convertible bond is protected against *dilution*. That is, his conversion privilege changes along with any material change in the outstanding common shares. For example, if a company should split its stock two for one, the conversion privilege of the bonds would also change proportionately, so that he could convert into twice as many shares as before the two-for-one split.

In some cases, a convertible bond is also a mortgage bond or a collateral trust bond, but more often it is a debenture with a claim on the general credit of the corporation. For a number of years, the American Telephone and Telegraph Company has sold a large number of convertible debenture bonds.

In several cases a convertible bond is a *subordinated debenture*, which is much the same as an ordinary debenture. *Interest and principal must be paid at the scheduled time.* An important difference is that, in the event of default of principal or interest by the issuer, the claims of the subordinated debenture holders must await satisfaction of the claims of the other debenture holders and perhaps of the bank creditors.

Some years ago sales finance companies started using *subordinated* debentures. They needed more capital than the banks were willing to extend, but were unwilling to sell stocks. Consequently, the banks agreed to allow the sales finance companies to sell more debentures provided they were *subordinated* to the bank debt and the outstanding debentures. These debentures were not convertible into common.

A number of industrial companies have issued subordinated debentures which were convertible into common stock; among them were the Dow Chemical Company, the General Portland Cement Company, and the General Tire and Rubber Company.

The holder of a convertible bond has in some respects double advantage. If, for example, the affairs of the company do not prosper, he is, as a bondholder, a creditor. Interest must be paid currently and principal at maturity. Thus the investor has assured income as long as the company is solvent and a bondholder's claim in the event of financial difficulty. On the other hand, if the affairs of the company prosper, the bondholder can convert to stock and benefit by increased principal and income.

As far as the corporation is concerned the convertible bond has at least two advantages. First, it can sell convertible bonds with a lower coupon than it could straight debentures or mortgage bonds. Convertible bonds are eagerly sought by institutions and by investors seeking fixed return with appreciation possibilities. Second, the convertible bond device enables the company to obtain more capital and still keep its capitalization balanced between common and preferred stock.

Income bonds, sometimes called *adjustment* bonds, are often issued by railroads that have been in financial difficulty. The principal of an income bond *must be paid at maturity.* But the interest depends on the earnings of the corporation. If the interest is earned the directors are, as a rule, required to pay it. On the other hand, if it is not earned it usually is not paid. Many indentures of income bonds provide that unpaid interest will accumulate. But this period of accumulation is often limited to a definite percentage—between 8 per cent and 12 per cent— or for a two or three year period. Sometimes the interest on income bonds does not accumulate at all. Due to the contingent nature of their interest payments, income bonds as a class are not considered as safe investments as fixed income securities. They are issued by companies with fluctuating earnings. Earnings which are good during the periods of boom become deficits in periods of low business activity. The income bond enables this type of company to defer interest without danger of bankruptcy in bad times. Further, the cumulative nature of the income bond permits the company to make up in part at least the back interest. There are few income bonds which are also convertible into stock. For example the New York, New Haven & Hartford Railroad Company general income 4½% bonds of 2,000 are convertible into ten shares of 5% preferred stock per $1,000 bond.

Guaranteed bonds are guaranteed by others than the corporation issuing the bonds. During the period of expansion in our country, a number of companies, particularly railroads, purchased other concerns not by cash but by guaranteeing or assuming their stocks and bonds. Usually the parent company guaranteed the payment both of the interest and the principal of the bonds. There are exceptions where the guaranteeing company assumed only the interest payments but did not promise to pay the principal of the bonds at maturity. However, since most of the securities guaranteed were an important part of the railroad system the principal was usually paid. If the interest or principal of a guaranteed bond is not paid the holder has a claim against the guarantor and against the company issuing the bonds.

For example, if the Pittsburgh, Cincinnati, Chicago, and St. Louis Railroad Company should default on its 5% bonds due in 1970, the trustee would sue first the Pennsylvania Rail Road Company which has guaranteed the principal and interest of the bonds. Failing to recover here the trustee might petition the court for a reorganization.

Other examples of guaranteed bonds are:

1. Cleveland, Cincinnati, Chicago and St. Louis Railway Co. 4% 1990—guaranteed principal and interest by the New York Central Railroad Company.

2. Joseph E. Seagrams & Sons 3% 1974—guaranteed principal and interest by Distillers Corporation-Seagrams Company.

Guaranteed stock should be considered under the heading of fixed income securities rather than as a stock, as its title implies. A guaranteed stock is a stock with dividends guaranteed at a fixed rate by a company other than the one issuing the stock. For example, the 5% preferred stock of the Carolina, Clinchfield and Ohio Railway Company is guaranteed unconditionally by the Atlantic Coast Line Railroad Company and by the Louisville and Nashville Railroad Company. This guarantee is joint and several. That means that if one railroad fails to pay its part of the guarantee, the other must pay the entire amount.

There are also guaranteed common stocks. Perhaps one of the strongest guaranteed common stocks is the Pittsburgh, Fort Wayne and Chicago Railway Company $7 stock guaranteed by the Pennsylvania Rail Road Company. This railroad controls 503 miles of main line between Pittsburgh and Chicago. It is therefore a vital link of the Pennsylvania Rail Road system. Against this line there are no bonds outstanding.

Mortgage or debenture bonds which are additionally secured by other securities placed with a trustee are collateral trust bonds. Collateral trust bonds are customarily issued by companies whose credit needs to be strengthened. The collateral deposited with the trustee is often the bonds or stocks of subsidiary companies. At times, the collateral is marketable listed securities. The holder of the collateral bond of an industrial or a public utility company has a bondholder's claim against the company, but he also can force the trustee, in the event of default, to sell the collateral and apply the proceeds to satisfy the claims of the bondholders. An example of a collateral trust bond of a public utility is the United Gas Corporation first and collateral trust 2¾% bonds due in 1970. The collateral deposited with a trustee as additional security to these bonds consists of shares of the United Gas Pipe Line Company and the Union Producing Company which are subsidiaries of the United Gas Corporation.

The trustee of the collateral of a railroad bond does not have the same freedom of action as industrial or public utility trustees. Railroads defaulting on bonds usually must go through complicated legal reorganiation. But the collateral behind a railroad bond is usually given consideration in any reorganization plan.

Equipment Trust Certificates

An equipment trust certificate is a serial bond since it matures in part at stated intervals, usually every six months. In addition, it is secured by the equipment of the railroad and sometimes of an industrial company. Let us assume that a railroad wishes to buy $10,000,000 worth of Diesel locomotives. The order is placed with the manufacturer, usually with the railroad advancing 20 per cent of the cost price in cash. The balance is raised by the investment bankers' selling equipment trust certificates to the investors, largely the commercial banks, the insurance companies, and the pension funds. These equipment trust certificates, when sold under the so-called "Philadelphia" plan, are guaranteed by the railroad as to principal and dividends. The dividends are at a fixed rate and must be paid the same as interest. In this case they are called *dividends* and not interest. The trustees, which must include a bank, hold title to the equipment for the benefit of the investors in the certificates. If the dividends or principal are not paid by the railroad, the trustee can sell the equipment for the benefit of the certificate holders. Equipment trust certificates also are sold under the "New York" plan which varies in detail from the "Philadelphia" plan although the basic security is the same.

It has been found that equipment trust certificates are excellent investments. First, they are serial maturities—a part of the total issue matures at stated intervals. Thus the railroad is paying off its debt as the equipment wears out. Second, the certificates are, as a rule, paid off *more rapidly* than the equipment depreciates. Third, the courts have recognized the first claim of the certificate holders to the equipment in reorganization. Among the types of companies issuing equipment trust certificates are the airlines, the meat packing industry, and the private car companies.

A *sinking fund bond* is not a distinct type or class of bond. A sinking fund is a provision in the indenture of the bond issue. Under this provision, the corporation agrees to set aside regularly sums sufficient to retire all or part of the debt prior to maturity. At stated intervals, the company or its agent calls by lot the numbers of a certain percentage of the bonds and then retires them from the proceeds of the sinking fund. Since sinking funds reduce the debt regularly over the life of the bonds, they often improve the credit of the company.

Industrial bonds usually have sinking funds which retire a substantial part of the bonds by maturity. Also, the maturity of an industrial bond is usually shorter than that of the bonds issued by the public utilities or railroads. For example, as explained in Chapter 2, the Union Carbide Corporation had a large number of bonds requiring heavy sinking-fund payments. Public utility bonds usually have funds requiring the company to retire their bonds at the rate of about 2 per cent a year.

Most of the railroad bonds were issued before the days when institutional investors were requesting sinking funds; consequently, many railroad bonds do not have sinking funds.

Municipal Bonds

"Municipals" is a general term applied to the obligations of states, cities, towns, school districts, and statutory authorities. Municipal bonds are sold to raise money to build public buildings, state roads, schools, subways, and streets. United States Government securities are not classed as municipal securities.

Municipal bonds are of two main types: *general obligations* (or unlimited tax bonds) and *limited obligations* (which include revenue and special assessment bonds).

General obligation or G.O. bonds are backed by the full faith and credit of the state, city, or town. The most important characteristic of a municipal bond is the fact that the interest is exempt from Federal income taxes. The exemption from taxation rests on a number of common law cases; the most famous is *McCulloch vs. Maryland*, 1819. Also, the present income tax laws do *not* require the taxpayers to report their income from municipal obligations; they may exclude it from their taxable income. It should be realized that Congress could change the laws and the Supreme Court of the United States could decide that municipal bonds *are* taxable. In other words, the exemption from federal income taxes is not written on the face of the bond and is not guaranteed. Whenever a municipal bond is issued, a law firm is asked to give a written legal opinion on the legality of the securities. This opinion says, among other things, that the bonds are legally issued and binding obligations of the state, city, or local government. Also the legal opinion states: "in the opinion of counsel the interest on these bonds is exempt from all federal income taxes under existing statutes as thus far construed by the courts." A copy of this legal opinion *must* go with every transaction of municipal bonds. Otherwise, the bond is not good delivery.

Sometimes municipal bonds are called "tax exempt" securities. This is a misleading title. Municipal securities are not exempt from inheritance taxes, nor are they exempt from state income taxes in many states. Nevertheless, exemption from federal income taxes has a distinct advantage not only to an individual in the high tax brackets but to corporations. An easy way to measure this advantage is *to take the difference between the tax bracket of the individual or corporation and 100 and divide it into the yield on the municipal bond to be purchased.* Let us suppose first that an individual must pay federal income taxes of 20 per cent on his income, that is, he is in the 20 per cent bracket. We would then subtract 20 from 100 which equals 80 (or the *supplement* of his tax bracket). Let us further assume he can buy a 4% municipal bond which is exempt from federal income taxes. To measure his advantage he would divide 4% by 80 which equals 5%. Thus an investor in the

20 per cent bracket would have to buy a corporate bond with a yield of 5 per cent to equal the 4 per cent yield on a municipal bond. The following summarizes this calculation:

Individual in 20% bracket pays tax of: 20%
Supplement of tax bracket: 100% minus 20% equals 80%
Offered Municipal Bond with yield of: 4.00%
Corporate yield equivalent: 4.00% divided by 80% equals 5.00%

The above can be proved by assuming the individual buys a 5% taxable security and applying a 20% tax. This would be 20% of 5% or 1%. Then, 5% less 1% would equal 4%. If an investor is in a 50% bracket and offered a 4% municipal the corporate equivalent would be 8%. A corporation in the 48% bracket would find a 4% municipal bond equivalent to a yield of 7.69% or 4.00% divided by 52.

It should not be believed that municipal bonds are riskless securities. During the depression years 1930–1941, millions of dollars' worth of bonds of cities, towns, and districts defaulted in their principal and interest, particularly in the states of Michigan, New Jersey, Arkansas, Florida, and Oklahoma. But most of these municipalities paid their bonds at maturity.

Almost all of the revenues of the municipalities and states are derived from taxes. The largest percentage of the income of states is from taxes on personal and corporate incomes. Cities, towns, and school districts rely more on real estate taxes. The power to tax is a large factor in reducing risk of default. General-obligation municipal bonds usually carry a lower interest rate than corporate bonds, due to this power to tax and to the exemption from federal income tax.

Municipal Revenue Securities

Statutory authorities are political subdivisions of the state. As such they issue revenue securities which are exempt from federal income taxes. They issue bonds to finance the construction of turnpikes, bridges, waterworks, airports, college dormitories or public utilities which are or will be income producing. The main difference between a revenue-obligation and a general-obligation bond is that the payment of interest and principal usually depends on the income or revenue of an electric public utility, a bridge, or a turnpike being financed. For example, the security of the bonds of the New York Thruway Authority depends on the income of the turnpike between New York City and Buffalo. The revenues of this turnpike are more than ample to cover the interest payments, and the bonds are considered sound investments. But the revenue of the West Virginia Turnpike is sufficient to cover only a part of the interest requirement. As of March 17, 1966, the West

Virginia 3¾% Turnpike bonds due 1989 were selling at 63. Sometimes, however, states and other public bodies guarantee the principal or interest of revenue obligations.

Since revenue securities are usually issued by authorities, or agencies of the state, the interest payments are also exempt from federal income taxes.

Special assessment bonds are issued by a district formed to construct a public improvement, such as a sewer or a water system. The interest and principal of these bonds are paid by special assessments, that is, taxes on the residents of the district. Sometimes the credit of the county or municipality is also pledged.

Tax anticipation notes are usually issued by cities in anticipation of the collection of taxes. They are short-term obligations either payable at a fixed maturity and guaranteed by the municipality, or maturing by numbers as the taxes are collected. In these cases, the security depends on the amount of the taxes collected being equal to the notes.

There are also United States Treasury tax anticipation *bills* and *certificates*. These are full-faith obligations of the government. They are issued in anticipation of income tax collections. Usually they are due one week after the tax date but acceptable at par for income taxes on the date the taxes are due. Thus the buyer of these bills or certificates gets one week's free interest if he uses them to pay income taxes.

Analysis of State, City, Town and Statutory Authority Bonds

STATE. Since a state is considered sovereign, it cannot be sued by its creditors without its consent. There are exceptions, however. New York State, for example, grants the right to bring certain suits against the state.

Therefore, the investor should investigate the past record of debt payment—willingness to pay as well as the state's wealth, population, industries—i.e., the state's ability to pay. A good measure of wealth is the per capita personal income of the various states. For example, the per capita income of New York State in 1964 was $3,162, whereas the Mississippi per capita income was only $1,438, compared with a national average of $2,566. Other criteria would be *net debt per capita*, which for the above mentioned states was about $63 and $56 respectively. The real test is the relationship of per capita debt to income. For example, the ratio of debt to income in New York is about 2 per cent but is about 3.9 per cent in Mississippi.

CITY AND TOWN. Sometimes called municipal bonds, these obligations are issued by cities, towns, school districts, and other political subdivisions of the states. The states must approve, and often limit, the issue of bonds by cities, towns, etc. Unlike states and the federal government, cities may be sued on default of principal or interest payment. Yet their analysis depends, as in state and federal obligations, on their ability and willingness to pay. Not all cities, towns, and so forth have as good a record as the federal government. In the 1930's, there were large numbers of defaults of municipal obligations, particularly in the South. In analyzing the credit of a municipality, the investor should consider the growth of the population, the diversification of industry, the type of city government, the overlapping debt—that is, the debt which the city is responsible for or guarantees. Important financial ratios would include the following (1) the net debt per capita; $300 is generally considered high; (2) the percentage of debt to full value, which should not be over 10 per cent; and (3) the interest and debt retirement charges which should not be over 25 per cent of the budget, i.e., gross income from taxes, etc.

MUNICIPAL REVENUE SECURITIES OR STATUTORY AUTHORITY BONDS. These can be analyzed first by the nature of the project and second by the financial figures. For example, an electric public utility such as the Los Angeles Department of Water and Power (popularly called Dewaps) has issued only revenue bonds and is an excellent public utility with high interest coverage and an Aa rating by Moody's Investors Service. Most public utility revenue bonds may be analyzed the same as privately owned public utilities, and most are in strong financial positions and have good interest coverage. The New York Thruway, serving many cities, has high traffic density and high interest coverage. The Kansas Turnpike, however, has a lower traffic density and interest coverage. The West Virginia Turnpike, as mentioned above, is in default. Generally speaking, a turnpike should cover its interest charges about two times, and its interest sinking fund or serial maturities about 1.25 times.

United States Treasury Securities

The total debt of the United States government in November, 1966, was $329.9 billion. Congress has set a temporary limit to the debt of $336.0 billion until June 30, 1968. This limit will undoubtedly be extended and perhaps increased. As far as the investor is concerned, the most interesting part of this debt is the marketable debt of about $217 billion. This marketable debt is divided into United States Treasury bills, certificates, notes and bonds. The nonmarketable debt consists largely of about $50.8 billion of savings bonds and $52.6 billion of special issues held by the United States government trust account. All of these issues are full-faith-and-credit obligations of the United States government (United States government securities should not be confused with municipal securities).

United States Treasury Bills are offered at competitive bidding to the large corporations with surplus funds, to the banks, and to others. Treasury bills are offered and traded at a discount from face amount. They are quoted on a yield to maturity basis. Treasury bills have a maturity of not more than one year. At maturity, usually ninety-one days from issue, the bills are paid off in cash. Sometimes the government will offer bills (as well as certificates discussed below) which may be used by corporations to pay taxes. Treasury bills are traded only over the counter.

United States Treasury Certificates are offered to the large bank and institutional investors at terms set by the United States Treasury. They are only traded in the over the counter market. Prices are quoted in 1/32nds. The maturity of certificates is not more than one year. They are issued with one coupon attached which is paid at maturity.

United States Treasury Notes are usually bought in large amounts by the commercial banks. Notes have maturity up to five years and have coupons attached. They may not be called by the Treasury. At maturity they are either paid off in cash or a new security is offered. By the note issue the Treasury has an opportunity to extend the average maturity of the government debt. They are quoted in 1/32nds and traded only over the counter.

Treasury bills, Treasury certificates, and Treasury notes are used for investment of short-term funds. Large investors in these obligations include commercial banks, large corporations and investment companies. Commercial banks with large demand deposits must keep liquid. Corporations with large taxes and dividend payments make a practice of accumulating funds and desire to obtain some income in the process. Investment funds often withdraw from the stock market a part of their funds awaiting a more favorable buying opportunity.

United States Treasury Bonds have a maturity of over five years. Under the present law (December 31, 1965) the Government cannot pay over $4\frac{1}{4}$ per cent on bonds. There is no limit on interest the Government can pay on bills, certificates, and notes. A number of the bonds have optional call dates—three to five years prior to maturity.

For example, U. S. Treasury $4\frac{1}{4}$s of 8/15/92–87 could be called by the Treasury on 8/15/87 provided it gave four months notice prior to that date. These are called optional call bonds as contrasted with *term* bonds, which have a single maturity. An example is the U. S. Treasury $3\frac{1}{2}$s of 11/15/98, which is the longest maturity outstanding.

About twenty-three of the bond issues of United States Treasury bonds may be accepted at face amount when presented for payment of estate taxes. However, these securities must be owned by the decedent at the time of his death. This is currently a desirable feature, since the bonds are selling at a deep discount from maturity value.

The government always pays its Treasury bills in cash at maturity.

But to the holders of the maturing Treasury certificates, Treasury notes, and Treasury bonds, the government often offers a new security: a certificate, note, or a bond. But the government must, of course, pay cash to investors not accepting the exchange.

Nonmarketable Issues

The most important of the nonmarketable issues are the United States savings bonds. These were first issued in 1935 and were designed principally for the savings of individuals. They were pushed hard in World War II and in the postwar period to stem inflation.

A number of series were sold with increasing interest rates, but the only ones being sold at present (August, 1966) are the series E and the Series H.

United States Savings Bonds Series E are issued only in registered form and are nontransferable. They are primarily for small savers, with a maximum purchase limit of $20,000 face value each year for an individual. In June, 1966, the investment yield was about 4.15 per cent per annum. They are issued on a discount basis at 75 per cent of their face and mature at par in seven years. The denominations range from $18.75 to $7,500. They may be redeemed according to a gradually increasing schedule at any time at the option of the owner. The appreciation is taxable as income and must be reported when redeemed at maturity if the holder is on a cash basis; otherwise the annual accrual is considered reportable taxable income.

United States Savings Bonds Series H are also issued only in registered form and are nontransferable. They are issued at par or $1,000 and mature at par or $1,000. Their maturity is in ten years with a yield to maturity of about 4.15 per cent in June, 1966. They may be redeemed by the holder after six months on one month's notice at par or $1,000. The maximum amount that may be purchased by one individual in a year is $30,000.

Trading of United States Government securities is conducted by a relatively few large money market commercial banks and a few large and small nonbank dealers. These dealers take a position, and make and maintain a market in governments. For the most part, they trade *net* in round lots. Round lots for U. S. Treasury bonds is $100,000 and for bills, certificates and notes it is $1,000,000. Any amount less than these is considered an odd lot.

As will be explained in Chapter 8, *stocks* are traded in dollars per share. Therefore one point is one dollar. But as was shown in Chapter 3, bonds are quoted in percent of par, which usually is $1,000. Thus a point in a bond is *one per cent* of $1,000 or $10. Corporate and municipal bonds are quoted in percent of par in fractions (1/8th to 7/8ths).

United States Treasury bills are quoted in 1/100th of a point (1 per cent). United States certificates, notes and bonds are quoted in 1/32nd of a point (1 per cent). Bills are usually traded on a yield basis.

The following is a *part* of a daily quotation sheet issued daily by Salomon Brothers and Hutzler, a leading government house:

UNITED STATES TREASURY SECURITIES
CLOSING TRADING QUOTATIONS 3:30 PM—JUNE 22, 1966
FOR JUNE 24 DELIVERY
TREASURY BILLS

Outstanding In Millions	# Days To Maturity	Due	Bid	Asked	Approx. Bond Equiv. Yield	Net Change In Yield	Current Market
3300	6	6/30/66	4.40	4.00	4.06		....
2300	13	7/ 7/66	4.40	4.00	4.07		....
2300	20	7/14/66	4.30	4.00	4.07	—10	....
2300	27	7/21/66	4.30	4.00	4.07	—10	....
2300	34	7/28/66	4.30	4.00	4.08	—10	....
1000	37	7/31/66	4.30	4.00	4.08	—30	....
2300	41	8/ 4/66	4.40	4.20	4.28	—10	....
2300	48	8/11/66	4.40	4.20	4.28	—10	....
2300	55	8/18/66	4.40	4.20	4.29	—10	....
2300	62	8/25/66	4.40	4.20	4.29	—10	....
2300	68	8/31/66	4.38	4.34	4.43	— 2	....

BONDS, CERTIFICATES, AND NOTES

Coupon		Maturity	Bid	Asked	Net Change	Current Mkt.	Yield to Mat.	Yield After Corp. • Tax	Approx. Corp. Tax Equiv.	Yield Value of 1/32	1966 High	Range Low	Outstanding in Millions
3	B	8/15/66	99-24	99-26....		...............4.27	2.22	4.27	.220	99-26	99- 1	699
4	N	8/15/66	99-29	99-31....		...............4.16	2.16	4.16	.220	99-31	99-15	8434
1½	N	10/ 1/66	99- 6	99-10....		...............4.06	2.11	4.06	.115	99-10	98-	357
3⅜	B	11/15/66	99-15	99-17....	+ 1	...............4.58	2.38	4.58	.080	99-17	98-25	1851
4	N	11/15/66	99-23	99-25....		...............4.55	2.37	4.55	.080	99-25	99- 7	2254
4¾	C	11/15/66	100-	100- 2....		...............4.57	2.38	4.57	.080	100- 2	99-26	1644
4	B	2/15/80†	92-16	92-24....		...............4.73	2.62	5.04	.003	94-14	91-14	2608
3½	B	11/15/80†	87-20	87-28....		...............4.66	2.69	5.17	.003	88-30	86-12	1912
3¼	B	6/15/83-78†	83-20	83-28....		...............4.63	2.72	5.23	.003	85-16	81-28	1581
3¼	B	5/15/85†	82-28	83- 4....		...............4.59	2.69	5.17	.003	85- 2	81-14	1126
4¼	B	5/15/85-75†	94- 4	94-12....		...............4.70	2.54	4.88	.003	97-	92-18	1218
3½	B	2/15/90†	84-	84- 8....		...............4.60	2.64	5.07	.003	85-30	81-22	4899
4¼	B	8/15/92-87†	93-26	94- 2....	— 4	...............4.65	2.50	4.80	.002	96-22	91-30	3818
4	B	2/15/93-88†	90- 8	90-16....		...............4.62	2.54	4.89	.002	92-26	88-22	250
4⅛	B	5/15/94-89†	92- 8	92-16....	+ 4	...............4.61	2.51	4.83	.002	94-24	90-	1560
3	B	2/15/95†	82-16	82-24....		...............4.02	2.32	4.46	.002	84-12	79-	2109
3½	B	11/15/98†	83- 8	83-16....		...............4.47	2.55	4.90	.002	84-30	80-12	4406

N Note   B Bond   C Certificate   All issues subject to all Federal taxes. Exempt under present laws from State income taxes. • Yield after corporate tax computed on basis of 22% Federal normal income tax and 26% surtax as those taxes apply to the yield shown for each issue. Net yields on obligations selling below par are computed at the 48% rate on the coupon with adjustment for long term capital gains. † Acceptable at par in payment of Federal estate taxes when actually owned by the decedent at time of his death. * Callable on any interest payment date on 4 month's prior notice. W Yield to call date.

It will be seen from the above quotations that bills of six days maturity are quoted to yield at asked price 4 per cent, whereas the bonds with coupon 3½ per cent due 11/15/98 yields 4.47 per cent. The difference is 47 *basis points*. A basis point is therefore 1/100 of a point. The above also shows the quotation variation of the different issues.

The credit of the United States Government throughout our history has fluctuated to a considerable degree, yet ever since the end of the Civil War in 1865 the obligations of the United States have been considered prime investments. Moody's Investors Service rates them Aaa—top quality with maximum safety. There seems no possibility of any default of principal or interest, since the government can always print money. If, on the other hand, a default *did* occur, the security holder could not *sue* for recovery since a sovereign government cannot be sued without its consent. Usually a government's credit depends on its willingness and ability to pay. The United States has never defaulted on its debt, and there appears to be no reason to expect any break in this tradition. Also, the United States has vast resources and revenue—$120 billion in the fiscal year ended June 30, 1965—which are substantial compared with interest charges of about $8.6 billion. Further, during the past eight years, the U. S. debt has not grown as fast as corporate or personal debt. In sum, in spite of frequent fiscal deficits, it is believed the United States debt has ample security of assets and earning power.

TAX STATUS.   The income on all United States government securities is subject to federal income taxes but exempt from state income taxes. Also, the appreciation of discount on Treasury bills and Series E Savings Bonds is taxable as income. The appreciation of Series E Savings Bonds may be reported annually or in total when the bond matures.

Agency securities of the United States government represent securities issued by corporations sponsored by the United States government. These include: (1) the Federal Land Banks which grant mortgages to farmers (2) the Federal Home Loan Banks which buys mortgages from mortgage-lending institutions such as savings banks (3) the Federal National Mortgage Association (Fanny Mae) which buys guaranteed and other mortgages from the institutions. All these agencies sell obligations to finance their activities. They are *not* guaranteed by the United States government. However, it is generally believed that the government will not allow these agencies to default and that it is morally responsible. During the Depression of the 1930's, the Federal Land Banks ran into considerable difficulty as a result of wholesale defaults of farm mortgages. However, the government supported the Federal Land Banks and they paid off their obligations.

Agency securities, therefore, are considered sound investments. They yield a little more than U. S. government obligations and are not rated by the rating services. The interest is fully taxable by the federal government but exempt from state income taxes.

The Role of the United States Treasury

The basic role of the United States Treasury is to manage the debt and fiscal policy of the government. It should manage the debt prudently. That is, it should meet the maturities as they come due—about 30 per cent of the total debt of the government comes due in one year. The Treasury must try to obtain the lowest cost in terms of interest payments, and manage the debt in the interest of the economy, according to inflation and deflation. Lastly, the Treasury has to defend the dollar in international markets.

The Role of the Federal Reserve System

The basic aim of the Federal Reserve System is to manage credit. That is, the Federal Reserve must make credit available to the banking system. In a broader sense, the Federal Reserve attempts to maintain a growing economy, full employment, and a rising level of consumption, at the same time trying to avoid inflation and overheating of the economy.

Late in 1965, the Federal Reserve—fearful of inflation—raised its discount rates from 4 per cent to 4½ per cent. (The discount rates are the rates the member banks pay to borrow money.) Thus, all the other rates were raised to include the so-called *prime rate*. The prime rate is the rate all credit-worthy companies must pay. In December, 1965, the prime rate was raised from 5 per cent to 5½ per cent and on August 16, 1966 to 6 per cent. Other rates were raised in the money market.

The Money Market

There is no specific building or marketplace where the money market is located. It is essentially wherever the demand and supply for *short-term* funds is met or meet. The money market may be distinguished from the capital market, which is for *long-term* funds.

The institutions of the money market are large banks, such as the Morgan Guaranty Trust Company; large government bond dealers, such as Salomon Brothers and Hutzler; commercial paper houses, such as Goldman, Sachs and Company; banker's acceptance firms, such as the Discount Corporation; federal funds firms, such as Garvin, Bantel and Company; and the Federal Reserve Bank of New York. These institutions, trading *shore-term* funds with each other—often by telephone or teletype—constitute the core of the money market in New York City.

Short-term instruments traded in the money market include:

1. *Short-term United States Government Securities.* As of March 31, 1966, there were outstanding $59.5 billion of United States Treasury bills and $1.7 billion of United States Treasury certificates. As explained above, these have maturities within one year and are virtually riskless.

2. *Commercial and Finance Paper.* As of February 28, 1966, total commercial and financial paper outstanding was $10.6 billion. Commercial and finance paper consists of a firm's signed promissory notes. A promissory note is a written unconditional promise to pay on demand and at a fixed date in the future a stated sum of money to a specified person or bearer. The maturities run from thirty to 270 days.

a. Commercial or dealer paper is sold to the banks and non-bank financing institutions by a dealer who receives a commission.

b. Finance paper is sold largely by the sales finance companies, such as Commercial Credit Corporation, *direct* to the buyers.

Commercial and finance paper are unsecured and nonrenewable. Therefore, these are considered a suitable and liquid money market instrument.

3. *Bankers Acceptances.* As of February, 1966, total bankers acceptances outstanding were $3.3 billion. These are the result of financing imports and exports. An example of foreign trade transaction might be as follows: Importer *A* in this country wishes to buy $10,000 of coffee from Brazil. He applies to his bank in New York for a commercial letter of credit. This permits the exporter in Brazil, on submission of shipping documents, etc., to draw a draft on *A*'s bank in New York. This draft or bill of exchange is an unconditional order in writing, requiring the bank to pay on demand $10,000. The bank *accepts* this, at which time it becomes a promise to pay by the bank. (Importer *A* is also bound to pay his bank.)

Thus, this banker's acceptance, which may be due up to 180 days, becomes a highly liquid money market instrument.

4. *Federal Funds.* Every member bank has to keep a balance at the Federal Reserve Bank. For example, in May, 1966, member banks in New York City had to keep a balance of 16½ per cent of their demand deposits and 4 per cent of their time deposits at the Federal Reserve Bank of New York. There are times, however, when some banks have more than is required and some less. These shortages and surpluses are telephoned daily into a federal funds house, like Garvin, Bantel and Company, and matched. Thus, a bank that is short of funds can borrow or exchange from a bank that is long. The buying bank gets an *immediate* balance at the Federal Reserve Bank and gives in return its own clearing house check (good the next business day) plus interest at the Federal Funds rate. Thus there are one-day or sometimes weekend loans. It is estimated that the total volume runs between $1 billion and $4 billion a day.

5. *Negotiable Time Certificates of Deposit.* Negotiable certificates are given by a commercial bank for a time deposit. The time deposit in May, 1966, was for at least thirty days and had a maximum interest of 5½ per cent. Thus the bank agreed to pay 5½ per cent and

had the use of the money for the time of the deposit, sometimes as much as a year. However, the holder of the certificates, usually in large denominations ($100,000 or more), could *sell* this certificate in the money market should it be necessary to obtain cash prior to the maturity of the certificate. In October, 1966, commercial banks could pay 5½ per cent on negotiable time certificates of deposit *only* on amounts of $100,-000 or more. For less than $100,000, the maximum amount was 5 per cent. The total volume of the negotiable time certificates of deposit in November, 1966, was about $16 billion.

     6. *Call Loans, or Brokers Loans.* These are an important part of the money market but do not constitute an instrument, strictly speaking. Commercial banks make call loans to brokers secured by listed securities for the purposes of carrying margin accounts and to dealers for the purpose of carrying securities which they are distributing. The term *call* loan is somewhat a misnomer. In the 1920's, there was a call money desk on the New York Stock Exchange, but this has been discontinued. Loans by commercial banks are made directly to brokers and dealers and at the end of 1966 amounted to $3.2 billion.

The following is a tabulation of the important money market rates as they appeared in the *Wall Street Journal* on November 22, 1966:

     Bankers acceptance rates for 1 day to Dec. 31, 5¾% to 5⅝%; Jan. 3 to 90 days, 5⅞% to 5¾%; 91 to 180 days, 6% to 5⅞%.

     Federal funds in the open market: Day's high 5½%; low 5¼%; closing bid 5¼%; offered 5½%.

     Call money lent brokers on Stock Exchange collateral by New York City banks, 6% to 6½%; by banks outside New York City, 6% to 6¼%.

     Call money lent on Governments to dealers by New York City banks 6% to 6½%; to brokers by New York City banks, 6% to 6½%; to brokers by banks outside New York City, 6% to 6¼%.

     Commercial paper placed directly by a major finance company was as follows: 30 to 270 days, 5⅞%.

     Commercial paper sold through dealers, 90 days and four to six months maturities, 6% to 5⅞%.

     Certificates of deposit: Rates paid at New York City banks, 30 days and longer, high 5½%, low 5½%.

Other money market rates which might be mentioned include:

1. The *discount rate,* which is the rate that the Federal Reserve Banks charge their member banks for temporary loans. This rate on November 22, 1966 was 4½ per cent.

2. The *prime rate,* which is the rate of interest that almost all large commercial banks charge their credit-worthy customers. This rate on November 22, 1966 was 6 per cent.

Analysis of Bonds

     In appraising the merits of a bond, the investor should consider safety, income, and maturity.

Safety of a bond is measured most easily by the service ratings. Moody's Investors Service and Standard & Poor's Corporation evaluate and rate almost all of the large bond issues.

The table illustrates how these two leading services group their bonds according to their ratings.

	Moody's	*Standard & Poor's*
Top quality—maximum safety	Aaa	AAA
Very high grade—high quality	Aa	AA
High grade—investment quality	A	A
Good grade—medium quality	Baa	BBB
Speculative grade	Ba	BB
Small assurance of continued payment of interest	B	B

Thus, an investor buying a bond with A or better rating can have some, but not complete, assurance that the interest and principal will be paid. If he buys a bond with a lesser rating, he must take great care in its selection.

Rating services also break down their ratings into Municipal bonds and Corporate bonds, which include industrials, utilities, and railroads.

The following are the ratings and comparative yields of Moody's Investors Service on August 4, 1966:

	Aaa	*Aa*	*A*	*Baa*
Municipals	3.79	3.89	4.12	4.34
Industrials	5.20	5.24	5.36	5.85
Public Utilities	5.26	5.37	5.53	5.72
Railroads	5.28	5.36	5.40	5.73
United States Government*	5.02	—	—	—

*Three issues.

Another measure of safety is the number of times the interest charges are earned or covered. For example, in the income account of the Lobuck Corporation, page 28, we showed an operating profit of $1,070,000, item 4-B and interest charges of $40,000, item 5. The interest coverage before taxes would be obtained by dividing operating income of $1,070,000 by $40,000 of interest, or 26.5 times. This is generally considered a high interest coverage. Often the interest coverage is calculated after taxes, as shown.

Item 4 B Operating Profit	$1,070,000
Less Federal Income Taxes	488,000
Balance for Interest	$ 582,000
Item 5 Interest on Bonds and Bank Loan	$ 40,000

Coverage for charges $582,000 divided by 40,000 equals 14.6 times

In order to qualify as investment bonds, interest charges should be covered over a *period of five years*, approximately as follows:

	Before Federal Income Taxes	After Federal Income Taxes
Industrial Bonds	7×	5×
Public Utility	4×	3×
Railroad	5×	4×

It is also important to note the record for coverage of interest. Has the interest coverage been steady? Is the number of times interest coverage improving? If the record for interest coverage is good even in a year of low business, the bond is more attractive than one that shows high coverage in very good times and low coverage in years of poor business. Also, the analyst should consider the outlook for the company.

Still another measure of safety may be obtained from the balance sheet. In an *industrial* bond, it is generally desirable *to have the bonded debt not in excess of the working capital*. There are exceptions to this rule, as in the case of certain chemical, aluminum, and air transport companies which are expanding rapidly.

In a public utility it is usually not desirable to have the debt exceed 50 per cent of the capitalization. The capitalization is defined as the sum of the bonds, preferred and common stock, and the surplus or retained earnings (see page 16).

While balance sheet items are important, it is earnings that pay the interest and eventually the principal.

Income and Interest Rates

At a given time, the relative yield obtained on a bond usually depends to a great extent on its quality. An *Aaa* bond will have a lower yield than a *Baa* bond. On the other hand, on occasions a shrewd buyer will find an *Aaa* bond with a *Baa* yield. This may be because there is a poor market for the bond or because it is an odd lot—under $5,000 worth of bonds.

Another determinant of the income of a bond is the money market. When interest rates are high, corporations—even those with high credit standing—must sell bonds with high coupon rates. In 1946, corporations with high credit standing could sell bonds at 2⅝ per cent; and in 1966 the same companies had to offer over a 6 per cent rate, yet their credit, if anything, had improved.

Interest rates are one of the most important factors affecting the price of high grade bonds. Take a simple case where an investor buys a 20-year 5 per cent high grade bond at face amount or at $1,000. Let us suppose that all other high grade bonds are selling at about the same yield basis or 5 per cent. Then let us suppose that money gets tight and corporations desiring to sell high grade bonds find they must offer bonds at 6 per cent. That is, all high grade bonds are selling on a 6 per cent basis. Obviously the investor who bought a 5 per cent bond at face amount will find it is no longer worth $1,000 in the current market but has declined. This may be calculated by referring to the bond yield table. It would be simply necessary to determine at what price a 20-year 5 per cent would sell to yield 6 per cent. The answer would be $884.44. A very rough calculation is sometimes made by dividing the new yield into the old. That is, 5 per cent divided by 6 per cent equals $833. In short, bond prices and yields move inversely to each other; that is, rising yields mean lower prices and the converse.

Many examples can be given of serious declines in prices of high grade bonds due to rising interest rates. In 1945, National Dairy Products Company sold at 101¾ bonds with 2¾ per cent coupon due 1970. On March 17, 1966, due only to money rates, the bonds were quoted at 90, a paper loss of over 11 points for those who bought the bonds when they were sold in 1945. This bond is also selling at a *discount* of 10 points from its maturity value of $1,000. Discount refers to the amount, in this case 10 points, by which securities—particularly bonds, and even preferred stocks—sell below par or face value.

By a careful selection of maturities the investor can in part protect himself against the drastic changes in interest rates. This can be done by the policy of spaced maturities. Spaced maturities means buying securities in a block coming due every year, every three years, or every five years. As the securities mature the proceeds can be invested in securities of longer maturity taking advantage of the higher rates.

Another similar way of arranging maturities is to have a certain percentage of securities in Treasury bills, certificates, or notes, and a part in longer bonds. Thus as interest rates rise the short-term obligations can be invested in the higher yielding short-term securities and the overall income improved.

Call Price of Redeemable Bonds

The call price is the price at which a company might call or pay off its bonds. Many times in the past companies have paid off their bonds before they came due or matured. Companies in the late 1920's sold 5 per cent and 6 per cent bonds. When interest rates declined in the 1930's, these companies were able to call their bonds and sell new ones with coupons as low as 2½ per cent. The call price is usually set at a premium over $1,000 of 4 or 5 points, declining as the maturity date approaches.

If the bond is callable at a price near maturity value, the company may call the bond and sell a lower coupon bond. This is often referred to as refunding, and is done to save interest costs. Thus an investor should choose if possible a bond with a high call price. For example, the American Telephone and Telegraph 4⅜s of 1985 are currently (June, 1966) callable at 103.28 until March 31, 1967, at 103.04 until March 31, 1968, and at declining prices thereafter. On March 4, 1966 these bonds were selling at 90. They were therefore selling at a *discount* from par or face amount of $1,000. Sometimes it is profitable for an investor to buy a high grade bond at a discount if lower interest rates are expected. But a call price places a ceiling on appreciation possibilities since a company might call the high coupon bonds with the proceeds of the sale of low coupon bonds. Therefore an investor might consider the purchase of a noncallable bond such as the Atchison, Topeka, and Santa Fe Railway Company 4s of 1995. On March 4, 1966 these bonds were selling at 88.

If an investor holds a convertible bond, he should watch carefully for a possible call. For example, many convertible bonds, as the affairs of the company improve, advance in price. Then the company might decide to call the bonds. The investor should then immediately sell his bonds or convert them into stock. An extreme case was that of the convertible bonds of the Interprovincial Pipe Line Company. These bonds, in June, 1953, were selling at about $5,080 a bond and called at $1,041. Thus a bondholder failing to see the public notice would lose $4,039 a bond. Notices are usually published in the recognized financial papers, such as the *Wall Street Journal*. Sometimes the entire issue is called, and sometimes only part of the issue is called. In the latter case, only the numbers of the bonds drawn for call by lot are published.

Marketability

Generally speaking, the larger the bond issue outstanding the greater its marketability. Marketability means that a security may be bought or sold in reasonable quantities at current prices. That is, there is a substantial volume of trades or transactions in a particular security. A large issue of bonds, over $20,000,000, usually has a good market, but there is no general rule. Sometimes the large investors will hold a substantial amount of a large issue and the marketability will be poor. Marketability usually does not apply to the investment merits of a bond. A bond could have a poor credit standing yet trade in substantial volume and have good marketability. Marketability is a desirable quality if the investor does not expect to hold the bond to maturity. Otherwise it can be ignored.

In summary, the investor analyzing a bond should examine its interest coverage over a period of years, its asset position, its call price, and its marketability. As a further check on the merits of a bond, the investor should look at the ratings of the services, such as Moody's and Standard & Poor's. Lastly, and possibly most important, he should look at the maturity of the bond, bearing in mind the possible effect of an increase in interest rates.

Interest Rates

Interest rates rise and fall in accord with the demand and supply of loanable funds. Early in 1966, it was clear that there was a heavy demand on the part of large corporations for capital goods. Consumers were also demanding durable goods such as automobiles, refrigerators, and the like. As a result, the bond market was flooded with new issues and commercial banks were pressed for loans. The outcome was that interest rates in general rose and bonds depreciated. The following table compares bond prices and yields, May, 1956 and May, 1966. It will be noted that the average price of bonds dropped from 97 to 76 or 21 points, and the yields increased from an average of 3.39 per cent, to 4.97 per cent.

| | | | MAY | | | |
| | | | 1956 | | 1966 | |
			Price	Yield	Price	Yield
Metropolitan Edison	3½	1986	100	3.25%	80	5.11%
Bell Telephone Co. of Pa.	3¼	1996	98	3.35	72	5.02
American Tel. & Tel. Co.	3¼	1984	97	3.42	77	5.13
Union Pacific Railroad	2½	1991	84	3.30	67	4.78
Norfolk & Western Railway	4	1996	108	3.62	87	4.83
Average			97	3.39	76	4.97

REVIEW QUESTIONS

1. Define a bond. What are the obligations of a company to a bondholder, as compared with its obligations to a stockholder?

2. Distinguish between nominal yield, current yield, and yield to maturity.

3. If you bought a 20-year 4½ per cent bond at 105, what is the *approximate* yield to maturity?

4. Calculate the *exact* yield to maturity on the above bond using the following bond yield table for 20 years at 4½ per cent:

Yield	Price
4.05	1.061
4.10	1.054
4.15	1.047
4.20	1.040

5. Distinguish between open end, closed end, and limited open end mortgages.

6. Describe debenture bonds. Are they necessarily weaker bonds than mortgage bonds? Explain.

7. What are two advantages of convertible bonds to the corporation and two advantages to the investor? What is meant by the term "conversion parity?"

8. Why are equipment trust certificates considered good investments?

9. What is the basis for exemption from federal income taxes of municipal securities?

10. If your client is in the 30 per cent tax bracket and is offered a 4.20 per cent municipal security, should he buy it if comparable corporate bonds yield 6.5 per cent? Show calculations.

11. What standards would you use in analyzing a general obligating medium sized city bond? Large turnpike revenue bond?

12. Describe the types of obligations issued by the United States. On what is the security of these obligations based?

13. Distinguish between the role of the United States Treasury and that of the Federal Reserve System. Do they work together?

14. Describe the important *institutions* and *instruments* of the money market.

15. What standards would you use in appraising the merits of a corporate bond? Describe three.

Economics

Chapter 5

Background

Economists may be divided into two schools: (a) the classical production, or micro economists and (b) the consumption, Keynesian or macro economists. The latter school is by far the predominant one.

The classical school runs back at least to Adam Smith (1723–1783), author of the renowned *Wealth of Nations* (1776). One of Smith's ideas was that the government should protect the individual from violence but let business alone. In other words, he advocated free enterprise of the *laissez faire* type. Perhaps this thought was best expressed by J. B. Say (1767–1832), who wrote that there is no such thing as over-production, since production creates its own demand and at a price the market will be cleared. Also, until the great depression of 1929, it was felt that the business cycle was a normal if painful process.

A business cycle generally consists of the following stages:

1. Rise in stock prices
2. Improving business
3. Speculation and booming stock prices
4. High interest rates and tight credit
5. Stock market crash
6. Decline in business and employment
7. Prolonged depression
8. Lower costs
9. Rise in stock prices
10. Improving business

We had especially severe business cycles starting in 1837, 1873, and 1929.

It was the general belief until the Great Depression (1929–1936) that little could be done about a business cycle by either business or government.

The worst part of the business cycle was the *depression*, which might be defined as a prolonged period of low business activity resulting in high unemployment, exhaustion of savings by many, low profits for business, and depressed stock prices.

The concept of *consumption economics* goes back to Lord Lauderdale (1759–1830), who claimed that overproduction is possible, based on under-consumption. Others of this thought might include J. C. L. S. Sismondi (1773–1842), who wrote that the national production must be consumed annually or equilibrium will be disturbed. By far the most important economist of this school was John Maynard Keynes (1883–1946). (Pronounce this name as if it were spelled "Kanes".) Lord Keynes was an Englishman trained under the conservativist economist Alfred Marshall. So great was Keynes's influence that a leading economist recently exclaimed that we are all Keynesians now. His great work was: *The General Theory of Employment, Interest and Money* (1936). Briefly, he advocated *spending* by the government and by industry for capital improvement in order to stimulate *consumption*, an important component of gross national product. He felt that spending was important and should exceed savings if the gross national product were to rise. In short, the following might summarize his thinking:

	Income, or Gross National Product	= Consumption	+ Investment	Savings
	Y	= C	+ I	S
(1)	100	= 80	+ 20	20
(2)	90	= 80	+ 10	20
(3)	110	= 80	+ 30	20

(1) Savings *equal* investment; therefore income is level
(2) Investment *less* than savings; therefore income falls
(3) Investment *greater* than savings; therefore income rises

The philosophy of spending to control the economy is the prevailing thought in this country today.

This should bring us to a clearer understanding of the *Gross National Product* or GNP. GNP might be defined as the sum at market price of the goods and services produced in the economy during a period. But it is also a measure of *expenditures* since all of the expenditures of the economy would equal the income. The following is a breakdown of the GNP by expenditures in 1965.

C	Personal Consumption Expenditures	$432,000,000,000
I	Gross Private Domestic Investment	107,000,000,000
G	Government Purchases and Miscellaneous	142,000,000,000
Y	Gross National Product or Expenditures	$681,000,000,000

New Economics. It is now the basic belief that the economy and the business cycle can be controlled and continued growth of our economy fostered by government intervention. This intervention takes the following forms:

1. *Monetary and credit control,* particularly by the Federal Reserve System and the U.S. Treasury. During times of depression both work to make money easy (low interest rates and available credit) and vice versa in boom times.
2. *Fiscal policy.* In times of slack business, taxes should be cut and government *expenditures* increased. In boom times taxes should be increased and government expenditures curtailed.
3. *Other forms of government intervention.* These would include direct controls over prices and wages. But the government has always been more willing and perhaps more able to control prices than wages. Also should be included the powers to reduce the unfavorable balance of payments (1) by controlling the investments abroad, (2) by controlling banks' loans abroad, (3) by taxing the flotation of foreign securities in the United States, or by other means.

But the *important* thing to keep in mind is that the Council of Economic Advisors, which advises the President of the United States, is determined (1) to prevent the recurrence of depression or even recession and (2) to keep the economy growing (i.e., increase consumption).

Here we might distinguish between a depression, which we have described above as a prolonged period of unemployment, poor business, and depressed stock prices, and a *recession.*

A recession is a *short-term* decline in stock prices, business activity and employment. In 1948, 1954, and 1957 we had short recessions. During these years the U. S. Government and the Federal Reserve System cut taxes and/or made credit easy in order to cure the recession and bring about recovery. In the main, they were successful.

Usually but not always the *stock market* forecasts a decline in business or a recession. However, there was one notable exception to this rule in 1962. For example, the stock market declined sharply in the first half of 1962 and in particular in May and June. However most of the business indicators (discussed in Chapter 18) did not decline. In other words, the market seemed to make a mistake. This was shown by the recovery of most stocks of their 1962 losses and new high in the following years.

However, in 1966, the country was concerned with inflation. Our country had gone through a period of unusual prosperity featuring heavy spending both by the Government—due to the war in Vietnam—and by private individuals. As a nation, we were spending more than we could earn by production. Prices were rising, and the purchasing power of the dollar was falling. In other words, we were faced with inflation.

Inflation might be defined briefly as too many dollars chasing too few goods, with resultant price rises. In more detail, inflation is a combination of *cost push* and *demand pull*. Cost push is a process where rising costs and prices interact with a spiral effect. This we saw clearly in 1966 when there were many wage demands. The demand pull also must be sufficient to keep the spiral moving. Demand pull is generated when the *expenditures* for consumption, for investment, for government purchases are in excess of the nation's capacity to produce.

Deflation, obviously, is the reverse of inflation and is feared by government, business, and the general public. Deflation occurs when demand falters and production is greater than demand. Hence prices fall. The government can dampen down demand by increasing both personal and corporate taxes, but it is generally conceded that the government fears deflation and depression more than inflation. Some economists have claimed that a certain amount of inflation is necessary if full employment and economic growth are to be sustained.

Balance of payments is a summary statement showing the receipts from and payments to foreign countries during the calendar year. The following is a summary of the receipts and payments in the balance of payments accounts in 1965.

Receipts (in billions)

Exports of merchandise	$26.3
Travel of foreigners in U.S.	1.2
Transportation, insurance, etc.	2.4
Investment income from abroad	5.6
Miscellaneous	3.5
Total	$39.0

Payments (in billions)

Imports of merchandise	$21.5
Travel of Americans abroad	2.5
Transportation, insurance, etc.	2.6
Investment payments	2.5
Military payments	2.8
Capital outflow	3.8
Grants in aid	4.3
Miscellaneous	.3
Total	$40.3
Balance of Payments *Deficit*	$ 1.3

The cumulative balance-of-payments deficit has amounted to about $31 billion between 1949 and 1965. This means that the deficit has been settled by loss of gold of more than $13.8 billion and by the building up of short-term balances of foreigners in this country to about $29.0 billion.

Balances of foreigners would include bank balances of foreign central banks, of foreign commercial banks, and of nonbanking concerns. In addition these have substantial holdings in short-term United States Treasury bills, notes, and certificates.

Attempts have been made to reduce this unfavorable balance of payments by inducing firms to curtail capital expenditures abroad, by deliberately high short-term money rates in the New York market, and by taxes.

REVIEW QUESTIONS

1. What is the difference between the *classical* and the *consumption* schools of economics?
2. Describe the components of the gross national product. What is the most important? How does *savings* affect gross national product?
3. What is the so-called *new economics*? Why is it important to the investor?
4. Distinguish between depression and recession and show how both are related to the *new economics*.
5. Define *inflation* and explain how it could affect corporate profits—favorably and unfavorably.
6. What is the effect of the spending policies of the government?
7. Show how monetary control, as well as fiscal policies, help stabilize the economy.
8. Define the balance of payments of the United States and discuss the significance of the cumulative deficit.
9. What is the business cycle? Is it outdated?

Preferred Stock

Chapter 6

Preferred stock, like common stock, is an equity or share in the earnings and assets of the corporation, but there are many distinguishing characteristics which should be discussed.

First—after the interest and all the operating expenses and bond interest have been paid, the preferred stockholder has priority over the common stockholder for dividends; but the preferred dividend is declared at the option of the board of directors.

The preferred stockholder has no claim against the company for dividends unless declared. He does not have any of the rights of a creditor or bondholder. He cannot throw the company into receivership for not paying preferred dividends. The only right inherent in preferred stock is the right to receive preferred dividends before the common stock dividends are paid. Preferred stock cannot be included when referring to funded debt.

In addition to preference over common for dividends, the charter may state that, *in liquidation*, preferred stock has preference over common. This is, of course, after the bond, trade, and bank creditors have been paid.

Second—the preferred stockholder receives dividends, usually quarterly, at a stated rate ranging from 3.5 per cent to 8 per cent ($3.50 to $8 of 100 par). The percentage rate is usually based on $100 par. While $100 par is the usual par value for preferred stocks, there are a number of preferred stocks of $50 par and as low as $10. Also there are no-par preferred stocks, as pointed out in Chapter 3. *The stated rate of a preferred stock is fixed as to maximum but not as to minimum.* This means that no matter how much money the company makes, the straight preferred stockholder usually receives only his stated rate (3 per cent to 8 per cent).

The exceptions to this rule might be the convertible and the participating preferreds discussed later. But if the earnings of the company fall, the directors may decide to pass the dividend for one quarter or a longer period.

Third—most but not all of the preferred stocks have *cumulative* features. These features are described in the charter of the corporation. They usually provide that if the full dividend is not paid each quarter, it accrues or accumulates to the benefit of the stockholders. Companies might have large accumulations of back dividends, or arrears, as they are called, yet be in no danger of insolvency. The dividend arrears are not carried as a liability on the balance sheet. However, *the company cannot pay dividends on the common stock until all the dividend accumulations are paid* to the preferred stockholders. Thus the holder of a cumulative preferred stock may or may not receive dividends for a quarter or even for years. At a later time, if the affairs of the company should improve, unpaid dividends will be paid, provided the preferred is cumulative.

Fourth—almost all preferred stocks are callable at the option of the corporation at a specified price. The charter states the terms under which a corporation may call its stock. These terms include the call price, the number of days' notice required and the place of payment. Usually the price is par or several points in excess of par, ranging from as high as $120 a share for the 4½% preferred stock of E. I. du Pont de Nemours Company to $100 a share of the W. T. Grant & Company 3¾% preferred. In no-par preferred stock, the call price is stated in dollars a share in the charter. There are some preferred stocks that are not callable at the option of the company. Most of these stocks were sold in the early part of the century when the demand for money was very great. Some of the companies had to pay a preferred dividend rate as high as 8 per cent and provide that the stock could not be called. An example of a noncallable stock is the United States Rubber Company 8% preferred.

Fifth—in contrast to a bond, a preferred stock does not have any maturity. Once a company has sold a preferred stock, the money received is in a sense permanent money. The corporation never has to pay it back.

Sixth—usually a preferred stockholder does not have the right to vote for the directors or have a voice in the management of the company. If, however, the company desires to issue senior securities, merge, or make any fundamental change in the corporate structure, the preferred stockholders usually have the right to vote on these issues. Under the rules of the New York Stock Exchange, preferred stockholders have a right to vote after the company has failed to pay six successive quarterly dividends.

Convertible Preferred Stock

Convertible preferred stock means that the owner has the right to exchange a preferred stock for a share or shares of common stock of the same company. As in the case of bonds, sometimes the number of shares of common are given. There are times when conversion is determined on the basis of par value. For example, a $100 par preferred might be convertible into common at $50 a share or two shares of common for each share of $100 par preferred. The holder of a convertible preferred stock usually has a stronger claim than the holder of a common stock to earnings and assets. In addition, if company earnings increase, the convertible preferred will rise in value. An example of a convertible preferred is the Kaiser Aluminum & Chemical Company $4\frac{1}{8}\%$ preferred. This stock is convertible into common stock of the company at $62.65 a share. Since the par value of the $4\frac{1}{8}\%$ preferred is $100 the conversion terms, or conversion ratio as it is sometimes called, are found by dividing 100 by $62.65 or 1.596. Thus the holder of the $4\frac{1}{8}\%$ preferred Kaiser Aluminum & Chemical Company may convert into 1.596 shares of common. Often the number of shares of common stock a preferred holder may obtain by conversion declines with the years.

A company might wish to call a preferred stock. Then the preferred stockholder must be given the required number of days notice. This will enable him to either convert into common or sell the stock. Since the preferred stock is registered in the name of the holder, the company will notify him of the call. This is *not* true of coupon convertible bonds (discussed in Chapter 4).

Participating Preferred

As its name implies, the holder of a participating preferred stock has the right to receive a stipulated dividend and then share in the earnings dividends at a specified rate along with the common stockholders. For example, the Chicago, Milwaukee & St. Paul Railroad Company has outstanding about 518,000 shares of 5% noncumulative series A, $100 par preferred. This stock on June 23, 1966 sold at $85 a share. A holder of this stock is entitled to a noncumulative dividend of $5 per share annually and to participate equally with the common up to $1 per share in addition to the $5. However, the preferred stockholder does not get the additional participation until the common stockholder receives $3.50 in dividends. Since 1951, the highest dividend paid the common stockholder of this railroad has been $2 a share.

Other railroads with participating preferreds include the Chicago and North Western Railway Company, the Alabama Great Southern Railroad Company, and the International Railways of Central America.

Selecting Preferred Stocks

There are several attributes of a preferred stock which an investor should seek before buying. These include: (a) steady past earnings, (b) strong financial condition, (c) good outlook, and (d) satisfactory yield.

Steady Past Earnings

Past earnings of a company should be examined by the investor to see if they have been steady. A number of companies have reported high earnings in some years and poor earnings in others. In the poor years, the preferred stockholder does not often receive dividends.

Earnings can be measured either on a *per share* basis or an *over-all* basis. In order to describe these two methods let us *assume* that a company has the preferred stock indicated below.

Preferred Stock Outstanding	$500,000
Dividend Rate on Preferred	5%
Dividend Requirement	$ 25,000
Number of Shares	5,000
Par Value	$ 100

Since the above $500,000 of preferred is $100 par, there would be 5,000 shares outstanding or $500,000 divided by 100. Also the dividend rate is 5 per cent. This means the preferred dividend requirement is $25,000 (or 5% × $500,000 equals $25,000).

Earnings per share of preferred as discussed on pages 26–7 are calculated by dividing into the net income the number of shares. In this example, we also might assume earnings and interest as shown.

Earnings before Interest	$180,000
Interest	60,000
Net Income	$120,000
Per Share of Preferred	$ 24.00

The net income of $120,000 divided by 5,000 shares equals $24 per share of preferred stock. This would seem to be fairly good earnings for a $5 dividend. As a matter of fact, it is—but the analyst should always look to the back years. If the earnings have been steady and have ranged between $20 and $30 a share it would appear that the dividend is reasonably secure. This is particularly true with the public utility preferred stocks.

A better way of measuring the dividend coverage is by the over-all basis.

The *Over-All Coverage* of preferred stock is figured by adding the interest and the preferred dividends and dividing the sum (of the interest and preferred dividends) into earnings before interest, as shown.

Earnings before Interest	$180,000
Interest	$ 60,000
Preferred Dividend Requirement	25,000
Total Interest and Preferred Dividend	$ 85,000

Over-all coverage 2.12 times

The over-all coverage is, therefore, the earnings before interest of $180,000 divided by the sum of the interest and the preferred dividend of $85,000 or 2.12 times.

Over-all coverage of a preferred stock should be at least 2 times in the case of a public utility and higher in railroads and industrials. It is often true that a company might have high per share earnings but *low* over-all coverage. This is true where there is a large amount of debt and a small number of shares of preferred. But in this situation the high per-share earnings of the preferred often fade quickly with any decline in business.

In weighing the merits of a preferred stock, the analyst should always consider the past record of a period of *four or five years* as well as the type of preferred. For industrial and railroad preferred, we suggest an average over-all coverage for a five-year period of between *four and five times*. For a public utility an average coverage of *two or three times* over a period of five years would be satisfactory, but the analyst should always observe the stability and trend of these coverages. An *average* coverage might be satisfactory due to high coverage in one year offsetting poor coverage in another. If coverage fluctuates sharply it is a danger signal. For example, the table below indicates that Fruehauf Trailer

	March 24, 1966			1965	
Investment Grade	Price	Call Price	% Yield	Per Share	Over-all Coverage
General Motors Corp. 5%	106	120	4.72	$749.60	147.9
E. I. duPont de Nemours & Co. 4½%	98	120	4.59	170.47	39.5
Gulf State Utilities Co. 4.40%	88	103	5.00	38.12	2.9
Medium Grade to Low Grade					
R. H. Macy & Co. 4¼%	86	107½	4.94	$ 59.44	2.3*
International Minerals & Chemical Co. 4%	80	110	5.00	206.90	4.3†
Fruehauf Corp. 4%	94	104½	4.25	410.00	8.1

*Year ended July 31, 1965.
†Year ended June 30, 1965.

Co. earned $410.00 per share of preferred in 1965. This seems like excellent earnings, but in 1958 the company reported a deficit of $68.91 a share of preferred.

Also, it is always reassuring to see an improving trend of dividend coverage. Each industry should be considered on its own merits, bearing in mind the more cyclical the industry the greater should be the coverage. The table on page 74 contains examples of the coverage of investment and medium-grade preferreds.

Strong Financial Condition

Although earning power is the first consideration in selecting a preferred, financial strength is also important. In an *industrial* concern, as illustrated in our chapter on bonds, the *net working capital* should be nearly as large as the debt. Where there is preferred stock, the *debt plus the preferred stock* of an industrial company should not greatly exceed the working capital. Also, in the case of the capitalization of an industrial company (explained in Chapter 2), the debt plus the preferred should not be much more than 40 per cent of the total of bonds preferred, common and surplus.

In utilities the working capital has little meaning. Very few public utilities have substantial working capital. In fact, the public utilities are on a cash basis, have no inventory problem, and therefore do not need working capital at all. It is not uncommon to see a working-capital deficit in a public utility, but the capitalization should not be topheavy with debt and preferred stock. For example, *debt plus preferred* should not exceed 70 per cent of the total capitalization.

In railroads, working capital is important but there are no established ratios. There are only a few investment-type preferred stocks of railroads. A number of these are noncallable and noncumulative. However, their earnings record over the years has been excellent. An example of an investment-type railroad preferred would be the Union Pacific Railroad Company's 40¢ preferred which was selling on March 24, 1966 at about $8 a share to yield 5%.

During the 1930's, many railroads could not pay their fixed charges. Their earnings were declining and their bonded debt was excessive. As a result, they were reorganized and new securities were issued. In many cases, preferred stocks were exchanged for junior bonds of the old railroad. As a result, these preferred issues are more speculative than the older and more seasoned preferred issues.

Good Outlook for Earnings

While the investor in a preferred stock may not receive a larger preferred dividend even if the earnings of the company improve, he cannot be indifferent to the outlook of the company. At present the outlook for the electric public utilities is good. Rates seem to be satisfactory, earnings of many companies are improving, and over-all coverage of the preferred dividend is increasing. Railroads are faced with a number of problems, including high labor costs, and declining business due to competition with trucks, canals, waterways, and airplanes. In industrial concerns, the outlook is varied. Some industrial preferreds such as those in the chemical, merchandising, food, and rubber industries have an excellent earnings outlook. But the outlook of other industries, such as oil, metal, amusements, coal, and tobacco is less clear.

Yields

We figure the yield on preferred stocks in the same way as the yield on common stocks (see pages 88–9). For example, on March 4, 1966 the $4\frac{1}{2}\%$ preferred stock of the Consumers Power Company, a high grade company, sold at 88. We calculate the yield by dividing the rate of $4.50 by the price of 88 or 5.11%. The $4\frac{1}{2}\%$ bonds of the Consumers Power Company on the same day sold at 92 to yield to maturity 5.09%.

In the late 1950's there was a tendency for high-grade preferreds to yield *more* than high grade bonds. Sometimes the difference ran as high as .5 per cent. It was reasoned that this yield difference in favor of the preferred was due to the lack of maturity of the preferred. The bondholder in theory obtained his money when the bond came due. The preferred stockholder never gets his principal back unless the company calls the stock or unless he sells the preferred in the market for as much as or more than he paid for it. Also, as has been pointed out, the company is not compelled to pay the preferred dividends to keep solvent, as it must with bond interest.

In recent years, the yield on high-grade preferreds has in most cases been lower than the comparable yield on high-grade bonds. First, the investment status of many preferreds has been improving due to higher earnings coverage. Second, preferred stocks, except those of electric public utility operating companies issued prior to October 1, 1942, have tax advantages when held by a corporation. These factors have broadened the market and increased the demand for preferred stocks.

In February, 1966 the average yield on high grade industrial preferreds was 4.26 per cent and on high grade Aa bonds was 4.91 per cent.

Taxes

A substantial portion of dividends received on preferred stocks held by corporations may be deducted when they compute their taxable income. Under existing federal income tax law, such investors (including, in certain cases, life insurance companies and mutual savings banks) are entitled to a deduction equivalent to 85 per cent of dividends received on certain preferred stockholdings. This 85 per cent deduction applies to income from all preferred issues other than issues of public utility operating companies, while income from public utility operating company preferred stocks is entitled to the 85 per cent deduction only if such preferred stocks are "new money" issues, meaning preferreds issued for "new money" purposes on or after October 1, 1942. For corporations in the 48 per cent tax bracket, with only 15 per cent of such dividend income taxable, 7.2 per cent of the dividends on such issues will be paid in taxes thus providing an after tax return equal to 92.8 per cent of the dividend. The deduction available to corporate investors on income from utility preferreds issued prior to October 1, 1942, or for the refunding of bonds, debentures or other preferred stocks issued prior to October 1, 1942, is only 60.20833 per cent. Such preferred issues are often termed "old money" issues. Thus, with 39.79167 per cent of the income from "old money" utility preferreds taxable at the 48 per cent rate, the effective tax rate thereon is 19.1 per cent; and 80.9 per cent of the dividend is available after taxes.

For corporations which have an effective tax rate of 20 per cent, dividends on preferred stocks (other than "old money" utility issues) are 97 per cent tax free. On "old money" utility issues slightly more than 92 per cent of the dividend is available to such corporations.

The following examples show how these calculations are made.

Type of Issue	Tax Rate		% Dividend Subject		% of Dividend (or Yield) Paid in Tax	% Remain. After Tax
New Money Utility (or other Pfd)	48%	×	15.00000	=	7.2	thus 92.80
Old Money Utility	48	×	39.79167	=	19.1	thus 80.90
New Money Utility (or other Pfd)	20	×	15.00000	=	3.00	thus 97.00
Old Money Utility	20	×	39.79167	=	7.96	thus 92.04

In summary, the investor in preferred stocks seeks a high yield or return on his money, plus a chance for appreciation. He should, however, also analyze the earnings record, the financial strength, the tax position of the issue, and the outlook for the company and industry.

REVIEW QUESTIONS

1. Discuss the rights of the preferred stockholder as to liquidation, dividends, call privileges, maturity, and voting. How do these rights compare with those of the bondholder?
2. Describe and distinguish between convertible preferred stock and participating preferred stock.
3. Given the net income of $1,000,000 and capitalization of $10,000,000 or $100 par, 5% preferred, and $20,000,000 of $100 per common, what are the earnings per share preferred and what is the balance for the common on a per share basis?
4. What is meant by over-all coverage of preferred stock dividends? Why is it important, and what would you consider standard for an industrial preferred?
5. What should be the relation of working capital of an industrial firm to the preferred stock; what about utility and railroad preferred stock?
6. In the selection of preferred stocks, what are the most important considerations?
7. Why are the yields of many high grade preferreds *lower* than the yields of comparable high grade bonds?
8. Discuss the tax status of preferred dividends when held by corporate investors.

Common Stock

Particularly in the last decade, common stocks have gained a greater degree of acceptance in the public mind. Increasing numbers of individuals are eager to buy shares listed on a stock exchange or traded over the counter, especially shares of investment companies. Colleges and trust funds, as well as life insurance companies and savings banks, are buying common stocks. More and more, common stocks are considered "investments." Nevertheless, the individual buying a common stock should understand its nature.

The common stock of a corporation is authorized in its certificate of incorporation, which is filed with a designated official of a state. This gives the number and type of identical units, called shares. Corporations issue common and sometimes preferred stock. Proprietorships and partnerships, as previously mentioned, do not issue stock. The holder of a share of common stock has a part ownership in the earnings and assets of the corporation. The stock representing ownership in a corporation is called capital stock. Preferred and common shares have no maturity dates and do not have any fixed claim on the assets or the earnings of the corporation. But in spite of these considerations, the common stockholder has certain rights and obligations.

Right to a Stock Certificate

A buyer of a share of stock of a company, whether it be direct from the company on its formation or from another stockholder, is entitled to an engraved stock certificate *evidencing ownership of a specified number of shares of a corporation.* Each stock certificate contains the following information:

a) the name, address, and number of shares of the holder
b) the number and type (common or preferred) of shares authorized

     c)   the name of the transfer agent and registrar

     d)   the signatures of the officers of the corporation authorized to sign the stock certificate

A stock certificate is, in short, the physical evidence of ownership in a corporation.

Every corporation has a stated amount of authorized shares which it may issue. Most of this stock is outstanding and in the hands of the public. But a part of the stock may have been reacquired by the company and held in its vault or treasury. This stock is usually acquired by purchase in the market or by private sale and is called *treasury stock*. Since *this* stock does not vote or receive dividends, it does not affect the voting control, the dividends, or the equity of the existing stockholders. It may be resold at any price, given to officers, or used to acquire new assets or companies. It is usually the case that pre-emptive rights, explained on pages 83–4, do not apply except in certain states. In most cases treasury stock is carried as a deduction from outstanding stock.

When stock is issued it may be $100 par, no par, or low par. In the nineteenth century and early in the twentieth, most stocks had $100 par value and were carried on the books of the company at that figure. Since many of these stocks were quoted at substantially less than $100 a share there was confusion and often the mistaken belief that the stocks were worth $100 or more. Also, under several state laws, no new stocks could be sold for less than par or $100. This made the raising of new common capital difficult by companies whose stocks had fallen below $100 a share.

At present, most states have laws which permit companies to issue either no-par or low-par stock.

No-par stock, as its name indicates, has no face amount. The stock certificate simply reads: no-par shares. However, the directors of the company prior to the issuance of this stock *designate* a stated value at which the shares are carried on the books of the company. Some states set a minimum amount which the corporations may designate as the stated value of their no-par stock.

Low-par stock has a face value of a definite amount, usually $1 to $25, and is carried on the books of the company at par value. Sometimes a corporation will find a *tax advantage* to itself and to the stockholders in issuing low-par stock rather than no-par. For the corporation, the state capital stock taxes are often lower; for the individual, the transfer taxes are sometimes lower.

It should be stressed that par value has no relation to the market value or to the intrinsic worth of a stock. For example, the stock of International Business Machines Corporation on March 24, 1966 had a par value of $5 a share and a market value of $500 a share. It had a book value of $72.88 a share at the end of 1965. (Book value was explained in Chapter 2, page 17).

Right to Buy and Sell Stock

If a stockholder desires to buy more stock, it is not necessary to obtain the permission of the company. He simply acquires it by purchase in the open market or privately. Conversely, if he desires to sell shares, he cannot demand that the company buy the stock. A stockholder is free, instead, to seek a buyer for the stock either in the markets or by private sale.

After the sale terms have been agreed upon, the mechanics of transfer are simple. The seller signs his name on the back of the stock certificate and delivers it to the buyer or his broker. A record is kept of these certificates by the company or by its duly appointed *transfer agent,* often a bank. The transfer agent has a record of the names and addresses of the stockholder and number of shares. After determining that the old certificate is in proper form for transfer, the transfer agent issues a new certificate to the new owner. Also, most companies have a *registrar.* The duty of the registrar is to double check the actions of the transfer agent and to prevent improper issue of stock or a fraudulent transfer.

Stock certificates should be kept in a safe place. If they are lost or stolen the stockholder has to go to considerable expense and trouble to obtain a new certificate. In some states, a surety bond must be posted.

Right to a Dividend if Declared by the Board of Directors

The declaration of a dividend is almost exclusively the right of the directors. In only a few cases have the stockholders forced the directors to declare a dividend. (*Dodge v. Ford Motor Co.,* 1919). The directors might decide, for example, to pay no dividend even if earnings were substantial, if the company needed the money to pay off bank and other debt or for expansion of plant and equipment. There is nothing on the common stock certificate which says the company is required to pay a stated dividend or any dividend at all. On the other hand, the directors might pay dividends *in excess* of the current earnings, particularly if the corporation is in strong financial condition or if the outlook for earnings is favorable. If, however, a *dividend has been declared by the board of directors of the company,* then and then only do the stockholders have a *right* to collect it from the company.

There are a number of circumstances when a board of directors *cannot* pay a dividend depending on the state laws of the state in which the company is incorporated. For example, in some states a dividend can only be paid from earned surplus. In other states, no dividend may be paid when the company is bankrupt.

FORMS OF DIVIDENDS. When the directors declare dividends the usual form is *cash*. This means that the company or its paying agents sends checks to all the stockholders whose names appear on the books of the company on the so-called record date. Each stockholder receives a definite amount of money per share owned. In short, a dividend is a pro rata distribution among the stockholders.

Frequently a company will declare a *stock* dividend. The company accomplishes this by reducing its surplus account and increasing its capital account by the amount of the stock dividend. In other words, the surplus is capitalized. Thus the stockholder having a share in both the capital and surplus *prior* to the stock dividend does not receive any additional interest in the company by the stock dividend; the size of his share of the corporate pie remains the same but he has more pieces. Usually a stock dividend is paid in order to satisfy the stockholders and at the same time to conserve cash. A stock dividend is ordinarily not taxable as income if it is *held* by the stockholder. On the other hand, if the stock dividend is sold it *is* taxable as a capital gain with the determination of cost by a complicated formula.

Stock splits are in many ways similar to stock dividends, but there are certain important differences. When a stockholder receives more than 25 per cent additional shares it is usually termed a "stock split." This is a rule of thumb used by the New York Stock Exchange. In this case, the number of shares is simply increased, usually by reducing the par value, or the stated value of no-par stock. The surplus account is unaffected. As in the case of stock dividends it results in no additional ownership in the assets or earnings of the corporation. If, for example, a $10 par stock is split two for one, the corporation usually sends the stockholder a new certificate of one new share of $5 par for each old share held and in addition sends a $5 par stamp to place on each old $10 par certificate. The new stock received by the stockholder as a result of the stock split is as a rule not taxable *unless sold*.

When the management recommends that the company split its stock or declare a stock dividend, the stockholders are usually pleased, for the following reasons:

1. Sometimes the over-all dividend received by the stockholders is larger.
2. It is management's expression of confidence that earnings and dividends will improve.
3. Further splits may be made.
4. The market is broader, owing to the lower-priced shares.

This last reason is perhaps the most important. For some reason the public seems reluctant to buy a high-priced stock even when the total dividends received on the higher-priced stock are larger. For example, many investors would prefer to buy 100 shares of a stock selling at 18 paying 60 cents a share or $60 a year than 10 shares of a similar company selling at 180 and paying $7 a share or $70 a year.

There are times when a company will have a *reverse* split. This usually occurs when a company's stock has declined substantially in price to around three or four dollars a share. In order to improve the collateral value of the shares and possibly to sell new shares, a company will authorize a *reverse split.* That is, it will increase the par value or stated value of the stock and offer to the existing shareholders fewer shares in exchange for their shares held. For example, for every three shares held which sell at about four dollars a share, the company would offer one share. In 1965, the Studebaker Corporation had a reverse split and offered its stockholders one share for each five held. In 1943 Standard Brands, Inc. offered its stockholders one share for each four held.

Rights to Information

Stockholders have a right to demand information about the company in which they hold stock. Legally, they can inspect the corporate books of the company. (The corporate books are the minutes of the directors' meetings, the list of the stockholders, etc.). But the best source of information is the annual report to the stockholders. The Securities and Exchange Commission requires all companies with over $1,000,000 in assets and 500 stockholders or more to file an annual report. This includes all companies listed on national securities exchanges. Annual reports contain comparative profit-and-loss statements and balance sheets. They often describe the business of the company during the past year—its problems and its outlook. Other items often discussed include capital expenditures, research projects, employee relations, foreign investments, affiliates, and changes in management. A complete list of the officers and directors is given, along with their affiliation.

In addition, the SEC requires that all companies listed keep their registration statements up to date (see Securities and Exchange Act 1934). These registration statements are on file and available to the public.

Last, a stockholder is entitled to attend the annual meeting of the stockholders and ask the management questions.

Pre-emptive Right

A pre-emptive right is simply the inherent right of the stockholder to maintain his proportionate share of the assets, earnings, and control of the corporation. It is a common-law right. In other words, the corporation in most, *but not all*, states must first offer a new stock to its own stockholders before offering it to the public. This is to prevent the company from offering stock to the public at a price substantially below its worth, thus lessening the interest of the old stockholders in the corporate pie. When a company offers new stock to its old stockholders, its price to them is usually set below the current market price. A stockholder has a right to subscribe for new shares proportionately for each share held. A certificate is sent to the stockholder stating the number of rights owned, which corresponds to the number of shares held. It will also specify the number of new shares to which the stockholder is entitled to subscribe and the per-share price of such subscription. This privilege to subscribe is of short-term nature, usually expiring in sixty days. On the certificate, the stockholder may indicate whether he wishes to sell the rights or to exercise the privilege of subscription. In the latter case, the money for the subscription price must accompany the certificate. The stockholder must take either course. If he allows the time limit to run out without acting, the rights become worthless.

There is a simple formula for calculating the value of rights. For example, let us suppose that a company offers to its shareholders one new share at $46 for each four shares held. This would mean that the stockholder would have to have four shares to have four rights. (For each share a stockholder has *one* right.) If the current market price for the stock is 56, the following procedure could be used in calculating the value of the right. We have therefore the following:

$$M \text{ equals the market price of the stock} \qquad 56$$
$$S \text{ equals the subscription price of the stock} \qquad 46$$
$$N \text{ equals the number of rights for one share} \qquad 4$$

Formula and solution:

$$\frac{M - S}{N + 1} \text{ equals } \frac{56 - 46}{4 + 1} \text{ equals } \frac{10}{5} \text{ equals } \$2.00$$

Thus, the value of each right is about $2.00.

After the stock sells *ex-rights* but before the rights expire, the formula is $\frac{M - S}{N}$. To repeat, after the rights expire they have *no value*.

Warrants are somewhat similar to rights. As explained above, the number of rights to which a stockholder is entitled is based on his present stock holdings. Warrants, on the other hand, when applied to the purchase of stocks, normally refer to the number of new shares a stockholder may buy. In other words, warrants represent privileges to buy securities at specified prices.

Warrants are customarily issued with bonds to make them more attractive. The buyer of bonds with warrants has a fixed claim as to interest and principal against the company. Also, he can buy stock of the company at a fixed price and participate in the future of the company. Warrants are usually detachable. This means they may be bought and sold apart from the security to which they were originally attached. Some warrants trade over the counter or on the American Stock Exchange. The warrants are good for a number of years, sometimes forever. The Tricontinental Corporation warrants, for example, are perpetual and entitle the holder to buy any time 2.54 shares of the common stock at $8.88 a share. More often, as in the case of Atlas Corporation warrants, the owner can buy stock at a stated price. Atlas Corporation warrants permit the holder to buy one share of common stock at $6.25. Warrants are usually protected against dilution through stock splits or dividends. If a stock is split, the exercise price of the warrant is reduced downward proportionately. For example, if a company has outstanding warrants entitling the holder to buy a stock at $6 a share, and splits its stock two for one, then the exercise price of the warrants is automatically reduced from six to three or split two for one.

Voting Rights

The stockholders have the right to select the board of directors, as well as to vote on any fundamental changes in the corporation such as dissolution, consolidation, or amendments to the charter or bylaws. But this right is largely theoretical. In most cases, the management determines the board of directors, and the basic changes to be made, at annual or special meetings. In advance of the meetings, the stockholders are sent notices of the meeting, statements setting forth the directors to be elected, other business to be approved, and proxies which they are asked to sign. The *proxy* is a document by which the stockholder authorizes another person (or a proxy committee usually appointed by the management) to vote his stock. In short, a proxy is a power of attorney granted by a stockholder authorizing another person to vote his stock.

Sometimes state laws or the charters of corporations provide for *cumulative voting* by stockholders for directors. Here the shareholder is able to multiply the number of his shares by the number of directorships to be elected and cast the *total* for one director or a selected group of directors. Let us assume a stockholder owns fifty shares of common stock and that there are ten directors to be elected. Under cumulative voting, he may cumulate his votes by multiplying his fifty shares times the ten directors to be elected, making 500. Then he may cast the entire 500 votes for only *one* director, or 250 each for two, or 100 each for five, and so forth.

The aim of cumulative voting is to permit minority stockholders to be represented on the board of directors. Under the regular or statutory voting method, the holder of fifty shares could cast only 50 votes for *each* of the 10 directors. He could not concentrate on one director. Under the statutory voting, the holder of 51 per cent of the stock can elect *all* of the directors but the holder of 49 per cent can elect none. Cumulative voting, required in some states, is supposed to correct this situation.

Usually, all of the proxies are tabulated and a single ballot is cast electing the board or approving the proposals. The stockholder has a right to attend the meeting and vote for or against the directors and proposals. Also, a stockholder can revoke his proxy at any time, provided it is done before the final vote is tabulated.

A proxy is sometimes confused with a *voting trust certificate*. These are usually issued by companies in financial difficulties. For example, the representatives of bank or bond creditors might feel that in return for additional money advanced or even for money already advanced they wished to supervise the management of the company. These creditors would persuade the stockholders to surrender to trustees their shares of common stock in return for an identical number of voting trust certificates. A stockholder having 100 shares of common would receive voting trust certificates for 100 shares. These certificates have all the rights of the common stock *except* the right to vote and hence to control the company. This power is held by the trustees representing the creditors. On the other hand, the voting trust certificates trade freely, receive dividends, and represent a proportionate interest in the earnings and assets of the corporation. Also, voting trust certificates usually have a maturity of four to eight years set by state laws. The holders of the certificates recover their voting rights at maturity.

When a brokerage house customer is buying securities on margin, the securities that he has pledged as collateral are not registered in his name but in a *"street name."* Thus, the proxy will go to the *"street name"* of the broker who, in theory, can vote the stock. The New York Stock Exchange, however, has complicated rules for brokers voting street-name stock without the instructions of the customer, particularly where there is a management contest in the company.

Right to Share in the Assets in the Event of Dissolution

It cannot be stressed too strongly that the common stockholder's claim to the assets of a corporation is *residual*. If a company is forced to liquidate its assets, the secured bondholders usually have first claim, followed by the unsecured bondholders and general creditors. After these claims are satisfied, the preferred stockholders, if any, are usually paid par or stated value per share before the common stockholder receives the final distribution. On page 17 it was illustrated how the book or liquidating value is determined.

These, then, are the principal rights of a stockholder. In addition, the stockholder in most states has the right to inspect the corporate books of the company. These include the list of stockholders and the minutes of the stockholder meetings. Also, the stockholder is entitled to an annual report.

The liabilities of a stockholder are, as a general rule, *limited*—that is, limited to their initial investment. For example, an investor might buy 100 shares of stock in the XYZ Corporation for $50 a share. If the corporation goes into bankruptcy, the investor has lost his investment, but the creditors, no matter what the debts of the XYZ Corporation are, cannot look to the investor for additional funds. There are few exceptions to this general rule. For example, the par value or stated value of the stock must be fully paid under the terms of the agreement to purchase of new stocks. If not, the creditors might insist on the full payment of the par or stated value.[1] Also, some states permit the stockholders to be assessed for back wages for a limited period if the assets are not sufficient. But by and large, the general rule holds that common stocks have the limited liability described above.

Selecting Common Stocks

In selecting common stocks, caution and thought should be exercised. It is not necessary, however, for the buyer to know the complicated techniques of the so-called security analysts. He need only follow a few simple rules.

In theory, an ideal common stock should have the following characteristics: (a) liquidity or marketability, (b) income, (c) appreciation possibilities and (d) safety. It is, of course, impossible to find a common stock possessing *all* these characteristics, but it is often feasible to find securities that approach this ideal in certain respects.

MANAGEMENT PERFORMANCE. This is one of the most important considerations in selecting a common stock. While it is difficult to evaluate management precisely, there are a few guideposts which may be followed. Perhaps the most significant is growth of sales and *earnings* over the years. Some authorities consider the stock of a company a "growth stock" if its earnings grow at the rate of 7 per cent or better a year. Other characteristics of good management performance and/or *growth* stock are large capital expenditures, extensive research, a large family of

[1]All stocks listed on the New York Stock Exchange are fully paid and nonassessable.

products, and an aggressive marketing organization. Unfortunately, growth stocks are usually selling at a high price-earnings ratio and have low yields. Dividends are low compared with earnings, since the companies usually choose to plough back earnings for future expansion. Examples of growth stock are Eastman Kodak Company and International Business Machines Company.

Sometimes good management is identified with companies with well-established strong concerns, steady earnings, and dividend records through good and bad times. These stocks are often referred to as *blue chip*. Examples would be General Electric Company and American Telephone & Telegraph Company.

MARKETABILITY OR LIQUIDITY. Marketability or *liquidity* is the quality that makes it possible for the holder of the common stock to convert it into cash within a few days. Most of the well-known stocks are listed on the New York Stock Exchange or the American Stock Exchange, and many have a broad market. This does not imply that *all* of these securities have a broad market; many listed stocks are difficult to buy or sell. However, generally speaking, listed companies have at least a reasonable market. The shares of open-end investment companies have marketability by law at current value. The issuing company usually contracts to redeem these shares on demand by the shareholders on any day the New York Stock Exchange is open.

Income

Income, or yield, is the return on investment. To a common stockholder, this means the dividends paid. The common-stock dividend of a company is relatively easy to determine. The current dividend rates of companies are estimated on the basis of past policies. For example, over the years a company might pay 50 per cent of its earnings in dividends. Another company might cling to a fixed dollar rate. The American Telephone and Telegraph Company for years paid a $9 dividend on its old stock even when earnings were less than that amount. Some companies, such as the E. I. du Pont de Nemours Company and General Motors Corporation, traditionally pay a high proportion of their earnings in dividends. Other companies that need money for expansion, such as Dow Chemical Company or Aluminum Company of America, pay out a low proportion of earnings.

The current return, sometimes called the "current yield," of a common stock is figured by dividing the dividends paid in the past calendar year by the current price. If we asume that a stock is selling on March 28, 1966, at $96 a share, and that in 1965 it paid dividends totaling $4.50, the current return would be calculated as follows:

1965 dividends of $4.50 divided by current price of 96 equals 4.69%.

The return has nothing to do with earnings. For example, in 1965 Deere and Company earned $3.68 a share but paid cash dividends of only $1.65 a share in that year. The return on the stock of Deere and Company purchased on March 28, 1966 at $60 a share would be cal-culated by dividing $1.65 by 60 a share, or 2.75%.

The current return changes with the change in dividends and in the price of the stock. For example, let us suppose that on March 28, 1966, John Jones purchased 100 shares of Deere and Company at $60 a share. If the price should rise to $70 a share and if the annual dividend rate should increase to $2.30 a share, the current return would be calculated in the same way by dividing $2.30 by $70, or 3.28%. In short, the current return is calculated by dividing the current price into the dividends for the year just past.

In recent years, most of the best stocks have been selling at a high price compared with their dividend and consequently have a low yield. As mentioned above, the payment of dividends is the right and duty of the directors. Directors, in declaring dividends are guided by the earnings, the assets, and the outlook of the company.

Appreciation

Appreciation is the increase in the market price of a stock. The appreciation possibility of a common stock is difficult to forecast. There are a number of reasons why the market price of a stock might go up.

First, when waves of optimism strike the country, a large number of the common stocks rise in price. This has occurred many times in our history, but particularly in 1924 to 1929, 1953 to 1959, and 1962–1965. Many *but not all* stocks bought in 1953 showed a substantial profit by 1966. Care should be taken in the individual selection of securities. To repeat, in bull markets the prices of many but not all stocks rise. Also, in a bear market, when most stocks fall, the fortunate investor might select a stock which either does not fall as much as the majority of the stocks or which goes against the trend of the market and rises.

Second, speculation breaks out in groups of stocks. This happened to the public utility holding company stocks in the 1920's, to the gold stocks in the 1930's, and the electronics stocks in the 1950's.

Third, the stocks of companies tend to rise if the growth of earnings over the years has been good. This earnings growth is usually the result of good management. Year after year the earnings of International Business Machines Corporation, of Eastman Kodak Company, and of Minnesota Mining and Manufacturing Company have shown steady growth. These companies have spent large sums on capital improvements, developed new products, and expanded sales.

Fourth, stocks appreciate when the *prospects* of an industry are good.

This is particularly true in the aluminum industry. It is believed by many in and out of the aluminum industry that the prospective demand for aluminum is very great, that aluminum will in many instances be used to replace copper, steel, and wood. Thus even though the earnings trend of many of the aluminum companies has not been impressive, the stocks sell at a high price compared with earnings. It is, of course, possible that too high a price will be paid for these stocks. In this case, the investor will have to wait until the earnings and dividends increase and cause the stock to move higher. There are, of course, situations where the price of stocks fails to reflect improved earnings and prospects, as well as where the prices of stocks over-discount the future. A skilled security analyst can often evaluate these situations. But no analyst, however skilled, can see into the future.

When the stock moves above his cost price, the investor has a paper or unrealized profit. Sometimes these are called book profits. Paper or book profits become realized profits only when the investor sells his stock.

Fifth, a stock might appreciate because it has *leverage*, which exists when borrowed money or senior capital (i.e., preferred stocks and bonds) is used to provide greater earnings for the common and hence stimulate *appreciation* of the stock. But by the same token leverage also can work against the common by a correspondingly greater degree of risk if the business of the company declines. In other words, leverage by the use of borrowed or senior money increases substantially the possibility of profits, but also increases to the same extent the possibility of loss. To show how leverage works both ways, let us assume that Jones Corporation issues $1,000,000 of 6% bonds and $1,000,000 of $100 par stock, or 10,000 shares. The result would be as shown.

Leverage	Normal Year	Bad Year	Good Year
Earnings after taxes and before interest	$120,000	$60,000	$240,000
Interest on bonds	60,000	60,000	60,000
Earned on stock	60,000	0	180,000
Per share (10,000 shares)	$ 6	0	$ 18

In a normal year, Jones Corporation must pay 6 per cent on its $1,000,-000 of bonds or $60,000, and has $60,000 left for the common or $6 a share ($60,000 divided by 10,000). In a bad year, the interest charges wipe out the earnings of the common. But in a good year, when net earnings after taxes and before interest are $240,000, or twice the earnings in the normal year, the per-share earnings are $18 or *three times* the $6 earnings in the normal year. Thus leverage magnifies the gains and declines in earnings.

In contrast, let us take the Smith Corporation, which issues only

$1,000,000 of common stock. Since it has no bonds, it does not have the same amount of capital working to generate earnings. Therefore, if we assume identical conditions for the Smith Corporation, the earnings in the three periods would be half as large as Jones Corporation in the three years.

Non-leverage	Normal Year	Bad Year	Good Year
Earnings after taxes and before interest	$60,000	$30,000	$120,000
Interest	0	0	0
Earned on stock, 10,000 shares	$ 6	$ 3	$ 12

From the above, note that the net earnings of the Smith Corporation in the normal year were the same as the Jones Corporation. In the bad year they declined sharply to $3, but did not disappear as did the earnings of the Jones Corporation. In a good year they doubled to $12, but did not increase as far as the Jones Corporation, which trebled to $18.

Safety

Safety concerns the avoidance of the risk of losing all or a part of an investment. Safety is, of course, relative. United States Treasury bonds would seem to have safety of principal as far as the interest and final payment at maturity are concerned. However, the prices of these bonds have in the past declined sharply as a result of higher interest rates.

As far as common stocks are concerned, their very nature as equities would seem to eliminate the element of safety. There are, however, several stocks which have shown a considerable amount of stability of market price and dividend payments. In this category might be placed the stocks of certain public utility, telephone, and consumer goods companies. Even in these cases, the price fluctuation over the years has been considerable.

Approaches to Selection of Common Stocks

Recognizing that common stocks have definite advantages and limitations, the thoughtful investor should proceed with his selection of common stocks. There are at least three possible approaches which have been used: (a) the diversification approach, (b) the industry approach, and (c) the undervalued stock approach. The first two of these might enable the investor to come closer to the ideals of marketability, income appreciation and relative safety.

The diversification approach is used when the investor concedes that it is not possible to select one or two outstanding stocks but desires to participate in the economic growth of the country. Thus the investor buys several of the leading stocks selected from any recognized list of stocks such as the 30 stocks of the Dow Jones Industrial Average. These stocks of well known companies such as General Motors Corporation, E. I. du Pont de Nemours and Company and the United States Steel Corporation are often referred to as "blue chip" stocks. The term "blue chip" should not be confused with Blue Sky laws of the various states concerning the selling of securities. The Blue Sky laws will be discussed in Chapter 15.

On the other hand, it is possible that the buyer has limited funds. In this case, it would not be advisable to buy a very few shares of a number of issues. The same purpose can be accomplished by the purchase of the shares of a well-known investment company. Much has been written about the importance of buying the stock of a growth company, but statistics have been developed showing that the purchase of a cross section of securities through an investment company has several advantages. The most important of these is that diversification is obtained. Further, the mutual funds investor has professional investment managers selecting the stocks in which he has an interest.

The industry approach has often proven more rewarding than the so-called diversification approach. Using the industry approach, the investor selects first the industry that has been growing and has a good outlook. Then he selects a common stock of the leading company or companies in that industry. There are, however, notable exceptions. For example, for years the paper industry has shown a poor earnings trend, yet due to excellent management, Scott Paper Company has forged ahead. In the years 1959 and 1960, the chemical industry was fairly prosperous, yet Virginia Carolina Chemical Company did not pay any dividends on its preferred stock.

One consideration in appraising the industry outlook should be: Are the products consumer-leisure-time oriented? This would include retail trade, air travel, photography, color television, packaged foods, and so on. If the answer is yes, they would be closely tied to the growing consumer expenditure for nondurable goods. This component of our gross national product has shown stability and a steady upward trend. Another industry, however, might be tied to the consumer durable goods such as automobiles, appliances, building materials, and the like. These items have had over the years a less steady demand and are more vulnerable to the downward swings in business.

Still another major area would include production of basic metals, petroleum, heavy equipment, and machine tools for plants. These fluctuate with business to a considerable extent.

In addition to the broad nature of the business, the analyst should consider the price structure in his industry, the competition, marketing policies, and in particular the amount spent on research. It is essential to develop new products to keep ahead of competition. Each company should attempt to develop a family of products so that it will not be too greatly dependent on any one item.

In some industries, especially public service, the regulatory climate is important. In an electric public utility, it is necessary to know the attitude of the state public service commission. As far as railroads are concerned, the attitude of the Interstate Commerce Commission is important. In recent years it has taken a more understanding attitude towards the problems of the railroads.

Characteristics of Principal Industries

AIR TRANSPORT. Continued growth of passenger travel is almost certain due to increasing population and the favorable attitude of youth toward flying. Regulations of the Federal Aviation Commission may force rate cuts. Labor unrest causes frequent strikes and higher costs.

AUTOMOBILES. Long-range predictions point to growing population and greater need for cars. Better roads and higher family income will also help. But the industry is inherently cyclical, harassed with safety regulations and expensive new models.

CHEMICALS. Steady growth during the past twenty years. Great stress placed on research, new products, and better processes. Competition and unsatisfactory prices are developing, particularly in textiles and plastics.

FOOD. Package or convenience foods are showing especially good growth due to the desire of housewives to cut down kitchen chores. Profits growth has been satisfactory in spite of keen competition. Intensive efforts have been made to expand product lines by developing new products.

INSURANCE. Fire and casualty has for years had an unsatisfactory underwriting record but good investment income. In 1967, there is hope for better underwriting due to higher insurance rates and lower fire losses. Life companies should benefit by higher interest rates as new money is invested. They have had a good underwriting record but suffer from keen competition.

METALS. Deposits of copper, lead, zinc, etc., are assets which are being depleted. The industry is subject to wide fluctuations. Much of the copper is located in Chile and Africa. Currently (1967) there is heavy demand for copper in particular, but equities are considered speculative.

PAPER. For years this product and industry has experienced over-capacity and unsatisfactory prices. As a result, profits growth—with one or two exceptions—has been disappointing. Most of the paper companies, however, have strong financial positions and ample timber reserves.

PETROLEUM. Steady increase in demand has taken place in the United States and faster increase in Europe. Domestic and international companies are facing greater competition and larger demands from a host of countries. Domestic companies with ample resources would seem safest.

PUBLIC UTILITIES. The electric public utilities have for years demonstrated a steady growth of about 6 per cent in net income. There seems to be no reason to believe this trend will not continue. Careful analysis should be made of the regulatory climate, territory, and breakdown of revenue by domestic, industrial, and commercial customers.

STEEL. This industry has a generally irregular earnings history. Even in a booming economy, it has been hampered by high labor and other costs. The demand for steel fluctuates sharply and is heavily dependent on the automobile and other durable goods industries.

In the past the chemical, drug, oil, public utility (gas, electric, telephone), and retail trade companies have shown steady growth. But the steel, automobile, and building concerns, which showed irregular growth during the 1960's, are in 1967 showing signs of decline. The air transport and railroad industries, which in early 1960's had an almost hopeless outlook, suddenly recovered and their stocks soared in the years 1965 and 1966. A new term came into use—*performance stock*. This applies to such spectacular performers as Syntex, Xerox, Fairchild Camera, and Polaroid.

It is, of course, possible that the investor following the industry approach might pay too high a price for a stock. In this case he might wait a long time for the earnings to increase enough to cause the stock to appreciate further. In other words, it is relatively easy to identify a growth company in a growing industry. Almost everybody knows that Eastman Kodak Company is the best camera company in a growing industry. Also, it produces a number of chemical products. But the difficult part is to determine that its price is not over-discounting the earnings growth and bright future.

There is a conventional method of measuring price in relation to earnings. This is the price-earnings ratio, or the price of the stock divided by the earnings. In the spring of 1966, the price of E. I. du Pont de Nemours and Company was $208 a share. In 1965, it earned $8.63 a share. Therefore its price-earnings ratio would be 208 divided by $8.63 or 24.1. A comparison of this price-earnings ratio with the price-earnings ratio of the other chemical companies is as shown.

	3/28/66 Price	1965 Per Share Earnings	Price/ Earnings Ratio
Allied Chemical Corporation	$ 48	$3.14	15.3
E. I. du Pont de Nemours and Company	208	8.63	24.1
Monsanto Chemical Company	79	3.89	20.3
Union Carbide Corporation	61	3.76	16.3
Eastman Kodak Company	123	3.07	40.1

On the basis of the price-earnings ratio table, the cheapest stock appears to be Allied Chemical Corporation, with a price-earnings ratio of 15.3, and the most expensive Eastman Kodak Company, with a ratio of 40.1.

The market obviously is willing to pay more for the earnings of Eastman than for Allied. Investors take into consideration growth of earnings, management, products, and the outlook for the company. Most of these are intangibles and defy measurement. But we *can* measure and compare the growth of earnings and the price-earnings ratios. The following table shows in column A the average earnings of Standard and Poor's list of 425 industrial stocks for the seven years ending in 1966. Next, in column B, we show the earnings of Eastman Kodak adjusted to the number of shares outstanding at the end of 1965. These two columns may be compared by taking a percentage of one by the other.

	A	B	C	D	E	F
	Standard & Poor's Corp. Average Earnings per Share*	Eastman Kodak Earnings per Share+	B ÷ A	Standard & Poor's Corp. Price/ Earnings Ratio*	Eastman Kodak Price/ Earnings Ratio	E ÷ D
1960	$3.39	$1.57	46%	18.1	34.2	189
1961	3.37	1.61	48	22.5	34.1	151
1962	3.87	1.74	45	17.0	29.9	176
1963	4.24	1.79	42	18.7	32.3	173
1964	4.83	2.32	48	18.6	30.1	162
1965	5.50	3.07	56	17.9	38.0	212
1966 # E	6.00 E	3.85	64	# 14.0	# 34.5	246

*425 Industrial Stocks
P Preliminary
E Author's Estimate
As of January 24, 1967

For example, in 1960, the per-share earnings of Eastman Kodak of $1.57 were about 46 per cent of the average of the Standard & Poor's earnings of $3.39 ($1.57 divided by $3.39 equals 46%). By using this method, we can see that the earnings of Eastman improved *more* than those of Standard & Poor since they were 46 per cent of the Standard & Poor's earnings in 1960 compared with 56 per cent in 1965 and an estimated 64 per cent in 1966 (see column C).

This is interesting, but it does not tell us anything about the *relative prices.* If, however, we compare the price-earnings ratio of the 425 stocks of Standard & Poor with the price-earnings ratio of Eastman Kodak, we might determine whether the price of Eastman Kodak has gone up more or less than the 425 stocks of the Standard & Poor average. In other words, there are some stocks which traditionally sell at a high price-earnings ratio. *It is only when they break out of this range that the investor* should try to determine if the stock is overdiscounting the future.

In the case of Eastman, the price-earnings ratio was 34.2 in 1960 compared with 18.1 for the average of Standard & Poor's. We have compared the two ratios by dividing column E by column D to find a *final comparative* ratio of 189 (see column F). It is significant to note that between 1960 and 1964 the percentage of Eastman earnings to the Standard & Poor improved slightly from 46 per cent to 48 per cent. Yet the final comparative ratio declined from 189 to 162 between 1960 and 1964 (see column F). This indicated that the price of Eastman was becoming more attractive relative to other stocks. In 1964, Eastman was selling as low as $58 a share. In 1964, earnings of Eastman improved, and the stock rose to $70 a share. In 1965, the earnings continued to improve, and the stock also increased to $116 a share at the end of the year. At this point, the stock was selling at 38.0 times earnings. On the basis of estimated earnings and market price of 133 on January 24, 1967, it was selling at 34.5 times estimated earnings. But, compared with other stocks, it was not nearly so attractive as it was in 1963.

The analyst may find this method useful, particularly if he plots columns C and F on three-cycle semi-log paper. This will show quite clearly that the earnings of Eastman were improving faster than the earnings of Standard & Poor's 425 stocks. Also, it will show that between 1960 and 1963 it was relatively more attractive than the Standard & Poor average, and in the years 1964–1966 it was less so.

The Undervalued Stock—A Special Situation

This approach is perhaps the most difficult for the average investor to follow. It means that through careful analysis a stock may be found which is selling at a price substantially less than its true worth based on earnings and outlook.

All the stocks in an industry may be undervalued. In 1964, the market was very pessimistic about the outlook for the airlines and the railroads. Careful analysts examined a long-term outlook for these industries and foresaw potential growth. Their heavy purchases of air transport and railroad stocks were most profitable.

There are also times when a *special situation* may be dug up by an analyst. Studebaker Corporation, for example, became a much more profitable concern after it got rid of its automobile manufacturing company. It is possible, too, for some large investors to buy control of a company at depressed prices and liquidate it at a profit. It is human nature to look for bargains. Even skilled analysts after much study make mistakes in their attempts to select undervalued stocks. There are many stories of fortunes made by buying cheap stocks, yet the millions lost in buying them far outweigh the gains. When a stock sells for a low price, there is usually a good reason.

This brings us to the distinction between investment and speculation. It is believed that in making an *investment*, the buyer is interested in trying to reconcile the objectives of safety of principal and stability of income as well as gradual appreciation of principal and income. These many objectives are difficult to obtain but the investor should strive for them. In *speculation*, a stock is subject to wide fluctuation and should be purchased by a person interested primarily in *capital gains* and willing to take a reasonable risk. There is nothing wrong with speculation provided the investor knows and weighs intelligently the facts and risks.

A person is *gambling* when he simply buys a stock on a tip without any investigation or knowledge of the company or its outlook.

Gambling is often done in the so-called *hot issues*. Hot issues might be described as securities—usually stocks—of little known value but with an attractive name which go up several points on the day that they are sold to the public. Any fortunate buyer of a hot issue makes an immediate profit, but this profit is not always retained and often turns into a loss. Also, a new "hot" issue might not attract widespread interest, and it may become necessary to stabilize the price during the period of distribution. In the middle 1950's, any stock with the name of uranium sold at an immediate premium over offering price. In 1961, in particular, there were a great many "hot" electronics issues.

The stocks of many of these companies not only depreciated substantially in value, but the companies themselves became insolvent, or bankrupt. The terms insolvency and bankruptcy are often used interchangeably. The purist might say that insolvency means that a corporation is unable to meet its debts as they come due, but hope is implied that, given time, the creditors will be paid and the company can continue to operate perhaps at a profit. The term bankruptcy is final; it implies that the affairs of the corporation are to be wound up and the creditors paid off any or part of their claims.

Portfolio Analysis

The basis for recommendations is that securities must be *suitable* for the customer on the basis of the facts disclosed. This is one of the most important of the NASD Rules of Fair Practice (see Article III, section 2.) Especially when the registered representative opens a new account, he should endeavor to find out as much as possible about the background of his customer. In particular, he should try to find his customer's ability to stand the loss of principal, his ability to stand loss of income, his tax position, his need for marketability, and the necessity for protection against inflation. (This applies largely to an institutional customer such as a fire insurance company.) In more detail, the registered representative should try to learn the following about his customer:

Personal
  Age and health
  Dependents, their age, and educational status
  Present employment, its stability and prospects
  Temperament and knowledge of investments

Present Portfolio
  Type of securities
  Balance of fixed income and equities
  Cash and savings

Financial
  Salary
  Other income
  Tax position
  Insurance
  Mortgage and other debts
  Surplus earnings available for investment
  Real estate or other investments
  Possible inheritance

The registered representative may have to use tact in finding out all of this information. Some customers are reluctant to disclose too much of what they consider their private affairs. But the registered representative should point out that the more information he has, the better he can advise the client.

Objectives or goals should be determined by mutual agreement between the customer and the registered representative. Almost all customers are interested in *appreciation* of their portfolio; some are interested in *tax exemption*; many are interested in *income*; some in protection against *inflation*; and almost all are interested in *protection of principal*. Nobody likes to see his capital diminish. It is obviously impossible to combine all these objectives. But it is the duty of the registered representative to *tailor* the investment program as nearly as possible to the particular objectives of the customer, taking into consideration his personal and financial background.

Starting with the objectives of the *senior citizens* (the retired and widowed), the registered representative should try to obtain as high an income as possible consistent with safety. Investments might include corporate bonds or municipal bonds, if he is in a high tax bracket, and sound common stocks with good yields and comfortable dividend coverage.

The *businessman*, if he has a large salary or other substantial income, might be encouraged to buy municipal securities and growth common stocks. Growth stocks have been defined as having an average growth of net income over the years of about 7 per cent as well as other characteristics.

The *young man starting out* on his career should first be encouraged to have a backlog of savings and ample insurance. Second, the registered representative and the customer should determine how much can be set aside for *growth* common stocks. A suggestion might be to use the M.I.P. (monthly investment plan) in stocks selected for appreciation by the firm's research department. The M.I.P. plans, developed by the New York Stock Exchange, are explained in greater detail in Chapter 12.

But it might be said here that basically the M.I.P. plans are methods of *dollar cost averaging*. This is periodic purchase of a fixed dollar amount. In dollar cost averaging, the average cost of the shares is always less than the average market price of the shares, because more shares can be bought at the lower market price. While dollar cost averaging has much to recommend it and has enabled many to build up a substantial fund over the past years, nevertheless it is not a riskless method of investment. The following are some of the conditions for successful dollar cost averaging. The customer

1. Must pick the right stock.
2. Must have steady income and keep buying.
3. Must *not* be in a steady downward trend of the market.
4. Must have fluctuation in stock picked but an upward trend over the years.

It should be stressed that *dollar cost averaging* should not be confused with *share cost averaging*. An example of share cost averaging would be a customer's buying more of a stock which has depreciated in order to lower his average cost. As an illustration, a customer might buy 100 shares of a stock at $60 a share and see it drop to, say, $30 a share. He then buys another 100 shares at $30, making his average cost 45. This, however, is often a dangerous practice. Before share cost averaging, the customer and the registered representative should determine the *reason* for the stock's decline. There may be a serious deterioration in the position of the company, or it may be a temporary situation.

REVIEW QUESTIONS

1. Discuss seven important rights of a stockholder. Does he have any liabilities?
2. Does a stock dividend add to a stockholder's *share* in the company's assets and earnings? Why does the price of the stock of a company usually rise when a stock dividend is declared?
3. What is a pre-emptive right and why is it important for a stockholder to have it?
4. Explain the difference between statutory voting and cumulative voting. What is a proxy?
5. What are the most important considerations in selecting a common stock?
6. How can management performance be evaluated?
7. If a common stock sells at 65 in March, 1967, earned $4.10 a share in 1966, and paid dividends of $3.50 in 1966, what is considered the current yield of the stock in March, 1967?
8. What are the advantages and disadvantages to a stockholder of buying a company with *leverage*?
9. What is meant by the industry approach to security analysis? Select and give reasons for your choice of three industries that have a favorable outlook and three that have an unfavorable outlook.
10. What are a growth stock, a performance stock, a blue chip, and a special situation?
11. What is the significance of a price/earnings ratio and how is it calculated?
12. Select a growth company of your choice and using the figures on page 95, figure:
    (a) the percentage earnings to Standard and Poor's average earnings over the years,
    (b) the price/earning ratio of your company over the years, and
    (c) the relationship of price/earnings ratios of your company to Standard and Poor's average price/earnings ratios over the years.
13. What are the most important considerations in making a *suitable* recommendation to a customer? What information should a registered representative try to find out from his customer?
14. How does dollar-cost averaging work? What are its wear points?

Stock and Bond Transactions

Chapter **8**

Every investor is familiar with the stock and bond quotation sections of the large newspapers, but few are familiar with the many small symbols and letters which appear in the quotation sheets. An investor should not only follow the price changes in his stocks and bonds but also should understand the financial terms used in buying and selling securities.

Stock Quotations

The large metropolitan papers usually publish every business day the stocks traded on the New York Stock Exchange and the American Stock Exchange. Stocks are traded and quoted in dollars a share in fractions of $\frac{1}{8}$, $\frac{1}{4}$, $\frac{3}{8}$, $\frac{1}{2}$, $\frac{5}{8}$, $\frac{3}{4}$, and $\frac{7}{8}$. The table on page 102 shows a sample of quotations published in *The Wall Street Journal* of stocks traded on the New York Stock Exchange on November 21, 1966.

From left to right, these quotations show for the current year, the high and the low price of stock traded, enabling the reader to compare the present price with the range for the year. Next is the name of the company, often in abbreviated form. Following the name of the company are the *dividend rate*, the volume of sales stated in units of 100 shares, the price at which the stock *first* sold or opened, the *high* or highest price and the *low* or lowest price on that day, and the *last* or the price of the last trade. The net change is the difference between the price the stock closed on Monday, November 21, 1966, and the price the stock closed the previous trading day—Friday, November 18, 1966. A glance at the stock tables on the following page will show how the market behaved on the previous day: whether it was strong, weak, or mixed.

101

THE WALL STREET JOURNAL
A-B-C

— 1966 — High	Low	Stocks Div.	Sales in 100s	Open	High	Low	Close	Net Chg.
16⅜	12¼	AbacusF .50t	3	13½	13½	13⅜	13½	....
48⅝	35⅛	Abbott Lab 1	73	45¼	45¾	44½	45¾	+ ¼
33	15¼	ABC Con .80	67	17⅛	17⅛	16½	16⅝	— ⅝
34¼	26⅞	Abex Cp 1.60	16	28⅝	28⅝	28¼	28⅝	— ⅛
54¾	35	ACF Ind 2.20	x47	41⅞	41⅞	41⅛	41⅛	— ⅛
57	38⅛	Acme Mkt 2b	18	39¼	39⅞	39¼	39½	+ ⅛
30½	26	AdamE 2.29e	11	28⅞	28⅞	28⅝	28⅝	....
19¼	12¼	Ad Millis .40b	3	14	14	13¾	13¾	....
77⅜	51⅛	Address 1.40	105	51⅞	51⅞	50½	51¼	— ½
55½	28¼	Admiral .50	351	30½	31⅝	30	31	— ¼
42¾	22¼	Air Prod .20	124	29⅞	29⅞	28	28⅜	— 1⅞
78½	51	Air Red 2.50	31	55⅜	55⅝	54	54⅞	— ½
7⅞	3	AJ Industries	46	3¾	3¾	3⅝	3⅝	— ½

In this table, we find that ACF Ind (Industries) in 1966 sold as *high* as 54¾ and as *low* as 35. It paid dividends of $2.20 a share in 1966. On November 21, 1966 it first traded or opened at 41⅞ which was also its high price for the day. It sold as low as 41⅛, which was also the same price at which it closed or the price of the last sale. It might be noted that ACF industries at 41⅛ was off about 25 per cent from its high price of the year. But Abbott Lab (Laboratories) at 45¾ was only off about 6 per cent from its high price of the year of 48⅝. The last column shows the *net change* of ACF Industries for the day of *minus* ⅛. This means that the stock closed ⅛ of a point lower on Monday, November 21, than it closed on the previous trading day or on November 18.

The stocks traded on the American Stock Exchange are quoted in a similar manner. It is quite possible that stocks might not be traded on the exchanges on a particular trading day. In this case, several of the large metropolitan papers publish about 400 bid-and-asked prices of the so-called inactive stocks. In general, the published bid on a listed stock is the highest public bid recorded on the books of the specialist, and the asked price is the lowest public offer recorded there. The difference between bid and asked prices is usually 1 to 3 points or dollars. Much, of course, depends on the number of shares to be bought or sold.

Some of the newspapers publish the bid-and-ask quotations of some of the industrial and utility stocks which are traded *over the counter*. In addition, many papers quote the over-the-counter bid-and-asked prices of leading banks, insurance companies, and mutual funds.

Commission on Stocks

The following are the commissions charged by the New York Stock Exchange and by the American Stock Exchange on round lots, and on round lots plus odd lots. *Round lots* usually, but not always, means 100 shares, and *odd lots* are 1 through 99 shares (less than the unit of trading).

Amount Involved	Commission*
$ 1 to $ 100	as mutually agreed
100 to 399	2% plus $3
400 to 2,399	1% plus $7
2,400 to 4,999	½% plus $19
5,000 to over	1/10% plus $39

*On odd lots the commission is the same as the above less $2.

Using the above schedule of commissions the following shows the calculation of a *round lot* and of an *odd lot*.

Round lot: 100 shares of ABC Corporation at $40 a share.

100 shares at $40 a share equals	$4,000.00
Commission:	
$4,000.00 times ½ of 1% equals	$ 20.00
Plus	19.00
	$ 39.00

Odd lot: 50 shares of XYZ Corporation at $40 a share.

50 shares at $40 a share equals	$2,000.00
Commission:	
$2,000.00 times 1% equals	$ 20.00
Plus	7.00
	$ 27.00
Less	2.00
	$ 25.00

In addition there are New York State transfer taxes as well as Securities and Exchange Commission fees, which must be paid *by the seller* in any transaction on the stock exchanges. There is no Securities and Exchange Commission fee on securities transactions in the over-the-counter market.

1. The New York State transfer taxes are as follows:

1¼¢ per share under $5
2½¢ per share between $5 and $10
3¾¢ per share between $10 and $20
5¢ per share over $20

2. The Securities and Exchange Commission fee is 1¢ for each $500 or fraction thereof.

The following is an example of the purchase and sale of 100 shares of common stock of Eastman Kodak Company.

Purchase:
100 Shares Eastman Kodak Company @ 105½ $10,550.00
Plus Commission:
    1/10% of $10,550.00 equals $10.55
                                                       39.00

                                                                        $ 49.55
                Total cost to buyer $10,599.55

Sale
100 shares of Eastman Kodak Company @ 105½ $10,550.00

Less Commission
    1/10% of $10,550 equals $10.55
    Plus   39.00

                                                                 $ 49.50

Less New York State tax
    5¢ per share times 100 equals $ 5.00
Less Securities Exchange Commission fee
    1¢ per $500 =
    22 times 1¢ or 22¢   .22

                                                                 $ 54.77
Net Proceeds to the seller $10,495.23

Put and Call Options

A *put option* is a negotiable bearer contract giving the buyer
the right at his option to deliver, or put, a specified number of shares
of stock at a stated price on or before a stipulated date. A put option
is generally bought by an investor who thinks a stock is overpriced and
will go down. For example, on June 2, 1960, a leading put-and-call
broker advertised that a put on 100 shares of Radio Corporation of
America could be bought for $475. This put gave the buyer the right
to sell or put the stock at 76⅝ until September 6, 1960. On July 28,
1960, Radio Corporation of America closed at 60. a share. The holder of
this put could either hold it until September 6, 1960, hoping the stock
would go lower or deliver the stock and receive the put price of 76⅝.
There will be two commissions since he will have to buy the stock
in the market for about 60 and sell it at the put price of 76⅝. Also he
will have to pay State transfer taxes on the sale. For details of commissions and taxes, see page 103.

The following would be the result of exercising a put on July 28,
1960, of Radio Corporation of America:

Sell: 100 shares at 76⅝ $7,662.50
        Less commission   46.66
        Less New York State tax   5.00
        Less Securities Exchange Commission fee   .16
        Total receipts $7,610.68

Buy:

	100 shares at 60	$6,000.00
	Plus commission	45.00
		$6,045.00
	Plus cost of option	475.00
	Total cost	$6,520.00
	Profit	$1,090.68

A call is just the reverse of the above. A call option is a negotiable bearer contract giving the holder the right to buy or call a stated number of shares of stock at a stated price on or before a stated date. A call is purchased in most instances by an investor who thinks the price of the stock is cheap and will rise. The cost of calls is usually a little higher than the cost of puts. Also, to exercise a call, two commissions and transfer taxes must be paid. In addition, state tax stamps based on the selling price must be affixed to call options, but not to put options.

Put-and-call options are made by about twenty members of the Put and Call Brokers and Dealers Association of New York. They are guaranteed by member firms of the New York Stock Exchange. Therefore, put and call options are confined largely to securities listed on the New York Stock Exchange. Puts and calls are made only in 100 share units and run for thirty days, sixty days, ninety days, six months and at times, for one year. The cost of the put or call varies with the market price and period of time of the option.

For example, on August 4, 1966, *puts* were offered by one put-and-call broker ranging from a 197-day put on Bethlehem Steel at 31½ for $150. to a 95-day put on Xerox at 225 for $1,875.

On the same day another put and call broker was offering *calls* ranging from a 97-day call on Microwave at 16 for $225.00 to a 75-day call on Fairchild at 190. for $1,275.00.

The risk of buying puts and calls is limited to the purchase of the options, but in order to make a profit, the stock must *move* up or down several points to cover the cost of the options, plus the commissions and taxes. There are several other uses for puts and calls. These include

1. The purchase of a put to protect a purchase
2. The purchase of a call to protect a short sale[1]
3. The purchase of a call to control additional shares.[1]

The National Uniform Practice Code

WHAT IT IS. The Board of Governors of the National Association of Securities Dealers, Inc. was authorized to adopt a uniform practice code to make uniform the customs, practices, and trading techniques

[1]For more complete explanation of puts and calls see Herbert Filer, *Understanding Put and Call Options* (New York: Popular Library, 1966). Copies may be obtained from Filer Schmidt and Company, 120 Broadway, New York, N.Y.

between members in the securities business. These include such matters as trade terms, deliveries, payments, rights, stamp taxes, computation of interest, due bills, and so forth.

The administration of the code has been delegated by the board to the National Uniform Practice Committee and the District Uniform Practice Committees. Any changes in the rules made by the district committees must be approved by the board. Any contract *between members* (except transactions executed on the national securities exchanges and transactions in exempt securities) is subject to the National Uniform Practice Code, and the code is part of the contract unless the parties to the transactions agree otherwise. Whenever a situation arises which is not covered by the code, it is referred to the appropriate District Uniform Practice Committee for action. In the case of a controversy with respect to interdistrict trade, it is handled by the National Uniform Practice Committee.

In the following pages, we will discuss certain important sections of the National Uniform Practice Code as it applies to various transactions.

DELIVERY OF SECURITIES (SECTION 4). For each security transaction, there are two dates of particular significance: (1) the trade date, and (2) the delivery date.

The trade date is simply the date on which the transaction takes place between two parties. All ordinary transactions must be confirmed by sending a written notice *on or before the first full business day following the date of transaction*. Confirmations of cash transactions (those in which the contract is settled on the same day the trade is made) shall be exchanged on the day of the trade. We will presently discuss cash transactions in greater detail.

Particular care should be taken on confirmations not only for cash sales but on all transactions. Confirmations should be compared on receipt, and any discrepancies should be checked immediately and corrected. A corrected confirmation should be sent by the party in error. Confirmations should include an adequate description of the security— if the security is a bond, the coupon rate and date of the maturity; if a stock, the class, common or preferred, and if preferred, the dividend rate. Also, it should be noted whether the confirmation is for "when as and if issued" or "when as and if distributed" securities, also the plan under which the securities will be issued or distributed should be stated.

The settlement date is simply the date on which a transaction was effected or accomplished.

The *delivery date* is the date on which the securities should be delivered to the customer. Deliveries are made "regular way," "delayed delivery," "seller's option," and "for cash."

Regular way delivery means that the seller contracts to deliver the securities to the office of the purchaser on the *fourth full business day following the date of the transaction*. This means that Saturdays, Sundays, and holidays, when the exchanges are closed, do not count. For example, if a trade is made on Friday, the securities should be delivered by the following Thursday, assuming no holidays intervene.

	Days Counted
Friday—trade day	
Saturday	0
Sunday	0
Monday	1
Tuesday	2
Wednesday	3
Thursday	4

If a seller delivers his securities before the fourth full business day the acceptance of their delivery is up to the buyer. If the buyer declines to let the seller deliver the securities before the fourth full business day, the seller still should deliver on the fourth day.

The four-day delivery rule applies to trades in securities over the counter, as well as on the New York and American Stock Exchanges. But exceptions are made when it is known at the time of the sale that the securities cannot be delivered on the date prescribed for a regular-way transaction. Here the seller must inform the buyer prior to the order that the securities cannot be delivered within the four-business-day period. In this case, the sale might be made for delayed delivery.

Delayed delivery means that the seller shall deliver the securities at the office of the buyer on the seventh calendar day following the date of the transaction. There is an exception to this rule when contracts mature on a Saturday or a holiday. Here the delivery may be made on the next full business day. Also, under "delayed delivery," delivery may be made on any full business day after the fourth full business day prior to the seventh calendar day following the date of the transaction.

Seller's option allows the seller to deliver up to sixty days. It is the long form of delayed delivery. For stocks and convertible bonds sold under sellers option, the delivery may not be before five business days or after sixty calendar days. On the day the option expires, the delivery shall be made at the office of the purchaser. Contracts maturing on a Saturday or a holiday carry over to the next full business day. The seller may deliver the security to the buyer after the fifth day from the transaction provided the seller gives written notice to the buyer a day in advance. *Seller's option* or *delayed delivery* is often requested by sellers who have difficulty in obtaining possession of their securities for any one of a number of reasons. For example, a man might be visiting New York City and decide to sell his securities which are in his safety deposit box in Los Angeles, California. At the time of the sale the seller *must* advise the buyer that delivery will not be made the regular way. The buyer is not required to enter the transaction if he desires to obtain delivery "regular way." For United States government securities, seller's option shall not be less than two business days nor more than sixty calendar days. For other bonds, it may be not less than eight nor more than sixty calendar days.

A buyer's option gives the buyer the option to receive securities at his office on a specific date, when the option expires. If the seller *wishes* to deliver prior to this time, the buyer must give his permission. The refusal of such delivery by the purchaser shall be without prejudice to his rights.

Cash sales means the security is sold and the contract settled on the same day the trade is made. Cash sales usually occur where a seller wishes to meet a special situation. For example, for tax reasons an individual or a company might desire to complete a transaction before the year end.

When a security is sold *for cash* the following must take place *on the day of the trade*:

    a.   The security shall be delivered to the office of the purchaser.
    b.   Confirmation of a cash transaction shall be exchanged.
    c.   The security transaction is settled by payment.

"When issued" securities, as their name implies, are usually shares of stock or of bonds which have been authorized by the corporation, but not yet delivered or issued. Often on the stock exchanges both the old and the "when issued" securities are quoted. For example, on July 28, 1960 the following quotation appeared:

	Close
Gen. Fds. (Foods)	126
Gen. Fds. wi	63½

On July 27, 1960, the stockholders of General Foods Corporation authorized a two-for-one stock split. The new stock was not delivered to the stockholders until August 23, 1960. A number of other companies have authorized stock splits, and prior to the issuance of these securities they trade on a "when issued" basis. These companies include American Telephone, Firestone Tire, Goodyear Tire, Inland Steel, and Eastman Kodak.

All trades in "when-issued" securities, as well as all profits and losses, are cancelled if for any reason the securities are not issued. All the trades are in contracts rather than in actual securities. When a company authorizes a split, there is very little chance that the securities will not be delivered.

In the past, however, when the railroads were being reorganized, "when issued" securities were used extensively. When the reorganization plans were well advanced, trading would start in the bonds and stocks on a "when issued" basis. Many speculators would buy the old securities and sell for future delivery, the "when issued" securities making a profit on paper. This was called "arbitrage." But if the reorganization was upset and a new plan approved, the arbitrager would find his "when-issued" contract cancelled and would still own the old securities. This happened in the reorganization of the Missouri Pacific Railroad.

Sometimes "when-issued" securities appear when a company offers to its stockholders rights to buy new securities. For example, the Consumers Power Co. in July, 1960 offered to its stockholders rights to subscribe to an issue of 4⅜ convertible debenture bonds due in 1975. The rights expired on August 12, 1960. On August 1, 1960, the bonds were selling on a "when issued" basis at about 108¾.

This illustrates one of the advantages of the "when issued" market. The holder of the old security can determine the value of a new security before he subscribes to it. In this case, the holder of 250 shares of Consumers Power common stock knows that he can buy for $1,000 a 4⅜ convertible worth 108¾.

Usually the buyer of "when issued" securities must pay the regular commission; and if he is buying on margin, must put up the regular margin as required for issued securities.

The difference in price between the old and the "when issued" securities is usually small, owing to the trading activities of the arbitragers, a highly skilled group of traders. They buy and sell the old and "when issued" securities, making a short-term profit on the transactions. Often it will appear from the quotation of the old and the new securities that there is an attractive spread. Sometimes it is possible for the layman to make a profit by selling and buying those securities. But these occasions are rare, and trading of this sort is best left to the experts.

"When, as and if issued" securities *are delivered at the office of the purchaser on the date declared by the Uniform Practice Committee of the district in which delivery is to be effected.* If no date is declared by the committee, the securities may be delivered at the office of the purchaser on the day after written notice has been delivered to the office of the purchaser. When open market "When, as and if issued" contracts in securities are being publicly offered through a syndicate, they shall be settled on the date the syndicate or selling group contracts are settled.

"When, as and if distributed" securities shall be delivered to the office of the purchaser on the date declared by the Uniform Practice

Committee of the District. If no delivery date is declared, the delivery may be made by the seller on the full business day following the day upon which the seller has delivered at the office of the purchaser written notice of conditions to deliver.

DIVIDENDS, EX-DIVIDENDS, EX-RIGHTS (SECTION 5). The *dividends* shown in the quotation sheets require some explanation. Sometimes they are shown as the annual rate, sometimes only the amount paid so far in the year, and sometimes only at the regular rate, not including extra dividends or stock dividends. At all events, these are usually explained by footnotes—a, b, c, and so on.

Each time a corporation declares a dividend there are four significant dates. These may be shown as follows:

Declaration Date	Ex-Dividend Date	Record Date	Payment Date

The board of directors of a corporation meet to *declare* a dividend on the common or preferred stock. Under most state laws, dividends can be paid only if there is a surplus.

Further, in many states the directors can declare dividends on the common stock *only* from earned surplus. Some states that permit dividend payments from capital surplus require that the directors inform the stockholders of the source. But as a general rule, dividends cannot be paid from capital. When the dividend is announced, the company designates a record date.

The record date is the day on which a list is made by the corporation of all the stockholders who will receive the declared dividends. As soon as a stock is purchased the name of the buyer should be recorded on the books of the company, usually kept by the bank that is the transfer agent. Often a company also appoints a bank as registrar. The registrar checks the transfer agent in order to prevent a fraudulent issue of the stocks. The service charges of the transfer agent are paid by the party at whose instance the record change is made. This is particularly true of small companies with limited resources. But the majority of the large nationally known companies such as General Motors Corporation pay the expenses of transferring their stock.

A buyer of a stock four days prior to the *record date* would have time to obtain delivery of this stock the *regular way* and have his name placed in the books of the company in time to become a holder of record to receive the dividend. In other words, the term *"dividend on"* signifies that the buyer is entitled to the dividend declared on a security.

Ex-dividend or ex-right date is the day on and after which the buyer of a common stock is not entitled to a previously declared dividend or right. In the example on page 102, the ACF Industries had an *x* before the number of sales made. This means that the shares were sold *ex-d* or *ex* a cash dividend of 55¢ on November 21, 1966 (Monday). Since the *record date* of the stock was Friday, November 25, a buyer of this stock on Monday, November 21 would not get delivery for four full business days, or until Monday, November 28. November 24 was Thanksgiving Day; November 26 was Saturday and November 27 was Sunday. The following shows the delivery date in detail:

November 21, 1966	Monday		Trade Date
November 22, 1966	Tuesday		1 Day
November 23, 1966	Wednesday		1 Day
November 24, 1966	Thursday	Thanksgiving Day—Holiday	
November 25, 1966	Friday	Record Date	1 Day
November 26, 1966	Saturday		Holiday
November 27, 1966	Sunday		Holiday
November 28, 1966	Monday	Delivery Date	1 Day
			4 Days

In short, a buyer of the stock of ACF Industries on Monday, November 21, would not get his stock until the following Monday—too late to get his name on the books of the company on the record date for the payment of dividends.

The basic rule in determining the ex-dividend date for cash or stock dividends is that securities shall be ex-dividend *on the third full business day* preceding the record date, if the record date falls on a business day and if announced sufficiently in advance of the record date.

If the record date falls on a holiday or any other day than a full business day, the ex date if the fourth full business day preceding the record date. To repeat, a buyer of shares of ACF Industries on or after November 21 is not entitled to the current dividend. It is paid to the seller. In the same manner, a security might trade *"ex rights."* When a security trades *"ex rights,"* the buyer does not get the rights, which remain the property of the seller.

Sometimes companies fail to give the public proper notice of the declaration of a dividend. In this case, the price of the stock reflects or trades as if the purchaser is entitled to the dividend, when as a matter of fact the purchaser has unwittingly bought the stock after it has passed the record date. In these circumstances the National Uniform Practice Code provides that if there was a late publication of a dividend, one that had not been announced sufficiently in advance of the record date to permit the security to trade ex-dividend in the usual way, then the security would trade *ex-dividend on the first full business day following the public notice.* Here the buyer would have public notice that the security he buys does not include the dividend.

Notwithstanding the above, the ex-dividend date on the stock of an *open end investment company* shall be the date designated by the issuer or its principal underwriter.

The *payable date* is the date the company or its agent pays its dividend. For example, the ACF Industries paid a dividend of 55¢ on December 15, 1966.

Occasionally, a security is sold *before* it trades ex dividend or ex rights but is delivered too late for the buyer to record his ownership on the company transfer records to get the dividend. Because the seller is still the holder of record, the company will pay the dividend or rights to him and he is *not entitled to keep it.* Under such circumstances the buyer can demand, and is entitled to receive from the seller, a promise to pay to him the distribution of dividends or rights when made. This promise is called *a due bill.*

SECTION 48 of the Uniform Practice Code provides that when a security is sold before it trades ex-dividend or ex-rights or ex-interest and is delivered too late for transfer on or before the record date, it must be accompanied by a *due bill* for the distribution made. Sometimes the term *due bill checks* is used. This means a due bill in the form of a check payable on the date of the cash dividend.

SECTION 6 of the Uniform Practice Code provides that bonds which are normally traded *flat* (that is, bonds whose interest does not accrue up to but not including date of delivery: See page 123) the record date means the date fixed by the trustee, registrar, paying agent or issuer. Ex-interest date on flat bonds is therefore the third full business day preceding the record date. It is on the fourth full business day preceding the record date if the record date falls on a day other than a full business day. It is also on the fourth full business day preceding the date on which interest is paid if no record date is set.

GOOD DELIVERY. All securities transactions must be for "good delivery." This means that the security is in such form that the record of ownership may be readily transferred. In short, the ownership must be clear. There are a number of qualifications to *good delivery.* Some of these are as follows and will be discussed in detail.

   a. Proper assignment
   b. Good condition of security
   c. *Not* in name of married women (in some states)
   d. *Not* in the name of a deceased person
   e. The proper number of units
   f. *Not* a called security
   g. At the proper time with taxes, etc., paid
   h. A permanent certificate if available

a) *Registered certificates* must be accompanied by an *assignment* to be good delivery. For example, if a stock certificate is registered in the name of John H. Jones he must endorse or sign it on the back *exactly:*

John H. Jones. The signature must correspond with the name written upon the certificate in every particular without alteration or enlargement or any change whatever except that "and" or &, Company or Co. may be written either way.

Sometimes the *power of substitution* is used. This may also be inscribed on the back of the certificate or as a separate power. Usually the proper signature on the certificate makes the certificate negotiable when guaranteed by a member, a member organization, or a bank. But sometimes, when there is risk of the loss of a certificate, it is desirable to designate the broker, an attorney, by *power of substitution.* This enables the broker to make good delivery. Most certificates are endorsed in blank and therefore negotiable. Many old certificates provided space for a witness, but in recent years the witness to an endorsement has not been required. The following is an example of an assignment and power of substitution appearing on the back of the stock of the *First Investors Fund for Growth, Inc.*

For value received _____ hereby sell, assign and transfer unto
Social Security Number _____

_____
(Please print or type name and address of assignee)
_____ shares
of the capital stock represented by the within Certificate, and do hereby irrevocably constitute and appoint

_____ Attorney to transfer
the said stock on the books of the within named Corporation with full power of substitution in the premises.
Dated _____

_____

Notice: The signature to this assignment must correspond with the name
written on the face of the certificate in every particular without
alteration or enlargement or any change whatever.

Sometimes a separate stock power is used. This is an assignment in form exactly like the one on the back of the stock certificate. It contains a full description of the security to which it may be attached, including the name of the company, the type of stock (common or preferred), its number, the amount of shares expressed in words and numerals. Each signature to an assignment may be witnessed by an individual and dated. However, many transfer agents do not insist that an assignment be witnessed as long as it is guaranteed, since the guarantor thus accepts the responsibility for the genuineness of the signature.

A stock power might be used by a registered stockholder who does not have the certificate available to place an assignment on its back. For example, let us assume a farmer living in Geneseo, New York wishes to sell 100 shares of the common stock of the United States Steel Corporation. Let us assume further that this stock is held by his banker in a custody account in New York City. The farmer can simply execute a stock power and send it along with a letter of instruction to sell the stock.

Sometimes a power is used in a similar manner to transfer registered bonds. It is not advisable, as a rule, to send a signed or endorsed certificate unregistered through the mails. As an alternative, the seller might send his stock certificate (never a bond) in one envelope and the signed stock power in another.

b) *The bond or stock certificate must be in good condition.* If it is mutilated in any way, it must be authenticated by the proper authority. This means that the proper authority must certify that the certificate is valid in spite of the mutilation and will be accepted as representing the equity or obligation it purports to be. The proper authority might be the transfer agent on the stock, an authorized company officer, or the trustee of an issue of bonds.

c) *A certificate in the name of a married woman is not good delivery under all circumstances.* For example, the laws of Texas, Arizona, New Mexico, and some foreign countries restrict the rights of married women. Some laws in these places provide that a certificate in the name of a married woman must be signed by the husband and wife and acknowledged before a notary public or other qualified officer.

A certificate of an unmarried woman is good delivery without the prefix "Miss" *only* if the assignment is accompanied by an acknowledgment in the proper form executed before a notary public or other qualified officer. Otherwise if the certificate is registered with the prefix "Miss," it is good delivery if it is signed "Miss."

A certificate in the name of a widow is good delivery only if the assignment is accompanied by an acknowledgment executed before a notary public or other qualified officer. (See section 35.)

An *acknowledgment,* as its name implies, is essentially a notarial acknowledgment by individuals, firms, corporations, married women, widows, and unmarried women. That is, a notary of public or qualified officer of the state swears under seal that he knows the parties named, that they have appeared before him, and that they have duly executed the assignment.

d) When a sales contract is for more than 100 shares, the delivery of the stock must be made in certificates *from which units of 100 shares each may be composed* to aggregate or add up to the highest multiple of 100 shares called for by the contract. This simply means that a seller must deliver either round 100 shares lots or smaller lots that add up to 100 shares. For example, a seller of 300 shares could deliver six certificates of fifty shares each. The buyer could turn around and sell the 300 shares in 100-unit lots. But the seller of 300 shares could not deliver four certificates of seventy-five shares each, since none of these lots add up to 100. This means that the seller of units that do not add up to the highest multiple of 100 shares must go to the company's transfer agent and perhaps *pay a fee* to have his shares consolidated.

Each delivery of stock should be in certificates aggregating the exact number of shares called for in the contract. Unless agreed at the time of the transaction, a certificate for more than 100 shares is not good delivery. Acceptance of any delivery not meeting the requirement explained above is at the option of the purchaser. If the purchaser accepts, a receipt should be given pending a transfer into suitable units. (See sections 15 and 16.)

e) A certificate in the name of a *deceased* person is *not* a good delivery even if properly assigned. Certificates in the name of deceased persons should be transferred by the executor to a street name before delivering it to the buyer. The transfer agent usually makes this transfer on receipt of several legal documents. Depending on the state, these documents usually include:

1. A certified copy of the will of the deceased
2. A certified copy of the court order appointing the executor of the estate
3. A death certificate
4. A tax waiver from the State showing the State taxes have been paid

The stock certificate must also be signed and witnessed by the executor.

In short, it is up to the seller, the executor, to get the certificate transferred out of the name of the deceased in order to deliver it to the buyer clean. Also not good delivery are certificates with an assignment or a power of substitution executed by a trustee, guardian, infant (except certificates registered under Statutory Gifts to Minors Acts), executor, administrator, receiver in bankruptcy, agent, or attorney. (See section 36.)

f) A *called* bond or called preferred stock is not good delivery unless the entire issue has been called. At times there are trades in "called stock" or "called bonds," but here it is known that they are called securities and dealt in specifically as such.

Every delivery of bonds, whether in bearer or registered form (see Chapter 3) shall be made in denominations of $500 or $1,000. But when a contract is for a principal amount which is not a multiple of $500 the parties shall agree at the time of the transaction concerning the proper units for delivery. (See section 17.)

g) Drafts accompanying the shipment of securities need be accepted only *on a full business day during business hours.* The acceptance of a draft prior to the settlement date is at the option of the drawee. Expenses of shipment, including insurance, postage, and collection charges, shall be paid by the seller. Failure to accept a draft in which no irregularities exist shall make the person on whom the draft is drawn liable for the payment of interest and miscellaneous expenses incurred because of the delay.

The securities should be *delivered* at the office of the buyer between the hours established by rule or practice in the community where the office is located. The seller on making the delivery shall have the right to *require* that the buyer pay upon delivery of the securities by a certified check, cashiers check, bank draft, or cash.

h) Temporary certificates (discussed in Chapter 3) are not good delivery when permanent certificates are available.

Under section 14 of the Uniform Practice Code the seller must furnish the buyer at the time of delivery a sale memorandum ticket to which shall be affixed and cancelled state transfer taxes which are required by the state in which the sale occurs, or the tax may be paid by the seller through the stock clearing corporations. See page 103 for New York State.

A certificate with an inscription to indicate joint tenancy, tenancy in common, or in the names of two or more individuals is *not* good delivery unless signed by the co-tenants or registered co-owners. (See sections 36 and 37.)

The Interest Equalization Act of 1964 provided for a tax to be imposed on American investors' purchases of foreign securities from foreigners. Purchases of foreign securities by an American from another American are not subject to the tax. The bill establishing the tax was signed into law by President Johnson on September 2, 1964, and was to expire December 31, 1965. In October, 1965, the interest equalization tax was extended through July 31, 1967.

Under terms of the extended law, the tax rates on foreign *bonds* range from 1.05 per cent of the purchase price for securities maturing in one year to 2.75 per cent of the purchase price for those maturing in three years. The rate schedule on longer maturities moves in graduated steps up to 15 per cent of the purchase price for bonds due in $28\frac{1}{2}$ years or more. The tax on new and existing issues of foreign *stocks* is a standard 15 per cent of the purchase price.

The law contains many exemptions. For example:

a. The U.S. President is allowed to exempt a foreign country's new securities from the tax if he thinks that such an exemption is necessary to avoid disrupting the international monetary system.

   b.   The tax does not apply if the funds being raised by the security issue are destined for use in an underdeveloped nation.

   c.   The tax does not apply if the funds being raised will be used for buying products from the United States.

The tax was implemented as part of the government's plan to reduce the nation's balance of payments deficit and thereby help curb the outflow of gold from the United States Treasury. The interest equalization tax imposed on American investors is intended to induce compensating price reductions by the foreign sellers, thus increasing by about 1 per cent their cost of raising capital in the United States.

DELIVERY UNDER GOVERNMENT REGULATION (See section 28.) A most important regulation is under the Interest Equalization Act of 1964. This provides, as stated above, for the payment of an excise tax imposed on the acquisition of foreign securities in order to equalize the costs of stock and long-term bond financing. Prior to 1964, the government felt that too many companies abroad were selling their securities for dollars and causing an outflow of capital and hence contributed to an unfavorable balance of payments. (See page 68.) Hence, the act imposes a tax which is paid on the acquisition of these foreign securities *when acquired from a foreign person.* Thus all sales by a member as a broker of stock of a foreign issuer or of debt of a foreign obligor which but for the *exemption of prior American ownership,* would be subject to the tax imposed by the Act.

A member effecting a sale shall have in his possession a Certificate of American Ownership or a blanket certificate relating to the account. If the sale is subject to the tax the selling member shall disclose same to the purchaser at the execution of the contract.

Other Sections of the Uniform Practice Code

   1. *Written confirmations or comparisons* must be exchanged on the day of a cash transaction, or on or before the first full business day following the transaction for other than a cash transaction. This does not apply to transactions cleared through the National Over the Counter Clearing Corporation. Confirmations shall include adequate description of the security and its price, as well as any other information deemed necessary. This would include such items as "ex warrants," "ex-stock," "registered," "flat," "part redeemed," etc. (See sections 9, 10, 11.)

   2. *Transfer fees.* The party at whose instance a transfer is made shall pay all service charges of the transfer agent. (See section 50.)

   3. *Marking to the market.* Perhaps the easiest way to under-

stand this concept is to consider what happens on a short sale. Here a customer sells a stock he does not own, hoping it will go down and he can buy it in to make delivery. Thus he will make a profit on the difference between what he sells his stock short and buys in to make delivery less taxes and commissions. However, if, after he has sold short, his stock goes up, then his broker will "mark his account to the market" and demand more collateral. This also occurs when there are market changes on *"when issued"* contracts. Here trading takes place but the settlement date is undetermined. Basically, marking to the market takes place during the period before the settlement date has been determined, if either party to the transaction is partially unsecured by reason of a change in the market that party may demand a deposit equal to the difference between the market price and the contract price. (See section 58.)

4. *Computation of Interest.* Interest is computed up to but not including the day of delivery. For corporate bonds it is on a thirty-day month, 360-day year. On United States Treasury bonds, it is calculated on the basis of the *exact number of days on a semiannual basis.*

But a more detailed discussion will be given of bonds in the following pages.

CLOSE-OUT PROCEDURE.   A contract which has not been completed by the *seller (section 59)* according to terms may be closed by the buyer after the first business day following the date the delivery was due.

Written notice of "buy in" shall be delivered to seller's office prior to twelve noon of the day preceding the execution of the proposed "buy in."

This notice shall contain details of the "buy in," that is, the date of the contract closed, quantity, and contract price of the securities as well as the demand. In case the notice is retransmitted to another broker/ dealer from whom the securities are due, the originator may not buy in the securities until twenty-four hours after the time indicated on the original "buy in" notice.

Upon failure of seller to effect delivery or to obtain a stay, the buyer may purchase for cash the securities in the best available market. If the "buy in" is not completed on the day specified, notice shall remain in force for five (5) full business days from date delivery is due.

Other parts of section 59 provide for partial delivery by seller, securities in transit, exempt securities, deferment of "buy in," and notice of the executed "buy in."

While a "buy in" notice is in force, the buyer shall accept during regular delivery hours any portion of the securities called for in the contract, provided the remaining portion undelivered at the time the buyer proposes to execute the "buy in" may be purchased for cash in the market or at the option of the buyer for guaranteed delivery no later than the settlement date.

If, prior to the closing of the contract on which a "buy in" notice has been given, the buyer receives from the seller written notice that the securities are in transfer or in transit or shipped that day giving certificate numbers, the buyer may not execute the "buy in" for a period not exceeding seven calendar days from date delivery was due under buy in. Upon request of the seller an additional seven calendar days may be granted by the Secretary of the National Uniform Practice Committee. In fact, a member or a representative of the National Uniform Practice Committee may defer a "buy in" whenever in his opinion circumstances justify such action.

The party executing the "buy in" shall, as promptly as possible on the day of the execution, by telephone, telegraph, or other means, notify the person for whose account the securities were bought, giving details; and shall promptly mail or deliver formal confirmation of purchase. A copy of this confirmation must be filed with the Secretary of the National Uniform Practice Committee. In addition, immediate similar notification shall be given to succeeding broker/dealer to whom a retransmitted notice was given.

The above "buy in" procedure shall not apply to contracts for warrants, rights, convertible securities, called securities, or any contract made for "cash" or made for or amended to include guaranteed delivery on a specified date.

Upon failure of the *buyer (section 60)* to accept delivery in accordance with the terms of the contract, the seller may without notice sell out all or any part of the securities called for in the contract in the best available market for the account and liability of the party in default.

The person whose account is sold out shall be notified promptly of the details of the transaction by mail or delivery of notice. A copy of this notice shall be filed with the Secretary of the National Uniform Practice Committee.

WRITTEN NOTICE. Written notice, as the term is used in the Uniform Practice Code, includes notice by letter, teletype, or telegraph.

Stock and Bond Transactions

BOND QUOTATIONS. Bonds are quoted on the New York and American Stock Exchanges in much the same manner as stocks. Here is a sample of some bonds quoted on the New York Stock Exchange from *The Wall Street Journal* of November 22, 1966.

CORPORATION BONDS

1966			Sales in				Net
High	Low	Bonds	$1,000	High	Low	Close	Chg.
95	81½	Ling TV 5¾s76	15	85	84⅛	84⅛	− ⅞
223¼	114½	Ling TV cv 5¾s76	60	167½	167	167½	....
91	52	Lionel cv 5½s80	22	85½	57½	58½	+ ½
215	144¼	Litton cv 3½s87	3	179	178	179	− 5
100	84	Mack Tr 5⅛s81	4	87	87	87	....
118½	87½	Macy cv 4¼s90	3	104	102	102	− 2
88¾	75	McCrory 5½s76	10	78½	77¾	78½	+ ¼
69	60⅛	McCrory 5s81	10	62½	61⅜	61⅜	− 1⅛
100¾	98	Mich CG 3⅞s67	226 99	98 13-16	98	29-32	+-3-32
95	91	Mich CG 3½s69	6	94½	94⅛	94½	+ ⅝
103	90	Mpls StL 6s85	9	90½	90½	90½	− 1
95	91	Mich CG 3½s69	7	93⅞	93⅞	93⅞	− ⅛
70⅜	55	MSPSSM gm4s91f	1	58	58	58	
100⅛	95¾	Minn MM 2¾s67	4	98	97⅛	98	+27-32

The high and low for 1966 to date are shown. The name of the bond is given in abbreviated form, as well as the interest rate and the maturity. Also shown are the volume of sales, the high, the low, the last sale of the day, and as with stocks the change from the close on the previous trading day. For example, the quotation shows that the bonds of R. H. Macy and Company have a 4¼% coupon and are due in 1990. On November 21, 1966, $3,000 bonds were traded. They sold at a high of 104 and as low as 102 at which price they closed. Since bonds are quoted in percent of par of $1,000, this would equal 104 per cent of $1,000 or $1,040 and 102 per cent of $1,000 or $1,020. Clearly, these bonds are selling at a *premium*, since their par value is $1,000. The premium in this case is $20 taken at the last price or the amount the bond is selling above the face amount of $1,000. But for most of the year 1966 the Macy bonds were selling below par or at a *discount*. The only reason the Macy bonds are selling at a premium when the level of interest rates for such bonds is over 6 per cent is that they are convertible into common stock. As indicated by the "cv" in the above quotation the bond of R. H. Macy is convertible into common stock at 60 or $1,000/60 equals 16.67 shares. Since the stock on November 21, 1966, sold at about 48, the bonds on the basis of conversion alone would be only worth about $800.16 or (16,67 × 48 equals $800.16). But if the earnings of Macy should improve, the convertible bonds could appreciate in value.

Although a considerable number of bonds are listed and traded on the New York Stock Exchange, by far the greatest volume is done on the over-the-counter market. Prices on the over-the-counter bonds are indicated by bid and asked prices published by the National Quotation Bureau and distributed to the subscribing members of the National Association of Securities Dealers. These quotation sheets are not available to the public. However, markets on over-the-counter bonds as well as stocks can usually be obtained by calling a broker who subscribes to these quotation sheets.

The majority of the bonds sell *with interest* or as sometimes stated *"and accrued interest,"* or *"plus accrued interest."* This means that the seller of the bond receives not only the sales price but in addition the accrued interest from the date of the last payment of interest. This interest is calculated from the date of the last interest payment but not including the date of delivery.

Let us assume that on Monday, November 21, 1966 an investor bought $1,000 of R. H. Macy and Company 4¼% of 1990 at 102.

$1,000 R. H. Macy and Co. 4¼ % of 1990	$1,020.00
Plus Commission $2.50 per bond	2.50
Plus Accrued interest	20.89
	$1,043.39

In this case, the commission to the broker would be $2.50. Interest on this bond is paid on June 1 and December 1, or $21.25 twice a year, making a total of $42.50 or 4¼ per cent of $1,000. Thus, a purchase on Monday, November 21, regular way would not be delivered until Monday, November 28, or at the *end of four full business days.* This is the same as regular way delivery for stocks as explained on page 106. *But interest accrues up to but not including the date of delivery.*

The following illustrates these points:

November 21, 1966	Monday	Trade Date
November 22, 1966	Tuesday	1 Day
November 23, 1966	Wednesday	1 Day
November 24, 1966	Thursday—Thanksgiving Day	Holiday
November 25, 1966	Friday	1 Day
November 26, 1966	Saturday	Holiday
November 27, 1966	Sunday—	
	End of Interest Accrual Period	Holiday
November 28, 1966	Monday—Date of delivery	1 Day
		4 Days

Interest is computed on the basis of a 360-day year, i.e., every calendar month shall be considered to be 1/12 of 360 days; every period from a date in one month to the same date in the following month shall be considered 30 days. The number of elapsed days shall be computed in accordance with the examples given in the following table:

> From 1st to 30th of the same month to be figured as 29 days.
> From 1st to 1st of the following month to be figured as 30 days.
> From 1st to 28th of February to be figured as 27 days.

Where interest is payable on the 30th or the 31st of the month:

From 30th or 31st to 1st of the following month as one day.

From 30th or 31st to 30th of the following month to be figured as 30 days.

From 30th or 31st to 1st of second following month to be figured as 1 month and 1 day.

In calculating the accrued interest on the Macy bonds, the analyst should consider first the fact that the interest payments are on June 1 and on December 1. Second, he should start counting each full month as thirty days plus the days in the month the bond was sold up to but not including date of delivery. The count should start from the date of the last interest payment, as follows:

June	30 Days
July	30 Days
August	30 Days
September	30 Days
October	30 Days
November	27 Days
	177 Days

In other words the seller of an R. H. Macy & Company 4¼% bond is entitled to interest for 177 days of 177/360 of a year's interest of $42.50. This amounts to $20.89.

In contrast to delivery *regular way*, which requires delivery on the fourth full business day after the trade date and accrued interest up to but not including the date of delivery, *delayed delivery* requires delivery on the seventh calendar day following the transaction date, but interest would accrue only up to but not including the date of delivery regular way. When parties to the contract specify *interest to run*, the interest accrues to but not including date of *actual* delivery. If delivery is *seller's option*, the interest accrues the same as regular way delivery.

No federal tax is paid by either the purchaser or the seller of bonds. But a Securities and Exchange fee is charged on the *sale* of bonds if the bond is traded on the exchanges. (No fee is paid if the bond is sold in the over-the-counter market.) This fee is 1¢ per $500 of market value or any multiple thereof.

Thus the seller of a $1,000 R. H. Macy & Company bond would receive the following:

$1,000 R. H. Macy & Company 4¼ of 1990 at 102	$1,020.00
Less Commission $2.50 per bond	2.50
Plus accrued interest	20.89
Less Securities and Exchange Commission fee	.03
	$1,038.36

While bonds of companies in sound financial condition usually sell with interest accrued, common and preferred stocks are sold without accrued dividends unless specified otherwise at the time the contract is made. In other words, they are sold flat.

Also, bonds which have defaulted on their interest payments sell flat because their future payments of interest are questionable. In other words, since the interest does not accumulate or accrue, the bonds are traded "f" or flat. There is no accrued interest, which might or might not be paid in the future.

In most cases, income bonds are traded flat. The reason for this is that the indenture of income bonds usually provides that no interest shall be paid unless and until it has been declared payable by the Board of Directors of the company issuing the bonds. Sometimes indentures provide that the directors may not declare the interest payable unless it has been earned.

However, there are several (about eight) income bonds listed on the New York Stock Exchange whose earnings record and surplus make declaration of interest a certainty. These bonds have been put in a special category by the exchange, which has ruled that these bonds shall trade with accrued interest even though they are income bonds. Sometimes, by agreement, bonds traded over the counter may be traded with accrued interest.

Also, the payment of interest on *income bonds* is somewhat uncertain, since interest payments depend on earnings. Therefore almost all income bonds are also quoted as "flat," that is, the interest does not accrue. Reference is made to the MSPSSM gm 4s 91f in the sample of domestic bond quotations on page 120. This is the Minneapolis, St. Paul and Sault Ste. Marie Railroad Co. (Soo Line) general mortgage 4% income bond due 1991. Since these are income bonds (discussed in Chapter 4) they are quoted flat as shown by the "f." However, almost all of the bonds traded are paying interest regularly and are therefore traded "and interest." When a company pays interest on a bond that normally trades flat, the situation is the same as in the case of a payment of a dividend discussed on page 110, except that the bonds trade ex interest instead of ex dividend on the third full day preceding the record date if the record date falls on a full business day.

Sometimes a company will be in reorganization for a long time and pays no interest on its coupons. As a result, the defaulted coupons would seem to have no value. But care should be taken of these defaulted coupons. If the bond is subsequently sold or exchanged for new securities, it must have all unpaid coupons attached (i.e., SCA—subsequent coupons attached) in order to be good delivery.

United States Government securities are usually quoted in the over-the-counter market. Only a very few United States Government bonds are traded on the New York Stock Exchange. All government securities are traded "and interest" and United States Treasury bills are quoted at discounts and gradually increase to face amount at maturity.

Government securities usually are traded net. This means no commission is charged since the dealer makes his profit by the difference between what he buys the securities for and what he sells them for. Sales made the regular way, require delivery the next business day.

AMERICAN DEPOSITORY RECEIPTS (ADR's). An American Depository Receipt is a form of registered security, which is fully negotiable and can be readily traded in the securities markets. ADR's are contracts which indicate that a specified number of shares of a certain foreign corporation have been deposited with the foreign branch or custodian of an American bank operating overseas. These deposited securities must remain on deposit as long as the ADR's are outstanding. The ADR is essentially an agreement between the bank as the depository and the holder of the ADR.

All ADR's must meet the United States disclosure rules established by the Securities Exchange Act of 1934. Under these regulations, American banks generally are permitted to sign a simplified form of registration statement in the name of the foreign issuer.

ARBITRAGE IN SECURITIES. Whenever securities are traded in two or more separate markets at the same time, it is possible for price discrepancies to develop. When such discrepancies exist it may be possible for a trader to make a profit by utilizing the technique of arbitrage.

Securities arbitrage may be defined as the simultaneous purchase and sale of the same security in order to take advantage of a price discrepancy. A person who engages in arbitrage is known as an arbitrager. If, for example, General Motors stock could be purchased in New York for $60 per share and sold at the same time on the Pacific Coast for $61 per share, the arbitrager making the simultaneous trades would make $1 per share profit (less expenses). Arbitrage performs the economic function of equalizing prices between markets by eliminating price differentials.

Arbitrage may also involve the purchase of rights to subscribe to a security, or the purchase of a convertible security—and the sale at about the same time of the security obtainable through exercise of the rights or of the security obtainable through conversion.

Arbitrage takes place in the money and commodity markets as well as in the securities markets.

REVIEW QUESTIONS

1. Assume that your broker bought for you 100 shares of a stock on the New York Stock Exchange for $5,625 and 50 shares of another stock for $2,125. What are the commissions for each transaction?

2. Describe a *put option* and a *call option*. What is the main advantage and disadvantage of each?

3. What is the *Uniform Practice Code* of the NASD and how is it administered?

4. Distinguish between delivery of a common stock regular way, delayed delivery, sellers option, and cash sales.

5. What does it mean when a stock sells ex dividend or ex rights? If a stock was bought on Monday, February 20, 1967, with a record date for dividend Friday, February 23rd, who gets the dividend? Explain.

6. What is meant by *good delivery*? Name six qualifications.

7. What are the requirements for the proper number of units of delivery?

8. Explain the background and importance of the *Interest Equalization Act of 1964*.

9. What is *marking to the market* as applied to a short sale and when issued securities?

10. Explain the *close-out procedure* when closed out by a buyer and by a seller.

11. Describe the calculation of accrued bond interest of a corporate bond and of a U.S. Government bond.

12. What does it mean when bonds are traded *"flat"*?

Technical Market Analysis

Chapter **9**

Fundamental Analysis vs. Technical Analysis

Security analysts have been divided for years into two schools of thought: the fundamental and the technical. The fundamental analyst considers the qualitative factors of a company, such as its outlook, its management, its research as well as the quantitative factors which include: its earnings, its balance sheet, its price, its dividend, and any number of ratios. The technical analyst is interested primarily in the action of the stock market in general and the price action of the particular company he is following. These price actions are recorded on charts.

Some analysts have been successful with one method, others with the other. But success seems to depend on the individual's interpretation of the data or charts. It is believed that a keen analyst should be well grounded in the fundamentals of a company but should not ignore the technical factors. The reason is that many follow the technical approach, so when a certain formation appears on the charts mass buying often follows if the formation is favorable, and mass selling if it is unfavorable.

Stock Averages

One of the best ways of following the day-to-day changes in the market as a whole is to watch one of the several stock averages. Perhaps the most generally used is the Dow Jones Average of thirty industrial stocks. This average is often used in conjunction with the Dow Jones Average of railroad stocks and the Dow Jones Average of Utility stocks. Others include the Standard and Poor's Average of 425 industrial stocks, the American Stock Exchange Price Index, the National Quotation Bureau Over-the-Counter Industrial index, and the

New York Stock Exchange Indexes. The following table shows these indexes as they appeared in *The Wall Street Journal* on November 22, 1966.

DOW-JONES CLOSING AVERAGES

	1966	Monday Changes		1965
Industrials	798.16	—11.24	—1.39%	946.38
Railroads	200.76	—3.01	—1.48%	236.21
Utilities	135.33	—1.51	—1.10%	156.18
Composite	282.77	—3.92	—1.37%	330.02

OTHER MARKET INDICATORS

	1966	Change	1965
N. Y. S. E. Composite	43.28	—0.61	49.18
Industrial	42.83	—0.63	....
Utility	44.70	—0.49	....
Transportation	45.36	—0.71	....
Financial	42.92	—0.54	....
Standard & Poor's Industrial	85.09	—1.30	97.50
American Exchange Price Index	$13.01	—$0.15	$13.43
N.Q.B. Over-Counter Industrial	223.96	—0.69	225.10

The most recent of these indexes was introduced by the New York Stock Exchange in July, 1966. This is the most comprehensive developed so far. It is based on 1280 or so common stocks which are listed on the New York Stock Exchange. As may be seen from the above tabulation, it consists of five indexes.

1,000 issues of *Industrial Companies* (Manufacturing, merchandising, mining, and service)

76 issues of *Transportation Companies* (Airline, shipping, and motor transport)

136 issues of *Utility Companies* (Operating and holding companies)

75 issues of *Finance Companies* (Closed end investment companies, real estate holding companies and stocks of Savings and loan companies.

1,287 issues of *Composite Companies* (All of the above)

The basis is 50, or the average price of all stocks as of December 31, 1965.

Stock splits and dividends have the effect of reducing the per-share price and are compensated for by simply increasing the number of shares divided into the value of the stocks which are calculated every half hour of a trading day.

The advantages of this index are two: first, it is much broader than any of the other indexes since it covers many more stocks; second, it tends to play down the wide swings of the other averages, in particular the Dow Jones average. For example, the above table shows that the composite average of the New York Stock Exchange on November 21, 1966, declined .61 or 61¢. But the Dow Jones industrial average declined 11.24 points or $11.24.

The Dow Theory

The average which is followed by many is the Dow Jones Average of thirty stocks. This average is given every half hour of each trading day. It is constructed by taking the market prices of thirty stocks and dividing by a divisor. This divisor is reduced each time a stock is split. For example, let us assume that the time is early 1959 and that there are only three stocks in the Dow Jones average.

	A	B
Eastman Kodak Company	140	70
Union Carbide Corporation	120	120
Allied Chemical Corporation	100	100
Total	360	290
Average of the three	120	96⅝

Let us further assume that Eastman Kodak Company splits its stock two for one. Then the average would be reduced to 96⅝ from 120 under *A*. Since there has been no change in prices, some adjustment must be made for the split. In other words, we know that the average is the same —that is, 120. Therefore, we simply find what number divided into 290 would equal 120.

$$\text{Thus, } 290 \div X = 120$$
$$\frac{290}{X} = 120$$
$$290 : X = 120 : 1.00$$
$$120\ X = 290$$
$$X = 2.417$$

Thus if the new total value of 290 of the three stocks is divided by 2.417, the average would be 120. In short, *to find the new divisor, the total value of the new stocks after the split* (in this case 290) *is divided by the old average price* (or 120). This gives the new divisor, as follows:

$$\frac{290}{120} = 2.417$$

The reason for this is to avoid the difficulty of raising and adjusting the number of shares of stock every time there is a stock split in the thirty stocks of the Dow Jones average. As of August 4, 1966, the thirty Dow Jones stocks were divided by 2.245.

From the Dow Jones average, many firms attempt to predict the future of the stock market by the so-called Dow Theory. Some of the principles of the Dow Theory are:

1. When the market is in a basic upward trend, the market will rise and fall in intermediate swings, *but the peak of each swing will be higher than the previous peak*. But it is impossible to determine when the peak of the cycle has been reached. See upper portion of the illustration which appears below.

2. When the market is in a basic downward trend, each decline will be followed by a recovery in price. But each recovery will not be as high as the previous peak. Here again, however, history has shown that it is not possible to determine when the bottom has been reached. This might be illustrated by the falling, irregular curve shown below.

3. At times another average such as the Dow Jones average of thirty railroads *confirms* the upward or downward movements of the thirty industrials. Then it is a bullish or a bearish signal.

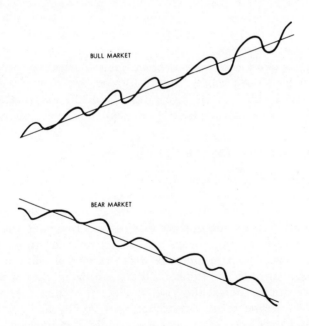

For example, the 1959 peak of the Dow Jones thirty industrial stocks was 678 in August, 1959. In January, 1960, the Dow Jones average broke through this level to 685. *However, the railroads did not confirm.* The 1959 high point of the Dow Jones railroad average was 173, but in January, 1960, it only reached 157. Thus, many Dow theorists interpreted this as a bearish signal and sold stocks. This is simply one example of when the Dow Theory seemed to work.

Many investors have charted these averages for years back and attempted to work out theories like the one explained. On the basis of these theories, many have endeavored to forecast the future course of the stock market. Some have been moderately successful, but the woods are full of people who have lost money trying to forecast the future of the stock market. It is believed that the averages are useful and interesting in showing the course of the market and for measuring changes, but not for forecasting the future.

The Odd Lot Theory

Another method of market forecasting is the *odd lot* theory. As explained, the buyers of odd lots and the New York Stock Exchange are buyers of one through ninety-nine shares or less than the unit of trading. The theory is that the odd-lot buyers are uninformed and therefore wrong. For example, when odd-lot purchases exceed sales, the theory holds that the market will go down, and vice versa. The odd-lot sales are reported daily by the two large odd-lot houses: Carlisle Jacquelin and de Coppet & Doremus. A simple ratio may be constructed by dividing the sales of odd lots by the purchases. Thus, if sales exceed purchases, the index will rise and indicate a bullish trend, and if purchases exceed sales, the index will fall. However, care should be exercised in using this index, as the so-called uninformed small investor is often *right*.

The Advance Decline Theory

Some market technicians place greater faith in the so called *advance decline* theory. This in effect measures the strength of a market's rise or fall. Each day the Wall Street Journal reports the number of issues that advance and the number that decline. By taking the cumulative balance each day, an index can be constructed. It is useful to compare this index with an index for the stock market and plot the two on the same chart. If, for example, the stock index rises rapidly and the advance decline index also rises rapidly, then the technician can feel *confident*. However, if the market rises rapidly and the advance decline index does *not* rise or rises less rapidly, this indicates that the rise in stock may not continue.

Closely related to the advance decline theory is the trading volume which is watched by some technicians. For example, traders like to see heavy volume in a rising market and dislike it in a declining market. Also, in a sharply declining market, if the volume does not increase, the feeling is that the selling will dry up and the decline may not continue. There are a number of chartists who follow the volume of transactions on individual stocks as well as for the market as a whole.

The Short Interest Theory

There are many technicians who watch the short interest position as reported in the middle of the month by the New York Stock Exchange. This is the total of the shares sold *short* on the Exchange. It is helpful to compare the total short interest with the average volume for the month and arrive at a ratio. For example, on July 15, 1966, customers were short 10,732,000 shares and the average volume for the month was 6,778,000 shares. Dividing the short interest by the volume equals 1.58. As a general rule, technicians consider a ratio of 2.00 as bullish, 1.50 as neutral, and 1.00 as bearish. The theory behind a heavy short interest compared with volume is that when a rally does take place, the short sellers will become anxious and seek to cover or buy in their stock. Thus a large short interest will cause a rally in the market to be more steep as the shorts run to cover. Short interest figures are available not only in the aggregate but for individual stocks.

Other Techniques

These would include the *point and figure* charts. These charts are constructed with an X every time a stock moves up a point, and an O every time it goes down. (Sometimes there are three-point and ten-point charts.) Only changes of the full point, three points or ten points are made. Every time the stock changes direction (moves up or down), the chartist moves to the right. No account is taken of time or of volume. But a pattern appears from which chartists claim they can tell which direction the stock is going.

Some even make predictions on such diverse factors as the price of seats on the New York Stock Exchange, insiders selling their stock, and margin changes.

INDIVIDUAL FORMATIONS. These are used in forecasting both the averages and the individual stocks.

The head and shoulders tops with a declining neckline is one of the most common. In this case the line chart would look as follows and indicate a *bearish* trend:

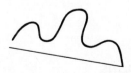

A bullish formation would be the reverse or a head and shoulders bottom and look as follows:

In both cases, the volume of buying and selling is watched. In the head and shoulders tops, for example, if the buying volume is weak on the up side and strong on the down, the formation is particularly unfavorable.

Another formation is a chart which shows a resistance point or support level. This is illustrated as follows:

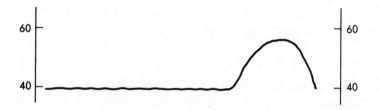

Thus for a long time the stock has sold around 40 and then gone up to around 60. When it falls back to 40 it will tend to stay there. The reason is that many have bought the stock at 40, have seen it go to 60 and fall back. When it goes below 40 they then have a loss and will be reluctant to sell. If it does go through it would be called a breakthrough. Also on the up side a breakthrough is when a stock or the average goes above a high point established some time in the not too distant past. (See chart on page 129.) When breakthroughs occur on the down side, the decline is accelerated.

All of these phenomena are interesting and should be understood because when they occur there are many who notice them and often take action in the securities market. Unfortunately, there is no technique yet discovered which can, with uniform accuracy, predict the market.

REVIEW QUESTIONS

1. Explain the difference between the fundamental and the technical analysis of stocks.

2. Describe the different stock indexes and averages. What are the advantages of the New York Stock Exchange average over the Dow-Jones average?

3. What is the Dow theory? What is meant by confirmation of averages? Head and Shoulders formation?

4. Explain the Odd Lot Theory. How would you follow this theory?

5. What is the Advance-Decline Theory and what does it measure? What is the importance of trading volume?

6. According to the Short Interest Theory, what would be the significance of a short interest of 14,700,000 shares in December, 1966 and average volume of 6,800,000 shares in that month?

7. Describe support levels and breakthroughs.

Taxes

Chapter 10

Tax laws are so complicated that great caution should be taken in advising customers. There are many competent professionals (lawyers and accountants) to whom problems should be referred. There are, however, some basic rules which might be kept in mind, particularly when advising customers on security trades.

Who Must File?

Everyone under 65 who has a gross income of $600 or more a year, or if over 65, $1,200, must file a federal income tax return. In making out the return, the taxpayer should be sure to fill in his Social Security number. A penalty of $5 is assessed for each failure to include this number unless a reasonable cause can be shown for not including it.

Records

Every taxpayer should maintain such records as will enable him to prepare a complete and accurate tax return. These will enable him to give proof of income and expenses in case the Internal Revenue Service makes an audit of the return.

The records which should be kept include:

1. Tax and income withholding statement, Form W-2.
2. Dividend payments reported by corporations as paid taxpayer, Form 1099.
3. Other income such as fees, bank interest, savings interest, trust income, rents and royalties.
4. Estate income. This must be reported even though the estate is not settled, unless tax is paid by the estate.
5. Brokerage reports of purchase and sale of securities.
6. Charitable contribution receipts.

7. Business expenses: travel, hotel, restaurant expenses which are necessary in the performance of employment.
8. Federal, state and real estate tax receipts or canceled checks.
9. Interest payments on mortgages, etc.
10. A clear copy of each tax return filed.
11. Receipted medical bills.

It should be stressed that medical expenses are deductible only to the extent that they exceed 3 per cent of adjusted gross income and drugs to the extent they exceed 1 per cent.

These records should be kept for as long as they may be material in the administration of the internal revenue law. Ordinarily, the statute of limitation for a return is three years from date return was due. However, the Internal Revenue Service cautions that there are instances where a taxpayer should retain his records indefinitely. As a practical hint, it is suggested that a large envelope be used for each year, and the return and all the receipts and records of contributions, taxes, security purchases and sales, etc., for the year be enclosed in separate smaller envelopes. Thus, if the taxpayer is called for an audit, he can easily assemble and verify his return.

Personal Income Taxes Are Progressive

Our federal income taxes are progressive. That is, the larger the income, the higher the rate of tax. This may be illustrated by the following tax rates in effect for the year 1966 for *married* taxpayers:

Schedule II. MARRIED TAXPAYERS FILING JOINT RETURNS and CERTAIN WIDOWS AND WIDOWERS

If the amount on line 11d, page 1, is:		Enter on line 12, page 1:				
Not over $1,000		14% of the amount on line 11d.				
Over–	But not over–					of excess over–
$ 1,000	—	$ 2,000	$ 140,	plus	15%	— $ 1,000
$ 2,000	—	$ 3,000	$ 290,	plus	16%	— $ 2,000
$ 3,000	—	$ 4,000	$ 450,	plus	17%	— $ 3,000
$ 4,000	—	$ 8,000	$ 620,	plus	19%	— $ 4,000
$ 8,000	—	$12,000	$ 1,380,	plus	22%	— $ 8,000
$12,000	—	$16,000	$ 2,260,	plus	25%	— $12,000
$16,000	—	$20,000	$ 3,260,	plus	28%	— $16,000
$20,000	—	$24,000	$ 4,380,	plus	32%	— $20,000
$24,000	—	$28,000	$ 5,660,	plus	36%	— $24,000
$28,000	—	$32,000	$ 7,100,	plus	39%	— $28,000
$32,000	—	$36,000	$ 8,660,	plus	42%	— $32,000
$36,000	—	$40,000	$10,340,	plus	45%	— $36,000

Schedule II (cont'd.)

*If the amount on
line 11d, page 1, is:*   *Enter on line 12, page 1:*

Over–	But not over–				*of excess over–*
$ 40,000	— $ 44,000	$ 12,140,	plus	48%	— $ 40,000
$ 44,000	— $ 52,000	$ 14,060,	plus	50%	— $ 44,000
$ 52,000	— $ 64,000	$ 18,060,	plus	53%	— $ 52,000
$ 64,000	— $ 76,000	$ 24,420,	plus	55%	— $ 64,000
$ 76,000	— $ 88,000	$ 31,020,	plus	58%	— $ 76,000
$ 88,000	— $100,000	$ 37,980,	plus	60%	— $ 88,000
$100,000	— $120,000	$ 45,180,	plus	62%	— $100,000
$120,000	— $140,000	$ 57,580,	plus	64%	— $120,000
$140,000	— $160,000	$ 70,380,	plus	66%	— $140,000
$160,000	— $180,000	$ 83,580,	plus	68%	— $160,000
$180,000	— $200,000	$ 97,180,	plus	69%	— $180,000
$200,000		$110,980,	plus	70%	— $200,000

These taxes are applied after deductions. Thus, a man with a net taxable income of $10,000 would pay on $8,000, $1,380 plus 22 per cent on $2,000 or $440, making a total of $1,820 or 18.2 per cent. However, a couple with a $220,000 income would pay $110,980 on $200,000 plus 70 per cent on $20,000 or $14,000, making a total tax of $124,980 or 56.6%.

Dividends

As pointed out on page 27 the corporations, for all practical purposes, pay taxes on their taxable income of about 48 per cent. After these taxes are paid, net income is reported. From this net income dividends are usually paid. (There are exceptions when a corporation pays dividends in excess of earnings—even where there are no earnings.) Thus, the stockholder being an owner of the corporation in effect pays 48 per cent of the taxable income to the government and in addition must report his dividends as taxable income. In effect there is *double* taxation of the stockholder.

The only recognition of this situation is the fact that in 1967 the taxpayer was allowed to *exclude* $100 from his dividends received. If his wife receives dividends, she also can exclude up to $100. For example, if a husband receives $120 and the wife $80 in dividends, the husband may exclude $100 but his wife only $80. Neither may consider any portion of the dividends received by the other for his own exclusion up to $100.

Ways of Easing the Tax Burden

As explained in Chapter 4, the income from municipal bonds (bonds of states, cities, towns and authorities etc.) are exempt from federal income taxes. Income from bills, certificates, notes and bonds issued by the United States Government are *not* exempt from federal income taxes but are exempt from the state income taxes.

There are some investors who can invest in oil wells and real estate ventures. These are speculative and only for the rich and well-informed. They do offer tax advantages, since heavy depreciation and depletion charges can be taken.

Some companies pay dividends which are entitled to special tax treatment and are sometimes called *tax-free* dividends. One group consists of companies holding a large amount of high-cost stock. These companies sell these shares and establish losses which offset other income. To the extent of the offset, earnings are paid tax free to stockholders. Some companies have large mineral resources which require many depletion charges. Some of these companies pay dividends which at least in part are considered a return of capital.

Some public utilities pay dividends which in part are considered tax free. This comes about through these companies' paying dividends in excess of the income reported for tax purposes.

Perhaps the best-known method of easing the tax burden is by switching securities. In switching securities, the investor can often accomplish a double purpose: (1) take a tax loss reducing his tax liability, and (2) improve his portfolio by selling the stock of a company with unsatisfactory outlook and buying one more favorable.

Basic Rules on Capital Gains and Losses

1. A *short-term gain* is taken when a security or capital asset such as a house is held six months or less. The holding period of a completed transaction starts on the day after the capital gain is purchased and ends with the date of sale. To determine if you have held property over six months, you begin counting on the day following the day you acquired the property. This same day of each succeeding month is the beginning of a new month, regardless of the number of days in the preceding month. In the computation you include the day you disposed of the property. For example, if a customer bought a stock on February 7, you start counting on February 8, and the 8th of each month is the beginning of a new month. Thus, you should sell your customer's stock on August 8 in order to have a long-term capital gain. If you sold it on August 7, it would be a short-term gain.

All the short-term gains are added to taxable income and taxed in brackets which run up to 70 per cent. Thus, our first rule might be to avoid short-term gains.

2. A *long-term gain* is one resulting from the sale or exchange of a security or a capital asset held *more than* six months. As in the case of short-term gains, the holding period of long-term gains and the

holding period of completed transactions begin on the day after the capital asset is purchased and end on the actual day of sale. Fifty per cent of long-term gains are taxable as income, but only up to a maximum of 25 per cent of the capital gain.

3. *Net short-term and long-term losses* may be applied as a deduction from ordinary income, but only up to $1,000. In the taxable year the losses taken as capital losses in excess of $1,000 may be carried over until exhausted.

4. *Rules affecting transaction.*

a. To establish a *loss* in a tax year a security may be *sold* up to and including the last business day of the year. For example, in the year 1966, a security might have been sold as late as Friday, December 31, 1966, even though delivery was not required until 1967.

b. However, to establish a gain in a tax year, a security must be sold so that the proceeds are *available* by the last business day of the year. Thus in 1966, to establish a gain, a security would have to have been sold on Friday, December 23, 1966 in order to be delivered and the proceeds available by Friday, December 31, 1966, the last day of the year. (The New York Stock Exchange was closed Monday, December 26). As explained in Chapter 8, delivery in the regular way requires four full business days. The security, of course, could be sold on Friday, December 31, 1966 for *cash*, which would mean that the funds would be *available* on that day.

c. Securities sold to establish a *gain* may be repurchased at once. For example, a security holder might aim to mark up the cost of his securities. This is often done by some institutional portfolio managers.

d. Sometimes an investor may wish to sell and buy back the same or substantially identical securities in order to establish a *loss* and retain his investment position. However, care must be taken to *have held* these securities at least thirty days and not to purchase them back until after thirty-one days from the sale date. The total period between acquisition, sale, and repurchase should cover at least sixty-one days.

However, a taxpayer may often accomplish the same purpose by selling one security to take a loss and buying at once the stock of *another* similar company. For example, he could sell at a loss Westinghouse Electric Company and buy General Electric Company.

Gains and losses from *short* sales are ordinarily considered to be short-term transactions. Stock dividends and rights are not taxable as income *unless sold* or distributed in discharge of preferred stock dividend for the current or preceding year. For example, if a company is in arrears for preferred dividends and pays to the preferred stockholders a common stock dividend to clear up the arrears, it would be taxable to the extent of the arrears of the preceding year. Also, stock dividends would be taxable where you have the option to receive cash or other property in place of such stock dividends.

When the new stock received as a dividend is identical with the old stock on which the dividend is declared, one can use a simple mathematical computation to arrive at a basis for the old and new stock. For example, if we assume you bought one share of common stock for $45, on which a dividend of two shares for each are held, you now have three shares with a basis of $15 a share. Arithmetically, this is worked when the new stock received as a dividend is identical with the old stock on which the dividend is declared; you should adjust the old price before calculating the capital gain on the sale of the stock dividend.

For example, let us suppose a customer bought a stock of the XYZ Company at 45 and it advanced to 60 in a year. At this point the company declares a stock dividend of 10 per cent. The customer sells the 10 per cent stock dividend at 60. He must figure his cost on an adjusted basis as follows:

$$\frac{\$45 \ \text{old cost}}{1.00 \ + \ .10 \ \text{dividend}} = \frac{\$45}{1.10} = \$40.909 \ \text{equals adjusted cost}$$

If at a later time the company pays, for example, a 5% dividend, the investor's new adjusted cost will be calculated as follows, using the last adjusted basis:

$$\frac{40.909}{1.00 \ + \ .05} = \frac{40.909}{105} = 38.952$$

Some Sample Examples of Purchases and Sales

The following assumptions might be made:

1. A *short-term* profit of $8,000. *Result*: the entire amount taken into income account and taxed in bracket.

2. A *long-term* profit of $10,000. *Result*: 50 per cent of this amount taken into income account and taxed in bracket up to but not exceeding 25 per cent of the total capital gain (or 50 per cent of one-half the total gain).

3. Where net short-term gains were greater than net short-term losses, 100 per cent of net short-term gains taxed as income:

100% of net short-term gain	$7,000
100% of net short-term losses	5,000
Taxed as income	$2,000

4. Where a net long-term gain is greater than a short-term loss, the balance is taxed as a long-term gain:

100% long-term gain	$5,000
100% short-term loss	2,000
Difference	$3,000
50% of long-term gain taken into income	$1,500

5. Short-term losses may be added to long-term losses, but only $1,000 may be taken off income in the year the loss occurs, with the

balance carried over to future years and applied against capital gains, if any, plus an additional $1,000 each year.

6. Care must be taken, however, to offset short-term capital gains before they become long term capital gains, *because long-term capital gains must be matched with long-term capital losses first.*

Let us assume the following:

Example A	
Short-term capital gain *taken*	$2,000
Short-term capital loss on paper but *not taken*	$2,000
Long-term capital gains *taken*	$2,000

The taxpayer should take his *short-term loss* before it becomes long term. In this case, his short-term gain would be offset by a short-term loss and he would pay a tax of only 50 per cent of his long-term capital gain of $2,000 or $1,000.

However, if he allows the short-term loss to go over six months and become a long-term loss, then he *must match* this long-term loss with the long-term capital gains leaving the short-term gain exposed. Thus, he would pay no tax on his long-term gains, but he would be forced to include the entire $2,000 of short-term gains as income.

Estate and Gift Taxes

As in the case of federal income taxes, federal estate taxes are highly progressive, as may be seen in the following table:

$ 60,000	No tax
100,000	$ 4,800
200,000	32,700
500,000	126,500
2,060,000	753,200
10,100,000	6,119,000

As the table shows, an estate of $500,000 would pay $126,500. An estate over $10,000,000 would pay over 60 per cent. In addition, the estate would be subject to state taxes, lawyers' fees, and executors' fees. For those with large assets, it is difficult to avoid these taxes by making gifts. For example, the gift taxes on $500,000 are $109,275, including the $30,000 life term exemptions of 86 per cent of the estate tax, $126,-500. One of the main advantages of making a gift prior to death is that the donor can be reasonably sure that his heirs have the money and that the transfer will not be held up by the expense or delay of administration.

Unless the donor remains alive for *three years* after the date of the gift, however, the Internal Revenue Service may claim that the gift was made in contemplation of death to avoid estate taxes.

It is also possible to give away $3,000 a year to each donee, plus a $30,000 lifetime exemption. Thus, a husband or wife could give each child $6,000 a year plus $60,000 in lifetime exemptions. An estate is a taxpayer. Therefore, it must pay taxes on the income collected and not distributable or distributed while the estate is being settled. If the estate is large, it might be advantageous to plan the administration of the estate in such a manner that the heirs pay the taxes even if they do not receive the income until the estate is settled.

The estate is valued at date of death or optionally, through election, one year after. This is to permit the executors of the estate to take the lower of the two figures. When the estate is settled, payments are made either in cash or in securities to the heirs. If securities are transferred, the heirs' cost of these securities is the same as established for estate appraisal purposes.

For example, if a man dies on January 20, 1967 with 100 shares of Eastman Kodak Company common stock which closed on that date at $133 a share, his executors may take this value or that of one year later. If one year later the stock sells at 103 a share, this value would be taken for estate tax purposes. If the stock is distributed to the man's wife, for example, her cost will be $103 a share. If she should sell the stock at $110 a share for example, she would have to pay a capital gains tax on 7 points since her cost price is $103 a share.

REVIEW QUESTIONS

1. Who should file income tax returns? What records should be kept?
2. Explain the double taxation of dividends.
3. Describe three ways a rich man might ease the burden of federal income taxes.
4. Distinguish between a short-term and a long-term capital gain. How are the holding periods calculated?
5. Explain how a gain or loss must be established in year-end transactions.
6. What is the required procedure in establishing a loss and buying the security back?
7. How should stock dividends be treated (1) if held by stockholder? (2) if sold?
8. What are the general principles of the corporate income tax? (See Chapter 3.)
9. Assume a distant uncle makes you a gift of $100,000, pays the gift taxes, but lives only one year after the date of the gift. What claims will the Internal Revenue Service make?
10. Assume that you received $300,000 in *securities* from your distant uncle on his death, how is the cost price of these securities *determined*?

Over-the-Counter
Securities Market

Chapter 11

The over-the-counter securities market handles most of the securities transactions that take place in the United States. In fact, its operations are so extensive that the easiest way to describe it is to indicate what it does not do in the way of securities transactions. The over-the-counter market does not handle the purchase or sale of securities that actually occur on securities exchanges. Everything else in the way of securities transactions, it does handle. Thus, securities not traded on a securities exchange are said to be traded over the counter.

Types of Securities Traded
Over the Counter

Many different types of securities are traded over the counter. These include:

1. Bank stocks
2. Insurance company stocks
3. U.S. government securities
4. Municipal bonds
5. Open-end investment company shares (mutual funds)
6. Railroad equipment trust certificates
7. Most corporate bonds
8. Stocks of a very large number of industrial and utility corporations including nearly all new issues
9. Securities of many foreign corporations

The over-the-counter market is not located in any one central place. Rather it consists of thousands of securities houses located in hundreds of different cities and towns all over the United States. These securities houses are called broker/dealers and they are engaged in buying and selling securities usually for their own account and risk. They also buy and sell securities for the account and risk of others and may charge a commission for their services. In order to transact their business, they communicate their buy and sell orders back and forth through a nationwide network of telephones and teletypes.

The exact size of the over-the-counter market cannot be determined, since the securities transactions that take place over the counter occur in many different places and are not reported to one central agency. However, it is known that in dollar volume, substantially more securities are traded in the over-the-counter market than on all national securities exchanges combined. Furthermore, it is estimated that tens of thousands of corporations have issued securities that are held by the public, and all of these securities with the exception of approximately 4,300 issues listed on the exchanges are traded over the counter.

Sometimes even securities *listed* on a registered securities exchange are traded over the counter. In fact, an over-the-counter dealer who has an order to buy or sell listed securities is not required to execute such orders on the exchange on which the securities are listed. However, since the main market for a listed security is usually on the exchange where that security is listed, it is generally traded on the exchange.[1]

The Third Market

Over-the-counter market transactions in securities listed on the New York Stock Exchange or other national securities exchanges are called "third market" transactions. The Report of Special Study of Securities Markets of the Securities and Exchange Commission released in July, 1963, indicated that the "third market's" share of all transactions in securities listed on the NYSE approximated 4 per cent in 1962. The report further noted that 10 per cent of the institutional transactions in listed securities which occurred that year took place in the "third market." In 1966 the "third market's" share of NYSE listed securities was estimated at 5 per cent.

Rule 17a–9 adopted under the Securities Exchange Act of 1934 provides a system for the identification of broker-dealers making off-board markets in common stocks traded on national securities exchanges whose sales of securities exceed $20,000,000 annually. The broker-dealers in the "third market" exist primarily to service the needs of institutional investors. The market has developed because of the ability of these

---

[1]Institutional investors interested in buying or selling large blocks of securities (listed and otherwise) do a substantial portion of their business in the over-the-counter market because: (1) Government and municipal bonds trade principally in the over-the-counter market. (2) New issues are first available in volume in the over-the-counter market. (3) Buying and selling can take place there without unduly affecting the price. (4) Large-block distributions can usually take place more efficiently in the over-the-counter market.

broker-dealers to perform a useful function under competitive cost conditions.

Prior to November, 1966, no New York Stock Exchange member firm could engage in stock transactions with a nonmember concern involving stocks listed on the exchange. On November 7, 1966, the New York Stock Exchange regulation Rule 394 (b) became effective. This rule provides that a New York Stock Exchange member holding a customer's round-lot order for the purchase or sale of stock listed on the exchange may solicit a "qualified" nonmember to participate in the transaction for the nonmember's account under specified conditions.

The Securities and Exchange Commission established standards for qualifying as a market maker eligible to participate in the off-board trades. A "qualified" market maker is required to maintain a net worth of at least $1,500,000, or a minimum net capital of $250,000 for each security in which he is qualified to make a market.

As indicated above, nothing in the law requires listed securities to be sold through a securities exchange. Any security owner can dispose of his securities in any way he sees fit. He can throw them away or burn them; he can give them away; he can sell them to anyone who happens to be passing his way—anyone, that is, who is able and willing to buy the securities. If, for example, Jim Bullen owns 100 shares of Anheuser-Busch stock (a stock traded over the counter) and Bill Jones, a friend attending a dinner party at Jim's home, indicated a desire to buy 100 shares of Anheuser-Busch stock, Jim Bullen could sell his stock directly to his friend, right there at the dinner table. Remember, however, that Jim would sell his stock to his friend only if they could arrive at a mutually agreeable price. This would then be an over-the-counter transaction.[2]

Obviously, the method suggested above is a far-from-satisfactory way of buying or selling securities. A brief analysis will show why this method is so unsatisfactory and so rarely used.

Let us suppose that Jim and his friend Bill negotiated with one another during the evening and agreed upon a price for the stock. The price they agreed upon was $28 per share. The big question is—how can either of them be sure that $28 was the "right price"? Perhaps Jim could have sold his 100 shares of Anheuser-Busch stock for much more than $28 per share if he had looked more actively for interested buyers. On the other hand, how does Bill know he couldn't have purchased 100 shares of Anheuser-Busch for less than $28 if he had looked more

[2]The reader should keep in mind that if Jim Bullen sold a stock listed on the New York Stock Exchange, or any other registered securities exchange, directly to his friend there at the dinner table this also would be an over-the-counter transaction.

actively for people with Anheuser-Busch stock for sale. The obvious answer is that neither can be sure that the price was "right."

Even if Jim and Bill, during their negotiations, had consulted the over-the-counter securities quotations printed in the daily paper, they still couldn't have been sure that the price they agreed upon was the "right" price. This is because published over-the-counter securities quotations are "bid and asked" prices which do not represent actual transactions. They are intended only as a guide to the approximate range within which these securities could have been sold (indicated by "bids") or bought (indicated by the "asked" price) at the time the prices were given.

The "Right" Price

How can a person buying or selling securities be sure the price he pays or receives is the "right" one? The "right" price for a security, or anything else for that matter, is the price that comes about through the interplay of the forces of supply and demand.

Two things must occur in order for the forces of supply and demand to work fully in a securities market. First, everyone who wants to sell a particular security must have an opportunity to make his offer known. Second, everyone who wishes to buy some shares of that same security must have an opportunity to make his bid known.

When the facilities of a stock exchange or the over-the-counter market are utilized in a securities transaction, the forces of supply and demand are given an opportunity to interact and set the price at which that security trades. For example, whenever a big supply of a security is offered for sale and investors want to buy only a very small quantity, its market price will tend to decline. On the other hand, if only a few shares of stock in a specific company are offered for sale, while the demand for the shares is large, the market price at which each successive transaction takes place will tend to be higher.

Of course, nothing is 100 per cent perfect, and even if the facilities of a stock exchange or the over-the-counter market are utilized, *some* potential buyers and sellers may be left out of the picture. However, by using the exchange facilities or the over-the-counter market facilities, the desires and wishes of a large percentage of the potential buyers and sellers are made evident. Thus, the price is generally more apt to be "right" than "wrong."

In our example, Jim Bullen could not be sure that he received the best possible price for his stock because he did not let the forces of demand enter into the transaction. All he knew about the demand for his stock was that his friend, Bill, would buy it if the price were low enough. Bill, on the other hand, could not be sure that the price he paid for the stock was the lowest possible price at which he could buy the stock. He could not be sure because he did not let the forces of supply enter into the transaction. All he knew about the supply of the stock was that his friend, Jim, had 100 shares that he would sell if he offered him a high enough price. If Bill and Jim had used the facilities of a stock exchange (if the stock had been listed) or the facilities of the over-the-counter market, for their stock deal, they could be much more certain that the price of $28 was the "right" price.

Although the interaction of supply and demand sets the price at which securities trade, both on stock exchanges and over the counter, the two markets are basically different. The basic characteristic of a stock exchange is that it is an "auction" market. In an "auction" market, the person making the highest bid is the one who buys the item being sold. In an "auction" market the person offering to sell at the lowest price is the one who is able to sell the item being offered.

The over-the-counter market, on the other hand, is primarily a "negotiated" market. Buyers and sellers negotiate prices on the most favorable basis they think they can achieve.

Jim Bullen and his friend Bill arrived at their price of $28 per share by negotiation, but they excluded from their negotiation all of the possible buyers and sellers, except themselves.

The Over-the-Counter Dealer

If Jim had called his broker when he wanted to sell his stock, the broker would have contacted the dealers "making a market" in Jim's stock and would have sold the stock at the highest possible price. The phrase "to make a market" means that the dealer creates and maintains a market in a security. A dealer is said to "maintain" a market in a security when he is known to be willing at all times to buy or sell that security usually for his own account and risk, at the prices he quotes.

When a broker, such as Jim's, calls the various "dealers" who "make a market" in a particular stock, he asks the dealer for a quotation on that stock. The dealer's quotation consists of his bid and asked prices. The price which the dealer will pay for a given security is called his "bid." The price at which a dealer will sell a given security is called his "*asked*" price or "*offer*." The differences between the bid and asked prices in any quotation is the "*spread*."

When a customer inquires how a security is quoted, it is *not* sufficient if the dealer tells him how he is offering that security. A quotation at all times must include both sides of the market even though one side may be nonexistent as, for example, "offered at 20, no bid" or "$20 bid, none offered."

It is not necessary for a dealer actually to have the securities he sells to his customers in his inventory at the time he sells them. A dealer may sell securities to a customer even though he does not own the securities at the time of the sale. However, once the dealer has sold them, he must obtain the securities and deliver them to his customer at the agreed price regardless of how much he has to pay to get them.

Firm or Subject Markets

In over-the-counter dealings, markets are quoted either as "firm" or "subject." A "subject market" is a quotation in which the prices are subject to confirmation. "Firm" market prices are those at which a security can actually be bought or sold. Firm market is sometimes referred to as "actual market".

"Firm bids" or "firm offers" are prices at which a dealer is committed to buy or sell a specified amount of securities, whether for a brief moment only or for a given period of time. "Offered firm" means that the seller has made an offering which is good for the period of time specified by the seller or until rejected.

In addition to the terms "firm" and "subject," the term "work-out" market is sometimes used in connection with the over-the-counter market. A "work-out" market represents an indication of prices at which it is believed a security can be bought or sold within a reasonable length of time.

One thing important to remember is that unless a dealer specifies to the contrary, the prices he quotes for a particular security are firm at the moment for amounts equivalent to the usual trading units for such a security. Examples of each type of quotation are as follows:

Firm Market

"the market is 65-70"
"it is 65-70"
"we can trade it 65-70"

Subject Market

"it is quoted 65-70"
"last I saw was 65-70"
"it is 65-70 subject"

"Size" of Market

When making a firm market to buy a security at a specified price, it is required that a dealer be prepared to complete the transaction.

Any dealer supplying a quotation as an "actual market" or claiming to have a "firm market" in a security, is expected to be ready and obligated to buy or sell at the prices quoted in amounts equivalent to what is commonly understood to be the trading unit or "size" in that security. The "size" is the actual number of shares or bonds represented in a bid or offering which comprises a given quotation. Unless the number of shares of a security named in a "firm bid" or "firm offer" is specified, it is understood to be the usual trading unit or size of the security. Unless a smaller or larger amount is specified when the "firm market" quotation is supplied, the usual size of the market is 100 shares of a stock, or 5 bonds.

Bid or Offering Wanted

Sometimes securities are offered for sale or sought for purchase by a dealer, but he doesn't receive any bids or offers. In such cases, the terms "bid wanted" or "offering wanted" are used. The term "bid wanted" or "BW" means a security is being offered for sale and prospective buyers are requested to submit a bid for that security. The term "offering wanted" or "OW" means the security referred to is being sought for purchase and anyone wishing to sell that security is requested to submit an offering. Dealers often use these terms when they advertise in the National Quotation Bureau "sheets."

Confirmation of Trade

A security trade over the counter is consummated by the statement, "we buy" or "we sell" and by the response, "we confirm."

When a customer gives an order to purchase any security accompanied by full payment, the transaction is not completed until the broker/dealer delivers the security to the customer or into his account.

Under all conditions, purchase and sale transactions must be confirmed to the customer *in writing* and the confirmation must contain certain specific information. See page 117 for a complete discussion of the information required on the confirmation.

When acting as agent for two principals, a broker must disclose on the confirmation the source and amount of any commissions received or to be received.

The Dealer's Markup

When a *dealer* sells securities to his customers, he does not charge them a commission. Commissions are charged only when an agency or brokerage relationship exists. A dealer makes his money from the markup on his merchandise. This *markup* is the difference between the amount the dealer pays for the securities when he buys them and the amount he receives for them when he sells them to his customers. For example, suppose a dealer buys 100 shares of General Chaos Corporation stock for $50 per share. He pays $5,000 for the stock. Later he sells his stock to one of his customers for $51½ per share. The customer pays the dealer $5,150 for the stock. The difference between what the dealer paid for the stock, $5,000, and what he got for the stock when he sold it, $5,150, is the markup. In this case, the markup is $150, or 3 per cent of what the dealer had to pay to acquire the stock in the first place.

Out of the $150 markup, the dealer must cover his costs of doing business. If any money is left after he covers his expenses, he has made a profit. If the markup does not cover his expenses, he has had a loss.

When a dealer makes a market (or "takes a position," as it is sometimes called) in a security he is taking a risk. He is taking a risk that the stock he owns will drop in price before he can sell it to someone.

In the example above, the dealer invested $5,000 of his capital in General Chaos Corporation stock. He marked the stock up 3 per cent and offered it for sale. He hoped to sell it to some customer for $5,150. However, assume that before he found an interested customer, some bad news concerning the corporation developed which caused interest in the stock to lag. Under these conditions, the following might occur: The dealer offered the stock for $51½ a share at first, and later for $50 a share, but found that no one was interested in the stock at either of those prices. Faced with this situation, the dealer can do one of two things. He can sell the stock for less than $50 per share, in which case he would lose part of his original capital investment; *or* he can hold the stock, hoping that some day investor interest in the stock will be renewed so that he can sell the stock at a price which will enable him to recover his original investment.

If he chooses the second course of action and continues to hold the stock, he is taking the risk of a further drop in price. Furthermore, by continuing to hold the stock, instead of selling it, he is tying up part of the money he needs to run his business. If this happens too often, the dealer may be forced to go out of business altogether, due to a lack of working capital.

As noted, if the dealer chooses the first course of action and sells his stock at a loss, he will lose part of his capital investment. However, by selling, even though at a loss, the dealer regains the use of the remaining capital. With this money, he can purchase other securities which he might be able to mark up successfully and sell at a profit.

Although a great deal depends upon the individual circumstances surrounding each case, many dealers, when faced with the above dilemma, feel it is best to take their loss and use the remaining capital elsewhere.

A dealer cannot afford to make many mistakes in selecting the securities he buys and marks up for resale. If he is wrong too often, he will be unable to continue in business.

In order for a dealer to continue successfully in business, he must be able to sell securities from his inventory at a markup high enough to cover his operating expenses, as well as any losses that occur on the stocks he holds in his inventory.

This is not as easy to accomplish as it sounds. In the first place, almost always there is more than one dealer making a market in any given security being traded over the counter. Very often there are several different dealers competing with one another. The dealers with the highest markups and prices for any given security will have a hard time selling any of these securities. Obviously, no one likes to pay a price higher than necessary for anything he buys.

The 5 Per Cent Markup Policy

Apart from the dealer competition, however, there is a second factor which in part determines how much the dealer markup will be; this is the 5 per cent markup policy adopted by the NASD. The Association's 5 per cent markup policy was adopted as a general guide to its members for their use in determining the prices that might be charged customers, which would be reasonably related to current market prices. The policy is based on Section 4, Article III of the Association's Rules of Fair Practice.

The 5 per cent markup is a general policy, and it is an extremely important one. Its importance is made clearly evident by a Securities and Exchange Commission decision covering broker/dealer markups. This SEC decision states that the sale of securities by a broker/dealer to an investor at prices that bear no reasonable relationship to the current market of those securities may constitute fraud.

The mere fact, however, that markups exceed 5 per cent does not in and of itself prove that the prices to the customer are unfair. As noted, the 5 per cent markup policy is intended to be used only as a general guide. It does not mean that the markup of a member may never exceed 5 per cent of his cost. Nor does the 5 per cent markup policy mean that a dealer is entitled to an over-all average of 5 per cent on his markup in sales to customers. Under certain conditions, markups of over 5 per cent may be justified. For example, a dealer selling a security which he has owned for a period of time should use current market prices, rather than cost, as a basis for computing markups.

Also, in the case of certain low-priced securities (such as those selling below $10), a somewhat higher percentage may be justified under special conditions.

On the other hand, however, it is equally true that under certain conditions, markups of *less* than 5 per cent may be unfair to the customer. For example, when a customer buys a security by selling another security through the same *member* firm at the same time, a 5 per cent markup or even a 3 per cent markup on both transactions would be unfair. In such a case, the *member* should consider the purchase and sale as one transaction, when determining his markup.

The most important point the broker/dealer should keep in mind when marking up securities for resale to investors is that the markup must not be *unfair*. Section 4, Article III of the NASD's Rules of Fair Practice indicates that securities shall be bought from or sold to customers at prices which are fair.

If a broker/dealer's markups are *unfair*, serious repercussions may result with appropriate action being taken by the NASD or the SEC.

Fair vs. Unfair Markups and Profits

In a free enterprise economy such as ours, practically every industry at one time or another is accused of making "excessive or unfair" profits. Sometimes a whole industry is accused of "profiteering"; at other times individual companies are singled out for condemnation.

Whenever these charges of unfair profits are leveled at an industry or a company, invariably the ensuing discussion revolves around the following questions:

How much profit is it *fair* for a company to make?

When does the amount of profit made by a company stop being *fair*, and become *unfair*?

Many laws, both federal and state have tried to define a "fair" level of profit. Many court decisions have been handed down in attempts to resolve this question. Regardless of these attempts, however, the term "fair level of profit" remains to a large extent a very general and vague expression.

"Fair level of profit" is an expression that in many cases is *open to individual interpretation*. A profit considered fair by one person or group may be considered excessive by a second individual or group. The term "fair level of profit" is also, certainly, an expression that is relative. Any attempt to determine whether or not a given amount of profit is fair must be made in relation to the circumstances surrounding the transaction which brought about the profit.

Irrespective of this difficulty in distinguishing a fair profit from an unfair one, the key to the NASD markup policy is *fairness*.

Fortunately, the NASD in administering the markup policy for its member firms has had the wisdom to base its rules and interpretations upon the premise that there is no acceptable definition or arbitrary answer that can be given to indicate the nature of a *fair* markup, as contrasted to an *unfair* markup, that will fit all situations. Thus a markup acceptable for one type of security under a given set of circumstances is not necessarily fair or justifiable for another type of security under the same set of circumstances; or even the same security under different circumstances.

The NASD contends that *all* of the different factors and circumstances surrounding a security transaction must be considered before the profit secured from that transaction can be intelligently labeled as fair or unfair.

Some of the factors and circumstances considered by the NASD in order to determine the fairness of a given profit or markup are:

1. The type of security involved in the transaction
2. The availability of the security in the market, and its degree of market activity
3. The price of the security
4. The cost to the dealer of obtaining the security and the amount of money involved in the transaction
5. The amount and type of service and effort involved in negotiating and consummating the transaction
6. Disclosure of markup
7. The pattern of the dealer's markups

Thus, it is obvious that no fixed maximum markup rate can be established by the Association. Furthermore, it is equally true that a *fixed* definition of fairness as it relates to security markups is not possible.

Historical Development of 5 Per Cent Markup Policy

The NASD's attempts to develop a markup guide for its members began shortly after the Association was formed. The question of fair markups or spreads was considered extensively both at the meetings of the Board of Governors and outside such meetings.

During this early period, numerous requests were sent to the board by NASD members, asking for an explanation of the term "a fair profit." No one seemed to be able to give a satisfactory explanation of the term. In fact, it was soon evident that no one even knew for certain what the general practice of the industry was concerning markups.

Recognizing that the *usual* amount of markup was at least a starting point from which an answer to the question could be sought, the NASD in 1943 conducted a membership-wide questionnaire examination of markup practices in retail or customer transactions.

In completing this questionnaire, members were asked to supply pertinent information on fifty consecutive principal transactions with customers. Certain types of transactions were excluded from this questionnaire. Examples of excluded transactions are as follows:

1. Initial public distributions of securities registered under the Securities Act of 1933 and made at the public offering price.

2. Transactions made at a price approved by an agency of the government, such as the Interstate Commerce Commission.
3. So called "secondary" and "special offerings."

The data compiled from the questionnaire were carefully studied by the NASD Board of Governors and ultimately became part of a statement it issued concerning member firm markup policies. An examination of the data showed that of the computable transactions reported in the questionnaire, 47 per cent were effected at a gross spread or markup, over the current market, of not over 3 per cent and 71 per cent at not over 5 per cent.

After numerous revisions and extensive discussions with the SEC, a letter setting forth the views of the NASD Board of Governors on securities markups was sent to the membership. This letter, dated October 25, 1943, stated in part:

> The Board wishes to refer to Section I of Article III of the *Rules of Fair Practice* which states: "A member, in the conduct of his business, shall observe high standards of commercial honor and just and equitable principles of trade."
>
> The Board of Governors has approved the following interpretation of the meaning of that rule: *"It shall be deemed conduct inconsistent with just and equitable principles of trade for a member to enter into any transaction with a customer in any security at any price not reasonably related to the current market price of the security."*
>
> The Board of Governors has the strongest possible conviction that it would be impracticable and unwise, if not impossible, to write a rule which would attempt to define specifically what constitutes a fair spread or fair profit, or to say in exact percentage of dollars, what would result in each and every transaction in a price to the customer which bears a reasonable relationship to the current market.

The Rules Require Observance of Ethical Rather than Legal Standards

The Maloney Act provides that one of the duties of the NASD is to enforce just and ethical principles of trade in the over-the-counter market. The NASD Board of Governors and the District Committees have repeatedly determined that members must adhere strictly to the ethical standards of the business.

According to the NASD Board, these ethical standards require that prices charged to customers must be *fair and reasonably related to the market. This is considered true even in cases where the member firm has disclosed the cost or the market, in some form, to the customer.*

Thus a price considered too high by a District Committee does not escape being a violation of the policy merely because the extent of the markup was disclosed to the customer.

Markup Policy Not Always Applicable

To help eliminate an apparent increasing misconception of what the 5 per cent policy actually is, the board has indicated the situations under which the policy is not applicable. These situations are:

1. The sale of securities sold in a public offering under a prospectus in which underwriting concessions and dealers' discounts are set forth.
2. The sale of shares of investment companies sold by prospectus.

Markup Policy Applicable

The 5 per cent policy is applicable and has been applied by the Business Conduct Committees of the Association to the following types of transactions:

1. A transaction in which a member buys a security to fulfill a sale of the same security previously made to a customer—

This transaction would include the so-called "riskless or simultaneous" transaction.

2. A transaction in which a dealer sells a security to a customer from inventory—

In such case the policy is applicable and has bearing only as a guide, both to the dealer and to the Association's Business Conduct Committees, in determining how much of a mark-up above the then current market is justified. This, of course, has no bearing upon market appreciation or depreciation from initial cost to the dealer.

3. The purchase of a security by a dealer from a customer—

In such case the policy is applicable again as a guide to the dealer and to the Business Conduct Committees of the Association, in determining the justification of price paid to a customer in relation to the then current market in that security.

4. A transaction in which the broker/dealer acts as agent—

In such a case, the commission charged the customer must not be unfair and should not exceed the amount which, were the member to act as a principal, would be in accord with the standard set forth.

5. Transactions wherein a customer sells securities to, or through a broker/dealer, the proceeds from which are utilized to pay for other securities sold to the customer by the broker/dealer—

In such instances the policy has been considered, as a guide only in determining the justification of the over-all return accruing to the broker/dealer from such a combination of transactions. In other words, the policy is again a guide to Business Conduct Committees and members and would, when applied, encompass these related purchases and sales as being embraced in one transaction.

The Association's 5 per cent markup policy is equally applicable to transactions of purchase or sale by a member with a customer in so-called oil royalty securities as to any other over-the-counter security.

Under the Securities Act of 1933 and the Securities Exchange Act of 1934, oil royalties, among others, are defined as securities and thus are subject to the NASD markup policy.

Profits Not Guaranteed

Section 4, Article III of the Rules of Fair Practice indicates that an NASD member firm is entitled to a profit. This is not a statement of principal, however; it is a statement of circumstance. A member firm is not entitled to an over-all net profit on its operations irrespective of the circumstances. If unreasonable expenses, such as excessive salaries to officers, excessive commissions to salemen, excessive telephone tolls, or excessive losses on inventory positions are incurred by a member firm, an over-all net loss could easily result. Under such circumstances, it is not proper for a member firm to apply excessive markups in its efforts to obtain an over-all net profit.

The case of one member firm whose books were examined by the Association in 1959 clearly illustrates the above point. An examination of the member firm's records indicated that the firm typically dealt in stocks selling for only $1 or $2 per share. The mark ups on these stocks had ranged from 7 per cent to 67 per cent, during the period under examination. Gross dollar profits had ranged from $14.25 on a 38-share transaction to $1,500.00 on a 4,000-share transaction.

A complaint was filed against the member firm and its principal officer by the appropriate Business Conduct Committee. The Committee charged that the markups of this firm, after taking into consideration all relevant circumstances, were not reasonably related to the current market value of the securities traded.

During the hearing which followed, the respondent member firm and officer contended that the Committee had *not* taken into consideration all relevant circumstances. According to the respondents, the Committee had failed to consider the current high cost of doing business; a cost so high, they pointed out, that the firm was operating at a loss.

The Business Conduct Committee, however, reasserted its claim of having given full consideration to all the relevant factors, including such things as the low price of the securities traded, the services performed for the customers by the firm, the expenses incurred by the firm, and so on. In view of all these and other related factors, the Committee claimed, the prices charged by the firm to its customers *were not fair* and *were not reasonably related to the current market*.

The penalties imposed by the District Business Conduct Committee were expulsion of the member firm from the NASD and revocation of the registration of the firm's principal officer.

The respondents appealed these penalties to the NASD Board of Governors. Upon review, the Board upheld the decision of the District Business Conduct Committee and the penalties were implemented.

The Broker/Dealer

A great many of the dealer firms act as brokers or agents as well as dealers. The terms "broker" and "agent" mean the same thing, that is, a person or firm executing orders for the account and risk of others. A broker/dealer registered with the Securities and Exchange Commission and engaged in the investment banking and securities business may buy and sell securities for his own account or risk, or as agent purchase and sell securities for the account and risk of others. As an agent, he may receive a commission for his services of buying or selling securities for the account and risk of his customers. However, whether or not a person or a firm charges for his services, he acts "as agent" when he executes orders for the account and risk of others.

A broker/dealer can handle purchase orders from a customer in any of three ways:

1. If the broker/dealer makes a market in a particular stock a customer wants to buy, he can sell him the stock out of his own inventory, *or*
2. When the broker/dealer gets the order, if he doesn't make a market in that particular stock, he can act as the customer's agent and buy it for him from some other dealer who does make a market in that stock, *or* from someone who owns the security and wishes to sell it *or*
3. When the broker/dealer gets the order, he can purchase the security for his own account from a dealer who does make a market in that security, or from someone who owns the security, and re-sell it to his customer.

Whenever the firm acts as an agent, it must disclose to its customer any commission charged in connection with the purchase or sale of the securities. The actual commission charged must be set forth in dollars and cents on the confirmation to the customer when a broker/dealer is acting as an agent.

Sometimes it happens that a broker acts for both the buyer and the seller in the purchase and sale of securities. When this occurs, the broker must disclose his total commission to the parties on both sides of the transaction.

In an agency transaction, the commission charged the customer by the broker/dealer must not be unfair, and should not exceed the amount which, were the broker/dealer to act as principal would be in accord with the 5 per cent mark-up policy.

As noted, under Association rules it is required that in agency transactions, commissions or service charges shall be fair. However, an NASD member who is acting as an agent for his customers may, within reasonable limits and using care to avoid discrimination, vary the commission charged to each, depending upon the circumstances relating to each transaction.

Over-the Counter Securities Market Quotations

The fact that over-the-counter securities transactions take place in thousands of different locations each day made it very difficult in past years for potential buyers and sellers to get representative, impartial quotations. However, with the formation of the NASD, a national organization for the first time was equipped to compile, distribute, and supervise the over-the-counter quotations in the nation's press. Before the NASD began this quotation service, the only over-the-counter quotations an investor could find were those supplied to the local press or sent out to customers by individual dealers and a few local dealer associations.

NASD Quotations Committees

In order to supervise closely the quotations on an estimated 4,000 over-the-counter securities regularly published in roughly 300 newspapers throughout the nation, the NASD has formed a group of Quotations Committees. These quotations committees operate on the local and national levels.

The National Quotations Committee of the NASD supervises the assembly and distribution of prices to the newspapers with respect to most over-the-counter securities in which there is national interest. Such quotations are also available to interested radio and television stations.

Any member of the NASD may file an application with a local quotations committee to have a security included on the Association's list of bid and asked prices. Not all of these applications are accepted, of course.

Qualifications for Quotation on National List

Securities traded over the counter must meet certain minimum requirements in order to be approved for quoting by the National Quotations Committee of the NASD. In order to be eligible for quotation on the national list, a security must meet the following qualifications:

1. Have a minimum of 1500 stockholders throughout the country.
2. Have a minimum of 100,000 shares of stock outstanding and in the hands of the public.
3. Have a minimum market value of $5 per share.
4. Have sufficient dealer interest to assure a realistic market.
5. Dividend declarations of the company listed must be published at least 10 days prior to the stock of record date and must be filed with the Secretary, Uniform Practice Committee.
6. It shall be the policy of the company to send to stockholders and to the National Association of Securities Dealers, Inc. its certified audited balance sheet and income statement at least once a year. Certain financial institutions may be exempted from the requirement of certification.
7. It shall be the policy of the company to disclose promptly to the public through the press, information with respect to company developments which may affect the value of the company's securities or influence investors' decisions.

Maintenance Requirements

1. Issues falling below $3 bid may be deleted from the National List and will be referred to the appropriate Local Quotations Committee for consideration for inclusion within their respective lists. Reinstatement to the National List will not be made until the issue again meets the qualifying market value requirement of $5 per share.
2. The company shall furnish to the Committee current stockholder-distribution data every two years.

Qualification for Quotation on Local List

The qualifications which must be met by a security in order for it to be eligible for local coverage are somewhat similar but less restrictive than those for the national list. Each local NASD quotations committee adopts minimum standards for the quotations lists under its jurisdiction. The specific standards established by each local quotations committee may be as stringent and comprehensive as local conditions warrant, and these standards become the basis for selecting the securities to be quoted. However, no set of minimum local requirements may be less comprehensive or less stringent than the NASD Minimum Standards for local lists established by the Board of Governors, unless an exception is approved by the National Quotations Committee.

Beginning in March, 1965, the following NASD Minimum Standards applied to all securities added to the quotations lists, unless it was determined that it was in the public interest to make an exception:

1. The market price at the time of acceptance for quoting must be at least $1.00 bid;
2. An issue falling below $.50 bid shall be deleted from the quotations list and may not be reconsidered for relisting until its market price is at least $1 bid;
3. The issue must have sufficient investor interest in an area to justify recommending to local newspapers that quotations on the issue be published. Each local quotations committee indicates the minimum number of area shareholders needed in the security to provide the necessary investor interest;
4. There must also be sufficient inter-dealer interest in the security issue to assure a realistic market;
5. Dividends declared on the security must be published at least ten days prior to the stock of record date and must be filed with the Secretary of the NASD Uniform Practice Committee;
6. The corporation which issued the security must send its balance sheet and income statement to its stockholders and to the Secretary of the NASD National Quotations Committee at least once a year;
7. The issuing corporation must have a policy of promptly disclosing to the public, through the press, any significant company developments which might influence investors' decisions.

By adoption of these standards and through other cooperative efforts, the NASD has been able to secure a wide coverage of over-the-counter quotations in the national press.

The Types of
Over-the-Counter Quotations

The prices published in the newspaper under the sponsorship of the NASD do not represent transactions of securities actually consummated. There is no ticker service reporting the prices of over-the-counter transactions as they occur, such as exists for the securities exchanges. In fact, there is no public record at all of actual over-the-counter transactions.

The NASD-sponsored quotations released for publication are interdealer quotations. Such quotations reflect a representative interdealer spread.

Quotations submitted on a "no bid, asked only" basis are not released for publication; however, a bid price only may be released when appropriate in the judgment of the committee.

Nominal quotations may not be released for publication.

Newspapers and other publications, and radio and television stations disseminating NASD quotations are required, as a condition for receiving the quotations, to include an explanatory statement disclosing the following information:

1. That the NASD is the source of the quotations.
2. The time of compilation.

3. The date of compilation if different from date of publication.
4. That the quotations are interdealer markets which do not include retail markup, markdown or commission.

The suggested masthead for published quotations of the NASD is:
"Quotations from the NASD are representative interdealer prices as of approximately ————A.M./P.M. Interdealer markets change throughout the day. Prices do not include retail markup, markdown or commission."
Quotations Committees make every effort to have the above full masthead used; however, if they find that the full masthead is rejected because of length, the following abbreviated masthead is acceptable:
"Representative interdealer quotations at approx. ————A.M./P.M. from NASD. Prices do not include retail markup, markdown or commission."

The NASD provides these inter-dealer quotations on some 1,300 nationally traded and active securities to major metropolitan newspapers.

Manipulative and Deceptive Quotations

NASD members must not be responsible in any way for the publication or circulation of any report of any securities transaction unless such a member knows, or has reason to believe, that such transaction was a bona fide transaction, purchase, or sale. To do so would be inconsistent with Sections 1, 5, and 18 of Article III of the NASD Rules of Fair Practice.

Similarly, it would be inconsistent with the above-cited sections for the member to be responsible in any way for the publication or circulation of any quotation for any security without having reasonable cause to believe that such quotation is a bona fide quotation, is not fictitious, and is not published or circulated for any fraudulent, deceptive, or manipulative purpose.

Policy with Respect to Firmness of Quotations

During 1965, in order to improve upon the mechanics of trading in the over-the-counter securities markets, the NASD Board of Governors developed a policy with respect to the firmness of the quotations supplied by NASD members. The policy states that under the usual circumstances of making a firm trading market in a security, a dealer is expected to buy or sell at least a normal unit of trading in the stock he quotes, at the price he quotes, unless he clearly designates that his quotation is "subject" or nominal or good only for less than a normal unit of trading.

Members of the NASD, and persons associated with them in the over-the-counter securities markets, make trading decisions and set prices for customers on the basis of telephone and wire quotations. The quotations in the National Quotation Bureau sheets are also used for this purpose.

In some instances in the past, a dealer's quotations, purportedly firm, were, in fact, so qualified upon further inquiry as to constitute "backing away" by the quoting dealer. Furthermore, dealers who had placed quotations in the sheets sometimes were found to be unwilling to make firm bids or offers upon inquiry. In some cases, their conduct was such as to raise doubt about the validity of the quotations they had originally inserted. Such "backing away" tends to disrupt the normal operation of the over-the-counter market, and the NASD Board of Governors' policy was designed to eliminate this disruptive practice. The policy takes into consideration the fact that NASD member broker/dealers change interdealer quotations constantly in the course of trading. Also, the policy recognizes that at times contemporaneous transactions or substantial changes in inventory might well require dealers to temporarily quote a "subject" market. Thus, in order to insure the integrity of the over-the-counter quotations, the board has ruled that every NASD member has an obligation to identify correctly the nature of the quotations they supply to others. In addition, each member furnishing quotations must be adequately staffed to respond to inquiries during his normal business hours.

Where to Find Quotations

Many financial publications provide extensive coverage of current over-the-counter quotations. Some examples are:

Barron's National Business and Financial Weekly
Moody's Bond Record
Bank and Quotation Record of the Commercial and Financial Chronicle
The Wall Street Journal
New York Times Financial Section

In addition, of course, investors desiring retail quotations on reasonably active over-the-counter securities can obtain them by calling their broker or their banker.

Wholesale Quotations

The National Quotation Bureau, a subsidiary of Commerce Clearing House Inc., with its principal offices in New York City, compiles and distributes "wholesale" or "professional" over-the-counter quotations. These wholesale quotations represent the prices at which securities can be traded between dealers. When a broker/dealer receives an order for a security in which he does not make a market, he can quickly determine the firms making a market in that security by consulting the daily wholesale quotation service issued by the National Quotation Bureau.

Bids and offers on various over-the-counter securities are listed by dealers making a market in such securities. Approximately 1,100 broker/dealers a year supply interdealer quotations in the daily "sheets." This information is compiled into a convenient form and redistributed to dealers subscribing to the service. The distribution of these wholesale quotations are confined to qualified securities dealers.

Currently, approximately 1,900 firms and their branch offices are using the wholesale quotations service for reference and to advertise their bids and offers.

The daily wholesale quotation service is issued every day the securities markets are open. It is published in three sections: the Eastern Section (New York); Western section (Chicago); and Pacific Coast section (San Francisco). On an average business day, the three sections combined will carry approximately 36,000 listings, with quotations on some 8,000 to 12,000 individual stock issues and approximately 1,800 bond issues. In the course of a year, an average of 30,000 different security issues will be covered in the daily service.

In addition to the daily serivce, the Bureau publishes monthly summaries in book form. These summarize the data on the issues of securities appearing in the daily service and include, as well, many thousands of issues that, due to their inactivity, rarely if ever appear in the daily sheets. The main purpose of the monthly summary is to enable the subscriber to review the past market performance of both the active and inactive issues and to determine the last published quotation.

New Security Issues

An important part of the over-the-counter securities market is the new-issue market. A new issue is one which generally has no history of bids and offers, must be sold at a fixed price, and is distributed initially only by those participating in the original sales effort.

Most new security issues are subject to regulation under the Securities Act of 1933. The act requires registration with the SEC of all securities covered by the act before such securities may be offered for public sale. Unless the security is exempt from the act, a registration statement must be filed which must become effective before the securities can legally be sold. Many provisions of the Securities Act of 1933 are extremely pertinent to any discussion of new security issues. See Chapter 15 for a discussion of the Securities Act provisions which relate to the registration of new security issues.

Generally, whenever a new security is issued and marketed, the issuing corporation seeks the advice and help of an investment banking firm.

Investment Banking

Investment bankers are not really bankers at all. The fact that the word banker appears in the name is partially responsible for many of the false impressions which exist regarding the functions performed by investment bankers. Investment bankers are not permitted to accept deposits from anyone. They may not provide checking account or savings account facilities for their customers, nor may they carry out other activities normally construed to be banking activities.

An investment banker is simply a business firm which specializes in helping other business firms (generally corporations) obtain the money they need on the most advantageous possible terms.

Business firms, of all types, must have adequate capital in order to operate successfully, and generally the more successful the business is, the more money it needs. In operating a business, money is needed to meet payrolls, to purchase and carry inventories, to finance accounts receivable, and to finance new plant and equipment expenditures.

Business firms often find it is necessary to employ larger amounts of money in their business in order to enlarge their facilities to the size needed to meet the growing demands of an expanding population.

When inflation occurs, the amount of money needed by a business firm increases. Additional money is needed by a corporation even if it conducts the same unit volume of business as it did before the inflation began, because of increased costs.

Investment bankers, with their specialized knowledge of finance, are often able to help these companies secure the money they need.

Many business firms obtain a large part of the money they need from their own earnings. During the past few years, a large proportion of corporate capital needs has been generated internally by retained earnings and depreciation. Some companies operate so successfully that their earnings cover all their costs and also provide the money they need to finance expansion. Most managements, however, must turn sooner or later to sources outside their own firms for a least a part of the money they require. Such companies can often profitably utilize the services of investment bankers.

Investment bankers generally do not help business firms secure short-term capital. Short-term business loans are usually obtained from commercial banks and, of course, do not involve underwriting or other services of investment bankers. However, long-term capital needs obtained from outside the business are generally raised through the sale of some type of security.

When a corporation obtains long-term funds by issuing and selling stocks or bonds, it can offer these securities to:

1. Its own stockholders or bondholders (perhaps through a direct rights offering).
2. The general public.
3. One or more institutional investors through a private sale.

The services of investment bankers can be utilized profitably, whichever method is chosen. In some cases, investment bankers underwrite the new security issues. In other cases, they function only in an advisory capacity.

Investment bankers help the corporation determine the best type of security to issue under prevailing money market conditions, the best method of offering these securities, the proper timing, the rate the corporation should pay for the money, and so on. They also perform a variety of other functions, all of which are designed to help the corporation obtain the money it needs. Some of the principal functions of the investment banker are:

1. To buy securities from an issuer and sell them to the public.
2. To distribute large blocks of securities held by a few persons or by a single large owner.
3. To provide the means for raising new capital for industry.
4. To buy and distribute securities of federal and state governments and of municipalities.

As noted, an investment banker is frequently an underwriter, and a new issue may be sold through a public offering underwritten by an investment banker. As an underwriter, the investment banker negotiates with corporations (called issuers) which plan to raise capital by issuing securities. Before it will agree to underwrite an issue, the investment banker makes a thorough investigation of the issuing corporation, and an analysis of the industry involved, in order to determine the investment merits of the proposed new securities issue.

After the terms of the offering have been agreed upon, the investment banker usually contracts to buy the securities at a specific price. Since the underwriting investment banking firm generally commits large sums of its own capital during the issuing process, it must be certain that the price paid the issuing corporation is a realistic one. The compensation (or underwriting spread, as it is generally known) received by the investment banker is the difference between the public offering price and the price paid the issuer by the investment banking group.

During negotiations with the issuer, arrangements can be made by the investment banker to buy the issue at a specified price (firm commitment) or to sell it on behalf of the issuer (best efforts). In a "best efforts" distribution the investment banker or broker/dealer acts as an agent and does not commit himself to buy any of the securities being distributed.

FORMATION OF THE SYNDICATE AND SELLING GROUPS. The investment banker negotiating with the issuing corporation is called the "managing underwriter." The managing underwriter generally assembles a group of other investment bankers into a syndicate to help underwrite the securities issue. A syndicate is a *joint venture*, which is a temporary form of organization created for the specific purpose of carrying through a particular transaction, and which is dissolved upon completion of the transaction. In terms of liability, most syndicates are *limited liability syndicates* or *divided-account syndicates* in which each member of the syndicate is responsible only for the amount of securities equal to his agreed upon participation.

The managing underwriter signs an *Underwriting Agreement* with the issuing corporation covering the terms of purchase. He also signs a contract with each underwriter in the syndicate. These contracts are called *Agreements Among Underwriters*, and they set forth the terms of the offering along with specific authorization for the managing underwriter to negotiate with the issuing corporation on behalf of each syndicate member.

About the time the managing underwriter forms the underwriting syndicate, he begins to seek from various securities dealers preliminary indications of interest concerning the new issue. The dealers ultimately combining their efforts in the distribution of a new issue are known as the *selling group*. Each selling group member is committed to purchase only the securities that are allotted to him or that he subscribes to at the time of the offering.

A special committee of the NASD Board of Governors, known as the Committee on Underwriting Arrangements, reviews new isues of securities to advise members as to the reasonableness and fairness of underwriting compensation.

As previously noted, a new securities issue must be registered with the SEC (unless it is exempt), and its registration statement must become effective before it may be offered for public sale. A twenty-day waiting period (or cooling-off period as it is often called) must elapse between the filing date and the date the registration statement becomes effective. Near the end of the cooling-off period, the managing underwriter will call a *due diligence meeting*. At the due diligence meeting, the underwriters, and the officers of the corporation issuing the securities, along with members of their legal and accounting staffs, will review the current status of the corporation. At this meeting, the group will also discuss various aspects of the registration statement and the prospectus in order to make certain that all material contained therein is complete and proper.

During this same general time period, the underwriters take the steps necessary to *qualify* the issue in states where they plan to offer the securities for sale. Many states have securities laws which require the registration of new issues before their sale. When such laws exist, the underwriters qualify or "blue-sky" the issue during the cooling-off period, so that there will be no delays when the twenty day waiting period has expired and the security is to be offered to the public. The various methods of qualifying securities under state laws are discussed in Chapter 15.

The actual underwriting does not take place until two or three days before the effective date. At this time, the public offering price is established. The final step in the underwriting procedure is when the underwriter hands the issuing corporation a check in payment for the amount agreed upon for the securities.

When the registration statement becomes effective, the prospectuses are distributed and the securities are offered for sale. The Securities Act of 1933 specifies that every purchaser of a registered issue, who buys the securities within a specified period of the offering date, must be given a prospectus.

Sometimes a new issue will not attract sufficient investor interest when it is first offered for sale. This lack of interest may be due to a variety of reasons, and when it does occur, it is necessary for the underwriting investment bankers to *stabilize the price* of the issue during the initial distribution period. This is accomplished by the syndicate manager making purchases of the issue in the market at, or below, the public offering price. The extent of the obligation of the underwriters to stabilize the price will be discussed in detail in the prospectus. Stabilization is not required, of course, in the case of so-called *hot issues.* Hot issues are those new issues which are in such great popular demand that once the initial public offering has been made, further transactions command a premium over the public offering price.

COMPETITIVE BIDDING. Another major type of underwriting activity is *competitive bidding.* Competitive bidding underwritings are those which are awarded entirely on the basis of prices (or in some instances, underwriting compensation) stated in sealed bids submitted at a specific time on a specified date. Competitive bidding in the corporate field is restricted to the sale of the securities of public utility companies and railroad companies, except for a few isolated instances. The steps followed in the sale of securities through competitive bidding is similar in many respects to the procedure used in the negotiated underwritings described above. The major difference between the two procedures is the manner in which the price of the issue is determined.

NASD Selling Group Restrictions

Selling group and selling syndicate agreements between members of the NASD must state the public offering price, or how it is determined, as well as to whom and under what conditions concessions may be allowed.

No NASD member firm may join with any nonmember broker/dealer in any syndicate or group in the distribution of an issue of securities to the public. This is true even though the nonmember broker/dealer is registered with the Securities and Exchange Commission. Furthermore, a member who is participating in the distribution of an issue of securities (other than exempted securities) as an underwriter or in a selling group, may not allow a selling concession to a bank or trust company.

Other NASD rules and regulations governing the sale and distribution of securities under both *primary* and *secondary* conditions are discussed in Chapter 13 under the Rules of Fair Practice.

Distribution of Securities

When an original offering of securities is sold to investors, it is called a *primary distribution*. A new security issue may be sold with or without an underwriter. In either case, if the securities have never before been issued, it is a primary distribution. Small corporations, or their organizers, frequently make their own primary distributions.

Secondary distribution is the term usually applied to the process wherby a large block of securities which has already been issued is sold and redistributed to others.

Private placement generally means the direct sale of an issue of securities to institutional investors. Corporations frequently raise capital by selling their securities directly to a financial institution such as an insurance company.

Free Riding

When a member firm of the NASD is participating in an initial public offering of securities, it is required to make a bona fide offering of the securities at the price specified in the prospectus. A member firm functioning as an underwriter or a member of a selling group is not permitted to set aside any of the firm's total allotment in a partners' account for the purpose of speculation. Any NASD member retaining his allotment of an initial public offering for himself, his family, his partners, or employees—instead of making a bona fide public offering of these securities—is said to be "free riding". Fundamentally, free riding is a dealer's holding back portions of the so-called "hot" issues for the benefit of himself or favored customers, instead of making bona fide efforts to distribute the new securities to the public. "Hot" issues are new securities issues which are expected to go to an immediate premium as soon as they are issued and traded over the counter or on an exchange.

The hot issues, of course, are the ones usually involved in the free-riding situations which develop.

Free riding first became a major issue in 1946. In April of that year, the SEC proposed the adoption of a rule designed to stop the practice of free riding. This rule would have (among other things) prohibited firms in the securities business from investing in new securities issues. Before the rule was to be adopted, representatives of the Board of Governors and various committees of the NASD conferred with the SEC concerning the most effective way to curtail this undesirable practice. After due deliberation, it was concluded that free riding was an area in which the NASD could most effectively apply the needed restraints.

Consequently, in 1946 the Board of Governors of the NASD, with SEC concurrence, wrote an interpretation of Article III, Section I, of the Rules of Fair Practice, which effectively left controls in this area in the hands of the Association. This interpretation on free riding was reviewed and published in revised form in 1957.

In 1966, the interpretation once again was reviewed and was published in revised form in August 1966 under the heading, "Interpretation with Respect to Free Riding and Withholding." As noted, these statements concerning free riding and withholding are interpretations under Article III, Section I, of the Rules of Fair Practice which states that:

> A member in the conduct of his business shall observe high standards of commercial honor and just and equitable principles of trade.

The interpretation states that the practice of free riding is a violation of this rule.

This failure of a member (whether functioning as an underwriter, a selling group member, or simply as a participant) to make a bona fide public offering at the public offering price when there is a great demand for an issue can be a factor in artificially raising its price. Not only is such a failure in contravention of ethical practices, but it impairs public confidence in the fairness of the securities business in general.

An NASD member firm is considered to be in a position of trust when it has information not generally known to the public with respect to a particular security, its indicated demand, and other factors bearing on its future price. To take unfair advantage of such a position as a participant in an offering is evidence of a lack of commercial honor.

Members have an obligation to make a bona fide public offering, at the public offering price, of securities acquired by a participation in any *distribution.*[3] This applies to securities acquired by the member firm as

---

[3]For purposes of this interpretation, the term "distribution" is defined to include all distributions, whether registered, unregistered, or exempt from registration under the Securities Act of 1933, or whether primary or secondary distributions, including intrastate offerings and Regulations "A" issues. The interpretation does not apply to exempted securities as defined in Section 3 (a) (12) of the Securities Exchange Act of 1934.

an underwriter or as a selling group member, and also to securities acquired from any other member participating in a distribution as an underwriter or selling group member.

A member with unfilled orders from the public for a security, or a member who has failed to make a bona fide public offering of the securities acquired as described above, is violating the interpretation if he directly or indirectly

1. Withholds any of the securities in his account;
2. Sells any of the securities to any officer, director, partner, employee, or agent of his firm, or to a member of the immediate family[4] of any such individual;
3. Sells any of the securities to any senior officer of a bank, of an insurance company, or of any other institutional type account; or to any person in the securities department of, or whose activities involve or are related to the function of buying or selling securities for a bank, insurance company, or any other institutional type account, or to a member of the immediate family of such persons;
4. Sells any of the securities to any account in which any person specified under (1), (2) or (3) has a beneficial interest;[5]
5. Sells any of the securities, at or above the public offering price, to any other broker or dealer.

A member may sell part of the securities to another member if the latter represents to the selling member, and is prepared to demonstrate, that such purchase was made to fill orders, as an accommodation and without compensation, for bona fide public customers at the public offering price. If such accommodation order is filled for any person in categories (2), (3) or (4) above, the member who fills the order for such person must represent to the selling member, and be prepared to demonstrate, that such sale was for bona fide investment in accordance with the normal investment practice of such person with the member.

It is not the object of the NASD Board of Governors to interfere with sales practices which do not conflict with a member's responsibilities and obligations as a participant in a distribution. The Board believes that NASD members and their partners, officers, directors, and employees have the right to invest in new issues and that sales to them for bona

---

[4]The term "immediate family", for purposes of this interpretation, is defined as the parents, mother-in-law or father-in-law, husband or wife, brothers or sisters, children, or any relative to whose support the NASD member, persons associated with the member, or other persons in categories (2) and (3) above contribute directly or indirectly.

[5]It should be noted that sales of "hot" issues to the accounts of banks, trust companies or other conduits for undisclosed principals shall not relieve a member of its responsibility to insure that the ultimate purchaser is not an account which is within the purview of the provisions of categories (2), (3) or (4).

fide investment in accordance with their "normal investment practices" does not constitute free riding or withholding.

The term "normal investment practice" is defined by the interpretation to mean the *history of investment* in an account with the member. The *history of investment* in an account is merely a record of the normal investment practice of that account over a reasonable period of time. This history should be a strong factor in determining the size and frequency of allotments of "hot issues." If the record discloses little or no investment or trading activity, or if it shows a practice of purchasing mainly securities of "hot issues," sales to such accounts should be carefully scrutinized. The practice of purchasing mainly hot issues in an account does not constitute a normal investment practice as the term is used in the interpretation.

If the account involved is that of the NASD member, it must be clearly an investment account and not a regular inventory or trading account.

Also, whenever a member allots a portion of any issue to members of his immediate family, the member should make certain that the aggregate of the securities so withheld and sold is insubstantial and not a disproportionate amount compared to sales to the public.

Whenever consideration of all pertinent facts results in the conclusion that a member is guilty of free riding, penalties may be imposed. The extent of the penalties *may* be related to the degree of profit realized by the participant, members of his official organization, or any immediate family members who may have profited by the violation. The penalties imposed *will* be based upon the seriousness of the violation, and may include censure, fine, suspension, expulsion, or the barring from association with any NASD member.

The statement on "free riding and withholding" is implemented by the NASD District Business Conduct Committees and the Board of Governors. The interpretation is applied to a given factual situation by individuals, serving on these committees and the Board, who are themselves in the securities business.

A knowledge of the provisions of the interpretation is essential to all registered representatives, since they are equally bound with their employing firms to make a bona fide public offering of all new issues.

REVIEW QUESTIONS

1. Describe the over-the-counter market, naming eight types of securities traded on it.

2. Distinguish between a "firm market," a "subject market," and a "work out market." What is meant by the term "size of market?"

3. Describe in general terms the 5 per cent markup policy. What are some of the circumstances that are considered by the NASD to determine the fairness of markups?

4. When does the 5 per cent markup policy apply? When does it *not* apply? What is the SEC attitude to the markup policy?

5. Describe the nature of over-the-counter quotations for the national and local lists.

6. Discuss *wholesale* quotation as compiled by the National Quotation Bureau. Where can an individual find quotations?

7. What is the NASD policy with respect to firmness of quotations?

8. Describe the main function of investment bankers.

9. Explain the formation of a syndicate and selling group.

10. When is competitive bidding used? What is the major difference between a negotiated and a competitive bidding deal?

11. What is *free riding*? Name four transactions which are considered violations of this rule.

Organized
Securities Exchanges

Chapter **12**

A securities exchange is an institution which provides facilities for its members to execute transactions in securities traded thereon for their own account and risk or for the account and risk of their customers.

Securities exchanges, or stock exchanges, as most of them are called, do not buy securities from anyone, nor do they sell securities to anyone. They simply provide a convenient centralized place where member firm brokers representing buyers of securities and member firm brokers representing sellers of securities, can meet and execute their customers' orders. As has been noted before, it may also be possible for member firms to execute transactions for their own account and risk.

The Number and Location of Securities Exchanges

On June 30, 1966 there were sixteen securities exchanges in the United States. Thirteen of these sixteen exchanges were registered with the Securities and Exchange Commission as national securities exchanges. These are as follows:

> American Stock Exchange
> Boston Stock Exchange
> Chicago Board of Trade

Cincinnati Stock Exchange
Detroit Stock Exchange
Midwest Stock Exchange
National Stock Exchange
New York Stock Exchange
Pacific Coast Stock Exchange
Philadelphia-Baltimore-Washington Stock Exchange
Pittsburgh Stock Exchange
Salt Lake Stock Exchange
Spokane Stock Exchange

The following three exchanges were exempted from registration with the Securities and Exchange Commission as national exchanges:

Colorado Springs Stock Exchange
Honolulu Stock Exchange
Richmond Stock Exchange

Under Section 5 of the Securities Exchange Act of 1934, exchanges may be exempted from registration if it is not necessary or appropriate in the public interest or for the protection of investors to require such registration.

The New York Stock Exchange and the American Stock Exchange are located in New York City, within two blocks of each other. Both exchanges have nationwide facilities, and about 85 per cent of their total memberships are members of both of these major exchanges. Many members of these two exchanges also hold memberships on one or more of the regional exchanges.

Securities traded on either the New York or the American Stock Exchange may be traded on one or more of the regional exchanges. This practice is known as "dual listing." However, no security issue is traded at the same time on both the New York Stock Exchange and the American Stock Exchange.

The New York Stock Exchange and the American Stock Exchange handle most of the trading in securities done through organized securities exchanges. For the thirty-one-year period from January 1, 1935, to December 31, 1965, the New York Stock Exchange handled annually from 82 to 89 per cent of the dollar volume and from 65 to 78 per cent of the share volume of all such transactions. The American Stock Exchange, during the same thirty-one-year period, transacted between 5 and 11 per cent of the total dollar volume and between 10 and 26 per cent of the total share volume handled through organized securities exchanges.

Comparative data covering the volume and value of securities transactions conducted through organized securities exchanges in 1964 are given in Table 12-1.

TABLE 12-1

DATA RELATING TO SECURITIES TRADED
ON
ORGANIZED SECURITIES EXCHANGES
DECEMBER 31, 1964

	New York Stock Exchange	American Stock Exchange	Other Exchanges*	Total
Stocks				
Number of Issues	1,606	1,022	445	3,073
Market Value (in millions)	$474,322	$28,220	$4,315	$506,857
Percent of Total Market Value	93.59	5.56	0.85	100.0
Percent of 1964 Share Volume Sales	72.54	19.35	8.11	100.0
Percent of 1964 Dollar Volume Sales	83.49	8.46	8.05	100.0
Bonds				
Number of Issues	1,186	91	23	1,300
Market Value (in millions)	$127,725	$ 1,267	$ 124	$129,116

*Includes only those securities which are not traded on the NYSE and AMEX.
Source: 31st Annual Report of the Securities and Exchange Commission, (Washington, D. C.: United States Government Printing Office, 1966), pp. 45-48.

As noted, the New York Stock Exchange and the American Stock Exchange combined handled all but 8.05 per cent of the total dollar volume, and all but 8.11 per cent of the total share volume of the stock transactions conducted through stock exchanges in 1964.

An examination of the data in Table 12-1 indicates that on December 31, 1964, the market value of stocks and bonds, both listed and unlisted admitted to trading, on one or more of the stock exchanges in the United States totaled approximately 636 billion dollars.

The 3,073 preferred and common stock issues indicated in Table 12-1 represented more than 11.4 billion shares, of which over 10.9 billion were included in the 2,872 issues *listed* on registered exchanges.

Auction Market

The various stock exchanges around the country work on an auction basis. Bids to buy securities and offers to sell securities are made openly on the floor of these exchanges. Whenever a trade takes place, the person or institution bidding the highest for a security becomes the buyer, and the person or institution making the lowest offer to sell a security is the seller. The prices at which such transactions take place on the New York Stock Exchange and on the American Stock Exchange are sent out to thousands of locations through the stock exchange ticker systems. These promptly and highly publicized prices give an indication to anyone interested in a particular security of the approximate price at which that security can be bought or sold. The latest bid and ask quotations also may be shown on the tape.

Functions and Services of Organized Securities Exchanges

Organized securities exchanges provide facilities where the forces of supply and demand for a given security have an opportunity to interact and set the price at which that security trades. When a security is traded on an organized exchange, both buy and sell orders for that security are funneled to the appropriate trading area on the exchange floor. Since a large percentage of the current potential buyers and sellers is represented at that trading post, the price at which the trade takes place is likely to reflect quite clearly existing supply and demand conditions.

The securities exchanges are not in themselves a source of new equity capital. However, unless exchanges and other efficient securities markets existed, many investors would be reluctant to purchase securities at all for fear they would be unable to sell them later when they needed their cash.

Thus the *liquidity* and *marketability* added to securities by the fact they are traded on an exchange are important factors which help facilitate the flow of new money to industry.

The New York Stock Exchange

The New York Stock Exchange is the nation's largest centralized market place for securities. Its huge trading floor is located in a building at the corner of Broad and Wall streets in New York City.

The Exchange has been in existence for a great many years. In fact, for its beginning, we must go back to the early period of our nation's history.

Before the Revolutionary War there was no centralized location where securities could be traded in New York. Any securities trading which did take place during this time was carried on in a variety of places, such as coffee houses, auction rooms, and offices. As a result the trading was rather spasmodic and disorganized.

Dissatisfied with the lack of facilities for trading securities, a group of merchants and auctioneers decided to establish a place in a centralized location, where they could meet daily at regular hours to trade securities. These men, who became the original members of the Exchange, held the first regular meeting of the Exchange on May 17, 1792.

At first, the Exchange members met out of doors under an old buttonwood tree on Wall Street, but in 1793 construction of the Tontine Coffee House was completed and they moved indoors.

In 1863, the name New York Stock Exchange was officially adopted. Four years later the stock tickers were installed and this method of publicizing the price at which securities trade on the Exchange has been used since that time.

Since those early years, business activity in the United States has grown tremendously and the Exchange has grown with it.

Today, New York Stock Exchange member firms have offices in hundreds of cities in forty-nine states and the district of Columbia. (As of late 1966, there are no member firms in Alaska.) There are also member firm offices in over 20 foreign countries.

The Board of Governors of the New York Stock Exchange consists of thirty-three individuals, thirty of which are elected by the Exchange members. Three board members are elected by the other governors and must be representatives of the public who have no direct connection with the securities business.

The Board of Governors has broad policy making and disciplinary powers. It sets the rules and regulations governing the conduct of all Exchange members and allied members. It also maintains complete control over the admission of new members. The policies of the board are administered by a staff headed by the Exchange president.

The New York Stock Exchange constitution makes provision for 1,375 members. Membership in the Exchange in 1966 totaled 1,366 individuals.

To be a member of the New York Stock Exchange, it is necessary to own a membership, or "seat," as it is popularly called. No one is permitted to transact business on the floor of the exchange without this seat. Regardless of how well qualified an individual may be for membership, he cannot become a member unless he can induce a present member to sell him his seat. Only individuals may own Exchange memberships.

An auction market exists in these seats, and their sale price is set by supply and demand. The price of the seats from the beginning of 1960 to August, 1966, has ranged from $38,000 to $270,000. Ordinarily, at any given time there are at least a dozen seats offered for sale at various prices by estates and by members who are thinking of retiring. In addition to the price of the seat, there is an initiation fee of $7,500 and annual dues of about $1,500.

Some individual members of the New York Stock Exchange trade for their own account exclusively and operate as sole proprietors. Other members are partners in one of the member firm organizations, or hold voting stock in one of the member corporations. At the beginning of 1966, there were 651 such member firm organizations, 499 partnerships, and 152 corporations. Before 1953, member organizations were limited to partnerships. Starting in May, 1953, corporations were permitted to become member organizations, provided such corporations were engaged primarily in the securities business as dealers or brokers and, in addition, were otherwise qualified.

ALLIED MEMBERS. In addition to the regular members of the New York Stock Exchange, there are several thousand allied members. The allied membership group is comprised of the partners in the member firms, and the holders of voting stock in the member corporations, who do not have seats on the Exchange.

Allied members may not do business on the trading floor, since national securities exchange regulations do not permit nonmembers to go on the floor of the Exchange to execute transactions. However, allied members are subject to the same rules and regulations as are members.

TYPES OF BROKERS, DEALERS AND TRADERS. There are several different types of brokers, dealers and traders among the members of the New York Stock Exchange. Each of these types performs certain specific functions, all of which contribute to the smooth operation of the Exchange auction market.

The Exchange makes a yearly tabulation of the classification of members based on the type of function in which they were predominately engaged. However, this can only be an estimate, since many members engage in more than one activity and also shift from one type of activity to another.

The most common classifications of brokerage and trading members functioning on the Exchange floor today are as follows:

1. Commission brokers
2. Specialists
3. Floor brokers
4. Floor traders
5. Odd-lot dealers

COMMISSION BROKERS. Commission brokers comprise approximately half of all the New York Stock Exchange members. This type of broker is the one best known to the average person because he is constantly doing business for his firm's customers. He also, of course, handles transactions for his firm and its registered representatives and partners.

The commission broker executes the orders to buy and sell securities sent in by the customers of his firm. For the performance of this agency service, the firm receives a commission.

There is no risk of security ownership involved for the commission broker, because he acts only on an agency basis in these transactions. In this important respect, the Stock Exchange commission broker differs markedly from the over-the-counter broker/dealer. The over-the-counter broker/dealer does not always act on an agency basis. Frequently he acts in the capacity of a principal rather than that of an agent or broker.

SPECIALISTS. Specialists are members who specialize in one or more listed stock issues. About one-fourth of all the New York Stock Exchange members function as specialists.

The specialist has two different major functions to perform on the Stock Exchange Floor. One of these functions is that of executing orders entrusted to him by other members of the Exchange. His other function is to maintain, insofar as reasonably practicable, fair and orderly markets in stocks which he services by dealing for his own account.

Very often an investor is interested in buying or selling a particular stock only at a price different from (or *away from*, as it is often called) the current market price of that stock. When this is the case, the investor gives a limited order to his broker to buy or sell that stock.

An investor giving his broker a limited order to buy a stock sets the maximum price he authorizes the broker to pay for that security. An investor giving his broker a limited order to sell a stock sets the minimum amount he authorizes his broker to accept for that security.

If an investor gives his broker an order to buy a stock currently selling for $50 a share, but limits the price he is willing to pay for the stock to $45 a share, the order obviously cannot be executed immediately. In fact, it cannot be executed at all until the stock trades at $45, and no one knows when that will next happen.

If the stock the investor wants at $45 stays around its current price of $50 or moves upward in price, it may be many weeks or months before the investor's limited order is executed, if it is executed at all. The broker receiving this limited order cannot possibly go to the appropriate trading post on the floor and wait for the stock to drop to $45 so that he can execute the limited order. However, the broker is expected to execute the order for his customer as soon as market conditions permit; this is where the specialist in that stock comes in.

The specialist is always standing at the post where his assigned stocks are traded. Brokers with limited orders *away from* the market price give the specialist these orders. The specialist enters these orders in his specialist's book.[1] Both limited orders to buy below the current market price and limited orders to sell above the current market price are written in the book. When trading in the stock reaches the price at which these orders can be executed, the specialist takes the appropriate action.

In our illustration, the $45 limited order would be written in the specialist's book and would be represented in the market by him *when* and *if* the price reached $45. If he executes the order, the specialist re-

---

[1] These limited orders *away from* the market are *open orders* (or good 'til cancelled orders as they are often called). An open or good 'til cancelled order (GTC) is an order entered at a specific price and is good until cancelled.

ceives a floor brokerage commission from the broker who gave him the order. The broker, in turn, receives the regular commission from his customer.

For the protection of the public, the specialist is prohibited by exchange rules, in transactions of the above nature, from buying stock for his own account at a given price, while he holds an order to buy at that price for someone else. Furthermore, the specialist may not buy stock for his own account at any price while holding an order to buy that stock "at the market." He is similarly prohibited from competing with a customer he represents on the sell side.

The responsibility of maintaining a fair and orderly market for a particular stock is charged to the specialist. His job is to see that price movements of the security in which he specializes are *reasonably orderly*. The role he plays is vital to the welfare of investors. Obviously, if stock prices typically jumped up several dollars on one transaction only to drop sharply on the next transaction, most people would be extremely reluctant to place any of their spare funds in the securities market.

To help avoid erratic price movements, the specialist is charged by the exchange with maintaining a market in his assigned stock. To do this, he often must risk his capital by buying stock for a price higher than others are willing to pay at that time. He also often has to sell that stock for less than others are willing to sell for at that time.

In performing this function, the specialist in certain respects is like a dealer in the over-the-counter market. He makes a market in the stock in which he specializes. A specialist often makes the best bid or the best offer in a stock for his own account. At other times, he makes both the best bid and the best offer. In either case, the "spread" is narrower than it would have been without him.

When there are a large number of market orders[2] to sell a given stock and few market orders, if any (or limited orders at a price reasonably close to the previous sale) to buy that stock, the specialist would normally buy in order to prevent the price from *dropping* too rapidly and too steeply between successive trades.

When there are a large number of market orders to buy a given security and few, if any, market orders (or limited orders at a price reasonably close to the previous sale) to sell that security, the specialist may sell in order to prevent the price from *increasing* too rapidly and too steeply between successive trades.

Thus, when the market price trend of the specialist's stock is *upward*, he usually *sells* stock from his inventory or sells short.[3] When the market

---

[2] A market order is an order to your broker to buy or sell a security (whichever it is you wish to do) at the best possible price.

[3] A short sale refers to the sale of securities which are not owned by the seller. The seller borrows the stock to make the delivery.

price trend of the specialist's stock is *downward*, he usually *buys* stock for his inventory. This type of trading action by the specialist has a *stabilizing effect* on the market price of the security. In recent years, approximately 85 per cent of the transactions made by specialists as dealers have been of this stabilizing nature.

Specialists participate as dealers on either the buy or sell side in about 30 per cent of all round lot transactions in maintaining orderly markets. Specialists also serve an important function in being ready to buy and sell inactive stocks if no public offers are reasonably close to the last sale.

The specialist is not expected to *prevent* a stock from declining or appreciating in price. It probably would be impossible for him to do so, even if it were expected of him. If a specialist were willing and *able* at all times to buy any and all shares of a particular company offered for sale at a fixed price, he could stop its market price from falling. If a specialist offered and was able to sell an unlimited quantity of these same shares to anyone wanting them at the same fixed price, he could stop its market price from going up. However, this activity could tie up tremendous amounts of money and would be of very little benefit to anyone.

Specialists *are* expected by their buying and selling actions to modify temporary supply and demand disparity existing in the Stock Exchange auction market. Their job, in other words, is to make every effort to keep the market price rises and declines fair and orderly for their securities insofar as is reasonably practical under the circumstances.

Sometimes immense sums of money are committed and great risks are taken by the specialists in their attempts to modify price swings of securities. To illustrate: On Saturday, September 24, 1955, President Eisenhower suffered a heart attack. The stock market the night before had closed at a record high. The shock and uncertainty created by the disheartening news caused a violent reaction in the stock market on Monday, September 26. Orders to sell poured into the market from all over the United States, and from many foreign countries. Round lot volume on the New York Stock Exchange reached 7,761,000 shares. The market as measured by the Dow Jones average of thirty industrial stocks dropped 31.89 points.

In performing their responsibilities to maintain an orderly market, specialists bought hundreds of thousands of shares during the day. By the time the New York Stock Exchange market closed for the day, specialists had increased their inventories by 595,550 shares of stock. Buying these shares increased their capital commitments by $25,500,000. It was a nerve-wracking day, filled with a great many risks; but the specialist's exemplary performance has been credited by many authorities with preventing a disastrous market collapse.

It is obvious that under the above conditions no specialist or group of specialists could have *prevented* the decline in the securities market by their buying activities.

The importance of the function performed by the specialist can be better appreciated by examining what could happen to investors placing *market orders* if it were not for the specialist. Assume that a corporation known as the B.B. Birkin Company is listed on the NYSE. The Birkin Company's ticker symbol is BBB. An investor named Betts is sitting in the board room of his broker in Ogden, Utah. He sees the symbol and number BBB 81½ come over the translux tape, so he knows that 100 shares of Birkin Company stock were just traded on the floor of the NYSE for $81.50 per share. Mr. Betts feels that the Birkin Company stock is an attractive buy at about 82 or 83, so he decides to purchase 100 shares. Having made this decision to buy the stock, Mr. Betts can place either of two types of orders with his broker for the stock. He can place either a *market order* or a *limited order*. The only way Mr. Betts can be certain of getting an immediate execution on an order for 100 shares of Birkin Company stock is by placing a *market order* for the 100 shares. Since, in our illustration, Mr. Betts is anxious to acquire the stock, he places a *market order* rather than a *limited order* with his broker.[4]

Upon receiving this market order, the broker can go to the appropriate trading post and bid for the stock at successively higher prices, i.e., 81⅜, 81½, 81⅝, 81¾, 81⅞, 82, and so on until he reaches a price at which someone is induced to sell 100 shares of Birkin Company stock. If Mr. Bett's market order should happen to arrive on the trading floor at a time when there are no market orders or limited orders to sell the stock at a price reasonably close to the previous sale, a very unpleasant situation could develop for him. His broker might have to bid for the shares at successively higher prices until he buys them at a price several dollars per share above the price Mr. Betts wanted to pay or expected to pay.[5] Here is where the specialist comes into the picture. Before the price of the Birkin Company stock goes up too much (due to the bidding of Mr. Betts' broker), it is probable that the specialist will sell 100 shares of BBB out of his inventory to Mr. Betts. Thus Mr. Betts won't have to pay several dollars more per share for the stock than he expected to pay.

As noted, a specialist often makes the best bid for a stock and/or the

[4]Assume that Mr. Betts places a limited order for the stock at 81½. If the stock does not trade at 81½ again, immediately, but moves upward in price, his order will not be executed. Even if the stock does trade at 81½ immediately or shortly after his order goes to the floor, Mr. Betts cannot be sure his order will be executed because other orders at 81½ may be ahead of his and thus have priority over his order.

[5]Similarly, of course, anyone trying to sell stock *at the market* at a time when there are not market orders to buy that stock might find his stock being offered by his broker at successively lower prices until it is sold for several dollars less per share than he wanted to sell it for.

best offer on a stock for his own account. In our illustration, the last
sale in BBB stock before Mr. Betts placed his order occurred at 81½.
Let us assume that after that sale, there were no unexecuted market
orders to sell BBB stock and that the best bid was 82 and the best
offer was 85. Assume the specialist, however, offers 100 shares from his
own account (inventory) at 82¾ thereby changing the quotation to
82-82¾. Mr. Betts's market order reaches the floor and is executed at
82¾. Thus, he has been able to buy the stock for 2 and ¼ points
(dollars) less than would have been the case without the specialist.

All stocks experience periods of inactive trading from time to time
regardless of how widely they are held. During these inactive periods
temporary supply and demand distortions often develop, which cause
the market price of a security to move upward or downward substantially in a very short time. It is during these inactive periods that the
function performed by the specialist becomes of such great importance
to the investor.

By maintaining a market in his stocks, the specialist greatly modifies
any erratic price swings caused by the temporary supply and demand
distortions which develop during a stock's inactive trading periods.

Most of the orders received by brokers on the floor before the opening
of the market are left with the specialist. Using these orders and also
dealing for his own account in varying degrees, the specialist arranges
the opening price in each of his assigned stocks. He arranges the opening
price as near as possible to the previous close, considering general market
conditions and market circumstances in the stock.

Floor Brokers.   Some members of the NYSE function as independent
floor brokers. These members, known a $2 brokers, assist the commis-
sion house brokers when the commission house brokers have too many
orders to handle by themselves. In effect, a $2 broker is a broker for a
broker.

Suppose that the Speedy Brokerage Company does a commission
house brokerage business and has two partners executing orders on the
floor of the Exchange. Further, suppose that the Speedy Company received simultaneously three market orders for stocks traded at different
trading posts. Obviously, the two Speedy Company men on the floor of
the Exchange cannot be in three places at one time. Nevertheless, all
Stock Exchange member firms are required to execute market orders
from their customers without delay.

With the assistance of a $2 broker, the solution to this problem is
simple. Two of the three market orders are handled by the Speedy
Company men, and the third is turned over to a $2 broker for execu-
tion. He goes to the appropriate trading post and acts as a broker for
the Speedy Brokerage Company. For this service, the $2 broker receives

the floor brokerage commission from the Speedy Company. The Speedy Company in turn receives a regular commission on the transaction from its customer.

The $2 broker also handles orders for other brokers when they have to leave the Exchange floor during business hours and for smaller firms outside New York who do not wish to keep their member in New York full time.

For many years the commission received by these brokers was $2 per 100 shares. As a result, the floor broker was commonly referred to as a "$2 broker." The name "$2 broker" is still in common usage, although the usual commission now ranges substantially above $2 per 100 shares, depending on the price of the stock.

NYSE FLOOR TRADERS.   Generally speaking, any member on the trading floor of the New York Stock Exchange who buys or sells for his own account any stock in which he is not registered as a specialist or odd-lot dealer is acting as a floor trader, or more properly today—a registered trader. A few members are primarily concerned only with trading for their own account. They do not deal with the public, nor do they regularly act as $2 brokers. Thus, they do not receive any income from commissions.

These registered traders roam the Exchange floor in search of trading opportunities which appear potentially profitable to them. They tend to buy and sell a given security within a short period of time. As a result, their transactions add liquidity to the market

Two distinct advantages accrue to the registered trader through his ownership of a seat on the Exchange. First, although he does have to pay a clearing fee and transfer taxes for each security trade he makes, he does not have to pay commissions to anyone unless he utilizes the services of the floor brokers or specialists. Second, the fact that he is able to move about the floor from post to post at will enables him to take immediate advantage, within the limitations of the rules, of any opportunities to buy or sell he discovers which appear particularly attractive to him. However, no news tickers are permitted on the Exchange floor, and the NYSE has stringent trading rules which are designed to prohibit transactions which may have a disruptive effect on the market, while at the same time permitting transactions that add to the orderliness of the market.

The New York Stock Exchange established several new regulations governing the activities of floor traders in 1964. Under these amended rules, members who wish to trade for their own accounts on the Floor of the Exchange must register separately with the Exchange and pass an Exchange-administered examination. The rules stipulate that at least 75 per cent of acquisitions and, with certain exceptions, 75 per cent of liquidations made by registered traders must be "stabilizing" in nature—that is, purchases at prices below or sales at prices above the last different price. Stabilization ratios are computed monthly by the Exchange. In general, destabilizing purchases at a price above the previous day's closing price of a stock are not permitted. Also, a registered trader may not trade for an account in which he has an interest and execute an off-floor order in the same stock during the same trading session. The amended rules require each registered trader to meet an initial capital requirement of $250,000.

The number of New York Stock Exchange members operating exclusively as registered traders has been declining steadily during the last few decades. The high cost of acquiring a seat on the Exchange, the initiation fee and annual dues, as well as other expenses, undoubtedly helped induce many floor traders to perform other floor activities in addition to their personal trading. As of November 1, 1966, 37 members qualified as registered traders.

ODD-LOT DEALERS.   Some Exchange members function as odd-lot dealers. Any investor wishing to buy or sell less than a "round lot" of any security listed on the NYSE will probably be serviced by one of these odd-lot dealers. On the American Stock Exchange, the specialist in the stock acts as the odd-lot dealer.

In most stocks, a round lot is 100 shares. When this is the case, an odd lot is any number of shares from 1 through 99. Some high-priced or particularly inactive stocks have a unit of trading of only ten shares.[6] In such cases, an odd lot would be any number of shares from one to nine.

The odd-lot member always acts as a dealer, never a broker. However, they do not accept orders direct from the investor. Rather, they stand ready to trade with any NYSE firm in any listed stock in any quantity from one through ninety-nine shares. When commission brokers have an order from a customer either to buy or sell less than a round lot of a given security, they buy the stock from or sell the stock to the odd-lot dealer for their customer. The odd-lot dealer strives to maintain the same free and open market for the trader in small lots as exists for the trader in round lots.

For his services, the odd-lot dealer receives a differential of one-eighth (12½¢) or one-quarter (25¢) of a point, on 100-share-unit stocks depending upon the price of the security. The differential is one-eighth on a stock selling for less than $55 a share. On stocks selling for $55 a share or over, the differential is one-quarter. In odd-lot transactions, both the odd-lot differential and the regular commission less $2 must be paid to

---

[6]A unit of trading (or trading unit) is the customary number of shares or bonds required for any single purchase or sale of a particular security.

the broker by the investor. However, none of the commission goes to the odd-lot dealer.

An investor buying or selling an odd lot of a security may place either a market order or a limited order.

When an odd-lot market order for a security is received on the floor of the Exchange, it is not executed until after the next round-lot transaction takes place. The price at which this round-lot transaction takes place becomes the base price for the odd-lot transaction. To this base price is added the odd-lot differential in the case of a buy order. From this base price is subtracted the odd-lot differential in the case of a sell order.

To illustrate:

An investor gives his broker an order to buy ten shares of J. C. Penney Co. stock at the market.[7] Just after this market order arrives at the appropriate trading post on the floor, a round lot of J. C. Penney stock trades at a price of 56½. To this base price of 56½ is added the odd-lot differential of ¼ (the differential is ¼ since the stock is trading for $55 a share or over). Thus, the price at which the odd-lot purchase takes place is 56¾. The execution price of an odd-lot as reported to the customer includes the differential. If the investor had been selling,[8] under the above conditions, instead of buying, the ¼ odd-lot differential would have been subtracted from the base price. Thus, instead of receiving 56½ per share for his stock when it was sold, the customer would receive 56¼ per share.

Limited orders placed for odd lots are also subject to the odd-lot differential. To illustrate:

An investor gives his broker a limited order to buy ten shares of Utah Power and Light Co. stock at 32. This limited odd-lot order to buy at 32 will not be executed until a round lot trades at 31⅞ or below. If the next round-lot trade is at 30, the odd-lot investor pays 30 plus the odd-lot differntial of ⅛ (the differential is ⅛ since the stock is trading for under $55.00 per share).

If the odd-lot investor had been selling under the above conditions instead of buying, his limited order to sell at 32 would not be executed until a round lot of the stock had traded at 32⅛ or higher. A limited order to sell, marked long, is filled on the first round-lot sale after the broker receives the order which is above the limited price by the amount of the applicable differential or by a greater amount.

---

[7] Taxes and commissions are excluded from these odd-lot illustrations.

[8] In this example, the order to sell at the market is marked "long"; it is not a short sale. An order to sell must be clearly marked "long" or "short." When it is not so marked, the dealer returns it to the originating firm for marking. The execution of an order to sell marked "short" received on the Exchange floor cannot take place until a round-lot sale takes place at a price higher than the last different round-lot price.

The odd-lot dealer will also fill an odd-lot order to buy "on offer." Such an order is executed at ⅛ (or ¼, depending on the price) above the round-lot offer prevailing at the time the order is received. Another type of order is the odd-lot order to sell "on bid" marked "long." Such an order is executed at ⅛ (or ¼, depending on the price) below the round-lot bid prevailing when the order is received. The odd-lot dealer cannot fill an order to sell "on bid" marked "short."

Subject to certain conditions and restrictions, odd-lot dealers also buy and sell odd lots after the close of the market at a price referred to as the "basis price." Basis prices are jointly arranged (on listed 100 share unit stocks) by the odd-lot dealers at the close of the market each trading day whenever closing bids and offers are two points or more apart and provided no round-lot sale took place that trading day. No "short" orders are executed on the "basis prices."

When his volume of odd-lot buying or selling in a particular security makes it necessary, the odd-lot dealer buys or sells in round lots to adjust his inventory.

The system of pricing odd lots as now practiced on the New York Stock Exchange serves as a guarantee to the odd-lot investor. It guarantees him the same reliability of market, fairness of pricing and accuracy as is accorded the round-lot investor. In addition, all odd-lot orders triggered by the round-lot sale are filled simultaneously because there is no priority or "stock ahead" which would prevent odd-lot orders from being executed.

TYPES OF ORDERS FOR SECURITIES. When an investor purchases or sells securities, he must make a variety of decisions regarding the type of order, or orders, he places with his broker. As noted, stocks may be purchased or sold in round lots or odd lots. Stocks may be sold short. A market order or a limited order may be placed for the purchase or sale of a security. When a limited order is placed, a time limit is used to determine the length of its life in case it is not executed right away. A limited order may be a day order; a week or month order; or an open or GTC order. A *day order* is one which expires at the close of the trading day in which it was entered. *Week orders* are those which expire at the end of the calendar week if they haven't been executed before that time, and unexecuted *month orders* (which are rarely used) expire at the end of the calendar month. *Open* or *GTC* (Good 'til Cancelled) *orders* remain in force until they are executed or cancelled, except that they must be confirmed at least every six months on the last business day of April and of October.

STOP ORDERS. There are several kinds of *special* orders used in connection with securities transactions. The most important type of special order is known as the *stop order* or *stop loss order*. A stop order is an order to buy or sell which becomes a market order as soon as the price of the stock reaches, or sells through, the price specified. A stop order may be used in an effort to protect a paper profit or to try to limit a possible loss to a certain amount. However, since the stop order becomes a market order when the stop price is reached, there is no guarantee that the order will be executed at the price.

To illustrate: if you bought stock at $65 a share, you could enter an order to sell at "60 stop." In the event the stock declines to $60 or below, your order automatically becomes a market order and is executed at the best possible price—which could be at $60, or below or above $60, depending upon the market in the stock at that time.

Or, if stock bought at $55 a share should rise to $90, the customer could enter a stop order to sell at $85. Should the stock decline to $85 or below, the stop order would automatically become a market order and the stock would be sold at the best price then available to him on the floor. Stop orders may also be used when buying stock.

When he gives his broker a limit order or stop order, the customer can specify that it is to be good for only one day. Or he can give a week order, or a month order. If the order is not executed during the period designated, it automatically expires.

SHORT SELLING. When an investor places an order with his broker to sell a security, the sell order must be marked either *long* or *short*. Ordinarily, if the investor owns the securities he sells and he intends to deliver these securities to the person he sells them to, the order will be marked *long*. If he does not own the securities, however, and must borrow them in order to make delivery, the sale will be marked *short*. A person sells short in the expectation that the security he is selling now (and borrowing to make delivery) will decline in price so that at some time in the future he can cover his short sale and make a profit.

To illustrate: Mr. Betts sells 100 shares of J. C. Penney Company stock short @ $72 a share. Through his broker he borrows the stock in order to make delivery. Within a few weeks the stock of the J. C. Penney Company is selling in the market for $60 per share. Mr. Betts covers his short sale by buying the stock for $60 per share and returning it to the person he borrowed it from. Mr. Betts would make capital gains of $12 per share (less expenses) on such a short sale transaction.

No short sale of a stock is permitted except on a rising price. Short sales must be plus tick or Zero-plus tick sales. A plus tick sale is a sale at a price above the previous sale price. A zero-plus tick is a sale at the same price as the previous sale but at a price above the last different sale price.

To illustrate: there might be four separate transactions in General Motors stock all at a price of $50 per share, but General Motors could not be sold short unless the price at which General Motors sold before these four transactions had been at 49⅞ or less.

THE MONTHLY INVESTMENT PLAN. The Monthly Investment Plan (MIP) is a creation of the New York Stock Exchange, and only stocks listed on the Exchange can be purchased under the plan. NYSE listed stocks selling in 10-unit shares may not be purchased through the MIP.

The MIP is designed primarily for the small investor, the man who wants to make periodic small investments in a particular stock. Essentially, it is a dollar-cost-averaging plan, and it permits investment of as little as $40 a quarter (every three months). The maximum investment under MIP is $1,000 monthly.

Under the MIP, the individual determines the amount of money he wishes to invest periodically and the particular stock he wants to buy. This information is entered on an MIP purchase order. The purchase order is not a contract, but rather a statement of intention on the part of the investor. The investor is not under any obligation to send the payments, and he can terminate the plan whenever he wishes. Only one stock may be purchased per MIP plan. If an individual investor wants to buy more than one stock, he opens a separate plan for each stock he wishes to buy.

When the investor's MIP payment is received by the broker, he subtracts the amount of the broker's commission and uses the balance to purchase stock for the investor's account. The broker purchases the exact number of shares that the remaining dollars will buy, figured to four decimal places. After each purchase, the investor is mailed a receipt for his money and a statement showing the number of shares purchased, the price, the commission paid, and the total number of shares held in the account. The investor owns these shares (even the fractional part of a share). He does not owe any balance and is not in debt for the shares.

Any dividends paid on the individual stocks held in the MIP are reinvested automatically unless otherwise specified on the purchase order.

Once an MIP is opened, the trades are handled by an odd-lot house. The odd-lot house takes care of the bookkeeping involved and holds the shares as custodian.

MIP purchases are made at the first odd-lot price of the stock established after the day the payment is credited to the investor's account.

A commission is charged on MIP purchases (including reinvested dividends) and on sales. The commission charge is 6 per cent on amounts of $100 or less; $1 plus 2 per cent (with a minimum of $6) on amounts between $100 and $399; and $5 plus 1 per cent on amounts between $400 and $1,000.

The investor can obtain the stock certificates he owns by requesting them or, automatically, upon termination of the MIP. There is no charge for delivery upon termination or when 50 shares or more are requested. When full shares in amounts of less than 50 shares are requested, there is a $1 charge plus mailing costs on each delivery.

THE TICKER TAPE. Whenever a trade takes place on the floor of the New York Stock Exchange, an Exchange employee sends a record of the transaction to the ticker department for transmission over the ticker network. This is done by placing a card designating the details of the transaction in an "optical card reader." This reader electronically transmits the report to the Market Data System which, in turn, automatically prints the information about the transaction on some 3,750 tickers and display devices in the U.S., Canada, and Europe.

Each stock listed on the New York Stock Exchange has a symbol of one, two, or three letters. Some well known examples are X for the United States Steel Corporation, GM for General Motors Corporation, and RCA for Radio Corporation of America. Sales are reported on the ticker tape by symbol, number of shares and price of transaction. To simplify reporting, the number of shares is omitted when 100-share transactions are put on the ticker tape. When transactions of 100-share multiples from 200 to 900 shares take place they are shown as 2s, 3s, 4s, etc. to 9s. Sales of 1,000 shares or more generally are printed on the tape in full.

The following are typical examples of the way transactions taking place on the floor of the New York Stock Exchange would appear on the ticker tape in a brokerage company's board room.

T	IBM	XRX	C	DDPr
55	3s316 ½	2000s158	36 ¾	3s89 ⅛

A translation of this "ticker talk" would be as follows:

> 100 shares of American Telephone and Telegraph Company common at $55 a share.
> 300 shares of International Business Machines common at $316.50 a share.
> 2,000 shares of Xerox common at $158 a share.
> 100 shares of Chrysler common at $36.75 a share.
> 300 shares of duPont preferred at $89.125 a share.

During periods of high volume trading the ticker tape sometimes falls behind in reporting transactions. Under such circumstances certain abbreviated forms of reporting are adopted.

BID AND ASKED QUOTATIONS. On a stock exchange, the bid and asked quotation is the highest bid and the lowest offer prevailing in the market at a specific time for a given security. The price which someone is willing to pay for a given security is called the *bid*. The price at which someone is willing to sell a security is called the *asked* price or *offer*. The difference between the bid and asked prices in any quotation is the *spread*.

Quotations are expressed with bid price given first followed by the offering price. This can take the form "30 bid, offered 30½" or "30, 30½" or "30 to a ½." Requests for quotations may also be in the form "quote and size" which asks that, in addition to the quotation, information be given on the number of shares for which the price is good.

Current quotations on New York Stock Exchange listed stocks are furnished through brokers to customers by the Quotations Department of the New York Stock Exchange.

SELF REGULATION OF THE EXCHANGE. The New York Stock Exchange has developed a very extensive and complex system of rules and regulations covering all phases of its members' operations. The business customs and ethics of the securities industry have been written paragraph by paragraph, over the years, into the 500-page Constitution and Rules of the New York Stock Exchange and its Company Manual of requirements for listed companies. In addition, of course, there are many regulations required under the various state and federal securities laws which are implemented by the Exchange.[9]

The conduct of member firms, both on and off the floor of the Exchange, is regulated by the Exchange authorities. Any member found guilty "of conduct or proceedings inconsistent with just and equitable principles of trade"[10] may be suspended or expelled.

The 500-page Constitution and Rules, mentioned above, deals principally with procedures and ethics in the following areas:

1. Protection of the interests of customers and shareowners.
2. The auction market on the Exchange floor.
3. Exchange contracts, their clearance, delivery, and settlement.
4. Personal qualifications of members of the Exchange, of partners or officers of member firms, and of member firm employees representing firms with the public.
5. Organization of a member firm, its capital, associations with nonmember firms, and business conduct.

The company Manual covers the requirements for listed companies. The manual codifies good corporate practices in relations with shareowners. It presents a wide variety of requirements ranging all the way from the printing specifications for stock certificates in order to prevent

---

[9]Many of the Exchange's provisions were written into the Securities Acts and SEC Rules now having the force of law. Its provisions are paralleled, too, in many instances, in the rules and regulations of the NASD.

[10]Quoted from the original constitution of the New York Stock Exchange.

counterfeiting, to the proxy requirements designed to make voting convenient and practical for all shareowners.

FLOOR RULES AND REGULATIONS.   There are several hundred rules regulating the activities of the brokers and dealers on the floor of the NYSE. These regulations are designed to insure that securities transactions on the floor will take place at prices arrived at fairly and openly.

The hours of trading on the Exchange floor are from 10.00 A.M. to 3:30 P.M. Monday through Friday. During the trading, bids and offers must be called out loud at the appropriate trading post. Bids and offers are made in multiples of the unit of trading (ordinarily 100 shares). The highest bid and the lowest offer for a given security have precedence over any other bids or offers for that security.

REGULATORY ACTIVITIES OF THE EXCHANGE.   Regulatory activities of the New York Stock Exchange include

1. reviewing all member firm legal documents
2. spot checking of advertising and market letters
3. checking the business history of each candidate for membership or registration
4. checking the market performance of each specialist
5. investigating unusual market activity
6. reviewing public complaints
7. enforcing the member firm capital requirements.

FINANCIAL REQUIREMENTS AND REPORTS.   Member firms are required to have a minimum amount of capital before carrying accounts for customers. Each such member firm must answer at least three financial questionnaires a year. These questionnaires are designed to enable the NYSE to check the firm's compliance with this minimum capital requirement. One of these three financial questionnaires is based upon a surprise audit made by independent public accountants.

Periodically, Exchange examiners go to the offices of each member firm, and spot-check their books, records and business practices.

Unless an exemption has been granted, NYSE regulations require that each member firm must report as required:

a. its position as an underwriter of securities
b. any money borrowed or loaned by the firm
c. any money borrowed or loaned by individual general partners, or in the case of member corporations, the holders of voting shares, unless a specific exemption is granted under Rule 420.

All customers of a member firm must be supplied with copies of the firm's latest financial statement upon request.

INSOLVENCY FUND.   The New York Stock Exchange instituted a $10,000,-000 Special Trust Fund in 1964, supplemented by a $15,000,000 indemnity bond or standby credit, available for use at the discretion of the Board of Governors in event of insolvency of a member organization. This $25,000,000 reserve is in addition to the $10,000,000 blanket bond the NYSE maintains covering fraud of employees, officers or partners of member organizations, and is intended to enable the Exchange to act in the case of any insolvency regardless of cause if it elects to do so.

STANDARDS OF ELIGIBILITY FOR LISTING ON THE NEW YORK STOCK EXCHANGE. The New York Stock Exchange has certain mathematical yardsticks which are used to measure a corporation's eligibility for listing common stocks. In order to meet these minimum qualifications for initial listing, a corporation should have:

1. A demonstrated earning power under competitive conditions of $2,000,000 annually before taxes, and $1,200,000 after all charges including federal income taxes. Three years of earnings at the $1,200,000 level will normally be looked for before a corporation is accepted for listing.
2. Net tangible assets of at least $10,000,000 and publicly held common shares with a total market value of $12,000,000 or more at the time of listing.
3. A minimum of 1,000,000 shares outstanding with a broad distribution of at least 700,000 publicly-held shares among not less than 2,000 shareholders. Each of at least 1,700 of the shareholders must own 100 shares or more.

In addition, to meet the initial listing requirements, the company must be a going concern, or be the successor to a going concern.

Each company must execute a listing agreement in which it undertakes to publish interim and annual financial information, solicit proxies for stockholders' meetings, have an independent registrar, give notice of setting of record dates, give notice of changes in officers or directors, charter or by-laws, and other pertinent information.

The listing agreement between the company and the Exchange calls for the distribution to stockholders of the company's annual report with financial statements certified by independent accountants at least fifteen days before the annual stockholder's meetings and not later than three months after the close of its fiscal year.

These initial listing standards are not applied inflexibly, but rather are considered together with various compensating factors. Some of the compensating factors which are taken into consideration in determining a security's eligibility for initial listing include:

1. The degree of national interest in the company
2. The character of the market for the corporation's products
3. The nature of the industry in which the corporation is operating (i.e., expanding or contracting)
4. The relative stability of the corporation, its position in its

industry, and its prospects of maintaining its position in the industry
5. The stock should have a sufficiently wide distribution to offer reasonable assurance that an adequate auction market will exist in its securities.

The existence of voting trusts or other voting restrictions may be a bar to listing. Since 1926, the NYSE has refused to list nonvoting common stocks, and all common stocks presently listed on the exchange carry the voting right. Exchange regulations permit it to refuse listing privileges to preferred stock not having the right to vote upon the default of the equivalent of six quarterly dividends.

SUSPENSION OF TRADING OR DELISTING SECURITIES. The Board of Governors at any time may suspend or delist a security if it believes that continued dealings in the security on the Exchange are not advisable. In each case under consideration for suspension or delisting, the board gives weight to all factors affecting the security and the company.

The suspension of trading or delisting of a common stock in the NYSE may be considered if:

1. There are less than 800 stockholders of record including not less than 700 round-lot shareholders.
2. There are 300,000 shares or less outstanding (exclusive of concentrated or family holdings).
3. The total market value of the common shares (exclusive of concentrated or family holdings) is less than $2,500,000.
4. The net tangible assets applicable to the common stock or total market value of the common stock has fallen below $5,000,000 and average net earnings after taxes have been below $400,000 for the last three years.
5. Liquidation of the company has begun, or substantially all of the company's assets have been sold.
6. The issuing corporation violates its agreements with the Exchange.

Preferred stock or guaranteed common stock will be considered for delisting if 10,000 or less shares are outstanding, or, if the value of the shares outstanding is $400,000 or less. Concentrated holdings are liminated in arriving at the above totals.

REQUIREMENTS FOR QUALIFICATION AS A REGISTERED EMPLOYEE OF THE NEW YORK STOCK EXCHANGE. Any individual wishing to become a customer's man, salesman, or securities trader for a member firm of the New York Stock Exchange must first be approved as a registered employee.

A candidate for employment as a registered employee must be at least 21 years of age and of good moral character. An investigation is made of each candidate's background in order to determine his eligibility. In addition, the candidate must either:

1. have had recent actual experience in the securities business (as a principal or employee) for a reasonable length of time, or
2. serve as a trainee in the office of a member firm for a period of time prescribed by the NYSE.

Registered employees of the NYSE may *not* be employed on a part-time basis.

The application for registration of any individual must be made by the sponsoring member firm employer. Any NYSE member firm seeking such approval for an employee must file an application form with the NYSE.

The NYSE has two registered representative categories for employees of member firms, one of which is temporary. These are:

1. *Full registration,* which entitles the registrant to handle all types of securities business on behalf of his member firm employer; and
2. *Limited registration,* which restricts the types of securities business the registrant may handle on behalf of his member firm employer to mutual fund shares or the Monthly Investment Plan.

A limited registrant may not solicit, service, or even so much as transmit an order involving securities other than mutual fund shares or those for Monthly Investment Plan accounts. A limited registration may be continued only for a period of up to seven months, during which time the trainee must spend at least half of his business time preparing to qualify for full registration.

The usual requirements for training candidates without previous actual experience are:

1. for full registration—six months
2. for limited registration—three months
3. for full registration via limited registration—eight months

The means of training is at the option of the sponsoring member firm employer, but the responsibility for the training program is placed directly on the employer. The training should include actual "on-the-job" training in the various departments of the office, and should be supplemented by a study of the rules of the Exchange and of other regulatory or supervisory authorities having jurisdiction over the securities business.

If the candidate for registration has had some previous actual experience in the securities business, the training period may be reduced or waived at the sole discretion of the NYSE.

NEW YORK STOCK EXCHANGE EXAMINATIONS. Written examinations prescribed by the Exchange are normally required unless the candidate for registration recently has been registered with the Exchange for some other NYSE member firm. Two different examinations for registered representatives are used by the NYSE. One is the Limited Registration Examination for those seeking limited registration. The other is the Standard Examination for those seeking full registration.

The Limited Registration Examination is designed to determine the extent of an applicant's knowledge in subjects considered essential to the work of a representative who gives investment service only on mutual funds and Monthly Investment Plans in a list of stocks recommended by his firm for this purpose.

The Standard Examination is designed to determine the extent of an applicant's knowledge in subjects considered essential to the work of a registered representative who gives general investment advice and service to his firm's customers.

Special examinations are given by the NYSE for persons whose principal work is in unusual fields.

The New York Stock Exchange and the National Association of Securities Dealers conduct a simplified examination program for the candidates for registration with both organizations, permitting candidates to satisfy the examination requirements of both the NYSE and the NASD at one test session rather than at two sessions.

Under the joint examination program, the NYSE accepts the 125-question NASD Examination in partial fulfillment of its own examination requirement. The NASD Examination consists of a 100-question General Securities Section and a 25-question NASD Section. To these, the Exchange adds a 50-question NYSE Section covering round-and-odd-lot trading, Exchange Constitution and Rules, corporate finance and security analysis. Candidates are scored on their answers to the combined total of 175 questions.

A study outline for NYSE Registration Examinations may be obtained by contacting the New York Stock Exchange, Publications Division, 11 Wall Street, New York, New York.

The American Stock Exchange

Before January 5, 1953, the American Stock Exchange was officially known as the New York Curb Exchange. In fact, many Wall Street regulars still automatically use the nickname "The Curb" when referring to the American Stock Exchange.

The name Curb developed in a natural way from the early origin of the American Exchange. The first brokers and traders to be associated with what was later to become the American Stock Exchange conducted transactions outdoors, standing on the curb of the street.

The trading of securities on the curb first started some time around the late 1840's or early 1850's. No one is certain of the exact date. Evidently, this curb trading was started by a group of traders and brokers who wanted to conduct transactions in unlisted securities rather than in the securities listed on the New York Stock Exchange. During the years before the American Exchange moved indoors, trading was conducted first on Wall and Hanover Streets in New York City, and later on William Street, Broad Street, and then Wall Street again.

At first, only a few securities transactions took place each day and these were handled by a relatively small number of brokers and traders. However, as the volume of transactions grew through the years and as the streets became more and more crowded with traders, brokers, customers, and sightseers, serious communication problems began to develop. Each year, as business expanded, it became increasingly difficult for the employees of the various brokers and traders to locate their employers in the crowd.

Wooden platforms were constructed out from the windows of the buildings lining the street where the trading was taking place. Order clerks sat on these platforms answering telephones and writing down the buy and sell orders as they came in from the firm's customers. Upon receipt of the orders, the clerks began their search for their firm's broker in the milling crowd of people below. After locating their men, the order clerks were faced with the almost impossible task of shouting the instructions concerning the orders loud enough for them to be heard above the roar of voices in the street. To overcome these communication problems, two unique practices were developed by the traders and brokers on the Curb, which were to delight New York sightseers for years to come.

To make it easier for their order clerks and partners to find them in the crowd, a few brokers began to wear brightly colored items of clothing while trading securities in the street. The clothing worn was so brilliant in color that the clerks and partners could find the man they wanted in the crowd no matter where he was. The idea caught on, and soon the Curb securities market began to look like a couturier's nightmare. Brokers wearing bright purple coats or bright plaid caps could be seen conducting securities transactions with other brokers who were wearing top hats of kelly green or a brilliant red.

An elaborate system of hand signals was worked out to enable the firm's order clerks to transmit buy and sell orders from the platforms above the street to the gaily attired brokers below. A busy trading day on the Curb was a fantastic sight to behold, and people came from miles around to enjoy it.

Notwithstanding its hectic, disorganized appearance, however, the "Curb" provided an effective market place for trading many types of securities.

During the early years of its operation, outside on the curb, there were no formal rules or regulations and no original supervision of the trading activities. However, a number of unwritten trading customs were adopted by the men trading securities on the curb.

At first, almost anyone could become a broker, but as the organization of the market and its trading activities became more formalized, certain membership requirements were adopted.

In 1908, the first official step toward establishing a regular securities exchange was taken by the formation of the New York Curb Agency.

In 1911, the New York Curb Market Association was established with offices at 25 Broad Street. An Association Board of Representatives was created, which developed and enforced some trading rules designed to govern the securities trading activities of Association members.

Memberships in the Association were limited in number and annual dues were required. A five-hour trading day was established and a listing department was created to admit qualified stocks to trading. Provision was made at this time for maintaining public records.

Trading on the outside curb reached its peak on Broad Street during the period from 1900 to 1921. Along with the great increase in the volume of transactions during this period, came the realization that an outdoor market place for securities had certain inherent disadvantages.

The Exchange authorities obviously could not observe and regulate the activities of its members out-of-doors as effectively as they could inside a building.

The brokers themselves realized that many improved methods and procedures could be adopted to help them more efficiently handle customer's orders, if they moved into a building. Furthermore, if the Exchange moved indoors, a ticker system could be put into operation. This would enable the Exchange to report promptly, to all parts of the country, the prices at which securities trades took place, and also quotations on listed securities.

All of these indoor advantages, coupled with the thought of the many past snowy and rainy days spent outside on the curb, formed an argument too strong to overcome. Consequently, at an open meeting on June 6, 1919, the members voted to move indoors.

Property was selected, and purchased with funds obtained by the sale of stock to Association members. The Association's Board of Representatives, on March 30, 1921, approved a new constitution which became effective on June 27, 1921, the date on which the exchange moved indoors.

The new market place was officially known as the New York Curb Market until 1929, when the name was changed to the New York Curb Exchange. On January 5, 1953, the present name, The American Stock Exchange, was officially adopted. The American Exchange is located at 86 Trinity Place, New York City, New York.

AMERICAN STOCK EXCHANGE MEMBERSHIP. The American Stock Exchange is a voluntary unincorporated association. The Exchange has a constitution which contains a statement of its primary objectives. These objectives are, "to provide a securities market place where high standards of honor and integrity shall prevail, and to promote and maintain just and equitable principles of trade and business."

This constitution is written in the form of a binding contract which must be signed by all Exchange members.

There were 650 regular members of the American Stock Exchange at the beginning of 1966. A regular membership sold at a price of $120,000 in June, 1966. This price was the highest membership price paid in over thirty-five years.

The American Stock Exchange has provided for associate memberships as well as regular memberships. Associate members do not have floor trading privileges but do have the right to reduced commissions on Exchange transactions. Associate memberships totaled 228 at the beginning of 1966.

The Board of Governors of the American Stock Exchange is charged with setting over-all Exchange policy. This board consists of thirty-two persons including three individuals not engaged in any phase of the securities business. These representatives of the public are generally prominent businessmen, educators, or other representative citizens.

The daily administration and operation of the Exchange is directed by the president, who is assisted by a staff of vice presidents and other special officers.

AMERICAN STOCK EXCHANGE LISTING REQUIREMENTS. The listing requirements of the American Stock Exchange differ from those of the New York Stock Exchange. The American Stock Exchange has adopted the following minimum standards for the determination of whether an applicant will qualify for listing:

Size (Net Worth):
   The applicant must have net tangible assets of at least $1,000,000.
Earnings:
   The applicant must have net earnings of at least $150,000 after all charges, including federal income taxes, in the fiscal year immediately preceding the filing of the listing application, and net earnings averaging at least $100,000 for the past three fiscal years.

The fact that an applicant meets all of the specified criteria will not necessarily result in approval by the Board of Governors of the listing application. Moreover, in special situations an application may be approved even though the applicant does not meet all of the specified criteria.

Distribution of Common Stock Issues:

a) In the case of common stock issues, the Exchange requires a minimum public distribution of 250,000 shares (exclusive of the holdings of officers and directors and other concentrated or family holdings) among not less than 750 holders, of whom not less than 500 must be holders of lots of 100 shares or more.

b) The total number of publicly distributed shares of common stock must have a minimum aggregate market value of $1,250,000. In the case of issues selling below $5 per share the aggregate market value of the publicly held shares must be substantially in excess of the prescribed minimum of $1,250,000. Generally, this will be interpreted on the basis of requiring 100,000 more publicly distributed shares for each 50¢ below $5 per share at which a stock is selling at the time the listing application is filed.

A company listing on the American Stock Exchange must make certain financial data available at the time of listing and periodically thereafter. Among other things, a company listing on the American Stock Exchange agrees to:

1. Furnish independently audited annual reports and, during the year, quarterly statements of sales and earnings.
2. Publicize promptly and notify the exchange of any action regarding dividend payments or nonpayments.
3. Solicit proxies in conformance with SEC rules so that stockholders not only have the material they need for investment decisions but also have the means of registering their votes.
4. Seek stockholder approval before issuing additional shares for certain types of acquisitions or before granting stock options to officers, directors, or key employees.

DELISTING CRITERIA. Under delisting criteria adopted in 1964, issues may be considered for removal from trading if the company has not operated at a profit in one of the last three years; or if:

a. Shares publicly held, exclusive of management or other concentrated holdings, decline below 100,000 shares, or
b. Shareholders of record are less than 300, or if there are less than 200 holders of lots of 100 shares or more, or
c. The aggregate market value of shares publicly held, exclusive of management or other concentrated holdings, is less than $500,000.

UNLISTED TRADING PRIVILEGES. Security issues already fully listed on the New York Stock Exchange are on occasion admitted to unlisted trading privileges on one or more of the regional Exchanges.[11] A security issue

11The New York Stock Exchange abolished its unlisted trading in 1910. By November, 1966, 89 per cent of the issues traded on the American Stock Exchange were listed, and no new isues have been admitted to unlisted trading privileges there since 1946.

is said to have unlisted trading privileges on a stock exchange whenever the exchange authorities permit the securities to be traded on that exchange without having received an application from, or having made an agreement with, the issuer of the securities.

Unlisted trading privileges for any security must be approved by the SEC. The SEC grants approval if it finds such action is necessary or appropriate in the public interest or is essential for the protection of investors.

The American Stock Exchange is the principal center of exchange trading on an unlisted basis.

According to the SEC, the reported volume of trading on the exchanges, in 1964, in stock admitted to unlisted trading only, was about 24.5 million shares. This was about 1.2 per cent of the total share volume transacted on all of the exchanges.[12] Over 96 per cent of this 24.5 million shares of unlisted trading took place on the American Stock Exchange.

During the fiscal year ending June 30, 1965, sixty-three applications by exchanges for unlisted trading privileges in stocks listed on other exchanges were granted by the SEC.[13]

REGISTRATION OF AMERICAN STOCK EXCHANGE EMPLOYEES. No American Stock Exchange member, member firm, or member corporation may permit any person to perform regularly any of the duties normally performed by a registered employee until that person has been approved by and registered with the Exchange.

To be approved by the American Stock Exchange as a registered employee, an individual must have adequate training and experience in the securities business to qualify for the duties to be assumed. The American Stock Exchange feels that a minimum of six months' experience is necessary for full registration. Employees engaged solely in the sale of mutual funds require only limited registration. Limited registration calls for a minimum of one month's intensive training in mutual funds. Employees approved by the Exchange for registration on a limited basis must become fully registered within six months of the date of limited registration approval. Registered employees of American Stock Exchange firms may not be employed on a part-time basis but must devote their entire time during business hours to the affairs of their member employer.

All prospective registered employees are required to pass an examination designed to test their qualifications. Questions in the examinations cover the following areas:

1. Conduct of the registered representative.

[12]31st Annual Report of the Securities and Exchange Commission, United States Government Printing Office, 1966, Washington, D.C.
[13]Ibid.

2. Fundamentals of securities.
3. Securities markets and firms.
4. Investment companies.

A study guide, giving an outline of the subject matter covered in the examinations, is available from the American Stock Exchange, 86 Trinity Place, New York City, New York 10006. The American Stock Exchange examination for prospective registered representatives is fully coordinated with the NASD examination. This also applies to the Pacific Coast Stock Exchange examination.

REVIEW QUESTIONS

1. What are the main functions and services of the organized securities exchanges?

2. On what basis do the organized exchanges work? How do they differ from the over-the-counter market?

3. What are the five types of brokers or dealers on the New York Stock Exchange?

4. Describe in some detail two important roles of a specialist on the New York Stock Exchange.

5. What is meant by the term "$2.00 broker" on the New York Stock Exchange?

6. Describe the function of the odd lot dealer on the New York Stock Exchange.

7. Assume a customer gives a broker an order to *buy* 10 shares of Continental Can. The next round lot trade after the order arrives on the floor is $42\frac{1}{2}$. At what price would the odd lot purchase take place?

8. Define and distinguish between: G.T.C. order, Day order, Week order, and stop or stop loss order.

9. When is selling short not permitted? At what price in the following sequence could a short sale be made: $47\frac{7}{8}$, $47\frac{3}{4}$, $47\frac{5}{8}$, $47\frac{3}{4}$, and $47\frac{5}{8}$?

10. Essentially, what is the main advantage of the M.I.P. plan?

11. What are the most important self-regulatory activities of the New York Stock Exchange?

12. Name three minimum standards for initial listing on the New York Stock Exchange. Are there any other considerations? What about delisting?

13. What are the important qualifications of requirements to be a registered representative on the New York Stock Exchange?

14. Contrast the American Stock Exchange with the New York Stock Exchange in regard to trading volume, listing requirements, membership, and administration.

The National Association of Securities Dealers, Inc.

Chapter 13

The National Association of Securities Dealers, Inc., is a registered national securities association. It was created pursuant to the provisions of federal law to adopt, administer, and enforce rules of fair practice in connection with over-the-counter securities transactions.

The NASD became a registered national securities association in August, 1939. It was organized under the Maloney Act, an amendment (Sec. 15 A) to the Securities Exchange Act of 1934.

The Maloney Act provides for the registration with the Securities and Exchange Commission of national securities associations and establishes standards for such associations. According to the act, the rules of these associations must be designed to promote just and equitable principles of trade and to meet other statutory requirements. The act also empowers these associations to require their members to maintain high standards of commercial honor.

The National Association of Securities Dealers, Inc., is the only association registered under the Maloney Act.

The act calls for the NASD to function as "a mechanism of regulation among over-the-counter brokers and dealers operating in interstate and foreign commerce or through the mails."

The Securities and Exchange Commission supervises the NASD operations. The SEC is authorized to review all disciplinary actions and decisions of the Association. It has the right to review the action taken on applications for membership and also to review any changes which are made in the rules of the NASD.

Legislative Background of the Maloney Act

Congressional hearings and reports on the Maloney Act make it clear that the NASD is intended to have the power to regulate the over-the-counter market in a manner comparable to the power of an Exchange to regulate the Exchange markets and members.

The SEC has indicated its belief that the NASD is authorized to exercise Exchange-type powers and controls and to establish *ethical* as well as legal standards.

The Congressional Committee that considered and reported favorably on the proposed Maloney Amendment clearly expressed the problem the amendment was intended to meet and the type of association needed to control the problem. In the committee report it was noted that:

> The problem of regulation of the over-the-counter markets has three aspects: First, to protect the investor and the honest dealer alike from dishonest and unfair practices by the submarginal element in this industry; second, to cope with those methods of doing business which, while technically outside the area of definite illegality, are nevertheless unfair both to customer and to decent competitor, and are seriously damaging to the mechanism of the free and open market; and, third, to afford to the investor an economic service the efficiency of which will be commensurate with its economic importance so that the machinery of the nation's markets will operate to avoid the misdirection of the nation's savings, which contributes powerfully toward economic depressions and breeds distrust of our financial processes.
>
> The Committee believes that there are two alternative programs by which this problem could be met. The first would involve a pronounced expansion of the organization of the Securities and Exchange Commission; . . . and a minute, detailed, and rigid regulation of business conduct by law. It might very well mean expanding the present process of registration of brokers and dealers with the Commission to include the prescription not only of the dishonest, but also of those unwilling or unable to conform to rigid standards of financial responsibility, professional conduct and technical proficiency.
>
> The second of these alternative programs which the committee believes distinctly preferable to the first . . . is based upon the cooperative regulation, in which the task will be largely performed by representative organizations of investment bankers, dealers, and brokers, with the Government exercising supplementary powers of direct regulation. In the concept of a really well organized and well conducted stock exchange, under the supervision provided by the Securities Exchange Act of 1934, one may perceive something of the possibilities of such a program.[1]

George C. Mathews, who as an SEC Commissioner testified in favor of the Maloney Amendment on behalf of the Commission, stated in his testimony:

> There is a vast field for the control of ethical practices in this business, which is not a field which the government can very well occupy. An association of this sort, if it is successful, must be able to control the practices of its members which, in the language of the stock exchange rules, are inconsistent with just and equitable principles of trading. I think if we have

[1]Securities Exchange Act Release No. 3734, September 14, 1945.

any hope that the securities business is to be put on that high professional plane, we must look to help from within the industry and I think, organized help.

. . . the bill . . . provides for voluntary associations, which it is hoped, will largely take over the problem of regulation of the business, subject to the safeguards which I shall later point out. . . .

I think that associations of this sort, if they are comprehensive enough and vigorous enough, can go a long way, although I do not expect that they will reach perfection, in assuring that people who are their members, and perhaps to some extent in assuring that others in the securities business have a proper standard of financial responsibility.[2]

NASD Rules Stress Ethical as Well as Legal Conduct

Through the NASD, the over-the-counter securities market is regulated in a way that would be difficult, if not impossible, to accomplish under straight governmental control. Government regulations generally concern themselves with the *legality* or *illegality* of a particular situation or action. The ethical conduct of the individual or of an organization, as contrasted to legal conduct, is generally considered outside the scope of governmental supervision.

The NASD is able to enforce ethical as well as legal standards among its members. Ethical standards are enforced by the simple method of denying membership in the association to any broker/dealer operating in an unethical or improper manner. Generally, loss of NASD membership prevents a broker/dealer from operating profitably in the over-the-counter securities market. Thus through the Association a more sensitive type of control can be exercised than would be possible under direct SEC supervision.

In adopting the legislation under which the NASD was organized, the Congress permitted the Association to adopt rules which, among other things, preclude a member firm from dealing with a nonmember firm except on the same terms and conditions as the member firm deals with the investing public. These rules were provided by the Congress as an incentive to membership in national securities associations. *More important, however, is the fact that these rules are essential and basic to the effective enforcement of ethical standards by the NASD.*

Because of these rules, membership in the NASD is a prerequisite to profitable participation in almost all underwriting and most over-the-counter trading. Only association members have the advantages of price concessions, discounts, and similar allowances. Loss or denial of membership in the NASD due to unethical business practices thus imposes a severe economic sanction on an organization.

2Ibid.

The Functions and
Objectives of the NASD

The NASD was originally established for the purpose of co-operating with the government in its efforts to prevent improper trans-actions in the securities business. To help provide effective guides to its operation, the NASD has indicated the functions it expects to perform and has formulated the objectives it hopes to attain. In the NASD Certificate of Incorporation, the Association's functions and objectives are indicated as follows:

1. To promote through cooperative effort the investment banking and securities business, standardize its principles and practices, promote high standards of commercial honor, and observance of federal and state securities laws.
2. To provide a medium through which its membership may be enabled to confer, consult, and cooperate with governmental and other agencies in the solution of problems affecting investors, the public, and the investment banking and securities business.
3. To adopt, administer, and enforce rules of fair practice and rules to prevent fraudulent and manipulative acts and practices, and in general to promote just and equitable principles of trade for the protection of investors.
4. To promote self-discipline among members, and to investigate and adjust grievances between the public and association members, and between association members themselves.

Geographical Division

Geographically, the NASD is divided into thirteen districts. Since over-the-counter securities transactions take place all over the country, the NASD has established district offices in many cities; they are presently located in: San Francisco, Los Angeles, Denver, Kansas City, Dallas, St. Louis, Chicago, Atlanta, New Orleans, Seattle, Cleveland, Washington, Philadelphia, New York, and Boston.

District Committees

A District Committe in each district acts as the agent for the Board of Governors in that area. This committee's main job is to provide sound local administration of the Association's affairs. These District Committees are elected by the membership in each district. Each individual on the District Committee is elected for a three-year term and, as a general rule, does not succeed himself.

Board of Governors

The Board of Governors, comprised of twenty-three members, administers and manages the affairs of the Association. Overall policy-making functions of the Association are granted to the board, and it has full power to act on behalf of the Association in most matters.

In the exercise of its powers, the Board of Governors may:

1. adopt, for submission to the membership, any new Bylaws or Rules of Fair Practice, or any changes or additions to existing Bylaws or Rules of Fair Practice that it deems necessary or appropriate
2. make any regulations, issue any orders, resolutions, interpretations and directions, and make any decisions that it deems necessary or appropriate
3. prescribe maximum penalties for violations of the provisions of the bylaws or the rules and regulations of the corporation; or for neglecting or refusing to comply with orders, directions, and decisions of the Board of Governors or any duly authorized NASD Committee.

Each district is represented on the Board of Governors by one or more members who are elected for a three-year term by the membership in the district they represent.

Both the Board of Governors and the District Committees have the right to hold meetings whenever they feel it is necessary. Also, action may be taken by mail, telephone, or telegraphic vote.

Members of the Board of Governors and District Committees do not receive any pay for the work they do for the Association. However, they are reimbursed for any out-of-pocket expenses incurred by them in the affairs of the Association. Without this voluntary contribution of time and effort on the part of the many elected board members and committee members, the Association could not operate.

Executive Committee

An executive committee created by the Board of Governors acts on its behalf in the period between meetings. Any disciplinary action of this committee, however, is not binding until approved by the board.

Officers of NASD are elected by the Board of Governors. The Board of Governors elects a chairman, one or more vice chairmen, and such other officers as it deems appropriate. Such officers may be removed at any time if twelve members of the board vote for their removal.

Chief Executive Officer and Other Administrative Personnel

The board selects a chief executive officer who is the principal administrative officer of the Association. The bylaws also authorize the board to employ counsel and hire any other paid officers it deems necessary. The chief executive officer is designated as president of the NASD corporation. The compensation of these administrative personnel is determined by the board.

District Committees, subject to the approval of the Board of Governors, may employ a district secretary and such other employees as are necessary and appropriate. Employment and compensation of these employees is at the pleasure of the Board of Governors.

Advisory Council

An Advisory Council, composed of the chairmen of the thirteen District Committees, aids the board in making policy relating to local problems. The Advisory Council is required to attend at least one meeting of the Board of Governors annually. District Chairmen are invited to participate freely in board meetings but are not permitted to vote. The main purpose of this Advisory Council is to help the board provide the best possible administration at the district level.

District Business Conduct Committees

Each district must appoint a District Business Conduct Committee. This committee has the major burden of enforcing the Association's Rules of Fair Practice.

At least one member of the District Business Conduct Committee must be a member of the District Committee itself. Actually, it is the general practice in all districts for the District Committee itself also to function as the District Business Conduct Committee.

When conditions make it necessary, the District Committee also appoints a number of Local Business Conduct Committees which function as subcommittees.

Primary responsibility for enforcement of the Association's ethical standards rests with the thirteen District Business Conduct Committees.

In carrying out their duty of determining conformance with the Association's rules and bylaws, these committees are authorized to examine the books, records, and business practices of member firms. These duties are assigned to examiners employed on the Association's staff.

Branch Offices

A branch office of an Association member is an office, other than the main office, located in the United States which is owned or controlled by the member and which is engaged in the investment banking or securities business.

Members are required to notify the NASD Board of Governors immediately upon opening or closing any branch office. All branch offices of an Association member must be registered with the NASD, and a fee must be paid for each branch office.

The NASD Board of Governors has established a number of standards for use in determining whether an office of a member firm or the operations of one or more of its registered representatives or principals constitutes a branch office operation and consequently require registration as a branch office.

In determining whether an office or the activities of a person associated with a member in an area constitutes a branch office of a member, the following standards shall be used:

1. It shall be considered a branch office if the member directly or indirectly contributes a substantial portion of the operating expenses of any place used by a person associated with a member who is engaged in the investment banking or securities business, whether it be commercial office space or a residence. Operating expenses, for purposes of this standard, shall include items normally associated with the cost of operating the business, such as rent and taxes.
2. It shall be considered a branch office if the member authorizes a listing in any publication or any other media, including a professional dealer's digest or a telephone directory, which listing designates a place as an office or if the member designates any such place with an organization as an office.

A branch office is not an "office of supervisory jurisdiction" unless it has been designated as such and has had specified supervisory activities assigned to it under the member's written procedures. If an office falls within the definition of both an office of supervisory jurisdiction, and a branch office, it must be designated to the NASD in each category.

Limited Liability of the Association

No officer, employee or member of the Board of Governors or District Committees is permitted to incur any liability larger than the amount specifically authorized or appropriated by the board, nor is anyone permitted to commit the Association for any charitable or political party or candidate.

No member shall use the name of the corporation on letterheads, circulars or other advertising matter or literature except to the extent authorized by the Board of Governors.

Changes in NASD Rules and Bylaws

While only the Board of Governors can propose changes in the Rules of Fair Practice, proposals for changes in the Association's bylaws may be made by:

a. A petition signed by any twenty-five member firms
b. A resolution of any District Committee
c. Any member of the Board of Governors

The Association members vote by secret ballot on each such proposal in order to indicate their approval or disapproval.

Changes in the bylaws and rules of the Association require a majority vote of the members and a majority of those voting must approve.

NASD Membership

Membership in the Association is open to all properly qualified brokers and dealers, whose regular course of business consists in actually transacting any branch of the investment banking or securities business in the United States under the laws of any state or the laws of the United States.

For NASD membership purposes, any individual, corporation, partnership, association, joint stock company, business trust, unincorporated organization or other legal entity is a

a. "broker" if engaged in the business of effecting transactions in securities for the account of others but does not include a bank.
b. "dealer" if engaged in the business of buying and selling securities for his own account through a broker or otherwise but does not include a bank or any person who buys or sells securities for his own account other than as part of a regular business.

Banks by definition are not broker/dealers and thus are not eligible for membership in the association.

WHO MAY NOT BECOME A MEMBER OF THE NASD. Not everyone wishing to engage in buying and selling securities is eligible for membership in the NASD.

One of the main purposes of the NASD has always been to promote high standards of commercial honor in the securities business. Obviously, with this basic objective, anyone convicted of a violation of the federal or state securities laws is barred from NASD membership, unless admittance is directed by the SEC.

Broker/dealers are denied NASD membership under the following conditions, unless the Securities and Exchange Commission specifically approves and orders such membership:

1. A broker/dealer who has been expelled from a registered securities association or from a registered national securities exchange for acts inconsistent with just and equitable principles of trade.
2. A broker/dealer whose registration with the Securities and Exchange Commission has been revoked or denied.
3. An individual who has been named a "cause" of a suspension,

expulsion or revocation, or one whose registration as a registered representative has been revoked by the Association or by a registered national securities exchange.

4. An individual who has been convicted within the preceding ten years of any crime:

   a. arising out of the securities business
   b. involving embezzlement
   c. involving fraudulent conversion
   d. involving misappropriation of funds
   e. involving the abuse or misuse of a fiduciary relationship.

5. A broker/dealer with any partner, officer, or employee who is not qualified for membership under any of the limitations of the bylaws of the Association.

6. A broker/dealer with officers, partners, or employees who are required to be registered representatives, but who have not become registered representatives.

Broker/dealers must be registered with the SEC and with state authorities if required by the law, in order to be eligible for membership in the NASD.

How to Become a Member of the NASD

It is a relatively simple matter to apply for membership in the National Association of Securities Dealers. Any broker or dealer desiring to join who is *lawfully* engaged in the investment banking or securities business may do so by completing and filing the necessary forms[3] and paying the necessary fees. Requests for the necessary forms should be addressed to:

> The National Association of Securities Dealers, Inc.
> 888 17th Street N.W.
> Washington, D. C. 20006.

When the Association sends the forms to the applicant, they also forward information about the obligations of membership. All NASD applicants are urged to read this material carefully.

The completed forms should be returned to the NASD office in Washington, D.C., for processing.

After admission to membership, the applicant will be billed for the assessment and branch office fees.

The Association warns new applicants that the above-mentioned forms must be completed with care. They will be returned for correction if they are not in order. This will delay the admission of an applicant to membership.

The forms indicated above, which applicants for membership must

[3]Specimen copies of these forms are shown in the appendix.

sign, contain a membership agreement. This membership agreement states that all applicants, if accepted, must abide by the bylaws and all other rules and regulations of the Association. Applicants also must agree to be bound by any ruling, directive or decision of, or penalty imposed by the Board of Governors or any duly authorized committee.

Processing of Applications

Membership applications are processed initially by the District Committee of the Association in the district in which the applicant is located. After the appropriate District Committee has decided that the applicant is lawfully engaged in the securities business and is eligible for membership, the committee recommends that admission to membership be granted.

If the District Committee denies membership to an applicant for any reason, he is notified of his ineligibility as promptly as possible and he is given an opportunity for a hearing before the District Committee. During this hearing the applicant is given a chance to discuss the specific grounds of disqualification which are barring his acceptance. A record is kept of this hearing. If a majority of the District Committee members feel the applicant is unqualified for membership, they send their negative recommendation (citing specific reasons) along with the record of the hearing to the Board of Governors. The Board of Governors, after reviewing the application and offering the applicant an opportunity for a hearing before a subcommittee of the board, either admits the applicant to membership or upholds the decision of the District Committee, whichever the circumstances justify.

If the board concurs with the District Committee and denies membership to the applicant, it must set forth in writing its specific reasons for disapproving the application.

After being turned down for membership by both the District Committee and the Board of Governors the applicant, if he still feels he is qualified, may appeal the decision. Provision is made in the law for an appeal to the SEC for an additional review. Thus, every effort is made to assure that all qualified broker/dealers seeking admission to NASD membership are granted admission.

Once admitted, the rights of membership may not be transferred from one organization to another, except in the case of change of name or merger.

SEC Broker or Dealer Registration

In addition to the filing of the above NASD forms, all NASD broker/dealers operating in interstate commerce are required to file a registration form with the SEC. This form, known as Form BD, is required in connection with registration under the Securities Exchange Act of 1934.

Form BD must be executed and filed, in duplicate, with the Securities and Exchange Commission, Washington, D.C., 20549. This form is customarily included by the NASD when it sends application forms to firms applying for Association membership. Registration with the SEC is required before NASD membership can be granted.

All broker/dealers operating in interstate commerce who are not members of the NASD are required to register with the SEC by filing forms SECO-2 and SECO-3. These forms may be obtained from the Securities and Exchange Commission, Washington, D.C., 20549. Specimen copies of these forms are shown in the appendix.

Broker/dealers operating entirely in intrastate commerce are not required to file with the SEC. Practically all broker/dealers doing business in the United States, however, do operate in interstate commerce. One reason for this fact is that any broker/dealer using the U.S. mail is classified for SEC purposes as a firm operating in interstate commerce.

Every broker or dealer filing the SEC application for registration must file with it, in duplicate, a statement of financial condition. This required financial statement must cover in detail the nature and amount of assets and liabilities and the net worth of the broker or dealer filing. Any securities in which the filing broker or dealer has an interest must be listed on a separate schedule. On this schedule the securities must be valued at the market as of a date within thirty days of the date on which the schedule is filed.

Brokers or dealers desiring to keep confidential the information provided on the above schedule of securities should bind the schedule of securities separate from the rest of their financial statement. Duly authorized persons, however, will have access to the schedule of securities regardless of its confidential nature.

Attached to the financial statement must be an oath or affirmation that such statement is true and correct to the best knowledge and belief of the person making the oath or affirmation. The oath or affirmation must be administered by a duly authorized person, for example, a notary public.

If the broker or dealer is a sole proprietorship, the oath or affirmation shall be made by the proprietor; if a partnership, by a general partner; if a corporation, by a duly authorized officer.

Assessment, Dues, Finances

The Association's bylaws provide for assessments annually by the Board of Governors to cover operating expenses. The board estimates each year how much money it will need to carry on the work of the Association. On the basis of this estimate, they determine the dues and charges to be assessed against the members.

Assessment rates for the fiscal year beginning on October 1, 1966 are as follows:

Basic assessment	$85.00
Personnel assessment to be determined upon the number of individuals in each member's organization as of June 30, 1966, or as of the date of application for membership after June 30, 1966	$ 4.50
Assessment on gross income, as defined for assessment purposes, for the year ended June 30, 1966	0.075%
The maximum assessment for any one member shall not exceed $15,000.[4]	

Assessment Instructions and Definitions

PERSONNEL Assessable personnel of a member of the Association includes an individual proprietor, partners, officers, registered representatives and other employees (including, but not limited to, bookkeepers, stenographers, typists, etc.) of the principal office and all branch offices who devote any time whatsoever to the over-the-counter securities business. Exclude only those persons who devote *all* of their time to:

1. Transactions in "exempted securities"[5]
2. Transactions executed on a registered national securities exchange and are employed by a member of such exchange; and
3. Commodities, insurance and other types of business that are not part of the over-the-counter securities business.

Affiliated organizations, such as a corporation and its subsidiary or a partnership and corporation controlled by the partnership, which are members of the Association and have the identical personnel or substantial duplications should report such personnel on only one member's assessment report to avoid duplication of personnel assessments. A brief explanation of the method of reporting, including the number of personnel dually employed by both members, should be noted on the assessment report of each member.

GROSS INCOME. Gross income from over-the-counter transactions in securities is defined for assessment purposes as the gross dollar amount of profits, commissions, concessions, fees, discounts, allowances and other income subject

[4]The fees and assessments charged by the NASD change from time to time. Consequently, the assessments schedule and the other fees and assessments given in this chapter must be regarded only as approximations.

[5]The term "exempted securities," as defined in Section 3 (a) (12) of the Securities Exchange Act of 1934, means those securities which are direct obligations of or are obligations guaranteed as to principal or interest by the United States, States, political subdivisions and municipalities or their agencies or instrumentalities.

to deductions and exclusions listed below but without any deductions for salaries, wages or other operating and overhead expenses.

INCLUDE in the amount to be reported as gross income:
Profits and/or commissions from principal and agency transactions; from over-the-counter transactions in listed securities; from participations in distributions as underwriters or as members of selling groups; from private placement fees; from proportionate interests in joint trading accounts; from transactions cleared through other firms acting as clearing agents; from transactions in warrants, rights, options, bonds and stocks; and from sales of shares of investment companies, including contractual plans, real estate investment trusts and real estate syndicates.

Gross income from sales of shares of investment companies shall include gross income from any shares repurchased and later redistributed and from sales of shares by said member represented by reinvestment of income dividends. In any case where gross income, net of deductions described below, from sales of investment company shares by a member acting as sponsor or underwriter (excluding sales to another member who is an underwriter or sponsor of a contractual plan for such shares) is less than 1.75% of such sales, then this amount shall be included as the minimum amount of gross income for the purpose of the assessment.

Profits from transactions in securities held primarily for sale to customers and other broker-dealers may be determined and may reflect profits and losses from inventory valuations on the basis shown by the member's books of account provided that the method of reporting is consistent from year to year.

DEDUCTIONS from the amount to be reported:
Any commissions, concessions or other allowances paid to another member in connection with the execution or clearance of such transactions. For example, a member acting as a clearing agent for another member shall deduct from its gross income net amounts allowed to the non-clearing member. The non-clearing member shall include in gross income the amount of such allowances.

Losses from underwritings and over-the-counter trading transactions (as opposed to transactions in investments referred to in the last item under "Exclusions") may be deducted from under-writing and trading profits to the extent of such profits but not in excess thereof.

EXCLUSIONS from the amount to be reported:
Interest and dividends.

Advisory fees, investment management fees and finders' fees not directly involving the offering of securities, proxy fees, vault service fees, safekeeping fees and transfer fees.

Commissions derived from transactions executed on a registered national securities exchange or a foreign securities exchange.

Profits or losses derived from transactions of which *both* the purchase and sale are executed on a registered national securities exchange or outside the territorial limits of the United States.

Profits and losses derived from transactions in "exempted securities" (see Note).

Profits and losses derived from transactions in commercial bank time certificates of deposit and commercial paper, which is defined to include drafts, bills of exchange, and bankers acceptances having maturities at the time of issuance of not exceeding one year.

Profits and losses derived from transactions in securities held for investment purposes, which are described in Section 1236 of the Internal Revenue Code as those securities designated within 30 days of acquisition and clearly identified in the dealer's records as being held specifically for investment and not primarily for sale to customers in the ordinary course of business.

Other fees established for the same period consist of the following:

1. Filing fee for each new membership application $150.00
2. Registration fee for each application for registration of a registered representative $ 30.00
3. Examination fee for each individual required to take the qualification examination for registration as a principal. This is in addition to the registration fee $ 25.00
4. Examination fee for each individual required to take the qualification examination for registration as a registered representative. This is in addition ot the registration fee. $ 20.00
5. Annual fee for each registered branch office $ 30.00

Assessments are levied on an annual basis.

The dues and assessment schedule is filed with the Securities and Exchange Commission each July for the coming fiscal year. The Commission may disapprove the schedule if it finds it does not provide an equitable allocation of costs among the member firms.

Member firms are required to furnish promptly all information and reports needed by the Board of Governors to determine member firm assessments and other charges. Membership in the Association may be suspended or cancelled for nonpayment of dues, assessments, or other charges or for failure to provide the information needed to determine such dues and other charges. Member firms are not liable for any fees or assessments greater than those set in advance by the board for that particular year.

As soon as practicable after the end of the fiscal year, the board is required to send each member firm a statement of receipts and disbursements for the fiscal year.

State Registration Forms and Information

Information about the securities laws and regulations of any particular state can be secured by contacting the proper state authority. Such information, and the forms needed for registering in the state as a securities broker or dealer, or as a securities agent, or securities salesman can be obtained by contacting the appropriate office indicated on pages 293–298.

Rules of Fair Practice

The NASD Board of Governors under Article VII of the Association's bylaws has adopted, and the members have approved, a series of regulations called the Rules of Fair Practice. These rules are designed to promote and enforce just and equitable principles of trade in the securities business. The Rules of Fair Practice constitute a guide to members in the ethical conduct of their business as distinguished from the legal conduct of business.

The NASD Board of Governors is empowered to make and issue interpretations of all Rules of Fair Practice. The board also determines procedures with respect to complaints of violation of the rules and prescribes the penalties for such violations.

NASD Member Firm Examinations

The NASD is required by law to enforce its own rules and regulations. In order to carry out this required program of enforcement, the Association makes periodic examinations of member firm books and records. Through these examinations the NASD strives to accomplish three basic objectives:

First, to uncover any unethical business practices or violations of the Association's rules by member firms or their employees.

Second, to obtain statistical information which will be useful to the Association and its member firms.

Third, to pursue the educational phases of its work.

In addition to its periodic examinations, special examinations are conducted, when needed, to obtain information about specific situations or complaints.

Examinations are carried out by a corps of trained examiners. The Association has expanded its corps of examiners so as to permit an annual examination of one-third of the membership.

METHOD OF EXAMINATION. NASD examination methods today are standardized. An established routine is followed by all Association examiners.

Examinations are conducted on a surprise basis. The NASD examiners walk into the office of member firms without notifying the firm of the impending visit. The examiners begin by interviewing the proprietor, or principal officer or partner of the firm. During this interview, the examiners seek information about the member firm's operating policies and the type of securities business being conducted by the firm.

An examination report form is used by the examiners. This form provides an outline for the conduct of the examination. It also is useful as a basis for the compilation of valuable statistical information.

Some of the items covered in the report form are:
1. The proportion of the member's business concerned with:
   a. underwriting new issues
   b. the sale of unlisted securities
   c. transactions in listed securities
   d. transactions in municipal securities
   e. the sale of investment company shares
2. Other business activities, if any, of the member, such as the sale of real estate or insurance
3. The number of branch offices
4. The firm's memberships, if any, on registered securities exchanges.

ITEMS COVERED BY EXAMINATION. During the examination the following items are among those checked by the NASD examiners:

1. The commissions charged to customers by the member firm
2. The pricing policies of the member firm

Member's transactions are reviewed to determine whether pricing policies are fair and reasonable and are generally in accord with the NASD's 5 per cent markup policy.

3. The adequacy of the firm's supervision of the sales methods of its salesmen

An examination is made to determine whether or not the member firm has properly endorsed all transactions conducted by its salesmen, and reviewed all correspondence by salesmen with customers.

Association examiners also check compliance with the rules requiring written confirmation containing certain disclosures to customers.

4. The records kept by the member firm

The examiners check to determine whether all required records are kept and properly maintained.

Recently, in certain districts, this has become a very serious problem, due to the increasing number of newly formed companies with inexperienced personnel.

5. The advertising policy of the member firm:

Since 1955, member firms have been required to maintain a file of all published material. This file is inspected by examiners to determine whether the material conforms to the NASD requirement that it shall not be misleading or contain flamboyant statements or employ "come-on" techniques.

When the individual member firm's type of operation makes such an examination appropriate, the following items are also checked:

1. The adequacy of the member firm's controls for safekeeping customers' securities accounts when customers' securities are in the members' possession.

Checks are made to assure that customers' securities are segregated from any securities belonging to members.

2. The transaction activity of the customers' accounts in which

the member firm has been given discretionary authority to effect transactions.

Examiners here look for evidence of "churning" or excessive "switching" of customers' investments from one security to another.

If the association's examiners uncover any evidence of overactivity when they sample the firm's transactions, a detailed analysis of such overactivity is compiled and presented to the appropriate Business Conduct Committee for its consideration.

3. The amount and conditions of member firm borrowing in order to determine whether securities belonging to customers have been improperly used as collateral against such borrowings.
4. The member firm's compliance with the board's "free-riding" policy in the case of member firm's handling new securities offerings.
5. The member firm's compliance with the SEC's Statement of Policy regarding investment company sales literature, which the Association administers for its members.
6. The amount and conditions of credit extended by member firms to customers.

Examiners check members' compliance with Regulation T of the Federal Reserve Board which imposes restrictions on the extension of credit by brokers and dealers to customers.

7. The compliance of member firms with federal and state requirements to affix or cancel the appropriate amount of sales or transfer tax stamps to cover specified securities transactions.
8. Member firms' relations with nonmember firms.

Examiners review books and records to determine whether any commissions or discounts have been paid to individuals not properly registered with the association, or whether members improperly have joined with nonmember broker/dealers in the distribution of a security.

In determining compliance with Association rules, any Association examiner duly authorized by the executive director, or by an appropriate Association committee, may require members to submit reports in writing with regard to a matter connected with any such member's business or business practices and may inspect the books, records, and accounts of members.

The NASD examinations do not involve a complete audit of its members' books. However, they do cover nearly all phases of the securities activities of the member firm and in the opinion of the District Committees and the Board of Governors are adequate to determine whether or not the member firm's conduct is ethical and proper.

Complaints

In the past the most frequent causes of complaints against member firms have been violations of NASD rules, in this order:

1. The basic ethical conduct rule (Section I of article III)
2. Rule requiring members to deal fairly with customers when marking up securities (Section 4)
3. Rule prohibiting fraudulent manipulative or deceptive activities (Section 18)
4. Rule prohibiting the misuse of customers' funds and securities (Section 19)
5. Rule relating to the keeping of books and records (Section 21)
6. Rules requiring certain disclosures on confirmations to customers (Section 12)
7. Rule relating to the supervision of employees (Section 27)
8. Rule relating to the propriety of recommendations for the purchase or sale of securities to or for customers (Section 2)

The amount of formal enforcement work has increased materially in recent years due to the rapid NASD membership growth. The fact that public interest in securities has widened has further contributed to the NASD enforcement task.

In addition to any improper practices of NASD member firms that may be uncovered by the Association's examination program, the Association learns of infractions of its rules and regulations in other ways. For example, the SEC as a matter of policy refers to the NASD any violations of the Association's rules disclosed by *its* inspection program which do not indicate fraudulent activities sufficient to warrant revocation proceedings by the Commission. In addition, complaints against member firms or their registered representatives received from various other sources by the NASD help it determine which member firms are violating the Association's standards. Charges of violations of one or more of the Rules of Fair Practice of the Association form the basis for these complaints.

When some evidence exists that an Association rule violation may have taken place, the District Business Conduct Committee may authorize an examination of members' books and records to determine whether a complaint should be filed. The committee also may require members to submit reports in writing on any matter involved in any investigation. Failures or refusal to supply such requested information is considered sufficient cause for suspending or canceling the membership of such members.

WHO MAY FILE COMPLAINTS. Complaints for violation of the Association's rules may be filed with District Committees by:

1. Any member of the public
2. Any member of the NASD
3. District Committees or the Board of Governors of the NASD

No member of the Board of Governors or any District Business Conduct Committee is permitted to participate in the determination of any complaint affecting his personal interest or the interests of any person in whom he is directly or indirectly interested. Where such interest is involved, the member must disqualify himself, or must be disqualified by the chairman of the board or committee.

CODE OF PROCEDURE FOR HANDLING TRADE PRACTICE COMPLAINTS. A code of procedure has been adopted by the NASD to govern the handling of complaints received by the Association. The procedure indicated in this code is followed regardless of the source of the complaint.

When a complaint is filed, on a form supplied by the Board of Governors, it must specify in reasonable detail the nature of the charges being made and the rule or rules allegedly violated by the member firm or its registered representatives.

NASD member firms and registered representatives are entitled to receive notice of the specific charge against them whenever a complaint is filed. Notification of any such charges are sent to the member as soon as possible after they are received by the District Business Conduct Committee.

WRITTEN ANSWER REQUIRED. Within ten business days after the accused member firm (respondent) is notified of the charges, he must file a written answer to these charges with the appropriate District Business Conduct Committee. If the respondent fails to answer within the prescribed ten business days, a second notice of the charges is sent, which must be answered within five business days. If the respondent fails to answer this second notice of charges, the committee may consider the allegations of the complaint as admitted by the respondent.

RIGHT OF HEARING. Any member firm or registered representative charged with a violation of the Association's rules is entitled to a hearing before the appropriate District Business Conduct Committee. At this hearing, respondents and complainants are entitled to be heard both by counsel and in person.

District Business Conduct Committees may authorize examination of members' book and records for the purpose of any hearing or any complaint.

Communications to the District Business Conduct Committees with respect to complaints against members are not privileged communications and may be considered in acting on complaints.

When all the evidence has been presented and the record completed, a decision is rendered by the proper District Committee. If it is found that the member firm has, in fact, violated the Association's rules, one or more penalties may be imposed.

A record must be kept of all hearings. Any determination reached in connection with a complaint must be by written decision and must set forth the specific findings of the committee.

These specific findings must include:

1. Any improper act or practice which the member has committed
2. The specific rule of the Association which the member is deemed to have violated by the act or practice, or omission to act
3. Whether the acts or practices of the member are deemed to constitute conduct inconsistent with just and equitable principles of trade
4. The penalty imposed

If the committee finds that no violation has occurred, the allegations are dismissed.

PENALTIES. Penalties which may be imposed on NASD member firms or their registered representatives or principals for violation of the rules are prescribed by the Board of Governors.

The penalties imposed may be one or more of the following:

1. Expulsion of the member firm from the NASD or revocation of the registration of any person associated with the member.
2. Suspension of the firm's membership or suspension, for a definite period, of the registration of a person associated with the member.
3. Censure of the member or any person associated with a member.
4. Imposition of a fine not in excess of $1,000 upon any member or person associated with a member.
5. Barring an NASD member firm or any person associated with that firm from associating with any other NASD member.

The seriousness of the violation committed by the member will, of course, determine the type of penalty imposed.

Expulsion from the Association is the most severe disciplinary action within the power of the NASD. This is true because, as noted, only Association members have the advantages of receiving price concessions, discounts, and similar allowances from other members. Loss of NASD membership prevents a broker/dealer from operating a profitable general securities business.

DECISION MAY BE APPEALED. Provision is made for appeal from a decision of a District Business Conduct Committee to the NASD Board of Governors. This appeal must be filed within fifteen days of the date of the decision. Should no appeal be filed by the member, the board can review the case on its own motion. Any review of a decision by the board on its own motion must be ordered within thirty days of the date of the decision.

In the review before the Board of Governors the parties again may appear and be heard by counsel and in person. After reviewing all of the admissible evidence, the board renders a written decision.

As a result of its review the board can:

1. Concur in the decision
2. Increase the penalty
3. Reduce the penalty
4. Modify the decision
5. Cancel the action taken
6. Remand the case to the appropriate Business Conduct Committee with instructions for further proceedings

The final decision by the Board of Governors concerning a disciplinary case may be appealed to the Securities and Exchange Commission. The SEC may concur in the decision or modify it but may not increase the penalty assessed.

Any action taken by the SEC concerning these cases may be appealed to the federal courts, up to the United States Supreme Court.

A penalty imposed by the NASD does not become effective until after the expiration of all periods of appeal or review.

NOTIFICATION OF EXPULSION OR SUSPENSION. When a member is suspended or expelled from the Association or becomes ineligible for further Association membership because of expulsion or suspension from a national securities exchange, notice must be sent forthwith to all members of the Association.

When a member firm is found to be ineligible for continuation in NASD membership, provision is made in the law for an appeal to the SEC.

The expelled firm may file a petition seeking review by the Securities and Exchange Commission of the decision to expel it by the Board of Governors. Filing this petition results in an automatic stay of the expulsion order of the Board of Governors. The expulsion order is stayed until the SEC studies the facts and rules on the member firm petition.

A notice of this stay is sent to the main offices and all registered branch offices of NASD members.

Voluntary Termination of NASD Membership

The only way a member firm may voluntarily terminate its NASD membership is to submit a formal resignation to the Association's Board of Governors. Unless proceedings are pending against the member firm, an examination of the firm is under way, or unless some indebtedness is due the Association, membership termination takes effect thirty days after the submission of the resignation.

Article III of the Rules of Fair Practice

Twenty-eight specific rules are set forth in Article III of the Rules of Fair Practice. All of the rules are designed to carry out the original intention of the Maloney Act.

BUSINESS CONDUCT OF MEMBERS (SECTION 1). Most basic of the Rules of Fair Practice is Section I, Article III, which sums up the fundamental philosophy of the Association. It states, "A member, in the conduct of his business, shall observe high standards of commercial honor and just and equitable principals of trade." Under Section 1, the Board of Governors has adopted an interpretation of the Rules of Fair Practice relating to "free riding" in connection with the distribution of original offerings of securities. This interpretation is discussed in detail in Chapter 11.

NASD MEMBER FIRM ADVERTISING. The advertising practices of NASD member firms are regulated by the Association's Board of Governors through an interpretation of Section 1, Article III of the Rules of Fair Practice. This interpretation provides principles to be used by the membership as a guide in the preparation and utilization of their advertising material.

For many years, the NASD board members were aware that certain advertising practices existed in the securities business which employed "come-on" techniques and contained statements that misled or tended to mislead investors. Consequently, a special committee was appointed by the chairman of the board to make a study of the advertising practices employed by the Association's members.

Ultimately, the Board of Governors adopted the following interpretation of Section 1 of Article III of the Rules of Fair Practice with respect to advertising:

> It shall be deemed a violation of Section 1 of Article III of the Rules of Fair Practice for a member, directly or indirectly, to publish, circulate or distribute any advertisement, sales literature or market letter that the member knows, or has reason to know, contains any untrue statement of a material fact or is otherwise false or misleading.

The NASD encourages the proper use of advertisements, sales literature, and market letters by their members to interest and inform the public concerning securities and available investment services. They also encourage the proper use of recruiting advertisements to publicize the existence of career opportunities within the securities business.

The NASD stresses the importance of basing all advertising, sales literature, and market letters on the principals of fair dealing and good faith. The material should be presented in such a way as to provide a sound basis for evaluating the facts in regard to any particular security or type of security. Further, it should provide a sound basis for evaluating the facts concerning any industry that is discussed or any service that is offered. No material fact or qualification may be omitted from the presentation if the omission in the light of the context of the material presented would cause the advertising or sales literature to be misleading.

Exaggerated, unwarranted, or misleading statements or claims are prohibited in all advertising, sales literature, market letters, and recruiting material sponsored by NASD members. In preparing such literature, members should keep in mind the fact that the risk of fluctuating prices, uncertainty of dividends, and uncertainty of rates of return and yield are inherent in the investment process.

Since this interpretation has been adopted, any NASD member using such prohibited advertising material, or employing such undesirable promotional practices, has been subject to disciplinary action by District Business Conduct Committees under the Rules of Fair Practice.

The NASD announced that as a matter of administration it would not examine communications taking place solely between issuers and underwriters. Nor does it examine advertising or sales promotion material relating to "exempted" securities and other securities transactions over which the association has no jurisdiction. The NASD also excluded from examination advertising or sales promotional material relating to investment company securities or to investment companies generally. This material is covered by the Securities and Exchange Commission Statement of Policy dated August 14, 1950, as amended, and is subject to the continuing NASD program of review established in that area. See Chapter 17.

As previously noted, NASD members may use the Association's name on advertising only to the extent authorized by the NASD Board of Governors. Specifically, members are prohibited from using the name of the Association in advertising or on the letterhead of letters that carry a discussion of a particular security or type of securities.

DEFINITIONS OF ADVERTISEMENTS. The NASD Board of Governors has determined for the purpose of administering this interpretation that *advertisements* will be considered to be "*any material for use in any newspaper, or magazine, or other public media, or by radio, telephone recording, motion picture or television.*" The board has also determined that *sales literature* and *market letters* will be considered to include notices, circulars, reports, newsletters, research reports, form letters, or reprints or excerpts of the foregoing, or reprints of published articles.

Advertisements, sales literature, and market letters will be considered as coming under this interpretation if they involve:

1. the offering of any security or type of securities or relate to or recommend the purchase or sale of any security or type of securities; or
2. the offering of any securities analysis or communication referred to above, or contain any securities analysis or investment advise or offer investment advise or any other service with regard to securities.

Since September, 1959, advertising designed to recruit sales personnel must also conform to the board's interpretation of Section I, Article 3 of the Rules of Fair Practice. Consequently, also included within this interpretation will be any of the above communications which:

1. offers any inducement or opportunity for employment as a registered representative or registered principal by a member; or
2. is used as a supplement to a prospectus or written offers which are not subject to the Securities and Exchange Commission's Statement of Policy on investment company sales literature.

EXCLUDED MATERIAL. The NASD board indicates that certain types of material are excluded from this interpretation. For example, letters addressed to an individual concerning only recommendations or advice relating to that individual, or others for whom he may be acting, would not come under this interpretation. Also excluded would be material addressed by a member to its branch offices or material that is not distributed to members of the public but is just used internally by a member organization.

So called *tombstone* advertisements, which do no more than identify the NASD member and/or identify an offered security, state its price, or offer literature about the security, also are exempted from the interpretation. Announcements relating solely to changes in the personnel of member organizations also are excluded. Material published in a prospectus or a preliminary prospectus which satisfies the rules of the SEC also are excluded as are advertisements and sales literature subjected to the SEC Statement of Policy.

All advertising material prepared by an NASD member should contain the name of the member, the person, or the firm preparing the material if other than the member firm. It should also include the date on which the material was first published, circulated, or distributed, and if the information contained in the advertising material is not current, this fact should be stated. The NASD points out that the name of the member does not need to be stated if the advertisement is one of the so-called blind advertisements used for the purpose of recruiting personnel.

The NASD indicates that when a member firm makes a recommendation (whether or not it labels the material as a recommendation) the member must have a reasonable basis for making such a recommendation and that the following facts must be disclosed:

1. the price at the time the original recommendation was made.
2. that the member usually makes a market in the issue, if such is the case.
3. that the member intends to buy or sell the securities recommended for the firm's own account and ownership if such is the case.
4. the existence of any options, rights or warrants to purchase any security of the issuer whose securities are recommended, unless the extent of such ownership is merely nominal.

The member must also provide or offer to furnish upon request available investment information supporting the recommendation.

NASD members may use material referring to past recommendations if the material sets forth all recommendations as to the same type, kind, grade or classification of securities made by the member within the last year. Longer periods of time may be covered in referring to past recommendations only if the years cited are consecutive and include the most recent year. When such material is used it must also name each security recommended, the date it was recommended and whether the customer was told to buy the security or to sell it. Additional information required in such a presentation includes the price at the time the recommendation was made; the price at which, or the price range within which, the recommendation was to be acted upon; and whether the period involved was one of a generally rising market or one of a generally declining market.

Advertisements, sales literature or market letters of NASD members must not contain promises of specific results, exaggerated or unwarranted claims or unwarranted superlatives, or give opinions for which there is no reasonable basis. Any forecasts presented by a member must be clearly labeled as forecasts and must not include any unwarranted statements. References to past specific recommendations may not imply that the recommendations were profitable to any person, or would have been profitable to any person, and that they are indicative of the general quality of a member's recommendations.

Testimonial material concerning the NASD member or concerning any advice, analysis, report, or other investment or related service rendered by the NASD member, must make clear that the experience cited in the testimonial is not necessarily indicative of future performance or results to be obtained by others. Testimonials must also state whether any compensation was paid to the maker directly or indirectly for giving the testimonial. If the testimony implies that the person making the statement is an expert and that his opinions are experienced or specialized, the qualifications of the person giving the testimonial should be given.

When an NASD member offers free services to his customers, he may not refer to the services as free services unless they are in fact entirely free and without condition or obligation. Consequently, the NASD member should not make a statement to the effect that any report, analysis, or other service will be furnished free unless this is actually the case.

NASD members may not claim or imply that they have research or other facilities beyond those which they actually do possess or have reasonable capacity to provide.

NASD regulations do not permit the use of cautionary statements, or *caveats* (often called hedge clauses) if they could mislead the reader or are inconsistent with the contents of the material.

Advertisements in connection with the recruitment of sales personnel must not contain exaggerated or unwarranted claims or statements about opportunities in the investment banking or securities business.

FILING REQUIREMENTS. A separate file of all advertisements, sales literature, and market letters, including the name or names of the person or persons who prepared them and/or aproved their use, shall be maintained for a period of three years from the date of each use, for the first two years in a place readily accessible to examination or spot checks.

Each item of advertising and sales literature and each market letter shall be approved by a signature, or initial, prior to use by an officer, partner or official of the NASD member designated to supervise all such matters.

Each NASD member shall file each "advertisement" for review with the executive office of the NASD in Washington, D. C., (within five business days after initial use). Material to be filed includes any presentation for use in any newspaper or magazine or other public media or by radio, telephone recording, motion picture or television, except tombstones and other excluded material as set forth above. Such advertisements do not have to be filed with the NASD if they have already received clearance from a registered stock exchange or other self-regulatory agency designated by the NASD Board of Governors as having substantially the same standards as set forth in this interpretation. Any member may file and ask clearance from the NASD Executive Office for any advertisement prior to use. When this is done, a second filing is not required.

Recommendations to Customers (Section 2)

Section 2 of Article III states that recommendations to customers concerning the purchase, sale, or exchange of securities should be based upon reasonable grounds that such recommendations are suitable for the customer.

A securities transaction should not be proposed to a customer unless the proposed transaction appears to serve the customer's best interest. The interest of the customer should be the controlling factor, not the interest of the salesman or the interest of the broker/dealer.

The decision concerning the advisability of making any specific recommendation to a customer should be based upon the facts concerning the customer's general financial situation and needs. Particular attention should be paid to the amounts and types of other securities the customer owns. Without the above information an intelligent decision concerning changes in a customer's security account is not possible.

Whenever a member recommends to his customer that a certain security should be purchased or sold, all essential information about that security must be supplied to the customer. However, a salesman does not completely discharge his obligation to his customer simply by disclosing all essential information about the security being recommended. The salesman, as noted, must consider and disclose all other pertinent factors when making a recommendation to his customer.

The following illustration indicates the importance of disclosing all essential information to a customer.

A customer has inherited $120,000 and with a salesman's assistance has selected the shares of five open-end investment companies, which he proposes to buy in approximately equal amounts. The offering prices of the shares of each of these five companies are reduced on purchases of $25,000 or more. Under these conditions it would be entirely improper for the salesman to sell the customer $24,000 worth of shares of each of the five mutual funds without first clearly pointing out the price advantage of making larger purchases of shares (over $25,000 each) in four of the five companies selected.

Break-point Sales

Dealers selling open-end investment company shares generally reduce their sales charge for customers who buy more than a specified number of shares. The quantity at which this sales charge reduction is granted is known as the "break-point."

The sale of open-end investment company shares by dealers in dollar amounts just below the point at which the sales charge is reduced on quantity transactions (as shown in above illustration), in order to share in the higher sales charges applicable on sales below the break-point, may subject the dealer to disciplinary action under the Rules of Fair Practice.

Letters of Intention

Investors buying investment company shares may take advantage of a device known as a *letter of intention*.

A letter of intention is an arrangement among the investment company share underwriter, the dealer, and the purchaser. This arrangement permits the purchaser to pay a reduced sales charge on the shares he buys, if certain conditions are met. In the letter, the customer states his intention of purchasing (over a period of thirteen months or less) a minimum of $25,000 worth of investment company shares. If he carries out this intention, the reduced sales charge applies on his entire purchase. There is no penalty if the customer does not make the purchases indicated in his letter of intention. To protect a customer's interest, the salesman should put him on notice that a letter of intention is available whenever there is any indication that the total amount of his purchases would make him eligible for a discount, were a *letter* in effect. SEC Rule 22d-1 indicates that letters of intention may not be backdated.

A member who induces the purchase, or makes the sale, of investment company shares by implying a rate of return based in whole or in part upon distributions of realized securities profits or who, without full explanation and disclosure, uses any impending dividend or distribution as an inducement for the purchase of such shares may be making representations contrary to the Rules of Fair Practice.

"Churning" Customers' Accounts

"Churning" is the improper practice of encouraging investors to make frequent purchases and sales of securities without adequate or proper justification.

Churning or excessive activity in customers' accounts by brokers for the purpose of earning additional commission is subject to disciplinary action under the NASD Rules of Fair Practice.

Excessive activity of customers' accounts is particularly questionable when investment company shares are involved. Investment company shares are designed for long-term investment purposes, not for short-term speculation. As noted, nothing about investment company shares makes them proper instruments for in-and-out trading.

Sometimes, of course, it is in a customer's best interest to sell part or all of the securities in his account, and purchase other securities or temporarily hold a cash balance. When there is no clear-cut advantage to the customer by taking such action, however, the securities in the customer account should be retained.

The NASD regards the churning of customers' accounts as highly unethical and improper—so much so, in fact, that in 1959 the Association imposed some of the most severe penalties in its history against a member firm for churning and related practices.

The violations came to light when a series of eight complaints were filed against a single member firm within a ten-month period. Upon receipt of the complaints the appropriate District Business Conduct Committee made an examination of the firm in question. During the examination some 2,300 principal transactions of the firm were reviewed. The Committee found that 2,100 of these transactions were same-day "riskless" transactions with over half of them executed at markups in excess of 10 per cent.

In numerous accounts examined for churning by the committee, customers were taken out of investment-grade securities and traded in and out of highly speculative stocks at excessive markups. The committee estimated that in eight of these accounts alone, the customers of the firm lost $216,000 while the firm and its representatives realized a profit of $181,500.

Transactions in one of these accounts resulted in rotating the customer's holdings three and one-half times within two years. The committee estimated that the loss to the customer in this case was $75,000 and the profit to the firm and its representatives was $61,000.

In its decision, the District Business Conduct Committee referred to the "built-in loss factor," inherent in these acts of churning. This built-in loss factor exists from the very inception of a transaction, owing to the excessive number of markups charged by the dealer. Because of these markups, the securities go into the account of the customer at a price considerably above the amount the customer could reasonably expect to obtain if he sold them in the current market. Many times these built-in losses were found to be "insurmountable."

In addition to the churning violations, the committee's examination further disclosed that several registered representatives of the firm had committed several other NASD rule violations including making *unsuitable recommendations* to customers without disclosing the material facts. These representatives had also offered *guarantees* to customers in connection with "switches" of securities. Furthermore, they had violated the law by converting customers' funds to the firm's use.

In its decision, the District Committee summarized the respondent's conduct as "utter and callous disregard for not only the Association's rules, but all accepted business ethics."

Accordingly, the District Committee imposed the following penalties which upon appeal were upheld by the Board of Governors, except for some modification of the fines.

1. The member firm was expelled from the Association and fined $25,000.
2. Fines totaling $62,300 were imposed against eleven registered representatives and the registrations of nine of these representatives were revoked.
3. Costs of the proceedings were also assessed against the member and its two principal officers.

Fair Dealing with Customers

NASD District Business Conduct Committees and the Board of Governors have taken disciplinary action and imposed penalties in many situations where members' sales efforts have exceeded the reasonable grounds of fair dealing.

Some practices that have resulted in disciplinary action under the Rules of Fair Practice and that clearly violate the member's responsibility for fair dealings are set forth below:

1. *Recommending speculative low-priced securities to customers without knowledge of the customers' other securities holdings, their financial situation, and other necessary data.* The fact that such information is not always readily available does not relieve the NASD member from his obligation to obtain adequate information about his customers' financial circumstances before he recommends speculative low-priced securities to the customer.

2. *Excessive activity in a customer's account, often referred to as "churning" or "overtrading".* There are no specific standards to measure excessiveness of activity in customer accounts because this must be related to the objectives and financial situation of the customer involved. See page 229.

3. *Trading in mutual fund shares, particularly on a short-term basis.* It is clear that normally these securities are not proper trading vehicles and such activity on its face may raise the question of rule violation. See pages 331–332.

4. Numerous instances of fraudulent conduct have been acted upon by the Association and have resulted in penalties against members. Some of these activities include:

   a. Establishment of fictitious accounts in order to execute transactions which otherwise would be prohibited. Examples would be the purchase of hot issues, or disguised transactions which are against firm policy.

   b. Transactions in discretionary accounts in excess of those authorized by customers or without actual authority from customers.

   c. The execution of transactions which are unauthorized by customers or the sending of confirmations in order to cause customers to accept transactions not actually agreed upon.

   d. Unauthorized use or borrowing of customers' funds or securities.

   e. Transactions by registered representatives which are concealed from their employers, or securities transactions outside registered representatives' regular employment,

even if disclosed to their employers, if such transactions
are in violation of federal or state law.

5. *Recommending the purchase of securities or the continuing
   purchase of securities in amounts which are inconsistent with
   the reasonable expectation that the customer has the financial
   ability to meet such a commitment.*

Under Section 1, Article III of the Rules of Fair Practice, the following transaction would be improper.

You offer to one of your customers, a country bank, a block of ABC
Corporation notes at 100 (quoted 99-100), suggesting that the bank sell
an equal amount of XYZ Corporation notes at 102 (XYZ notes being
quoted 102-102½). The banker tells you he would like to make the
switch, but the XYZ notes cost him 104 and he doesn't want to show a
loss on his books. He suggests that if you will pay him 104 for his
XYZ notes, he will buy your ABC notes at 102, which will give him the
same differential as your suggested exchange.

A great deal depends on the specific circumstances of a particular
situation. However, the following examples appear to violate NASD
rules as written and interpreted or federal securities laws and administrative rules and regulations:

A broker/dealer buys 100 shares of LMN common on Monday @ 100⅛
on Friday he sells to customer @ 103, when the market is 92 bid, offered
@ 95.

A salesman urges his customer to purchase shares of XYZ Mutual Fund
as a "good buy" solely because a dividend has been declared and will be paid
to holders of record shortly.

A broker/dealer tells a new customer, "The price of this stock is going
up quickly—you can buy today for $10 a share. Next week when payment
is due I will sell the stock you buy today, deduct the purchase price and
send you my check for the difference."

A broker/dealer's salesman offers to pass back one-half of the sales
charge on XYZ Mutual Fund as an inducement to the customer to buy.

A Dealer sells 100 shares XYZ Corp. common @ 95 to customer at
10:00 A.M. He then buys 100 shares XYZ Corp. common over-the-counter
for 85 at 10:01 A.M. His confirmation states, "As Dealer (Principal) and for
our own account, we confirm Sale to you of 100 shares XYZ @ 95."

The following example does not appear to violate NASD rules as written
or interpreted or federal securities laws and administrative rules and
regulations as written and interpreted:

A dealer who has no position in the security sells 100 shares XYZ
Corp. common @ 95 to customer at 11:05 A.M. and confirms. He buys 100
shares XYZ Corp. common for 94 at 11:10 A.M.

The following statements are examples of the type of comments which
may properly be made by security salesmen, assuming there are no con-
tradictory facts:

We feel this security has excellent speculative features.

My firm is the only firm making a market in this security so we know more about the market than anyone else. The market this morning is 26 bid, 27 offered.

While this security has some speculative features, we feel the higher return available due to its present low price makes it attractive for long-term investment.

The following statements are examples of the type of comments which may never be properly used by security salesmen regardless of the circumstances:

We will refund your purchase price if you wish to sell out when the market value is below the purchase price.

This security will be issued in one week. Give me your order today before our allotment is sold out.

Get in on the ground floor. I know the price of this security will double in three months.

Charges for Services Performed (Section 3)

Section 3 of Article III of the Rules of Fair Practice states that charges made by members for services performed must be reasonable and not unfairly discriminatory between customers.

Services performed by member firms for their customers include such things as:

1. Collection of monies due for principal, dividends, or interest
2. Exchange or transfer of securities
3. Appraisals of securities
4. Safekeeping or custody of securities

Fair Prices and Commission (Section 4)

Section 4 of Article III of the Rules of Fair Practice states that members buying securities for, or selling securities from, their own accounts shall buy or sell at prices which are fair. Furthermore, members shall not charge customers more than a fair commission when acting as their agent.

See Chapter 11 for a detailed discussion of this regulation.

Publication of Purchases and Sales (Section 5)

Section 5 of Article III of the Rules provides that no member of the Association shall circulate information based upon fictitious transactions or quotations. According to the above rule, only bona fide securities transactions should be reported. Also, quotations of bid and asked prices must be clearly marked as *nominal quotations*, unless they are known to be bona fide bids and offers.

Section 5 also states that it is improper to circulate misinformation about securities transactions or quotations by communications of any kind, including by notice, circular, advertisement, newspaper article, or investment service. See Chapter 11 for a detailed discussion.

Offers at Stated Prices (Section 6)

Section 6 of Article III of the Rules indicates that no member shall make an offer to buy from or sell to any person any security at a stated price unless such member is prepared to purchase or sell, as the case may be, at such price and under such conditions stated at the time of such offer to buy or sell.

This rule is discussed in Chapter 11.

Disclosure of Price and Concessions (Section 7)

Section 7 of Article III of the Rules states that selling syndicate agreements or selling group agreements shall set forth the price at which the securities are to be sold to the public or the formula by which such price can be ascertained, and shall state clearly to whom and under what circumstances concessions, if any, may be allowed.

Securities Taken in Trade (Section 8)

Section 8 of Article III of the Rules provides that whenever an NASD member firm is a member of a selling syndicate or a selling group, it shall purchase securities taken in trade at a *fair* market price. The purchase price (of the securities taken in trade) shall be determined by conditions existing at the time the NASD member purchases such securities.

Use of Information Obtained in Fiduciary Capacity (Section 9)

Section 9 of Article III of the Rules forbids use by an NASD member of any confidential information acquired by a member while acting in the capacity of paying agent, transfer agent, trustee or in any other similar capacity.

Information obtained by Association members (while acting in any of the above capacities) as to the ownership of securities, shall under no circumstances be used for the purpose of soliciting purchases, sales or exchanges of such securities except at the request and on behalf of the issuer.

Influencing or Rewarding Employees of Others (Section 10 and Section 11)

Under Section 10 of Article III of the Rules, members are forbidden to give anything of value to the employee, agent, or representative of another person, as a reward in relation to the business of the employer of the recipient without the prior knowledge and consent of the employer.

Association members are not permitted to attempt to influence the business decisions of the employees of others, either directly or indirectly.

Section 11 deals with influencing or rewarding the employees of others in connection with published material about securities.

Information about a security placed in newspapers, investment services, and the like, often is intended to have an effect upon the market price of that security. Under such circumstances, it is highly improper to attempt to influence the decision concerning the desirability of publishing certain data.

Section 11 does not apply to published material which is clearly distinguishable as paid advertising.

Disclosures Required (Sections 12, 13, and 14)

Section 12 of Article III of the Rules requires a member acting as a broker or dealer to notify customers in writing at or before the completion of each transaction whether he is:

1. acting as the customer's broker
2. acting as a dealer for his own account
3. acting as a broker for some other person
4. acting as a broker for the customer and also for some other person

When acting as an agent, a broker/dealer is required to disclose to his customer the source and amount of any commission or other remuneration received. Also, upon request he must disclose the date and time of the transaction and the name of the person from whom the security was purchased or to whom it was sold.

A member, when acting as a dealer (principal) is not required to disclose to his customer the amount of profit he made on the transaction.

Section 13 of Article III of the Rules requires the disclosure to the customer of any control existing between an Association member and an issuer of a security. The disclosure should be made in writing by the member before entering into any contract with, or for, a customer for the purchase or sale of the security.

Section 14 of Article III of the Rules requires a member participating in (or having a financial interest in) a primary or secondary distribution to give a written notification of this fact to customers under the following conditions:

  a. when the member acts as an agent for the customer *or* receives a fee from him for financial advice
  and
  b. when the customer is purchasing the security in which the member is participating or has a financial interest

The written notification of the member's participation or interest must be made *before* the completion of any such transaction with the customer.

Discretionary Accounts (Section 15)

A discretionary account is an account in which the customer gives the broker or dealer discretion, either complete or within specified limits, as to the purchase and sale of securities, including selection, timing, and the price to be paid or received.

Section 15 of Article III of the Rules of Fair Practice states that members vested with discretionary power over a customer's account must not make security purchases or sales which are excessive in size or frequency in view of the financial resources and character of the customer's account. NASD members or their registered representatives or principals are not permitted to exercise discretionary power in a customer's account at all, unless the customer has given his prior written authorization and the account has been accepted in writing by a properly designated representative of the member firm.

Each discretionary order must be approved in writing by an authorized official of the member firm. Furthermore, all discretionary accounts must be reviewed at frequent intervals in order to detect and prevent transactions which are excessive in size or frequency in view of the financial resources and character of the account.

Discretionary account transactions must be recorded, and these records must be maintained by the NASD member for a minimum of two years.

Offerings "At the Market" (Section 16)

Section 16 of Article III of the Rules states that a member having a financial interest in the distribution of an over-the-counter security may not say he offers the security "at the market," when he or his associates maintain the only active market in the security, without disclosing that fact.

Solicitation of Purchases on an Exchange to Facilitate a Distribution of Securities (Section 17)

Section 17 of Article III of the Rules of Fair Practice relates to the activities of NASD members who are participating in, or are otherwise financially interested in a *primary* or *secondary* distribution of securities.

Section 17 states it is improper for an NASD member to influence by solicitation (or in any other manner) purchases of securities on an exchange for the purpose of facilitating a distribution of securities in which he is interested.

Use of Fraudulent Devices (Section 18)

Section 18 of Article III of the Rules prohibits the use, by NASD members, of any manipulative, deceptive, or other fraudulent device or contrivance to effect or induce the purchase or sale of securities. See the section on fair dealing with customers, page 231.

Hypothecation of Customer's Securities (Section 19)

Section 19 of Article III of the Rules states that members shall not make improper use of a customer's securities or funds.

Members may not borrow a customer's securities without first securing written permission. A member is also required to obtain written authorization from a customer before he may lend a customer's securities to anyone or use the customer's securities in any other way.

Regardless of the nature of the agreement between the member and his customer, the member is never justified in pledging more of his customer's securities than is fair and reasonable in view of the indebtedness of the customer to the member.

Hypothecation is the practice of the pledging of customer's securities as collateral by brokers and dealers in order to obtain loans. There are a number of important SEC rules concerning hypothecation practices which have been adopted under the Securities Exchange Act of 1934.

Basically, these rules provide that a broker or dealer may not hypothecate or pledge securities carried for the account of their customers:

1. in such a way as to permit the securities of one customer to be *commingled* with the securities of other customers unless he first obtains the written consent of each such customer.
2. under a lien for a loan made to the broker or dealer in such a way as will permit such securities to be *commingled* with the securities of any person other than a bona fide customer.

The rules further provide that a broker or dealer may not hypothecate securities carried for the account of his customers in such a way as to permit the liens or claims of pledges thereon to exceed the aggregate indebtedness of all such customers in respect of securities carried for their account.

Installment or Partial Payment Sales (Section 20)

Section 20 of Article III of the Rules prohibits members from carrying accounts for, or conducting transactions for, customers where payments are made on an installment basis except under the following conditions:

1. When acting as an agent for the customer, the member must actually buy the security for the account of the customer, take delivery in the regular course of business, and maintain possession or control of the security for as long as he remains under obligation to deliver the security to the customer.
2. When acting as a principal, the member must actually own the security at the time of such transaction and must maintain possession or control of the security for as long as he is under obligation to deliver the security to the customer.
3. The member must satisfy any applicable provisions of Regulation T.

Under the type of transactions indicated above, the member must not pledge or hypothecate any security involved for any sum larger than the amount the customer owes him.

Required Books and Records (Section 21)

Section 21 of Article III of the Rules indicates that each member must maintain books and records in accordance with all applicable federal and state laws.

Records required of NASD member firms are specified by the Securities and Exchange Commission. These records are also required of all members of national securities exchanges and any broker or dealer transacting a business in securities through such members.

These required books and records are:

A. Blotters (or other records of original entry) containing an itemized daily record of:
   1. all purchases and sales of securities
   2. all receipts and deliveries of securities (including certificate numbers)
   3. all receipts and disbursements of cash
   4. all other debits and credits
   5. the account for which each transaction was effected
   6. the name and amount of securities
   7. the unit and aggregate purchase or sale price (if any)
   8. the trade date
   9. the name or other designation of the person from whom purchased or received or to whom sold or delivered

These records must be preserved for at least six years, the first two years in an easily accessible place.

B. Ledgers (or other records) reflecting all assets and liabilities, income and expense and capital accounts.

These records must be preserved for at least six years, the first two years in an easily accessible place.

C. Ledger accounts (or other records) itemizing separately:
   1. each cash and margin account of every customer and of such member, broker, or dealer and partners thereof
   2. all purchases, sales, receipts, and deliveries of securities and commodities for such accounts
   3. all other debits and credits to such accounts

These records must be preserved for at least six years, the first two years in an easily accessible place.

D. Ledgers (or other records) reflecting the following:
   1. securities in transfer
   2. dividends and interest received
   3. securities borrowed and securities loaned
   4. monies borrowed and monies loaned (together with a record of the collateral thereof and any substitutions in such collateral)
   5. securities failed to receive and failed to deliver

These records must be preserved for at least three years, the first two years in an easily accessible place.

E. A securities *record* or *ledger* reflecting separately for each security as of the clearance dates all "long" or "short" positions (including securities in safekeeping) carried by such member, broker, or dealer for his account or for the account of his customers or partners and showing the location of all securities long and the offsetting position to all securities short and in all cases the name or designation of the account in which each position is carried.

These records must be preserved for at least six years, the first two years in an easily accessible place.

The records described under F, G, H, I, J, and K must be preserved for a period of not less than three years, the first two in an easily accessible place.

F. A memorandum of each brokerage order, and of any other instruction, given or received for the purchase or sale of securities whether executed or unexecuted. Such memorandum shall show:
   1. the terms and conditions of the order or instructions and of any modification or cancellation thereof
   2. the account for which entered
   3. the time of entry
   4. the price at which executed and
   5. to the extent feasible, the time of execution or cancellation

Orders entered pursuant to the exercise of discretionary power by such member, broker or dealer, or any employee thereof, shall be so designated.

The term "instruction" shall be deemed to include instructions between partners and employees of a member, broker, or dealer.

The term "time of entry" shall be deemed to mean the time when such member, broker, or dealer transmits the order or instruction for execution or, if it is not so transmitted, the time when it is received.

G. A memorandum of each purchase and sale of securities for the account of such member, broker, or dealer showing the price and, to the extent feasible, the time of execution.

H. Copies of confirmations of all purchases and sales of securities and copies of notices of all other debits and credits for securities, cash, and other items for the account of customers and partners of such member, broker, or dealer.

I. A record in respect of each cash and margin account with such member, broker, or dealer containing the name and address of the beneficial owner of such account and, in the case of a margin account, the signature of such owner. In case of a joint account or an account of a corporation, such records are required only in respect of the person or persons authorized to transact business for such an account.

J. A record of all puts, calls, spreads, straddles, and other options in which such member, broker, or dealer has any direct or indirect interest or which such member, broker, or dealer has granted or guaranteed, containing, at least, an identification of the security and the number of units involved.

K. A record of the proof of money balances of all ledger accounts in the form of trial balances. Such trial balances shall be prepared currently at least once a month.

Members of a national securities exchange are not required to make or keep such records of transaction cleared for such member by another member as are customarily made and kept by the clearing member.

Brokers or dealers registered pursuant to Section 15 of the Securities Exchange Act of 1934, as amended, are not required to make or keep such records reflecting the sale of United States Tax Savings Notes, United States Defense Savings Stamps, or United States Defense Savings Bonds, Series E, F, and G.

Such records shall not be required with respect to any cash transaction of $100 or less involving only subscription rights or warrants which by their terms expire within ninety days after the issuance thereof.

The following material must be preserved by registered broker/dealers for a period of not less than three years, the first two years in an easily accessible place:

1. All checkbooks, bank statements, cancelled checks, and cash reconciliations

2. All bills receivable or payable (or copies thereof), paid or unpaid, relating to the business of such broker or dealer as such

3. Originals of all communications received and copies of all communications sent by such broker or dealer (including interoffice memoranda and communications) relating to his business as such

4. All trial balances, financial statements, branch office recon-

ciliations, and internal audit working papers, relating to the business of such broker or dealer as such

5. All guarantees of accounts and all powers of attorney and other evidence of the granting of any discretionary authority given in respect of any account, and copies of resolutions empowering an agent to act on behalf of a corporation

6. All written agreements (or copies thereof) entered into by such broker or dealer relating to his business as such, including agreements with respect to any account

Every such broker/dealer must preserve for a period of not less than six years after the closing of any customer's account any account cards or records which relate to the terms and conditions with respect to the opening and maintenance of such account.

Every such member broker/dealer must preserve during the life of the enterprise (and of any successor enterprise) all partnership articles or, in the case of a corporation, all articles of incorporation or charter, minute books, and stock certificate books.

After a record or other document has been preserved for two years, a photograph thereof on film may be substituted therefore for the balance of the required time.

Any person required to keep the above records must continue to preserve the records for the period of time specified, even if he discontinues operating as a securities broker or dealer.

Disclosure of Financial Condition (Section 22)

Section 22 of Article III of the Rules states that a bona fide customer for whom a member holds cash or securities has the right to inspect the current financial statement of the member.

Net Prices to Persons Not in Investment Banking or Securities Business (Section 23)

Section 23 of Article III of the Rules requires that transactions between members and persons not actually engaged in the securities business must be confirmed by members at a net dollar or basis price. Under no circumstances may a concession, discount, or allowance be granted.

Selling Concessions (Section 24)

Section 24 of Article III of the Rules of Fair Practice states that selling concessions, discounts, or other such allowances are permitted only if they are given for services rendered in a distribution. Furthermore, they must not be allowed to anyone other than a broker or dealer actually engaged in the investment banking or securities business.

NASD Member Firm Relations With Nonmember Firms (Section 25)

Section 25 of Article III of the Rules states that all NASD members must deal with nonmember broker/dealers on the same terms as they would with members of the general public. This means that a member may not sell an over-the-counter security to a nonmember of the Association at a discount from the price available to the public. This is true regardless of whether or not the nonmember firm is registered with the SEC.

A member may not pay a commission to any nonmember broker or dealer for executing a brokerage order in the over-the-counter market but may execute over-the-counter an order for a nonmember and charge a commission.

Section 26 of Article III of the Rules of Fair Practice is discussed in detail in Chapter 17. This section relates to the activity of NASD members in connection with the securities of investment companies.

Supervision of Registered Representatives (Section 27)

Section 27 of Article III of the Rules of Fair Practice discusses the supervision of the registered representatives of NASD members. This material is discussed in detail in Chapter 14.

Transactions for Personnel of Another Member (Section 28)

Section 28 of Article III of the Rules of Fair Practice requires NASD members to diligently avoid executing a transaction for a partner, officer, or employee of another member, which would be adverse to the interests of the other member. The executing member can fulfill this obligation by notifying the employer-member prior to the execution of the order.

The executing member must notify his customer's employer that he proposes to open an account for this customer and, if asked to do so, the executing member must send copies of confirmations of individual transactions or of monthly statements to his customers' firms.

REVIEW QUESTIONS

1. Describe the background, functions, and objectives of the NASD.

2. Describe the administration, the board of governors, and the committees of the NASD.

3. Who may be a member of the NASD?

4. Who may *not* become a member of the NASD?

5. Discuss the procedure involved in becoming a member of the NASD and in registration with SEC.

6. What are the Rules of Fair Practice of NASD?

7. What are some of the items covered by an NASD examination of member firms?

8. Discuss the *Code of Procedure* for handling trade practice complaints. Who may complain? What are most frequent complaints? What are the obligations and rights of the accused?

9. What are five possible penalties imposed on a NASD member for violation of rules?

10. What are the filing requirements for all advertisements, sales literature, market letters, and so forth.

11. What is the single most important rule to follow in making a recommendation to a customer?

12. What is meant by *"churning"* customers' accounts? Illustrate.

13. List four instances of fraudulent conduct by a securities dealer.

14. What disclosures are required by a member acting as an agent?

15. Discuss the requirements a registered representative must keep in mind in handling a discretionary account.

Registered Representatives and Registered Principals of NASD

Chapter **14**

Every business firm with a sales force is continually faced with the problem of how best to supervise the activities of its sales personnel. No reputable business wants its sales force to mislead or misinform its customers about the firm's products and services. However, all companies *do* want their sales force to present the most favorable picture possible to the customers in order to induce them to buy.

Proper supervision of *securities* salespeople is particularly difficult for a number of reasons. One is the rather intangible nature of the services or products offered by the securities companies. When a home appliance or automobile is offered for sale, the salesman can quickly and easily point out the special features or advantages of his company's product over the competitor's product. The salesman can explain clearly what this product can do and what it cannot do. Furthermore, the customer can look and actually see these differences and in many cases can even try out the products or see them demonstrated before he buys. Although exaggerated and extravagant claims may be made for a product, the extent of the salesman's exaggeration is often quickly evident to the prospective buyer.

An extravagant or overenthusiastic claim made in order to sell a security, however, is not so easily recognizable by potential buyers. Since the purchaser is often ignorant of the basic factors giving value and strength to a security, he can much more easily be misled. Furthermore, while a vacuum cleaner, dishwasher, or washing machine is obviously going to be used for one specific purpose, securities are acquired for many different reasons. One type of security may be able to accomplish a specific purpose, while another security, which is virtually indistinguishable from the first by the unsophisticated purchaser, would be completely unable to accomplish the same purpose.

Another complication is the fact that, even if the investor selects the security to match his objective, no one can *guarantee* the security bought will accomplish the intended purpose.

If a vacuum cleaner does not clean your rug properly, it is immediately evident. You take it back and get one that will. If a security designed to provide adequate income for your old age fails to do so, you generally don't discover this fact until it is too late for you to exchange it for one that will.

Two other factors make supervision of sales personnel in the securities business a particularly difficult task.

One is the large number of new salespeople entering the securities business each year. With a continuous flow of new and inexperienced individuals entering the securities business, the task of supervising their activities properly is bound to be difficult.

The other factor is the fact that many people regard speculating in securities as a possible way of making a great deal of money in a short period of time. Given the proper psychological conditions, this lure of a chance to "get rick quick" is a very effective sales theme for any unscrupulous salesman to use in separating a speculator from his money.

Improperly trained and ill-informed salespeople can cause the employing broker/dealer, as well as his customers, a great deal of trouble. It is essential for the reputation of the individual broker/dealer and for the reputation of the securities business as a whole that registered representatives fully understand the products and services they are offering their customers. They must understand why one type of security or mutual fund is suitable for a particular customer and why certain other types of securities or mutual funds are completely unsuitable for that customer.

An ill-informed security salesman dealing with an uninformed customer can create a portfolio hodge-podge which might permanently destroy the customer's interest in securities as an investment vehicle.

Obviously, sales personnel in the securities field need constant and careful supervision, and effective training for securities sales personnel should be stressed for the protection of the investing public.

NASD Sales Supervision

The NASD has been concerned with the problem of adequate supervision of member firm sales personnel since its beginning. This problem has proved to be a very difficult one to resolve and has required a great deal of study and experimentation.

In 1941 and 1945, a series of studies was undertaken by the NASD to determine the most effective ways to provide this essential sales supervision.

These studies indicated that the supervision of salesmen by member firms would become much more effective if the NASD itself had the power to control and discipline individual salesmen connected with member firms. (The Association's control actually extended at that time only to the member firms and not to the firm's individual salesmen.)

Accordingly, the committee recommended, and the board approved, a change in the bylaws and rules which extended the Association's authority to include action against salesmen.

New Rule Required Registration

The new rule required the registration of partners, officers, employees and other representatives of the member firms with the NASD as registered representatives. The rule also required individuals applying as registered representatives to sign an agreement to abide by all of the bylaws, regulations, and rules of the Association and to submit to disciplinary action in the event of violation.

Thus registered representatives are placed under the same duty and obligation to abide by the Rules of Fair Practice as the member firms. They are also subject to the same disciplinary penalties for failure to fulfill these duties and obligations.

Registration of Principals

The NASD Board of Governors, in September 1965, established a second category of registration for individuals associated with member firms.

This new regulation required all persons associated with NASD member firms (unless exempt) to register either as a "registered representative," or as a "principal."

The NASD further indicated that all persons associated with an NASD member who were designated as principals were required to pass a "Qualification Examination for Principals" before their registration could become effective. "Principals" were identified as those persons associated with an NASD member who are actively engaged in the management of the member's investment banking or securities business. Included were those involved in supervision, solicitation, the conduct of business or the training of persons associated with the member firm.

"Principals" include such persons as:

1. Sole Proprietors;
2. Officers;
3. Partners;
4. Managers of Offices of Supervisory Jurisdiction; and
5. Directors of Corporations.

Any person who was registered with the NASD, on or before, October 1, 1965, and was designated as one of the above principals, was not required to pass the Qualification Examination for Principals unless his most recent registration had been terminated for a period of two years or more immediately preceding the filing of a new application.

Any individual associated with an NASD member firm as a Registered Representative whose duties are changed by the same member firm after October 1, 1965 so as to require his classification as a Principal is allowed a reasonable period of time following such a change to pass the Principal's Examination.

Who Must Become a Registered Representative

As noted, every officer, partner, director, or manager of an office of supervisory jurisdiction of an NASD member firm must register as a registered principal. In addition, all other persons associated with member firms who are engaged in the management, supervision, solicitation, trading, or handling of transactions in listed and unlisted securities are required to be registered with the Association. Every employee engaged in the solicitation of subscriptions to investment advisory or to investment management services furnished on a fee basis must also become registered. Registration is also required of anyone to whom has been delegated general supervision over foreign business, or who is engaged in the sale of listed or unlisted securities on an agency or principal basis. Employees of member firms who are not involved in any of the above activities need not become registered representatives. Thus, those whose duties are solely clerical and ministerial need not become registered.

The NASD warns that a member must not permit any person to transact any branch of the investment banking or securities business as its representative unless such person is registered with the NASD as a registered representative or registered principal of that member. This is a significant restriction in that it prohibits the use of unregistered trainees and office personnel as order takers or salesmen and in client contact assignments.

Registration is not required of employees who are engaged solely in the handling or selling of

1. exempted securities, including federal, state, and local government obligations;
2. cotton, grain, or other commodities, provided they are registered with a recognized national cotton or commodities exchange;
3. securities on a national securities exchange, provided they are registered with a national securities exchange.

By resolution, the NASD Board of Governors has determined that any member who fails to register a qualified employee may be suspended from the association.

Bank Employees as Registered Representatives

It is generally felt that a person should not be an employee of a commercial bank and at the same time be working in the securities business. Many bank employees have the responsibility of selecting appropriate investments for the various trust funds being administered by the bank and, obviously, a conflict of interest may develop if an individual is both a bank employee and a registered representative of a securities firm.

To prevent any such conflict of interest involving individuals under its jurisdiction, the Board of Governors of the Federal Reserve System has decreed that no employee or director of a bank that is a member of the Federal Reserve System may be employed by a securities firm. Officials of the Federal Deposit Insurance Corporation have informed the NASD that no employee of a FDIC-insured bank should be engaged in the securities business.

Qualifications of a Registered Representative

Individuals who become, or are associated with, an NASD member firm may become registered representatives if they:

1. possess all of the qualifications for membership in the Association[1], and
2. have passed the NASD Qualification Examination for Registered Representatives.

Before new employees may become registered representatives, the member firm must certify to the adequacy of the training, and the experience of these new employees. This certification must be based on adequate investigation.

A member who employs a registered representative must have reason to believe, upon the exercise of reasonable care, that the individual hired is qualified by training or experience to perform the functions and duties to which he is assigned.

The determination of the training and experience of the registered representative is solely the responsibility of the member. Improper or unwarranted certification by a member constitutes conduct contrary to high standards of commercial honor and may result in disciplinary action.

A registered representative of a member firm does not have to devote his entire time during business hours to the business of the member. A large number of registered representatives sell securities on a part-time basis.

[1]The qualifications for membership in the Association are discussed in the section covering NASD membership requirements.

The Application

Application for registration must be made on the prescribed form,[2] which requires, among other things, the applicant to agree to abide by all of the provisions of the Certificate of Incorporation, the By-Laws, the Rules and Interpretations of the Association.

Restrictions Applicable to Registration

No person shall be registered who:

1. is subject to an order of the Association suspending or revoking his registration as a registered representative;
2. is subject to an order of the Securities and Exchange Commission denying or revoking his registration as a broker/dealer;
3. was named as a cause of suspension currently in effect, or of an expulsion or revocation by the Association or the SEC;
4. is subject to an order of a national securities exchange revoking or suspending his registration with the exchange for conduct inconsistent with just and equitable principles of trade;
5. has been convicted within the preceding ten years of a felony or misdemeanor involving the purchase or sale of any security;
6. has been convicted within the preceding ten years of any felony or misdemeanor which the Association finds involved embezzlement, fraudulent conversion, misappropriation of funds or abuse or misuse of a fiduciary relationship.

By resolution, the NASD Board of Governors has determined that the filing of information with respect to registration which is incomplete, inaccurate or which could in any way tend to mislead officers or committees of the Association, provides sufficient cause for disciplinary action.

New Employees of NASD Member Firms

Member firms hiring new personnel without adequate experience in the securities business are expected to train them in the securities field. This training should be quite extensive and certainly must be comprehensive enough to enable the employees to determine what may properly be done and what may not properly be done in the securities business.

The training of new sales personnel should cover the basic securities fundamentals, the basic securities laws, and the NASD bylaws, rules, regulations, and codes as well as the sales approaches and methods of the company.

---

[2]Application for Registration as Registered Representative must be filed by all individuals required to be registered representatives. See section on "How to Become a Member of the NASD," Chapter 13.

Salesmen, in order to be effective, need a great deal of training. Obviously, securities salesmen cannot do a good job for their company's customers without thoroughly understanding how and why the company's products or services will help the customer attain his investment objectives.

In addition to the fact that it makes good business sense to train sales personnel properly, another factor makes sound employee training important to the member firms. This second factor is the fact that *member firms are legally responsible for the actions of their registered representatives.*

Close Supervision Required after Registration

After the new employees become registered representatives, the member firms must supervise their purchase and sales methods. This sales supervision should not be loose or haphazard.

In order to protect its own interests and reputation, a member firm's supervision of its sales personnel should be detailed and methodical. Each member is responsible for all transactions made by its employees.

The high degree of sales supervision desired by the NASD is illustrated by their rule requiring a responsible official of a member firm to evidence in writing his approval of every transaction made by the firm's registered representatives. This approval must be written on the original memorandum or other record of the transaction by either a partner, executive, or branch office manager of the member in order to be valid. If the member firm official disapproves of a transaction, he may reject it, even if it is a customer's order to purchase a security which has been accepted by an employee.

Office of Supervisory Jurisdiction

Section 27 of Article III of the Rules of Fair Practice provides that each NASD member shall establish, maintain and enforce *written* procedures so as to supervise properly the activities of its registered representatives and other persons associated with the member firm. A partner, officer, or manager must be designated in each *Office of Supervisory Jurisdiction* to be responsible for supervising the activities of others. Appropriate records must be kept for carrying out the member's supervisory procedures.

An "office of supervisory jurisdiction" is any office which has been specifically designated as directly responsible for the review of the activities of registered representatives or associated persons in such office and/or in other offices of the NASD member. The office of supervisory jurisdiction is the member's center of supervision.

Each NASD member must review all transactions and correspondence pertaining to the solicitation or execution of any securities transaction by its registered representatives.

Each member must consistently review the activities taking place in each of its offices. The member must make annual inspections of its various offices, and must periodically examine customer accounts to detect and prevent irregularities or abuses.

A "Guide to Supervision Practices" is available from the NASD's Executive office in Washington, D.C.

Termination of Registration by Resignation

Registered representatives of member firms may voluntarily terminate their registration at any time, but only by formal resignation in writing addressed to the Board of Governors.

Upon receipt of such a request, the Board of Governors immediately notifies the member firm involved.

The resignation does not take effect until thirty days after it is received by the board, or so long as there is any complaint or action pending against the registered representative.[3]

Termination Without Resignation

A member firm must notify the Board of Governors promptly in writing whenever any of their registered representatives are no longer employed by them.

The registered representative may have terminated his employment with the member firm at his own option or at the option of the member firm. In either case, the termination becomes effective thirty days after the above notification is received by the board unless:

a.   The board terminates the registration sooner, or
b.   The registered representative is a respondent in a complaint or action against a member firm.

Registration Not Transferable

Registered representatives are not permitted to transfer their registration from one member firm to another. A representative of one member firm who leaves that firm and goes to work for another member firm must go through the registration process all over again.

[3]A registered representative is subject to any complaint or action in which he has been named a respondent brought against any member with whom he was formerly registered.

Penalties Applicable to
Registered Representatives

The bylaws of the Association prescribe penalties applicable to registered representatives who violate the Association's regulations. These penalties include censure, levying of fines and costs of proceedings, and suspension and revocation of registration.

When the suspension or revocation of a registered representative's registration occurs, formal notice of the action taken is sent to all member firms.

Growth of Registered Representatives

By December 31, 1946, one year after the registration requirement discussed above was implemented, 24,843 persons had been registered with the NASD as registered representatives of members.

The number of registered representatives had grown to 44,488 by the end of 1955. Thus, in nine years there was an increase of 19,645 registered representatives. This was an increase of almost 80 per cent over the nine-year period.

The rate of growth was even greater from 1956 through 1960. During the five-year period, from the beginning of January, 1956, to the end of December, 1960, the number of registered representatives increased from 44,488 to 93,828, an increase of 110%. At the end of 1966, there were 87,806 registered representatives.

The growing interest in the securities market after World War II brought a rapid increase in the number of member firms and their registered representatives. As this trend gained momentum, the NASD Board of Governors became more and more concerned over the number of inexperienced individuals entering the securities business. A special study committee was appointed by the board to determine how to develop standards for admission into the securities business.

Minimum Qualification Standards Established

After considering several possible solutions, the committee concluded and ultimately recommended that certain minimum qualification and experience standards should be imposed as a condition of membership in the NASD. Consequently, in the fall of 1955 the board adopted the following minimum qualification standards as a condition of membership or registration as registered representatives:

1. that all officers, partners, proprietors and other registered representatives of members, who on June 1, 1956, did not have at least one year's experience in the investment banking or securities business, must pass a qualification examination in order to remain in the business;

2. that after June 1, 1956, all applicants for membership and all applicants for registration as officers, partners or other registered representatives of members, must pass an examination before becoming registered, unless they have had at least one year's experience in the securities business in the capacity of a registered representative.

The above qualification examination program was formally established by amendments to Article I, Section 2 of the NASD Bylaws. In the fall of 1955, the membership approved the amendments by formal vote.

The NASD's Board of Governors was authorized to prescribe all the details pertaining to any examination for determining the qualification of applicants for membership or registration as a registered representative.

Ultimately, a bank of 441 questions was prepared for use in the NASD Qualification Examination. These questions were constructed by members of the NASD Board of Governors and its staff working in consultation with the authors of the present book, in their capacity as faculty members from the Graduate School of Business Administration, New York University. The NASD has been giving a qualification examination to employees of member firms since the fall of 1956.

The Qualification Examination for membership or registration in the NASD was originally composed of 100 questions selected from the bank of 441 questions. The questions were all either of the true-false or the multiple-choice type. The examination took one hour.

The purpose of the qualification examination was to require applicants for registration to demonstrate that they have the technical proficiency and knowledge of the securities business necessary to perform properly their duties as registered representatives.

The first examinations were given in the fall of 1956. At that time, a grade of only 65 per cent was needed in order for the applicant to pass the examination and qualify as a registered representative. Later the passing grade was raised to 80 per cent. Despite this higher minimum passing grade, however, the NASD recognized the need for a stiffer qualification examination, and ultimately a more difficult qualification examination was constructed.

Examination for Qualification as a Registered Representative

The Examination for Qualification as an NASD Registered Representative is now a 125-question, two-hour, multiple-choice examination. There are several forms of this examination, each of which requires equal knowledge. This examination is not scored on the curve, and all questions are given equal weight. The subject matter covered in the examination is presented in a booklet entitled "Study Outline for Qualification Examination for Registered Representatives and Registered Principals," which is available from the NASD headquarters in Washington, D.C.

NASD Qualification Examination for Principals

As noted, the National Association of Securities Dealers requires that all persons associated with a member who are designated as Principals must pass a Qualification Examination for Principals and be registered as a Principal with the Association.

The examination for Principals is subjective and includes multiple choice, short answer, and paragraph essay questions. A maximum of three hours is allowed to complete the examination. The examination is scored on the basis of a point value which has been assigned to each question.

The subject matter of the questions in the examination is drawn from the Study Outline for Qualification Examinations for Registered Representatives and Registered Principals.

Subject Matter of Examination for Principals

All the subjects covered in the Examination for Principals are listed in the Study Outline for Qualification Examinations for Registered Representatives and Registered Principals. Questions in the examination for Principals generally delve deeply into the subjects covered and require a high level of understanding of the subject matter. For example, in the examination for Principals, questions on financial statements could:

1. require the candidate to compute such items as "book value of common stock," "current ratio," "earnings per share," and other pertinent ratios using sample financial statements.
2. require the candidate to indicate what immediate effect, if any, actions such as stock dividends or redemption of preferred stock at a premium, could have on a corporation's working capital or its retained earnings or on shareowner's equity.
3. require the candidate to compare the performance of open-end investment companies having the same investment objectives, using data from financial statements.

Subjects of particular importance to those who will be acting in a managerial capacity are also covered in the examination for Principals.

Report of Results of Examinations

The results of the examinations are reported to the applicant's firm in the following manner. If the applicant passes the examination, the member firm will receive notice of the applicant's registration. This notice will give the examination grade as either A (excellent), B (good), or C (fair). If the applicant fails the examination, a notice of failure will be sent to the member firm along with an analysis of the examination paper.

Applicants who fail the examination the first time they attempt it, may not try again for thirty days. A sixty-day waiting period is required for those who fail it in their second attempt. A ninety-day waiting period is required before each additional attempt for those who have failed the test three or more times.

The Qualification Examinations for Registered Representatives or Principals are given only to individuals who have submitted applications for registration, or to those registered representatives whose title or designation is being changed to that of Principal. An examination fee of $25 must be paid every time the Qualification Examination for Principals is taken. An examination fee of $20 must be paid each time the Qualification Examination for Registered Representatives is taken.

The president of the NASD may, in exceptional cases and where good cause is shown, waive the applicable Qualification Examination upon written request by the member, and accept other standards as evidence of an applicant's qualifications for registration. Advanced age, physical infirmity, or experience in fields ancillary to the investment banking or securities business will not individually of themselves constitute sufficient grounds to waive a qualification examination.

Examination Centers

Examinations are given in approximately seventy cities throughout the United States. A certificate of admission to the examination centers is mailed to the applicant's firm after the application and fees have been processed by the executive office. Applicants for examination may then report to any of the examination centers. Details of times and places for examination sessions are stated in a schedule which is mailed with the certificate of admission.

Coordination with Exchanges

The Examination for Qualification as a Registered Representative of the NASD is coordinated with the Full and Limited Registration Examinations of the New York and American Stock Exchanges. An applicant for registration with a firm holding membership in any combination of these three organizations may qualify for registration with all at a single examination session. When the application for NASD registration is received, a certificate of admission for the coordinate portion of the NASD-Stock Exchange Examination is mailed by the

NASD to the appropriate stock exchange. The applicant will receive, from the exchange, certificates of admission for all examinations he must take to qualify with the NASD and the appropriate stock exchange (s) .

The Examination for Principals is coordinated with the New York Stock Exchange Examination for Members and Allied Members, and applicants required to take both of these examinations may qualify their examination requirements at a single examination session by taking a coordinate form of these examinations. Arrangements for this may be made by contacting the NASD or NYSE. NASD examinations also are coordinated with the Pacific Coast Stock Exchange examinations.

Coordination with the States

The NASD examination program is now coordinated to varying degrees with the programs of certain states. An applicant for NASD registration may make arrangements to sit for the State Securities Law Examination required by the states of Oklahoma, Kansas, Missouri, and Texas at the NASD examination center (s) located in each of these states. At the NASD test centers in Missouri, both the Missouri and Kansas Securities Law Examinations are administered. There is no charge by the NASD for the administration of any State Securities Law Examination. Thus an applicant for NASD registration may qualify with the NASD, the New York or American Stock Exchanges, and a state at the same examination session.

NASD examinations are also given overseas.

Necessary forms and information on these procedures may be obtained from the NASD Executive Office, Qualification Examination Department, 888 17th Street N.W., Washington, D.C.

REVIEW QUESTIONS

1. What are the reasons why supervision of sales people is difficult? Explain how the NASD has attempted to solve the supervision problem.
2. Who must register as a representative and what are the rules he must obey?
3. Who in the securities business does *not* have to register?
4. Are bank employees permitted to become registered representatives?
5. Who must certify, to the Board (NASD) the business repute, training, and experience of the prospective registered representative?

6. Does a registered representative of a member firm have to devote his entire time during business hours to the business of the member firm:
    a. if the firm is only an NASD member?
    b. if the firm is a New York Stock Exchange Member?

7. List the circumstances under which a person may *not* be registered as NASD registered representative.

8. Explain how a registered representative may terminate his registration with, and without, resignation.

9. Define the term *principals.* Whom do they include? (Name six.)

10. How does the examination for *principals* compare with the one for *registered representatives?*

Federal
and State Securities
Regulation

Chapter 15

The securities business is one of the most highly regulated industries in the United States. A wide variety of federal and state legislative acts have been enacted to govern the activities of the individuals and institutions engaged in this economic area. The products handled by the securities business (stocks and bonds) are regulated from the cradle to the grave, so to speak. The services supplied by the individuals and institutions in the securities business are subject to this same intensive and extensive regulation.

From the time a corporation gives birth to a new security issue until the time that issue dies (through refunding or retirement, merger, consolidation, reorganization, or dissolution of the corporation) the issue is watched, controlled, studied, observed, evaluated, checked and double checked. Furthermore, all individuals and institutions involved in its conception, birth, active life, old age, and death are subject to codes, rules, regulations, laws, and restrictions of many types and from many sources.

In addition to the regulatory details spelled out by the federal and state statutes, securities and security issuers, underwriters, brokers, dealers, and salesmen are subject (when applicable) to the extensive regulations, rules, and codes of:

1. The National Association of Securities Dealers, Inc.
2. The New York Stock Exchange
3. The American Stock Exchange
4. Various regional securities exchanges
5. The orders and interpretations of a variety of regulatory agencies, such as:
   a. The Securities and Exchange Commission
   b. The Interstate Commerce Commission
   c. The Federal Power Commission
   d. The Federal Reserve System's Board of Governors

6. Individual firms in the securities business
7. Various securities associations and institutes

The extent of the regulation existing in the securities business is clearly illustrated by taking the example of the broker/dealer. Under certain conditions an individual operating as a broker/dealer has to apply, qualify, and register in five separate places as follows:

1. *With the Securities and Exchange Commission.* All broker/ dealers operating in interstate commerce are required (under provisions of the Securities Exchange Act of 1934 and the 1964 amendments) to file a registration form with the SEC. A qualification examination is required by the Federal Government.
2. *With the appropriate agency of the state in which the broker/ dealer has his principal place of business.* In some states (New York, for example) certain requirements for qualification are more stringent than for registration with the SEC. In some states a qualification examination is required.
3. *With the National Association of Securities Dealers Inc.* Requirements for qualification are given in Chapter 14. Note, however, that a qualification examination is required.
4. *With the New York Stock Exchange.* A qualification examination is required.
5. *With the American Stock Exchange.* A qualification examination is generally required.

It is interesting to note that as many as four or five separate qualifying examinations may be required to effect registration in all of the required places.

Federal Securities Regulation

Any securities business being conducted on an interstate basis is subject to the provisions of the federal securities laws. Generally speaking, the federal securities laws are more comprehensive and more stringent than their state counterparts. However, some state laws appear in certain respects to be more restrictive and detailed than the various federal provisions designed to regulate the same general area. In some cases, it appears obvious that the state legislative bodies have not provided statutes governing a given area of the securities business because of their feeling that the federal securities laws were already adequately supplying any needed restrictions in that area.

The Securities and Exchange Commission

The Securities and Exchange Commission (SEC) organized July 2, 1934, is the U.S. Government Agency which administers the federal securities laws. The commission consists of five men appointed by the president for five year terms.

The Act of Congress which created the SEC is called the Securities Exchange Act of 1934.

The commission administers seven major pieces of federal legislature all of which relate to the nation's securities business. These are:

1. The Securities Act of 1933[1]
2. The Securities Exchange Act of 1934
3. The Public Utility Holding Company Act of 1935
4. The Trust Indenture Act of 1939
5. The Investment Company Act of 1940
6. The Investment Advisers Act of 1940
7. The Securities Acts Amendments of 1964

The SEC also serves as an advisor to the federal courts in the corporate reorganization proceedings under Chapter X of the National Bankruptcy Act.

Securities Act of 1933

The Securities Act of 1933 was the first of a series of federal legislative acts passed to regulate the interstate activities of the securities business. This act has two basic objectives:

1. "to provide full and fair disclosure of the character of securities sold in interstate and foreign commerce and through the mails."
2. to prohibit certain fraudulent acts and practices in the sale of securities generally, and to prohibit statements, acts, and practices which tend to misrepresent the facts or deceive the investor.

The Securities Act is often referred to as the "truth in Securities Act," and attempts to assure that the investing public will have adequate information with which to make an accurate informed evaluation of a security being offered for sale.

Registration of Securities

One of the main provisions of the Securities Act of 1933 deals with the registration of securities. The act requires registration with the SEC of all securities covered by the act before these securities may be

---

[1]This act was administered by the Federal Trade Commission until September, 1934.

offered for public sale by an issuing company or by any person in a "control" relationship to such a company.

To meet this registration requirement, specified information dealing with many aspects of the corporation must be presented in detail in a registration statement and filed by the issuer with the SEC.

Exemptions

Certain securities issues are exempt from registration with the SEC. Some of the major exemptions are:

1. Securities issued or guaranteed by the U.S. Government, any state government or territory or any of their public instrumentalities.
2. "Small" issues of new securities where a total amount of $300,000 or less is issued in any one year. (These are known as Regulation A offering.[2])
3. Security issues sold entirely on an intrastate basis.
4. Private placements where securities are sold to a limited number of investors.
5. National or State bank issues.
6. Securities issued by common carriers, e.g. railroad securities, the issuance of which is subject to the Interstate Commerce Act.
7. Securities issued by nonprofit organizations.
8. Securities exchanged by the issuer with its existing security holders exclusively where no commission or other remuneration is involved.

The registration statement filed with the SEC generally contains much more information about the issuing company than the typical investor will take time to read. Ordinarily, the registration statement contains information about the type of business, the purpose of the securities issue, comparative balance sheets and income accounts, statements about suits pending against the corporation, compensation of the promoter, the underwriting spread, and the price at which the security will be issued, among numerous other things.

Under the Securities Act of 1933, an abbreviated form of the registration statement (called a prospectus) must be delivered to all initial buyers of registered securities. The act also states that every written communication soliciting an order of open-end investment company shares must be accompanied or preceded by a prospectus. The prospectus

[2]Although Regulation A offerings are exempt from registration with the SEC, it is necessary for the issuer to file a circular or specified content with the commission at least fifteen days before the proposed date of offering. Also, an offering circular generally must be used in connection with the sale of such securities and their sale is subject to the Rules of Fair Practice of the NASD.

contains the most important information covered in the registration statement.

When the SEC examines the registration statement covering a particular security issue, it looks primarily for false or misleading statements (or omissions) of a material nature. The act provides penalties of fine or imprisonment or both for any such misleading statements or omissions. All persons signing the registration statement are liable for misleading statements or omissions of fact. Criminal penalties of five years in prison and/or $5,000 fine may be imposed. Civil suits may be brought for recovery within three years of offering, and one of discovery.

It is important to remember that the SEC does not approve securities registered with it and offered for sale. In fact, the SEC does not even guarantee the accuracy of the disclosures made in a prospectus or registration statement. Nor does it pass on the merits of a particular security covered by a registration statement. The individual investor, not the SEC, must make the ultimate decision concerning the value or worth of the security.

In order to make certain that the role of the SEC in reviewing the registration statement of a new issue is not misunderstood, the Securities Act requires a statement on each prospectus indicating the limitation of the SEC's authority. This statement, which must be printed in heavy type on the prospectus cover, is as follows:

THESE SECURITIES HAVE NOT BEEN APPROVED OR DISAPPROVED BY THE SECURITIES AND EXCHANGE COMMISSION NOR HAS THE COMMISSION PASSED UPON THE ACCURACY OR ADEQUACY OF THIS PROSPECTUS. ANY REPRESENTATION TO THE CONTRARY IS A CRIMINAL OFFENSE.

Effective Date of the Registration Statement

A twenty-day waiting period (or cooling-off period as it is often called), must elapse between the filing date and the date the registration statement becomes effective. Once the registration statement becomes effective, the securities may be sold.[3] This minimum interval, which may be extended or shortened by the SEC, is necessary in order to give the commission time to examine the registration statement and call for any

---

[3]During 1965, the average length of time needed by the SEC to "clear" a registration statement was about thirty-six days. This change from the average of twenty days needed in 1950 is primarily due to two factors as follows:
  a) The total number of registration statements being filed with the SEC was about three times as large in 1965 as in 1950.
  b) Registration statements for new issues (which are harder to clear) made up a much larger proportion of the total registrations in 1965 than they did in 1950.

additional required information from the issuer. The SEC asks for this supplementary material by issuing a deficiency letter which outlines to the company any additional information needed and any changes which must be made. When the additions and changes called for by the deficiency letter have been prepared, they are presented in an amended registration statement and filed with the SEC.

Preliminary Prospectus

Until the registration statement becomes effective, no confirmation of a sale may be made. However, during this waiting period, a preliminary prospectus (referred to in the past as a "Red Herring" prospectus) may be used. A preliminary prospectus is one which is complete except for amendments as to price and any additional required information. It may be used to acquaint potential investors with essential facts in order to obtain indications of interest prior to the effective date of a registration statement.

The outside front cover of the preliminary prospectus must bear the caption "Preliminary Prospectus" in red ink. It must also show the date the prospectus was issued, and must have the following statement printed in prominent type:

> A registration statement relating to these securities has been filed with the Securities and Exchange Commission but has not yet become effective. Information contained herein is subject to completion or amendment. These securities may not be sold nor may offers be accepted prior to the time the registration statement becomes effective. This prospectus shall not constitute an offer to sell or the solicitation of an offer to buy nor shall there be any sale of these securities in any state in which such offer, solicitation or sale would be unlawful prior to registration or qualification under the securities laws of any such state.

The public offering price and the underwriting spread are not decided until shortly before the actual offering. When they are decided, a final amendment (setting forth the public offering) is filed with the SEC. If everything is acceptable to the commission, the registration statement will be ordered effective and the securities will be released for actual sale.

Stop Orders

A stop order suspending the effectiveness of a registration statement can be entered by the SEC whenever it appears that the registration statement contains any untrue statement of a material fact or any misleading omission of a material fact. An opportunity is given for a hearing before the stop order is imposed.

The Securities Exchange Act of 1934

The Securities Exchange Act of 1934 is one of the most important federal statutes regulating the securities business. It was enacted following a number of congressional investigations which uncovered the existence of a variety of undesirable and improper practices in the securities markets of the early 1930's.

The Exchange Act became law on June 6, 1934, and had the express objective of establishing and maintaining fair and honest markets for securities.

As a result of the stock market crash in 1929, and the confusion which followed, American investors generally lost confidence in securities as a safe and profitable investment medium. Such a situation is a calamity in a capitalistic society which depends on private capital for the machines required to sustain industrial health and promote economic growth. Congress knew it was essential that this lost confidence be restored as quickly and as completely as possible.

The Securities Act of 1934 was the statute Congress offered to help the securities business place its house in order and keep it there. Its provisions were designed to outlaw the misrepresentations, manipulations, and other abusive practices which had been preventing the functioning of just and equitable principles of trade in the securities markets. From its provisions and amendments, the Securities and Exchange Commission and the National Association of Securities Dealers Inc. were created to help with its enforcement.

EXCHANGE REGISTRATION. The Securities Exchange Act of 1934 provides for the registration and regulation of securities exchanges, and the registration of the securities listed on such exchanges. To insure fair and orderly markets, all exchanges, unless exempt, must register with the SEC.[4] Under the Securities Acts Amendments of 1964, the Exchange Act also provides for the registration and regulation of certain securities traded over-the-counter. See page 278.

One primary objective of the Exchange Act is to provide the investing public with reliable information regarding securities listed on national securities exchanges and the corporations which issued such securities. To provide this information, detailed registration statements must be filed by each corporation listing its shares on an exchange. The Exchange Act forbids trading in any nonexempt security on a national exchange unless the security is registered. Data contained on the registration form must include all pertinent material facts and must be set forth in such a manner so as not to be misleading. The Exchange Act

[4]A detailed discussion of the organization, operation and regulation of registered securities exchanges is presented in Chapter 12.

establishes financial and other reporting requirements for issuers of securities registered under the act.

BROKER/DEALER REGISTRATION. The Exchange Act also requires the registration of securities brokers and dealers. Unless a securities broker/dealer is registered with the SEC, he is denied the use of the mails or of any instrumentality of interstate commerce, to effect any securities transaction.

PROXY SOLICITATIONS. The Exchange Act also concerns itself with proxy statements and the regulation of proxy solicitations of issuers of securities registered under the act. Under provisions of the act, the SEC insists that all proxies must be detailed and truthful and must avoid false or misleading statements of material fact. Furthermore, the proxy statement must not omit any material fact necessary to make statements already made not false or misleading. The proxy statement must disclose all pertinent information concerning the matter to be decided by the proxy vote, and a place should be provided on the proxy to enable the shareholder to vote yes or no.

INSIDER TRADING RESTRICTIONS. The Exchange Act also establishes reporting requirements and imposes trading restrictions on the directors, officers and principal securities holders of corporations whenever such persons are trading in the securities of their own companies. Principal securities holders subject to these provisions are those shareholders who are beneficial owners of more than 10 per cent of the outstanding securities of a registered class of stock. Under the regulations, all such "insiders" must report their initial holdings to the SEC, and must report any change that takes place in their beneficial ownership within ten days after the end of each calendar month in which any change occurs.

Corporate insiders, by virtue of their position, may have information of a company's condition and prospects which is unavailable to the general public. This inside knowledge may be used by such persons to their personal advantage in trading in the company's securities. Thus regulations have been promulgated which remove the profit incentive in short-term trading by permitting the corporation or its stockholders to bring suit for the recovery of profit from insiders on transactions completed within six months. "Short" sales and "sales against the box" are also prohibited by such persons by the Exchange Act regulations.

Several sections of the Securities Exchange Act contain provisions which specifically prohibit manipulation of securities prices and fraudulent and deceptive practices in the securities markets.

Securities transactions designed to give a misleading appearance of active trading are illegal. Two such prohibited fictitious practices are:

1. "Wash Sales," where one person purchases and sells the same

stock at about the same time in order to give the impression
of activity in the stock, and

2. "Matched Orders" where transactions between individuals
acting in concert to "paint the tape" record a price and give
the impression of delivery without a true change of ownership.

The Exchange Act also prohibits pool devices used to manipulate
markets and the spreading of rumor or false information.

PERSONNEL RECORDS. Under the provisions of Section 17 of the Securities Exchange Act of 1934 certain records are required to be kept by
brokers and dealers who are registered with the SEC. Beginning in 1962,
such brokers and dealers were required to maintain personnel records
showing the following information for each of their registered representatives:

1. name, address, social security number, and the starting date of
employment or other association with the member, broker, or
dealer;
2. date of birth;
3. the educational institutions attended and degree or degrees granted;
4. a complete, consecutive statement of all business connections for
at least the preceding ten years, including the reason for leaving
each prior employment, and whether the employment was part-
time or full-time;
5. a record of any denial of membership or registration, and of any
disciplinary action taken, or sanction imposed upon the registered
representative by any federal or state agency, or by any national
securities exchange or national securities association, including any
finding that he was a cause of any disciplinary action or had violated
any law;
6. a record of any denial, suspension, expulsion, or revocation of
membership or registration of any member, broker, or dealer with
whom he was associated in any capacity when such action was taken;
7. a record of any permanent or temporary injunction entered against
the representative or any member, broker, or dealer with which he
was associated in any capacity at the time such injunction was
entered;
8. a record of any arrests, indictments, or convictions for any felony
or other misdemeanor, except minor traffic offenses of which he
has been subject;
9. a record of any other name or names by which the registered representative has been known previously or which he has used in
the past.

Credit Extension to Customers
by Brokers and Dealers

The Board of Governors of the Federal Reserve System prescribes the regulations which determine the amount of credit brokers

and dealers may extend to their customers. These regulations are contained in the Federal Reserve Board's *Regulation T*. Regulation T was adopted by the FRS Board of Governors under the provisions of the Securities Exchange Act of 1934 (as amended).

Regulation T relates to the extension of credit to customers by brokers and dealers doing business through the medium of a member of a national securities exchange. Initial margin requirements are established under Regulation T and have ranged from 40 to 100 per cent. Regulation T does not permit the extension of credit on unlisted stocks by brokers or dealers. Regulation T is considered one of the most important federal regulations affecting the day-to-day activities of registered representatives.

Regulation U applies to the extension of credit on registered securities by banks. It deals with loans by banks for the purpose of purchasing or carrying registered stocks.

The Effect of Credit on Securities Prices

The general market level of securities prices is determined by the supply of securities in relation to the over-all demand for these securities. The greater the demand for a given quantity of securities the higher the general market prices of the securities will tend to become.

The demand for securities, at any given time, is determined by the number of shares investors desire to buy and *are able to buy*. The demand for a product, securities included, is not determined alone by the desires and wishes of individuals and institutions. *Demand couples desire with purchasing power.* (Most people probably would enjoy owning a yacht. However, the demand for yachts is rather limited because few people have the necessary money to acquire and operate a yacht.)

Individuals and institutions acquiring securities in the market obviously have to pay for these securities. The amount of money they have, plus the amount of money they can borrow, will determine the upper limits to their total potential demand for securities. Thus one of the major elements in the over-all level of demand for securities is the amount of credit in the securities markets.

The excessive use of securities market credit can have unpleasant repercussions in the market. Excessive use of credit in the past introduced extreme instability into the securities markets and ultimately brought about severe market price declines.

During the 1920's, investors in the market could buy securities for as little as 10 per cent down, with 90 per cent of the purchase price of the security being advanced to the customer by the broker. The broker in turn would secure money from banks to lend to his customers. Thus with $500, an investor could purchase 100 shares of stock selling for $50 a share. (Five hundred dollars bought a total of $5,000 worth of stock.) This practice of using other people's money to make money for themselves appealed to a great many speculators, and as long as the price trend in the market was strongly upward, the practice was profitable indeed. So profitable, in fact, that a great many people with very limited financial resources viewed the stock market as a golden medium for quick riches and, of course, were attracted to it.

The dangers of an excessive amount of credit in the securities market became forcefully evident, however, when the general price trend in the market changed to downward. Stocks purchased on a 10 per cent-down basis began to drop in price. Soon the 10 per cent of the securities purchase price (the margin) put up by the investor was gone. Brokers called for additional margin, and whenever it wasn't immediately forthcoming, the customer's securities were quickly sold to protect the broker's capital. During severe price downturns, the 10 per cent margins provided by the purchasers were quickly wiped out, and the flood of sell orders from brokers attempting to protect their capital caused the market prices to drop more and more sharply.

These sharp drops in securities prices forced the selling of additional shares by investors and brokers in order to protect their interests. Thus, a chain reaction was set in motion, which caused extremely rapid and precipitous downward changes in securities prices. Many investors lost their entire capital investment in a matter of a few hours or in some cases, within a very few minutes.

As a measure to prevent a recurrence of the great stock market crash of 1929, margin regulations and other types of controls were introduced.

The percentage of the total purchase price of securities which investors must provide from their personal funds is now determined by Regulation T. The percentage has varied in recent years from 100 per cent to 50 per cent.

Special Cash Account
Provisions of Regulation T

Regulation T as it applies to transactions in over-the-counter securities is concerned primarily with "cash account" transactions with customers. The "cash account" (technically termed the "special cash account") described in Regulation T is one in which customers' transactions are effected with the understanding that they will be settled promptly. "Promptly" means within the two or three days required by use of the usual transmittal facilities. Thus the over-the-counter dealer is in the unique position of being able to cite his responsibilities under federal law when requiring customers to pay promptly for over-the-counter securities. Furthermore, Regulation T prohibits an over-the-counter dealer from seeking a competitive advantage over another dealer by negotiation with a customer regarding extension of credit.

Under Regulation T, broker/dealers can purchase any security for, or sell any security to, any customer with a special cash account, provided:

1. sufficient funds for the purpose are already held in the account, or
2. the broker/dealer accepts a statement of the customers, in good faith, that he will "promptly" make full cash payment for the security and does not contemplate selling the security prior to making such payment.

Thus the following suggested securities transaction would be prohibited by Regulation T:

> The buyer for a large insurance company to whom you have offered a block of bonds which your firm owns, tells you on December 17 that his company has "closed" its books on new investments for the balance of the year, but he will buy the securities you have offered, if your firm will deliver them against payment on January 2 in the new year.

Broker/dealers can sell any security for, or purchase any security from, any customer with a special cash account provided:

1. the security is held in the account, or
2. the broker/dealer accepts, in good faith, a statement that the customer or his principal owns the security and that the security is to be promptly deposited in the account.

Customers purchasing securities (other than an exempted security) in the special cash account should make full payment within seven full business days unless the transaction is a C. O. D. transaction. If full payment is not made within this specified seven-day period, the broker/dealer must cancel or otherwise liquidate the transaction, unless an extension of time for payment for good cause has been granted. Extensions of time for payment may be granted, for good cause, by a committee of the NASD or by the appropriate authority from any registered national securities exchange.

In the case of unissued securities, payment is due within seven full business days after the date on which the security is made available by the issuer for delivery to purchasers.

If the security when purchased is a "when distributed" security which is to be distributed in accordance with a published plan, payment is due seven days after the date on which the security is distributed.

When a customer owes a broker/dealer less than $100 in connection with a purchase transaction in a "special cash account," the broker/dealer may disregard the provisions of Regulation T.

Failure of underwriters to insist upon prompt payment by dealers for open-end investment company shares which dealers have sold to customers is contrary to the generally accepted standards of the business and may contribute to misuse of customers' funds by the dealers involved.

A dealer may not arrange for a bank loan for his customer or in the name of his customer for the purpose of purchasing and carrying securities using over-the-counter securities as collateral.

If a purchase is made by a customer with the understanding that payment is to be made on delivery, the broker/dealer may treat the transaction as one in which the applicable period is not seven full business days but thirty-five calendar days. However, the broker/dealer has the obligation to deliver and obtain payment as soon as possible. He may not delay delivery. Delivery to a bank for the account of a customer is equivalent to delivery to the customer.

If any shipment of securities is incidental to the consummation of the transaction, the seven-full-business-day period is extended by the number of days required for such shipments, but not for more than seven additional full business days.

Frozen Accounts

All purchases must be paid for by the account owner as specified by Regulation T. The account must be paid before the purchased securities may be sold.[5] Failure to settle the account promptly will result in the account being frozen for a period of ninety calendar days. An account must be frozen for ninety days if through failure to make prompt settlement the transaction is cancelled or liquidated. When an account is frozen, subsequent purchases can be effected only if cash is on hand prior to the execution of the transaction. However, this restriction may be disregarded in the following instances:

1. Whenever, in the case of a sale without prior payment, full payment is received before the expiration of the seven full business days and provided the proceeds of the sale have not been withdrawn on or before the day on which payment is received.
2. Whenever, in the case of delivery to another broker/dealer, the delivering broker obtains from the receiving broker a written statement that the securities are being accepted for a Special Cash Account of the customer in which there are already sufficient funds to make full cash payment for the securities so received.

If the last day of either the thirty-five or ninety calendar day period falls on a Saturday, Sunday, or holiday, such period extends to the next full business day.

[5]Cancellation of a transaction for a reason other than to correct an error is deemed to constitute a sale.

Extensions of Time

If properly authorized, an extension of time may be granted which will modify this frozen account cash requirement. Whenever any exceptional circumstance has prevented payment for securities within the periods specified in the regulation, an application for a limited extension of time to obtain such payment may be made to any national securities exchange or to the NASD. The authority of appropriate committees of the NASD to grant extensions of time is limited to transactions in special cash accounts. A special NASD form, obtainable at the district offices of the Association, must be used for any such application.

The regulation is clear in its statement that applications for extensions must be based on exceptional circumstances, and a clear recitation of those circumstances is necessary. If the periods of time alloted by the regulation have expired, a violation has already occurred, and no authorization exists to grant an extension on such a transaction. In fact, an extension erroneously granted after a violation has occurred is of no value.

A broker or dealer is prohibited from extending or maintaining, or arranging for the extension or maintenance of, credit to or for a customer with respect to any transaction in any security which was a part of a new issue in which the broker or dealer participated as a member of a selling group within thirty days prior to such transaction.

There are many other provisions in Regulation T which are very important to any broker/dealer whose business involves other than merely cash transactions. Copies of Regulation T may be obtained from any Federal Reserve Bank or from the office of the Securities and Exchange Commission.

Public Utility Holding Company Act of 1935

The Public Utility Holding Company Act passed in 1935 gave the Securities and Exchange Commission regulatory powers over holding companies controlling electric and gas operating companies. Under provisions of the act, the SEC's jurisdiction also extends to natural gas pipeline companies and other nonutility companies which are subsidiaries of registered holding companies. The purpose of the act was to eliminate abuses that have characterized the formation, financing, and operation of public utility holding companies.

A holding company, for purposes of the act, is defined as any company which owns or controls 10 per cent or more of the outstanding voting securities of an electric or gas public utility company.

All public holding companies having electric and gas subsidiaries in more than one state are subject to the act and are required to register with the SEC.

Under provisions of the act, the SEC required the break up of scattered groups of public utilities and limited holding companies to a single integrated simplified system. Before the implementation of the act corrected these abuses, the capital structure of various holding companies had been unduly complicated, and the distribution of voting power among the stockholders had been unfair and inequitable.

The holding company structure is limited by the act to three layers of corporate entities. This means that a holding company cannot have a subsidiary which in turn has a subsidiary which is a holding company.

In order to prevent undue concentration of control of public utility companies, the SEC must approve the purchase or acquisition of the securities or assets of a public utility by a holding company before such a transaction can take place.

In order to prevent unwarranted expansion, a registered holding company or any of its subsidiaries may not issue securities without first receiving the approval of the SEC. Furthermore, "upstream loans" or borrowing by holding companies from their subsidiaries is prohibited by the act.

Trust Indenture Act of 1939

The Trust Indenture Act, passed in 1939, established specific statutory standards for trust indentures. A trust indenture (or deed of trust, as it is often called) is a contractual agreement between a corporation issuing bonds and a trustee or trustees representing the investors who own the bonds. The trust indenture indicates in detail the rights and privileges of the bondholders and how these may be enforced. It also gives a detailed description of rights, privileges, and liabilities of the debtor corporation. Under a trust indenture, the trustee (generally a bank or trust company) represents all of the bondholders and deals with the corporation on their behalf.

The Trust Indenture Act applies only to those trust indentures under which more than $1,000,000 of securities may be outstanding at any one time. Most debt securities, such as mortgage bonds, debentures, notes, and so on, are issued pursuant to a trust indenture.

SEC studies made prior to the passage of the Trust Indenture Act disclosed that many trust indentures failed to provide the minimum protection needed to prevent losses to debt security holders. In addition, the studies revealed that many corporations neglected to provide an independent trustee to protect the bondholder's investment. The act was specifically designed to prevent losses brought about by these conditions.

The following elements are among those which must be included in order for a trust indenture to qualify under the act:

1. Provision for a financially responsible corporate trustee with a minimum combined capital and surplus of $150,000.
2. Provision for a trustee free from conflicting interest so that nothing will interfere with his obligation to protect the bondholders.
3. A statement specifying the action to be taken by the trustee in case the corporation fails to live up to the terms of the indenture agreement.
4. Provision for the submission of an annual report from the trustee to the bondholders.

The Trust Indenture Act requires the indenture trustee to use the same degree of care and skill in carrying out his indenture duties as a "prudent man" would use in the conduct of his own affairs.

The trustee has a variety of duties to perform under the provisions of the act, all of which are designed to protect the interests of the bondholders.

The trustee authenticates the bonds but in no way guarantees the payment of interest on the bonds nor the return of the bondholders' principal.

The trustee is required to check performance of the covenants of the indenture. He must see that interest and taxes are paid when due, and must notify the bondholders within ninety days in the event of default.

The trustee must see that the sinking fund and collateral covenants of the indenture are met, and must submit annual reports to the bondholders.

The trustee can be sued for negligence if conditions warrant.

The corporation issuing the securities covered by the bond indenture is required to keep the trustee furnished with an up-to-date list of all bondholders. The issuing corporation must also supply the trustee with evidence of recording the indenture.

Under the Act, *exculpatory clauses* formerly used to eliminate all liability of the indenture trustee are outlawed.

Securities issued under an indenture covered by the act must also often be registered under the Securities Act of 1933. The registration statement of such securities is not permitted to become effective unless the indenture is qualified under the Trust Indenture Act and unless necessary information as to the trustee and the indenture is contained in the registration statement.

Investment Advisers Act of 1940

The Investment Advisers Act of 1940 sets the statutory standards which govern the activities of individuals or organizations who engage in the business of advising others (either directly or in writing) with respect to their securities transactions. Unless exempt from the act, all organizations and individuals who receive compensation for giving such advice must register under this act.

The basic purpose of the act is to protect investors from practices based on fraud or deceit.

The major points of control established by the act are as follows:

1. It is unlawful for registered investment advisers to engage in fraudulent or deceitful practices in connection with clients or potential clients.
2. Investment advisers are required to disclose the nature of their interest, if any, in transactions executed for their clients.
3. Investment advisers are prohibited from entering into profit sharing arrangements with clients. (This means that an investment adviser may not base his compensation upon a share of the capital gains or appreciation of his client's funds.)
4. Investment advisers are not allowed to assign investment advisory contracts without their client's consent.

Most investment counselors and securities services are covered by the Act; however, certain exemptions exist, such as:

1. newspapers
2. magazines of general circulation
3. brokers and dealers giving gratuitous and incidental advice
4. banks and government security houses
5. individuals such as attorneys, accountants, engineers, and teachers who are giving advice which is purely incidental

Under certain conditions, investment advisers are not required to register under the act. Some examples are:

1. When the investment adviser furnishes advice only to investors who are residents of the state in which he maintains his principal place of business, and he does not give advice about securities listed on a national securities exchange, or admitted to unlisted trading privileges on such an exchange.
2. When the investment adviser has only investment companies and insurance companies as clients.
3. When the investment adviser has had fewer than fifteen clients in the last twelve months and does not represent himself to the public generally as an investment adviser.

The SEC may deny registration as an investment adviser to unqualified individuals. The commission may also revoke the registration of an investment adviser for violation of certain provisions of the Investment Advisers Act.

Under the Investment Advisers Act, the SEC has the authority to investigate violations of the act and to secure information by subpoena or by inspecting the books and records of an investment adviser.

Registration of an investment adviser may be denied or revoked under the following conditions:

1. When an investment adviser has been enjoined from furnishing investment advice or conducting a securities business by a court of competent jurisdiction or
2. When he has been convicted in the past ten years of a crime involving securities, the securities business, or certain related activities or
3. When he has falsified his application for registration or has otherwise violated certain provisions of the act.

Any individual denied registration, or any investment adviser faced with revocation of his registration, is permitted a hearing.

The Investment Company Act of 1940

The Investment Company Act of 1940 is the most important piece of federal legislation relating to investment company activities. The act provides for the registration and regulation of companies primarily engaged in the business of investing, reinvesting, owning, holding, or trading in securities.

The organization, operation and regulation of investment companies is discussed in detail in Chapter 16 and Chapter 17.

The Securities Acts Amendments of 1964

The Securities Acts Amendments of 1964 became law on August 20, 1964. This legislation extensively revised the Securities Exchange Act of 1934. It also amended one aspect of the Securities Act of 1933. The amendments contained in this new law affect the legal obligations of both broker/dealers and the issuers of securities. The 1964 Amendments stemmed from the *SEC's Report of Special Study of the Securities Markets* and are considered the most significant statutory advance in federal securities regulation and investor protection since 1940, when the Investment Advisers Act was passed.

The 1964 amendments strengthen the standards of entrance into the securities business. They also make the disciplinary controls of the SEC more effective. Further, they strengthen the rules of the NYSE, the NASD, and other self-regulatory securities organizations relating to brokers and dealers and persons associated with them.

The 1964 amendments provide shareholders in publicly held companies whose securities are traded over the counter the same fundamental disclosure protections as have been provided to investors in companies whose securities are listed on an organized securities exchange.

This has been accomplished by extending the registration, periodic reporting, proxy solicitation and insider reporting and trading provisions of the Exchange Act to a substantial portion of the securities not listed on organized securities exchanges.

"OTC Registered" Securities. Unless specifically exempted by the 1964 amendments, the new provisions apply to those non-listed companies engaged in interstate commerce with assets in excess of $1,000,000 and with 750 or more shareholders of record of one class of their stock. Such companies must file a registration statement with the SEC. Securities of issuers registered under these new requirements are referred to as "OTC registered." During the course of the first year in which the 1964 amendments were in effect, over-the-counter issuers filed a total of 1,508 registration statements with the SEC.

On July 1, 1966, the "OTC registered" securities requirements were extended to include nonexempted corporations engaged in interstate commerce with total assets in excess of $1,000,000 and with 500 or more shareholders of record of one class of their stock. Under the terms of the 1964 amendments, corporations are considered to be engaged in interstate commerce if they are in a business affecting interstate commerce, or if their securities are traded by use of the mails or by any other means or instrumentality of interstate commerce.

Termination of Registration. The 1964 amendments provide that an "OTC registered" issuer may terminate registration of a class of securities by filing a certification with the SEC indicating that the securities are held of record by less than 300 persons. Registration will be terminated ninety days after an issuer files the certification or within such shorter time as the SEC directs, unless the Commission determines, after notice and opportunity for hearing, that the certification is untrue.

An "OTC registered" issuer will continue to be subject to the periodic reporting, proxy solicitation and insider trading provisions of the act until registration has been terminated for each class of its registered equity securities. Any class of securities for which registration has been terminated thereafter will be subject to registration if on the last day of any fiscal year the class of securities are held of record by the requisite number of persons and the issuer has total asset in excess of $1,000,000.

Securities Exempted from the 1964 Amendments. As noted, securities listed and registered on any national securities exchanges are exempted from the 1964 amendments. The following types of securities also are exempted:

1. securities issued by registered investment companies
2. securities of savings and loan associations and similar institutions, (other than stock generally representing non-withdrawable capital)
3. securities of certain nonprofit organizations operated exclu-

> sively for religious, educational, benevolent, fraternal, charitable, or reformatory purposes
> 4. securities of certain agricultural marketing cooperatives
> 5. securities of certain nonprofit mutual or cooperative organizations which supply a commodity or service primarily to members
> 6. direct obligations issued or guaranteed by the United States or any State or political subdivision thereof.

INSURANCE COMPANY EXEMPTION.   Insurance companies are exempt from the new registration requirements provided the company is regulated by its state of incorporation in all three of the following respects:

> 1. It is required to (and does) file annual reports with a state official or agency substantially in accordance with the requirements prescribed by the National Association of Insurance Commissioners;
> 2. It is regulated in the solicitation of proxies in accordance with the requirements prescribed by the National Association of Insurance Commissioners; and
> 3. The purchase and sale of securities, issued by the insurance company, by beneficial owners, directors or officers of the company are subject to regulation (including reporting and trading) substantially in the manner provided in section 16 of the Exchange Act of 1934.

REGULATION OF BANK SECURITIES.   The Securities Acts Amendments of 1964 state that the registration, periodic reporting, proxy solicitation, and insider reporting and trading provisions of the Exchange Act relating to all bank securities, both listed and unlisted, henceforth will be administered and enforced by the following agencies:

> 1. Securities issued by national banks and District of Columbia banks will be regulated by the Comptroller of the Currency.
> 2. Securities issued by state banks which are members of the Federal Reserve System will be regulated by the Board of Governors of the Federal Reserve System
> 3. Securities issued by state banks which are not members of the Federal Reserve System but are insured by the Federal Deposit Insurance Corporation will be regulated by the Federal Deposit Insurance Corporation.
> 4. Securities issued by state banks which are neither members of the FRS nor insured by the FDIC will be regulated by the Securities and Exchange Commission.

GENERAL EXEMPTION.   Under the 1964 amendments, the SEC has the power to exempt, in whole or in part, any issuer or class of issuers from the registration, periodic reporting and proxy solicitation provisions and to grant exemption from the insider reporting and trading provisions if such exemption is not inconsistent with the public interest or the protection of investors.

Pursuant to this authorization, the SEC exempted from registration any interest or participation in an employee stock bonus, stock purchase, profit sharing, pension, retirement, incentive, thrift, savings, or similar plan if the interest or participation is not transferable except in the event of death or mental incompetency. Any security which is issued solely to fund such plans also is exempted.

FOREIGN SECURITIES EXEMPTION. In addition to the above exemptions, the 1964 amendments specifically authorize the SEC to exempt securities of foreign issuers (and certificates of deposits issued against such securities) from the various registrations requirements if it finds that such action is in the public interest and is consistent with the protection of investors.

TYPE OF INFORMATION REQUIRED. An over-the-counter corporation required to register under the 1964 Amendments must furnish the SEC with information relating to its business, its capital structure, the terms of its securities, the persons who manage or control its affairs, the remuneration paid to its officers and directors, and the allotment of options, bonuses and profit-sharing plans. The corporation also must file material contracts not made in the ordinary course of business, and must notify the SEC of: major changes in control; important acquisitions or dispositions of assets; the institution or termination of important legal proceedings; and important changes in the issuer's capital securities or in the amount thereof outstanding. Current regulations require most issuers to file balance sheets, and statements of profit and loss and surplus for the preceding fiscal years, certified by an independent public accountant. In general, an account is not deemed to be independent if, during the period covered by his certification, he had any direct, or material indirect, financial interest in the issuer, its parent, or its subsidiaries, or had any other relationships or arrangements which might affect the exercise of his independent judgment.

PERIODIC REPORTING. The information provided by the "OTC registered" corporation on the registration statement must be kept current by filing:

1. an appropriate annual report, within 120 days after the end of each fiscal year, containing certified financial statements and various other pertinent information;
2. a report within ten days after the end of any month during which certain major events occur and;
3. where applicable, specified semi-annual reports concerning operating results.

PROXY SOLICITATIONS. The 1964 amendments contain provisions extending proxy regulations and rules to "OTC registered" securities. These amendments provide that whenever the management of "OTC registered" corporations solicit proxies with respect to an annual meeting of security holders at which directors are to be elected, the proxy statement used must be accompanied or preceded by an annual report. This report to security holders must contain financial statements for the last fiscal year which will (in the opinion of management) adequately reflect the financial position and operations of the issuer. If these statements, accompanying the proxy solicitation, differ materially from those filed with the SEC, an explanation must be given concerning the effect of the differences.

OVER-THE-COUNTER TRADING SUSPENSION. Under the 1964 amendments, the SEC has been granted the authority to summarily suspend trading in any "OTC registered" security. These suspensions can be for a maximum of ten days and broker/dealers are prohibited from trading in any such security during its period or periods of suspension.

INSIDER REPORTING AND TRADING. Under the 1964 amendments, each officer and director of an "OTC registered" issuer and each beneficial owner of more than 10 per cent of the outstanding securities of a registered class of such an issuer must file a report with the SEC showing his holdings in the company's equity securities. The report must be filed on the effective date of the registration statement or within ten days after the individual becomes a director, officer, or beneficial holder. After the initial report, each such person must file an additional report each time any change takes place in his beneficial ownership of the "OTC registered" securities. This report is due within ten days after the end of each calendar month in which any transaction takes place.

The 1964 amendments indicate that profits realized by any such persons, from transactions completed within six months in the equity securities of "OTC registered" issuers, may be recovered by, or on behalf of, the issuing corporation. The regulations also prohibit such persons from selling such securities "short" or "selling against the box."

PROSPECTUS DELIVERY REQUIREMENTS. The 1964 amendments indicate that a prospectus must be delivered in connection with transactions in securities registered under the act for ninety days from the effective date of the registration statement or the date the security was bona fide offered to the public.

The ninety-day prospectus delivery requirement applies only to the securities of an issuer which has not previously sold securities pursuant to an earlier effective Securities Act registration statement. Those companies which have previously sold securities which were registered as indicated above, are subject to the traditional forty-day prospectus delivery requirement.

The SEC is empowered to shorten the forty- or ninety-day period if it determines it is in the public interest to do so.

ENLARGED DISCIPLINARY AUTHORITY. The Securities Acts Amendments of 1964 modified in important respects the provisions of the Exchange

Act relating to disciplinary action against brokers and dealers and persons associated with them. For the first time the SEC and the NASD are authorized to proceed directly against individuals associated with broker/dealer firms and to impose sanctions on such individuals, including suspension. They also may bar an individual from being associated with a broker/dealer.

The sanctions which may be imposed upon broker/dealers were expanded to include censure and suspension of registration for up to twelve months. Furthermore, the statutory disqualifications which bar an individual from being registered as a broker/dealer or from being associated with a broker/dealer were expanded to include certain additional types of injunctions, convictions, and violations.

QUOTATIONS. The Securities Acts Amendments of 1964 provided as statutory basis for the NASD to adopt rules designed to produce fair and informative quotations and to prevent fictitious and misleading quotations as well as to promote orderly procedures for collecting and publishing such quotations.

Net Capital Rule of Securities and Exchange Commission

The Securities and Exchange Commission has prescribed rules governing the capital position of registered brokers and dealers. These rules make particular reference to the ratio of the dealers' net aggregate indebtedness to the capital position. Under these net capital rules, which are enforced for the SEC by the National Association of Securities Dealers, the ratio of aggregate indebtedness to net capital of a broker/dealer must not exceed twenty to one. These SEC rules setting the maximum ratio of indebtedness to net capital were the only SEC rules governing the capital position of registered brokers and dealers for many years.

A special study of the securities markets was concluded by the SEC in 1963. This broad study was designed to determine the adequacy of investor protection in the nation's securities markets. The Report of the Special Study indicated that the SEC net capital rule, as then constituted, did not provide adequate investor protection and recommended the adoption of a minimum net capital requirement for securities broker/dealers. It was felt that such a minimum requirement was one approach to assuring a broker/dealer community of principals and firms qualified in terms of responsibility and commitment. The Report of the Special Study recommended that the financial requirement need not, and should not, be a uniform one for all firms, but should be appropriately scaled to reflect the size and type of business in which different firms were engaged.

Based on the above recommendations, the Securities and Exchange Commission Rule 15c3-1 (commonly referred to as the Net Capital

Rule) was amended on May 26, 1965, to become effective on December 1, 1965. This rule now specifies that a registered broker/dealer must not permit its "aggregate indebtedness" to exceed 2000 per cent (twenty times) of its "net capital," and must not permit its net capital to fall below a minimum of $2,500 or $5,000 depending on the type of business conducted. It is interesting to note that this rule adopted by the SEC in 1965 was almost identical to a minimum net capital requirement proposed by the NASD in 1942.[6]

The NASD has provided the following material as a general clarification of the application of the SEC's Net Capital Rule under normal circumstances.[7]

MINIMUM NET CAPITAL REQUIREMENT. The minimum net capital requirement which must be maintained is $5,000 for a member broker/dealer operating a general securities business. To qualify for the $2,500 minimum net capital requirement level, a member broker/dealer must deal exclusively in mutual fund shares and/or share accounts of insured savings and loan associations, except for the sale of other securities for the account of a customer to obtain funds for immediate reinvestment in mutual fund shares, or as a broker or dealer transacting business as a sole proprietor. A registered broker/dealer also may effect occasional transactions in other securities for his own account with, or through, another registered broker/dealer.

A broker or dealer operating under the $2,500 minimum must promptly transmit all funds and deliver all securities received in connection with his activities as a broker or dealer, and may not otherwise hold funds or securities for customers, or owe money or securities to customers. The minimum capital requirements do not exempt a broker/dealer from insuring that its aggregate indebtedness does not exceed 2,000 per cent of its net capital, but rather, the rule requires net capital of either 5 per cent of aggregate indebtedness or the minimum capital amount, whichever is greater.

EXEMPTIONS. Certain broker/dealers have been exempted from the rule. Generally speaking, the exemption applies only to members in good standing of specified registered securities exchanges who are subject to

---

[6]An analysis was made by the NASD of the disciplinary actions against member firms involving unfair prices, misuse of customer's funds or securities, and improper recommendations. This analysis showed that the above violations tended to be most prevalent in firms whose net capital was small or inadequate. Consequently, the NASD Board, in May, 1942, adopted a new rule which was to establish minimum capital requirements as a requisite for membership in the NASD. The proposed requirement called for a minimum of $5,000 capital for members doing a general securities business and $2,500 for those firms not handling customers' funds or securities, but working on a cash basis only. This rule was submitted to the membership in June, 1943, and was approved by the membership. There was opposition to this proposal from some groups in the securities business and the rule was subsequently disapproved by the Securities and Exchange Commission.

[7]The complete text of the Net Capital Rule is given in the Appendix.

the capital requirements of the particular exchange, and to those broker/ dealers who, upon written application, satisfy the commission that the nature of their business is such that an exemption is warranted. Brokers who limit their business to effecting transactions in variable annuity contracts as a general agent for the issuer are also exempt, if they meet certain specified conditions.

AGGREGATE INDEBTEDNESS DEFINITION. Aggregate indebtedness is defined as the total money liabilities of a firm, with certain exclusions. The exclusions may be summarized as follows:

1. Liabilities "adequately collateralized" by securities or spot commodities owned by the broker/dealer or by exempted securities (An adequately collateralized liability is one which would be considered a fully secured loan by banks in the community making comparable loans to broker/dealers. For example, if banks generally were lending 50 per cent of the value on collateral consisting of common stock, a $10,000 liability secured by at least $20,000 of common stocks would be "adequately collateralized.")

2. Liabilities for securities failed to receive for the account of the broker/dealer and which have not been resold by him;

3. Liabilities fully secured by fixed assets, e.g., real estate or any other asset which is not included in the computation of "net capital" under the rule;

4. Liabilities on open contractual commitments, e.g., firm commitment underwritings contracted for but for which settlement has not been made (Usually these are not recorded on the firm's general ledger.)

5. Liabilities subordinated under a "satisfactory subordination agreement." (A satisfactory subordination agreement is defined in subsection (c) (7). The terms of such an agreement operate to make the liability, in effect, a part of the firm's capital.) If the period of time for which the agreement was written has elapsed and by its termination the member's capital would be below that required by the rule, the lender is "locked in" until such time as the capital of the member has improved to where the subordinated debt is no longer needed for the firm to comply with the rule; and

6. Amounts segregated in accordance with the Commodity Exchange Act.

NET CAPITAL DEFINITION. Net capital is the net worth (gross capital) of a broker/dealer, with certain adjustments which are designed generally to reflect the current liquid position of a firm. The adjustments may be summarized as follows:

a. The addition of unrealized profits and the deduction of unrealized losses in any firm accounts;

b. The deduction of all assets which cannot be readily converted into cash, i.e., non-liquid assets. Where indebtedness is secured by any such asset, the deduction made is the excess of the value of the asset over the amount of the indebtedness;

c. The deduction of specified percentages ranging up to 30 per cent (called a "haircut") of the market value of all securities (except exempted securities) and commodities futures contracts in long or short positions in firm accounts, including the net long or net short positions in open contractual commitments, and a deduction of 1½ per cent of the market values of the total long or total short futures contracts in each commodity, whichever is greater, carried for all customers;

d. The exclusion of liabilities subordinated under a satisfactory subordination agreement (as related above, this effectively makes such liabilities a part of capital); and

e. For sole proprietors, the deduction of the excess of liabilities not incurred in the securities business over assets not used in the business.

[For purposes of the rule, firm accounts include "accounts of partners," which are considered partnership property, as covered in sub-section (c) (4).]

The following are illustrative examples showing the computation of aggregate indebtedness and net capital, with accompanying explanations, from the balance sheets of hypothetical broker/dealers.

EXAMPLE NO. 1

Firm conducting a general securities business with adequate capital above minimum requirement of $5,000.00 or 1/20th of aggregate indebtedness, whichever is greater.

ABC INVESTMENTS CO.
BALANCE SHEET
DECEMBER 31, 19....

Assets		Liabilities	
Cash	$ 5,000.00	Bank Overdraft	$ 2,000.00
Customers Cash Accounts		Customers' Cash Accounts	3,000.00
Secured	4,000.00	Fails to Receive (for account of customers)	
Unsecured	6,000.00		9,000.00
Fails to Deliver	10,000.00	Inventory Account Common Stocks Short	
Inventory Account Common stocks long (market)	12,000.00	(market)	3,000.00
Investment Account Common stocks long		Deposit on Firm Securities Loaned	3,000.00
(market)	5,000.00	Taxes Payable	1,000.00
Real Estate	15,000.00	Mortgage Payable	10,000.00
Exchange Memberships	5,000.00	Total Liabilities	$31,000.00
Prepaid Expenses	1,000.00	Partnership Capital	35,000.00
Goodwill	3,000.00	Total Liabilities and	
Total Assets	$66,000.00	Capital	$66,000.00

ABC INVESTMENTS CO. (Cont'd.)

Aggregate Indebtedness

Bank Overdraft	$ 2,000.00
Customers' Cash Accounts	3,000.00
Taxes Payable	1,000.00
Fails to Receive (for account of customers)	9,000.00
	$ 15,000.00
	x.05
	$ 750.00

Minimum Capital Required
($5,000.00 or 1/20 of aggregate in-
debtedness, whichever is greater) $5,000.00

Computation of Net Capital

Capital		$35,000.00	
Deduct: Real Estate (less Mortgage			
Payable)	$5,000.00		
Exchange Membership	5,000.00		
Customer Cash Accounts			
(unsecured)	6,000.00		
Prepaid Expenses	1,000.00		
Goodwill	3,000.00		
30% of Inventory Account			
($12,000.00)	3,600.00		
30% of Investment Account			
($5,000.00)	1,500.00		
30% of Common Stocks—			
short ($3,000.00)	900.00		
Total Deductions		$26,000.00	
Net Capital			$9,000.00
Net Capital Above			
Minimum Requirement			$4,000.00
Allowable aggregate indebtedness:	$180,000.00		
Actual aggregate indebtedness:	15,000.00		

EXPLANATION:

Of the liability accounts, only Deposit on Firm Securities Loaned, Common Stocks (short) and Mortgage Payable are not considered aggregate indebtedness, because Deposit on Firm Securities Loaned account reflects the cash deposit repayable to the borrowing broker/dealer when he returns the securities and is thus secured by the securities which are owned by the firm. Mortgage Payable Account is excluded because it is adequately secured by a fixed asset for which no credit is given in the firm's net capital. Common Stocks (short) is reduced by a 30 per cent "haircut" with the "haircut" being deducted from capital. The account is not considered aggregate indebtedness under Rule 15c3-1.

The rule specifies that aggregate indebtedness must not exceed twenty times (2000%) the net capital. Conversely, required minimum net capital should be at least one-twentieth (5%) of the aggregate indebtedness, or $5000, whichever is greater under Rule 15c3-1.

The computation of net capital begins with the inclusion of the firm's net worth (called "capital" in this example). Adjustments are then made in accordance with the rule. The adjustments called for here are deductions of Real Estate less Mortgage Payable, any Exchange Memberships, unsecured customer debits, all prepaid expenses, Goodwill Accounts, (all assets which are not readily converted into cash), 30 per cent "haircuts" on the market values of the Inventory Account (long), Investment Account (long) and common stocks (short).

The assets for which full credit is given are Cash, Customers' Secured Cash Accounts and Fails to Deliver. The Fails to Deliver are considered, in this example, to be for contracts with other firms who are able and willing to pay for the securities covered thereunder. In exceptional circumstances, such as where the buying firms may be unwilling or unable to honor the contracts for any reason, this asset might not be allowed for purposes of the rule, and would be shown as a deduction from net capital.

The Customers' Cash Accounts (secured) are considered here to be debit balances in bona fide special cash accounts of customers, payments for which are expected promptly in the normal course of business. Debit balances arising from the cancellation or liquidation of transactions pursuant to Regulation T would normally not be an allowable asset and would be shown as a deduction from net capital.

EXAMPLE NO. 2

Firm conducting a general securities business with adequate capital above minimum requirement of $5,000.00 or 1/20th of aggregate indebtedness, whichever is greater.

THE BIG CORPORATION
BALANCE SHEET
DECEMBER 31, 19

Assets		Liabilities	
Cash	$ 25,000.00	Fails to Receive:	
Fails to Deliver (firm account)	50,000.00	Account of Firm	$ 40,000.00
		Account of Customers	30,000.00
Customer Cash Accounts— (debit balances)	50,000.00	Collateral Loan (secured by firm securities)	50,000.00
Customers' Future Commodities	19,000.00		
Contracts (regulated commodities)		Common Stocks Trading (market value $5,000.00)	10,000.00
Common Stocks Trading (market value $100,000)	60,000.00	Customers' Future Commodities	
Securities Borrowed	10,000.00	Contracts - Short (regulated commodities)	11,000.00
Advances to Salesmen	5,000.00	Subordinated Loan from Officers	50,000.00
Furniture and Fixtures	15,000.00	Total Liabilities	$191,000.00
		Common Stock $33,000.00 Outstanding	
		Earned Surplus 10,000.00	
		Capital	$ 43,000.00
Total Assets	$234,000.00	Total Liabilities and Capital	$234,000.00

NOTE: Contractual commitment for Firm Account not recorded in a ledger account for money underwriting—10,000 shares Acme Motor Corp.: $50,000.00.

Customers' Future Commodities Contracts

Quantity	Long Commodity	Market	Quantity	Short Commodity	Market
5 MBU	Soybeans	$ 7,500.00	4 MBU	Soybeans	$ 6,000.00
4 MBU	Corn	4,000.00	5 MBU	Corn	5,000.00
5 MBU	Wheat	7,500.00			
		$19,000.00			$11,000.00

Aggregate Indebtedness:

Fails to Receive account of customers	$30,000.00	
Commodities Futures Contracts—Short (account of customers)	11,000.00	
Minimum capital required ($5,000.00 or 1/20th of aggregate indebtedness, whichever is greater).	$41,000.00 x.05 $ 2,050.00	$ 5,000.00

Computation of Net Capital:

Total Capital		$43,000.00
Add: Subordinated Loan from Officers	$50,000.00	
Unrealized Profit on Trading (long)	40,000.00	
Unrealized Profit on Trading (short)	5,000.00	
Total additions		$95,000.00
Total		$138,000.00
Deduct: 30% of Trading - long (market)	$30,000.00	
30% of Trading - short (market)		
1½% of customers commodities	1,500.00	
Futures contracts ($20,000.00)	300.00	
Advances to Salesmen	5,000.00	
Furniture and Fixtures	15,000.00	
30% of Open Contractual Commitment	15,000.00	
Total Deductions		$ 66,800.00
Net Capital		$ 71,200.00
Net Capital above minimum requirement		$ 66,200.00
Allowable Aggregate Indebtedness	$1,424,000.00	
Actual Aggregate Indebtedness	41,000.00	

EXPLANATION:

In this example the Subordinated Loan from Officers is not only excluded from aggregate indebtedness, but is actually added to the firm's net capital since it is covered by a satisfactory subordination agreement. [See Rule 15c3-1 (c) (7)].

The difference (in this case a profit) between the market value and book values of the firms's long and short trading accounts is also shown as an addition to net capital.

Besides the haircut on the market value of the Trading Account, and the non-liquid assets (Advances to Salesmen and Furniture and Fixtures), there is also a deduction of a haircut on the firm's open contractual commitment, even though this item has not yet been recorded to the regular accounts of the firm.

A deduction from Net Capital is made of 1½ per cent of the market values of the total long or short future conrtacts *in each commodity*, whichever is greater, carried for customers. For this example, since the long commodity futures contracts in Soybeans is $7,500 and the short futures contracts are $6,000.00, the firm takes the long account of $7,500. The long futures contracts in Corn are $4,000.00 and the short contracts are $5,000 so the firm would therefore take the short account of $5,000. In the wheat futures there is only long future contracts of $7,500 with no short account so the long future contracts of $7,500 is taken. The resulting amount of $20,000 is used for the 1½% deduction.

The breakdown of Customers Commodities Futures Contracts as shown on the balance sheet is for illustrative purposes only and need not be shown this way on a firm's balance sheet. A supporting schedule of commodities futures contracts should, however, be attached to and made a part of, the Form 17A-5 as would ordinarily be done with securities in an inventory or investment account.

The Securities Borrowed Account is included as an allowable asset because in this example it is considered that the broker/dealer has paid cash to, or deposited securities with, the lending broker equivalent to the market value of the borrowed securities. If he had not done so, that amount for which no equivalent value was paid or credited would be a liability, and would also be included in aggregate indebtedness if the securities were borrowed for any purpose other than for delivery against customers' sales.

EXAMPLE NO. 3

Firm dealing exclusively in mutual funds with capital slightly in excess of the minimum requirement of $2,500.00 or 1/20th of aggregate indebtedness, whichever is greater.

GHI & CO.
BALANCE SHEET
DECEMBER 31, 19 ...

Assets		Liabilities	
Cash in Bank	$2,600.00	Due To Mutual Fund	
Petty Cash	50.00	Underwriters	$ 300.00
Due From Customers	475.00	Notes (unsecured)	1,750.00
Due From Mutual Fund		Note (secured)	250.00
Underwriters	225.00	Commissions Payable To	
Investment Account (market)	2,250.00	Salesmen	50.00
Furniture and Fixtures		Total Liabilities	$2,350.00
(depreciated)	200.00	Capital	3,450.00
		Total Liabilities and	
Total Assets	$5,800.00	Capital	$5,800.00

Aggregate Indebtedness:	
Due To Mutual Fund Underwriters	$ 300.00
Notes (unsecured)	1,750.00
Commissions Payable To Salesmen	50.00
Total	$2,100.00
	x.05
	$ 105.00

Minimum Capital Required ($2,500.00
or 1/20th of aggregate indebtedness, whichever is greater) $2,500.00

Computation of Net Capital

Capital		$3,450.00
Deduct:		
Furniture and Fixtures	$ 200.00	
30% of Investment Account ($2,250.00)	675.00	875.00
Net Capital		$2,575.00
Net Capital above minimum requirement		$ 75.00
Allowable Aggregate Indebtedness:	$50,000.00	
Actual Aggregate Indebtedness:	2,100.00	

EXPLANATION:

As to the liabilities, the Notes (secured) Account is excluded from aggregate indebtedness because under the Rule adequately secured liabilities (those secured by firm securities or spot commodities) are not considered part of such indebtedness.

In the net capital computation, the Furniture and Fixtures Account is excluded because such an account is not readily converted into cash. The Investment Account of securities is given the regular 30 per cent "haircut" and that reduction is deducted from capital.

In this example the allowable aggregate indebtedness exceeds the actual aggregate indebtedness by $47,900 and the firm has net capital of $2,575 which is slightly above the minimum required capital of $2,500.

EXAMPLE NO. 4

Firm requiring minimum net capital of $5,000.00 or 1/20th of aggregate indebtedness, whichever is greater, with a net capital violation.

JKL & CO.
BALANCE SHEET
DECEMBER 31, 19 ...

Assets		Liabilities	
Cash in Banks	$ 19,200.00	Notes Payable (unsecured)	$ 32,500.00
Fails to Deliver		Due to Customers	28,500.00
(firm account)	30,500.00	Fails to Receive (for ac-	
Customers Cash Accounts	18,000.00	counts of customers)	45,000.00
Investment Account-Munic-		Taxes Payable	5,000.00
ipal Bonds (market)	26,250.00	Total Liabilities	$111,000.00
Inventory Account (market)	31,500.00	Capital	15,250.00
Advances to Salesmen	300.00		
Furniture and Fixtures			
(depreciated)	500.00	Total Liabilities and	
Total Assets	$126,250.00	Capital	$126,250.00

Aggregate Indebtedness:	
Notes Payable (unsecured)	$ 32,500.00
Due to Customers	28,500.00
Fails to Receive	
(for accounts of customers)	45,000.00
Taxes Payable	5,000.00
	$111,000.00
	x.05
	$ 5,550.00

Minimum Capital Required ($5,000.00 or 1/20th of aggregate indebtedness, whichever is greater). $ 5,550.00

Computation of Net Capital

Capital		$ 15,250.00	
Deduct:			
Advances to Salesmen	$ 300.00		
Furniture and Fixtures	500.00		
30% Long Inventory	9,450.00	10,250.00	
Net Capital			$5,000.00
Net Capital needed to meet minimum requirement			$ (550.00)
Allowable Aggregate Indebtedness		$100,000.00	
Actual Aggregate Indebtedness		$111,000.00	

EXPLANATION:

In the computation, Advances to Salesmen is excluded from net capital because the account is not secured. The Furniture and Fixtures Account is excluded because under the Rule such an account cannot be readily converted into cash. The Inventory Account which is here carried at market, is reduced by 30 per cent under the Rule and this reduction is deducted from net capital. The Investment Account is carried at full market price with no reductions because municipal bonds are an exempted security.

In this example, even though the firm has the minimum required capital of $5,000 under Rule 15c3-1, the aggregate indebtedness of the firm is sufficiently large so as to require $5,550 net capital in order to cover such indebtedness. This results in a deficiency of $550.

State Regulation of the Securities Business

State governments, in the United States, have been regulating various aspects of securities for well over 100 years. Massachusetts, for example, had a statute attempting to control the stock and bond issues of common carriers in that state as early as 1852. This was long before any federal government attempts were made to regulate the securities industry. Federal securities legislation of general applicability did not appear until 1933, by which time forty-seven states had laws governing the activities of the securities firms operating within their boundaries.

BLUE SKY LAWS. State statutes regulating the offering and sale of securities within the jurisdiction of the respective states are commonly referred to as "blue sky laws". "The name that is given to the law," said Justice McKenna in *Hall vs. Geiger-Jones Co.*, 242 U.S. 539, 550 (1917), "indicates the evil at which it is aimed; that is, to use the language of a cited case, 'speculative schemes which have no more basis than so many feet of blue sky.' "

All states except Delaware had some type of blue sky law in force in 1966. There is no local blue sky law in the District of Columbia. Securities transactions there are governed by the federal statutes.

The first blue sky law was adopted by Kansas in 1911. During the next several years, many of the other states adopted similar laws. The variations in state laws, however, made it difficult for investment bankers to market issues on an interstate basis. Consequently, in 1929, a Uniform State Securities Act was approved by the Conference of Commissioners on Uniform State Laws and by the American Bar Association, and served as a basis for numerous new state securities laws.

The Investment Bankers Association prepared three model blue sky laws, in 1948, which brought the 1929 Uniform State Securities Act up to date and coordinated it with the existing Federal securities laws. As a result, a new Uniform State Securities Act was approved in 1956 by the Conference of Commissioners on Uniform State Laws and the American Bar Association.

The provisions of the forty-nine state blue sky laws currently on the books vary tremendously. Although space does not permit individual treatment of these laws in this book, broker/dealers and registered representatives are urged to become fully cognizant of the securities regulations of the state in which they operate, since their professional lives may very well depend on such knowledge. Furthermore, registered representatives might advise customers to consult with legal counsel with respect to the interpretation of the technicalities of certain state laws and their application in individual circumstances.

Although the provisions of the forty-nine blue sky laws vary widely, they generally utilize three distinct types of regulatory devices.

1. The blue sky laws in most states have anti-fraud provisions, which prohibit deceitful and fraudulent securities activities. Those states which do *not* have anti-fraud provisions generally have provisions prohibiting misrepresentation or misleading statements.
2. All but a few states require the registration or licensing of certain persons engaging in the securities business in their respective state. Approximately half of the states require some form of registration or licensing of investment advisers. It is important for a registered representative to remember

that registration or licensing as a salesman in the state in which you conduct your principal activities does not automatically permit you to make sales in other states where registration is required. Similarly, registration of a broker/dealer under the Securities Exchange Act of 1934 or its amendments does not exempt that broker/dealer from state registration requirements.

3. Most states have provisions in their blue sky law calling for the registration or licensing of nonexempt securities.

State registration may be effected by:

1. *Notification.* Under this method, registration statements for securities which meet certain specified standards become effective after a long period of time unless the registration is denied by the State Security Administrator.

2. *Coordination.* Under this procedure, copies of the prospectus filed under the Securities Act of 1933 may be filed with the appropriate State Security Administrator in lieu of a state registration statement. State registration becomes effective at the same time federal registration becomes effective.

3. *Qualification.* Under this method, a registration statement must be filed with the appropriate State Security Administrator who in turn must approve or disapprove the registration statement. In many states the Security Administrator has broad authority to refuse to permit particular security offerings for a variety of reasons. This broad power of the state administrator to approve or disapprove a specific security issue can be more restrictive than the SEC power under the Securities Act of 1933, since the federal law is primarily a "disclosure" statute rather than an "approval" statute.

Registration of securities under the Securities Act of 1933 does not automatically exempt a security from state registration requirements.

GENERAL CORPORATION LAWS. Most corporations, operating in the United States, are incorporated under the general corporation law of some state. These state laws are important to individuals in the securities business, since the conduct of an individual business firm's corporate affairs will be determined, in part, by the corporate laws of the state from which it received its corporate charter.

Since a corporation is an artificial person created by the state, its whole character and most of its activities depend upon the conditions of its charter. The amounts and kinds of securities that may be issued by a corporation will be indicated by its charter.

PRUDENT MAN RULE. In forty states or more, trustees operate under some form of Prudent Man Rule. Under this rule, trustees are relatively free to select the securities they feel are best for their customers. No specific group of securities are designated as legal investments for trustees in "Prudent Man Rule" states.

The term "Prudent Man Rule" stems from a Massachusetts Court decision in 1930 which stated in part that "all that can be required of a trustee . . . is that he shall conduct himself faithfully and exercise a sound discretion. He is to observe how men of prudence, discretion and intelligence manage their own affairs, not in regard to speculation, but in regard to the permanent disposition of their funds, considering the probable income as well as the probable safety of the capital to be invested."

A trustee operating under the Prudent Man Rule obviously must be careful in his selection of securities. The task of such a trustee is much more difficult than that of a trustee operating in a state where authorized trusteed investments are specifically designated by the state's "legal list."

LEGAL LISTS. Some states designate classes and groups of investments that may legally be purchased by a trustee operating in that state. This compilation of eligible securities is known as a "legal list."

In "legal list" states, the state banking department, or commission, annually publishes a list of securities (often called "legals") considered eligible for investment by institutional investors such as life insurance companies, mutual savings banks, commercial banks, trust companies, and restricted trust funds, operating in that state. Traditionally, the investments of such institutions have been limited, by the legal lists, to high-grade bonds, high-grade preferred stocks, and well-secured first mortgages on real estate. In recent years, however, many states have moved toward a liberalization of investment practices. These states now permit a portion of restricted trust funds to be invested in common stocks, and permit some investment in the shares of investment companies by these funds.

Partial control is exercised over the investment practices of fire and casualty insurance companies in some states. Typically, these regulations call for the investment of an established portion of the institutions funds in high grade bonds, while permitting remaining funds to be invested at the discretion of the company management.

Ordinarily, unrestricted trust funds, endowments of educational institutions, and philanthropic foundations, and the funds of investment companies are not subject to state control insofar as investment portfolio holdings are concerned.

Uniform Gifts to Minors Act

Gifts of securities to minors became possible through the passage of legislation sponsored by the New York Stock Exchange and the Association of Stock Exchange Firms. A "model law" was designed which made it possible to make an outright gift of securities to a minor child by using prescribed words of registration while reserving the power of management for a "custodian" until the child reached twenty-one years of age. This "model law" was enacted in a number of states.

A "Uniform Gifts to Minors Act" was prepared in 1956 and was adopted by the National Conference of Commissioners on Uniform State Laws. This Uniform Act broadened the old "model law," and permits gifts of money as well as securities. It also permits purchase of securities with money delivered to a custodian account for a child, and enlarges the choice of custodians.

Although the Uniform Act is in effect in almost every state, the various state laws do not follow the standard version in every respect. Consequently, individuals should be advised to consult legal counsel as to provisions existing in a particular state.

Information About State Securities Laws

Information about the securities laws and regulations of any particular state can be secured by contacting the proper state authority. Such information and the forms needed for registering in the state as a securities broker or dealer, or as a securities agent, or securities salesman can be obtained by writing or contacting the appropriate office indicated below:

Securities Commissioner
State Securities Commission
250 Administrative Building
Montgomery, Alabama 36014

Commissioner of Commerce
Division of Banking & Securities
Department of Commerce
Alaska Office Building
Pouch "D"
Juneau, Alaska 99801

Director of Securities
Arizona Corporation Commission, Securities Division
1688 West Adams
Phoenix, Arizona 85007

Securities Commissioner
State Bank Department, Securities Division
1515 West 7th Street
Suite 305
Little Rock, Arkansas 72202

Commissioner of Corporations
Division of Corporations
1020 N Street
Sacramento, California 95814

Securities Commissioner
Department of Law
Division of Securities
State Office Building
Denver, Colorado 80203

Director of Securities
Securities Division, Department of Banking
State Office Building
Hartford, Connecticut 06115

Since Delaware has no securities
law, there is no state authority
to contact.

Director, Securities Commission
424 Carlton Building
Tallahassee, Florida 32304

Secretary of State
Commissioner of Securities
214 State Capitol Building
Atlanta, Georgia 30334

Commissioner of Securities
Department of Regulatory Agencies
P.O. Box 40
Honolulu, Hawaii 96810

Commissioner of Finance
Department of Finance
State House
Boise, Idaho 83702

Securities Commissioner
Office of the Secretary of State
Securities Division
State Capitol Building
Springfield, Illinois 62706

Securities Commissioner
201 State House
Indianapolis, Indiana 46209

Superintendent of Securities
Securities Department
State Office Building
Des Moines, Iowa 50319

Securities Commissioner
Securities Division, State Corporation Commission
Fourth Floor, State Office Building
Topeka, Kansas 66612

Director, Division of Securities
Department of Banking & Securities
102 Mero Street
Frankfort, Kentucky 40601

Commissioner of Securities
108 Louisiana State Office Building
New Orleans, Louisiana 70112

Director, Securities Division
Department of Banks and Banking
State Office Building
Augusta, Maine 04330

Securities Commissioner
State Law Department
Division of Securities
One Charles Center
Baltimore, Maryland 21201

Supervisor, Division of Investigation of Securities
Department of Public Utilities
100 Cambridge Street
Boston, Massachusetts 02202

Director, Corporation and Securities Bureau
Department of Commerce
Corr Building
P.O. Drawer C
Lansing, Michigan 48904

Commissioner of Securities
Securities Division
Department of Commerce
260 State Office Building
St. Paul, Minnesota 55101

Secretary of State
Securities Division
Room 120 New Capitol
Jackson, Mississippi 39205

Commissioner of Securities
Office of Secretary of State
Securities Department
Capitol Building
Jefferson City, Missouri 65101

Investment Commissioner
Capitol Building
Helena, Montana 59601

Department of Banking, Bureau of Securities
1310 State House
Lincoln, Nebraska 68509

Secretary of State
Division of Securities
Capitol Building
Carson City, Nevada 89701

Insurance Commissioner, Securities Division
State House Annex
Concord, New Hampshire 03301

Chief, Bureau of Securities
Department of Law and Public Safety
744 Broad Street Room 607
Newark, New Jersey 07102

Commissioner of Securities
Department of Banking
Securities Division
113 Washington Avenue
Santa Fe, New Mexico 87501

Assistant Attorney General
Department of Law
Bureau of Securities
80 Centre Street
New York, New York 10013

Securities Deputy
Securities Law Administration
Department of State
State Capitol Building
Raleigh, North Carolina 27602

Commissioner of Securities
401 State Capitol
Bismarck, North Dakota 58501

Commissioner of Securities
Division of Securities
417 Ohio Departments Building
Columbus, Ohio 43215

Administrator,
Oklahoma Securities Commission
Will Rogers Memorial Office Building
Room 403
Oklahoma City, Oklahoma 73105

Corporation Commissioner
Department of Commerce
Corporation Division
158 12th Street NE
Salem, Oregon 97310

Chairman, Pennsylvania Securities Commission
P.O. Box 249
471 Education Building
Harrisburg, Pennsylvania 17120

Securities Examiner
Department of Business Regulation
Securities Division
49 Westminster Street
Providence, Rhode Island 02903

Deputy Securities Commissioner
Department of State
Securities Division
State Life Building, 104 Palmetto
Columbia, South Carolina 29201

Commissioner of Securities
Department of Securities
State Capitol Building
Pierre, South Dakota 57501

Director, Division of Securities
Department of Insurance and Banking
114 State Office Building
Nashville, Tennessee 37219

Securities Commissioner
State Securities Board
Sam Houston State Office Building
P.O. Box 12306 Capitol Station
Austin, Texas 78711

Director, Securities Division
Department of Business Regulation
330 East Fourth South Street
Salt Lake City, Utah 84111

Commissioner, Department of Banking and Insurance
Division of Banking
State Office Building
Montpelier, Vermont 95602

Director, Securities Division
State Corporation Commission
P.O. Box 1197
Richmond, Virginia 23209

Securities Administrator
Department of Motor Vehicles
Division of Profession Licensing
Securities Section
P.O. Box 648
Olympia, Washington 98102

Commissioner of Securities
State Auditor's Office
State Capitol Building
Charleston, West Virginia 25305

Director, Department of Securities
538 Hill Farms State Office Building
Madison, Wisconsin 53702

Secretary of State
State Capitol Building
Cheyenne, Wyoming 82001

REVIEW QUESTIONS

1. What are the five separate places where a broker/dealer under certain conditions must apply, qualify and register?

2. List at least five acts now administered by the SEC.

3. Under the Securities Act of 1933, what is the purpose of the registration statement and what does it include?

4. What is a preliminary prospectus (Red Herring) and how does it differ from a final prospectus.

5. Name four important provisions of the Securities Act of 1934.

6. Explain the special cash account provision of Regulation T. How does Regulation T apply to extension of credit to customers by brokers and dealers who are *members* of a national exchange?

7. Much of the work of the SEC has been *completed* under the Public Utility Holding Company Act of 1935, namely the breaking up holding companies. What are the present supervisory concerns of the SEC under this act?

8. Under the *Trust Indenture Act* of 1939, what are the liabilities, rights, and privileges of (1) the issuing corporation, (2) the trustee, and (3) the bondholders?

9. Under the Securities Acts Amendments of 1964, a nonexempt corporation with assets in excess of ————, and with ———— or more shareholders must register with the SEC and be subject to the same rules as a listed company.

10. What are the most important securities which are exempt from the Securities Acts Amendment of 1964?

11. What is the net capital of the SEC? Define the aggregate indebtedness. Describe the firm's assets allowed in the computation and their appraisal.

12. Discuss state regulation of the securities industry, including Blue Sky laws.

13. What is the "prudent man" rule and how does it relate to the legal lists?

Investment Companies

Chapter **16**

An investment company is either a corporation (or a trust) through which investors pool their funds in order to obtain diversification and supervision of their investments. Simply put, an investment company is a financial institution engaged in the business of investing in securities.

Not every company which invests in securities is an investment company, however. Many kinds of institutions, financial and otherwise, with a variety of objectives in mind, invest at least a part of the funds they own, or hold, in securities.

Banks buy investments, for example, but their main functions are to make loans, provide checking account facilities, and safeguard the deposits of their customers. Operating corporations buy the securities of other corporations which do produce things. The objective of the holding company purchase, however, may not be investment, but control.

Insurance companies buy tremendous quantities of securities, but insurance companies are in the business of insurance, not the business of investing. The investment activities of insurance companies are designed to provide, in part, the dollars they need to pay the claims and annuities they are obligated to pay to their policy holders.

The investment company, however, has investing as its sole business activity and its sole reason for existence. Thus, investment companies are among the few types of institutions which spend all of their time and effort on investment activities.

An investment company is generally a business corporation holding a charter similar to that issued to any ordinary business corporation. It has the right to issue and sell bonds and both common and preferred stocks. The typical investment company, however, obtains its investment funds by selling its own common stocks to anyone wishing to buy them. (Very few investment companies have raised investment funds by issuing bonds or preferred stocks.) [1] The money thus obtained is reinvested by the investment company in a large variety of securities issued by other corporations.

The list of the securities purchased and held by the investment company is called its investment portfolio. The prices of investment company shares are related to the market value of the securities in the investment portfolio.

The Development of Investment Companies in the United States

The concept of the investment company has been known and extensively used in Europe for many decades. Investors in England and Scotland have utilized investment trusts, in one form or another, for collective investment purposes for at least the past century. However, when investment companies were first introduced into the United States, they did not catch the imagination nor much of the money of the American investor. During this early period, people seemed to regard investment companies with a high degree of suspicion, and by 1924 only about $15,000,000 had been used by American investors to buy the shares of domestic investment companies.

About this time, however, Americans embarked upon what turned out to be the greatest securities speculation binge in the history of this country, perhaps of any country. Securities of all shapes, sizes, colors, and description; securities that were good, bad, and indifferent, were indiscriminately snapped up by an ever-growing number of speculators.

Volume on the New York Stock Exchange rose from 1,029,145 shares per day average in 1924, to an average daily volume in 1929 of 4,276,808.[2] Stock prices became astronomically high. Some stocks which had not paid dividends in years were selling at market prices over $400 per share. During this period, anything remotely connected with the securities markets drew favorable glances from the public. Investment companies, particularly closed-end companies, were no exception, and from 1924 to 1929, their growth was extremely rapid. Many of the closed-end investment companies formed during this period were closely affiliated with investment banking houses and stock brokerage firms and are still active and successful today.

By 1929, new investment companies were being formed at the rate of about one a day, and the total funds invested in them approached $7 billion. In October, 1929, the artificially supported pyramid of the stock

---

[1] Some investment companies provide for limited borrowing, when this is judged desirable, to further their investment objectives. The Investment Company Act of 1940 limits the amount of borrowing to 33 per cent of net assets.

[2] The New York Stock Exchange Fact Book, 1959, p. 39.

market collapsed, dashing down with it the hopes and dreams of speculators and investors alike.

The economic chaos wrought by the speculative excesses of this period was instrumental in inducing the Congress to examine thoroughly the entire securities business. This investigation ultimately ended in the passage of a series of legislative acts designed to clear up the inclement investment climate of the United States. During the same period, the Securities and Exchange Commission was created to administer these new securities laws.

Several years later, in 1940, after another investigation, the Investment Company Act was passed. This act, along with the Securities Act of 1933, provides the basic statutory framework for the rules and regulations under which investment companies operate today.

Definition and Classification of Investment Companies

The Investment Company Act of 1940, as amended August 10, 1954, classifies and defines the various types of investment companies and establishes the requirements for their regulation. The act divides investment companies into three principal classes. These are: face-amount certificate companies; unit investment trusts; and management companies. The act defines these three types of investment companies as follows:

1. "Face-amount certificate company" means an investment company which is engaged or proposes to engage in the business of issuing face-amount certificates of the installment type, or which has been engaged in such business and has any such certificate outstanding.
2. "Unit investment trust" means an investment company which
   a. is organized under a trust indenture, contract of custodianship or agency, or similar instrument
   b. does not have a board of directors
   c. issues only redeemable securities, each of which represents an undivided interest in a unit of specified securities, but does not include a voting trust.[3]
3. "Management company" means any investment company other than a face-amount certificate company or a unit investment trust.

The management companies are by far the most common type in use today. There are two basically different types of management investment companies. One is the closed-end investment company. The other type is known as the open-end investment company or, more popularly, as the mutual fund. These companies are called management companies because they manage a diversified portfolio of various types of securities in accordance with certain specified investment objectives.

[3]Most contractual plans are unit investment trusts.

The Investment Company Act of 1940 defines these two types of management companies as follows:

1. "open-end company" means a management company which is offering for sale or has outstanding any redeemable security of which it is the issuer.
2. "closed-end company" means any management company other than an open-end company.

Management companies are further divided into diversified companies and nondiversified companies.

Practically all mutual funds and the majority of the closed-end investment companies are registered as "diversified" companies under the Investment Company Act of 1940. To qualify as a registered diversified company, an investment company must have 75 per cent or more of its total assets invested so that:

1. not more than 5 per cent of its assets is invested in any one corporation, and
2. not more than 10 per cent of the voting securities of any corporation is held by the investment company.

Specifically the Investment Company Act of 1940 indicates that a "diversified company" means a management company which meets the following requirements:

At least 75 percentum of the value of its total assets is represented by cash and cash items (including receivables). Government securities, securities of other investment companies, and other securities for the purpose of this calculation limited in respect of any one issuer to an amount not greater in value than 5 percentum of the value of the total assets of such management company and to not more than 10 percentum of the outstanding voting securities of such issuer.

The foregoing definition divides the assets of diversified investment companies into two components. One segment, which must amount to at least 75 per cent of total assets, must be diversified. The other segment, which may amount to as much as 25 per cent of total assets, need not be diversified. This 25 per cent of the investment company's assets may be invested in a single security. This enables a diversified investment company to commit substantial portions of its resources to special situations without losing its diversified status.

"Nondiversified company" means any management company other than a diversified company.

There are a number of differences between closed-end and open-end investment companies. The most important and clear-cut distinction that can be made between an open-end investment company and a closed-end investment company is the fact that the open-end company or mutual fund does not have a fixed number of shares in the hands of the public, as is the case with a closed-end company, but rather is continually offering new shares to the public. Consequently, the number of its shares outstanding is constantly changing.

Closed-end investment companies obtain their investment funds in the same way an ordinary business corporation obtains capital to finance its production and distribution. It determines how much money it wants to manage and it offers securities for sale in that amount to the general public. Usually, the services of an investment banker are employed, and once the issue is sold no more securities are offered to the public, at least for a period of time. Thus a characteristic feature of closed-end investment companies is that they do not continually offer their securities for sale, whereas open-end companies do. Once the total number of authorized shares of a closed-end investment company have been sold, anyone wishing to purchase some of these shares must buy them from someone who owns them and is willing to part with them for the right price. Closed-end investment company shares are not redeemed by the issuer and thus have no redemption price.[4] Their shares are traded in the open market by broker/dealers, are often listed on securities exchanges, and often sell at varying relationships to net asset value. Thus the cost of buying closed-end investment company shares comprises the market price demanded by the owner of the shares plus the brokerage fees involved in their purchase. The amount received by the owner when the shares are sold is the market price of the shares less the required brokerage fees.

Normally a mutual fund stands ready to redeem any of its shares at the current net asset value per share, whenever a shareholder wishes to turn his securities back to the company.

A mutual fund with an effective sales organization, a sales organization which is continually inducing individuals to purchase more of the mutual fund shares than are being turned in for redemption by other shareholders, can continue to increase its assets year after year. There is generally a sales charge connected with the purchase of mutual fund shares.

Recent Growth of Investment Companies

The Investment Company Act of 1940 has had an extensive over-all impact on the operations and growth of investment companies. Since the act, it has been possible to differentiate more clearly among the various types of investment companies so that more accurate statistical compilations and comparisons are possible.

---

[4]However, closed-end companies do sometimes purchase their own shares in the market when they can buy them at a discount from their net asset value per share.

During the past twenty-five years, investment companies in the United States have grown and developed at an extraordinary rate. The data presented in Table 16-1 illustrates the striking growth of the assets of investment companies since the enactment of the Investment Company Act of 1940.

Table 16-1.
INVESTMENT COMPANIES REGISTERED
UNDER THE INVESTMENT COMPANY ACT OF 1940
SELECTED DATA 1941-1965

Fiscal Year (Ended June 30)	Number Registered at Beginning of Year	Number Registered During Year	Number Terminating Registration During Year	Number Registered at End of Year	Estimated Total Market Value of Assets at End of Year (in millions)
1941	0	450	14	436	$ 2,500
1942	436	17	46	407	2,400
1943	407	14	31	390	2,300
1944	390	8	27	371	2,200
1945	371	14	19	366	3,250
1946	366	13	18	361	3,750
1947	361	12	21	352	3,600
1948	352	18	11	359	3,825
1949	359	12	13	358	3,700
1950	358	26	18	366	4.700
1951	366	12	10	368	5,600
1952	368	13	14	367	6,800
1953	367	17	15	369	7,000
1954	369	20	5	384	8,700
1955	384	37	34	387	12,000
1956	387	46	34	399	14,000
1957	399	49	16	432	15,000
1958	432	42	21	453	17,000
1959	453	70	11	512	20,000
1960	512	67	9	570	23,500
1961	570	118	25	663	29,000
1962	663	97	33	727	27,300
1963	727	48	48	727	36,000
1964	727	52	48	731	41,600
1965	731	50	54	727	44,600

Source: Securities and Exchange Commission.

The estimated total market value of the assets of all investment companies registered under the Act in 1965 totaled $44.6 billion. This was almost eighteen times greater than the value of such assets in 1941. The number of registered investment companies increased during this same period from 436 to 727.

Some of the more comprehensive statistical presentations of investment company activities are compiled and presented by the Investment Company Institute.

In 1940, according to the ICI, sixty-eight open-end investment companies were members of the Investment Company Institute. By the end of December, 1965, the membership had increased to 170 open-end investment companies. The total value of the assets of these member mutual funds increased from about $448,000,000 at the end of 1940, to $35.2 billion by the end of December, 1965. The number of shareholder accounts in open-end companies showed a phenomenal increase during this same period, growing from 296,056 to 6,709,343, an increase of over 2200 per cent.

The use of shareholder accounts to depict the growing popularity of investment companies tends to give a somewhat distorted impression. This distortion appears because of the fact that many investors—individuals as well as institutional—buy and hold shares in more than one investment company. Each different investment company in which an investor holds shares lists him as a separate shareholder account. This results in a great deal of duplication whenever the aggregate shareholder account figures are tabulated. Thus 6,000,000 shareholder accounts might represent the investment activity of 3,000,000 investors, if each has invested in an average of two different investment companies, or even only 1,000,000 investors if each has invested in an average of six different investment companies. The most widely accepted estimate of the total number of different individuals and institutions holding mutual fund shares is about 3,500,000.

Irrespective of the duplication in shareholder account figures, however, the expanding acceptance of open-end investment companies as an investment vehicle remains impressive. In the short space of about twenty-five years, the attitude of a great many Americans towards investment companies has changed from one of suspicion or almost complete indifference to enthusiastic acceptance. In order to understand this great shift of attitude, it is necessary to look at the underlying factors that brought about this change.

Factors Behind Investment Company Growth

The extremely rapid expansion of the net assets of investment companies during the past twenty-five years has been due to a variety of factors. Not the least of these has been the growing public confidence in investment company shares as an investment medium. As noted, more and more people have been putting some of their surplus funds into these shares. Also, there has been a general appreciation, since 1950, of the market value of the securities held in the investment companies' portfolios.

Another major factor behind investment company growth, of course, has been the tremendous amount of savings accumulated by the American people. Without these savings to divert into the investment company area, no such growth could possibly have taken place.

Savings and the Problem of
What to Do with Them

The accumulation of a substantial amount of savings by the "middle income" citizens of a country is a relatively recent phenomenon. During the early period of world history only a very few people, a tiny percentage of the total population, could save even so much as a few small coins. The overwhelming majority of people considered themselves lucky indeed if they were able to keep themselves warm, halfway dry and reasonably free from hunger. Any savings or surplus that occurred during this early period usually took the form of an accumulation of extra grain, corn, or other commodities, and were exchanged quickly (before they spoiled) for various comforts and products the wealthy people enjoyed during that day and age.

Thus the early problem of where to invest a surplus in order to provide protection for old age was quickly solved by the simple process of trading the surplus for luxuries, which were promptly consumed— besides, what with the black plague, smallpox, assorted one-eyed dragons, and wars between the manors, who lived long enough in those days to have an old age about which to worry?

Today in the United States the savings picture couldn't be in sharper contrast to the period just described, even if the twentieth century American had come from outer space. By the year 1966, instead of having a society with just a few very wealthy people with savings, we find a large proportion of U.S. families able to accumulate at least something in the form of savings. Today more and more people have surplus funds available for investing.

Accompanying these savings, of course, has been the problem of how to safeguard and preserve them for future use. The big problem here is to find a place to invest the extra money without running too much risk of losing it.

In any sort of savings program, it is obvious that first things must come first. If total savings consist of only a few hundred extra dollars, obviously the place for these dollars is in a bank account, where they will be readily available as cash in case of emergency. Also, an adequate insurance program should be in force to provide living necessities to dependents in case of the breadwinner's premature death.

Assuming, however, that adequate cash reserves have been set aside and adequate insurance protection exists, the problem of investing surplus funds without incurring undue risk must be resolved.

WHERE TO INVEST SURPLUS SAVINGS. Due to a lack of fundamental knowledge about the securities business or because of past sad investment experiences on the part of friends and relatives, some people still feel uneasy about having anything to do with the securities market. They seem to view the securities market facilities as some sort of gigantic slot machine, which, after snatching away their hard-earned cash, only rarely sees fit to let them "win" a stock or bond of any real value. Thus, securities are all too often eliminated from some people's minds as a possible place to invest their savings.

"It is too risky to buy stocks or bonds," they say. "There are too many to choose from, and I don't understand enough about finance to tell the good stocks and bonds from the bad ones." Consequently, they select an alternate place for their savings.

Some of these surplus funds are placed in savings accounts in commercial banks. Others may be deposited in mutual savings banks, saving and loan associations, or credit unions. Still other individuals prefer to save through the medium of U.S. government savings bonds or through various types of "non-term" insurance programs.

Many people feel that by putting their extra money in any one of the above institutions, they can avoid all the risks of losing it. Unfortunately, this is not true. Risk is an inherent part of the modern fast-paced world in which we live, and with savings—just as is true with life itself—it is impossible to avoid all the risks. No matter where savings are kept, some risk of loss still remains. For example, the distrust of banks which developed as an aftermath of the banking crisis of the early 1930's vastly increased the popularity of hoarding. However, this so-called "riskless" activity of hoarding soon lost much of its popularity, because of numerous robberies and fires in which houses went up in smoke taking the money with them.

It is also ironical that at least some of the savings that individuals put into banks or other savings institutions in order to avoid investing them in securities may be invested by the financial institutions involved in the very securities the savers are trying so hard to avoid.

INFLATION AND THE INVESTOR. When money is saved and put away, complete or partial loss of savings can occur in either or both of the following two ways: First, the saver may not get back as many actual dollars, at the time he decides to withdraw and use his savings, as he had at the time he originally saved them and put them away. Second, the saver may not get back as much in purchasing power at the time he decides to withdraw and use his savings as he had at the time he originally saved and put the money away.

When inflation occurs in a country, the amount of goods and services each dollar of savings will buy decreases. This means that when savings are withdrawn for use, the purchasing power of all the money received will be less than the same or smaller dollar amount was at the time the money was originally saved and put away.

In the years immediately following World War II, a period of rapid inflation developed. During this period many people experienced, for the first time in their lives, a big loss in the purchasing power of their savings. It wasn't a pleasant experience for any of them, and since that time more and more people have been seeking ways to reduce the risk of the purchasing power loss of their savings dollars. It was soon evident that the securities markets were probably the best available place to hedge against inflation. Thus many people who had previously ruled out the securities market as a place for part of their surplus cash reconsidered because of inflation and decided to "give it a try."

Price trends in the United States in the middle 1960's continue to be upward. There is evidence to indicate that gradual inflation, at least, will continue in this country for many years to come. It is most likely that the securities markets will continue to be one of the investment areas attracting those people who are attempting to avoid the purchasing-power loss in their savings.

THE DESIRE FOR DIVERSIFICATION. Each individual saver who finally became convinced that he should "give the securities markets a try" was faced with the problem of deciding which of the many thousands of securities offered for sale would be best for him to buy. Although it was true that security prices in general tended to move to higher levels as inflation progressed, it was equally true that the prices of all securities did not go up at the same time, nor did they go up the same amount. In fact, the prices of some securities didn't go up at all, but rather moved downward to a lower level and stayed there.

One solution to this problem of finding the best securities to buy is to have enough money to be able to buy some of the securities of all of the biggest and most profitable companies. If an investor's funds were spread among the best companies in a wide variety of industries, adverse conditions developing in any one company or industry would have only a moderate effect on his over-all investment results.

Obviously, few individuals have investment funds large enough to obtain by themselves the extremely wide diversification of holdings suggested above. However, more and more people each year are finding that by combining part of their savings with the extra funds of thousands of other people, through the purchase of investment company shares, it is possible to diversify widely their holdings in the common stocks of American corporations. Since each investment company shareholding represents a proportionate interest in the widely diversified assets held by the investment company, the average person through these shareholdings is able to share the growth, profits, and risks of the American economy with considerably less wear and tear on the nerves.

Thus, to many people, one answer to the complex problem of investing in the securities market is to take advantage of the diversification and professional management provided by investment companies. Since risk cannot be avoided, one way to handle an individual investment problem is to pick a solution which offers a chance for the attainment of objectives while assuming as little risk as possible.

Professional Investment Management

The growing popularity of investment companies in America is easy to explain in general terms. The reasons are both basic and simple. Investment companies provide desired services to American investors for a price they are willing to pay. As long as this continues to be true, their popularity and growth will continue. When this ceases to be true, their popularity will diminish and their rate of growth will be slowed or will stop altogether. Just what are these services being offered by the investment companies which are so attractive to such a wide variety of investors?

Investment companies provide professional investment management to individuals who otherwise would not be able to afford that service. Further, investment companies enable the small or medium investor to diversify his investment so as to reduce his over-all investment risk. They also relieve investors from most of the bothersome details involved in a diversified investment program.

Few people outside the field of investments have the time or background knowledge necessary to select and manage successfully a portfolio of individual corporate securities. Supervising a list of securities effectively enough to arrive anywhere near the predetermined goal is a full time, rigorous task, which generally can only be accomplished by professionals.

Only a small proportion of individuals have investment funds large enough to justify incurring the fees investment counselors charge for handling individual investment accounts. For most people with relatively modest saving accumulations, the investment company provides one of the most efficient devices for obtaining professional investment management.

Liquidity and Marketability

Investment company shares enjoy a high degree of marketability. This is particularly true of mutual fund shares, since the issuing fund stands ready to redeem the shares at the net asset value per share any time the securities markets are open. The net asset value per share is generally computed twice a day, and is published daily in financial columns of the newspaper, so it is easy to determine the value of each share. There is no question that the immediate redeemability of mutual fund shares, at liquidating value, in good markets and in bad, has been a feature attracting a great many investors to mutual funds.

Closed-end investment company shares are sold in the open market, often through securities exchanges and, thus, are also readily marketable. The diversification of the closed-end company's portfolio is often a factor enhancing the overall marketability of its shares.

How Mutual Funds are Organized, Managed and Sold

The typical mutual fund organization in the United States consists of two or three entities. These are, the fund itself, the investment adviser and frequently the principal underwriter.

The mutual fund itself is usually a corporation which owns the investment portfolio and whose shares are in turn owned by the investing public. An open-end investment company organized as a corporation will have officers and directors to carry out the normal activities of the corporate officers.

A mutual fund operating as a common law trust will not have officers, directors, or an advisory board. The investment management function of such a fund will be handled by the trustee under the terms of the trust agreement.

Each mutual fund utilizes the services of an investment adviser. The investment adviser is usually a partnership or corporation separate from the mutual fund itself but which, by contract with the fund, undertakes to give advice concerning the purchase and sale of securities for the fund's portfolio.

The investment adviser also renders various management services, subject, of course, to the approval and general supervision of the fund's board of directors. The typical advisory contract calls for the investment adviser firm to bear the expense of many of the corporate costs of the fund, and to pay the salaries of the fund's officers and staff. The investment adviser is paid a continuing fee by the fund for these services. The mutual fund prospectus will present the essential elements of these arrangements.

Most mutual funds utilize the services of a principal underwriter. The principal underwriter is a firm (either partnership or corporation) which by contract has the exclusive right to purchase new shares from the fund. These contracts always permit the underwriter to buy these shares at net asset value. Frequently the principal underwriter and the investment adviser are the same.

The principal underwriter makes contractual arrangements with securities dealers in states where the investment company's shares are registered and can be sold. Under the terms of these contracts, the dealers may continually offer the fund's shares to the public.

These dealers buy shares from the underwriter. They charge their customers a commission on these shares out of which they compensate their sales representatives who deal with the public. The principal underwriter retains the smaller part of the total selling commission. The dealer and his representatives receive the major portion of the commission. It should be noted that the mutual fund itself always receives the full net asset value per share for its shares when they are issued and that all selling commissions are paid by the incoming shareholder.

Most mutual fund shares are distributed as noted above, that is: from mutual fund—to underwriter—to dealer—to investor. However, there are other ways in which the shares of open-end investment companies are distributed. For example, some mutual fund shares are sold directly to the public by the underwriter without utilizing the services of dealers.

Under another distribution method, the fund sells its shares directly to investors by advertising. Shares sold in this way may involve a reduced sales charge, or there may be no sales charge at all, in which case they are called "no load" funds.

The so-called "no-load" funds are offered to the public for subscription at net asset value, without the payment of commissions to underwriters, dealers, or salesmen. This type of mutual fund often is associated with a firm engaged in the business of rendering investment advice to private clients on a fee basis, thus providing a parallel source of income which enables the advisory firm to supervise the associated mutual fund as though the latter were merely an additional individual client.

In recent years, subscriptions to the shares of the "no-load" type of fund have accounted for less than 5 per cent of the annual sales of all new mutual fund shares. This fact emphasizes the importance of the sales representative, or securities salesman, in the growth of mutual funds in the United States.

Still other mutual funds sell their shares through exclusive regional or national organizations of sales representatives. These representatives deal directly with the public. Several of these groups are very large and important, and their sales represent a significant percentage of all new mutual fund shares sold.

Mutual funds shares are sometimes distributed by the underwriter to a "plan company," which in turn sells these shares to individual investors. Plan companies are usually connected with the contractual plan method of distributing mutual funds. The prospectus of the fund, or of the plan company, will describe the method of distribution.

However, no matter what method of distributing new shares is used, the fee structure as between the mutual fund and its investment adviser is based, in common practice, on a percentage of the net assets of the fund, rather than on a percentage of the fund's income.

Thus, an individual investor, wishing to buy mutual fund shares ordinarily would buy them from the issuing company or a dealer and underwriter, not from a present shareholder. The offering price of these new shares would be the same as the net asset value per share of the shares currently outstanding, plus a sales charge. This sales charge on each purchase of mutual fund shares ranges from 1 per cent up to 9 per cent of net asset value per share. The sales charge involved in the acquisition of the shares of any specific mutual fund must be stated in the fund's prospectus as a percentage of the public offering price. It is important to remember that the sales charge is a charge of the selling organization, not of the fund itself.

Mutual fund shares are normally sold in dollar amounts not share amounts. An investor would typically order $1,000 worth of Buckley Fund shares, not 100 shares of Buckley Fund. The precise number of shares and fractional shares bought for the $1,000 would be determined by the amount remaining for investment after deducting the sales charge. For example, if the sales charge is 7 per cent for a $20,000 investment, $18,600 remains for the actual purchase of shares after the deduction of the commission.

Types of Mutual Fund Accounts

Both individuals and institutions purchase the shares of investment companies. Although there are a number of different types of institutions which have found the services of investment companies useful for their investment purposes, the big majority of investment company shareholders are individuals.

Individuals buying investment company shares are classified as either regular account holders or as accumulation plan holders.

REGULAR ACCOUNT HOLDERS. Regular account holders are those individuals who have made "lump sum" investments, but have not indicated any intention of making periodic investments of additional sums of money. Regular account holders should be made aware of the fact that most mutual fund underwriters reduce their sales charges when quantity purchases of from $5,000 to $25,000 are made. The details for any given fund will appear in the prospectus.

The purchase need not be a single lump-sum purchase to qualify for the reduced sales charge if the investor signs a *Letter of Intention* signifying his intent to purchase the required dollar amount within a period not to exceed thirteen months.

To qualify for a reduced sales charge on a lump-sum purchase, or through use of the letter of intent, the purchaser must be:

1. an individual, or
2. an individual, his spouse and children under the age of 21, or
3. a trustee or other fiduciary of a single trust estate or single

fiduciary account or a pension or a profit-sharing plan qualified under Section 401 of the Internal Revenue Code.

This means that investment clubs or other groups of individuals cannot band together for the purpose of obtaining reduced sales charges on purchases of investment company shares.

ACCUMULATION PLAN HOLDERS. Accumulation plan holders are those investors who make formal arrangements to purchase mutual fund shares on a continuing basis. The money used to buy these shares often comes from the investor's current income. Purchase of additional shares are generally made every month or every quarter.

The term accumulation plan holder refers only to those investors who purchase the shares of open-end investment companies. Since closed-end investment company shares are generally listed on the New York Stock Exchange, most formal arrangements calling for regular and periodic purchases of such shares are handled under the New York Stock Exchange's Monthly Investment Plan.

An accumulation plan can be either a voluntary, (informal or level charge) plan or a contractual plan.

LEVEL CHARGE OR VOLUNTARY ACCUMULATION PLANS. Many funds permit investors to start a voluntary plan requiring only an initial minimum purchase of a stated amount and an indication of the investor's wish to invest monthly (or at some fixed interval) at least a minimum stated annual amount. The exact amount of the initial investment required and of the subsequent minimum monthly and/or annual investment will be stated in the prospectus.

Voluntary accumulation plans are just what the name suggests. The person with this type of account does not make any *binding* commitment as to the total amount he will ultimately invest, nor does he indicate when he will invest additional funds in the plan. This plan is very much like a type of open account, where the investor has indicated his intention of buying some securities over a period of time and has opened an account for that purpose but has not committed himself to a time schedule nor a total investment figure.

CONTRACTUAL PLANS. Contractual accumulation plans involve a definite commitment on the part of the investor. Under this type of plan the investor commits himself to a specific time schedule of periodic investment, as well as to a total intended investment amount.

An investment company contractual plan holder can terminate his plan at any time, although in doing so he may incur a penalty. The penalty depends in part on the length of time he has participated in the plan. These plans are also often referred to as penalty, or prepaid charge, or front-end load plans.

Plan companies and some underwriters and distributors offer contractual plans under which an investor makes investments of a fixed dollar amount at regular intervals, usually monthly, for a fixed number of years, usually ten years. Essentially, it is a dollar-cost-averaging plan. Details are given in the plan prospectus, but a typical contractual accumulation plan might call for a $10,000 total investment accumulated through equal monthly or quarterly investment installments over a 10-year period.

A sales charge is involved in both the voluntary and in the contractual plan. The voluntary accumulation plan holder pays the sales charge at the regular rate on each investment. The contractual holder, however, pays a substantial portion of the sales commission applicable to his total planned investment out of the money invested during the first few years of the program. In many such plans, 50 per cent or more of the first year's payments will not be used to buy investment company shares for the investor but rather will go to pay part of the sales charges.

The Investment Company Act of 1940 limits sales charges on investment company shares to a maximum of 9 per cent of the total investment, but permits, as to contractual plans, up to 50 per cent of the first year's payments to be deducted for sales charges. The concentration of sales charges in the first year and the resulting likelihood that a plan discontinued during the first year or so will show a loss, account for the terms "penalty," "prepaid charge," or "front-end load" which are given these plans.

The holder of a contractual plan normally pays a custodial fee for various services performed by the custodian or the despositor-sponsor. Where applicable, this fee would be deducted from the dividends credited to the investor's account. Service charges of various kinds may also be charged to investors in voluntary accumulation plans. Usually 1 to 2½ per cent of the sales charge is retained by the fund sponsor, distributor, or underwriter as described in the fund prospectus and the balance goes to the selling dealer.

Dividends from net investment income and distributions from other sources are automatically used to purchase additional fund shares under contractual accumulation plans. It should be noted that these payments are taxable to the shareholder despite the fact that they are reinvested. This is true of all distributions of investment companies whether reinvested or taken in cash.

The use of the contractual plan method of selling mutual fund shares is illegal in a few states. Securities representatives should check the statutes of the state in which they operate to determine what restrictions, if any, are imposed on the distribution of mutual fund shares through contractual plans.

Contractual plans are not eligible for sale in the state of Illinois because of a statutory provision of the Illinois Securities Law of 1953 which prohibits the sale of investment company shares if the net asset value of the shares is not at least 90 per cent of the public offering price of such shares. As noted, an investor who enters into a contractual plan could, upon withdrawal from the plan, suffer a forfeiture on his investment which could exceed the 10 per cent limitation imposed under the Illinois law. Thus, the state does not permit their use.

Contractual plans in Ohio are not deemed to be regulated by the Securities Act but are regulated by the Bond Investment Company Act. Such plans may be sold in Ohio only if the contractual plan sponsor is able or willing to meet the substantial deposit requirements of $100,000.00 as a condition precedent to certification.

The contractual plan method of distributing mutual fund shares has never been permitted in Wisconsin. The Wisconsin statute, in specifically referring to mutual funds, provides that they shall be "registered and sold in this state only upon compliance with such terms and conditions as the department may prescribe as necessary or appropriate in the public interest or for the protection of investors." This wording of the law gives the Wisconsin Department of Securities broad statutory authority in regulating the distribution of mutual fund shares. According to John K. Kyle, the director of the Wisconsin Department of Securities, it has been the position of his department that "contractual plans do not meet the standards set by our legislature for the following reasons:[5]

1. It is unfair to the investor who, for some reason, has to withdraw his shares during the early years to subject him to loss of up to 50 per cent of the amount invested.
2. It is equally unfair to the man who completes his contract within ten or fifteen years because only from 50 per cent to possibly 80 per cent of his money is invested in shares of American industry during the early years of his investment program. Our statute, by Rule 2.03, limits the maximum commission which may be collected for the sale of mutual fund shares to 8½ per cent."[6]

A number of funds have declining term group life-plan-completion insurance available to purchasers of contractual or voluntary plans.

[5]This information was taken from a letter written to the authors by John K. Kyle dated October 21, 1966.
[6]It should be noted, however, that due to the dollar-cost-averaging aspect of the contractual plan method it is possible that the investor could have acquired more total fund shares over the years of the plan by virtue of the front-end load then he would have acquired with a level sales charge. Only an analysis, after the fact, would indicate which would have resulted in the greatest acquisition of shares and largest total share value.

Under these group insurance plans, the contractual planholder pays a premium for the assurance of completion of his program in the event of death. This coverage is much like that taken out by home owners to assure the payment of the mortgage in case of premature death.

In the event of death prior to completion of the plan, insurance proceeds equal to the unpaid cash balance due on the plan are paid by the insurance company to the custodian and, after the usual deductions, are applied to the purchase of fund shares. No part of the proceeds of the insurance are paid directly to the estate or to the beneficiary of the plan holder, since this function is performed by the custodian at the direction of the new owners of the shares.

Contractual plan completion insurance is not available to the purchasers of mutual fund shares in all states. (Again, each securities representative is urged to check the regulations of the state in which he operates.) The state of North Carolina, for example, does not permit insurance coverage on a contractual plan when such an insurance policy is a group policy as defined in North Carolina General Statute 58-210 (2). This is a rule by the North Carolina Commissioner of Insurance which states there is no debtor-creditor relationship; consequently there would not be an insurable interest.[7]

The state of South Carolina does not permit the sale of contractual plans with plan completion insurance. This is due to an opinion given by the states' Insurance Department that insurance of that type may not be legally sold in the state. In Virginia, contractual plans that carry an insurance feature are limited to $10,000 of insurance per company.

How AN INVESTOR SELLS HIS MUTUAL FUND SHARES. Mutual fund investors can sell the shares they hold in mutual funds at any time they wish. Ordinarily a shareholder wishing to dispose of his shares would sell them back to the issuing fund through the same securities dealer or underwriter through which he purchased them in the first place. Since a great proportion of mutual fund shares are purchased through a particular salesman of a dealer, or an underwriter which has a sales agreement with an issuing mutual fund, it is only natural that the same firm should be contacted by the investor when he wishes to convert his shares back into cash. This process of converting mutual fund shares into cash by selling them back to the issuing company is known as *redemption*.

It is not mandatory that a mutual fund shareholder go through the same channels to sell his shares as he did to buy them. If he wishes to do so, an investor can take his shares directly to the issuing company or send them to the company through the mail, and the company will

---

[7]This information was taken from a letter to the authors from William W. Coppedge, Securities Deputy, State of North Carolina, dated October 20, 1966.

repurchase the shares directly from the shareholder. Mutual funds also will generally redeem shares in the possession of their shareholders upon presentation of these shares in proper order at the custodial bank of the mutual fund.

The shares of no-load mutual funds are generally sent through the mail for redemption. Since no salesmen are employed by such funds, and their shares are originally sold directly to the investing public through the mail, that is how they are redeemed.

Briefly stated then, a mutual fund shareholder may redeem his shares by depositing his stock certificate, properly endorsed at the office of the issuing mutual fund, its distributor, or its custodian. The stock certificate should be accompanied by an irrevocable offer to sell the shares back to the issuing mutual fund at the net asset value per share.

The specific redemption procedures and provisions for any mutual fund will be found outlined in detail in the funds prospectus.

REDEMPTION PRICE IS THE NET ASSET VALUE PER SHARE. When a mutual fund shareholder turns his shares back to the company for redemption, the amount he receives is determined by dividing the total number of shares the company has outstanding into the total net assets of the company at that time. This redemption price is called the net asset value per share.

Some mutual funds require the payment of a redemption fee when shareholders turn their stock back to the company for redemption. This redemption fee may be nominal, or it may run to 1 or 2 per cent of the net asset value per share. Redemption fees are most typically charged by no load mutual funds; i.e. those without a sales charge. When a redemption fee *is* charged, the redemption price is the net asset value per share minus the redemption fee.

COMPUTATION OF NET ASSET VALUE PER SHARE. During the days when the New York Stock Exchange is open for business, mutual funds normally compute their net asset value per share twice daily. Typically, the net asset value per share is determined on the basis of securities prices in existence at about 1:00 P.M. and again on prices existing at around 3:30 P.M.[8]

In order to compute its net asset value per share the mutual fund has to be able to determine the value of each of the different securities in which it has invested its shareholders' money. Ordinarily in the computation, each mutual fund portfolio security is valued at its latest reported sale price. If no sale of a particular security has taken place since the last time the fund computed its net asset value per share,

---

[8]The net asset value per share computed as of 1:00 P.M. is effective for orders placed with the underwriter between 2:00 P.M. and 4:30 P.M. of that day. The net asset value per share computed as of 3:30 P.M. is effective from 4:30 P.M. of that day until 2:00 P.M. on the next day the New York Stock Exchange is open.

the average of the latest bid and asked prices are used as the value of the security in the portfolio. When no market quotations at all are available, securities are valued at their "fair market value."

After the value of each portfolio security is determined, these values are totaled. Added to this aggregate value of the portfolio securities is the dollar amount of the mutual funds cash and accounts receivable. Next, all of the mutual funds liabilities and accrued expenses must be subtracted in order to arrive at the total net asset value of the fund. Reduced to its simplest terms, the above means that the fund totals the value of everything it owns (except buildings, supplies, and equipment, etc., which normally would never be converted into cash in the normal operation of its business), it subtracts the amount of everything it owes and the remainder is the amount the mutual fund is worth. Using this "total of worth," it is a simple matter to arrive at the mutual fund's net asset value per share. It is computed by dividing this "total of worth" by the number of shares the fund has outstanding.

The computation of the net asset value per share for a mutual fund can best be shown with a hypothetical example. Table 16-II shows that the Fictitious Mutual Fund Company holds six different security issues in its portfolio. (The typical mutual fund, of course, generally invests in a great many more than six different security issues.) The latest reported sale price of each portfolio security at 1:00 P.M. on April 12, 1966, is given in Table 16-II along with the number of shares the mutual fund owns in each company. The total value of these securities at 1:00 P.M. is $1,420,000. In addition to the portfolio securities valued at $1,420,000, the Fictitious Mutual Fund has cash in the bank of $60,000 and has accounts receivable of $20,000. Thus total assets equal $1,500,000.

TABLE 16-II

FICTITIOUS MUTUAL FUND COMPANY
(100,000 SHARES OUTSTANDING)

APRIL 12, 1966

Portfolio Security	Number of Shares Owned	Market Value at 1:00 p.m.	Total Market Value
Able Company	1,000	@ $19	$ 19,000
Baker Company	2,000	@ 40 ½	81,000
Charley Company	4,000	@ 30	120,000
Dog Company	5,000	@ 60 ¾	303,750
Easy Company	10,000	@ 50	500,000
Fox Company	5,000	@ 79 ¼	396,250
Total			$1,420,000

Liabilities of the Fictitious Mutual Fund on April 12, 1966, total $20,000. These $20,000 in liabilities consist of $5,000 in accrued wages, which the fund owes to its employees but has not yet paid, and $15,000 in taxes which it owes but has not yet paid.[9]

Subtracting the $20,000 in liabilities from the $1,500,000 in assets leaves $1,480,000 as the total net asset value of the Fictitious Mutual Fund.

Calculation of the net asset value per share of the Fictitious Mutual Fund Company is as follows:

	$1,420,000	Total value of portfolio securities
plus	80,000	Cash in bank and accounts receivable
	$1,500,000	Total value of assets
minus	20,000	Liabilities (accrued wages and taxes)
	$1,480,000	Net value of assets

$1,480,000 ÷ 100,000 (number of shares outstanding) =
$14.80 net asset value per share.

When a mutual fund shareholder liquidates or redeems his shares, he almost always will receive for these shares a dollar amount different from the amount he paid for them. The dollar amount received by the shareholder for these shares may be more or less than they cost, depending upon the market value of the portfolio securities held by the fund at the time of the redemption.

REDEMPTION PROCEEDS PAID IN FEW DAYS. Usually the mutual fund will pay the investor for his shares in cash within one to five days after the shares are duly presented for redemption. Legally, the mutual funds can take somewhat longer in redeeming their shares.

Under the provisions of the *Investment Company Act of 1940,* mutual fund redeemable shares must ordinarily be redeemed within seven days after they are tendered (that is, offered for redemption). However, under the act's provisions, the board of directors of the issuing mutual fund may suspend this right of redemption and postpone payment of the redemption price during any period:

1. When trading on the New York Stock Exchange is restricted or when the NYSE is closed for other than weekends and holidays.
2. When the Securities and Exchange Commission has by order permitted the mutual fund to suspend the redemption right for the protection of shareholders.
3. When an emergency exists that makes disposal of the funds portfolio securities or the valuation of its net assets not reasonably practicable.[10]

[9] The reader should realize that these wages and taxes have not been paid as yet because the time has not come to pay them, not because the fund is unwilling or unable to pay them.

[10] Such existing emergency must be one as defined by rules and regulations of the Securities and Exchange Commission or any succeeding governmental authority.

Only once since the passage of the Investment Company Act of 1940 has the New York Stock Exchange closed its door due to an emergency. This was on the day of the assassination of President John F. Kennedy, Friday, November 22, 1963. Investors hearing the shocking news of the President's death deluged the floor of the New York Stock Exchange with orders to sell their securities. Sell orders came in so rapidly and in such large quantities that it was impossible to handle them all. The stock market as measured by the Dow Jones Industrial Average dropped 20 points in 20 minutes. Everyone wanted to sell. No one wanted to buy. At 2:22 Friday afternoon the emergency closing of the New York Stock Exchange was ordered. The Exchange remained closed Monday, November 25, 1963, which was declared a day of national mourning due to President Kennedy's funeral. The New York Stock Exchange reopened for business as usual on Tuesday, November 26.

During this emergency period, the mutual funds had difficulty accurately determining the value of their portfolio assets. Mutual funds ordinarily compute their net asset value per share twice daily whenever the New York Stock Exchange is open. On this particular Friday, however, most mutual funds acting under the provisions of the Investment Company Act of 1940 decided it would be in their shareholders best interests to ignore whatever the net asset value of their shares appeared to be late Friday afternoon. Most fund directors felt that due to the crisis, the market values of the individual securities making up the mutual fund portfolios could not be realistically determined at that time. For investors who wanted to buy or redeem shares during this period, most funds decided that the fairest way was to use the "next price" rather than the Friday afternoon price as the basis for the transactions. By "next price" was meant, whatever the net asset value per share would be on Tuesday, November 26, around 12:00 o'clock noon.

The stock market rallied sharply beginning Tuesday morning. Consequently, based on this "next price" method, mutual fund shareholders who liquidated their shares on the weekend of President Kennedy's assassination received more for their shares than they would have received if the redemption price had been determined on the basis of Friday afternoon's stock prices.

Some few mutual funds, however, were not so generous to their shareholders. These funds calculated the net asset value of each of their shares as of 2:22 Friday afternoon, November 22. Although they attempted to discourage any shareholders who wanted to cash in their shares during this emergency period, they did redeem some shares at these reduced prices. Investors purchasing the shares of these same funds during that weekend and on Monday, November 25, however, were able to *buy* at this reduced price. All orders from new investors for shares in these funds were consummated at Friday afternoon's prices which were below the price at which such orders could be accepted after a new net asset value per share had been computed on Tuesday. One mutual fund group even used this emergency, its price decline, and the anticipated rebound, as a sales line in pushing for new business. As a result, they claim their salesmen had the most productive day in their history bringing in millions of dollars in new business.

REDEMPTION IN "KIND." It is legally mandatory that mutual funds redeem their shares when called upon to do so by their shareholders. Frequently, however, mutual funds reserve the right under unusual circumstances to make redemption payments in something other than cash.

When so stated in its prospectus, and when faced with an emergency, the board of directors of a mutual fund can make redemption payments to the fund's shareholders, in securities, or in other assets of the fund. However, this "payment in kind" as it is frequently called, seldom takes place. Almost 100 per cent of the time, mutual fund shareholders sending shares in for redemption receive cash in payment from the fund.

Closed-end Investment Companies

PREMIUMS AND DISCOUNTS. The shares of closed-end investment companies generally sell at a price different from their net asset value per share, while the shares of mutual funds do not. Sometimes closed-end shares sell at a price higher than or above the net asset value per share, in which case they are said to be selling at a "premium." The term "discount," as applied to closed-end investment company securities, means the amount the securities are selling below the net asset value per share. These premiums and discounts develop because closed-end investment company shares are traded in the open market by broker/dealers, or through a securities exchange and, as a result, the price at which they trade depends not only upon the net asset value of each share but also upon supply and demand conditions. Since there are a fixed number of these shares outstanding, the price at which the shares trade depends upon the number of shares in a particular investment company offered for sale in relation to the number of these same shares buyers want to purchase at that same time. Thus, closed-end investment company shares generally sell at varying relationships to net asset value per share.

For example:

An investor purchased 100 shares of the Buckley Company, a closed-end investment company, on January 1, 1966 for $10.40 per share. On that same date, the net asset value of the Buckley Company was $10.80 per share. Thus the company's shares were selling at a 40 cent *discount* per share. One year later the market price was $12.20 per share. On that same date the net asset value per share of the Buckley Company was $11.90.

Thus the market price of the shares had moved from a discount of 40 cents per share to a premium of 30 cents per share due to supply and demand conditions.

By way of contrast, mutual fund shares do not sell at a discount or a premium in relation to net asset value per share. They do not because the price of the shares offered for sale by the holder is not directly determined by the supply and demand for the mutual fund shares themselves, but instead is a price which is based upon the fluctuating market prices of the securities in the fund's portfolio.

The fact that the prices of mutual fund shares are not related to the supply and demand for the shares themselves, but rather to the supply and demand for the securities held in their portfolios, is one of the many unique things about them. Regardless of how many shares are offered at any one time by the shareholders of a mutual fund, the company is obligated to redeem them at their net asset value per share. Obviously, if the issuing company is willing at any time to redeem the securities at their net asset value per share (and this figure is generally computed twice a day by the company) no one in his right mind would be foolish enough to sell these shares to anyone at a price less than the net asset value per share.

Investment Company Share Quotations

It is generally a simple matter to find the current redemption price and the current offering price of most mutual fund shares. These prices can be found by checking the bid and asked quotations of mutual fund shares printed in the daily newspapers. The net asset value per share and the "bid" price for mutual fund shares in the newspapers are one and the same. The net asset value per share, plus the sales charge, is the same as the "asked" price in the newspapers. The "public offering price" is the same as the asked price. It is computed, as provided in the fund prospectus, by determining the net asset value per share and adding the sales charge.

Finding the current market price of most closed-end investment company shares is also simply a matter of looking in the daily newspaper. Since many closed-end investment company shares are listed on securities exchanges, the daily stock market quotations will generally reveal the day's prices of these shares. The day's last trading price is the approximate price an individual would expect to pay for these shares if he planned to buy them the next day, or, if he planned to sell the shares, the approximate price he would expect to receive for them. Quotations on closed-end investment company shares not listed on securities exchanges generally can be found in the over-the-counter quotation lists carried in many newspapers.

The sales charge of a particular mutual fund's shares can easily be determined from the newspaper bid and asked quotations. The actual dollar amount of the sales charge per share can be found by subtracting the bid price per share from the asked price per share. The actual dollar amount of the sales charge divided by the asked price per share will show the percentage sales charge.

To illustrate: The Fictitious Mutual Fund Company shares are quoted in the newspaper as "bid $18.40, asked $20.00":

$20.00 minus $18.40 = $1.60 (The actual dollar
amount of sales charge)

$1.60 divided by $20.00 = 8% (The percentage sales
charge)

Fundamental Investment Policies of Investment Companies

There are several hundred different investment companies currently operating in the United States. Small wonder the average investor tends to become bewildered and confused when confronted with the task of selecting the one best investment company to meet his specific investment need. It is the responsibility of the trained securities representative to help a customer interested in acquiring investment company shares to place his funds in the securities of a company with a good performance record and with a fundamental investment objective which matches that of the customer.

Every investment company has a fundamental investment policy. This policy must be specifically stated in the company's SEC registration statement and its prospectus, and cannot be changed without approval by its shareholders.

While investment objectives, methods, policies and degrees of risk vary materially from company to company, the following is descriptive of some of the broad classifications of investment companies currently in existence.

DIVERSIFIED COMMON STOCK FUNDS. A diversified common stock fund is a fund which has a portfolio consisting primarily of common stocks. The various diversified common stock funds operating in the United States today have a wide variety of investment objectives and policies. For example, some funds concentrate their investments in "blue chip" stocks, while others invest largely in the securities of growth companies.

Growth investment companies are companies whose stated objective is to seek long-term growth of capital. They attempt to accomplish this by investing in the securities of companies which plow back a substantial part of earnings for expansion, research, or development purposes.

In recent years, more and more investors have indicated an interest in obtaining growth securities. This has been particularly true of people who have been in a position to forego current income in order to obtain capital appreciation. As a result of this increasing interest in growth securities, many new investment companies have adopted "growth" as their stated portfolio objective.

The stated investment objective of a diversified common stock fund might well call for both reasonable growth of capital and reasonable current return on invested capital. Such a company may reserve the right in its registration statement to take defensive positions in cash, bonds, and other senior securities, whenever current conditions indicate such action is warranted. This policy would enable the company to retain maximum flexibility in the management of its portfolio through avoiding any restrictions on the proportion of various classes of securities to be held.

BALANCED FUNDS. A balanced fund is an investment company whose stated policy is at all times to have some portion of its invested assets in bonds and preferred stocks, as well as in common stocks.

The fund is "balanced" in such proportions of each type of security as seem desirable in light of investment considerations as they exist at any given time. During periods that appear favorable for increased market prices for equities, a higher proportion of the assets will be invested in common stocks and other equity types of securities. At other times, when the bond market appears right, a higher proportion of bonds, short-term securities, and cash may be held. There is always some relationship of "balance" between the two classes however.

Generally, a balanced fund may be expected to follow a more conservative investment policy than a common stock fund. Because the prices of the securities held in its portfolio are less volatile in a rising market, the balanced fund will not show as much gain as would be expected of a common stock fund. Conversely, in a declining market, the net asset value per share of the balanced fund should decline less than that of a common stock fund.

A balanced fund would be suitable for a investor who is seeking an investment which provides a reasonable conservation of capital with a relatively high quarterly income. Many people in their retirement years would be expected to have an investment objective comparable to that of a balanced fund because there would be expected appreciation during times of inflation with a related increase in current income.

INCOME FUNDS. Some investment companies have the stated management objective of maximum current income. These are known as income funds. People who must live on the current income they receive from their investments often select this type of investment company which strives to provide a higher-than-average investment return.

Income funds attempt to achieve an above average investment return by investing in securities which are characterized by relatively high dividend payout. Frequently these securities have below average growth potential and are considered to be of above average risk.

SPECIALIZED FUNDS. An investment company which invests in the securities of companies in a single industry or in allied industries is called a specialty fund. This type of fund is also referred to as an industry investment company.

Specialty funds exist in the automobile, chemical, electronic, steel, tobacco, and railroad as well as numerous other industry areas. Many of those specialty funds have done extremely well during certain phases of the market. Some of these specialized funds seek to achieve their investment objective by investing in a specific geographical area. These funds typically have an investment objective of long-term capital growth, which they hope to be able to attain by concentrating their investments in certain growth industries.

BOND AND PREFERRED STOCK FUNDS. An investment company which has all bonds, or primarily bonds, in its portfolio is known as a bond fund. The investment objective of a bond fund typically would be that of providing income stability to its shareholders.

Some of these funds offer a diversified portfolio of senior securities, including both bonds and preferred stocks. Others specialize in railroad bonds and preferreds, high grade, medium grade and low-priced bonds.

Investment Company Earnings and Distributions

Investment companies have two main sources of earnings. These are investment income and income realized by taking capital gains. Investment income consists of the dividend and interest payments investment companies received from the corporations whose securities they hold in their portfolio. Capital gains are the profit investment companies make by selling a security for more than it originally cost to acquire. Payments to investment company shareholders generally are made from funds obtained from one or both of these two sources. Investment companies are required by law to indicate to their shareholders the sources of each distribution they make. Dividends and capital gains can never be added together when calculating the yield on a mutual fund. Only the dividend income portion of distributions may be used to calculate yield.

Most investment companies pay all of their income, after expenses, to their shareholders. By paying out all net income, investment companies are able to avoid federal income taxes.

Internal revenue authorities, under certain conditions, regard investment companies simply as conduits or pipelines between their shareholders and the corporations whose securities the investment companies hold. Whenever investment companies function simply as a type of passageway through which dividends and interest payments flow on their way from the corporation to the investor, they see no logical basis for taxation of the investment company. However, individual investors receiving the income from the investment company must report it as personal income and pay the regular tax rates on that income. Whenever the investment company appears to function as a haven designed to protect investors from taxation, however, it is a different matter, and the internal revenue authorities view the investment company's tax liability differently.

It should be noted that not all investment income distributed to mutual fund shareholders is qualified for the dividend exclusion provision of the federal income tax law. Usually the interest income which is distributed as part of the investment income does not qualify. Interest income would be found in the distributions of a balanced fund, for example. The dividend exclusion under federal law is currently (1967) $100 per shareholder. If a shareholder of an investment company receives $120 of qualified income, he will pay taxes at ordinary income rates only on the $20. If a husband and wife both own shares and the husband should receive $150 of qualified income dividends and the wife only $80, the husband would report $50 and the wife would report no dividends for taxable income. The husband could not use the additional $20 of the dividend exclusion which the wife did not use.

In order for an investment company to qualify for the special tax treatment permitted under the Federal Internal Revenue Code it must qualify as a "regulated" investment company.

To qualify as a "regulated" company, an investment company must be registered under the Investment Company Act of 1940 for the entire taxable year and, among other things, must distribute at least 90 per cent of its net investment income to its shareholders.[11] "Regulated" investment companies are not required to pay federal income taxes on net income or capital gains paid out to shareholders. Nor are they required to make provision for taxes on unrealized net appreciation of investments.

Investment companies, regulated or not, must make provision for and pay federal income taxes on any net income or capital gains they secure during the year which they do not pay out to their shareholders. In other words, if a regulated investment company, after paying out 90 per cent of its income in order to qualify as regulated investment company,

---

[11]There are a number of additional technical requirements which must be met in order for an investment company to qualify as a regulated company, but they are of a rather minor nature. Actually, almost all open-end companies and a majority of closed-end investment companies are registered as regulated investment companies.

retains the remaining 10 per cent of its investment income, it would be taxed on this 10 per cent. Furthermore, it would be taxed (at capital gains rates) on any capital gains it had realized during the year but had not distributed to its shareholders.

SPECIAL CAPITAL GAINS TAX FEATURE. Under certain conditions, the Federal Revenue Act permits investors to pay taxes on some types of income at a rate lower than the rate required on regular income. For example, any profit received by an investor from the sale of a capital item such as real estate or securities) is taxed at a maximum rate of 25 per cent, if the investor has owned the capital item for longer than six months at the time he sells it. This tax is known as the *capital gains tax*.

Investment company shareholders can regard a capital gains distribution from the investment company as a long-term capital gain even if the shareholder has only held the shares for one or two days. This is an exception to the standard rule which indicates that a capital item must be held by the investor for longer than six months in order for any profit from its sale to be eligible for the lower tax rate applicable to long-term capital gains.

Investment company shareholders taking dividends in additional shares of stock (in lieu of cash) in most instances do not relieve themselves of the necessity of paying income taxes on such dividends.

Capital gains distributions, when available, normally are declared annually and are considered a return of capital which should be reinvested in order to keep the original investment intact. The reinvestment of capital gains distributions from an investment company (as distinguished from taking them in cash) does not enable the investor to avoid the capital gains tax.

COSTS OF OPERATING A MUTUAL FUND. All business firms have operating and other expenses. Mutual funds are no exception. Since mutual funds usually are corporations, most of them must pay incorporation fees, filing fees, taxes, and various other levies when they are originally formed. During the course of the funds operation, it incurs and must pay executive salaries, directors' fees, costs of holding stockholders' meetings and preparing financial reports, accounting fees, secretarial salaries, bills for postage, stationery costs, and printing expenses. In addition, there are costs involved in collecting income, paying dividends and capital gains distributions, providing custodian services, and paying federal, state, and local taxes. All of these expenses must be paid either directly or indirectly by the fund.

A major item of expense for most mutual funds is the payment made to management companies for the investment advice the fund receives. These fees, paid annually to the mutual fund's investment adviser, (management company) are known as management fees. The amount of this fee will vary from one fund to another, but typically it is about ½ of 1 per cent of the fund's assets. This fee is often subject to sliding scale reductions as assets increase. The staff of a management company usually consists of economists, industry specialists, and investment analysts as well as the administrative and clerical personnel. Obviously, the services of such a professional staff cannot be obtained without incurring substantial expense.

Just as with any other corporate operation, the more income it takes to cover the expenses of operation, the less there is left to distribute to the shareholders. All management fees, operating expenses, and other costs must be paid out of the mutual fund's gross income before the net income available for payments to shareholders can be determined. Once the expenses have been provided for, dividends can be distributed to the investment company shareholders. Of course, the operating expenses of mutual funds vary from company to company. Some have greater expenses than others. However, operating expenses of investment companies are usually less than 1 per cent per annum of the average net assets of the reporting company.

Operating expenses of investment companies may also be calculated as a percentage of the companies' annual earnings. Some mutual funds have such large annual expenses that, after they are paid, little is left out of their income for distribution to the shareholder. In selecting a mutual fund, an investor should give substantial thought and consideration to this aspect of the mutual fund's operation. The factor of cost should not be considered alone, however, since the ultimate test of a mutual fund is how well it accomplishes its shareholders' investment objective.

MUTUAL FUND CUSTODIANS.   Every mutual fund retains a national bank, trust company, or other qualified institution to act as its custodian. The name of the custodian and the functions it is to perform for the mutual fund will be specifically stated in the fund's prospectus.

The institution functioning as the mutual fund's custodian will hold the cash and the securities of the fund and will, in addition, perform a variety of essential clerical-type services for the fund and its shareholders.

Services performed by the custodian may include functioning:

1. as the transfer agent of the fund
2. as a registrar of the fund shares
3. or as dividend disbursing agent of the fund.

The custodian also receives investor payments and invests those payments in shares of the fund. It keeps custody of the fund shares of individual owners when requested to do so, or when legally required to do so. The custodian also keeps a variety of necessary books and records.

The custodian does *not* perform any management, supervisory, or investment functions, nor does it take part in the sale or distribution of fund shares. The activities of the custodian cannot in any way provide protection against a decline in the net asset value per share of mutual fund securities.

DIVIDEND AND CAPITAL GAINS REINVESTMENT PLANS. Many mutual funds have dividend and capital gains reinvestment plans. Under these plans, the mutual fund shareholder does not take (or does not keep) his distributions from the mutual fund in cash, but rather reinvests all of the dividends and capital gains distributions he receives in new shares of the fund. Mutual funds have found that the various reinvestment plans are popular. In some funds as high as 95 per cent of the capital gains and dividend distributions made to shareholders are reinvested by the shareholders in additional shares of the same fund.

Many mutual fund underwriters offer *automatic dividend reinvestment* plans. In an *automatic* plan, the shareholder does not receive a cash dividend. When declaring a dividend, under such a plan, the mutual fund, or its underwriter, simply notifies the shareholder that his dividends have purchased him X number of additional shares. If the investor does not utilize an automatic reinvestment plan, or if the fund of which he is a shareholder does not have such a plan, he can nevertheless usually reinvest his dividends simply by sending the fund his money either directly or through its representatives and by making his wishes known.

Some funds will permit their shareholders to reinvest their dividends in new shares at net asset value per share. In other words, without requiring a sales charge. Other funds, however, require the full customary sales charge on shares purchased by dividend reinvestment. Some mutual funds fix minimum limits on the shareholder accounts for which the dividend reinvestment privilege without charge is extended. The policies of each individual fund regarding the dividend investment privilege and other matters can be found in its prospectus.

Under some circumstances dividend reinvestment without the imposition of a sales charge can be a valuable privilege for an investor. The existence of this privilege, or the lack of it, should be one of the factors weighed by an investor when he is deciding which mutual fund can best serve his needs.

Most mutual funds give their shareholders an option to receive capital gains distributions in cash or in additional shares of the fund. The reinvestment of capital gains distributions is generally required by the fund if dividends are reinvested. All mutual funds permit their shareholders to reinvest capital gains distributions at the net asset value per share, i.e., without imposing a sales charge. The capital gains distributed by a mutual fund to an investor are considered a partial return of his capital. It represents the net realized capital gains from the fund's portfolio transactions. Thus the option to take additional mutual fund shares instead of cash is important to an investor since its exercise automatically assures that the full amount of his capital remains invested and continues to earn. Nearly all funds encourage their shareholders to reinvest any capital gains distributions they receive. Many companies automatically declare capital gains distributions in shares unless the shareholder specifically requests cash.

SYSTEMATIC WITHDRAWAL PLANS. Some mutual funds provide their shareholders with a service known as a systematic withdrawal plan. Under this plan, a mutual fund shareholder can receive payments from the fund at regular intervals over a period of time. These payments may be in fixed amounts or may be calculated on one of several other bases. Withdrawal plans are designed for investors who wish to supplement their income for current needs, or who wish to meet commitments of a specified goal, such as college education for their children or their own retirement. - A shareholder generally must have a certain minimum amount invested in the fund before such a withdrawal plan can be instigated. A $10,000 minimum investment is fairly typical. When the minimum amount required is on deposit and the shareholder indicates the amount he periodically wishes to receive the payments are begun.

Dividend and capital gains distributions are used to make the payments required under a withdrawal plan in so far as is possible. However, if the scheduled payments are larger than the amounts of dividend and capital gains distributions the investor has coming for that period, some of the investors' shares will be liquidated in order to make the payments. If the investor chooses not to disturb the capital amount, he must either accept a smaller fixed amount or be prepared to accept a variable amount reflecting the level of investment income. The investor should be aware of the extent to which, if any, his shares are being liquidated to meet his payments.

Since by their very nature withdrawal plans carry the risk of exhausting invested capital, any discussion of withdrawal plans or any presentation to the public should be handled with care. See Chapter 17 for a discussion of the SEC's Statement of Policy regarding the presentation and use of withdrawal plan sales literature.

EXCHANGE OR CONVERSION PRIVILEGES. Some mutual fund management organizations manage a group of several mutual funds rather than a single mutual fund. Typically, each fund in the management group has a different portfolio composition and investment objective from each other fund. By managing funds with a variety of investment objectives, the mutual fund management organization is able to offer appropriate investment vehicles to many different people with a wide variety of investment objectives. Thus, a mutual fund salesman representing a group of funds has a fund that he can recommend to an individual who desires growth or capital appreciation, and a different fund sponsored by the same group which he can offer to a person who needs current income.

Sometimes the investment objective of an individual changes. For example, an investor holding shares in a growth fund may find, upon retirement, that he needs more current income from his investment than the growth fund is able to provide. Under such circumstances it would be advantageous for the mutual fund shareholder to be able to exchange his growth shares for the income shares of another fund without paying a sales charge for the privilege. Some mutual fund organizations permit such exchanges within their group of funds. This privilege is known as an *exchange* or *conversion privilege*.

The investor should be given a word of caution at this point. The U.S. Internal Revenue Service considers the exchange or conversion of the shares of one fund for those of another the same as a redemption and a new purchase. In this case, a shareholder who has considerable appreciation in the value of his shares will be liable for a capital gains tax when he redeems them. The fact that he then goes on to exchange them or convert them into new shares has no bearing on the transaction's taxability.

Mutual Funds as Short-Term Investments

The fact that open-end investment company (mutual fund) shares are redeemable does not make them good vehicles for short-term investment. In fact, nothing about them makes them a proper instrument for in-and-out trading.

In the first place, the initial sales charge makes the shares relatively expensive to acquire, particularly if the purchaser is going to turn them in for redemption after a short period. In addition, it should be remembered that some mutual funds charge a redemption fee. However, the most important reason mutual fund shares are not good short-term trading vehicles is the very nature of the mutual fund shares themselves.

Investment companies generally buy a large number of different securities with the money they obtain when they sell their own shares to the public. If the market prices of the portfolio securities held by the investment company go up, the net asset value of the shares will go up. If the market prices go down, the net asset value of the shares will go down. But here is the catch, as far as the short-term investor is concerned: while the market prices of some of the securities in the portfolio are increasing, the market prices of other securities in that same portfolio will remain unchanged, or go down. Thus, the change in the net asset value of the mutual fund shares actually shows the *average* amount the market prices of all the securities in the mutual fund portfolio increased or decreased during a given period. The redemption price, (which is equal to the net asset value per share) being an *average* price, will go up or down less than the market prices of some of the individual security issues in the portfolio which are used to compute this average.

Table 16-III shows the original cost and market prices on June 1, 1966, of the securities held in the portfolio of the Fictitious Mutual Fund Company. It also shows the market prices and total market value of these same portfolio securities as of July 1, 1966, and August 1, 1966. To simplify the illustration, it is assumed that the company started investing for the first time on June 1, 1966, and holds only six different security issues in its portfolio (the typical investment company generally holds a great many more than six different security issues). It is further assumed that these securities are held (not sold) from June 1, 1966, the time they were purchased, through August 1, 1966, the latest date used in the illustration.

Thus we find that 27,000 shares of stock were purchased by the company on June 1, 1966, for a cost of $1,420,000 exclusive of brokerage fees. By July 1, 1966, the total market value of these shares had appreciated to $1,490,000, an increase of $70,000 on a $1,420,000 original capital investment. This is an increase of just a little less than 5 per cent on the original capital investment.

Although this would not be the usual situation, since the number of mutual fund shares outstanding are constantly fluctuating, for purposes of illustration we are assuming that the Fictitious Mutual Fund has 100,000 shares of stock outstanding on each of the three separate dates. Further assuming that cash and other nonportfolio assets will cover any outstanding liabilities, the total net asset value of the company on June 1, 1966, will be the same as the total market value of the portfolio securities held by the company (i.e., $1,420,000).

On June 1, 1966, the redemption price of each share would have been $1,420,000 divided by 100,000 shares or $14.20. One month later, July 1, 1966, the redemption price would have increased to $14.90 per share, ($1,490,000 divided by 100,000 shares) an increase of just slightly under 5 per cent. A 5 per cent appreciation of capital in one month is not at all a bad deal. It is certainly much better than having a loss. However, there are two things the short-term investor should keep in mind while analyzing the situation.

NET UNREALIZED APPRECIATION AND LOSS. First, the gain of $70,000 (which averages about 5 per cent per share on the redemption price) is a *net unrealized appreciation*. Unrealized securities profits are often termed "book" or "paper" profits. This net unrealized appreciation is the difference between the cost and market value of the securities held in the company's portfolio. It is entirely possible that the $70,000 net unrealized appreciation could become a loss before the portfolio securities are ever sold.

Table 16-III shows how the Fictitious Company's net unrealized appreciation of $70,000 had changed to a net unrealized loss of $20,000 by August 1, 1966, without a purchase or sale of the underlying portfolio

TABLE 16—III.

FICTITIOUS MUTUAL FUND COMPANY—100,000 SHARES OUTSTANDING

Corporate name	June 1, 1966			July 1, 1966			August 1, 1966	
	Number of shares held	Original purchase price	Total original cost	Market price	Total market value	% change	Market price	Total market value
Able Co.	1,000	@ $20.00	$ 20,000	@ $40.00	$ 40,000	+100	@ $30.00	$ 30,000
Baker Co.	2,000	@ $40.00	80,000	@ $20.00	40,000	− 50	@ $30.00	60,000
Charley Co.	4,000	@ $30.00	120,000	@ $40.00	160,000	+ 33⅓	@ $40.00	160,000
Dog Co.	5,000	@ $60.00	300,000	@ $80.00	400,000	+ 33⅓	@ $70.00	350,000
Easy Co.	10,000	@ $50.00	500,000	@ $40.00	400,000	− 20	@ $40.00	400,000
Fox Co.	5,000	@ $80.00	400,000	@ $90.00	450,000	+ 12½	@ $80.00	400,000
Total	27,000		$1,420,000*		$1,490,000	+ 5		$1,400,000

*Excluding brokerage fees, etc.

securities by the investment company management. This net unrealized loss developed simply because the existing securities in the portfolio dropped enough in market price from July 1, 1966, to August 1, 1966, to put the total market value below the original cost.

REALIZED APPRECIATION OR LOSS. The only way the Fictitious Mutual Fund Company could actually have realized the $70,000 gain shown on July 1, 1966, was by selling the securities. Furthermore, the only way an investor could have secured the additional 70¢ added to the net asset value per share of the Fictitious Mutual Fund shares he owned, was to have turned the shares back to the company for redemption. Since it probably cost the investor between 6 per cent and 9 per cent to acquire the shares just one month before, the 5 per cent appreciation on his capital does not appear even to cover the initial cost of acquiring the shares. Actually, the investor may have less total capital if he sells his shares at this time, than he had before he purchased the Fictitious Mutual Fund Shares.

There is a second factor the short-term investor should keep in mind when analyzing the 5 per cent increase in the redemption price indicated above. It is that a short-term investment during the same one-month period in any one of four individual securities in the Fictitious Company portfolio would have resulted in a much greater capital appreciation than 5 per cent for the shareholder. An investment in Able Company stock would, for example, have shown a capital appreciation of 100 per cent; an investment in Charley Company 33⅓ per cent; in Dog Company 33⅓ per cent and in Fox Company 12½ per cent. After payment of the brokerage fees involved in buying and selling these securities, the short-term investor would still clearly have had much more capital appreciation than he would have obtained had he purchased the Fictitious Company shares themselves.

However, a short-term investment during the same one-month period in either one of the two portfolio securities which went down instead of up, would have resulted in a loss to the investor. A capital investment in Baker Company stock would have shown a loss of 50 per cent and an investment in Easy Company a 20 per cent loss. The losses illustrated above would be somewhat larger after the brokerage fees incurred for buying and selling were included and, of course, would only be paper losses (unrealized losses) unless the securities were actually sold at those deflated prices.

By buying Fictitious Mutual Fund Company shares, the investor avoided the large capital losses which would have resulted had he invested in the stocks of either Baker Company or Easy Company. In order to avoid these losses, however, the investor had to forego the rapid appreciation in the market prices of the other four stocks in the portfolio. Foregoing this possible rapid appreciation in some of the individual portfolio stocks is part of the price the mutual fund share-holder must pay for the diversification which reduces his over-all investment risk.

Closed-End Investment Companies as Short-Term Investments

Both mutual funds and closed-end investment companies suffer from the basic defect described above as far as short-term trading is concerned. Both types of investment companies, as a general rule, purchase and hold a wide variety of different security issues in their portfolios. Consequently, in closed-end portfolios, just as in mutual fund portfolios, some individual securities are going up, while others are going down, or standing still.

One important difference, however, is the fact that closed-end investment shares do *not* have a redemption price. They are traded either over the counter or through a stock exchange. The price at which they trade is determined only partially by the market value of the securities held in the portfolio. In part, the trading price of closed-end shares reflects the supply and demand conditions for the closed-end shares themselves. Thus, it is possible for closed-end shares to be selling at a substantial discount from net asset value per share and to move rapidly upward to a market price substantially above the net asset value per share. It is equally possible, of course, for the market price of the shares to move from a premium down to a discount in a short period of time.

Almost always however, during any given period, the market prices of at least some of the individual security issues in the portfolio increase or decrease a greater amount, percentage-wise, than the market price of the closed-end shares. This is true even though the closed-end shares may have substantial leverage. Consequently, in order to secure the rapid market price appreciation the short-term investor is always seeking, an individual security issue is generally far superior to the closed-end shares. The brokerage fees incurred in buying and selling either closed-end shares or individual security issues are generally less than the mutual fund sales charge for an equivalent investment.

Investment Company Shares vs. Stock Market Averages

The prices of investment company shares do not move up and down in direct relation to stock market averages. The various stock market averages published regularly in the daily papers are computed in a wide variety of ways (see Chapter 9). Each of these different averages has its own "portfolio," so to speak. Although they do not actually purchase any securities, each one includes in its average a certain quantity of specific stocks. For example, the Dow Jones Industrial Average uses thirty different securities for computation purposes; while the Standard and Poor's Industrial Average includes 425 different securities. When stock splits, stock dividends, and the like occur, the necessary adjustments are made.

The only possible way any investment company's shares could move up and down in a direct relationship with any one of the stock market averages would be for it to hold the identical security issues in the exact proportions they exist in a specific stock market average. However, even under the above conditions closed-end investment company shares generally would not move in direct relationship to a stock market average, since they usually sell at either a premium or a discount.

Swap or Tax-Free Exchange Funds

Tax-free exchange funds (or swap funds, as they are popularly called) are open-end investment companies which allow an investor to exchange his individual securities holdings for the fund's shares without incurring the immediate tax liability on capital gains profits which would have been incurred if the individually held securities had been sold. The capital gains tax is due and payable eventually, of course, whenever the investor sells his fund shares, since the tax cost of the mutual fund shares he acquired is the same as the tax cost of his original holdings. Thus the swap fund investor does not eliminate the capital gains tax but only postpones paying it until the swap fund shares are sold.

The swap fund concept has special appeal to wealthy individuals with large holdings of a single stock or a relatively few stocks which have appreciated substantially in value since they were first purchased. The owners of such securities are said to be "locked in" the securities position they have, because of their reluctance to incur the large capital gains taxes which the sale of such securities would bring about. However, continuing to hold indefinitely securities which have gone up in price can result in the unpleasant experience of watching the unrealized gains (paper profits) shrink, disappear, or, worst of all, ultimately turn into a loss. This can be particularly serious if all or a large part of the investor's money is tied up in only one security or a relatively few securities. This dilemma can be resolved, under certain circumstances, by the use of a swap fund.

A properly created swap fund provides a vehicle which allows these individuals to diversify their holdings and obtain continuous professional management of their investment funds by pooling their shares with those of other individuals in the tax-free swap. The Internal Revenue Service originally approved this concept in 1960 when the first tax-free exchange fund was offered. By mid-July, 1966, when the Internal Revenue Service decided that future swaps no longer would be tax free, more than twenty swap funds with assets totaling some $750,000,000 had been organized.

Swap funds were granted a limited extension of life by a new law passed in late 1966. This new law permits a tax-free exchange of corporate stock (until July 31, 1967) for the shares of any new swap mutual funds that meet three standards:

1. They must file their registration statement with the Securities and Exchange Commission by the end of 1966;
2. They must collect investors' individual stock holdings by May 1, 1967, and;
3. They must have completed the entire transaction by July 1, 1967.

The tax situation is all important for exchange or swap funds, of course. If an investor incurred a capital gains tax in the exchange for mutual fund shares, it would defeat his purpose. Under such conditions he could just as well have sold his securities and purchased outright the shares of a typical mutual fund or invested in some other type of security.

Swap mutual funds do not make a continuous offering of their shares to the public. Securities to be "swapped" must be held in escrow during the period in which the new mutual fund corporation is being organized. All such securities are exchanged for shares of the swap fund in a single transaction.

The performance of some swap funds has been disappointing in the past. Some critics claim that certain swap funds have had trouble performing well because they accept stock in exchange that other people want to eliminate from their portfolios. Accordingly, better results could have been obtained by the funds if they had been able to go into the market and buy the most attractive stocks for their investment portfolios. In an effort to solve this problem, many swap funds have limited the stocks they will accept in exchange for their shares to those on an approved list.

No-Load Mutual Funds

No-load mutual funds are open-end investment companies whose shares may be purchased without the payment of a sales commission or charge. There are currently about forty no-load funds in existence in the United States.

Generally, when mutual funds shares are purchased, a sales charge or commission of from 2 to 8 per cent is involved. Ordinarily, this sales charge (or load as it is often called) is not a charge of the mutual fund itself. As previously noted, it usually is collected by a mutual fund underwriter or sales organization which is independent from the mutual fund whose shares it sells. The sales charge or load is the compensation to the salesman for his efforts in bringing the investor and the mutual fund together.

Many mutual funds are extensively advertised by their management company in order to stimulate investor interest. Television, radio, newspaper, and magazine advertising are all frequently employed by mutual fund management companies in their promotional efforts. No-load mutual funds, on the other hand, usually do not employ salesmen, either directly or indirectly. Furthermore, although no-load mutual fund shares are usually sold by mail, they are generally the subject of only a limited amount of advertising.

The initial advantage of the no-load fund to the investor is obvious. By buying shares in a no-load mutual fund, the investor obtains all of the typical mutual fund benefits without incurring or paying the loading charge (or sales commission) which is taken out of his capital whenever he buys shares in a fund with a sales load. The following illustration graphically points out this initial no-load fund advantage.

Mr. Betts has $8,000 of extra savings, and he has concluded that he would like to invest this money in mutual fund shares.

He has done a good bit of reading about various mutual funds and has come to the conclusion that a common stock fund with some growth potential would be most advantageous for him. For sake of illustration, let us assume that the two particular growth mutual funds which appeal to him the most are both selling for $16 per share at the time he is considering the purchase. One mutual fund, the S. C. Mutual Fund, has a sales charge of 8 per cent on purchases of $10,000 worth of shares or less. The other fund under consideration is the N. L. Mutual Fund, which has no sales load whatsoever.

The number of shares Mr. Betts could acquire with his $8,000 in each of the two mutual funds he is considering, is as follows:

N. L. Mutual Fund

(no-load)
$8,000   (Investment ÷ $16 (price per share) = 500 shares acquired

S. C. Mutual Fund

(sales charge)
$8,000   Investment
− 640   (Sales Charge 8 per cent of $8,000)
$7,360   Amount available for the purchase of shares
$7,360 ÷ $16 (price per share) = 460 shares acquired

Assuming that each of the two funds are equally successful in building up their net asset value per share over a period of years, the conclusions are inescapable. The no-load fund shares considered by Mr. Betts in our illustration would have 8 per cent greater total value at the end of any appreciation period than would the shares of the S. C. Mutual

Fund. This means that in order to overcome the initial disadvantage of the 8 per cent sales charge the net asset value per share of the S. C. Mutual Fund would have to appreciate at a rate faster than that of the N. L. Mutual Fund.

No-load mutual funds incur a variety of operating expenses, just as do mutual funds with sales charges. No-load funds must pay management fees and in addition have to cover all of the other expenses typically involved in operating a mutual fund. See pages 326–329. These expenses must be paid before distributions may be made to the mutual fund shareholders.

There is no reason to assume that the expenses involved in operating a no-load mutual fund will be any less, (or any more, for that matter), than the expenses incurred in the operation of a mutual fund which has an initial sales charge. The only difference as far as the mutual fund shareholder is concerned is that it does not cost anything to acquire the no-load shares.

The value of a mutual fund to an investor depends entirely upon its performance. If the fund performs well and fulfills the investment objective of its shareholders, it is a good fund to own. If the fund consistently performs poorly due to high operating expenses and management fees, and/or poor or mediocre portfolio results, it obviously is not a good fund to own. No-load funds are no bargain if they perform badly, regardless of the fact they initially cost nothing to acquire.

Some mutual funds require the payment of a redemption fee by the investor when they redeem their shares. A redemption fee is, in a sense, a delayed load and should be considered by the investor as a cost factor influencing his investment decision.

Redemption Fees

Mutual fund shareholders are generally entitled to redeem their shares at their full net asset value per share. Some mutual funds, however, impose a redemption fee upon their shareholders when they cash in their shares.

A redemption fee is usually stated as a certain percentage of the net asset value per share of the redeemed shares. If a redemption fee is imposed by a mutual fund, it is generally one per cent or less of the net asset value per share.

The following illustration shows the effect of a redemption fee upon the amount received by a mutual fund shareholder when he cashes in his shares.

Mr. Betts owns 1,000 shares of the RF Mutual Fund. He wishes to sell his shares, so he sent them to the RF Mutual Fund for redemption. At the time Mr. Betts turned his shares in for redemption, the net asset value per share was $8.50. The RF Mutual Fund requires payment of a redemption fee of one per cent. Thus the price per share paid by the RF Mutual Fund to any shareholder redeeming his shares in the net asset value of each of its shares minus the redemption charge of one per cent.

Under the above conditions, the net amount Mr. Betts would receive for his shares would be as follows:

	1,000	(Shares: RF Mutual Fund)
times	$8.50	(Net asset value per share)
	$8,500	
less	85.	(one per cent redemption fee)
	$8,415	(net proceeds to Mr. Betts)

The Tax-Exempt Bond Fund or Municipal Bond Fund

The tax-exempt bond fund (or municipal bond fund, as it is frequently called) is a mutual fund which invests its shareholders' money in municipal securities.[12] Municipal securities are bonds or other interest-bearing obligations issued by the governments of any of the fifty states or any of their governmental subdivisions. Bond issues of counties, boroughs, municipalities, cities, towns, or governmental authorities thereof, such as school districts, water districts, toll roads, etc., are called municipal bonds. The interest paid to the holder of these obligations, (in this case the mutual fund), is exempt from federal income taxes. The income distributions passed on to the municipal bond fund shareholder by the mutual fund likewise are exempt from personal federal income taxes. Consequently, the investor's return on the money he has invested in the shares is not reduced by federal income taxes.

However, if the tax-exempt bond fund sells some of the municipal securities it owns and realizes a capital gain on the sale, a capital gains tax may have to be paid by the fund. Any distribution of capital gains made to the shareholder will be subject to the capital gains provision of the federal income tax laws. Thus it should be carefully noted and remembered that the tax-exempt feature of municipal bonds relates only to the interest payments made by the municipality to the security holder and does not eliminate the owner's need to pay a federal capital gains tax if conditions of sale require such a payment.

An individual investor could purchase municipal bonds on his own of course, and obtain the same tax exemption that he gets when he buys shares in a tax-exempt bond fund. However there are so many thousands

---

[12]Technically, the tax-exempt bond funds now in existence are a series of trusts. These funds do not make a continuous offering. While investment units are being sold in one trust, bonds are being purchased for another.

of different municipal issues in existence it is difficult for the average individual to identify them, let alone evaluate their investment worth. Also, since municipal issues are almost always unlisted, obtaining information about their current prices requires a phone call to a broker who in turn must often go to a substantial amount of effort in order to track down information about the issue.

Small investors are at a particular disadvantage in municipal-bond investing, since the small standard commission received on a municipal-bond transaction by a broker frequently makes him reluctant to do the necessary research for small customers. Another complication for the typical small investor is the fact that a single municipal bond costs approximately $1,000. Consequently, the small investor usually cannot, by himself, obtain both tax exemption on his investment income and the lesser risk supplied by diversification.

The tax-exempt bond fund device enables the small investor to obtain both of these advantages in one package. After the initial offering of the trust units of a municipal bond fund has been completed, the units begin trading over the counter.

REVIEW QUESTIONS

1. Define an investment company and explain the important advantages to the investors of holding stocks of investment companies.
2. Describe and distinguish between: a management company, an open end company, a closed end company, and a diversified company.
3. What are two reasons for the substantial growth of investment companies in recent years? Give detailed reasons.
4. In what way are investment companies a hedge against inflation?
5. Explain how mutual funds are organized, managed, and sold.
6. What is meant by the term "load"? What is a no load fund?
7. Describe regular account holders and accumulation plan holders.
8. Differentiate between level charge and contractual plans.
9. Describe how a holder of mutual fund shares may redeem them. How is the redemption price calculated?
10. Where can an investor in a mutual fund find the redemption and offering prices for his shares?
11. Explain the investment policies of a diversified common stock fund, a specialized fund, a balanced fund, and an income fund.
12. Explain in detail a regulated investment company and show how the fact that it is a "regulated" company affects the tax position of the holder.

13. What are the costs of operating a mutual fund? About what per cent are these costs of the fund's assets? About what per cent are these costs of the fund's annual income?

14. Why are mutual funds poor vehicles for short-term investments?

15. What is a tax exempt fund? Explain its advantages.

16. Describe some of the privileges available to the holders of mutual funds.

Investment Company Regulation

Chapter 17

Investment companies in the United States are very closely regulated at both the federal and state levels. State blue sky laws are applicable to the activities of investment companies as are the general corporate statutes of the various states. At the federal level, a variety of statutes and regulatory agencies govern the operations of investment companies. These include:

1. The Securities Act of 1933.
2. The Securities Exchange Act of 1934.
3. The Investment Company Act of 1940.
4. The Investment Advisers Act of 1940.
5. The Internal Revenue Service, through the application of portions of the Internal Revenue Code.
6. The Federal Reserve Board, through the application of Regulation T.
7. The Securities and Exchange Commission Statement of Policy, in respect to investment company sales literature.
8. Numerous other rules and regulations of the NASD and of the various securities exchanges.

The most important single piece of federal legislation relating to investment company activities, of course, is the Investment Company Act of 1940. The act provides for the registration and regulation of companies primarily engaged in the business of investing, reinvesting, owning, holding, or trading in securities.

As previously noted in Chapter 16, provisions of the Investment Company Act of 1940 provide the definitions of various types of investment companies. These provisions also permit the classification of companies and indicate the requirements for the registration of investment companies. The act attempts to reduce investment company selling abuses and assure the availability of adequate factual information about investment companies.

It is important to remember that the registration of an investment company under the Investment Company Act of 1940 does not involve any supervision by federal or state authorities of the management of the company or of the company's investment practices or policies.

The Investment Company Act of 1940 requires that some "outsiders" must be on each investment company's board of directors. Not more than 60 per cent of the board of directors of an investment company may be its own officers or employees, or its banker, underwriter, or investment adviser.

The act also places restrictions on transactions with persons or underwriters affiliated with the fund. For example, a mutual fund may not purchase the securities of any company if one or more of the officers or directors of the fund (or its investment adviser) owns more than 1/2 of 1 per cent of the securities of that company, or if together such officers or directors own more than 5 per cent of the securities of the company. Officers, directors and larger stockholders of closed-end companies must report their transactions in the shares of the company to the SEC.

Investment advisory contracts signed by investment company boards must be approved by majority vote of the stockholders according to provision of the Investment Company Act of 1940. Management contracts usually are approved initially for a two-year period but thereafter are renewed annually. These contracts may be cancelled by directors or stockholders on 60 days' notice.

All investment companies must comply with SEC rules in relation to the solicitation of proxies for voting on matters concerning the company. Furthermore, since 1960, all proxy statements issued by investment companies are required to list the details of the company's contract with its investment adviser and the relationships which exist between the adviser and the investment company officers.

Investment company shareholders must receive complete financial reports from the companies whose shares they hold at least semi-annually. All financial reports sent to shareholders by investment companies must be filed with the SEC.

The capital structure provisions of the Investment Company Act of 1940 limits the borrowing practices of investment companies. A mutual fund may issue only common stock but is permitted to borrow temporarily from a bank as long as it maintains a 300 per cent asset coverage on all money borrowed. A closed-end company, on the other hand, may utilize bank loans *and* senior securities, again subject to the asset coverage provisions. This asset coverage requirement has the effect of keeping the capital structure leverage factors of investment companies at relatively low levels.

Other curtailments on investment company activities include those restricting short sales and those requiring margin purchases to be made in accordance with SEC rules.

Provisions of the Investment Company Act of 1940 relating to sales charges involved in the distribution of investment company shares, the payment of redemption proceeds and the operation of contractual plans are covered in Chapter 16. This chapter also contains material relating to the application of Subchapter M of the Internal Revenue Code to investment company earnings.

Regulation T, administered by the Board of Governors of the Federal Reserve System, also applies to investment company activities. Regulation T does not permit the extension of credit on unlisted securities by brokers and dealers. Since the shares of an open-end investment company are not listed on national securities exchanges, the prohibition against extension of credit applies to transactions in mutual fund shares. The effect of Regulation T is to bar brokers and dealers from granting credit or arranging for credit to enable customers to buy or carry the securities of any open-end investment company.

NASD members who sell investment company shares must transmit the funds received in payment to the appropriate underwriter (or custodian) promptly after the date of the transaction. If payment is not received within ten business days, the underwriter must immediately notify the dealer and the Association's office in the district where the dealer's office is located. As noted, transactions in investment company shares between NASD members and their customers are subject to Regulation T of the Federal Reserve Board.

Investment Company Registration and Prospectus Required Under Securities Act of 1933

Any corporation planning to make a public distribution of its shares must comply with the registration requirements of the Securities Act of 1933 prior to issuing its shares. Open-end investment companies (mutual funds) are not exempt from this regulation.

Mutual funds issue new shares continuously, and these shares must be properly registered with the SEC before they may be offered for public sale. Furthermore, there can be no offer made to sell mutual fund shares to anyone unless the offer is accompanied by a current copy of the company's prospectus. A prospectus is an abbreviated form of registration statement, and a copy of this prospectus must be given to a potential mutual fund customer before, or at the time, he purchases the fund's shares. Every thirteen or fourteen months, a new group of mutual fund shares is registered by the company and a new, revised or updated prospectus is used.

The mutual fund prospectus contains a great deal of information of vital importance to the potential investor and should be read carefully before a decision is made regarding the purchase of the shares. The law requires an investment company to clearly define its fundamental investment policy in its prospectus as well as in its registration statement. This policy cannot be changed without majority stockholder approval, but may be altered under certain circumstances to meet emergency market conditions. It is not mandatory that the prospectus mention the names of the specific securities or industries in which the investment company has invested its money, but it frequently does include this information. The prospectus should give complete and up-to-date information about the investment company's management, advisers, and distributors.

It is important for the potential investment company shareholder to remember that the SEC does not guarantee the accuracy of the information contained in the prospectus. Any representation to the contrary is a criminal offense. The significance of the registration of a security under the Securities Act of 1933, and the issuance of a prospectus, is discussed in detail in Chapter 15.

Investment Companies and the Securities Exchange Act of 1934

Both the Securities and Exchange Commission and the National Association of Securities Dealers Inc., play key roles in the regulation of the investment company industry. These two regulatory bodies developed from the provisions and amendments of the Securities Exchange Act of 1934.

Investment Company Rule

Section 26 of Article III of the Rules of Fair Practice applies exclusively to the activity of NASD members in connection with the securities of investment companies. Section 26 states that an NASD member who is the underwriter or sponsor of an investment company's shares may not execute a sales agreement with any securities dealer unless such dealer is a member of the NASD.

Furthermore, he may not sell any such securities to any dealer or broker at any price other than the public offering price unless such dealer or broker is a member of the NASD and a sales agreement is in effect between the parties. The sales agreement must set forth, among other things, the concession to be received by the dealer.

An NASD member underwriting the shares of an open-end investment company may not sell the shares if the public offering price includes an unfair gross selling commission or load.[1] The fairness or un-

---

[1]The gross selling commission or load is the difference between the public offering price and the price received by the issuer.

fairness of the gross selling commission or load should be determined after taking into consideration all relevant circumstances, including the current marketability of the security and all expenses involved.

Section 26 also states, "No member who is an underwriter shall accept a conditional order for securities of an open-end investment company on any basis other than at a specified definite price." This means that no underwriter for an open-end investment company may accept an order except at the current offering price or at a specified definite price. This prohibits an underwriter from accepting orders placed on the basis of "best-of-day prices" or "next advance."

Section 26 has the effect of prohibiting underwriters from accepting, after the effective time of a price change, any orders at a previous price. In other words, no orders can be accepted after the price change dead-line, with the sole exception of orders received by telegram, where the time stamped on the telegram is prior to the price change and the buyer is therefore entitled to an earlier price.

A member who is a party to a sales agreement may not, as principal, purchase shares from a record holder at a price below the bid price then quoted by the issuer.

An investment company underwriter may not repurchase its shares from a dealer (acting as principal) who is not a party to a sales agreement with the underwriter *unless* the dealer is the record owner of the shares. This dealer may, however, acting as agent, sell the shares to the underwriter at the current bid price for the account of the record owner and charge a fair commission for handling the transaction.

Section 26 also provides for the following:

A dealer may purchase open-end company shares from the underwriter only for the purpose of covering purchase orders already received from customers or for his own investment.

Members must never withold customers' orders in order to profit from the withholding.

Underwriters are required to calculate the public offering price at least once each business day at 3:30 P.M. the closing time of trading at the New York Stock Exchange. Most underwriters, however, calculate the price twice a day.

Mutual fund shares normally must be redeemed by the issuer at net asset value on any day the New York Stock Exchange is open.

The sales agreement between the investment company underwriter and the dealer must provide that if a customer redeems shares within seven business days after purchase, the dealer must refund to the underwriter the full concession received on the original sale.

In principal transactions between dealers and customers in shares of open-end investment companies, the current public offering price must, by law, be maintained.

SELLING DIVIDENDS.   Any NASD member who uses an impending investment company dividend or distribution as an inducement for the purchase of investment company shares may be making representations contrary to the provisions of *Article III, Section 1 of the Rules of Fair
Practice.* It is essential that the potential purchaser of investment company shares be made aware of the effect that the payment of these
distributions will have on the price of his shares. The investor must
not be misled.

No advantage accrues to the buyer of investment company shares
by purchasing the shares just before a distribution. Before it is distributed, the amount of the distribution is included in the price the
investor pays for the shares. When the distribution is paid out to the
shareholders, the shares decline in price (on their ex-distribution date)
by the amount of the distribution.

Selling dividends is the name given to the process of getting investors
to buy investment company shares just before a distribution on the false
assumption it will benefit them.

INTERPRETATION WITH RESPECT TO SPECIAL DEALS.   The NASD Board of
Governors has adopted the following interpretation of the Rules of
Fair Practice with regards to "special deals":

> It shall be deemed conduct inconsistent with just and equitable prin-
> ciples of trade and in violation of Section I of Article III of the Rules of
> Fair Practice for a principal underwriter or an associated or affiliated person
> of a principal underwriter in connection with the sale or distribution of
> investment company shares to give directly or indirectly to a member or to
> a registered representative or other associated person of a member, or for
> a member or an associated person of a member to accept anything of *material
> value* in addition to the discounts or concessions set forth in the currently
> effective prospectus of the investment company.

For purposes of this *special deals interpretation* anything of material
value means:

1. Gifts amounting in value to more than $25 per person per
   year.
2. Gifts of management company stock or other security, or
   making such a security available on a preferential basis.

Regulation of Investment Company
Sales Literature

In 1950, the SEC, with the assistance of the NASD, reviewed
samples of advertising and supplemental sales literature used in pro-
moting the sale of investment company shares. This review revealed
(to use the words of the SEC) "the existence of many practices in connection with the use, form and content of certain advertising and sales
literature which, in the opinion of the Commission might violate sta-

tutory standards, including provisions of the Securities Act of 1933 and the Investment Company Act of 1940."[2] Furthermore, it was noted, much of the literature and advertising material examined had not been filed with the commission.

Motivated by the information uncovered by the above review, the SEC issued a *Statement of Policy* in respect to investment company sales literature. The Statement of Policy was issued, stated the commission, "so that issuers, underwriters and dealers may understand certain of the types of advertising and sales literature which the Commission considers may be violative of the statutory standards."[3]

The SOP is, in effect, the SEC interpretation of the fraud sections of the Securities Act of 1933 as applied to investment company sales literature.

The Statement of Policy was issued on August 11, 1950, and was amended on November 5, 1957. Its basic purpose is to create standards to govern the quality and truthfulness of investment company sales literature. There is no intention or desire on the part of the SEC or the NASD to prevent broker/dealers from presenting a fair and accurate picture to their customers or potential customers.

NASD Administers SEC Statement of Policy

The SEC, along with leaders in the investment company area of the securities business, felt that the SOP should be administered by the NASD. As a logical and needed further step in the process of self-regulation, such action was taken.

In 1950, the NASD Board of Governors gave the Association's Investment Companies Committee the authority and duty to supervise member firm sales literature and advertising relating to the shares of open-end investment companies. Also, where applicable, similar material relating to the securities of closed-end companies is supervised by the NASD. The NASD thus has the responsibility of regulating the sales literature of member firm distributors and dealers of investment company shares.

The SEC enforces the SOP when the material is prepared by investment company underwriters and sales organizations which are not members of the NASD.

By agreement, any seemingly improper sales material of NASD member firms that comes to the attention of the SEC is referred to the NASD. In return, any nonmember firm sales material discovered by the NASD that does not appear to conform with the standard is referred to the SEC.

The NASD's task of supervising member firm sales literature has

2Securities and Exchange Commission, Washington, D. C. Statement of Policy (as amended November 5, 1957).
3Ibid.

proved to be extremely time consuming and difficult. One reason is that most NASD members are actively engaged in selling investment company securities. These companies have issued a tremendous volume of literature which is subject to the Statement of Policy.

The last year the NASD attempted to review literature prepared by "outsiders" for sale to member firms was 1958. The volume of books, articles, brochures, sales training guides, and so on became so large that the board of governors directed a discontinuance of this part of the review service in order to avoid impairing the over-all quality of the review program.

Investment Company Sales Literature
Filing Requirements

All NASD members must file with the Association in Washington, D. C., within three days after its first use or publication, all sales literature prepared by (or especially for) them, having to do with investment company shares.

Members may submit such sales material in advance of use or publication with a request for comment as to whether such material seems to meet the requirements of the Statement of Policy. However, this is not required. If advance comment is requested, a revised copy must be filed for final check prior to publication. Furthermore, the member must still file any material actually used or published within three days after it is first utilized.

Since literature of members or questions regarding its preparation and use should be submitted to the Investment Companies Department, National Association of Securities Dealers, Inc., 888 Seventh Street N.W., Washington, D.C. 20006.

Type of literature which must be filed includes any communication used by an issuer, underwriter, or dealer to induce the purchase of shares of an investment company. This includes, among other material:

1. All newspaper, magazine, radio, or television advertising or scripts
2. All form letters including postal cards with form messages
3. All individually typed sales letters which repeat the theme of the same central idea
4. Most reports and brochures
5. All telephone recordings and motion picture advertising presentations

Annual and quarterly reports sent to company shareholders which do not contain an express offer are not considered sales literature but must nevertheless conform to the SOP.

Communications between issuers, underwriters, and dealers are defined as sales literature for SOP purposes if the communications are:

1. passed on, either orally or in writing
2. shown to prospective investors
3. designed to be employed in either written or oral form in the sale of securities.

Member firm dealers need not file sales material prepared by sponsors of investment companies, but must file the material they prepare themselves or have prepared for their use by outside agencies.

Sales material prepared by sponsors or issuers of investment company shares must be filed with the SEC as well as the NASD by the firm preparing the material.

Statement of Policy Sections

The Statement of Policy comprises eighteen sections which cover many of the major abusive forms of investment company sales literature. The SEC warns, however, that the eighteen sections do not attempt to cover all of the possible abuses, and that literature which complies with the SOP may not be used if it is, in fact, misleading. The SEC stresses the fact that nothing in the SOP is intended to prevent the use of factual statements, fairly presented, concerning fundamental investment policies and objectives, investment restrictions, or other characteristics of a particular investment company.

For SOP purposes, investment company sales literature is considered materially misleading if it:

1. Includes an untrue statement of a material fact, or
2. Omits a material fact which is needed to make the literature clear and not misleading
3. Fails to conform with any of the sections of the statement of policy itself.

RATES OF RETURN. Section *A* of the Statement of Policy (SOP) forbids the presentation of percentage rates of return on investment company shares in general. It prescribes precise formulae for calculating percentage rates of return on income dividends paid by individual investment companies in past periods.

In computing rates of return on investment company shares, on the basis of dividends in the last twelve months, all of the following elements must be shown:

1. The current offering price of the shares
2. The total amount of income dividends paid
3. The change in asset value which occurred in the period covered
4. A disclaimer as to future results

Section *A* provides that rates of return of investment company shares may be expressed only in either of the following two ways: on a historic basic, or on a current basis.

Rates of return expressed on a historic basis may relate dividends paid from net investment income during a fiscal year to the average monthly offering price existing during that same fiscal year. If any year prior to the most recent fiscal year is selected for this comparison, however, the rate of return of all subsequent fiscal years similarly calculated must also be shown. Thus the statement made in question 422 is improper.

Rates of return expressed on a current basis may relate dividends paid from net investment income during the last 12 calendar months before publication to an offering price current at date of publication.

Example: *Historic Basis*

Dividends from Income for fiscal 1965	$ 0.75
Average Monthly Offering Price for fiscal 1965	$18.75
Rate of Return ($.75 divided by $18.75)	4%

Example: *Current Basis*

Dividends from Income during calendar months (July 1, 1965 to July 1, 1966)		$ 0.80
Offering Price, July 15, 1966	$19.20	
Capital Gain Distribution, Dec. 1965	+ .50[4]	
Adjusted Offering Price		$19.70
Rate of Return ($.80 divided by $19.70)		4.06%

In either case, the net asset value per share at the beginning and end of the periods, or the percentage increase or decrease, must be shown. It may be indicated, either where the rate of return is shown, or by reference in the same text to an historical table elsewhere in the same piece of literature.

Capital gains distributions may never be included with income in computing a percentage yield or dollar return on investment company shares.

Compound interest tables may not be used to express or imply rates of return on investment companies.

Percentage return or yield figures should not be used in advertisements or general sales literature of an institutional type, involving investment company shares, since such information can be given in conformance with the Statement of Policy only with respect to specific companies.

SALES LITERATURE FEATURING INCOME. Section *b* of the Statement of Policy makes it improper to combine into one amount distributions from investment company income and distributions from capital or any

---

[4]This simple adjustment of adding back to the current offering price the per share amount of capital gains distributions is not precisely accurate; nevertheless it is usually a sufficient adjustment to prevent misleading rate of return.

other source. It is also improper for sales literature or a salesman to represent or imply an assurance that an investor will receive a stable, continuous, dependable, or liberal return or that he will receive any special rate or rates of return in the future. This is true even when the past record of the company appears to support such a statement.

Dividends from income and distributions from capital gains and from other sources must be shown under separate headings in investment company sales literature rather than under a common heading. Thus it is improper to show distributions from various sources under a single heading such as "Distributions During the Past 12 Months." (This rule is not intended to bar the traditional historical per-share table of asset value, dividends from income, and distributions from other sources, so long as there is no common heading over the distributions.)

Sponsors and underwriters using sales literature featuring "income programs" or "check-a-month" plans must limit such presentations to listing the amounts of dividends from income that would have been received during the past twelve months on an investment of a certain sum or sums one year ago. The computation may be based on:

1. The number of shares that would have been acquired at the offering price or prices in effect at the time of the investment, plus any shares that would have been acquired had capital gains distributions been accepted in additional shares, or
2. If capital gains distributions are assumed to have been received in cash, the amounts of such distributions may be shown as a footnote unrelated to the tabulation of income distributions.

In either case, asset value of the investment at the beginning and end of the period must also be shown as an integral part of such presentation.

Sales literature, prepared by underwriters, containing blank spaces to be filled in with data about capital values, capital gains distributions, dividends from income, and other similar performance data at the time of presentation to customers may not be used. Such material was found to be susceptible to misuse and erroneous computations and consequently had misleading implications within the meaning of the SOP.

Sales presentations by dealers relating to estate planning, investment programming, and the like must conform in all respects to the Statement of Policy.

EXPLANATION OF RISKS. Section *c* of the Statement of Policy requires an explanation of the risk of the market fluctuation that is involved in investment company shares when any of the following is discussed:

1. Appreciation and profit possibilities
2. Preservation of capital
3. Protection against loss of purchasing power

4. Accumulation of an estate
5. Diversification of investments

REFERENCES TO FEDERAL REGULATION. Section *d* of the Statement of Policy forbids references to federal regulation of investment companies unless such statements are properly qualified.

While it is true that investment companies are subject to federal and state regulation, this regulation does not involve supervision of the investment companies' management activities.

Investment company managements make their own investment decisions. They decide which stocks and bonds to buy and when to buy them. They decide which securities to sell and when to sell them. Neither the SEC nor the state blue sky laws regulate such decisions. Thus, in order to avoid creating a misimpression about the nature of investment company regulation, the SOP requires that any mention of federal or state regulation of investment companies must be properly qualified. "Proper qualification" requires an explanation that such regulation does not involve supervision of the company's management, investment practices or policies.

CUSTODIAL SERVICE OF BANKS. Section *e* of the Statement of Policy forbids any implication that the employment of banks as custodians provides the investor any service beyond a clerical operation.

Banking institutions are frequently retained by investment companies and other corporations to perform a variety of clerical-type services for the corporations and their stockholders. Such services include:

1. Holding the cash and securities of the company in custody for safekeeping
2. Functioning as the company's transfer agent
3. Functioning as the company's dividend disbursing agent

When such arrangements have been made with a bank, it is perfectly acceptable for the investment company to make a statement of these specific facts in its sales literature. However, when referring in a general way to a bank as the company's custodian, care must be exercised to avoid creating a misimpression.

Under section *e* of the SOP there is no objection to statements which say no more than the following:

1. "The XYZ Bank is custodian."
2. "The cash and securities of the investment company are held in custody of the XYZ Bank."
3. "The cash and securities are held by the XYZ Bank as custodian."

Anything beyond a simple straightforward statement such as these, however, requires an explanation of the limited role played by a custodian bank.

In pointing out the limited role of the custodian bank, the literature should clearly indicate that the bank does not in any way supervise the investment activities of the investment company's management. The managers of the investment company decide which securities it should buy, which securities it should sell and the timing of these transactions. The management also determines when dividends will be paid, what form these dividends will take, and the amount of dividends that will be paid.

The sales literature should also make it clear that the custodian bank does not guarantee the earnings or capital of the investment company nor does it provide any sort of trusteeship protection.

Thus, the custodian bank does not provide any protection for investors against possible depreciation of the investment companies' assets.

Since many investors are unaware of the traditional services embodied in the custodial relationship, failure to mention the above limitations under the prescribed circumstances, may be misleading and thus constitute a violation of the Statement of Policy.

REDEMPTION DISCUSSION. Section *f* of SOP requires that discussions of the redemption feature of open-end investment shares must be accompanied by an explanation that the redemption price may be more or less than the price paid for the shares.

Some investors have the impression that a redemption price of a security is something entirely different from a sales price. The fact that the issuing company stands ready at all times to redeem the shares (as is the case with the shares of mutual funds) evidently gives some purchasers the idea that they will be able to get *all* of their money back, whenever they wish to turn their shares back to the issuing company for redemption.

This is a very unrealistic attitude for several reasons. To begin with, the purchase price of the mutual fund shares generally includes a sales charge. This part of the investor's money (up to 9 per cent) is not used to purchase securities at all, but is used to pay the commissions and expenses of the sales organization through which the investor purchased the open-end investment company shares. Without any change at all in the market prices of the portfolio securities which provide the underlying value of each share, an investor turning his shares in for redemption, would receive less for them than he originally paid, due to this sales charge alone. If a redemption fee is charged by the company buying back its shares the net amount received by the investor would be even less.

The market prices of the portfolio securities held by the mutual fund are constantly changing. Since the total assets of the company are always fluctuating in value it is obvious that the redemption price (which is equal to the net asset value per share) will also always be changing. An increase in the value of the portfolio securities (if it is large enough) can increase the amount of net assets available for each share to a point high enough to more than offset any sales charge or redemption fee the investor had to pay. Under these conditions, the investor will receive more for his shares upon redemption than he paid to acquire them. Under any other conditions, he will not.

To avoid creating any false impressions, Section *f* of the SOP requires a clear presentation of how the above factors will influence the redemption price of mutual fund shares.

COMPARISONS WITH ALTERNATIVE INVESTMENTS. Section *g* of the State ment of Policy forbids any implication that investment company shares are similar to government bonds, insurance, or savings accounts, or that investment companies have any restrictions such as those governing savings banks and insurance companies.

Investment company shares do not provide investors with a *guaranteed* fixed income over a period of time. Some investment companies, due to successful investment activities, are able to pay the same amount of income per share for several quarters in succession. However, there is no assurance that this will happen in the future.

Furthermore, there is no way to guarantee that the investor can ultimately recapture his original principal investment in the investment company's shares. No guarantee is possible, because the money used to buy investment company shares is reinvested by the investment companies in securities which fluctuate in price. Due to these price fluctuations, the investor may not be able to realize as much money from the sale of the investment company shares as he originally spent to acquire them. On the other hand, he may actually get more money back than he originally used to buy the investment company shares. The fluctuating dollar value of investment company shares is one important way these shares differ from some alternative investment media and from savings accounts and life insurance.

Savings deposits in a savings account of a commercial bank, savings and loan association, or other such savings institution, generally carry some sort of assurance that the depositor will be able to recapture or withdraw the full amount deposited whenever he wishes to do so. This is true, because his savings account is generally insured by an agency of the United States Government. One agency, known as the Federal Deposit Insurance Corporation, insures individual savings in bank accounts up to $10,000.00 per individual account and will return the depositor's savings if the institution is unable to do so.

Annuities or other types of insurance contracts are also, theoretically at least, safer than investment company share purchases. Annuity payments and life insurance disbursements are contractual in nature and are determined on an actuarial basis. These two facts offer the purchaser greater assurance that he will receive the specified amount at the proper time. Furthermore, the investment media in which assets of life insurance companies may be placed are carefully controlled by the individual states in which these companies are incorporated or operate. Generally, these laws are designed with protection of the beneficiary uppermost in mind.

Numerous safeguarding restrictions, which do not exist as far as investment company operations are concerned, regulate and govern many phases of bank and insurance company operations.

Finally, it should be noted that insurance purchases are generally made for the purpose of protection and not for the purpose of investment.

U. S. Government obligations, of course, are fully guaranteed by the U. S. Government both as to principal if held to maturity and interest and thus from a safety standpoint are without peer. The U. S. Government, with its extensive power to tax and its vast ability to borrow, can easily raise the money needed to fullfill its obligations. And the U. S. Government's right, if ultimately necessary, to resort to the printing press for needed funds assures that it will never have to default on any of its outstanding obligations.

Thus, it is obvious that investment company shares are not basically the same as insured savings accounts, U. S. government bonds, or insurance contracts. Any suggestion or intimation that they are similar is improper and a violation of the SOP.

COMPARISONS WITH MARKET INDEX OR OTHER SECURITY. Section *h* of the Statement of Policy specifies standards for comparison of investment company shares with other securities.

When comparing an investment company security with any other security or medium of investment or any security index or average, the differences or similarities of the subjects compared must be made clear. This section also requires that the purpose of the comparison must be given. For example, if investment company shares were compared to savings bank deposits, it must be made clear that the investment company shares are subject to market fluctuations and that their dividends vary, whereas savings bank deposits, although affording no opportunity for capital gain, are relatively safe and the interest paid thereon relatively stable. It would also be necessary to show that the purpose of the comparison was to point out the advantages of investment company shares for capital gains purposes in rising markets, or to keep pace with the increase in living costs, and so on, and that they would be disadvantageous in periods of falling markets.

Comparisons including charts and tables must comply with the provisions of Section *j* of the SOP as well as of Section *h*.

Any comparisons of one investment company with another investment company not under the same management or sponsorship, must be filed with the NASD.

NEW CAPITAL.   Section *i* of the SEC Statement of Policy forbids the representation or implication that investment companies in general are direct sources of new capital to industry.

An individual investment company claiming to be a direct source of capital to any industry must disclose the extent of such investments. This rule stems from the fact that, generally, funds obtained by investment companies when they sell their shares to investors are used to purchase securities which are already outstanding rather than new security issues just being offered.

However, it should be remembered that by buying securities already outstanding in the market, investment companies are putting cash in the hands of people who can use this cash to buy part of a new securities offering if they so choose. Also, many of the large investment companies carefully analyze new security issues coming into the market. Whenever a new security seems particularly attractive to these companies they buy it for their portfolios.

To the extent that individual investment companies actually do provide new capital to an industry they may advertise the fact.

PERFORMANCE CHARTS AND TABLES.   Rigid standards for investment company performance charts and tables are prescribed in Section *j* of the SOP.

Section *j* prohibits the use of any chart or table which is inaccurate in factual detail or tends to create a false or misleading impression. This includes charts or tables relating to any material aspect of the investment company's past performance or of an assumed investment of any investor in the investment company, or any material which appears to represent that the investment company's past performance or investor experience will be repeated in the future. Charts or tables which conform to the "Approved Charts and Tables" described below and illustrated in the Appendix[5] will not be regarded by the Commission as materially false and misleading in the absence of facts or circumstances which make such charts or tables or their use in fact false and misleading in a particular use. Persons using other charts and tables must assume responsibility that they are not materially false or misleading. Any such chart or table may be submitted to the Commission for its views in advance of its use.

(1)   Approved charts should conform with the following:

(i) The text, graphic detail and arrangement of any such chart should be substantially as shown on sample charts A, B, C, and D in the Appendix, whichever is applicable.

(ii) Each chart should be drawn to scale which should be shown on the side of the chart and the same scale should be used for all segments of the chart. Appropriate shading or coloring should

[5]Reproduced on pp. 366–373 of this book.

be added to distinguish between the different elements of the chart.

(iii) Charts A and B may not be used to show the reinvestment of dividend income.

(iv) The caption of sample chart B may, if desired, be changed to read as follows:

RECORD OF .... FUND IN TERMS OF NET ASSET VALUE PER SHARE, AND ILLUSTRATION OF AN ASSUMED INVESTMENT IN ONE SHARE WITH CAPITAL GAINS DISTRIBUTIONS ACCEPTED IN ADDITIONAL SHARES

(v) Chart C should be accompanied in the same piece of literature by Table 1 and Chart D should be so accompanied by Table 2. These tables should be prepared on the same assumption and cover the same period as the related chart, and should appear in a manner and location which permit easy reference from the chart to the corresponding table.

(2) Approved tables should conform with the following:

(i) The text, detail and arrangement of any table illustrating a dividend reinvestment or continuous investment program should be substantially as shown on Tables 1 and 2 in the Appendix, whichever is applicable. Tables prepared in accordance with the requirements for a table prescribed for use in the investment company's prospectus, or tables containing the same information as is shown on Charts A and B, may also be employed.

(ii) Any table designed to show any other investment program should contain comparable information. *(Contractual plan companies must use Sample Tables 3 and 4)*

(iii) When Table 1 is used with Chart C or when Table 2 is used with Chart D in accordance with subparagraph (1) (v), above, such table need not contain any specific reference to the sales commission. When such table follows immediately after the chart, on the same page as the chart, the caption of the table and any notes thereto which are contained in the chart may be omitted from the table.

(3) Approved charts and tables should conform with the following:

(i) Charts and tables may be set up on a per share basis, or in amounts other than those shown on the attached samples, provided the charts and tables give effect to the maximum sales commission currently charged. The amounts used in constructing the chart or table should be amounts capable of being invested under the particular program being described. Any chart or table may be accompanied, in the same piece of literature, by a chart or table (which may be in summary form) illustrating investments in larger amounts at reduced sales commissions.

(ii) Any chart or table which reflects either the acceptance of capital gains distributions in additional shares or the investment of dividends from investment income should not be captioned or characterized as the record of the fund, except as permitted in subparagraph (1) (iv).

(iii) The period covered by such chart or table should be the most recent period ending with the latest available fiscal or calendar year and embracing:

A. The life of the company or the life of the issuer of the underlying investment company shares, or,

B. The duration of any plan or contract of the type referred to in Section 27 (a) of the Investment Company Act of 1940, or,

C. The immediately preceding 10 years, or,

D. Periods longer than 10 years but less than the life of the company or the duration of such plan or contract, if such additional periods are multiples of five years;

provided that a portion of the current year may be added to the period ended with the last fiscal or calendar year. In no event should such chart or table relate to a period that exceeds the life of the company or the life of the issuer of the underlying shares.

(iv) Charts A, B, C, and D and Tables 1 and 2 may be accompanied in the same piece of literature by summary tables for the same period covered by the chart or table showing the end results which would have been obtained if alternative assumptions had been made as to the acceptance of capital gains distributions in shares or the reinvestment of dividends from investment income or both.

(v) Charts and tables may be accompanied in the same piece of literature by summary tables prepared on the same basis as the chart or table they accompany as follows:

A. A summary table showing the end results depicted in the chart or table.

B. Successive summary tables showing the end results over several periods of equal length, provided that the latest 10-year or longer period as well as every other such period within the total time span covered by the chart or table is included and that the chart or table and the summary tables are presented on the same page or on facing pages.

C. Successive summary tables showing the end results over several periods of unequal length, provided that such unequal periods start with each successive year and end with the last date shown on the chart or table, that every such period of unequal length within the total time span covered by the chart or table is included, and that the chart or table and summary tables are presented on the same page or on facing pages.

(vi) In depicting the end results in any summary or successive summary tables provided for in (iv) and (v) above, the total of initial and periodic investments, total dividend reinvestment cost, total investment cost, total of capital gains distributions accepted in shares, and ending total asset value shall be shown separately to the extent applicable. The total capital gains distributions accepted in shares may be shown in a footnote. Summary tables need not contain any specific reference to sales commission.

(vii) Any approved chart or table may be prepared on a basis which does not reflect the acceptance of capital gains distributions in shares or the reinvestment of dividends from investment income, or both, provided that no chart or table should reflect the reinvestment of dividends from investment income unless it also reflects the acceptance of capital gains distributions in shares.

(viii) Any chart or table should be preceded or accompanied by a prominent statement of any additional information or explanation of material significance to investors in appraising the figures shown, when necessary in a particular case to provide adequate and accurate disclosure of material facts.

(ix) Other relevant data in addition to that shown on the Approved Charts or Tables, such as the number of shares of stock acquired through assumed investments or the price of the shares so acquired, may be included, if the addition of such data does not result in a false and misleading presentation.

EXTRAVAGANT MANAGEMENT CLAIMS. Section *k* of the Statement of Policy forbids any extravagant claims regarding investment company management ability.

INVESTMENT COMPANIES NOT COOPERATIVES. Section *l* of the SEC Statement of Policy bans any suggestion that investment companies are operated as cooperatives or nonprofit enterprises.

Investment companies are formed and operated for the purpose of providing a profitable investment vehicle for individuals with surplus funds. They are not operated as cooperatives or nonprofit organizations and are not granted the special tax consideration provided in the revenue acts for such institutions. Any suggestion that investment companies are similar to such enterprises may create a misimpression in the minds of investors concerning investment companies' tax and other liabilities. Consequently, any such intimation is improper and a violation of the SOP.

INVESTMENT COMPANIES USED BY FIDUCIARIES. Section *m* of the SEC Statement of Policy forbids any representation that investment company shares generally have been selected for investment by fiduciary groups or institutions.

A fiduciary is a person, group, or institution holding something in trust. Under a trust agreement a person or institution, *called the trustor*, gives all or part of his property to another person or institution *called the trustee* to hold and manage for the benefit of a third party *called the beneficiary*.

The use of the word *trust* as the name of the above noted arrangement stems from the definition of the word itself. To trust someone, means to rely on their judgment and to have confidence that they will act honestly and properly.

The trustee or fiduciary is expected to manage the affairs of the trust wisely and honestly so that the beneficiary will prosper.

Due to the extensive use of the trust device and the serious consequences in case of improper administration, most state laws carefully spell out the duties and obligations of anyone acting as a trustee in that state. These laws often specify exactly what type of securities can be purchased by a fiduciary or trustee in that state. Investment company shares are permissable investments for trustees or fiduciaries in certain states, but in some other states they may not generally be purchased by trustees or fiduciaries. Thus, any general suggestion that investment company shares have been selected for investment purposes by fiduciary groups or institutions gives the impression that investment companies' shares have been approved in general by state laws. Such an implication is improper and a violation of the SOP.

CONTINUOUS INVESTMENT PROGRAMS.   Section n of the Statement of Policy establishes certain warning statements which must be made on investment company sales literature when describing the advantages of continuous investment or multiple purchase (dollar cost averaging) plans.

The section prohibits the use of the phrases "dollar averaging" or "averaging the dollar" in referring to any plan of continuous investment in the shares of an investment company, at stated intervals, regardless of the price level of the shares. However, the phrases "dollar cost averaging" or "cost averaging" may be used when referring to such plans.

Dollar cost averaging means investing equal sums of money at regular intervals regardless of price levels. Dollar cost averaging, of course, does not protect the investor against loss in the value of his securities declining markets. It does, however, enable the investor in a declining market to purchase more shares of a particular security with a given amount of money since the average price of each share is declining.

When discussing or portraying any Periodic Payment Plan referred to in section 27 (a) of the Investment Company Act of 1940 (or when discussing the merits of dollar cost averaging) the sales literature must make the following points clear:

1. That the investor will incur a loss under such a plan if he discontinues the plan when the market value of his accumulated shares is less than his cost
2. That the investor is putting his funds primarily in securities subject to market fluctuations and that the method of investing being used involves continuous investment in such shares at regular intervals regardless of the price levels and trends
3. That the investor before committing himself to such a plan must take into account his financial ability to continue the plan through periods of low price levels

4. That such plans do not protect against loss in value in declining markets

Discussions of the advantages of voluntary or noncontractual plans for the periodic purchase of investment company shares must include an explanation that such plans cannot assure profits nor protect against losses.

When shares of open-end investment companies are offered under a so-called "contractual plan," the sales literature must disclose that up to half of the sales charge payable on all purchases during the life of the plan (usually ten years) is collected in the first year.

SALES COMMISSIONS. Section *o* of the Statement of Policy requires disclosure that there is a sales charge involved in the purchase of investment company shares.

The sales charge is in substance the acquisition cost, usually a stated percentage of the public offering price, charged to a buyer of open-end investment company shares.

In sales literature, which does not include the actual rate or amount of commission, the SOP requires a clear reference to the prospectus or prospectuses of investment companies for information concerning the sales commission and other information such as the latest schedule of investments and the financial condition of the company.

The reference is most appropriate whenever the purchasing of shares is discussed. However, the reference is not required in communications which deal only with routine business matters or in communications which do not discuss or describe any investment company or investment company security.

The reference is not required in normal letters of transmittal, which enclose literature carrying the reference; nor is it required in newspaper, magazine, radio or television advertising of limited length.

Reports of issuers when transmitted only to shareholders, that do not contain an express offer, need not include the statement required by Section *o*, but must otherwise conform with the SOP. Reports used for sales purposes, however, must include the sales commission reference if the report does not state the amount or rate of the sales charge.

SALES CHARGE WARNING. Section *p* of the Statement of Policy states that a warning must be included in any sales literature which is designed to encourage investors to switch from one investment company to another, or from one class of security of an investment company to another class.

The required warning should contain the substance of the following statement and should appear in the sales literature in a separate paragraph in type as large as that used generally in the body of the piece:

Switching from the securities of one investment company to another or from one class of security of an investment company to another, involves a sales charge on each such transaction, for details of which see the prospectus. The prospective purchaser should measure these costs against the claimed advantage of the switch.

COMPARISONS OF INDUSTRY PERFORMANCE TO COMPANY PERFORMANCE. Section *q* of the Statement of Policy forbids the use of material indicating that an investment company will necessarily duplicate the performance of any industry.

REPRINTS.   Section *r* of the Statement of Policy states that a reprint of a published article relating to investment companies must comply with the Statement of Policy if it is to be used as sales literature. Furthermore, any such material used must not be taken out of context in a manner which alters its intended meaning.

CONTRACTUAL PLAN TABLES

Under Section *j* of the Statement of Policy, hypothetical tables used by contractual plan company underwriters in supplemental sales literature must conform to Sample Table 3 and 4 on the following pages.

These tables are prepared on the basis of an assumed investment of $10 monthly. This is to meet the requirement that such tables must be prepared on the basis of assumed investments involving the smallest permissable monthly payment and carrying the largest sales charge. Anyone wishing to do so may also include in sales literature containing tables such as these, additional tables or summaries based on larger monthly payments and carrying smaller sales charges; but no such additional tables or summaries may be used except when published in the same literature that contains tables on the basis of the largest sales charge.

The sample tables contain summary results. Such summaries are not required. They are included in the samples simply to make clear that, at the minimum, any such summaries must include at least the following: total payments, total dividends reinvested, total investment cost, total capital gains reinvested, and total liquidating value.

Where a particular type of contractual plan does not wholly fit the details of the samples, such tables may be adapted to be applicable to the particular plan being shown. However, the over-all format and text of the tables must be followed as closely as possible.

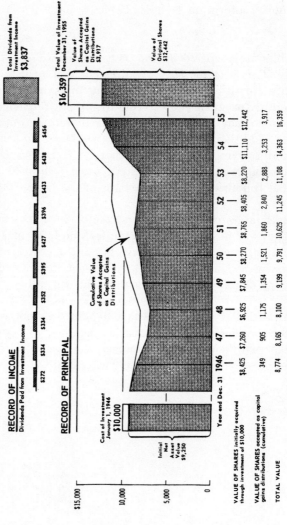

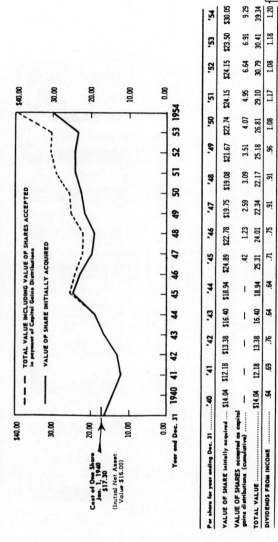

Sample Chart B

ILLUSTRATION OF AN ASSUMED INVESTMENT IN ONE SHARE
with Capital Gains Distributions Accepted in Additional Shares

The chart below covers the period from January 1, 1940 to December 31, 1954. This period was one of generally rising common stock prices. The results shown should not be considered as a representation of the dividend income or capital gain or loss which may be realized from an investment made in the fund today.

- - - TOTAL VALUE INCLUDING VALUE OF SHARES ACCEPTED
in payment of Capital Gains Distributions

——— VALUE OF SHARE INITIALLY ACQUIRED

Cost of One Share
Jan. 1, 1940
$17.30

(Initial Net Asset
Value $16.00)

Per share for year ending Dec. 31	'40	'41	'42	'43	'44	'45	'46	'47	'48	'49	'50	'51	'52	'53	'54
VALUE OF SHARE initially acquired	$14.04	$12.18	$13.38	$16.40	$18.94	$24.89	$22.78	$19.75	$19.08	$21.67	$22.74	$24.15	$24.15	$23.50	$30.05
VALUE OF SHARES accepted as capital gains distributions (cumulative)	—	—	—	—	—	.42	1.23	2.59	3.09	3.51	4.07	4.95	6.64	6.91	9.29
TOTAL VALUE	$14.04	12.18	13.38	16.40	18.94	25.31	24.01	22.34	22.17	25.18	26.81	29.10	30.79	30.41	39.34
DIVIDENDS FROM INCOME	.64	.69	.76	.64	.64	.71	.75	.91	.91	.96	1.08	1.17	1.08	1.18	1.20

Total 13.32

Initial net asset value is the amount received by the fund after deducting from the cost of the investment the sales commission as described in the prospectus.

No adjustment has been made for any income taxes payable by stockholders on capital gains distributions accepted in shares. The dollar amounts of capital gains distributions accepted in shares were: 1940-1944 - none; 1945 - $0.34; 1946 - $0.92; 1947 - $2.58; 1948 - $0.57; 1949 - none; 1950 - $0.35, 1951 - $0.59; 1952 - $1.63; 1953 - $0.45; 1954 - $0.35. Total - $7.78.

Sample Chart C

ILLUSTRATION OF AN ASSUMED INVESTMENT OF $10,000
with Dividends Reinvested and Capital Gains Distributions Accepted in Shares

The chart below covers the period from January 1, 1946 to December 31, 1955. This period was one of generally rising common stock prices. The results shown should not be considered as a representation of the dividend income or capital gain or loss which may be realized from an investment made in the fund today.

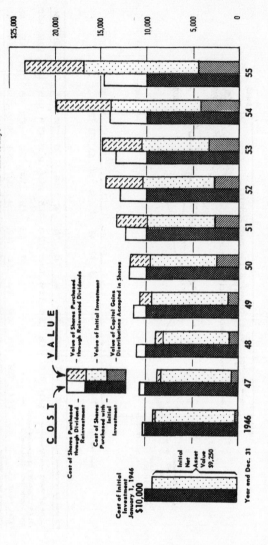

Initial net asset value is the amount received by the fund after deducting from the cost of the investment the sales commission as described in the prospectus. Income dividends were assumed to have been reinvested in additional shares at the public offering price which includes a sales commission of 7 1/2%, as described in the prospectus.

No adjustment has been made for any income taxes payable by shareholders on capital gains distributions and dividends reinvested in shares.

NOTE: See table ___ on page ___ for dollar amounts represented by this chart.

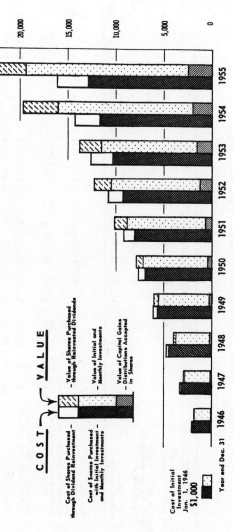

Sample Chart D

ILLUSTRATION OF A CONTINUOUS INVESTMENT PROGRAM

in terms of an Assumed Initial Investment of $1,000 and Subsequent Investments of $100 Per Month
with Dividends Reinvested and Capital Gains Distributions Accepted in Shares

The chart below covers the period from January 1, 1946 to December 31, 1955. This period was one of generally rising common stock prices. The results shown should not be considered as a representation of the dividend income or capital gain or loss which may be realized from an investment made in the fund today. A program of the type illustrated does not assure a profit or protect against depreciation in declining markets.

Total cost for each year represents the initial investment of $1,000 plus the cumulative total of monthly investments of $100 per month plus the cumulative amount of income dividends reinvested. The cost for all shares so purchased includes sales commissions of 7 1/2% as described in the prospectus.

No adjustment has been made for any income taxes payable by shareholders on capital gains distributions and dividends reinvested in shares.

NOTE: See table___ on page___ for dollar amounts represented by this chart

Sample Table 1

ILLUSTRATION OF AN ASSUMED INVESTMENT OF $10,000
with Dividends Reinvested and Capital Gains Distributions Accepted in Shares

The table below covers the period from January 1, 1946 to December 31, 1955. This period was one of generally rising common stock prices. The results shown should not be considered as a representation of the dividend income or capital gain or loss which may be realized from an investment made in the fund today.

Year Ended Dec. 31 -	1946	1947	1948	1949	1950	1951	1952	1953	1954	1955
AMOUNT OF DIVIDENDS FROM INVESTMENT INCOME REINVESTED ANNUALLY	$ 275	$ 349	$ 361	$ 397	$ 463	$ 791	$ 227	$ 565	$ 594	$ 637
CUMULATIVE COST OF SHARES PURCHASED THROUGH INVESTMENT OF INCOME DIVIDENDS	275	624	985	1,382	1,845	2,636	2,863	3,428	4,022	4,659
TOTAL COST, INCLUDING REINVESTED DIVIDENDS	$10,275	$10,624	$10,985	$11,382	$11,845	$12,636	$12,863	$13,428	$14,022	$14,659
VALUE OF SHARES:										
a. Initially Acquired	$ 8,434	$ 7,268	$ 6,962	$ 8,120	$ 7,240	$ 7,189	$ 7,699	$ 7,391	$ 9,871	$11,473
b. Accepted as Capital Gains Distributions (cumulative)	320	860	1,090	1,120	2,400	2,600	2,890	3,220	4,170	4,350
SUB-TOTAL	$ 8,754	$ 8,128	$ 8,052	$ 9,240	$ 9,640	$ 9,789	$10,589	$10,611	$14,041	$15,823
c. Purchased Through Reinvestment of Income (cumulative)	260	580	925	1,370	2,100	3,450	3,910	4,250	5,800	7,400
TOTAL VALUE	$ 9,014	$ 8,708	$ 8,977	$10,610	$11,740	$13,239	$14,499	$14,861	$19,861	$23,223

The total cost figure represents the initial cost of $10,000 plus the cumulative amount of income dividends reinvested, and includes sales commissions of 7 1/2%, as described in the prospectus, on all shares so purchased. The dollar amounts of capital gains distributions accepted in shares were: 1946 - $334; 1947 - $594; 1948 - $220; 1949 - none; 1950 - $1,148; 1951 - $147; 1952 - $258; 1953 - $210; 1954 - $171; 1955 - $436. Total - $3,518.

No adjustment has been made for any income taxes payable by shareholders on capital gains distributions and dividends reinvested in shares.

Sample Table 2

ILLUSTRATION OF A CONTINUOUS INVESTMENT PROGRAM

in terms of an Assumed Initial Investment of $1,000 and Subsequent Investments of $100 Per Month
with Dividends Reinvested and Capital Gains Distributions Accepted in Shares

The table below covers the period from January 1, 1946 to December 31, 1955. This period was one of generally rising common stock prices. The results shown should not be considered as a representation of the dividend income or capital gain or loss which may be realized from an investment made in the fund today. A program of the type illustrated does not assure a profit or protect against depreciation in declining markets.

Year Ended Dec. 31 -	1946	1947	1948	1949	1950	1951	1952	1953	1954	1955
AMOUNT OF DIVIDENDS FROM INVESTMENT INCOME REINVESTED ANNUALLY	$ 38	$ 89	$ 139	$ 201	$ 286	$ 372	$ 403	$ 501	$ 572	$ 649
CUMULATIVE COST OF SHARES PURCHASED THROUGH INVESTMENT OF INCOME DIVIDENDS	$ 38	$ 127	$ 266	$ 467	$ 753	$ 1,125	$ 1,528	$ 2,029	$ 2,601	$ 3,250
TOTAL OF INITIAL AND MONTHLY INVESTMENTS	2,100	3,300	4,500	5,700	6,900	8,100	9,300	10,500	11,700	12,900
TOTAL COST, INCLUDING REINVESTED DIVIDENDS	$ 2,138	$ 3,427	$ 4,766	$ 6,167	$ 7,653	$ 9,225	$10,828	$12,529	$14,301	$16,150
VALUE OF SHARES:										
a. Acquired Through Initial and Monthly Investments	$ 1,816	$ 2,559	$ 3,706	$ 5,506	$ 6,863	$ 8,404	$ 9,432	$10,113	$14,237	$15,941
b. Accepted as Capital Gains Distributions (cumulative)	25	147	198	218	340	548	1,152	1,430	2,005	2,592
SUB-TOTAL	$ 1,841	$ 2,706	$ 3,904	$ 5,724	$ 7,203	$ 8,952	$10,584	$11,543	$16,242	$19,533
c. Purchased Through Reinvestment of Income (cumulative)	30	108	225	425	790	1,237	1,753	2,272	3,511	4,790
TOTAL VALUE	$ 1,871	$ 2,914	$ 4,129	$ 6,149	$ 7,993	$10,189	$12,337	$13,815	$19,753	$24,323

The total cost figures represent the initial investment of $1,000 plus the cumulative total of monthly investments of $100 per month plus the cumulative amount of income dividends reinvested, and include sales commissions on all shares so purchased of 7 1/2%, as described in the prospectus. The dollar amounts of capital gains distributions accepted in shares were: 1946 - $33; 1947 - $129; 1948 - $76; 1949 - none; 1950 - $86; 1951 - $178; 1952 - $575; 1953 - $181; 1954 - $161; 1955 - $436; Total $1,855.

No adjustment has been made for any income taxes payable by shareholders on capital gains distributions and dividends reinvested in shares.

Sample Table 3

ILLUSTRATION OF A TWENTY YEAR CONTRACTUAL PLAN FOR INVESTMENT IN _____

This illustration is in terms of an assumed investment of $10 per month (minimum monthly payment plan) for ten years, with dividends reinvested and capital gains distributions accepted in shares, followed by an additional ten years during which dividends from investment income and distributions from capital gains on accumulated shares continue to be received in shares.

The period covered, from January 1, 1938 to December 31, 1957, was one of generally rising common stock prices. The results shown should not be considered as a representation of the dividend income or capital gain or loss which may be realized from an investment made in the fund today. A program of the type illustrated does not assure a profit or protect against depreciation in declining markets.

ACCUMULATION PERIOD
(1st through 10th years)

Year End	MONTHLY PAYMENTS Annually	Cumulative	Annual Div'd. Income Reinvested	Total Cumulative Cost (a)	DEDUCTIONS Sales Charge	Custodian Fee	BALANCE INVESTED AFTER DEDUCTIONS Annually	Cumulative	Annual Capital Gains Dists. Reinvested	Value of Accumulated Shares	Total Shares Accumulated
1938	*$130.00**	*$ 130.00*	*$ 1.44*	*$ 131.44*	*$ 65.00**	*$ 3.25**	*$ 61.87*	*$ 61.87*	*$ 1.08*	*$ 43.40*	*6.9*
1939	120.00	250.00	5.12	256.56	4.80	3.00	117.32	179.19	1.16	179.17	25.6
1940	120.00	370.00	6.93	383.49	4.80	3.00	119.13	298.32	9.76	320.97	44.5
1941	120.00	490.00	13.39	516.88	4.80	3.00	125.59	423.91	9.03	439.68	64.6
1942	120.00	610.00	25.38	662.76	4.80	3.00	138.08	561.99	6.74	529.49	86.3
1943	120.00	730.00	31.58	814.34	4.80	3.00	143.78	705.77	10.87	743.62	111.1
1944	120.00	850.00	38.69	973.03	4.80	3.00	150.89	856.66	23.43	1,047.76	133.4
1945	120.00	970.00	42.19	1,135.22	4.80	3.00	154.39	1,011.05	41.51	1,373.90	156.6
1946	120.00	1,090.00	43.32	1,298.54	4.80	3.00	155.62	1,166.57	84.21	1,817.35	181.5
1947	110.00	1,200.00	45.89	1,454.43	4.40	2.75	148.74	1,315.31	79.87	1,872.27	205.0
			$254.43		$107.80	$30.00			$267.66		

(a) Reflects the cumulative total of monthly payments, plus the cumulative amount of income dividends reinvested.

Under the terms of this plan, out of the initial payment of $20, $10 is deducted as a sales charge, with $5 being deducted as a sales charge from each of the next 11 payments. Additional deductions include $.50 from the initial payment, and $.25 from each of the next 11 payments for custodian fees, with $1.32 also being deducted, from the initial payment only, for Federal issuance tax. Total deductions from the first 12 payments equal $69.57, or 53.5% of the total of the first 12 monthly payments. If all of the first 10 years' payments are made, total sales charge and other deductions amount to 11.5% of the total agreed payments.

=== **END OF PAYMENT PERIOD** ===

RETAINED INVESTMENT PERIOD
(11th through 20th years—Distributions Accepted in Shares)

Year Ended	Annual Div'd. Income Reinvested	Total Cumulative Cost (b)	DEDUCTIONS Sales Charge	Custodian Fee	BALANCE INVESTED AFTER DEDUCTIONS Annually	Cumulative	Annual Capital Gains Dists. Reinvested	Value of Accumulated Shares	Total Shares Accumulated
1948	$ 60.53	$1,514.96	—	$ 2.40	$ 58.13	$1,373.44	$ 44.04	$1,805.14	216.9
1949	71.70	1,586.66	—	2.40	69.30	1,442.74	39.04	1,872.10	229.9
1950	91.25	1,677.91	—	2.40	88.85	1,531.59	26.19	2,178.45	243.4
1951	98.94	1,776.85	—	2.40	96.54	1,629.13	37.70	2,452.40	257.8
1952	104.91	1,881.76	—	2.40	102.51	1,730.64	66.38	2,752.56	274.9
1953	111.78	1,993.54	—	2.40	109.38	1,840.02	70.61	3,052.82	292.4
1954	118.70	2,112.24	—	2.40	116.30	1,956.32	69.27	3,107.43	311.0
1955	129.30	2,241.54	—	2.40	126.90	2,083.22	100.60	4,064.16	330.4
1956	145.51	2,387.05	—	2.40	143.11	2,226.33	148.69	4,692.64	352.5
1957	158.78	2,545.83	—	2.40	156.38	2,382.71	162.41	4,894.43	376.7
	$1,091.40			$24.00			$765.00		

(b) Based on total cumulative cost at beginning of 1948 of $1,454.43, plus income dividends reinvested for the period 1948-1957.

No allowance has been made for any income taxes payable by planholders on capital gains distributions and dividends reinvested in shares for the 20-year period.

SUMMARY

		Shares
Total Payments	$1,200.00	141
Income Dividends Reinvested	1,345.83	135
Total Investment Cost	$2,545.83	276
Capital Gains Distributions Reinvested	$1,032.00	100
Total Liquidating Value (Dec. 31, 1957)..	$4,894.43	376

Sample Table 4

ILLUSTRATION OF A TWENTY YEAR CONTRACTUAL PLAN FOR INVESTMENT IN ――――――――

This illustration is in terms of an assumed investment of $10 per month (minimum monthly payment plan) for ten years, with dividends reinvested and capital gains distributions accepted in shares, followed by an additional ten years during which dividends from investment income and distributions from capital gains on accumulated shares are received in cash.

The period covered, from January 1, 1938 to December 31, 1957, was one of generally rising common stock prices. The results shown should not be considered as a representation of the dividend income or capital gain or loss which may be realized from an investment made in the fund today. A program of the type illustrated does not assure a profit or protect against depreciation in declining markets.

ACCUMULATION PERIOD
(1st through 10th years)

Year End	MONTHLY PAYMENTS Annually	MONTHLY PAYMENTS Cumulative	Annual Div'd. Income Reinvested	Total Cumulative Cost (a)	DEDUCTIONS Sales Charge	DEDUCTIONS Custodian Fee	BALANCE INVESTED AFTER DEDUCTIONS Annually	BALANCE INVESTED AFTER DEDUCTIONS Cumulative	Annual Capital Gains Dists. Reinvested	Value of Accumulated Shares	Total Shares Accumulated
1938	$130.00*	$ 130.00	$ 1.44	$ 131.44	$ 65.00*	$ 3.25*	$ 61.87	$ 61.87	$ 1.08	$ 43.40	6.9
1939	120.00	250.00	5.12	256.56	4.80	3.00	117.32	179.19	1.16	179.17	25.6
1940	120.00	370.00	6.93	383.49	4.80	3.00	119.13	298.32	9.76	320.97	44.5
1941	120.00	490.00	13.39	516.88	4.80	3.00	125.59	423.91	9.03	439.68	64.6
1942	120.00	610.00	25.38	662.76	4.80	3.00	138.08	561.99	6.74	529.49	86.3
1943	120.00	730.00	31.58	814.34	4.80	3.00	143.78	705.77	10.87	743.62	111.1
1944	120.00	850.00	38.69	973.03	4.80	3.00	150.89	856.66	23.43	1,047.76	133.4
1945	120.00	970.00	42.19	1,135.22	4.80	3.00	154.39	1,011.05	41.51	1,373.90	156.6
1946	120.00	1,090.00	43.32	1,298.54	4.80	3.00	155.62	1,166.57	84.21	1,817.35	181.5
1947	110.00	1,200.00	45.89	1,454.43	4.40	2.75	148.74	1,315.31	79.87	1,872.27	205.0
			$254.43		$107.80	$30.00			$267.66		

(a) Reflects the cumulative total of monthly payments, plus the cumulative amount of income dividends reinvested.

Under the terms of this plan, out of the initial payment of $20, $10 is deducted as a sales charge, with $5 being deducted as a sales charge from each of the next 11 payments. Additional deductions include $.50 from the initial payment, and $.25 from each of the next 11 payments for custodian fees, with $1.32 also being deducted, from the initial payment only, for Federal issuance tax. Total deductions from the first 12 payments equal $69.57, or 53.5% of the total of the first 12 monthly payments. If all of the first 10 years' payments are made, total sales charge and other deductions amount to 11.5% of the total agreed payments.

No allowance has been made for any income taxes payable by planholders on capital gains distributions and dividends reinvested in shares during the first 10 years.

SUMMARY

		Shares
Total Payments	$1,200.00	141
Income Dividends Reinvested	254.43	32
Total Investment Cost	$1,454.43	173
Capital Gains Distributions Reinvested	$ 267.66	32
Total Liquidating Value (Dec. 31, 1947)..	$1,872.27	205

==== END OF PAYMENT PERIOD ====

RETAINED INVESTMENT PERIOD
(11th through 20th years—Distributions Received in Cash)

Year Ended	Total Cumulative Cost	Dividends from Investment Income	DEDUCTIONS Sales Charge	DEDUCTIONS Custodian Fee	Net Dividends from Investment Income Received in Cash	Capital Gains Received in Cash	Value of Accumulated Shares	Total Shares Held
1948	$1,454.43	$ 59.47	—	$ 2.40	$ 57.07	$ 43.06	$1,706.16	205.0
1949	1,454.43	66.63	—	2.40	64.25	35.89	1,669.25	205.0
1950	1,454.43	79.98	—	2.40	77.58	22.56	1,835.35	205.0
1951	1,454.43	82.03	—	2.40	79.63	30.76	1,950.19	205.0
1952	1,454.43	82.03	—	2.40	79.63	51.26	2,052.73	205.0
1953	1,454.43	82.03	—	2.40	79.63	51.26	2,140.90	205.0
1954	1,454.43	82.03	—	2.40	79.63	47.16	2,048.63	205.0
1955	1,454.43	84.08	—	2.40	81.68	64.60	2,522.33	205.0
1956	1,454.43	89.20	—	2.40	86.80	90.23	2,729.45	205.0
1957	1,454.43	91.25	—	2.40	88.85	92.28	2,663.83	205.0
		$798.75		$24.00	$774.75	$529.06		

WITHDRAWAL PLAN TABLES

The Investment Companies Committee of the NASD Board of Governors has completed negotiations with the SEC staff on means of presenting hypothetical results of assumed investments under withdrawal plans. As a result, the commission staff will not object under the Statement of Policy to presentation of such results if they conform with the provisions of the Statement of Policy and with the sample tables which follow.

Any person wishing to show withdrawal plan results on any other basis must obtain prior clearance through the Association's Investment Companies Committee.

The NASD warns that underwriters and sponsors should be alert to discourage any effort by their wholesalers, dealers, or registered representatives to promote such plans on an indiscriminate, broadside basis. Care must be exercised to insure that such plans are offered only when their use is in the best interest of the customer in the light of known facts. Any discussion of withdrawal plans should include the warning that such plans carry the risk of exhausting invested capital.

The two sample tables on pages 375 and 377 differing only in heading and footnote language, are to be used as formats in demonstrating each of the two major mechanical means of handling withdrawal plans: Sample Table 1 applies if income dividends are held in cash and supplemented with liquidation of shares as needed to meet withdrawal payments. Sample Table 2 applies if income dividends are automatically invested in shares at net asset value, and sufficient shares liquidated to meet each withdrawal payment.

In either situation, hypothetical tables used to demonstrate withdrawal plan results must conform to the appropriate sample table. The hypothetical initial investment and withdrawal amounts must be amounts permitted to be invested and withdrawn, respectively, under the terms of the current prospectus of the fund used.

For purposes of illustration only, the assumption must be made that if total income in any year exceeds the established yearly total withdrawal rate, all income is paid out during that year. However, this will not prevent actual withdrawal plans being handled in such a way as to maintain the established withdrawal rate and carry excess income forward in the form of cash or shares.

The annual withdrawal amount may not be discussed in such a way as to imply a rate of return on the shareholder's investment. Rather, it must be pointed out that withdrawals normally represent both income and return of principal, and involve depletion of principal to the extent that withdrawals exceed income dividends.

The withdrawal period demonstrated must be either ten years or the life of the fund, whichever is less, and material showing a pay-in or holding period with a subsequent withdrawal period may not be used. The results of a withdrawal plan initiated at the beginning of the last year covered by the full table must appear as shown in the sample tables.

The tables may be up-dated to include the most recent calendar quarter during the current year. Thus, the "ten-year" table may cover up to 10¾ years.

Members may, if they desire, include in sales literature discussing withdrawal plans additional tables based on larger initial investments and carrying smaller sales charges, but no such additional tables may be used except when published in the same literature that contains tables based on the largest sales charge.

No summary results may be used.

Generally, all pertinent provisions of the Statement of Policy, as currently interpreted, continue to apply in promotion of withdrawal plans. Material supplementing the table must state the minimum investment amount acceptable under the plan, and if any limitation is placed on withdrawal amounts, it must be pointed out that it is not a recommended amount, and may not be desirable in all situations.

Where a particular withdrawal plan does not wholly fit the details of the sample table, the table may be adapted to the particular plan being shown. However, the over-all format and text of the table must be followed as closely as possible, and tables which do not conform to the sample tables must be submitted to the Association's Investment Companies Committee for comment prior to publication.

No devices such as type size, color, etc., may be used to emphasize one or more columns as compared with any other. The explanatory text which precedes the table must appear in a uniform type size, as must the footnotes.

(SAMPLE WITHDRAWAL PLAN TABLE #1)
ILLUSTRATION OF AN ASSUMED INVESTMENT OF $10,000
BASED ON INITIAL NET ASSET VALUE OF $9,150 WITH
$50 WITHDRAWN EACH MONTH

The table below covers the period from January 1, 1954 to December 31, 1963. It was assumed that shares were purchased at the beginning of the period at a cost of $10,000 and that $50 was withdrawn each month. This was a period during which common stock prices fluctuated, but were generally higher at the end of the period than at the beginning. The results reflect the operation of a withdrawal plan under the terms of which all investment income dividends are held in cash until needed to meet a withdrawal payment, such payments being made first from investment income dividends to the extent available and then by liquidation of shares to the extent necessary to provide for such payment (*plus the bank's service charge). Continued withdrawals in excess of current income will eventually exhaust principal, particularly in a period of declining market prices.

To be included only if applicable.

The results shown should not be considered as a representation of the dividend income, capital gain or loss, or amount available for withdrawal from an investment made in the Fund today. Only that portion of the total amount withdrawn designated "From Investment Income Dividends" should be regarded as income; the remainder represents a withdrawal of principal.

AMOUNTS WITHDRAWN (1)   REMAINING VALUE OF SHARES (1)

Year Ended 12/31	From Investment Income Dividends	From Principal	Annual Total	Cumulative Total	Value of Remaining Original Shares	Value of Shares Acquired Through Capital Gain Distribution (2)	Total Value of Shares Held at Year-End
1954	$ 350	$ 250	$ 600	$ 600	$11,416	$ 131	$11,547
1955	357	243	600	1,200	12,462	430	12,892
1956	369	231	600	1,800	11,974	873	12,847
1957	397	203	600	2,400	10,846	1,440	12,286
1958	440	160	600	3,000	12,653	2,592	15,245
1959	454	146	600	3,600	12,435	3,086	15,521
1960	509	91	600	4,200	12,353	3,970	16,323
1961	519	81	600	4,800	14,082	4,770	18,852
1962	529	71	600	5,400	12,651	4,843	17,494
1963	546	54	600	6,000	13,414	5,417	18,831
	$4,470	$1,530	$6,000				

Results If Plan Had Commenced January 1, 1963

1963	$ 279	$ 321	$ 600	$ 600	$ 9,416	$ 135	$ 9,551

(1) The figures in this illustration are based on the assumption that withdrawals were made first from income for the year, then from principal. Any cash balance remaining at the year-end was assumed to be part of the "Value of Remaining Original Shares" and of "Total Value of Shares Held at Year-End." Withdrawals from principal representing the sale of shares were assumed to have been in the order shares were acquired. († Shares acquired through capital gain distributions were assumed to have been liquidated only when investment income dividends for the year plus the remaining original shares were insufficient to provide for the amount to be withdrawn.)

(2) Amounts of capital gain distribution accepted in shares were as follows: 1954-$105; 1955-$253; 1956-$437; 1957-$632; 1958-$721; 1959-$493; 1960-$800; 1961-$192; 1962-$543; 1963-$245; Total—$4,421. For the one-year period: 1963-$128.

Note: These results reflect the payment of a service charge of $0.50 per monthly payment.

No adjustment has been made for any income taxes payable by shareholders on investment income dividends and capital gain distributions or of any net capital gains realized on the liquidation of shares in connection with periodic withdrawals. (‡ The fund (underwriter) supplies shareholders with information after the end of each year as to the amount of any capital gains or losses realized on such liquidations, based on the assumption that shares are liquidated in the order acquired.)

‡To be included only if and to the extent applicable; if tax basis used for shareholder information differs from that stated in the above language, appropriate modification of language should be made.

(SAMPLE WITHDRAWAL PLAN TABLE #2)

ILLUSTRATION OF AN ASSUMED INVESTMENT OF $10,000
BASED ON INITIAL NET ASSET VALUE OF $9,150 WITH
$50 WITHDRAWN EACH MONTH

The table below covers the period from January 1, 1954 to December 31, 1963. This was a period during which common stock prices fluctuated, but were generally higher at the end of the period than at the beginning. It is assumed that shares were purchased at the beginning of the period at a cost of $10,000 and that $50 was withdrawn each month. The results reflect the operation of a withdrawal plan under the terms of which all investment income dividends and capital gain distributions are invested in additional shares at net asset value and sufficient shares are sold from the shareholder's account at the time of each withdrawal payment to provide for such payment (*plus the bank's service charge). Continued withdrawals in excess of current income will eventually exhaust principal, particularly in a period of declining market prices.

To be included only if applicable.

The results shown should not be considered as a representation of the dividend income, capital gain or loss, or amount available for withdrawal from an investment made in the Fund today. Only that portion of the total amount withdrawn designated "From Investment Income Dividends" should be regarded as income; the remainder represents a withdrawal of principal.

AMOUNTS WITHDRAWN (1)   REMAINING VALUE OF SHARES (1)

Year Ended 12/31	From Investment Income Dividends	From Principal	Annual Total	Cumulative Total	Value of Remaining Original Shares	Value of Shares Acquired Through Capital Gain Distributions (2)	Total Value of Shares Held at Year-End
1954	$ 350	$ 250	$ 600	$ 600	$11,416	$ 131	$11,547
1955	357	243	600	1,200	12,462	430	12,892
1956	369	231	600	1,800	11,974	873	12,847
1957	397	203	600	2,400	10,846	1,440	12,286
1958	440	160	600	3,000	12,653	2,592	15,245
1959	454	146	600	3,600	12,435	3,086	15,521
1960	509	91	600	4,200	12,353	3,970	16,323
1961	519	81	600	4,800	14,082	4,770	18,852
1962	529	71	600	5,400	12,651	4,843	17,494
1963	546	54	600	6,000	13,414	5,417	18,831
	$4,470	$1,530	$6,000				

Results If Plan Had Commenced January 1, 1963

1963	$ 279	$ 321	$ 600	$ 600	$ 9,416	$ 135	$ 9,551

(1) The figures in this illustration are based on the assumption that withdrawals were made first from income for the year, as measured by the investment income dividends reinvested that year, and then from principal, as represented by the original shares acquired. (†Shares acquired through capital gain distributions were assumed to have been liquidated only when investment income dividends for the year plus the remaining original shares were insufficient to provide for the amount to be withdrawn.)

†To be included only if in the accompanying illustration, the original shares are exhausted.

(2) Amounts of capital gain distribution accepted in shares were as follows: 1954-$105; 1955-$253; 1956-$437; 1957-$632; 1958-$721; 1959-$493; 1960-$800; 1961-$192; 1962-$543; 1963-$245; Total—$4,421. For the one-year period: 1963-$128.

Note: These results reflect the payment of a service charge of $0.50 per monthly payment.

No adjustment has been made for any income taxes payable by shareholders on investment income dividends and capital gain distributions or on any net capital gains realized on the liquidation of shares in connection with periodic withdrawals. (‡The fund (underwriter) supplies shareholders with information after the end of each year as to the amount of any capital gains or losses realized on such liquidations, based on the assumption that shares are liquidated in the order acquired, rather than in the manner assumed in this illustration.)

‡To be included only if and to the extent applicable; if tax basis used for shareholder information differs from that stated in the above language, appropriate modification of language should be made.

REVIEW QUESTIONS

1. Enumerate the federal acts, state laws, and various other governmental and nongovernmental regulations under which investment companies are regulated.

2. What are two important purposes of the Investment Company Act of 1940?

3. What is the purpose of the *"outsiders"* provision of the Investment Company Act of 1940?

4. Why are advisory contracts regulated under the Investment Company Act of 1940?

5. Is it possible under the Act for an *open end* investment company (1) to issue bonds, (2) to borrow from banks, (3) to issue preferred stock? What about a *closed end* investment company?

6. Explain the terms "break point sales" and "letter of intention" as applied to the sales of open end investment companies (see Chapter 13).

7. What in particular does the prospectus of a mutual fund contain? About how often must a prospectus be revised?

8. What is the *investment company* rule? Explain three important provisions.

9. Explain the term *selling dividends* as applied to investment companies.

10. What is the interpretation of the Board (NASD) of the Rules of Fair Practice in regard to *special deals?*

11. What is the purpose of the so-called *Statement of Policy* of the SEC in respect to investment companies?

12. Describe the administration, the material covered, and the filing requirement under the *Statement of Policy*. What is considered materially misleading sales literature?

13. Explain two alternatives allowed in the calculation of rate of return on investment company shares under the Statement of Policy.

14. Comment on the sections of the Statement of Policy covering sales literature featuring (1) income, (2) the explanation of risks, (3) reference to federal regulation, (4) the custodial service provided by banks, (5) redemption, and (6) comparison with alternate investments.

Financial
Information

Chapter 18

Many years ago, the great philosopher Ralph Waldo Emerson wrote an essay praising "Self Reliance"; his scholarly and inspiring advice is even more valid today. Our current catch-phrase, "Do it yourself," applies in many respects to the securities business. Many people value the opinions of economists, industrialists, and security analysts about the current business situation and outlook. Few realize that it is not too difficult to become well informed on the general business picture as well as the more detailed fundamentals of a number of basic industries. It is commonly believed that the investor should follow closely not only the securities in which he is interested, but also business activity, earnings of companies, banking trends, and even political events. While this seems like a large order, it requires only a little regular reading of the right literature to be well informed. A detailed discussion of some of the chief sources of financial information might be helpful to the reader.

The Daily Papers

A great many large metropolitan newspapers, such as *The New York Times*, regularly publish valuable information needed by the informed investor. In particular, *The Wall Street Journal*, a publication of Dow Jones & Company, is devoted almost exclusively to business information of this type.

Weekly Figures

The most sensitive business indicators include the weekly figures of production of automobiles, electric power, steel, and carloadings. These are published in *The Wall Street Journal* and most of the large newspapers. *The New York Times* publishes these figures on week-days and has a summary of these and other figures in its Sunday edition. The conscientious investor might keep a loose-leaf notebook in which he could record this weekly data. Thus he can follow the figures week by week and, on a cumulative basis, compare them with previous year. Some of the more important weekly figures are:

1. *Carloadings* show the actual weekly movement by the railroads of agricultural, forest, and mineral products, as well as manufactured items.
2. *Electric power production* is reported by the Edison Electric Institute. It shows the weekly kilowatt hours produced by the electric power companies. Here is a very sensitive index, since almost all householders as well as commercial and industrial firms have to use power.
3. *Steel production* is given in tons of steel produced in per cent of the industry capacity to produce. Since steel is used in almost all the basic industries, this would seem to be a good indicator.
4. *Automobile production* is reported not only in total passenger automoibles produced but by individual makes of cars. Both weekly and cumulative figures are given. This enables the analyst to see what makes of cars are being produced faster than others.
5. *Department store sales* are reported by the Board of Governors of the Federal Reserve System and published in the large newspapers. They show the percentage change of sales weekly and on a cumulative basis. Further, the sales are given by areas, making it possible to see where in the country sales are gaining or declining on a comparative basis.
6. *Other weekly indicators* would include (A) the production and stocks on hand of oil and gasoline, (B) the bank loans of leading New York City banks (Friday papers) and out-of-town banks (Thursday papers) .
7. *Weekly Indices of Business Activity* are published by *The New York Times. Business Week*, a magazine published by McGraw-Hill, Inc., also has an index of business activity.

Monthly Indicators

There are also a number of monthly indicators which may be obtained from *The Wall Street Journal* and *The New York Times*. Some of the most meaningful of these are:

1. *Machine Tools.* New orders and shipments of machine tools placed by manufacturers are useful in forecasting an increase or decline in business activity. As the manufacturers anticipate an increase in business, they naturally buy more tools for their plants. The reverse is true when they expect a decline. The 1957-1958 decline in business could have been

clearly forecast by watching these statistics. These are usually published in *The Wall Street Journal.*

2. *Consumer Credit* outstanding shows the amount of credit advanced to purchase automobiles, for repair and modernization loans, for personal loans, and charge accounts. While total consumer credit outstanding is usually reported in the daily press, the detailed figures are found in the *Bulletin* of the Board of Governors of the Federal Reserve System.

3. *Money Supply* is the sum of the money in circulation plus the total deposits of commercial banks. *The Federal Reserve Bulletin* publishes this figure monthly. As it increases, the greater are the inflation possibilities unless production also increases. A check on these figures can be made by looking at the index of wholesale commodity prices also reported in the *Federal Reserve Bulletin* as well as in the *Index of Production.*

4. An *Index of Production* is a measure of the business health of the nation. Perhaps one of the best indices is the *Federal Reserve Index of Production.* This index is usually published in *The Wall Street Journal* and other leading newspapers. The *Index* has been revised, and all back figures to 1919 are available in the December, 1959, *Bulletin* of the Board of Governors of the Federal Reserve System.

Industry Information

For those interested in a particular industry, there are a number of trade magazines, special services, and government publications which are helpful. Some of the better known of these sources are:

1. *Automobiles: Ward's Automotive Reports* (service, weekly) Detroit, Michigan
2. *Chemicals: Chemical Week* (weekly magazine) McGraw-Hill, Inc., New York, N.Y.
3. *Electric Public Utilities: Public Utilities Fortnightly* (monthly magazine) Public Utilities Report, Inc. Washington, D.C.
4. *Oil: Oil & Gas Journal* (weekly magazine) Petroleum Publishing Co., Tulsa, Oklahoma
5. *Railroads: Railway Age* (weekly magazine) Simmons-Boardman Publishing Corp., New York
6. *Steel: Iron Age* (weekly magazine) Chilton Company, Philadelphia
7. From a statistical standpoint, a most useful monthly publication is the *Survey of Current Business*, published by the United States Department of Commerce. This is particularly useful in following the monthly production of the different chemicals, metals, paper, food, petroleum, and rubber products. Also, it has many monthly business indicators as well as the component parts of the gross national product.

Bank Letters

A number of the leading banks in New York City and in other cities publish monthly letters. These are very informative, since they have statistical studies and comments on general business conditions, on earnings of industries, on international trade, on employment, on commodity prices, and on money and banking matters. Some of the better known of these letters are:

1. *Business in Brief* (bi-monthly), Chase Manhattan Bank, New York
2. *Business and Economic Conditions* (monthly), The First National City Bank, New York
3. *Business and Economic Review* (monthly), The First National Bank, Chicago
4. *The Morgan Guaranty Survey* (monthly), Morgan Guaranty Trust Co., New York

Other monthly letters are published by the Cleveland Trust Company of Cleveland, Ohio; the Security First National Bank of Los Angeles; the Bank of Montreal, Montreal, Canada. In addition, the Federal Reserve Bank of New York publishes an excellent monthly letter on banking matters.

Brokerage Reports

Many investment banking and brokerage concerns publish for their own and prospective customers reports on stocks. Also, on occasion, these companies publish statistical surveys. These would include studies on bonds, on industries, on electrical and natural gas public utilities, and on railroads. Some of the reports are short, and some are very detailed. These reports, as a rule, are available on request. *The Wall Street Journal* usually publishes, in its section called "Abreast of the Market," a list of the reports which have been written and the names of the brokerage concerns which have produced them.

Magazines

There are a wide variety of magazines devoted to financial and business matters. Some have articles on particular companies; others discuss stock-market technique and industry trends. Some of the better known of these magazines are:

1. *Barron's* (weekly), Dow Jones & Co. Inc., New York
2. *Business Week* (weekly), McGraw-Hill, Inc., New York
3. *Commercial & Financial Chronicle* (weekly), W. B. Dana & Co., New York

4. *Financial Analysts Journal* (bi-monthly), National Federa-
   tion of Financial Analysts, New York
5. *Fortune* (monthly), Time, Inc., New York
6. *Magazine of Wall Street* (weekly), Ticker Publishing Co.,
   New York
7. *U.S. News & World Report* (weekly), U.S. Publishing Co.,
   New York

Annual Reports

The annual report of a company often has a large amount of
current information on its products and recent activities. Of course every
stockholder receives an annual report. But often companies will send
copies of their reports on request. Also, they are generally available
in the large libraries. Annual reports usually contain a detailed income
account and balance sheet for the most recent and previous year. In addition, there are sometimes comments of interest on the trend of sales,
the products of the companies, as well as the problems and outlook.
The names of the officers and the directors are given. Often a comparative table is given for a number of years back showing the growth of
the income and assets. These tables enable the investor to see the
progress of the company.

Registration Statement and Prospectus

Whenever a company sells to the public over $300,000 of securi-
ties, it must file a registration statement with the Securities and Exchange Commission. A copy of this registration statement is on file at
the office of the Securities and Exchange Commission and the New
York Stock Exchange. The registration statement often contains a great
deal of valuable information about the company. This would include
such items as reserves of oil, iron ore and nonferrous metals, subsidiary
earnings, and important (over 10 per cent) stockholders and the stockholdings of the officers.

A prospectus is a summary of a registration statement. This can often
be obtained by asking or writing to the leading underwriters. However,
since they are not required to give a prospectus beyond a limited period,
it is often difficult to obtain a copy of a prospectus if the underwriting
is over a year old. Nevertheless, prospectuses are on file at the New
York Stock Exchange and at the office of the Securities and Exchange
Commission.

Financial Services

The two leading financial services are Moody's Investors' Service
and Standard and Poor's Corporation of New York. Both publish large

manuals which give a detailed description of the business of railroad, utility, industrial, and financial companies. Comparative balance sheets and income accounts for a number of years are reproduced. These manuals are generally available in the large libraries. Also, Standard and Poor's Corporation publishes basic analyses of about twenty-five industries. These give the background, problems, a large amount of industry statistics, ratios, and comparative income of industrial figures. Both Standard & Poor's Corporation and Moody's Investors' Service publish weekly newsletters discussing the outlook for industries and individual companies as well as recent financial news of the leading companies.

Textbooks

Some of the textbooks which might be useful in explaining the theory and technique of investment and security analysis are as follows:

1. *Industry Analysis:* Dr. Lester V. Plum has edited a book written by a number of industry specialists entitled *Investing in American Industries* (New York: Harper & Row, Publishers, 1960). Here a detailed discussion is given of the background, problems, statistics, and outlook for the aircraft, business machine, chemical, electric utility, insurance, nonferrous metal, petroleum, paper, steel, and railroad industries.

2. *Security Analysis:* There are a number of textbooks written on security analysis. The following are some of the more helpful books:

   a. American Bankers Association, *Investment Fundamentals* (New York: The American Bankers Association, 1966).

   b. Douglas H. Bellemore, *Investments, Principles, Practices, and Analysis* (New Rochelle, New York: South-Western Publishing Company 1966).

   c. Ralph E. Badger, Harold W. Torgerson, and Harry G. Guthmann, *Investment Principles and Practices* (Englewood Cliffs, N.J.: Prentice-Hall, Inc., 1961).

   d. John H. Prime *Investment Analysis* 4th ed. (Englewood Cliffs, N.J.: Prentice-Hall, Inc., 1967).

3. *General Reading:* Some of the books which might be of interest in the fields of finance and the security markets are as follows:

   a. J. I. Bogen, *Financial Handbook*, 4th ed. (New York: The Ronald Press Company, 1964).

   b. Hugh Bullock, *The Story of Investment Companies* (New York: Columbia University Press, 1960).

   c. I. Friend, W. Hoffman, and W. J. Winn, *The Over-the-Counter Market* (New York: McGraw-Hill Book Company, 1958).

   d. George L. Leffler, and Loring C. Farewell, *The Stock Market* (New York: The Ronald Press Company, 1963).

> *e.* W. H. Steiner, Eli Shapiro, and Ezra Solomon, *Money and Banking* (New York: Holt, Rinehart and Winston, Inc., 1958).
>
> *f.* Arthur Wiesenberger and Company, New York, N.Y. *Investment Companies* Annual Manuals, privately printed.

We have listed a large array of sources of information, not to suggest that all or a substantial part of these books, services, and magazines be read. We wish, however, to show the sources in order that the reader may follow his line of interest. Basically, it is believed an investor can keep well informed by regular reading of one newspaper such as *The New York Times* or the *Wall Street Journal* and one weekly business magazine. He can, without cost, ask for the bank letters. If he finds reading of these not too burdensome, he can subscribe to the *Commercial and Financial Chronicle*, Moody's *Stock Survey* or the *Investment Outlook* of Standard and Poor's Corp. If he is statistically inclined and wishes to follow particular businesses, it is suggested that he subscribe to one of the *Industry Surveys* of Standard & Poor's Corp., and the *Survey of Current Business*.

APPENDIX

Important Provisions & Rules of Securities Act of 1933

1. Called Truth in Securities Act—to prevent fraud.
2. Does not approve, recommend or guarantee accuracy of figures of securities.
3. All offerings over $300,000 must file *registration statement* with SEC unless exempt, i.e., municipals.
4. Statement contains type of business, purpose of issue, balance sheets, income accounts, suits, spread, price, officers and directors, underwriters, large stockholders, and counsel.
5. No sale before effective date, usually twenty days, exceptions.
6. SEC stop order, when untrue statement.
7. SEC deficiency letters, when data inadequate.
8. Prospectus—summary of important facts of registration statement—must be given on all offerings, or sale of security.
9. "Red herring" is preliminary prospectus without price amendment—not an offer to sell.
10. *Penalties:* criminal—five years and/or $5000; civil, difference between price paid and sold, must be brought in three years.
11. *Liable:* All signers of registration statement directors, underwriter, controlling pensions (person with influence on management). A mistatement or withholding a material fact.
12. No secret profits—profits made by promoter not disclosed to corporation.

13. Administered by Federal Trade Commission until 1934 Securities Exchange Act.

Important Provisions & Rules of Securities Exchange Act 1934

1. *Registration and Regulation* of national securities exchanges, listed securities, all brokers and dealers (Sec. 156).
2. To control trading practices, proxies, dealings by insiders.
3. To prevent manipulation of markets.
4. 1964 amendment: All over-the-counter securities with 500 or more stockholders and $1,000,000 of assets must file registration statements. (All other provisions of the act apply to these companies as to proxies, etc.).
5. Insiders: directors, officers, and owners of 10 per cent or more must report initial holdings and monthly changes thereafter to SEC.
6. Proxies must be approved by SEC—truthful, with complete and clear information.
7. No misleading appearance of active trading, no pool, no fictitious transactions by matching orders or wash sales. No spreading rumors (Sec 15C 1).
8. No short selling by officers or directors in own stock.
9. All stock must be marked long or short. Short sales must be executed at a higher price than the last sale, (plus tick), or at a price the same as the last sale which is higher than the preceding price (zero plus tick).
10. Formation of NASD under Maloney Act Amendment 1938—Section 15A.
11. Formation of the SEC—five members appointed by President.
12. Exchanges, broker/dealers must keep records, make reports too and be examined by SEC. (Sec 17a–5).
13. No action of SEC a Federal Reserve to be construed as approving merits of issue. (Sec 26).
14. Board of Governors of the Federal Reserve System to set the margin requirements of brokers' loans to customers buying on margin under Regulation T, and for banks making collateral loans under Regulation U.

Important Provisions & Rules of Investment Company Act of 1940

1. To provide registration full disclosure, and regulation of investment companies to prevent speculative abuses.
2. Not more than 60 per cent of board may be officers, em-

ployees of investment company, its advisers, bankers or underwriters (except no-load).

3. May not buy security if any one of employees or its adviser own ½ per cent of securities or combined 5 per cent.

4. Investment policy must be in prospectus, prospectus updated every 14 months. An investment policy can't be changed without majority vote.

5. Management contracts—two years with approval by shareholders. Renewed annually; may be cancelled by directors or stockholders on 60 days' notice.

6. Redemption required in seven days at net asset value.

7. SEC regulates proxies.

8. Capital adequacy:
   a. Minimum net worth $100,000 to start fund.
   b. Open end—common only, may borrow from bank—300 per cent coverage.
   c. Closed end may issue debt 300 per cent coverage; preferred 200 per cent.

9. Investors must receive complete financial reports at least semi-annually (SEC quarterly reports).

10. To register as diversified investment company, must have at least 75 per cent of assets invested in securities with not more than 5 per cent of assets in securities of one issuer or more than 10 per cent of vote.
    (Thus one segment of the fund must amount to 75 per cent of total assets; must be diversified. The other 25 per cent need not be diversified and may indeed be invested in securities of a *single issuer*. This statement is subject to modification depending on the state which might have a more strict regulation. California sets a maximum of 10 per cent in any one security.)

11. Prospectus given on every offering on sale of shares of investment company (management, securities, adviser, custodian, performance etc.).

12. Maximum load, 9 per cent of offering price; on contractual plans may charge up to 50 per cent of first year's payments.

13. Margin purchases unlawful unless in accord with rules of SEC.

14. Short sales restricted.

15. Transaction between dealers and customers require public offering price be maintained as defined in prospectus.

16. All sales in compliance with Securities Act 1933 and Securities Exchange Act 1934 as well as blue-sky state laws, SEC regulates proxies.

17. Securities cash must be kept by bank or broker, member of national securities exchange.

18. Must not claim any federal agency is involved in management of funds.

Important Provisions of the Investment Advisers Act of 1940

1. Requires all persons engaged in the business of advising others in regard to securities to register with the SEC.
2. Covers all individuals or organizations who for compensation engage in the business of advising others.
   a. All services, investment counsels, and investment advisory service of brokerage firms who charge a fee.
   b. Exempts newspapers and magazines and brokers who give advice incidentally or gratuitously, banks, and government security houses, attorneys, accountants, engineers, and teachers.
3. Unless exempt must *register* with SEC giving
   a. Education and affiliations for ten years
   b. Reports of any changes
   c. Control over accounts.
4. Investment counsel confined to registered investment advisors.
5. SEC power limited to investigations and may enjoin.
6. *May not give advice on basis of capital gains.*

Important Provisions of the Trust Indenture Act of 1939

1. Administered by the SEC.
2. All trust indentures on bonds sold must conform to this act.
3. Trustees must have certain qualifications which are:
   a. One or more must be a corporation
   b. Corporation must have capital funds of $150,000
   c. Any conflict of interest the trustee must remove the conflict or notify security holders of their rights.
4. Duties of trustee defined:
   a. Must submit annual reports to bondholders
   b. Must notify bondholders in the event of default within ninety days
   c. In the event of a default, must act as a prudent man
   d. To authenticate the bonds
   e. To check performance of covenants: interest, taxes, sinking funds, collateral
   f. To protect the interest of bondholder.
   (Note: The trustee in no way guarantees the payment of interest or principal of the bonds, but can be sued for negligence).
5. Duties of corporation defined:
   a. Furnish trustees with evidence of recording indenture.
   b. Furnish trustee with list of bondholders and keep it up to date.

Important Provisions of the Public Utility Holding Company Act of 1935

1. *Purpose*: To prevent abuses in the operation and financing of public utility holding companies administered by SEC.
2. All public utility holding companies were required to register with SEC.
3. SEC compelled breakup of scattered group of public utilities. Required each be an *integrated* system.
4. SEC has control over issuance of securities of holding companies and their subsidiaries to prevent unwarranted expansion.
5. SEC must approve acquisition of securities and utility assets of utility holding companies.
6. SEC approves all financial transactions of public utility holding companies and upstream loans, etc.

Amended Net Capital Rule

Following is the text of the Amended Rule:

NET CAPITAL RULE

Rule 15c3-1
of the General Rules and Regulations under the
Security Exchange Act of 1934

Net Capital Requirements for Brokers and Dealers

(a) Every broker or dealer shall have the net capital necessary to comply with all the following conditions:

    (1)   his aggregate indebtedness to all other persons shall not exceed 2,000 per centum of his net capital; and

    (2)   he shall have and maintain net capital of not less than $5,000; except that the minimum net capital to be maintained by a broker or dealer meeting all of the following conditions shall be $2,500:

        (A)   his dealer transactions (as principal for his own account) are limited to the purchase, sale and redemption of redeemable shares of registered investment companies; except that a broker or dealer transacting business as a sole proprietor may also effect occasional transactions in other securities for his own account with or through another registered broker-dealer;

        (B) his transactions as broker (agent) are limited to: (i) the sale and redemption of redeemable securities of registered investment companies; (ii) the solicitation of share accounts for savings and loan associations insured by an instrumentality of the United States; and (iii) the sale of securities for the account of a customer to obtain funds for immediate reinvestment in redeemable securities of registered investment companies; and

(C) he promptly transmits all funds and delivers all securities received in connection with his activities as a broker or dealer, and does not otherwise hold funds or securities for, or owe money or securities to, customers.

(b) exemptions

(1) The provisions of this rule shall not apply to any broker who is also a licensed insurance agent under the laws of any State or the District of Columbia, whose securities business is limited to effecting transactions in variable annuity contracts as general agent for the issuer, who promptly transmits all funds and delivers all variable annuity contracts received in connection therewith, and who does not otherwise hold funds or securities for or owe money or securities to customers, if the issuer files with the Commission an undertaking satisfactory to it that the issuer will assume responsibility for all valid claims arising out of all activities of such agent in effecting transactions in such variable annuity contracts; *provided, however,* that a broker transacting business as a sole proprietor who meets all other conditions of this subparagraph (b) (1) may also effect occasional transactions in other securities for his own account with or through another registered broker-dealer.

(2) The provisions of this rule shall not apply to any member in good standing and subject to the capital rules of the American Stock Exchange, the Boston Stock Exchange, the Midwest Stock Exchange, the New York Stock Exchange, the Pacific Coast Stock Exchange, the Philadelphia-Baltimore-Washington Stock Exchange, or the Pittsburgh Stock Exchange, whose rules, settled practices and applicable regulatory procedures are deemed by the Commission to impose requirements more comprehensive than the requirements of this rule; *provided, however,* that the exemption as to the members of any exchange may be suspended or withdrawn by the Commission at any time, by sending ten (10) days written notice to such exchange, if it appears to the Commission to be necessary or appropriate in the public interest or for the protection of investors so to do.

(3) The Commission may, upon written application, exempt from the provisions of this rule, either unconditionally or on specified terms and conditions, any broker or dealer who satisfies the Commission that, because of the special nature of his business, his financial position and the safeguards he has established for the protection of customers' funds and securities, it is not necessary in the public interest or for the protection of investors to subject the particular broker or dealer to the provisions of this rule.

(c) Definitions—For the purpose of this rule:

   (1) The term "aggregate indebtedness" shall be deemed to mean the total money liabilities of a broker or dealer arising in connection with any transaction whatsoever, including, among other things: money borrowed; money payable against securities loaned and securities "failed to receive"; the market value of securities borrowed (except for delivery against customers' sales) to the extent to which no equivalent value is paid or credited; customers' free credit balances; credit balances in customers' accounts having short positions in securities; and equities in customers' commodities futures accounts; but excluding

   (A) indebtedness adequately collateralized, as hereinafter defined, by securities or spot commodities owned by the broker or dealer;

   (B) indebtedness to other brokers or dealers adequately collateralized, as hereinafter defined, by securities or spot commodities owned by the broker or dealer;

   (C) amounts payable against securities loaned which securities are owned by the broker or dealer;

   (D) amounts payable against securities failed to receive which securities were purchased for the account of, and have not been sold by, the broker or dealer;

   (E) indebtedness adequately collateralized, as hereinafter defined, by exempted securities;

   (F) amounts segregated in accordance with the Commodity Exchange Act and the rules and regulations thereunder;

   (G) fixed liabilities adequately secured by real estate or any other asset which is not included in the computation of "net capital" under this rule;

   (H) liabilities on open contractual commitments; and

   (I) indebtedness subordinated to the claims of general creditors pursuant to a satisfactory subordination agreement, as hereinafter defined.

   (2) The term "net capital" shall be deemed to mean the net worth of a broker or dealer (that is, the excess of total assets over total liabilities), adjusted by

   (A) adding unrealized profits (or deducting unrealized losses) in the accounts of the broker or dealer and, if such broker or dealer is a partnership, adding equities (or deducting deficits) in accounts of partners, as hereinafter defined;

   (B) deducting fixed assets and assets which cannot be readily converted into cash (less any indebtedness secured thereby) including, among other things, real estate; furniture and fixtures; exchange memberships; prepaid rent, insurance and expenses; good will; organization expenses; all unsecured advances and loans; customers' unsecured notes and accounts; and deficits in customers' accounts, except in bona fide cash accounts within the meaning of Section 4 (c) of

Regulation T of the Board of Governors of the Federal Reserve System;

(C)   deducting the percentages specified below of the market value of all securities, long and short (except exempted securities) in the capital, proprietary and other accounts of the broker or dealer, including securities loaned to the broker or dealer pursuant to a satisfactory subordination agreement, as hereinafter defined, and if such broker or dealer is a partnership, in the accounts of partners, as hereinafter defined:

    (i)   in the case of non-convertible debt securities having a fixed interest rate and a fixed maturity date which are not in default, if the market value is not more than 5% below the face value, the deduction shall be 5% of such market value; if the market value is more than 5% but not more than 30% below the face value, the deduction shall be a percentage of market value, equal to the percentage by which the market value is below the face value; and if the market value is 30% or more below the face value, such deduction shall be 30%;

    (ii)   in the case of cumulative, non-convertible preferred stock ranking prior to all other classes of stock of the same issuer, which is not in arrears as to dividends, the deduction shall be 20%;

    (iii) on all other securities, the deduction shall be 30%; *provided, however*, that such deduction need not be made in the case of (i) a security which is convertible into or exchangeable for other securities within a period of 30 days, subject to no conditions other than the payment of money, and the other securities into which such security is convertible, or for which it is exchangeable, are short in the accounts of such broker or dealer or partner, or (ii) a security which has been called for redemption and which is redeemable within 90 days;

(D)   deducting 30% of the market value of all "long" and all "short" future commodity contracts (other than those contracts representing spreads or straddles in the same commodity and those contracts offsetting or hedging any "spot" commodity positions) carried in the capital, proprietary or other accounts of the broker or dealer and, if such broker or dealer is a partnership, in the accounts of partners as hereinafter defined;

(E)   deducting, in the case of a broker or dealer who has open contractual commitments, the respective percentages specified in subparagraph (C) above of the value (which shall be the market value whenever there is a market) of each net long and each net short position contemplated by any existing contractual commitment in the capital, proprietary and other accounts of the broker or dealer and, if such broker or dealer is a partnership, in accounts of partners, as hereinafter defined; *provided, however*, that this deduction shall not apply to exempted securities, and that the deduction with respect to any individual commitment shall be reduced by the unrealized profit, in an amount not greater than the percentage deduction provided for in subparagraph (C), (or increased by the unrealized loss) in such commitment; and that in no event shall an unrealized profit on any closed transactions operate to increase net capital;

(F) deducting an amount equal to 1½% of the market values of the total long or total short futures contracts in each commodity, whichever is greater, carried for all customers;

(G) excluding liabilities of the broker or dealer which are subordinated to the claims of general creditors pursuant to a satisfactory subordination agreement, as hereinafter defined; and

(H) deducting, in the case of a broker or dealer who is a sole proprietor, the excess of (i) liabilities which have not been incurred in the course of business as a broker or dealer over (ii) assets not used in the business.

(3) The term "exempted securities" shall mean those securities specifically defined as exempted securities in Section 3 (a) of the Act.

(4) The term "accounts of partners," where the broker or dealer is a partnership, shall mean accounts of partners who have agreed in writing that the equity in such accounts maintained with such partnership shall be included as partnership property.

(5) The term "contractual commitments" shall include underwriting, when-issued, when-distributed and delayed delivery contracts, endorsements of puts and calls, commitments in foreign currencies, and spot (cash) commodities contracts, but shall not include uncleared regular way purchases and sales of securities and contracts in commodities futures; a series of contracts of purchase or sale of the same security conditioned, if at all, only upon issuance may be treated as an individual commitment.

(6) Indebtedness shall be deemed to be "adequately collateralized" within the meaning of this rule, when the difference between the amount of the indebtedness and the market value of the collateral is sufficient to make the loan acceptable as a fully secured loan to banks regularly making comparable loans to brokers or dealers in the community.

(7) The term "satisfactory subordination agreement" shall mean a written agreement duly executed by the broker or dealer and the lender, which agreement is binding and enforceable in accordance with its terms upon the lender, his creditors, heirs, executors, administrators, and assigns, and which agreement satisfies all of the following conditions:

(A) it effectively subordinates any right of the lender to demand or receive payment or return of the cash or securities loaned to the claims of all present and future creditors of the broker or dealer;

(B) the cash or securities are loaned for a term of not less than one year;

(C) it provides that the agreement shall not be subject to cancellation by either party, and that the loan shall not be repaid and the agreement shall not be terminated, rescinded or modified by mutual consent or otherwise if the effect thereof would be to make the agreement inconsistent with the conditions of this rule or to reduce the net capital of the broker or dealer below the amount required by this rule;

(D) it provides that no default in the payment of interest or in the performance of any covenant or condition by the broker or dealer shall have the effect of accelerating the maturity of the indebtedness:

(E) it provides that any notes or other written instruments evidencing the indebtedness shall bear on their face an appropriate legend stating that such notes or instruments are issued subject to the provisions of a subordination agreement which shall be adequately referred to and incorporated by reference;

(F) it provides that any securities or other property loaned to the broker or dealer pursuant to its provisions may be used and dealt with by the broker or dealer as part of his capital and shall be subject to the risks of the business; and

(G) two copies of such agreement, and of any notes or written instruments evidencing the indebtedness, are filed, within 10 days after such agreement is entered into, with the Regional Office of the Commission for the region in which the broker or dealer maintains his principal place of business, together with a statement of the full name and address of the lender, the business relationship of the lender to the broker or dealer, and whether the broker or dealer carried funds or securities for the lender at or about the time the agreement was entered into. If each copy of such agreement is bound separately and clearly marked "Non-Public" such agreements shall be maintained in a non-public file; *provided, however,* that they shall be available, for official use, to any official or employee of the United States or any State; to any national securities exchange and any registered national securities association of which the broker or dealer filing such agreements is a member; and to any other person to whom the Commission authorizes disclosure in the public interest.

(8) The term "customer" shall mean every person except the broker or dealer; *provided, however,* that partners who maintain "accounts of partners" as herein defined shall not be deemed to be customers insofar as such accounts are concerned.

NATIONAL ASSOCIATION OF SECURITIES DEALERS, INC.

APPLICATION FOR MEMBERSHIP
OR
AMENDMENT TO APPLICATION

PLEASE TYPEWRITE

(Check appropriate blocks)

A. This is an APPLICATION FOR MEMBERSHIP .... ☐
Complete in full, file with Assessment Report, Statement of Financial Condition, Application for Registration of Branch Office, if any, an Application for Registration as Registered Principals for each principal and an Application for Registration as Registered Representatives, if any. Appropriate fees for each category must accompany application.

B. This is an AMENDMENT TO APPLICATION FOR MEMBERSHIP to:

(1) Correct and keep current answers in previous applications, in accordance with requirements of the certification on last page of this form. .... ☐

(2) Record change of name of applicant. .... ☐
State exact name under which you are presently registered

_____

(3) Record change of form of organization. .... ☐
Presently registered as a _____

(4) Record consolidation, reorganization or merger of two or more members to one successor organization. .... ☐
Names of predecessor firms. _____

If B (3) or (4) has been checked, this AMENDMENT must be completed in full, including a financial statement for the successor organization. The successor organization should answer all questions below.

C. Forward in duplicate to National Association of Securities Dealers, Inc., 888 17th Street, N. W., Washington, D. C. 20006. If additional space is needed for any answer, attach a separate sheet with a proper cross reference to the question it supplements.

---

1. State exact name of applicant.

_____
     (Name should be identical to that registered with the Securities and Exchange Commission)

2. (a) State the address of the main office of the applicant.

_____
   (Street)   *(City)*   *(County)*   *(State)*   *(Zip Code)*

(b) Is the main office located in: (a) a separate business office ☐; (b) a business office shared with others ☐; or, (c) a private residence ☐?
If (b), indicate: the name(s) of the firm(s) with whom you share office space and the type(s) of business in which such firms(s) are engaged:

3. Designate the name, address and title of the Executive Representative* and Substitute Representative of the applicant.

Executive Representative _____
                                       (Name and Title)

_____
                                     (Business Address)

Substitute Representative _____
                                       (Name and Title)

_____
                                     (Business Address)

4. List those offices, other than the main office, which are designated as Offices of Supervisory Jurisdiction** along with the name of each manager:

_____   _____
       (Street)   *(Street)*

_____   _____
  (City and State)   *(Zip Code)*   *(City and State)*   *(Zip Code)*

_____   _____
   (Name of Manager)   *(Name of Manager)*

* See By-Laws, Article I, Section 5.
** See Rules of Fair Practice, Article III, Section 27 and see Page G-51 of NASD Manual.

5. Attach to this application a list of all branch offices of the applicant showing the address and the name and title of the person to whom correspondence should be directed.*** In addition, list the names of all registered principals and registered representatives assigned to each office. (Use the Application for Registration of Branch Office form.)

6. Are you registered as a broker-dealer with the Securities and Exchange Commission? Yes ☐ No ☐. Complete the following:

_____   _____
(Date of Filing or Effective Date of Registration with SEC)   *(SEC File Number)*

7. List states in which applicant is registered or in which registration is pending and so indicate:

State	Effective Date	Pending	Date Filed

8. Attach in duplicate a statement of financial condition which is attested under oath or affirmation that it is true and correct to the best knowledge and belief of the person making such oath or affirmation. Such financial statement shall contain such detail as will disclose the nature and amount of assets and liabilities and the net worth of the applicant and should be as of a date within 30 days of the date on which this application is filed. This statement is required only in the case of an application for membership or in the case of an amendment to the application for membership, if boxes B (3) or (4) are applicable.

9. Attach a complete résumé of applicant's business experience and a similar résumé for all persons designated as principals,**** regardless of whether they must be registered. (Use the completed Application for Registration as a Registered Principal form.)

10. Is applicant presently engaged in, or does it intend to engage in, business activities other than the securities business? .... Yes ☐ No ☐
If "yes," describe type of business and give approximate percentage of time devoted thereto annually.

_____
_____
_____

11. (a) State the applicant's form of organization, sole proprietor, partnership, corporation or other.

_____

   (b) If applicant is other than a sole proprietor, partnership or corporation, attach a statement showing in detail the nature of the organization and indicate the persons who control such organization.

TO BE FILLED OUT ONLY IF APPLICANT IS A PARTNERSHIP

12. List full names of all general, limited and special partners and indicate their relationship to the partnership:

_____
_____
_____
_____
_____

*** See definition of the term "branch office," By-Laws, Article I, Section 11 and Page G-51 of NASD Manual.
**** See Schedule "C," Page C-61 of NASD Manual.

13. (a) State date and place of incorporation. _____

(b) List full names of all officers, directors and other persons with similar status or functions:

Full Name	Designate Title of Each Officer	Designate Directors by stating "Director"	Active in Operation of Business
			Yes ☐ No ☐
			Yes ☐ No ☐
			Yes ☐ No ☐
			Yes ☐ No ☐
			Yes ☐ No ☐
			Yes ☐ No ☐

(c) List all owners, including those who, directly or indirectly, are beneficial owners, of 10 percent or more of any equity security of the applicant, showing the class and number of shares held:

Full Name	Number of Shares Owned	Class of Security	Total Shares Outstanding

14. Does any person not named hereinbefore directly or indirectly through agreement or otherwise exercise or have power to exercise control of the business of applicant? .... Yes ☐ No ☐

If yes, list name(s) of individual(s) and the basis of his power to exercise controlling influence:

_____

_____

15. (a) Are you also applying for registration or are you registered with a national securities exchange? .... Yes ☐ No ☐

(b) If "yes", please indicate: NYSE ☐   ASE ☐   MSE ☐   PBS ☐   PCS ☐   Other _____

16. Indicate the types of securities business in which you have been, or intend to be engaged:

Underwriting
☐ Corporate
☐ Municipal
☐ Investment Company

Trading
☐ Corporate
☐ Municipal

Retailing
☐ Over-the-counter
☐ Listed
☐ Municipal

Investment Company Shares
☐ Underwriting
☐ Retailing of Shares
☐ Sale of contractual plans

Other
_____
(Specify)

17. (a) Have you ever been suspended or expelled from a national securities association, registered pursuant to Section 15A of the Securities Exchange Act of 1934, as amended, or from a national securities exchange, registered pursuant to Section 6 of the same Act, or have you ever been barred or suspended from being associated with any member of such association or exchange, for violation of any rule of such association or exchange which prohibits any act or transaction constituting conduct inconsistent with just and equitable principles of trade, or requires any act, the omission of which constitutes conduct inconsistent with just and equitable principles of trade? (See Article I, Section 2 of the By-Laws) .... Yes ☐ No ☐

(b) Are you subject to an order of the Securities and Exchange Commission denying, suspending or revoking your registration pursuant to Section 15 of the Act, or expelling or suspending you from membership in a registered securities association or national securities exchange, or barring or suspending you from being associated with a broker or dealer? (See Article I, Section 2 of the By-Laws) .... Yes ☐ No ☐

(c) Have you, by your conduct while associated with a broker or dealer, been a cause of any suspension, expulsion or order of the character described in (a) or (b) above, which order is in effect with respect to such broker or dealer? (See Article I, Section 2 of the By-Laws) .... Yes ☐ No ☐

(d) Do you have any person associated***** with yourself whom you know is a person who, if such person were a broker or dealer, would be ineligible for admission to or continuance in membership under questions (a), (b) or (c)? (See Article I, Section 2 of the By-Laws) .... Yes ☐ No ☐

***** See By-Laws, Article I, Section 3 (f).

(e) Have you or any person associated with you ever been suspended or expelled from a national securities exchange or barred or suspended from being associated with any member of such exchange, for violation of any rule of such exchange? (See Article I, Section 2 of the By-Laws).. Yes ☐ No ☐

(f) Have you or any person associated with you (A) ever been convicted within the ten years preceding the filing of this application or at any time thereafter of any felony or misdemeanor which involved the purchase or sale of any security or which arose out of the conduct of the business of a broker, dealer or investment adviser; or which involved embezzlement, fraudulent conversion, or misappropriation of funds or securities, or which involved mail fraud, or fraud by wire, radio, or television; or, (B) ever been permanently or temporarily enjoined by order, judgment, or decree of any court of competent jurisdiction from acting as an investment adviser, underwriter, broker, or dealer, or as an affiliated person or employee of any investment company, bank or insurance company, or from engaging in or continuing any conduct or practice in connection with such activity, or in connection with the purchase or sale of any security? (See Article I, Section 2 of the By-Laws) .... Yes ☐ No ☐

If your answer to question 17(a), (b), (c), (d), (e), or (f) is "yes", or if any such action is pending, set forth on a separate sheet, in reasonable detail, the facts with respect thereto.

CERTIFICATION

The undersigned, a broker and/or dealer authorized by law to transact and whose regular course of business consists in actually transacting one or more branches of the investment banking or securities business in the United States of America, hereby applies for membership in the NATIONAL ASSOCIATION OF SECURITIES DEALERS, INC. (hereinafter referred to as the Corporation), a non-stock, non-profit, membership corporation organized under the laws of the State of Delaware and registered with the Securities and Exchange Commission as a national securities association under the Securities and Exchange Act of 1934, as amended, and, if admitted to membership, the undersigned hereby agrees:

(1) To accept, abide by, comply with, and adhere to all the provisions, conditions, and covenants of the Certificate of Incorporation, the By-Laws, the Rules of Fair Practice, and the Code of Procedure for Handling Trade Practice Complaints of the Corporation as they are or may from time to time be adopted, changed, or amended (copies of which Certificate of Incorporation, By-Laws, Rules of Fair Practice and Code of Procedure for Handling Trade Practice Complaints have been received and read by the undersigned applicant and which are made a part of this Application for Membership and Agreement by reference thereto); and to accept, abide by, comply with, and adhere to all rulings, orders, directions and decisions of, and penalties imposed by, the Board of Governors of the Corporation or any duly authorized committee of the Corporation;

(2) To pay such dues, assessments and other charges in the manner and amount as shall from time to time be fixed by the Board of Governors pursuant to the By-Laws;

(3) That neither the Corporation, nor any officer or employee thereof, nor any member of the Board of Governors or of any District or other Committee, shall be liable, except for wilful malfeasance, to the applicant or to any member of the Corporation or to any other person, for any action taken by such officer or member of the Board of Governors or of any District or other Committee in his official capacity, or by any employee of the Corporation while acting within the scope of his employment or under instruction of any officer, board or committee of the Corporation, in connection with the administration or enforcement of any of the provisions of the By-Laws, any of the rules and regulations as they are or may from time to time be adopted, changed or amended, or any ruling, order, direction, decision of, or penalty imposed by, the Board of Governors of the Corporation or any duly authorized committee of the Corporation;

(4) To keep the answers to the information called for herein accurate and up-to-date by supplementary written notices to the Secretary of the Corporation and further agree that the address listed in reply to question 2 shall be kept current and shall be the address of record for the receipt of all Corporation communications.

The undersigned further certifies that the statements made in this application which includes the Assessment Report and Statement of Financial Condition are true and complete. The undersigned understands that penalties may be imposed under Section 32 of the Securities Exchange Act of 1934, as amended, or under the Corporation's Rules of Fair Practice in the event false or misleading information is given on the application with respect to any material fact or if there are material omissions of fact therein.

Subscribed and sworn to before me

this _____ day of _____ _____
                                                                                                  (Name of Applicant)

19____ .

_____ _____
            (Notary Public)   (Title)

My Commission expires _____   Dated: _____

FORM BD

Revised
March 2, 1959

SECURITIES AND EXCHANGE COMMISSION
WASHINGTON, D.C., 20549

**FORM OF APPLICATION FOR REGISTRATION AS A BROKER AND DEALER OR TO AMEND
SUCH AN APPLICATION UNDER THE SECURITIES EXCHANGE ACT OF 1934**

- -

THIS IS AN APPLICATION FOR REGISTRATION.

**CHECK
ONE
BOX**

Instructions—All Items in the Form must be answered in full. If this is an application by a predecessor
on behalf of a successor broker-dealer not yet formed or organized, see instruction 7 below.

THIS IS AN AMENDMENT TO AN APPLICATION.

**APPLICANT OR REGISTRANT REPRESENTS THAT TO THE EXTENT THAT INFORMATION PREVIOUSLY
FILED IS NOT CORRECTED, SUCH INFORMATION IS TRUE, CORRECT, AND COMPLETE.**

Instructions—If Items 3 (b) or 3 (c) are amended, they must be answered in full. With respect to any
other items, furnish only the corrected information.

**FULL NAME OF APPLICANT OR REGIS-
TRANT** . . . .

**NAME UNDER WHICH BUSINESS WILL BE
CONDUCTED** . . . .

**ADDRESS OF PRINCIPAL PLACE OF BUSI-
NESS.** (Complete address of actual location) . . . .

**IF NAME, OR NAME UNDER WHICH BUSI-
NESS WILL BE CONDUCTED, IS HEREBY
AMENDED, SHOW PREVIOUS NAME
HERE** . . . .

GENERAL INSTRUCTIONS

1. This Form must be executed and filed in duplicate with the Securities and Exchange Commission, Washington 25, D. C.
An exact copy should be retained by the applicant or registrant.

2. If the space provided for any answer is insufficient, the complete answer shall be prepared on a separate sheet which
shall be attached to the Form and identified as "Answer to Item ...." and reference thereto shall be made under the
item on the Form.

3. Individuals' names shall be given in full.

4. A Form which is not prepared and executed in compliance with applicable requirements may be returned as not
acceptable for filing. However, acceptance of this Form shall not constitute any finding that it has been filed as
required or that the information submitted is true, correct, or complete.

5. Rule 15b–8 requires a statement of financial condition to be filed in duplicate with every application for registration.
Consult Rules 15b–7 and 17a–7 to determine whether any non-resident of the United States named in the Form is
required to file a consent and power of attorney, or a notice or undertaking with respect to books and records.

6. Rule 15b–2 (b) requires that if the information contained in the application, or in any supplement or amendment thereto,
is or becomes inaccurate for any reason, an amendment must be filed promptly on Form BD correcting such information.

7. If the Form is filed as an application by a predecessor broker-dealer on behalf of a successor not yet formed or organized, the information furnished shall relate to the successor to be formed. The Form shall be executed by the predecessor. Section 15 (b) of the Securities Exchange Act of 1934 and Rule 15b–3 provide that registration shall terminate
on the forty-fifth day after the effective date unless prior thereto the successor shall adopt the application as its own.
This procedure cannot be used where the successor is a sole proprietor.

DEFINITIONS

Unless the context clearly indicates otherwise, all terms used in the Form have the same meaning as in the Securities
Exchange Act of 1934 and in the General Rules and Regulations of the Commission thereunder.

1

1. IS APPLICANT OR REGISTRANT TAKING OVER SUBSTANTIALLY ALL OF THE ASSETS AND LIABILITIES <u>AND</u> CONTINUING THE BUSINESS OF A REGISTERED BROKER OR DEALER?

YES ☐   NO ☐

IF SO, NAME OF PREDECESSOR: _____

ADDRESS OF PREDECESSOR: _____

DATE OF SUCCESSION: _____

2.   TO BE FILLED OUT ONLY IF APPLICANT OR REGISTRANT IS A SOLE PROPRIETOR

FULL NAME _____

RESIDENCE ADDRESS _____

3.   TO BE FILLED OUT ONLY IF APPLICANT OR REGISTRANT IS A CORPORATION

(a) STATE OR PLACE IN WHICH INCORPORATED_____

DATE OF INCORPORATION _____

(b) COMPLETE LIST OF OFFICERS AND DIRECTORS, AND PERSONS WITH SIMILAR STATUS OR FUNCTIONS:

Full Names	Designate Titles of Each Officer	Designate Directors by Stating "Director"

(c) IS ANY PERSON, DIRECTLY OR INDIRECTLY, THE BENEFICIAL OWNER OF 10 PERCENT OR MORE OF ANY CLASS OF ANY EQUITY SECURITY OF APPLICANT OR REGISTRANT?

YES ☐   NO ☐

IF SO,   As to each such person state:

Full Name	Class of Security

4.   TO BE FILLED OUT ONLY IF APPLICANT OR REGISTRANT IS A PARTNERSHIP

(a) LIST FULL NAMES OF GENERAL PARTNERS | RESIDENCE ADDRESS OF EACH GENERAL PARTNER WHO DOES NOT RESIDE IN THE UNITED STATES

(b) LIST FULL NAMES OF LIMITED OR SPECIAL PARTNERS | LIMITED OR SPECIAL PARTNERS (Continued)

2

5. TO BE FILLED OUT ONLY IF APPLICANT OR REGISTRANT IS <u>OTHER THAN</u> A SOLE PROPRIETOR, PARTNERSHIP OR CORPORATION.

TYPE OF ORGANIZATION OR ASSOCIATION: --

FULL NAME OF EACH PERSON, INCLUDING A TRUSTEE, WHO DIRECTS, MANAGES OR PARTICIPATES IN DIRECTING OR MANAGING ITS AFFAIRS, AND THE RESIDENCE ADDRESS OF ANY SUCH PERSON WHO DOES NOT RESIDE IN THE UNITED STATES.

Full Name	Residence Address if Non-Resident

6. DOES ANY PERSON NOT NAMED IN ITEMS 2 TO 5, INCLUSIVE, DIRECTLY OR INDIRECTLY, CONTROL BUSINESS OF APPLICANT OR REGISTRANT?

YES ☐   NO ☐

¹F SO, Furnish Full Name	Business Address	Residence Address of Any Such Person Who Does Not Reside in the United States

7. LIST EACH PERSON NAMED IN ANSWERS TO ITEMS 2 TO 6, INCLUSIVE, AND WITH RESPECT TO EACH FURNISH THE FOLLOWING INFORMATION CONCERNING ANY CONNECTION WITH OR FINANCIAL INTEREST IN ANY BROKER OR DEALER (OTHER THAN REGISTRANT OR APPLICANT OR ANY PREDECESSOR) WITHIN THE PAST 10 YEARS. IF ANY SUCH PERSON HAS HAD NO SUCH CONNECTION, THE WORD "NONE" SHALL BE STATED WITH RESPECT TO SUCH PERSON:

Full Name	Name of Broker-Dealer	From Month	Year	To Month	Year	Exact Nature of Connection or Interest

3

FORM BD - - ITEM 8 (As Revised September 15, 1964)

8. STATE WHETHER THE APPLICANT OR REGISTRANT, ANY PARTNER, OFFICER, DIRECTOR OR BRANCH MANAGER OF APPLICANT OR REGISTRANT (OR ANY PERSON OCCUPYING A SIMILAR STATUS OR PERFORMING SIMILAR FUNCTIONS), ANY PERSON DIRECTLY OR INDIRECTLY CONTROLLING OR CONTROLLED BY APPLICANT OR REGISTRANT, INCLUDING ANY EMPLOYEE:

(a) HAS BEEN FOUND BY THE COMMISSION TO HAVE WILLFULLY MADE OR CAUSED TO BE MADE IN ANY APPLICATION FOR REGISTRATION OR REPORT REQUIRED TO BE FILED WITH THE COMMISSION UNDER THE SECURITIES EXCHANGE ACT OF 1934, OR IN ANY PROCEEDING BEFORE THE COMMISSION WITH RESPECT TO REGISTRATION, ANY STATEMENT WHICH WAS AT THE TIME AND IN THE LIGHT OF THE CIRCUMSTANCES UNDER WHICH IT WAS MADE FALSE AND MISLEADING WITH RESPECT TO ANY MATERIAL FACT, OR TO HAVE OMITTED TO STATE IN ANY SUCH APPLICATION OR REPORT ANY MATERIAL FACT WHICH WAS REQUIRED TO BE STATED THEREIN. **YES** ☐ **NO** ☐

IF SO, FURNISH THE FOLLOWING INFORMATION WITH RESPECT TO EACH SUCH PERSON

Full Name of Person	Position with Applicant or Registrant	Title of Action

(b) HAS BEEN CONVICTED, WITHIN 10 YEARS, OF ANY FELONY OR MISDEMEANOR (i) INVOLVING THE PURCHASE OR SALE OF ANY SECURITY; (ii) ARISING OUT OF THE CONDUCT OF THE BUSINESS OF A BROKER, DEALER, OR INVESTMENT ADVISER; (iii) INVOLVING EMBEZZLEMENT, FRAUDULENT CONVERSION, OR MISAPPROPRIATION OF FUNDS OR SECURITIES; OR (iv) INVOLVING VIOLATION OF SECTION 1341, 1342 OR 1343 OF TITLE 18 UNITED STATES CODE (MAIL FRAUD; FRAUD BY WIRE (INCLUDING TELEPHONE, TELEGRAPH, RADIO OR TELEVISION).) **YES** ☐ **NO** ☐

IF SO, FURNISH THE FOLLOWING INFORMATION WITH RESPECT TO EACH SUCH PERSON:

Full Name of Person	Position with Applicant or Registrant	Name and Location of Court and Date of Conviction

(c) IS PERMANENTLY OR TEMPORARILY ENJOINED BY ORDER, JUDGMENT, OR DECREE OF ANY COURT FROM ACTING AS AN INVESTMENT ADVISER, UNDERWRITER, BROKER, OR DEALER, OR AS AN AFFILIATED PERSON OR EMPLOYEE OF ANY INVESTMENT COMPANY, BANK, OR INSURANCE COMPANY, OR FROM ENGAGING IN OR CONTINUING ANY CONDUCT OR PRACTICE IN CONNECTION WITH ANY SUCH ACTIVITY, OR IN CONNECTION WITH THE PURCHASE OR SALE OF ANY SECURITY. **YES** ☐ **NO** ☐

IF SO, FURNISH THE FOLLOWING INFORMATION WITH RESPECT TO EACH SUCH PERSON:

Full Name of Person	Position with Applicant or Registrant	Title of Action Name and Location of Court, and Date of Judgment or Order

(Continued on reverse side)

(d) HAS BEEN FOUND BY THE COMMISSION OR ANY COURT TO HAVE VIOLATED ANY PROVISION OF THE SECURITIES ACT OF 1933, OR OF THE SECURITIES EXCHANGE ACT OF 1934, OR OF THE INVESTMENT ADVISERS ACT OF 1940, OR OF THE INVESTMENT COMPANY ACT OF 1940, OR OF ANY RULE OR REGULATION UNDER ANY OF SUCH ACTS.

YES ☐ NO ☐

IF SO, FURNISH THE FOLLOWING INFORMATION WITH RESPECT TO EACH SUCH PERSON:

Full Name of Person	Position with Applicant or Registrant	Title of Action and, if by a Court, Name and Location, and Date of Judgment or Order

(e) HAS BEEN FOUND BY THE COMMISSION OR ANY COURT TO HAVE AIDED, ABETTED, COUNSELLED, COMMANDED, INDUCED OR PROCURED THE VIOLATION BY ANY OTHER PERSON OF THE SECURITIES ACT OF 1933, OR THE SECURITIES EXCHANGE ACT OF 1934, OR THE INVESTMENT ADVISERS ACT OF 1940, OR THE INVESTMENT COMPANY ACT OF 1940, OR OF ANY RULE OR REGULATION UNDER ANY OF SUCH ACTS, OR TO HAVE FAILED REASONABLY TO SUPERVISE ANOTHER PERSON WHO COMMITTED SUCH A VIOLATION.

YES ☐ NO ☐

IF SO, FURNISH THE FOLLOWING INFORMATION WITH RESPECT TO EACH SUCH PERSON:

Full Name of Person	Position with Applicant or Registrant	Title of Action and, if by a Court, Name and Location, and Date of Judgment or Order

(f) IS SUBJECT TO AN ORDER OF THE COMMISSION ENTERED PURSUANT TO PARAGRAPH (7) OF SECTION 15 (b) OF THE SECURITIES EXCHANGE ACT OF 1934, AS AMENDED, BARRING OR SUSPENDING THE RIGHT OF SUCH PERSON TO BE ASSOCIATED WITH A BROKER OR DEALER, WHICH ORDER IS IN EFFECT WITH RESPECT TO SUCH PERSON.

YES ☐ NO ☐

IF SO, FURNISH THE FOLLOWING INFORMATION WITH RESPECT TO EACH SUCH PERSON.

Full Name of Person	Position with Applicant or Registrant	Title of Action

651966

DS-4572

9. APPLICANT OR REGISTRANT CONSENTS THAT NOTICE OF ANY PROCEEDING BEFORE THE COMMISSION IN CONNECTION WITH THE APPLICATION OR WITH REGISTRATION THEREUNDER MAY BE GIVEN BY SENDING NOTICE BY REGISTERED MAIL OR CONFIRMED TELEGRAM TO THE PERSON NAMED BELOW, AT THE ADDRESS GIVEN:

NAME _____

ADDRESS _____

EXECUTION

THE APPLICANT OR REGISTRANT SUBMITTING THIS FORM AND THE PERSON BY WHOM IT IS EXECUTED HEREBY REPRESENT THAT IT CONTAINS A TRUE, CORRECT, AND COMPLETE STATEMENT OF ALL INFORMATION REQUIRED TO BE FURNISHED.

Dated the _____ day of _____, 19_____

Sole proprietor . . . . _____
(Proprietor)

Partnership or other unincorporated organization
_____
(Name of Partnership (or Organization))

By _____
(General Partner (or Managing Agent))

_____
(Name of Corporation)

Corporation . . . . By _____

_____, a principal officer.
(Title)

If this form is filed by a sole proprietor, it shall be signed by the proprietor; if filed by a partnership, it shall be signed in the name of the partnership by a general partner; if filed by an unincorporated organization or association which is not a partnership, it shall be signed in the name of such organization or association by the managing agent, i. e., a duly authorized person who directs or manages or who participates in the directing or managing of its affairs; if filed by a corporation, it shall be signed in the name of the corporation by a principal officer duly authorized.

☆ U.S. GOVERNMENT PRINTING OFFICE: 1965—O—792-038

FORM SECO-2

U.S. SECURITIES AND EXCHANGE COMMISSION
Washington, D.C. 20549

PERSONNEL FORM

(submit in duplicate) (see instructions on reverse side of form)

NAME OF ASSOCIATED PERSON *(last, first, middle name)*	NAME AND ADDRESS OF BROKER OR DEALER *(No. & St., City, State, Zip Code)*

DATE OF EMPLOYMENT OR APPOINTMENT	POSITION *(also indicate full-time or part-time)*	DATE OF BIRTH	SOCIAL SECURITY NUMBER

STATE OR STATES (INCLUDING THE DISTRICT OF COLUMBIA) IN WHICH YOU ARE REGISTERED OR LICENSED TO ENGAGE IN THE SECURITIES BUSINESS

1. Educational institutions attended *(high school and above)* and whether or not you graduated.

NAME	CITY AND STATE

GRADUATED YES ☐ NO ☐	NO. OF YEARS COMPLETED	DEGREE RECEIVED

NAME	CITY AND STATE

GRADUATED YES ☐ NO ☐	NO. OF YEARS COMPLETED	DEGREE RECEIVED

2. Furnish below all prior business connections for the preceding ten years, including the reason for leaving each employment. *(list last position first).*

DATES OF EMPLOYMENT *(month, year)* FROM TO	POSITION	FULL-TIME OR PART-TIME
NAME AND ADDRESS OF EMPLOYER *(firm, organization, etc.)*	KIND OF BUSINESS OR ORGANIZATION *(accounting, insurance, broker-dealer, etc.)*	REASON FOR LEAVING

DATES OF EMPLOYMENT *(month, year)* FROM TO	POSITION	FULL-TIME OR PART-TIME
NAME AND ADDRESS OF EMPLOYER *(firm, organization, etc.)*	KIND OF BUSINESS OR ORGANIZATION *(accounting, insurance, broker-dealer, etc.)*	REASON FOR LEAVING

3. Have you ever been denied or barred from membership or registration, or has any disciplinary action been taken or sanction been imposed upon you, by any Federal or State agency or by any national securities exchange or national securities association, including suspension or expulsion from membership, suspension or revocation of registration, fine, censure, or finding that you have been a cause of any disciplinary action or have violated any law or rule? . . . .   YES ☐ NO ☐

4. Has any broker or dealer with which you were associated in any capacity when such action was taken, ever had its membership or registration denied, suspended, expelled or revoked? . . . . . .   YES ☐ NO ☐

5. Has any permanent or temporary injunction ever been entered against you or any broker or dealer with which you were associated in any capacity at the time such injunction was entered? . . . .   YES ☐ NO ☐

6. Have you ever been the subject of any arrests, indictments or convictions for any felony or misdemeanor, except minor traffic offenses? . . . .   YES ☐ NO ☐

If your answer to any of the above questions (Questions 3-6) is "Yes," furnish the following information on a separate sheet: Name of Federal or State agency or agency of the District of Columbia, national securities exchange, or national securities association; name and location of broker or dealer with which you were associated and capacity in which you were associated; designation of statutes, rules or regulations which you or the broker or dealer you were associated with were charged with violating and nature of charges made; and nature and date of judgment, decision or other findings made, and sanction imposed.

7. Furnish any other name *(including maiden name)* by which you have been known that is necessary to complete a check of your previous business connections. _____

I hereby certify that the above answers are true and complete to the best of my knowledge. I consent that notice of any proceeding before the Commission may be given by sending notice by certified or registered mail or confirmed telegram at the address given below or at such substituted address as I may hereafter furnish the Commission.

Date _____   Signature of Associated Person _____

Address _____

(over)

DS-4688

406

CERTIFICATION BY BROKER OR DEALER

The company certifies, on the basis of a due and diligent inquiry made of the background of the person named on this form and other information available, that it has reason to believe that such person is of good character and reputation and is qualified to perform his functions and duties as a person associated with this firm. Such person has fulfilled the examination requirement of Rule 15b8-1, if such requirement is applicable to him. *(see instruction number 3.)*

If the examination requirement is applicable, complete questions 1, 2 and 3.

1. Examination(s) successfully completed _____

2. Date _____

3. Examining authority_____

Dated the_____day of _____,19____

(NAME OF CORPORATION, PARTNERSHIP, SOLE PROPRIETORSHIP OR OTHER ORGANIZATION)

_____   _____
(MANUAL SIGNATURE OF PRINCIPAL OFFICER, GENERAL PARTNER, SOLE PROPRIETOR OR MANAGING AGENT)   (TITLE)

INSTRUCTIONS

1. This form must be filed by every nonmember broker or dealer registered under Section 15 of the Securities Exchange Act of 1934 ("Act"), for every associated person engaged directly or indirectly in securities activities, for or on behalf of such nonmember broker or dealer, before such person engages in any such activities on behalf of such nonmember broker or dealer; except (A) that with respect to each associated person to whom the examination requirement of Rule 15b8-1 is applicable and who is an associated person on July 1, 1966, not later than July 1, 1966 and (B) with respect to each associated person to whom such examination requirement is not applicable and who is an associated person engaged directly or indirectly in securities activities on October 15, 1965, not later than November 30, 1965.

2. Page 1 of this form must be completed and signed by the associated person for whom it is filed. Page 2 is a certification to be completed and signed by the broker or dealer.

3. The term "associated person" is defined in subparagraph (c)(2) of Rule 15b8-1. Associated persons subject to the examination requirement are described in subparagraph (a)(1)(A) of Rule 15b8-1.

4. The examination requirement may be fulfilled by successful completion of one of the examinations deemed by the Commission, on the basis of its content and administration, to be a satisfactory alternative to the Commission examination.

5. If this form is filed by a sole proprietor, the certification on page 2 shall be signed by the proprietor; if filed by a partnership, it shall be signed in the name of the partnership by a general partner; if filed by an unincorporated organization or association which is not a partnership, it shall be signed in the name of such organization or association by the managing agent, i.e., a duly authorized person who directs or manages or who participates in the directing or managing of its affairs; if filed by a corporation, it shall be signed in the name of the corporation by a principal officer duly authorized.

6. If the space provided for any answer is insufficient, the complete answer should be prepared on a separate sheet which should be attached to the form and identified as "Answer to Item___."

7. Pursuant to Rule 15b8-1, if the information contained in Form SECO-2 is or becomes inaccurate or incomplete for any reason, a new Form SECO-2 must be filed promptly by the nonmember broker or dealer correcting such information.

8. Failure to include or file information required to be reported or the making of any false statements may result in the institution of administrative or civil proceedings. Moreover, intentional misstatements or omissions of material facts constitute federal criminal violations punishable by up to five years imprisonment and fines up to $10,000 for each offense. (See 18 U.S.C. 1001 and Section 32(a) of the Act.)

GPO 896-309

407

NATIONAL ASSOCIATION OF SECURITIES DEALERS, INC.

888 SEVENTEENTH STREET N. W. WASHINGTON, D. C. 20006

NOTICE OF TERMINATION OF REGISTRATION
REGISTERED PRINCIPAL ☐   REGISTERED REPRESENTATIVE ☐

(All questions must be answered)

1. _____
(Name of Individual)

2. _____
(Home Address)

3. _____
(Capacity)

4. _____
(Name of Firm)

5. _____
(Office of Employment)

6. State the reason for discontinuance:

Voluntary resignation	_____	
Permitted to resi	_____	*
Discharged	_____	*
Deceased	_____	
Other	_____	*

* Give full details on the reverse side for any answer which is marked by an asterisk.

7. Within your knowledge and/or within the records of your firm, was the individual the subject of any of the following within the past **five** years:

	Yes	No
(a) Any investigation or proceeding conducted by any regulatory body which has jurisdiction over the securities industry?	☐	☐
(b) Any disciplinary action by any regulatory body which has jurisdiction over the securities industry in which such individual was found to have violated any securities law, rule or regulation?	☐	☐
(c) Any complaint, as defined in Article III, Section 21(d) of the Rules of Fair Practice, filed by a customer of your firm?	☐	☐
(d) Any disciplinary action taken by your firm?	☐	☐
(e) Aside from the foregoing, do you know of any reason why the above named individual should not be employed by another member of the Association?	☐	☐

Give full details on the reverse side for any "yes" answer.

Date _____   _____
(*Signature of Executive Representative or*)
(*Registered Principal of Member*)

NATIONAL ASSOCIATION OF SECURITIES DEALERS, INC.

888 SEVENTEENTH STREET N. W. WASHINGTON, D. C. 20006

REQUEST FOR QUALIFICATION EXAMINATION FOR PRINCIPALS

This is not an application for registration. Applicant must be presently registered.

This form is used in connection with Schedule "C", Part 1, No. 3 (See Page C-61, NASD Manual): "Any person associated with a member as a representative whose duties are changed by the same member after October 1, 1965, so as to require his classification as a Principal will be allowed a reasonable period of time following such change to pass a Qualification Examination for Principals."

This form should be sent to NASD accompanied by an examination fee of $25.00. Examination fees are not refundable. (See Page H-4, NASD Manual.)

Please Typewrite or Print

1. _____
Principal's Last Name   First   Name   Middle   Name

2. _____
Name of Member Firm

3. _____
Office where Principal is located

4. (a) Are you becoming a member or allied member of a national securities exchange? Yes ☐ No ☐ (b) If yes, please indicate: NYSE ☐ ASE ☐ MSE ☐ PBS ☐ PCS ☐ Other_____

5. _____
Social Security Number

6. Indicate
☐ Partner
☐ Officer _____
                    Title

☐ Director
☐ Manager of OSJ
☐ Other _____
                    Specify

Date _____

_____
(Signature of proposed Principal)

_____
(Signature of Qualified Partner or Executive)

DO NOT WRITE IN THIS SPACE — For use by National Association of Securities Dealers, Inc.

Issued_____   Examination Fee Received_____

Date Taken_____   Records: Member_____

Grade_____   Individual_____

Satisfactory_____   Approval Forwarded_____

O. K. TO FILE: _____

Do Not Detach

IMPORTANT — MUST BE COMPLETED   Indicate amount of payment enclosed $_____

Firm Name_____

Principal's Name_____

NATIONAL ASSOCIATION OF SECURITIES DEALERS, INC.

888 Seventeenth Street, N. W.
Washington, D. C. 20006

APPLICATION FOR REGISTRATION

AS A REGISTERED PRINCIPAL * ☐   AS A REGISTERED REPRESENTATIVE * ☐

This application must be accompanied by a registration fee of $25. In addition, if an examination is required, enclose: (a) $20 for any applicant who is applying for registration as a Representative or (b) $25 for any applicant who is applying for registration as a Principal. Registration and examination fees are not refundable.

If the applicant has been registered previously in the same category and such registration has not been terminated for two years or more preceding the filing of this application, the applicant is not required to take and pass an examination. Complete and accurate answers to every question will eliminate delay and assist in prompt handling of the application.** Please make sure that the tear sheets are completed.

PLEASE TYPEWRITE

1. _____   2. _____
   (Applicant's Last Name)   (First Name)   (Middle Name)   *(Social Security Number)*

3. _____   4. _____
   (To Be Employed by)   *(Date applicant was employed or associated)*

5. _____
   (Location of office where employed—Specify street, city, county, state, zip code.)

6. (a) Specify Full Time ☐   Part Time ☐
   (b) If Part Time, specify nature of other business activities:
   _____

   (c) Proposed Title or Position (Check Applicable Box)

Principal		**Representative**
☐ Sole Proprietor		☐ Assistant Officer
☐ Officer_____ *(Specify)*		☐ Registered Representative
☐ Partner		☐ Other_____ *(Specify)*
☐ Manager of Office of Supervisory Jurisdiction		
☐ Director		
☐ Other_____ *(Specify)*		

7. (a) Have you ever been registered as a principal or a representative of a member of the NASD prior to filing this application? .... Yes ☐   No ☐
   (b) Are you applying for registration with a national securities exchange? ....Yes ☐   No ☐
   (c) If "yes", please indicate: NYSE ☐ ASE ☐ MSE ☐ PBS ☐ PCS ☐   Other_____
   (d) In what state(s) are you applying for a license or registration?

DO NOT WRITE IN THIS SPACE. FOR USE BY NASD.

Examination Required:	Registration Fee Received ....
Principal ☐ Representative ☐	Examination Fee Received ....
Issued	Records: Member ....
Date Taken	Individual ....
Grade	Acceptance Forwarded ....
FILE:	

---

* For designations and examination requirements, see Schedule "C" of the By-Laws.
** Complete and accurate information is required, even in the case of a re-registration. A copy of this application, properly maintained by the member, will satisfy the requirements of SEC Rule 17 a-3 (a) (12).

8. _____

(Applicant's home address—specify street, city, county, state, zip code.)

9. _____ 10. ☐   ☐
    (Date of birth)   (Male) (Female)   (If married, give maiden name.)

11. _____

(Place of birth—Specify city, state and country)

12. Are you a citizen of the United States: Yes ☐   No ☐   If "no," specify _____

13. Educational Institutions attended: Elementary ☐   High School ☐   College ☐   Graduate School ☐
    Specify highest year completed.   ☐ ☐ ☐   ☐ ☐ ☐ ☐   ☐ ☐ ☐ ☐   ☐   ☐   ☐
                                            6   7   8   9 10 11 12   1   2   3   4   1   2   3

Name of Institution and Address	From Mo.	Yr.	To Mo.	Yr.	Course	Did You Graduate	Degree

14. The following is a complete, consecutive statement of my business history for the past ten years:
    Note: Account for all time and list all residence addresses during periods of unemployment. If presently associated with the member in any capacity, give starting date of such association and position held.

List Latest Position First

From Month	Year	To Month	Year	Name of Employer Address (Street, City and State)	Position Held	Part Time or Full Time	Reason For Leaving

If more space is needed, attach separate sheet.

15. (a) Have you ever been refused bond by a surety company? .... Yes ☐   No ☐

    (b) Has any surety company paid out any funds on your coverage? .... Yes ☐   No ☐
        If your answer is "yes" to either question, attach details.

16. (a) Have you ever been subject to an order of the NASD, any national securities exchange or any federal or state agency involving the expulsion, suspension, revocation or denial of your registration as a broker-dealer or of your membership or of your registration as a registered representative, or involving the barring or suspending of your association with any member or any broker-dealer, or the imposition of any other disciplinary action, including any finding that you were a cause of any disciplinary action or had violated any law? (Reference, Article I, Section 2 of the By-Laws) .... Yes ☐   No ☐

    (b) Do you know or to your knowledge have you ever been associated in any capacity with a broker-dealer who has been subject to an order of the NASD, any national securities exchange or any federal or state agency involving the suspension or expulsion from membership therein, or who was barred or suspended from associating with any broker-dealer or who was refused membership therein, or who withdrew an application for membership, or whose registration as a broker-dealer with any federal or state agency has been denied, for conduct found to have occurred in a period during which you were associated with such broker-dealer? (Reference, Article I, Section 2 of the By-Laws) .... Yes ☐   No ☐

    (c) Have you ever been enjoined permanently or temporarily or have you ever been associated in any capacity with any broker-dealer who during the period of your association with such broker-dealer has been enjoined permanently or temporarily by order, judgment, or decree of any court of competent jurisdiction from acting as an investment adviser, underwriter, broker or dealer, or an affiliated person, or employee of any investment company, bank or insurance company or from engaging in or continuing any conduct or practice or in connection with such activity, or in connection with the purchase or sale of any security? (Reference, Article I, Section 2 of the By-Laws) .... Yes ☐   No ☐

NATIONAL ASSOCIATION OF SECURITIES DEALERS, INC.

NOTICE OF ACCEPTANCE OF REGISTRATION

AS A REGISTERED PRINCIPAL ☐ AS A REGISTERED REPRESENTATIVE ☐

(Name of Applicant)

(Enter name and address of member to which Notice of Registration should be directed)

When validated by National Association of Securities Dealers, Inc., this will be your notice of acceptance of registration with the National Association of Securities Dealers, Inc., while in the employ of the member named on left side of this page.

TEST SERIES 1

GENERAL AND NASD SECTIONS
2 HOURS
WHITE COVERED BOOKLET

Note: Validation Stamp Required

REQUIRED BY   NASD ☐   NYSE ☐   ASE ☐

The candidate named below is authorized to take the examination described on this Admission Certificate during the THIRTY DAYS following the date listed below when validated.

(Enter full name of Applicant)

(Enter name and address of member to which this certificate should be directed)

(See Reverse Side)

Applicant _____

Member _____

(Enter full name of applicant and member)

**FOR NASD USE ONLY.
DO NOT WRITE IN THIS SPACE.**

Candidate qualified with NASD by previous exam.

DATE ....

SCORE ....

NASD Examination Not Required ☐

Do Not Detach

Indicate amount of payment enclosed $_____

Member _____

Applicant _____

(Enter full name of member and applicant)

(d) Have you been convicted within ten years preceding the filing of this application of any felony or misdemeanor which involved the purchase or sale of any security or which arose out of the conduct of the business of a broker, dealer or investment adviser; or which involved embezzlement, fraudulent conversion or misappropriation of funds or securities; or which involved mail fraud, or fraud by wire, radio or television? (Reference, Article I, Section 2 of the By-Laws) .... Yes ☐ No ☐

If your answer to question 16 (a), (b), (c) or (d) is "yes", or if any action is currently pending, supply the following information on an attached sheet:

Action taken by whom and the nature of it; the date of such action; the name of broker-dealer subject to such action and the nature of your association with such broker-dealer; the designation of such statute, rule or regulation alleged to have been violated; and the nature and date of judgment, decision or other findings made, and sanction imposed.

17. Have you ever been arrested, indicted or convicted for any felony or misdemeanor, except minor traffic offenses? .... Yes ☐ No ☐

If your answer is "yes", attach details.

18. Are you at present involved in any litigation connected with the securities business or are there any unsatisfied judgments outstanding against you arising out of the securities business? .... Yes ☐ No ☐

If your answer is "yes", attach details.

19. Have you ever been known personally by any other name, or have you ever conducted business or carried brokerage or bank accounts in any other name than that shown in questions 1 or 10 above? .... Yes ☐ No ☐

If your answer is "yes", attach details and dates of other names used.

APPLICANT'S CERTIFICATION

I hereby apply for registration as a registered principal or registered representative of a member of the NATIONAL ASSOCIATION OF SECURITIES DEALERS, INC., in accordance with Articles I and XV of the By-Laws of the Association, and attest that I have read the Association's Certificate of Incorporation, By-Laws, Rules of Fair Practice and Code of Procedure for Handling Trade Practice Complaints, and hereby (1) accept and agree to abide by, comply with and adhere to all the provisions, conditions and covenants of the Certificate of Incorporation, the By-Laws, the Rules of Fair Practice and the Code of Procedure for Handling Trade Practice Complaints of the Association, and regulations of the Association as they are, or may from time to time be adopted, changed or amended, and all rulings, orders, directions and decisions of, and penalties imposed by, the Board of Governors or any duly authorized committee; and (2) agree that neither the Association nor any officer or employee thereof, nor any member of the Board of Governors or of any District or other Committee, shall be liable, except for wilful malfeasance, to the applicant, for action taken by such officer or member of the Board of Governors or of any District or other Committee in his official capacity, or by any employee of the Association while acting within the scope of his employment or under instruction of any officer, board or committee of the Association, in connection with the administration or enforcement of any of the provisions of the By-Laws, any of the rules and regulations as they are, or may from time to time be adopted, changed or amended, or any ruling, order, direction, decision of, or penalty imposed by the Board of Governors or any duly authorized committee and (3) agree to notify the Association promptly of my termination of association with the member and my intention to terminate my registration and (4) agree that the information contained herein shall be kept current and that either address as shown in answer to questions 5 and 8 shall be considered the address of record for the receipt of all Association communications.

I CERTIFY TO THE BOARD OF GOVERNORS OF THE NASD THAT THE STATEMENTS MADE HEREIN ARE TRUE AND COMPLETE. I UNDERSTAND THAT I AM SUBJECT TO THE IMPOSITION OF PENALTIES UNDER SECTION 32 OF THE SECURITIES EXCHANGE ACT OF 1934, AS AMENDED, OR ASSOCIATION RULES OF FAIR PRACTICE IN THE EVENT FALSE OR MISLEADING INFORMATION IS GIVEN ON THE APPLICATION OR IF THERE ARE OMISSIONS OF MATERIAL FACTS. I FURTHER CERTIFY THAT I WILL AT ALL TIMES KEEP THE ANSWERS TO THE INFORMATION CALLED FOR HEREIN ACCURATE AND UP TO DATE BY SUPPLEMENTARY WRITTEN NOTICES TO THE SECRETARY OF THE CORPORATION.

_____   _____
(Date)   *(Signature of applicant)*

_____   _____
(Witness)   *(Title)*
(Witness must be either registered principal or registered representative—Please indicate)

MEMBER'S CERTIFICATION

I certify to the Board of Governors of the National Association of Securities Dealers, Inc., that I, on behalf of the member, based upon an investigation made by me of the applicant's background, have reason to believe that the applicant named herein is a person of good character and good business repute and is qualified by experience or will be qualified by training to perform the functions and duties required of the applicant.* I further certify that the applicant will not undertake any act that a registered individual can perform until such time as registration of the applicant is made effective by NASD and the state in which he expects to do business. In the event the applicant has been/or is presently associated with a firm in the securities business other than this firm, I have advised the applicant's latest employer in the securities business of the applicant's employment with this firm, by communicating with:

Mr. _____
        (Name)   *(Position)*   *(Firm)*

Method Used: Telephone_____ Interview_____ Letter_____

In addition, I have exercised reasonable care to verify that the statements contained in this application are accurate and there are no material omissions of fact.

_____   _____
(Date)   *(Signature of Registered Principal)*

* See Article III, Section 27(e) of the Rules of Fair Practice.
IMPORTANT . . . PLEASE COMPLETE THE FOLLOWING TEAR SHEETS BUT DO NOT DETACH

Examinations are conducted at the Examination Centers at the locations and times indicated on the enclosed NASD EXAMINATIONS CENTERS SCHEDULE.

The candidate should report to any one of the examination centers within THIRTY DAYS after the date on the reverse side and present this Certificate for admission to an examination session. If a candidate is not able to take the examination within that period, the member should request another Certificate of Admission from the Association.

The candidate will not be admitted to an examination center without this Certificate. Examinations will start promptly and *no candidate will be admitted to the examination room after the scheduled starting time.*

The candidate should plan to arrive at the examination center at least 15 minutes before the scheduled starting time.

CANDIDATE NOTE:

Make sure that the Test Series Number on the test booklet you receive is Series Number 1.

HOLIDAY SCHEDULE:

Examination sessions falling on national holidays will take place on the next business day unless exceptions are noted in the NASD EXAMINATIONS CENTERS SCHEDULE. Refer to page G-48—NASD Manual.

Index

419

423

425